W9-AEX-963

The Sporting News

CHRONICLE OF

BASEBALL

Baltimore Orioles Manager
Earl Weaver (right) with
Yankee boss Billy Martin.

New York Giants Manager
John McGraw.

Casey Stengel as
manager of the
New York Yankees.

Bill McKechnie as manager
of the Cincinnati Reds.

RON SMITH

The Sporting News

CHRONICLE OF
BASEBALL

Bucky Harris as manager of the Washington Senators.

Leo Durocher as manager of the New York Giants.

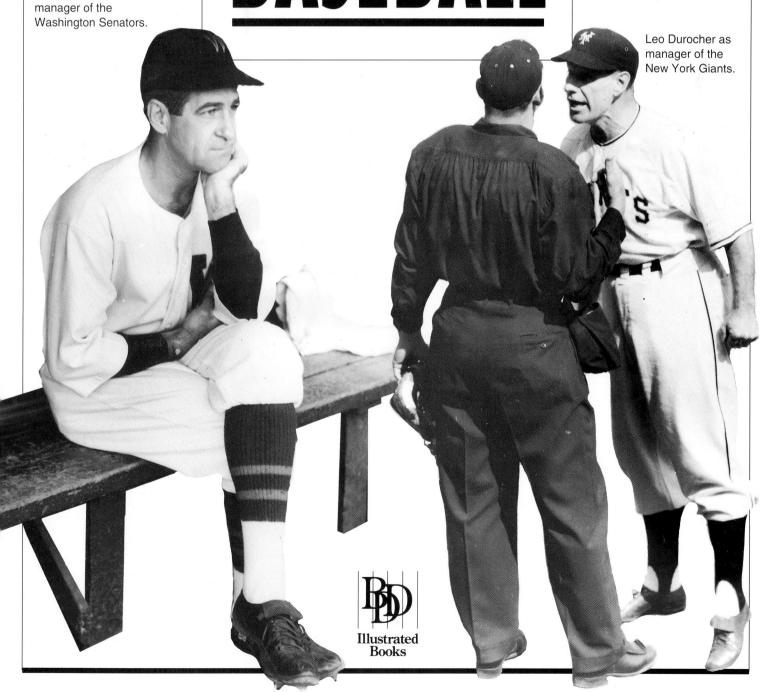

BDD

Illustrated
Books

Sparky Anderson as
manager of the
Cincinnati Reds.

Joe McCarthy as
manager of the
New York Yankees.

BDD Illustrated Books
An imprint of BDD Promotional Book Company, Inc
1540 Broadway
New York, N.Y. 10036

BDD Illustrated Books and the accompanying logo are trademarks
of the BDD Promotional Book Company, Inc.

Copyright © 1993 The Sporting News Publishing Company
Design © 1993 Reed International Books Limited

First Published in the United States of America in 1993 by
BDD Illustrated Books

ISBN 0 7924 5849 4

All rights reserved

Produced by Mandarin Offset
Printed in China

Photographic Acknowledgements
The photographs in this book were obtained from
The Sporting News and The Bettmann Archive.

Los Angeles Dodgers
Manager Tom Lasorda.

Contents

New York Yankees
Manager Miller Huggins.

Philadelphia Athletics
Manager Connie Mack.

Brooklyn Dodgers Manager
Walter Alston.

INTRODUCTION

by John D Rawlings, Editor of *The Sporting News*

Baseball and The Sporting News. The Sporting News *and baseball.
No matter how you say it, the message comes out the same. Like the vines
that grace the outfield walls at Chicago's Wrigley Field, the fortunes of these
two sports icons have been intertwining for more than a century.*

The symbiotic relationship began in 1886 when *The Sporting News* started publishing under the direction of Alfred Spink. It intensified over the years as baseball's popularity grew and society expressed an appetite for a national sports perspective. Through the formation of the American League, the dead-ball era, periods of prosperity, The Great Depression, world wars, unbridled growth and big-business evolution, *TSN* has served as baseball's watchdog, its champion, its comrade and its biggest critic.

It is no wonder that the publication that was there should be chosen to chronicle the charm, grace, deeds and misdeeds baseball has heaped upon society since the turn of the century. Historian and educator Jacques Barzun once said, "Whoever wants to know the heart and mind of America had better learn baseball," and those words are

Walter Johnson 1907   Christy Mathewson 1915   Ty Cobb 1927

reawakened by every word, every headline, every classic photograph in this book.

The format is simple and easy to follow. A year-by-year chronicle of baseball's formative years to start out, followed by monthly breakdowns of yearly events as the sport becomes more sophisticated and complex. All of the game's great moments are analyzed along with the behind-the-scenes developments, ironies, accomplishments, failures, fun, excitement and statistical data that have made baseball America's National Pastime.

Babe Ruth, Ty Cobb, Walter Johnson, Christy Mathewson, Lou Gehrig, Joe DiMaggio, Ted Williams, Bob Feller, Willie Mays, Mickey Mantle, Pete Rose, Nolan Ryan – all the great names and personalities are brought back to life for one more swing, one more pitch on the nostalgic fields of **our** dreams. Never before have so many memories been triggered and relived between the covers of one baseball volume.

So enjoy this stroll through yesteryear and cheer once more for the long-gone, but never forgotten, glories of generations past. As you browse, remember that baseball's enduring charm is that it never stops amazing even those who "have seen everything".

And make no mistake – much of baseball's best **is** yet to come. Alfred Spink knew that in 1886 and baseball has proven it, over and over, for more than a century.

Joe DiMaggio 1949   Willie Mays 1967   Pete Rose 1964

The 1900s

Like a newborn colt stumbling uncertainly on wobbly legs, baseball staggered innocently into the 20th century.

The emerging National Pastime turned the corner with roots firmly entrenched but lacking in direction and discipline. More than anything else, it needed a heavy dose of respectability — and a firm hand to bring order out of growing chaos.

Byron Bancroft Johnson had such a hand and he wielded it like a sword — with all the subtlety of a Roman gladiator. He rose into prominence in 1901 with the announcement that his new American League was ready to challenge the established National League as a major circuit and he proceeded to bully his rivals into submission, stealing their players, luring away fans in their key markets and outwitting them at every turn. When National League owners pressed for peace in 1903, Johnson dominated the talks and dictated the terms of coexistence. He would continue to dictate until his retirement in 1927.

With baseball fighting its most serious battle against itself, Johnson's arrival was fortunate. The game was stagnating because of its growing

NATIONAL LEAGUE

League Batting Leaders

Average

Year	Player-Team	Avg.
1900	Honus Wagner, Pit.	.381
1901	Jesse Burkett, St. L.	.382
1902	Ginger Beaumont, Pit.	.357
1903	Honus Wagner, Pit.	.355
1904	Honus Wagner, Pit.	.349
1905	Cy Seymour, Cin.	.377
1906	Honus Wagner, Pit.	.339
1907	Honus Wagner, Pit.	.350
1908	Honus Wagner, Pit.	.354
1909	Honus Wagner, Pit.	.339

Home Runs

Year	Player-Team	HR
1900	Herman Long, Bos.	12
1901	Sam Crawford, Cin.	16
1902	Tommy Leach, Pit.	6
1903	Jimmy Sheckard, Bkn.	9
1904	Harry Lumley, Bkn.	9
1905	Fred Odwell, Cin.	9
1906	Tim Jordan, Bkn.	12
1907	Dave Brain, Bos.	10
1908	Tim Jordan, Bkn.	12
1909	Red Murray, N.Y.	7

RBIs

Year	Player-Team	RBI
1900	Elmer Flick, Phil.	110
1901	Honus Wagner, Pit.	126
1902	Honus Wagner, Pit.	91
1903	Sam Mertes, N.Y.	104
1904	Bill Dahlen, N.Y.	80
1905	Cy Seymour, Cin.	121
1906	Jim Nealon, Pit.	83
1907	Sherry Magee, Phil.	85
1908	Honus Wagner, Pit.	109
1909	Honus Wagner, Pit.	100

League Pitching Leaders

Winning Percentage

Year	Pitcher-Team	W-L	Pct.
1900	Jesse Tannehill, Pit.	20-6	.769
1901	Jack Chesbro, Pit.	21-10	.677
1902	Jack Chesbro, Pit.	28-6	.824
1903	Sam Leever, Pit.	25-7	.781
1904	Joe McGinnity, N.Y.	35-8	.814
1905	Christy Mathewson, N.Y.	31-8	.795
1906	Ed Reulbach, Chi.	19-4	.826
1907	Ed Reulbach, Chi.	17-4	.810
1908	Ed Reulbach, Chi.	24-7	.774
1909	Christy Mathewson, N.Y.	25-6	.806
	Howie Camnitz, Pit.	25-6	.806

Earned-Run Average

Year	Pitcher-Team	ERA
1900	Rube Waddell, Pit.	2.37
1901	Jesse Tannehill, Pit.	2.18
1902	Jack Taylor, Chi.	1.33
1903	Sam Leever, Pit.	2.06
1904	Joe McGinnity, N.Y.	1.61
1905	Christy Mathewson, N.Y.	1.27
1906	Mordecai Brown, Chi.	1.04
1907	Jack Pfiester, Chi.	1.15
1908	Christy Mathewson, N.Y.	1.43
1909	Christy Mathewson, N.Y.	1.14

Strikeouts

Year	Pitcher-Team	SO
1900	Rube Waddell, Pit.	130
1901	Noodles Hahn, Cin.	239
1902	Vic Willis, Bos.	225
1903	Christy Mathewson, N.Y.	267
1904	Christy Mathewson, N.Y.	212
1905	Christy Mathewson, N.Y.	206
1906	Fred Beebe, Chi.-St. L.	171
1907	Christy Mathewson, N.Y.	178
1908	Christy Mathewson, N.Y.	259
1909	Orval Overall, Chi.	205

WORLD SERIES

Year	Winner	Pennant Winner	Games
1903	Boston Red Sox	Pittsburgh Pirates	5-3
1904	No series		
1905	New York Giants	Philadelphia Athletics	4-1
1906	Chicago White Sox	Chicago Cubs	4-2
1907	Chicago Cubs	Detroit Tigers	4-0-1
1908	Chicago Cubs	Detroit Tigers	4-1
1909	Pittsburgh Pirates	Detroit Tigers	4-3

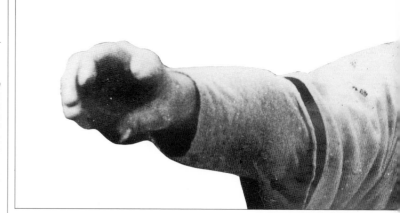

Chicago Cubs righthander Mordecai (Three Finger) Brown.

Final Standings

1900

	W	L	PCT.	GB
Brooklyn	82	54	.603	--
Pittsburgh	79	60	.568	4.5
Philadelphia	75	63	.543	8
Boston	66	72	.478	17
Chicago	65	75	.464	19
St. Louis	65	75	.464	19
Cincinnati	62	77	.446	21.5
New York	60	78	.435	23

1901

	W	L	Pct.	GB
Pittsburgh	90	49	.647	--
Philadelphia	83	57	.593	7.5
Brooklyn	79	57	.581	9.5
St. Louis	76	64	.543	14.5
Boston	69	69	.500	20.5
Chicago	53	86	.381	37
New York	52	85	.380	37
Cincinnati	52	87	.374	38

1902

	W	L	Pct.	GB
Pittsburgh	103	36	.741	--
Brooklyn	75	63	.543	27.5
Boston	73	64	.533	29
Cincinnati	70	70	.500	33.5
Chicago	68	69	.496	34
St. Louis	56	78	.418	44.5
Philadelphia	56	81	.409	46
New York	48	88	.353	53.5

1903

	W	L	Pct.	GB
Pittsburgh	91	49	.650	--
New York	84	55	.604	6.5
Chicago	82	56	.594	8
Cincinnati	74	65	.532	16.5
Brooklyn	70	66	.515	19
Boston	58	80	.420	32
Philadelphia	49	86	.363	39.5
St. Louis	43	94	.314	46.5

1904

	W	L	Pct.	GB
New York	106	47	.693	--
Chicago	93	60	.608	13
Cincinnati	88	65	.575	18
Pittsburgh	87	66	.569	19
St. Louis	75	79	.487	31.5
Brooklyn	56	97	.366	50
Boston	55	98	.359	51
Philadelphia	52	100	.342	53.5

1905

	W	L	Pct.	GB
New York	105	48	.686	--
Pittsburgh	96	57	.627	9
Chicago	92	61	.601	13
Philadelphia	83	69	.546	21.5
Cincinnati	79	74	.516	26
St. Louis	58	96	.377	47.5
Boston	51	103	.331	54.5
Brooklyn	48	104	.316	56.5

1906

	W	L	Pct.	GB
Chicago	116	36	.763	--
New York	96	56	.632	20
Pittsburgh	93	60	.608	23.5
Philadelphia	71	82	.464	45.5
Brooklyn	66	86	.434	50
Cincinnati	64	87	.424	51.5
St. Louis	52	98	.347	63
Boston	49	102	.325	66.5

1907

	W	L	Pct.	GB
Chicago	107	45	.704	--
Pittsburgh	91	63	.591	17
Philadelphia	83	64	.565	21.5
New York	82	71	.536	25.5
Brooklyn	65	83	.439	40
Cincinnati	66	87	.431	41.5
Boston	58	90	.392	47
St. Louis	52	101	.340	55.5

1908

	W	L	Pct.	GB
Chicago	99	55	.643	--
New York	98	56	.636	1
Pittsburgh	98	56	.636	1
Philadelphia	83	71	.539	16
Cincinnati	73	81	.474	26
Boston	63	91	.409	36
Brooklyn	53	101	.344	46
St. Louis	49	105	.318	50

1909

	W	L	Pct.	GB
Pittsburgh	110	42	.724	--
Chicago	104	49	.680	6.5
New York	92	61	.601	18.5
Cincinnati	77	76	.503	33.5
Philadelphia	74	79	.484	36.5
Brooklyn	55	98	.359	55.5
St. Louis	54	98	.355	56
Boston	45	108	.294	65.5

Detroit slugger Sam Crawford.

reputation as a rowdy, pugilistic sport played by unsavory characters who preached hooliganism, and watched by uncivilized fans who behaved violently. That image was acceptable for the largely agrarian society baseball had been trying to entertain, but it repulsed much of the gentility that might ordinarily have been attracted to the sport. With the country taking its first steps toward industrialization, this would have to change.

Johnson understood and began demanding decorum from his players, better ballpark security from his owners and respect for his umpires. He dealt harshly with those who transgressed his standards of good conduct and he paved the way for growth and prosperity with his unyielding determination. By the end of the decade, Johnson's efforts were showing results.

As baseball went about the business of refining its personality, it also organized into a strong, stable unit that would exist without so much as a franchise shift for 50 years. As officials and owners quit fighting among themselves and began working for the common good, the game prospered. Uniform rules were drawn up, a three-man commission was established to act as final authority over both leagues and an annual World Series to determine an undisputed champion was introduced.

The American League's Boston Red Sox were the first such champions in 1903 and the New York Giants, Chicago White Sox, Chicago Cubs and Pittsburgh Pirates all took turns before the decade closed.

While the game searched frantically for an identity, it did not lack for gate attractions. Such greats as John McGraw, Cy Young, Christy Mathewson, Nap Lajoie, Honus Wagner, Jimmy Collins and Kid Nichols helped usher in the new century while such youngsters as Walter Johnson, Ty Cobb, Tris Speaker and Eddie Collins exploded into prominence at mid-decade.

Their rising stars would light the way into an era of prosperity.

AMERICAN LEAGUE

League Batting Leaders

Average

Year	Player-Team	Avg.
1901	Nap Lajoie, Phil.	.422
1902	Ed Delahanty, Wash.	.376
1903	Nap Lajoie, Cle.	.355
1904	Nap Lajoie, Cle.	.381
1905	Elmer Flick, Cle.	.306
1906	George Stone, St. L.	.358
1907	Ty Cobb, Det.	.350
1908	Ty Cobb, Det.	.324
1909	Ty Cobb, Det.	.377

Home Runs

Year	Player-Team	HR
1901	Nap Lajoie, Phil.	13
1902	Socks Seybold, Phil.	16
1903	Buck Freeman, Bos.	13
1904	Harry Davis, Phil.	10
1905	Harry Davis, Phil.	8
1906	Harry Davis, Phil.	12
1907	Harry Davis, Phil.	8
1908	Sam Crawford, Det.	7
1909	Ty Cobb, Det.	9

RBIs

Year	Player-Team	RBI
1901	Nap Lajoie, Phil.	125
1902	Buck Freeman, Bos.	121
1903	Buck Freeman, Bos.	104
1904	Nap Lajoie, Cle.	102
1905	Harry Davis, Phil.	83
1906	Harry Davis, Phil.	96
1907	Ty Cobb, Det.	116
1908	Ty Cobb, Det.	108
1909	Ty Cobb, Det.	107

League Pitching Leaders

Winning Percentage

Year	Pitcher-Team	W-L	Pct.
1901	Clark Griffith, Chi.	24-7	.774
1902	Bill Bernhard, Phil.-Cle.		
		18-5	.783
1903	Cy Young, Bos.	28-9	.757
1904	Jack Chesbro, N.Y.	41-12	.774
1905	Andy Coakley, Phil.	20-7	.741
1906	Eddie Plank, Phil.	19-6	.760
1907	Bill Donovan, Det.	25-4	.862
1908	Ed Walsh, Chi.	40-15	.727
1909	George Mullin, Det.	29-8	.784

Earned-Run Average

Year	Pitcher-Team	ERA
1901	Cy Young, Bos.	1.62
1902	Ed Siever, Det.	1.91
1903	Earl Moore, Cle.	1.77
1904	Addie Joss, Cle.	1.59
1905	Rube Waddell, Phil.	1.48
1906	Doc White, Chi.	1.52
1907	Ed Walsh, Chi.	1.60
1908	Addie Joss, Cle.	1.16
1909	Harry Krause, Phil.	1.39

Strikeouts

Year	Pitcher-Team	SO
1901	Cy Young, Bos.	158
1902	Rube Waddell, Phil.	210
1903	Rube Waddell, Phil.	302
1904	Rube Waddell, Phil.	349
1905	Rube Waddell, Phil.	287
1906	Rube Waddell, Phil.	196
1907	Rube Waddell, Phil.	232
1908	Ed Walsh, Chi.	269
1909	Frank Smith, Chi.	177

Final Standings

1901

	W	L	Pct.	GB
Chicago	83	53	.610	- -
Boston	79	57	.581	4.
Detroit	74	61	.548	8.5
Philadelphia	74	62	.544	9
Baltimore	68	65	.511	13.5
Washington	61	73	.455	21
Cleveland	55	82	.401	28.5
Milwaukee	48	89	.350	35.5

1902

	W	L	Pct.	GB
Philadelphia	83	53	.610	- -
St. Louis	78	58	.574	5
Boston	77	60	.562	6.5
Chicago	74	60	.552	8
Cleveland	69	67	.507	14
Washington	61	75	.449	22
Detroit	52	83	.385	30.5
Baltimore	50	88	.362	34

1903

	W	L	Pct.	GB
Boston	91	47	.659	- -
Philadelphia	75	60	.556	14.5
Cleveland	77	63	.550	15
New York	72	62	.537	17
Detroit	65	71	.478	25
St. Louis	65	74	.468	26.5
Chicago	60	77	.438	30.5
Washington	43	94	.314	47.5

1904

	W	L	Pct.	GB
Boston	95	59	.617	- -
New York	92	59	.609	1.5
Chicago	89	65	.578	6
Cleveland	86	65	.570	7.5
Philadelphia	81	70	.536	12.5
St. Louis	65	87	.428	29
Detroit	62	90	.408	32
Washington	38	113	.252	55.5

1905

	W	L	Pct.	GB
Philadelphia	92	56	.622	- -
Chicago	92	60	.605	2
Detroit	79	74	.516	15.5
Boston	78	74	.513	16
Cleveland	76	78	.494	19
New York	71	78	.477	21.5
Washington	64	87	.424	29.5
St. Louis	54	99	.353	40.5

1906

	W	L	Pct.	GB
Chicago	93	58	.616	- -
New York	90	61	.596	3
Cleveland	89	64	.582	5
Philadelphia	78	67	.538	12
St. Louis	76	73	.510	16
Detroit	71	78	.477	21
Washington	55	95	.367	37.5
Boston	49	105	.318	45.5

1907

	W	L	Pct.	GB
Detroit	92	58	.613	- -
Philadelphia	88	57	.607	1.5
Chicago	87	64	.576	1.5
Cleveland	85	67	.559	8
New York	70	78	.473	21
St. Louis	69	83	.454	24
Boston	59	90	.396	32.5
Washington	49	102	.325	43.5

1908

	W	L	Pct.	GB
Detroit	90	63	.588	- -
Cleveland	90	64	.584	.5
Chicago	88	64	.579	1.5
St. Louis	83	69	.546	6.5
Boston	75	79	.487	15.5
Philadelphia	68	85	.444	22
Washington	67	85	.441	22.5
New York	51	103	.331	39.5

1909

	W	L	Pct.	GB
Detroit	98	54	.645	- -
Philadelphia	95	58	.621	3.5
Boston	88	63	.583	9.5
Chicago	78	74	.513	20
New York	74	77	.490	23.5
Cleveland	71	82	.464	27.5
St. Louis	61	89	.407	36
Washington	42	110	.276	56

★1900★

Three rule changes

National League officials adopted three rule changes in March that affected play in 1900. The most significant involved the reshaping of home plate.

Instead of the 12-inch square design, the plate is now a five-sided figure, 17 inches wide. The move expanded the strike zone for the pitcher while creating more pressure for the hitter trying to put the ball in play.

Other changes: The N.L. reverted back to one umpire after experimenting with two and the balk rule was changed to allow only the baserunner to advance while not affecting the batter.

The rumblings of war

The year opened with National League officials glancing nervously over their shoulders and ended with them declaring war against a renegade with grandiose plans to create a second "major league." Byron Bancroft (Ban) Johnson was the target of their disaffection and his new American League the object of their concern.

Johnson, the long-time president of the successful Western League, renamed his 1900 circuit the American League and opened the campaign with eight teams in Chicago, Kansas City, Minneapolis, Milwaukee, Detroit, Indianapolis, Cleveland and Buffalo. In late October, the former Cincinnati sportswriter declared that his A.L. had attained major league status, a notion quickly rejected by N.L. officials.

N.L. officials had fought this battle before, but not against a take-no-prisoners executive like Johnson, who was clever, well organized and confident of success. He already had promised to ignore the reserve clause in N.L. contracts while introducing provisions in A.L. contracts that seemed sure to attract many of the senior league's star players.

Johnson also announced that long-time N.L. star John McGraw will head a new team in Baltimore next year and he reportedly has considered placing franchises in other current N.L. cities.

Brooklyn captures another N.L. pennant

The Brooklyn Superbas walked away with their second straight National League pennant, but second-place Pittsburgh gathered most of the individual honors in the first baseball campaign of the new century.

Brooklyn finished with an 82-54 record, outdistancing the Pirates by 4½ games and giving Manager Ned Hanlon his fifth pennant in seven years. Hanlon had guided Baltimore to consecutive titles in 1894, '95 and '96.

Pittsburgh's consolation was the performances turned in by Honus Wagner and pitchers Jesse Tannehill and Rube Waddell. Wagner captured his first batting title with a .381 mark while Tannehill led the league in winning percentage (20-6, .769) and Waddell led in earned-run average (2.37) and strikeouts (130). The key for Brooklyn was tireless righthander Joe McGinnity, who topped the N.L. with 29 victories and 347 innings pitched.

Brooklyn's Wee Willie Keeler led the league with 208 hits, Boston's Herman Long took home run honors with 12 and Philadelphia's Elmer Flick topped the charts with 110 runs batted in.

Brooklyn Manager Ned Hanlon: five pennants in seven years.

SEASON LEADERS

National League		
Avg.	Honus Wagner, Pit.	.381
HR	Herman Long, Bos.	12
RBI	Elmer Flick, Phi.	110
SB	Jim Barrett, Cin.	46
W-L Pct.	Jesse Tannehill, Pit. 20-6,	.769
ERA	Rube Waddell, Pit.	2.37
SO	Rube Waddell, Pit.	130

CAUGHT ON THE FLY

APRIL
Doc Amole got the new American League off to a rousing start when he fired an Opening Day no-hitter and defeated Detroit, 8-0.

JULY
Kid Nichols, the Boston Braves' 30-year-old righthander, became the youngest pitcher ever to win 300 games when he beat the Chicago Cubs, 11-4.

Cincinnati lefthander Noodles Hahn allowed five walks but did not give up a hit in pitching the Reds to a 4-0 victory over Philadelphia.

DECEMBER
The New York Giants traded 241-game winner Amos Rusie to the Cincinnati Reds for a young righthander with potential — Christy Mathewson.

Brooklyn's Willie Keeler captured National League honors with 208 hits.

★1901★
JANUARY-DECEMBER

Chicago rules in A.L.

Charles Comiskey's Chicago White Stockings captured the first American League pennant, but hard-hitting Napoleon Lajoie ran away with individual honors after shifting his allegiance from the National League's Philadelphia Phillies to the A.L.'s Philadelphia Athletics.

With Clark Griffith leading the way as manager and ace pitcher, the White Stockings compiled an 83-53 record and finished four games ahead of second-place Boston. Griffith fashioned a 24-7 record and league-best .774 winning percentage and Chicago surprised everybody by outdrawing the cross-town Cubs at the turnstiles. The Cubs finished sixth behind Pittsburgh in the N.L.

Lajoie feasted on American League pitching; he captured a Triple Crown with an unprecedented .422 batting average, 13 home runs and 125 runs batted in. The righthanded hitter also led the A.L. in runs scored (145), hits (229), doubles (48) and fielding percentage (.963).

Philadelphia's Napoleon Lajoie started his American League career by winning a Triple Crown.

SEASON LEADERS

	American League		National League	
Avg.	Nap Lajoie, Phi.	.422	Jesse Burkett, St.L.	.382
HR	Nap Lajoie, Phi.	13	Sam Crawford, Cin.	16
RBI	Nap Lajoie, Phi.	125	Honus Wagner, Pit.	126
SB	Frank Isbell, Chi.	48	Honus Wagner, Pit.	48
W-L Pct.	Clark Griffith, Chi.	24-7, .774	Jack Chesbro, Pit.	21-10, .677
ERA	Cy Young, Bos.	1.62	Jesse Tannehill, Pit.	2.18
SO	Cy Young, Bos.	158	Noodles Hahn, Cin.	239

CAUGHT ON THE FLY

APRIL
Chicago hosted the A.L.'s first major league game and celebrated with an 8-2 victory over Cleveland.

Detroit's A.L. debut was amazing: The Tigers rallied for 10 runs in the bottom of the ninth inning and defeated Milwaukee, 14-13.

Eight days after the National League Phillies drew 4,500 fans in their Philadelphia opener, the Athletics played before 16,000 Philadelphia fans in their American League debut.

JULY
Christy Mathewson pitched his first major league no-hitter, blanking St. Louis, 5-0.

N.L. meets its match

The National League, in operation since 1876 and secure in its monopoly, was not prepared to meet the challenge of Ban Johnson and his new "major league." Other entrepreneurs had folded quickly after organizing outlaw circuits that tried to trade blows with the established N.L.

But a year after Johnson's declaration of war, it appears the N.L. hierarchy has underestimated his guile and determination. The American League is alive and well after its first season of head-to-head competition and panic-stricken N.L. officials are desperately looking for ways to defend their once-sacred territories.

The A.L. began play April 24 with eight franchises, three of which Johnson had the audacity to place in N.L. strongholds — Chicago, Boston and Philadelphia. The rosters of those teams and the others located in Detroit, Baltimore, Washington, Cleveland and Milwaukee were laced with star players pirated from the rosters of N.L. teams.

Cy Young, Joe McGinnity, Napoleon Lajoie, Jimmy Collins, John McGraw, Chick Stahl, Buck Freeman, Clark Griffith and Wilbert Robinson were a few of the name players who opened the season in A.L. uniforms. And the defections continued in October, when seven St. Louis Cardinals, including batting champion Jesse Burkett, jumped leagues.

The A.L.'s biggest advantage is its leadership. Johnson is a powerful personality who commands respect and knows how to get what he wants. He is backed by Charles Comiskey, owner of the Chicago franchise, and Connie Mack, owner and manager of the Philadelphia Athletics. The N.L. lacks a forceful hand at the top and is splintered in its approach to solving the American League problem.

As a result, A.L. officials are taking full advantage of the $2,400 yearly salary ceiling in N.L. contracts, a ceiling the senior circuit has stubbornly refused to eliminate. And they are offering five-year limits on the reserve clauses in player contracts.

Johnson capped his first season with a daring move. He shifted the A.L.'s Milwaukee franchise to St. Louis to do head-to-head battle with the Cardinals.

Ban Johnson, the brains behind the American League.

★ 1902 ★

JANUARY-DECEMBER

CAUGHT ON THE FLY

JUNE

Corsicana of the Texas League defeated Texarkana, 51-3, as Nig Clarke belted an incredible eight home runs.

JULY-AUGUST

Baltimore Manager John McGraw, unhappy with Ban Johnson's dictatorial manner, left the A.L. to take over the N.L. New York Giants, taking five players with him. A month later, the Giants had a new owner, too — John T. Brush.

SEPTEMBER

The Chicago Cubs' infield took on a poetic look when shortstop Joe Tinker, second baseman Johnny Evers and first baseman Frank Chance played their first game together.

DECEMBER

National League owners elected Harry Pulliam as the circuit's president.

The A.L. announced plans for a franchise in New York.

Lajoie jumps again

National League officials, unable to stop a mass defection of their star players to the American League, went to court and won an early battle — before losing the war.

The Pennsylvania Supreme Court upheld the legality of the reserve clause and barred Napoleon Lajoie, Chick Fraser and Bill Bernhard from playing for the Philadelphia Athletics or any team other than the N.L.'s Philadelphia Phillies. Other former Phillies, such as Elmer Flick and Ed Delahanty, also were affected by the decision.

But A.L. President Ban Johnson was undaunted by the setback. He simply transferred Lajoie's contract to the Cleveland Indians and the 1901 Triple Crown winner was back in uniform by June. He could not play in games at Philadelphia, but the A.L. kept its brightest star.

Even the Philadelphia ban was lifted by early July, when a series of federal court rulings established the legitimacy of the new contracts league jumpers were signing.

SEASON LEADERS

	American League		National League	
Avg.	Ed Delahanty, Wash.	.376	Ginger Beaumont, Pit.	.357
HR	Socks Seybold, Phi.	16	Tommy Leach, Pit.	6
RBI	Buck Freeman, Bos.	121	Honus Wagner, Pit.	91
SB	Topsy Hartsel, Phi.	54	Honus Wagner, Pit.	43
W-L Pct.	Bill Bernhard, Phi.-Cle.	18-5, .783	Jack Chesbro, Pit.	28-6, .824
ERA	Ed Siever, Det.	1.91	Jack Taylor, Chi.	1.33
SO	Rube Waddell, Phi.	210	Vic Willis, Bos.	225

Pirates win by 27½

Pittsburgh, one National League team that managed to survive the bidding wars and keep most of its players, cruised to a final 103-36 record (an incredible .741 winning percentage) and won its second consecutive pennant by a whopping 27½ games over Brooklyn.

Fred Clarke's Pirates rode the big bat of Honus Wagner and the strong arm of Jack Chesbro to an early lead and never let up in their one-sided pursuit of a championship. Wagner batted .329 and led the league in runs scored (105) and runs batted in (91) while Chesbro compiled a 28-6 record and league-best .824 winning percentage. Pirates center fielder Ginger Beaumont batted a league-leading .357.

Connie Mack's Philadelphia Athletics managed only 83 victories, but that was enough to insure a final five-game lead over St. Louis in the American League. The A's boasted the 1-2 pitching punch of lefthanders Rube Waddell and Eddie Plank, both 20-game winners.

Lefthander Rube Waddell won 23 games for the Philadelphia Athletics.

Honus Wagner, N.L.-champion Pittsburgh's hit man.

★1903★

JANUARY - DECEMBER

The peace treaty

Peace talks between the rival American and National leagues opened in January and Ban Johnson quickly demonstrated just how powerful he has become. Backed by such strong owners as Charles Comiskey (Chicago) and Connie Mack (Philadelphia), the A.L. president controlled the proceedings and came away with every important concession.

First, Johnson squelched the National League's idea of a merger arrangement. Then he demanded and received: recognition of the A.L. as a major league, respect from N.L. owners for the reserve clause in A.L. player contracts, permission to keep the players pirated from the National League, and the right to place a franchise in New York

Giants Owner John T. Brush and Manager John McGraw protested the final point, but N.L. officials reluctantly agreed to everything. Johnson's only concession was a promise not to put an A.L. team in Pittsburgh.

The result was a National Agreement that brought the rival factions under one administrative arm and ensured peaceful coexistence. A three-man national commission (Johnson, Cincinnati Owner Garry Herrmann and N.L. President Harry Pulliam) was formed to rule on all disputes.

SEASON LEADERS

	American League		National League	
Avg.	Nap Lajoie, Cle.	.355	Honus Wagner, Pit.	.355
HR	Buck Freeman, Bos.	13	Jimmy Sheckard, Bkn.	9
RBI	Buck Freeman, Bos.	104	Sam Mertes, N.Y.	104
SB	Harry Bay, Cle.	46	Frank Chance, Chi.	67
			Jimmy Sheckard, Bkn.	67
W-L Pct.	Cy Young, Bos.	28-9, .757	Sam Leever, Pit. 25-7, .781	
ERA	Earl Moore, Cle.	1.77	Sam Leever, Pit.	2.06
SO	Rube Waddell, Phi.	302	Christy Mathewson, N.Y.	267

CAUGHT ON THE FLY

APRIL

The New York Highlanders, a new A.L. entry, played their first home game before 16,000 fans, beating Washington, 6-2.

AUGUST

New York Giants iron man Joe McGinnity recorded victories in both ends of a doubleheader against Philadelphia, the third time in the month he accomplished the feat.

Twelve persons were killed and more than 250 injured when an overhang atop the left-field bleachers at Philadelphia's Baker Bowl collapsed during a game.

SEPTEMBER

Veteran Philadelphia righthander Chick Fraser fired a no-hitter against the Chicago Cubs and the Phillies recorded a 10-0 victory.

WORLD SERIES REPORT

RED SOX PULL SHOCKER

Pittsburgh Owner Barney Dreyfuss and Boston Owner Henry Killilea punctuated baseball's recently signed National Agreement when they officially buried the hatchet and agreed to stage a "world championship" postseason playoff between the pennant-winning teams of the rival National and American leagues. The Red Sox used that stage to bury a different kind of hatchet, with fiendish delight, into the notion of National League superiority.

This surprising championship duel, ending almost three years of N.L.-A.L. warfare, figured to be a mismatch. The Pirates, powerful, experienced and sure of victory, had won 91 times en route to their third straight N.L. pennant. The Red Sox, also 91-game winners and 14½-length victors in the A.L., relied heavily on the strong right arms of Bill Dinneen and 36-year-old Cy Young.

The best-of-nine series opened true to form October 1 with Pittsburgh workhorse Deacon Phillippe pitching a six-hitter, right fielder Jimmy Sebring hitting an historic home run and the Pirates prevailing, 7-3, over Young and the Red Sox at Boston. After the Red Sox had evened the count on Dinneen's three-hit, 3-0 shutout the next day, Phillippe pitched the Pirates to 4-2 and 5-4 victories and a commanding three games to one lead. Phillippe's second series win came October 3 at Boston, and No. 3 came three days later at Pittsburgh. But the rest of the fall classic belonged to the Red Sox.

Young pitched Boston to 11-2 and 7-3 victories in Games 5 and 7 and Dinneen went the distance in 6-3 and 3-0 Red Sox wins in Games 6 and 8.

The two pitchers combined to pitch 69 of 71 innings, recorded all five Boston victories and compiled 1.59 (Young) and 2.06 (Dinneen) earned-run averages. Just as heroic, however, was the performance of Phillippe, who pitched five complete games and worked an incredible 44 innings.

Sebring, who hit Pittsburgh's only home run, led all Series regulars with a .367 average, but Pirate shortstop Honus Wagner, the N.L. batting champion at .355, was held to six hits and a .222 mark. Center fielder Chick Stahl led Boston with a .303 average while left fielder Patsy Dougherty belted two Game 2 homers and drove in five runs in baseball's first World Series — a major league shocker.

Veteran Cy Young won two games for Boston in baseball's first "World Series."

Game 1	Pittsburgh	7	Boston	3
Game 2	Boston	3	Pittsburgh	0
Game 3	Pittsburgh	4	Boston	2
Game 4	Pittsburgh	5	Boston	4
Game 5	Boston	11	Pittsburgh	2
Game 6	Boston	6	Pittsburgh	3
Game 7	Boston	7	Pittsburgh	3
Game 8	Boston	3	Pittsburgh	0

★ 1904 ★

Sox get 'Brushoff'

New York Giants Owner John T. Brush and the team's Manager John McGraw, chastising the American League as a "minor" circuit and its pennant winner as unworthy to step on the same field with the National League-champion Giants, flatly rejected the challenge of the Boston Red Sox to a second "World Series."

Boston, which shocked Pittsburgh last year in the first post-season confrontation between the two rival leagues, issued the challenge after winning its second straight pennant. But the Giants, 106-game winners in the N.L., would have none of it.

"Why should we play the upstarts?" asked an indignant McGraw. "When we won the National League pennant, we became champions of the only real major league."

Brush was equally defiant, asserting there was no reason why "the dignity of the pennant of the National League" should be "cheapened" by playing the best club of a "minor league."

The rejection reflects the intense dislike Brush holds for A.L. President Ban Johnson and the similar bad blood that exists between Johnson and McGraw. The McGraw-Johnson feud dates back to 1902 when McGraw jumped the A.L. ship for a job with the Giants.

Baseball's iron men

You can look at the American League pennant race two ways. Theory 1: the New York Highlanders finished 1½ games behind Boston because of the heroic workmanship of strong-armed pitcher Jack Chesbro. Theory 2: the Highlanders finished 1½ games behind Boston because of Chesbro's final-day wild pitch.

Theory 1 works best because Happy Jack was nothing short of sensational in compiling a 41-12 record and 1.82 earned-run average while pitching in 55 games and logging 454⅔ innings. He also pitched six shutouts and completed 48 of his 51 starts.

But Chesbro's performance was forever marred on the final day of the season when the right-hander uncorked a ninth-inning wild pitch that allowed Boston to break a 2-2 tie and score the pennant-winning run in the first game of a doubleheader at New York's Hilltop Park. A victory in that game and another in the nightcap would have given the Highlanders a pennant.

Chesbro was not the only New York iron man in 1904. Right-handers Joe McGinnity and Christy Mathewson combined for 64 percent of the Giants' 106 league-leading wins, McGinnity finishing 35-8 and Mathewson 33-12. McGinnity logged 408 innings, pitched nine shutouts and fashioned a 1.61 ERA while Matty pitched 367⅔ innings with a 2.03 ERA.

CAUGHT ON THE FLY

APRIL
Brooklyn, circumventing Sunday Blue Laws by not charging admission while making purchase of a program mandatory, played its first-ever Sunday home game, beating the Boston Braves, 9-1.

JULY
The Philadelphia Phillies' 6-5 victory snapped New York's 18-game winning streak, but the Giants still topped the N.L. with a commanding 53-18 record.

AUGUST
Boston lefthander Jesse Tannehill's best effort of the season: A 6-0 no-hit victory over the Chicago White Sox.

OCTOBER
St. Louis Cardinals pitcher Jack Taylor set a major league record with 39 consecutive complete games and Boston's Bill Dinneen set an A.L. mark with 37.

Cy Young is perfect

Boston's Cy Young, a veteran of 14 major league seasons, reached perfection May 5 when he pitched the first perfect game of the century, retiring all 27 Philadelphia Athletics in a 3-0 victory at Boston.

The 37-year-old righthander struck out eight batters and allowed only six balls to be hit out of the infield. He was in control all the way and no Philadelphia player came close to getting a hit. The first-place Red Sox collected 10 themselves but managed only a single run in the sixth and two more in the seventh off A's starter Rube Waddell.

Young's perfecto was the first in major league history from the 60-foot, 6-inch pitching distance. Two previous perfect games were recorded in 1880 when pitchers worked 45 feet from the batter.

SEASON LEADERS

	American League			National League	
Avg.	Nap Lajoie, Cle.	.381		Honus Wagner, Pit.	.349
HR	Harry Davis, Phi.	10		Harry Lumley, Bkn.	9
RBI	Nap Lajoie, Cle.	102		Bill Dahlen, N.Y.	80
SB	Harry Bay, Cle.	42		Honus Wagner, Pit.	53
	Elmer Flick, Cle.	42			
W-L Pct.	Jack Chesbro, N.Y.	41-12, .774		Joe McGinnity, N.Y.	35-8, .814
ERA	Addie Joss, Cle.	1.59		Joe McGinnity, N.Y.	1.61
SO	Rube Waddell, Phi.	349		Christy Mathewson, N.Y.	212

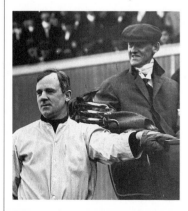

Giants Owner John T. Brush (in carriage) and Manager John McGraw (standing) refused to meet A.L. champion Boston in a second World Series.

New York iron man Joe McGinnity: 408 innings and 35 victories.

Brush relents, helps set up Series rules

Apparently trying to mend fences after torpedoing a 1904 world championship series between his New York Giants and the Boston Red Sox, John T. Brush did an abrupt about-face and played a major role in formulating the rules that would govern an annual, mandatory World Series between the champions of the American and National leagues.

The John T. Brush Rules, under the umbrella of the National Commission, established the World Series as a best-of-seven classic and set up a revenue-sharing formula for the teams involved. Assuming a seven-game Series, each team will act as host three times with the National Commission to decide the site of Game 7. Two umpires, one from each league, will work the contests.

SEASON LEADERS

	American League		National League	
Avg.	Elmer Flick, Cle.	.306	Cy Seymour, Cin.	.377
HR	Harry Davis, Phi.	8	Fred Odwell, Cin.	9
RBI	Harry Davis, Phi.	83	Cy Seymour, Cin.	121
SB	Daniel Hoffman, Phi.	46	Art Devlin, N.Y.	59
			Bill Maloney, Chi.	59
W-L Pct.	Andy Coakley, Phi. 20-7, .741		Christy Mathewson, N.Y. 31-8, .795	
ERA	Rube Waddell, Phi.	1.48	Christy Mathewson, N.Y.	1.27
SO	Rube Waddell, Phi.	287	Christy Mathewson, N.Y.	206

CAUGHT ON THE FLY

JUNE

Christy Mathewson was almost perfect — two batters reached on errors — as he pitched his second no-hitter in a classic duel with Chicago's Mordecai (Three Finger) Brown, which New York won, 1-0.

JULY

No-hitter: Journeyman righthander Weldon Henley pitched the Philadelphia Athletics to a 6-0 victory over the St. Louis Browns.

AUGUST

Detroit's Ty Cobb collected a double off New York's Jack Chesbro in his major league debut as the Tigers beat the Highlanders, 5-3.

SEPTEMBER

Two more no-hitters: Chicago's Frank Smith stopped Detroit, 15-0, and Boston's Bill Dinneen beat Chicago, 2-0.

THE SHUTOUT CLASSIC

The New York Giants, a year after refusing the challenge of American League-champion Boston to play a second "World Series," were willing participants in the formalized 1905 fall classic and showed why they were 105-game winners during the regular season. Pitching, pitching and more pitching.

With the sensational Christy Mathewson leading the charge, the Giants captured the best-of-seven postseason battle against Connie Mack's Philadelphia Athletics in five games — all shutouts. Mathewson blanked the A's three times over a six-day span, allowing only 14 hits while walking one and striking out 18. Joe McGinnity pitched a 1-0 Game 4 shutout and Philadelphia righthander Chief Bender fired a four-hit, 3-0 shutout in Game 2.

Giants Manager John McGraw used only three pitchers, with Red Ames, a 22-game regular-season winner, working one scoreless inning. McGinnity surrendered three unearned runs in Game 2 and the Giants finished the Series with a 0.00 earned-run average. Philadelphia pitchers Andy Coakley, Eddie Plank and Bender allowed only four earned runs and finished with a combined 0.84 ERA, but that sterling effort was not good enough.

Mathewson, New York's fabled Big Six, won the October 9 opener in Philadelphia, 3-0, and then followed with a 9-0 Game 3 shutout after two days of rest and a 2-0 Game 5 clincher after one day off.

Philadelphia's Chief Bender earned the Athletics' only World Series win with a Game 2 shutout.

The 1905 season belonged to Giants great Christy Mathewson, who capped his 31-win year with three World Series shutouts.

Game 1	New York	3	Philadelphia	0
Game 2	Philadelphia	3	New York	0
Game 3	New York	9	Philadelphia	0
Game 4	New York	1	Philadelphia	0
Game 5	New York	2	Philadelphia	0

THE WORLD SERIES

The Classic of Classics

The World Series approaches its 90th birthday in 1993 as a showcase for modern technology and a window to a not-so-high-tech past. Baseball's technology stands in stark contrast to humble roots that trace all the way back to the turn of the century, a "stone age" era when hungry athletes played the game with frenzied abandon.

What is the World Series? It is the First Lady of American championship events, a revered rite of autumn, the classic of the classics. It is the grand finale to yet another wonderful summer of baseball.

It is Christy Mathewson's three shutouts, Grover Cleveland Alexander striking out Tony Lazzeri, Babe Ruth's called shot, Mickey Owen's passed ball, Cookie Lavagetto's no-hit-ruining double. It is Billy Martin's shoetop save, Don Larsen's perfect game, Sandy Amoros' perfect catch, Bill Mazeroski's home run. It is Bob Gibson's strikeout binge, Carlton Fisk's foul-pole blast, Reggie Jackson's three-homer rampage, Kirk Gibson's one-homer miracle, a San Francisco earthquake.

It is massive state-of-the-art stadiums, huge crowds, exploding scoreboards, instant replay screens, millions of television viewers, artificial surfaces, top-line equipment, six-man umpire crews and hordes of media representatives.

The World Series approaches its 90th birthday in 1993 as a showcase for modern technology and a window to a not-so-high-tech past. Baseball's technology stands in stark contrast to humble roots that trace all the way back to the turn of the century, a "stone age" era when hungry athletes played the game with frenzied abandon.

The turn-of-the-century player was tough, poor, uneducated and combative, always ready to settle disputes with his fists. He was most likely the product of an agrarian society that was trying to make the transition from horse-drawn carriage to automobile while suffering the early growing pains of urbanization and industrialization. Meager pay, rowdyism and a reputation as an undignified pursuit made the game unattractive to the gentility that baseball officials were hoping to attract.

Players were generally considered foul-mouthed bums who were too lazy to work for a living. Alcoholism often resulted from a difficult lifestyle that sometimes included criminal activity and violence. Daughters were prohibited from contact with these unsavory characters and some of the finer hotels issued strict bans against baseball teams.

The players' tough, spikes-high style of play naturally attracted fans of the same ilk. Free-for-alls on the field were an open invitation to jump out of the stands and enter the fray. The situation was complicated by the sale of hard liquor at most parks and umpires (two worked each game) who were as angry and pugilistic as the players they were trying to control.

This is not to say that baseball was without redeeming social value. Not all players fit the tough-guy mold and some, like Mathewson, even had college educations. The game's leaders, particularly American League President Ban Johnson, were continually increasing discipline in an effort to raise the image of their sport.

The game itself was suffering growing pains. Johnson had established his American League as a new major circuit in 1901 and declared war on the 26-year-old National League with a series of player raids and territorial battles that lasted for two difficult years. The leagues finally signed a peace treaty in early 1903 and agreed to coexist under a three-man National Commission that decided policy and devised the rules under which the game was played. Much of that policy and many of those rules were understandably geared toward helping the pocketbooks of the men who paid the bills.

The "Dead Ball" era was a result of that approach. Baseballs were expensive at $1 apiece and tightfisted owners kept them in play, no matter what. Balls fouled into the stands were retrieved by ushers willing to use strong-arm tactics if necessary. When a ball was hit completely out of a stadium, it sometimes was chased down and returned to play.

By the third or fourth inning, a new baseball might resemble a brown, rotting apple. It was spit upon, cut, gouged, darkened with tobacco juice or mutilated by any other method a pitcher believed might give him an edge.

Some hurlers made the ball heavy by putting it in an icebox overnight. To complicate matters, the balls had a rubber center that made them much less resilient than today's cork-centered variety.

"When I was batting, they used the emery ball and a lot of other freak pitches," said Hall of Fame Pittsburgh shortstop Honus Wagner, a turn-of-the-century superstar. "And they never threw out a ball as long as it would hold together. That gave the pitcher a big advantage."

With the odds stacked against them, hitters were left to their own creative devices. It naturally followed that they would disdain power and develop bat control, choking up and punching or slashing the ball to all fields. They also learned to bunt and run the bases aggressively. Players like Wagner, Ty Cobb and Nap Lajoie turned this style of play into an artform.

Home runs most often were inside-the-park drives that got past shallow-playing outfielders. Pittsburgh's Tommy Leach led

Cy Young (left) and Bill Dinneen (right) combined to pitch 69 of 70 innings while winning all five games for Boston, the champion of baseball's first World Series.

Pittsburgh's Deacon Phillippe pitched 44 innings and won three times in the first World Series, but it wasn't enough.

the N.L. in 1902 with six. The leader for each of the next three seasons had nine. Would-be power hitters were further stymied by stadiums with extremely deep outfields.

Fielders played with tiny gloves and were forced to throw slick, lopsided balls. Infielders often complemented their normal duties with sneaky strategy, such as tripping an opposing runner when the umpire wasn't looking or grabbing his belt to slow him down. Nothing was sacred when it could mean the difference between winning or losing.

It was into such conditions that the World Series was born. It was the product of two ambitious owners, Pittsburgh's Barney Dreyfuss and Boston's Henry Killilea, who agreed to have their pennant-bound teams meet in a best-of-nine world champ-ionship playoff at the end of the 1903 campaign, the first

under the new peace agreement.

The N.L.'s Pirates, featuring Wagner, Leach and workhorse pitcher Deacon Phillippe, were heavily favored to defeat the upstart Red Sox, who were anchored by Chick Stahl and pitchers Cy Young and Bill Dinneen. Bets were openly made and money exchanged hands in Boston hotels before the Series opened.

It caught everybody by surprise when 16,242 fans showed up for the first game at Boston's Huntington Avenue Grounds. Nobody had anticipated such interest and since the stadium's wooden grandstand seated only 9,000, the overflow crowd was positioned in roped-off areas along the sidelines and around the outfield.

The series, as expected, was decided by pitching, and the Boston underdogs had more than Pittsburgh. Phillippe was phenom-enal, working 44 innings and recording three victories.

But he tired at the end and did not get any help from his teammates. Dinneen and the 36-year-old Young combined to pitch 69 of the 71 innings logged by Boston pitchers and recorded all five victories. Four of the wins came consecutively after the Pirates had jumped to a three games to one advantage.

That first modern World Series was chronicled by a handful of writers who attended the games while hordes of interested fans crowded around the newspaper offices in both cities to get inning-by-inning updates. The interest was beyond everybody's expectations and Boston basked in the glow of victory.

But that interest was not enough to insure a followup in 1904. That's because New York Owner John T. Brush and Manager John McGraw, still feuding with A.L. President Johnson, refused to let their N.L.-champion Giants meet the winner (Boston again) of a

"minor league" in a postseason series. But Brush, reacting to severe criticism, changed his tune in 1905 and helped draw up the rules that would govern future "World Series."

When Brush's Giants defeated the Philadelphia Athletics in the all-shutout Series in 1905, the fall classic was on its way to becoming an enduring American institution. The classic of all classics.

The Pirates, who played in baseball's first World Series in 1903, were led by 'Dead Ball' era stars (left to right) Honus Wagner, Tommy Leach and Fred Clarke.

WORLD SERIES REPORT

THE 'HITLESS WONDERS'

The Chicago White Sox, the American League's "Hitless Wonders," finished off their shocking six-game World Series upset of the cross-town Cubs October 14 when they posted an 8-3 victory at South Side Park and burst the West Siders' aura of invincibility.

The Cubs, winners of a record 116 games, were prohibitive favorites to walk all over the White Sox in baseball's first one-city World Series. The Sox had scrambled to a three-game A.L. edge over the New York Highlanders with a team that posted only a .228 batting average and their lineup appeared to be easy pickings for an excellent Cubs pitching staff that featured Mordecai (Three

Finger) Brown, Jack Pfiester, Ed Reulbach and Orval Overall.

But it was the White Sox's staff that ruled in this Series. With Ed Walsh winning twice and Nick Altrock and Doc White once apiece, the Sox posted a 1.67 earned-run average and held the hard-hitting Cubs to a .196 average. The White Sox managed only a .198 mark, but got enough offense from George Rohe, Jiggs Donahue, Frank Isbell and George Davis to make the difference.

After the teams had fought to a 2-2 four-game standoff, the Sox took control with 8-6 and 8-3 victories, White pitching a seven-hitter in the Series clincher.

Chicago lefty Doc White.

Chicago White Sox ace Ed Walsh helped deflate the powerful Cubs with a pair of World Series victories.

Game 1	White Sox	2	Cubs	1
Game 2	Cubs	7	White Sox	1
Game 3	White Sox	3	Cubs	0
Game 4	Cubs	1	White Sox	0
Game 5	White Sox	8	Cubs	6
Game 6	White Sox	8	Cubs	3

A's capture marathon

Philadelphia struck for three runs in the top of the 24th inning and Jack Coombs set down the Boston Red Sox in the bottom of the frame to give the Athletics a 4-1 victory September 1 in the longest game in major league history.

With darkness closing in, 18,000 Boston fans watched the A's erupt for three runs after 20 scoreless innings. Run-scoring triples by Socks Seybold and Danny Murphy were the key two-out hits that spoiled an outstanding pitching performance by Bos-

ton righthander Joe Harris, who went the distance in the four-hour, 47-minute marathon.

Harris, who walked two, struck out 14 and allowed 16 hits, was touched for a single run in the third inning and then shut down the Athletics until the 24th. Coombs, who walked six, struck out 18 and allowed 15 hits, was touched for a solo run in the sixth. Both pitchers worked out of numerous jams.

Three previous major league games had lasted 20 innings.

SEASON LEADERS

	American League			National League	
Avg.	George Stone, St.L.	.358		Honus Wagner, Pit.	.339
HR	Harry Davis, Phi.	12		Tim Jordan, Bkn.	12
RBI	Harry Davis, Phi.	96		Jim Nealon, Pit.	83
SB	John Anderson, Wash.	39		Frank Chance, Chi.	57
	Elmer Flick, Cle.	39			
W-L Pct.	Eddie Plank, Phi.	19-6, .760		Ed Reulbach, Chi.	19-4, .826
ERA	Doc White, Chi.	1.52		Mordecai Brown, Chi.	1.04
SO	Rube Waddell, Phi.	196		Fred Beebe, Chi.-St.L.	171

CAUGHT ON THE FLY

MAY/JULY
Two no-hitters: Philadelphia's Johnny Lush baffled Brooklyn, striking out 11 in a 1-0 Phillies victory, and Dodgers righthander Mal Eason downed St. Louis, 2-0.

JUNE
Newcomers at the Polo Grounds ticket windows: Women and new ticket-selling machines.

OCTOBER
The Chicago Cubs finished the season with an amazing team earned-run average of 1.76.

Boston's massacre

While Chicago's White Sox and Cubs were wheeling their way to pennants and a one-city World Series date, the two Boston teams were heading in a different direction. The Red Sox, American League champions in 1903 and '04, finished a dismal campaign in last place with a 49-105 record while the Beaneaters settled at the bottom of the National League with a 49-102 mark.

When the Red Sox defeated Chicago, 3-0, May 25 on Jesse

Tannehill's two-hitter, they ended an A.L.-record 20-game losing streak that tied for third on the all-time list. Cleveland dropped 24 straight games in 1899, Pittsburgh lost 23 in 1890 and Louisville fell 20 straight times in 1894. Amazingly, the Red Sox lost 19 of their 20 at home.

The Beaneaters almost matched the Red Sox, but a 6-3, June 9 victory over St. Louis ended their losing streak at 19, fifth on the all-time list.

Baseball's ugly side

The popularity of baseball is on the rise, but the game's rowdy element presents a serious obstacle to the sport's general acceptance as the National Pastime.

When unruly fans stormed the field in the ninth inning of the Giants' April 11 opener against Philadelphia at the Polo Grounds, umpire Bill Klem awarded a forfeit victory to the Phillies. Fans standing in the roped-off outfield section had pelted players with snowballs the entire game and the Phillies' 3-0 lead was enough to trigger their late-game outburst.

But that was merely a prelude to a full-scale riot that occurred May 21 at the Polo Grounds. When the Chicago Cubs took over first place from the Giants with a 3-2 victory, more than 10,000 fans stormed on to the field and began throwing anything within grasp at umpires Hank O'Day and Bob Emslie. Police rushed to their aid and players formed a circle around the arbiters as they edged their way toward the clubhouse.

But it was not until a Pinkerton man fired a gunshot into the air that the crowd dispersed enough to let the umpires through. It was something of a miracle that nobody was seriously injured.

Other ugly incidents: American League umpire Billy Evans needed a police escort after Tigers Manager Hughie Jennings incited the crowd to a riotous situation in Detroit; Chicago Cubs Manager Frank Chance, bombarded by empty bottles in Brooklyn, was suspended indefinitely after throwing two of them back into the stands and getting mobbed by angry fans; Evans was felled by a bottle during a Browns-Tigers game in St. Louis and had to be carried from the field and hospitalized, and on-field and in-stands fights were commonplace.

Until baseball can control these kinds of incidents, the game's reputation will continue to suffer.

SEASON LEADERS

	American League		National League	
Avg.	Ty Cobb, Det.	.350	Honus Wagner, Pit.	.350
HR	Harry Davis, Phi.	8	Dave Brain, Bos.	10
RBI	Ty Cobb, Det.	116	Sherry Magee, Phi.	85
SB	Ty Cobb, Det.	49	Honus Wagner, Pit.	61
W-L Pct.	Bill Donovan, Det. 25-4, .862		Ed Reulbach, Chi. 17-4, .810	
ERA	Ed Walsh, Chi.	1.60	Jack Pfiester, Chi.	1.15
SO	Rube Waddell, Phi.	232	Christy Mathewson, N.Y.	178

CAUGHT ON THE FLY

APRIL
New York Giants catcher Roger Bresnahan introduced his newest innovation: wooden shin guards to protect his legs from pitches in the dirt.

MAY
No-hitter alert: Boston's Frank Pfeffer overpowered the Cincinnati Reds, 6-0, in a game at Boston.

CUBS TAME TIGERS

Mordecai (Three Finger) Brown pitched a seven-hitter and Harry Steinfeldt collected three hits and drove in a run to lead the Chicago Cubs to a 2-0 victory over Detroit and their first World Series championship.

The October 12 win at Detroit was the powerful Cubs' fourth straight and provided a fitting conclusion to their 107-victory regular season. But the most important World Series game for the National League champions might have been the one they did not win.

The Tigers were on the verge of taking Game 1 in Chicago when a strange twist of fate worked in the Cubs' favor. Chicago, trailing 3-2 in the bottom of the ninth inning, had runners on first and third with two out and light-hitting pinch-hitter Del Howard facing 25-game winner Bill Donovan. Howard was overmatched and Donovan struck him out. End of game.

Wrong. Detroit catcher Charlie Schmidt failed to catch the ball and Howard reached first safely as Steinfeldt scored the tying run. The game remained tied through three extra innings and was finally called because of darkness.

The Tigers never recovered from that turnaround and the Cubs, atoning for their 1906 Series upset loss to the cross-town White Sox, rolled to 3-1, 5-1, 6-1 and 2-0 victories. Pitchers Brown, Ed Reulbach, Orval Overall and Jack Pfiester combined for a 0.75 earned-run average and Steinfeldt batted a lofty .471. Jimmy Slagle drove in four runs for the winners.

Chicago Cubs righthander Ed Reulbach.

Chicago's biggest World Series bat was wielded by third baseman Harry Steinfeldt.

Game 1	Detroit	3	Chicago	3
Game 2	Chicago	3	Detroit	1
Game 3	Chicago	5	Detroit	1
Game 4	Chicago	6	Detroit	1
Game 5	Chicago	2	Detroit	0

Joss has perfect day

Cleveland righthander Addie Joss joined Cy Young as the only modern-era pitchers to throw perfect games as he set down all 27 Chicago batters he faced October 2 in a 1-0 victory.

Joss struck out three en route to his 24th victory in the Indians' second-to-last game of the season. He lowered his earned-run average to a sparkling 1.16 and outdueled Big Ed Walsh in a great pitching duel.

Walsh, the White Sox's workhorse and 40-game winner, allowed only four hits, struck out 15 and walked one in eight innings. Cleveland's only run was scored in the third when Joe Birmingham singled, stole second, advanced to third on an errant throw and scored when catcher

Ossee Schreckengost committed a passed ball.

Young pitched his perfecto against Philadelphia in 1904.

Cleveland's Addie Joss was perfect in a game against Chicago.

SEASON LEADERS

	American League		National League	
Avg.	Ty Cobb, Det.	.324	Honus Wagner, Pit.	.354
HR	Sam Crawford, Det.	7	Tim Jordan, Bkn.	12
RBI	Ty Cobb, Det.	108	Honus Wagner, Pit.	109
SB	Patsy Dougherty, Chi.	47	Honus Wagner, Pit.	53
W-L Pct.	Ed Walsh, Chi.	40-15, .727	Ed Reulbach, Chi.	24-7, .774
ERA	Addie Joss, Cle.	1.16	Christy Mathewson, N.Y.	1.43
SO	Ed Walsh, Chi.	269	Christy Mathewson, N.Y.	259

CAUGHT ON THE FLY

APRIL

Henry Chadwick, 'The Father of Baseball,' died in Brooklyn at age 85 after a long career as a reporter, commentator, scorer and goodwill promoter of the game.

JUNE

Boston veteran Cy Young recorded his third career no-hitter and became the oldest player ever to turn the trick, beating New York, 8-0, at age 41.

JULY

New York Giants lefty Hooks Wiltse had to go overtime to complete his no-hitter, beating Philadelphia, 1-0, in 10 innings at the Polo Grounds.

MERKLE'S 'BONER'

It's official. The Chicago Cubs are World Series champions for the second straight year, courtesy of a September baserunning blunder by New York's Fred Merkle that cost the Giants a National League pennant. The Cubs' five-game Series triumph over the Detroit Tigers is a culmination of the most heated controversy in baseball history.

With the Cubs and Giants engaged in a torrid pennant race, a September 23 confrontation at New York's Polo Grounds went into the bottom of the ninth inning tied 1-1. With Moose McCormick stationed on third base and Merkle on first with two out, Al Bridwell singled to center for an apparent game-winning hit.

But Merkle, eager to avoid the crush of jubilant fans pouring onto the field, went halfway to second base, turned and headed for the center-field clubhouse. Chicago's Johnny Evers noticed the indiscretion, secured a ball and stepped on second base, appealing to umpire Hank O'Day for the force out. O'Day agreed, negating the run.

But with spectators thronging the field and most of the players already retired to their respective clubhouses, continuation of play was impossible. Confusion reigned, the Giants claiming victory and the Cubs insisting the game had ended in a tie.

Eventually the matter was turned over to the National League officials who ruled in favor of the Cubs. They also determined that in the unlikely event the teams were deadlocked at the end of their 154-game schedules, the game would have to be replayed.

Amazingly, that's exactly what happened. Both the Giants and Cubs finished the regular campaign with 98-55-1 records and squared off October 8 at the Polo Grounds to decide the pennant. With the stadium packed and thousands of fans watching from the bluffs overlooking the field, Mordecai (Three Finger) Brown outdueled Christy Mathewson and Chicago prevailed, 4-2. Cubs shortstop Joe Tinker delivered a key triple in Chicago's four-run third inning.

The Cubs were National League champions and Merkle's boneheaded play would go down in baseball infamy.

Game 1	Chicago	10	Detroit	6
Game 2	Chicago	6	Detroit	1
Game 3	Detroit	8	Chicago	3
Game 4	Chicago	3	Detroit	0
Game 5	Chicago	2	Detroit	0

Fred Merkle's baserunning blunder cost the Giants a pennant.

★1909★

WORLD SERIES REPORT

TIGERS FALL AGAIN

Rookie righthander Babe Adams wrote a happy ending to his post-season script October 16 when he fired a six-hit Game 7 shutout at the Detroit Tigers and gave Pittsburgh its first World Series championship.

Adams' 8-0 victory ended the first seven-game fall classic and provided a fitting conclusion to Pittsburgh's 110-victory regular season. The World Series loss was the third straight for the Tigers.

Adams got the Pirates off to a good start October 8 when he allowed six hits in a 4-1 victory. But the Tigers, sparked by Ty Cobb's steal of home, bounced back for a 7-2 Series-tying win behind the pitching of Bill Donovan. The victory-swapping pattern continued with Pittsburgh recording 8-6 and 8-4 triumphs in Games 3 and 5 and Detroit winning Games 4 and 6, 5-0 and 5-4.

That set up a Game 7 showdown

and Donovan was no match for Adams. Known as Wild Bill, Donovan lived up to his nickname by hitting the game's first batter and walking six in the first two innings.

Leading Pittsburgh's offensive charge was veteran Honus Wagner, who batted .333 while Cobb, Triple Crown winner in the A.L., was held to a .231 Series average.

Pittsburgh's Honus Wagner and Detroit's Ty Cobb.

Game 1	Pittsburgh	4	Detroit	1
Game 2	Detroit	7	Pittsburgh	2
Game 3	Pittsburgh	8	Detroit	6
Game 4	Detroit	5	Pittsburgh	0
Game 5	Pittsburgh	8	Detroit	4
Game 6	Detroit	5	Pittsburgh	4
Game 7	Pittsburgh	8	Detroit	0

SEASON LEADERS

	American League		National League	
Avg.	Ty Cobb, Det.	.377	Honus Wagner, Pit.	.339
HR	Ty Cobb, Det.	9	Red Murray, N.Y.	7
RBI	Ty Cobb, Det.	107	Honus Wagner, Pit.	100
SB	Ty Cobb, Det.	76	Bob Bescher, Cin.	54
W-L Pct.	George Mullin, Det.	29-8, .784	Christy Mathewson, N.Y.	25-6, .806
			Howie Camnitz, Pit.	25-6, .806
ERA	Harry Krause, Phi.	1.39	Christy Mathewson, N.Y.	1.14
SO	Frank Smith, Chi.	177	Orval Overall, Chi.	205

Cobb triples pleasure

Statistically speaking, the 1909 baseball season belonged to young Detroit outfielder Ty Cobb. The 22-year-old Georgia Peach batted .377 with nine home runs and 107 runs batted in, becoming only the second Triple Crown winner of the century.

En route to capturing his third straight American League batting title, Cobb also led the A.L. in runs (116), hits (216), slugging average (.517), total bases (296) and stolen bases (76). Not surprisingly, the Tigers captured their third consecutive pennant in his fourth full major league season.

Cobb follows in the footsteps of Napoleon Lajoie, who won a Triple Crown while playing for Philadelphia in the A.L.'s 1901 debut as a major league. All nine of Cobb's home runs were inside-the-park blasts.

CAUGHT ON THE FLY

FEBRUARY

Boston traded veteran Cy Young to Cleveland and 'Iron Man' Joe McGinnity was released by the New York Giants.

JULY

Detroit's Ed Summers and Washington's Bill Gray dueled for 18 innings in a game that was finally stopped as a 0-0 tie.

N.L. President Harry Pulliam, unable to cope with the stress of his office, shot himself to death with a pistol.

Shibe, Forbes open

Philadelphia's Shibe Park and Pittsburgh's Forbes Field, baseball's first steel-and-concrete super-stadiums, have opened their gates to rave reviews.

Shibe Park, the creation of Athletics Owner Ben Shibe, entertained an April 12 opening-day throng of 30,162 and thousands more were turned away at the gate. The A's, behind Eddie Plank's six-hit pitching, christened their new home with an 8-1 victory over Boston.

The Pirates dedicated their $2

million park on June 30, four months after Owner Barney Dreyfuss had presided over ground-breaking ceremonies. An overflow crowd of 30,338 was disappointed when the Pirates dropped a 3-2 decision to the Chicago Cubs.

Shibe Park has a symmetrical configuration that measures 360 feet down the lines, 393 feet in the power alleys and 420 feet to center. Forbes Field has irregular dimensions of 360 feet to left, 376 to right and 462 to center.

An overflow crowd, dressed to kill, turned out for the first game at Philadelphia's Shibe Park.

The 1910s

As a more mobile America pulled up its agrarian roots and advanced toward a new urban industrial order, enterprising baseball officials watched with growing fascination.

What they saw was a healthier, wealthier society that was interested in expanding its sports and entertainment horizons. The result was an explosion of large steel and concrete stadia that would help fuel the popularity of the game while promoting a regional identity for the teams and their ever-increasing legions of fans.

Philadelphia's Shibe Park and Pittsburgh's Forbes Field were the first new-era ballparks to open their gates in 1909, and by 1916, seven more teams had constructed and unveiled large, attractive and inviting new facilities. The ballpark entrepreneurs were quickly rewarded by the sight of fans streaming through their turnstiles.

They also were rewarded by the sounds of cheers cascading from the stands, coins clanging into their cash boxes and predictions of even happier, more prosperous days in the future. All they had to do was supply the talent and hungry fans would infect others with their contagious baseball fever.

NATIONAL LEAGUE

League Batting Leaders

Average

Year	Player-Team	Avg.
1910	Sherry Magee, Phil.	.331
1911	Honus Wagner, Pit.	.334
1912	Heinie Zimmerman, Chi.	.372
1913	Jake Daubert, Bkn.	.350
1914	Jake Daubert, Bkn.	.329
1915	Larry Doyle, N.Y.	.320
1916	Hal Chase, Cin.	.339
1917	Edd Roush, Cin.	.341
1918	Zack Wheat, Bkn.	.335
1919	Edd Roush, Cin.	.321

Home Runs

Year	Player-Team	HR
1910	Fred Beck, Bos.	10
	Frank Schulte, Chi.	10
1911	Frank Schulte, Chi.	21
1912	Heinie Zimmerman, Chi.	14
1913	Gavvy Cravath, Phil.	19
1914	Gavvy Cravath, Phil.	19
1915	Gavvy Cravath, Phil.	24
1916	Dave Robertson, N.Y.	12
	Cy Williams, Chi.	12
1917	Dave Robertson, N.Y.	12
	Gavvy Cravath, Phil.	12
1918	Gavvy Cravath, Phil.	8
1919	Gavvy Cravath, Phil.	12

RBIs

Year	Player-Team	RBI
1910	Sherry Magee, Phil.	123
1911	Frank Schulte, Chi.	121
1912	Heinie Zimmerman, Chi.	103
1913	Gavvy Cravath, Phil.	128
1914	Sherry Magee, Phil.	103
1915	Gavvy Cravath, Phil.	115
1916	Heinie Zimmerman, Chi.-N.Y.	83
1917	Heinie Zimmerman, N.Y.	102
1918	Sherry Magee, Cin.	76
1919	Hy Myers, Bkn.	73

Most Valuable Players

Selected by Chalmers

Year	Player-Team	Pos.
1911	Frank Schulte, Chi.	OF
1912	Larry Doyle, N.Y.	2B
1913	Jake Daubert, Bkn.	1B
1914	Johnny Evers, Bos.	2B

League Pitching Leaders

Winning Percentage

Year	Pitcher-Team	W-L	Pct.
1910	King Cole, Chi.	20-4	.833
1911	Rube Marquard, N.Y.	24-7	.774
1912	Claude Hendrix, Pit.	24-9	.727
1913	Bert Humphries, Chi.	16-4	.800
1914	Bill James, Bos.	26-7	.788
1915	Grover Alexander, Phil.	31-10	.756
1916	Tom Hughes, Bos.	16-3	.842
1917	Ferdie Schupp, N.Y.	21-7	.750
1918	Claude Hendrix, Chi.	19-7	.731
1919	Dutch Ruether, Cin.	19-6	.760

Earned-Run Average

Year	Pitcher-Team	ERA
1910	George McQuillan, Phil.	1.60
1911	Christy Mathewson, N.Y.	1.99
1912	Jeff Tesreau, N.Y.	1.96
1913	Christy Mathewson, N.Y.	2.06
1914	Bill Doak, St. L.	1.72
1915	Grover Alexander, Phil.	1.22
1916	Grover Alexander, Phil.	1.55
1917	Grover Alexander, Phil.	1.86
1918	Hippo Vaughn, Chi.	1.74
1919	Grover Alexander, Chi.	1.72

Strikeouts

Year	Pitcher-Team	SO
1910	Earl Moore, Phil.	185
1911	Rube Marquard, N.Y.	237
1912	Grover Alexander, Phil.	195
1913	Tom Seaton, Phil.	168
1914	Grover Alexander, Phil.	214
1915	Grover Alexander, Phil.	241
1916	Grover Alexander, Phil.	167
1917	Grover Alexander, Phil.	201
1918	Hippo Vaughn, Chi.	148
1919	Hippo Vaughn, Chi.	141

WORLD SERIES

Year	Winner	Pennant Winner	Games
1910	Philadelphia Athletics	Chicago Cubs	4-1
1911	Philadelphia Athletics	New York Giants	4-2
1912	Boston Red Sox	New York Giants	4-3-1
1913	Philadelphia Athletics	New York Giants	4-1
1914	Boston Braves	Philadelphia Athletics	4-0
1915	Boston Red Sox	Philadelphia Phillies	4-1
1916	Boston Red Sox	Brooklyn Dodgers	4-1
1917	Chicago White Sox	New York Giants	4-2
1918	Boston Red Sox	Chicago Cubs	4-2
1919	Cincinnati Reds	Chicago White Sox	5-3

Chicago Cubs third baseman Heinie Zimmerman.

Final Standings

1910

	W	L	PCT.	GB
Chicago	104	50	.675	--
New York	91	63	.591	13
Pittsburgh	86	67	.562	17.5
Philadelphia	78	75	.510	25.5
Cincinnati	75	79	.487	29
Brooklyn	64	90	.416	40
St. Louis	63	90	.412	40.5
Boston	53	100	.346	50.5

1911

	W	L	Pct.	GB
New York	99	54	.647	--
Chicago	92	62	.597	7.5
Pittsburgh	85	69	.552	14.5
Philadelphia	79	73	.520	19.5
St. Louis	75	74	.503	22
Cincinnati	70	83	.458	29
Brooklyn	64	86	.427	33.5
Boston	44	107	.291	54

1912

	W	L	Pct.	GB
New York	103	48	.682	--
Pittsburgh	93	58	.616	10
Chicago	91	59	.607	11.5
Cincinnati	75	78	.490	29
Philadelphia	73	79	.480	30.5
St. Louis	63	90	.412	41
Brooklyn	58	95	.379	46
Boston	52	101	.340	52

1913

	W	L	Pct.	GB
New York	101	51	.664	--
Philadelphia	88	63	.583	12.5
Chicago	88	65	.575	13.5
Pittsburgh	78	71	.523	21.5
Boston	69	82	.457	31.5
Brooklyn	65	84	.436	34.5
Cincinnati	64	89	.418	37.5
St. Louis	51	99	.340	49

1914

	W	L	Pct.	GB
Boston	94	59	.614	--
New York	84	70	.545	10.5
St. Louis	81	72	.529	13
Chicago	78	76	.506	16.5
Brooklyn	75	79	.487	19.5
Philadelphia	74	80	.481	20.5
Pittsburgh	69	85	.448	25.5
Cincinnati	60	94	.390	34.5

1915

	W	L	Pct.	GB
Philadelphia	90	62	.592	--
Boston	83	69	.546	7
Brooklyn	80	72	.526	10
Chicago	73	80	.477	17.5
Pittsburgh	73	81	.474	18
St. Louis	72	81	.471	18.5
Cincinnati	71	83	.461	20
New York	69	83	.454	21

1916

	W	L	Pct.	GB
Brooklyn	94	60	.610	--
Philadelphia	91	62	.595	2.5
Boston	89	63	.586	4
New York	86	66	.566	7
Chicago	67	86	.438	26.5
Pittsburgh	65	89	.422	29
Cincinnati	60	93	.392	33.5
St. Louis	60	93	.392	33.5

1917

	W	L	Pct.	GB
New York	98	56	.636	--
Philadelphia	87	65	.572	10
St. Louis	82	70	.539	15
Cincinnati	78	76	.506	20
Chicago	74	80	.481	24
Boston	72	81	.471	25.5
Brooklyn	70	81	.464	26.5
Pittsburgh	51	103	.331	47

1918

	W	L	Pct.	GB
Chicago	84	45	.651	--
New York	71	53	.573	10.5
Cincinnati	68	60	.531	15.5
Pittsburgh	65	60	.520	17
Brooklyn	57	69	.452	25.5
Philadelphia	55	68	.447	26
Boston	53	71	.427	28.5
St. Louis	51	78	.395	33

1919

	W	L	Pct.	GB
Cincinnati	96	44	.686	--
New York	87	53	.621	9
Chicago	75	65	.536	21
Pittsburgh	71	68	.511	24.5
Brooklyn	69	71	.493	27
Boston	57	82	.410	38.5
St. Louis	54	83	.394	40.5
Philadelphia	47	90	.343	47.5

Boston's Smoky Joe Wood.

Finding new talent was not a problem. Such stars as Ty Cobb, Walter Johnson, Christy Mathewson, Tris Speaker, Eddie Collins and Joe Jackson already were playing the game with amazing grace and reckless abandon and more help was on the way. The most notable newcomer would make his pitching debut in 1914 with the Boston Red Sox, although the massive impact of George Herman Ruth would not be felt until the next decade.

More immediate impacts were made at the team level, with Connie Mack's Philadelphia Athletics becoming the first three-time World Series champions while winning four American League pennants in five years (1910-14) and the Miracle Braves of Boston capturing the country's imagination with their rags-to-riches comeback story of 1914. Another Boston team, the Red Sox, earned three World Series titles while many Americans in other parts of the world were fighting a different kind of battle.

Overall, this was a decade of discovery and innocence, of transition and survival. While baseball was greedily expanding its horizons and testing how deep the roots of its popularity had grown, it also was adjusting to a new social order and fighting against forces that threatened its very existence. First, the game had to deal with a rival major league. Then World War I threw a serious and depressing shroud over the nation, calling away athletes and drastically reducing its schedule. As the decade came to a close in 1919, rumors of a World Series "fix" were being circulated with alarming concern and a long-running investigation was taking root.

But not even the ominous shadows of a world war or scandal could hide the sports prosperity that lay just around the corner. And when athletes, coaches and fans returned from their war-time duties, the time was right for a new order of commitment. The first "Golden Age of Sports" was at hand.

AMERICAN LEAGUE

League Batting Leaders

Average

Year	Player-Team	Avg.
1910	Ty Cobb, Det.	.385
1911	Ty Cobb, Det.	.420
1912	Ty Cobb, Det.	.410
1913	Ty Cobb, Det.	.390
1914	Ty Cobb, Det.	.368
1915	Ty Cobb, Det.	.369
1916	Tris Speaker, Cle.	.386
1917	Ty Cobb, Det.	.383
1918	Ty Cobb, Det.	.382
1919	Ty Cobb, Det.	.384

Home Runs

Year	Player-Team	HR
1910	Jake Stahl, Bos.	10
1911	Frank Baker, Phil.	11
1912	Frank Baker, Phil.	10
	Tris Speaker, Bos.	10
1913	Frank Baker, Phil.	12
1914	Frank Baker, Phil.	9
1915	Braggo Roth, Chi.-Cle.	7
1916	Wally Pipp, N.Y.	12
1917	Wally Pipp, N.Y.	9
1918	Babe Ruth, Bos.	11
	Tilly Walker, Phil.	11
1919	Babe Ruth, Bos.	29

RBIs

Year	Player-Team	RBI
1910	Sam Crawford, Det.	120
1911	Ty Cobb, Det.	144
1912	Frank Baker, Phil.	133
1913	Frank Baker, Phil.	126
1914	Sam Crawford, Det.	104
1915	Sam Crawford, Det.	112
1916	Del Pratt, St. L.	103
1917	Bobby Veach, Det.	103
1918	Bobby Veach, Det.	78
1919	Babe Ruth, Bos.	114

Most Valuable Players

Selected by Chalmers

Year	Player-Team	Pos.
1911	Ty Cobb, Det.	OF
1912	Tris Speaker, Bos.	OF
1913	Walter Johnson, Wash.	P
1914	Eddie Collins, Phil.	2B

League Pitching Leaders

Winning Percentage

Year	Pitcher-Team	W-L	Pct.
1910	Chief Bender, Phil.	23-5	.821
1911	Chief Bender, Phil.	17-5	.773
1912	Joe Wood, Bos.	34-5	.872
1913	Walter Johnson, Wash.	36-7	.837
1914	Chief Bender, Phil.	17-3	.850
1915	Joe Wood, Bos.	15-5	.750
1916	Ed Cicotte, Chi.	15-7	.682
1917	Reb Russell, Chi.	15-5	.750
1918	Sam Jones, Bos.	16-5	.762
1919	Ed Cicotte, Chi.	29-7	.806

Earned-Run Average

Year	Pitcher-Team	ERA
1910	Ed Walsh, Chi.	1.27
1911	Vean Gregg, Cle.	1.81
1912	Walter Johnson, Wash.	1.39
1913	Walter Johnson, Wash.	1.09
1914	Dutch Leonard, Bos.	1.01
1915	Joe Wood, Bos.	1.49
1916	Babe Ruth, Bos.	1.75
1917	Ed Cicotte, Chi.	1.53
1918	Walter Johnson, Wash.	1.27
1919	Walter Johnson, Wash.	1.49

Strikeouts

Year	Pitcher-Team	SO
1910	Walter Johnson, Wash.	313
1911	Ed Walsh, Chi.	255
1912	Walter Johnson, Wash.	303
1913	Walter Johnson, Wash.	243
1914	Walter Johnson, Wash.	225
1915	Walter Johnson, Wash.	203
1916	Walter Johnson, Wash.	228
1917	Walter Johnson, Wash.	188
1918	Walter Johnson, Wash.	162
1919	Walter Johnson, Wash.	147

Final Standings

1910

	W	L	PCT.	GB
Philadelphia	102	48	.680	--
New York	88	63	.583	14.5
Detroit	86	68	.558	18
Boston	81	72	.529	22.5
Cleveland	71	81	.467	32
Chicago	68	85	.444	35.5
Washington	66	85	.437	36.5
St. Louis	47	107	.305	57

1911

	W	L	PCT.	GB
Philadelphia	101	50	.669	--
Detroit	89	65	.578	13.5
Cleveland	80	73	.523	22
Chicago	77	74	.510	24
Boston	78	75	.510	24
New York	76	76	.500	25.5
Washington	64	90	.416	38.5
St. Louis	45	107	.296	56.5

1912

	W	L	PCT.	GB
Boston	105	47	.691	--
Washington	91	61	.599	14
Philadelphia	90	62	.592	15
Chicago	78	76	.506	28
Cleveland	75	78	.490	30.5
Detroit	69	84	.451	36.5
St. Louis	53	101	.344	53
New York	50	102	.329	55

1913

	W	L	PCT.	GB
Philadelphia	96	57	.627	--
Washington	90	64	.584	6.5
Cleveland	86	66	.566	9.5
Boston	79	71	.527	15.5
Chicago	78	74	.513	17.5
Detroit	66	87	.431	30
New York	57	94	.377	38
St. Louis	57	96	.373	39

1914

	W	L	PCT.	GB
Philadelphia	99	53	.651	--
Boston	91	62	.595	8.5
Washington	81	73	.526	19
Detroit	80	73	.523	19.5
St. Louis	71	82	.464	28.5
Chicago	70	84	.455	30
New York	70	84	.455	30
Cleveland	51	102	.333	48.5

1915

	W	L	PCT.	GB
Boston	101	50	.669	--
Detroit	100	54	.649	2.5
Chicago	93	61	.604	9.5
Washington	85	68	.556	17
New York	69	83	.454	32.5
St. Louis	63	91	.409	39.5
Cleveland	57	95	.375	44.5
Philadelphia	43	109	.283	58.5

1916

	W	L	PCT.	GB
Boston	91	63	.591	--
Chicago	89	65	.578	2
Detroit	87	67	.565	4
New York	80	74	.519	11
St. Louis	79	75	.513	12
Cleveland	77	77	.500	14
Washington	76	77	.497	14.5
Philadelphia	36	117	.235	54.5

1917

	W	L	PCT.	GB
Chicago	100	54	.649	--
Boston	90	62	.592	9
Cleveland	88	66	.571	12
Detroit	78	75	.510	21.5
Washington	74	79	.484	25.5
New York	71	82	.464	28.5
St. Louis	57	97	.370	43
Philadelphia	55	98	.359	44.5

1918

	W	L	PCT.	GB
Boston	75	51	.595	--
Cleveland	73	54	.575	2.5
Washington	72	56	.563	4
New York	60	63	.488	13.5
St. Louis	58	64	.475	15
Chicago	57	67	.460	17
Detroit	55	71	.437	20
Philadelphia	52	76	.406	24

1919

	W	L	PCT.	GB
Chicago	88	52	.629	--
Cleveland	84	55	.604	3.5
New York	80	59	.576	7.5
Detroit	80	60	.571	8
St. Louis	67	72	.482	20.5
Boston	66	71	.482	20.5
Washington	56	84	.400	32
Philadelphia	36	104	.257	52

★ 1910 ★

CAUGHT ON THE FLY

APRIL

President William Howard Taft became the first chief executive to throw out a ceremonial first ball at an Opening Day contest in Washington.

Cleveland's Addie Joss pitched his second career no-hitter, stopping the White Sox, 1-0, at Chicago.

APRIL/JULY

Two new ballparks opened, in Cleveland — League Park — and Chicago — Comiskey Park — but both A.L. teams were beaten.

AUGUST

New York Highlander hurler Tom Hughes was unhittable for 9⅓ innings, but Cleveland broke through in the 11th and walked away with a 5-0 victory at Hilltop Park.

Cobb tops Lajoie

American League President Ban Johnson, furious over the controversy surrounding his circuit's 1910 batting championship, officially declared Detroit's Ty Cobb the winner over Cleveland's Nap Lajoie October 16 and made it perfectly clear he will not tolerate any sideshow conspiracies.

Cobb, batting .383, enjoyed a comfortable lead over Lajoie — .376 — and decided to sit out the Tigers' final game. It was not until the next day that he received word that Lajoie had collected eight hits in as many at-bats during a doubleheader in St. Louis, lifting his final average to .384.

When details of Lajoie's big finale reached Johnson, the A.L. boss hit the roof. In his first at-bat of the day, Lajoie tripled. But in his subsequent seven at-bats, he bunted safely for base hits. St. Louis rookie third baseman Red Corriden had been ordered to play deep by Browns Manager Jack O'Connor, ostensibly to protect the youngster from Lajoie's powerful line drives. It is more likely the Browns helped Lajoie beat out the unpopular Cobb.

Johnson met with the principals, banished O'Connor from baseball and ordered a check of Cobb's official average. He then announced a discrepancy had been found and Cobb's mark, authenticated by the A.L., was .385 — one point above Lajoie.

American League stars Nap Lajoie (Cleveland) and Ty Cobb (Detroit) posing in a Chalmers automobile, given annually to the league batting champions. Their final 1910 averages were so close that Chalmers awarded them both a new car.

WORLD SERIES REPORT

A'S SHUT DOWN CUBS

When Philadelphia lefthander Eddie Plank was forced to sit out the World Series with an arm problem, the Chicago Cubs became heavy favorites to capture their third fall classic in four years. The Cubs had won 104 regular-season games and an incredible 530 over the last five years.

But Athletics Manager Connie Mack had a simple solution. He unleashed righthanders Chief Bender and Jack Coombs on the Chicago hitters and Eddie Collins, Frank Baker and Danny Murphy on Cubs pitchers. With Bender and Coombs pitching every inning and the team hitting a blistering .316, the A's, winners of 102 regular-season games, earned their first championship.

Bender got the A's off to a fast start October 17 in Game 1 when he allowed only three hits in a 4-1 victory. Coombs won the next two games, 9-3 and 12-5, as Philadelphia hitters teed off on Chicago starters Mordecai Brown, Ed Reulbach, Orval Overall and Jack Pfiester. After Chicago rebounded for a 4-3 victory, Coombs closed out the Series with a 7-2 triumph.

Collins (.429) and Baker (.409) were the hottest Philadelphia hitters, but Murphy drove in eight runs.

Philadelphia's Jack Coombs, a three-time World Series winner for the champion Athletics.

Game 1	Philadelphia	4	Chicago	1
Game 2	Philadelphia	9	Chicago	3
Game 3	Philadelphia	12	Chicago	5
Game 4	Chicago	4	Philadelphia	3
Game 5	Philadelphia	7	Chicago	2

Young wins 500th

Baseball's "Grand Old Man," 43-year-old Cy Young, stepped into uncharted territory July 19 when he recorded his 500th victory — a feat that may never be approached.

Young showed traces of old form when he pitched Cleveland to an 11-inning 5-2 victory over the Senators in the second game of a doubleheader at Washington. His four-hitter lifted his career mark to 500-302 — 287 victories as a National Leaguer and 213 in the American League. Kid Nichols and Pud Galvin are tied for second on the all-time win list with 361.

Young, a five-time 30-game winner in his outstanding career, has topped the 20-victory plateau 16 times.

SEASON LEADERS

	American League		National League	
Avg.	Ty Cobb, Det.	.385	Sherry Magee, Phi.	.331
HR	Jake Stahl, Bos.	10	Fred Beck, Bos.	10
			Frank Schulte, Chi.	10
RBI	Sam Crawford, Det.	120	Sherry Magee, Phi.	123
SB	Eddie Collins, Phi.	81	Bob Bescher, Cin.	70
W-L Pct.	Chief Bender, Phi.	23-5, .821	King Cole, Chi.	20-4, .833
ERA	Ed Walsh, Chi.	1.27	George McQuillan, Phi.	1.60
SO	Walter Johnson, Wash.	313	Earl Moore, Phi.	185

★ 1911 ★

WORLD SERIES REPORT

A'S GET REVENGE

Chief Bender pitched a four-hitter and Philadelphia batters broke loose for 13 hits October 26, giving the Athletics a 13-2 victory over the New York Giants and their second consecutive World Series championship.

Connie Mack's forces broke open a 1-1 Game 6 tie with a four-run fourth inning and coasted to their Series-ending victory. It was sweet revenge for Mack, who had watched his team lose to New York in 1905.

Christy Mathewson defeated Bender in a Game 1 pitching duel, 2-1, but dropped 3-2 and 4-2 decisions in Games 3 and 4. Bad weather had delayed Game 4 by six days.

The A's offensive star was third baseman Frank Baker, who batted .375 and hit a pair of timely home runs. His two-run blast off Rube Marquard in the sixth inning of Game 2 gave Philadelphia a 3-1 victory and his solo ninth-inning homer the next day off Mathewson tied the score 1-1. The A's prevailed in 11 innings.

The Athletics, who used only two pitchers while beating Chicago in the 1910 Series, needed only three this time. Bender, who won twice, combined with Jack Coombs and Eddie Plank to hold six New York regulars under .190. The Giants, who set a modern league record with 347 stolen bases, swiped only four against the A's.

Frank (Home Run) Baker connected twice in Philadelphia's six-game World Series win over the New York Giants.

Game 1	New York	2	Philadelphia	1
Game 2	Philadelphia	3	New York	1
Game 3	Philadelphia	3	New York	2
Game 4	Philadelphia	4	New York	2
Game 5	New York	4	Philadelphia	3
Game 6	Philadelphia	13	New York	2

SEASON LEADERS

	American League			National League	
Avg.	Ty Cobb, Det.	.420		Honus Wagner, Pit.	.334
HR	Frank Baker, Phi.	11		Frank Schulte, Chi.	21
RBI	Ty Cobb, Det.	144		Frank Schulte, Chi.	121
SB	Ty Cobb, Det.	83		Bob Bescher, Cin.	81
W-L Pct.	Chief Bender, Phi.	17-5, .773		Rube Marquard, N.Y.	24-7, .774
ERA	Vean Gregg, Cle.	1.81		Christy Mathewson, N.Y.	1.99
SO	Ed Walsh, Chi.	255		Rube Marquard, N.Y.	237

CAUGHT ON THE FLY

JUNE

The Detroit Tigers staged the biggest comeback in major league history, roaring back from a 13-1 deficit after 5½ innings to defeat the Chicago White Sox, 16-15.

Two months after a fire destroyed their stadium, the New York Giants opened their new horseshoe-shaped Polo Grounds ballpark.

Giants players inspect what is left of the fire-ravaged Polo Grounds.

AUGUST

Another no-hitter: Chicago's Big Ed Walsh was only one walk away from perfection in his 5-0 victory over Boston at Comiskey Park.

SEPTEMBER

Cy Young, released earlier in the year by Cleveland and signed by the Boston Braves, recorded his 511th and final big-league victory with a 1-0 shutout of Pittsburgh.

Baseball picks MVPs

Detroit's Ty Cobb and the Chicago Cubs' Frank (Wildfire) Schulte were named baseball's first Most Valuable Player award winners October 11 and were presented new cars by automaker Hugh Chalmers.

The American League voting, handled by a committee of baseball writers, was easy. Cobb fell one home run short in his bid for a second Triple Crown, but he topped the charts with a phenomenal .420 batting average and led in runs batted in (144), runs scored (147), hits (248), doubles (47), triples (24), total bases (367), slugging average (.621) and steals (83). Chicago righthander Ed Walsh (27-18), the man who stopped Cobb's A.L.-record 40-game hitting streak in July, finished second in the voting.

National League voters selected Schulte over New York ace Christy Mathewson (26-13). The Chicago outfielder batted .300 and led the league with 21 homers and 121 RBIs, becoming the first major leaguer to collect more than 20 doubles (30), triples (21) and homers in the same season.

TY COBB

Winning at all costs

"He was the most violent, successful, thoroughly maladjusted personality ever to pass across American sports . . . "

Ty Cobb biographer Al Stump

History reverently chronicles the baseball deeds of Ty Cobb and remembers him affectionately as the "Georgia Peach." But to his contemporaries, the former Detroit star was anything but peachy. He was a raging wildcat and the master of cutthroat baseball, a mean, nasty, intimidating, antagonistic and devilish practitioner of his chosen profession.

It followed, naturally, that Cobb would reign for 24 seasons as the most hated man in baseball. But those same contemporaries, as well as the writers who watched him carve out an incredible career ledger filled with mind-boggling numbers, also admitted a grudging admiration for the man who seemed obsessed in his mission to set standards by which future generations could judge the sport.

"The greatest ballplayer was Ty Cobb — though none of us was very crazy about him when he played," said former Boston Red Sox outfield star Duffy Lewis in 1950. "However, you had to admire him for his ability. . . . There didn't seem to be anything he couldn't do."

A quick glance at Cobb's record reveals that this was no ordinary demon. He played from 1905 to 1928 with the Tigers and Philadelphia Athletics, recording an amazing .367 career average (the highest in history) and setting an incredible 90 all-time records. Among those marks were stolen bases (892), hits (4,191), runs scored (2,245) and games played (3,033). He also won the American League batting title a record 12 times, nine in succession, and topped the sacred .400 plateau three times, including a whopping .420 mark in 1911. Cobb retired at age 42 following his second season with Connie Mack's A's, after batting .323.

That's just the tip of the man's offensive iceberg, but the legacy of Tyrus Raymond Cobb goes beyond mere numbers. His story is one of an indomitable will to succeed, an obsession with winning. He approached every inning of every game as if it was a war that had to be won at all costs, and he attacked the opposition with the hell-bent ferocity of a wounded tiger backed into a corner. He showed no mercy and asked for none in return, and he ran the basepaths with intimidating abandon, often leaving a bloody trail of success. Cobb did not aim to maim, but

Cobb, playing his final season with Philadelphia, poses with New York Yankee great Babe Ruth.

woe to the man who dared block his path. The spikes were as sharp as his tongue and nobody was spared in the heat of battle.

Herschel Cobb had wanted 17-year-old Ty to travel a different life course in 1904. The Royston, Ga., school superintendent viewed baseball as a forum for hoods, gamblers and drunks and wanted his son to attend law school. But when Ty passionately pleaded for a chance at the profession of his choosing, Herschel relented, with the warning, "You can go, Tyrus, but I don't ever want to see your face again — unless you've made good."

Ty had no intention of doing otherwise. He played parts of the 1904 and 1905 seasons with Augusta of the South Atlantic League before his contract was purchased by the Tigers. He made his major league debut on August 30, 1905, and doubled off New York ace Jack Chesbro, setting in motion a career that could be described as borderline psychotic.

"When I came up to Detroit," Cobb said after retirement, "I was just a mild-mannered Sunday school boy. But as soon as I started to get some publicity, the old-timers began to work on me. They practically put a chip on my shoulder, hazed me unmercifully. . . . If I became a snarling wildcat, they made me one."

They also made him realize that his obstacles to greatness could be found inside his own locker room as well as on the field. He answered the challenge of his own teammates with closed-door fights that inevitably left his opponent pleading for mercy, and he answered the challenge between the white lines with a take-no-prisoners, swashbuckling style that earned him the contempt of both peers and fans.

But if that bothered Cobb, he never let anybody know. He spent his baseball life as a loner and swaggered around the field with an air of superiority, willingly squaring off with anybody who challenged that notion. He got away with it because, in terms of talent, fighting ability and smarts, he *was* superior.

"He was the most violent, successful, thoroughly maladjusted personality ever to pass across American sports," said author Al Stump, who collaborated with Cobb on his autobiography. "It is a historic irony that the very best baseball player who ever lived was widely and passionately hated," added Josh Greenfield, another writer.

Catchers and other infielders had to be alert when Cobb was running loose on the basepaths.

Master baserunner Cobb was a man of many slides.

As a hitter, Cobb had no peers. He choked up on the bat with a split grip and merely hit the ball anywhere he wanted. He was to bat control what Babe Ruth was later to home runs. He could punch or pull the ball at will, and he could muscle up when he wanted and hit for power. He was an excellent bunter who could lure head-hunting pitchers into his path along the first-base line for a quick lesson in intimidation.

But it was on the basepaths that Cobb earned his battle scars. He was daring, aggressive and even reckless — but never out of control. Pitchers shuddered when Cobb reached base and infielders stood their ground at risk of life and limb. Lots of blood flowed from Cobb-delivered spike wounds — and vice versa.

Those who saw Cobb stripped down were aghast at the mass of raw flesh that covered his almost-skinless legs during the course of any season. But that never stopped him from hitting the dirt with one of his inventive fadeaway slides or perfectly executed hooks. He was tough beyond description, had an incredible threshold for pain and an even more incredible desire to succeed at all costs.

His baserunning feats go beyond stolen bases and intimidation. The speedy Cobb once scored from first on an infield out, he often raced around to score from first on singles and he sometimes went from first to third on sacrifice bunts. He was clever and always a step ahead of the opposition, prompting St. Louis Cardinal front-office man Branch Rickey to observe, "Cobb has brains in his feet."

He also was an above-average outfielder with a reasonable arm that produced 30 assists in the 1907 season.

"He could do everything better than any player I ever saw," said Washington pitching great Walter Johnson. "He was always the first one to detect weaknesses or mistakes by the opposition and benefit by the same."

Johnson was not alone in his opinion.

"He could do all that any player should do and had great competitive spirit and the willingness to take chances at all times," said former Boston and Cleveland great Tris Speaker.

"He surpassed all the players that I remember," said former Philadelphia A's Manager Mack, who saw plenty in his 60-plus-year career.

Like or dislike Cobb's philosophies, there is no denying that he attained a level of success that most men can only dream about. He played in only three World Series (batting .262) and he retired without close ties or friendships with anybody in the game, but he considered that the price of success. And success, obviously, was all that counted.

The indomitable spirit never waned, as evidenced by a conversation Cobb had shortly before his death in 1961.

"What do you think you would hit against present-day pitching?" an interviewer asked.

"Oh, about .300, I'd guess," Cobb said.

"Is that all?" the interviewer replied.

"Well," Cobb responded seriously, "you must remember I'm almost 74 years old."

Detroit Manager Cobb with Tigers Owner Frank Navin.

The stroke that resulted in 12 American League batting titles.

★ 1912 ★

CAUGHT ON THE FLY

APRIL
Three new parks: The Cincinnati Reds opened Redland Field, the Boston Red Sox dedicated Fenway Park and Detroit opened Navin Field.

JUNE
New York Giants ace Christy Mathewson recorded his 20th victory of the season and the 300th of his outstanding career with a 3-2 decision over the Chicago Cubs. It marked Matty's 10th straight 20-win campaign.

JULY
New York Giants lefthander Rube Marquard outpitched Brooklyn's Nap Rucker and won his major league-record 19th straight game, a 2-1 decision at the Polo Grounds in New York.

OCTOBER
Chicago Cubs third baseman Heinie Zimmerman won the N.L. Triple Crown, batting .372 with 14 home runs and 103 RBIs.

SEASON LEADERS

	American League		National League	
Avg.	Ty Cobb, Det.	.410	Heinie Zimmerman, Chi.	.372
HR	Frank Baker, Phi.	10	Heinie Zimmerman, Chi.	14
	Tris Speaker, Bos.	10		
RBI	Frank Baker, Phi.	133	Heinie Zimmerman, Chi.	103
SB	Clyde Milan, Wash.	88	Bob Bescher, Cin.	67
W-L Pct.	Joe Wood, Bos.	34-5, .872	Claude Hendrix, Pit.	24-9, .727
ERA	Walter Johnson, Wash.	1.39	Jeff Tesreau, N.Y.	1.96
SO	Walter Johnson, Wash.	303	Grover Alexander, Phi.	195

Amateur Tigers fall

One of Detroit's losses in a bleak 69-84 campaign will be remembered for more than its artistic merit. It was recorded on May 18 at Philadelphia, a day on which team Owner Frank Navin commissioned local semipros to do battle with the powerful Athletics while his Tigers were on strike.

It all started May 15 in New York when Detroit's Ty Cobb entered the stands to fight a heckler and was suspended indefinitely by American League President Ban Johnson. The next day was an open date, but the Detroit players met in Philadelphia and voted to strike the May 18 game if Cobb's suspension was not lifted. A telegram containing the signature of each Tiger player was sent to Johnson in Chicago.

Navin, realizing that he would be liable for a $5,000 fine each day the club did not field a team, sent Manager Hughie Jennings in search of substitutes.

With Aloysius Travers yielding 26 hits and pitching the entire game, the pseudo-Tigers dropped a 24-2 decision to the A's. Johnson traveled to Philadelphia, summoned the striking players to his hotel suite and threatened them with lifetime suspensions. At Cobb's urging, the real Tigers returned to uniform.

Each player was fined $100 and Cobb, who sat out 10 days, forfeited $50.

WORLD SERIES REPORT

GIANTS BLOW SERIES

New York Giants fans, still reeling from a 1908 baserunning blunder by Fred Merkle that cost them a National League pennant, were horrified October 16 by news that the Giants had given away another championship — this time in the eighth game of the World Series at Boston's Fenway Park.

When Merkle delivered a run-scoring single in the top of the 10th inning to give New York a 2-1 lead, John McGraw's Giants were three outs away from their second World Series victory, with Christy Mathewson on the mound.

But center fielder Fred Snodgrass inexplicably dropped an easy fly ball by Boston's Clyde Engle for a two-base error. Snodgrass partially atoned when he made a great running catch to rob Harry Hooper of a hit, but Engle tagged and advanced to third, where he remained as Steve Yerkes drew a walk.

Mathewson then induced Tris Speaker, a .383 hitter during the regular campaign, to lift a foul pop between home plate and first base. But catcher Chief Meyers and Merkle let the ball drop and Speaker promptly singled home Engle with the tying run.

With Yerkes at third and Speaker on first, Duffy Lewis was walked intentionally. Larry Gardner's fly ball scored the Series-winning run and made a three-game winner out of Smokey Joe Wood, who pitched three innings in relief of starter Hugh Bedient.

The loss ended the Giants' hopes of becoming the first team to recover from a three games to one deficit and win a best-of-seven Series. Boston, winner of an A.L.-record 105 games during the regular season, had captured Games 1, 4 and 5, with the second game, tied 6-6, being stopped after 11 innings because of darkness. But the New Yorkers, led by the pitching of Rube Marquard (two wins), recovered for 5-2 and 11-4 wins in Games 6 and 7.

Game 1	Boston	4	New York	3
Game 2	New York	6	Boston	6
Game 3	New York	2	Boston	1
Game 4	Boston	3	New York	1
Game 5	Boston	2	New York	1
Game 6	New York	5	Boston	2
Game 7	New York	11	Boston	4
Game 8	Boston	3	New York	2

Fred Snodgrass dropped a fly ball and the New York Giants dropped a World Series heartbreaker to Boston.

Rube Marquard's two victories were not enough to get the Giants back into the World Series winner's circle.

★ 1913 ★

WORLD SERIES REPORT

GIANTS FALL AGAIN

Philadelphia lefthander Eddie Plank, a 10-inning, 3-0 loser to New York's Christy Mathewson in Game 2, fired a two-hitter and outdueled Mathewson in the Game 5 finale October 11, beating the Giants, 3-1, and giving the Athletics their third World Series championship in four years.

Plank was masterful and Frank (Home Run) Baker drove in two runs as the A's handed the Giants their third straight fall classic defeat. Baker batted .450 and finished the classic with a home run and seven runs batted in. Second baseman Eddie Collins batted .421 and Wally Schang batted .357 with six RBIs.

The Athletics won the opener, 6-4, behind Chief Bender. They lost the next day to Mathewson, but then rolled to three straight victories. Joe Bush, a 20-year-old rookie, pitched a five-hitter and won Game 3, 8-2, while Bender captured his second decision the next day, holding off the Giants, 6-5.

Game 1	Philadelphia	6	New York	4
Game 2	New York	3	Philadelphia	0
Game 3	Philadelphia	8	New York	2
Game 4	Philadelphia	6	New York	5
Game 5	Philadelphia	3	New York	1

Feds declare war

The Federal League, an 'outlaw circuit that just completed its first season, announced that it will play its 1914 schedule as a third major league.

The Federals already have signed St. Louis Browns Manager George Stovall to direct the Kansas City franchise and the Chicago Whales reportedly are close to signing former Cubs shortstop Joe Tinker. President Jim Gilmore says his ownership groups will do what it takes to make the new circuit work, including the pirating of players from the American and National leagues.

The new league will begin the 1914 campaign with eight franchises: Chicago, St. Louis, Brooklyn, Baltimore, Kansas City, Pittsburgh, Buffalo and Indianapolis. Each team will be responsible for building new ballparks and having them ready for opening day.

Joe Tinker as manager of the Federal League's Chicago Whales.

Johnson is masterful in a streaky season

Fireballer Walter Johnson completed the season with an armload of statistical honors and selection as the American League's Most Valuable Player.

The Washington righthander compiled a phenomenal 36-7 record with an amazing 1.09 earned-run average. He also led the A.L. in innings (346), complete games (29), shutouts (11) and strikeouts (243) and won 14 straight games at midseason, falling two short of tying the major league record he shares with Smokey Joe Wood.

But the highlight was the major league-record 56-inning shutout streak he compiled from Opening Day, when the New York Yankees scored a first-inning run against him, to May 10, when he yielded a fourth-inning run to the St. Louis Browns. Between runs, Johnson pitched shutouts against the Yankees, Boston, Philadelphia and Chicago. He also pitched 8⅔ scoreless innings in relief.

American League MVP Walter Johnson, 36-7 with a 1.09 ERA for Washington, ran up a record 56-inning scoreless streak.

CAUGHT ON THE FLY

APRIL

Cold weather limited the crowd to 12,000 and Philadelphia righthander Tom Seaton spoiled the dedication of Brooklyn's new Ebbets Field with a 1-0 victory over the Dodgers.

In their first official game as "Yankees," the former New York Highlanders dropped a 2-1 Opening Day decision to Washington and Walter Johnson at Griffith Stadium.

DECEMBER

John K. Tener, former pitcher, Congressman and Governor of Pennsylvania, was elected to a four-year term as National League president.

SEASON LEADERS

	American League		National League	
Avg.	Ty Cobb, Det.	.390	Jake Daubert, Bkn.	.350
HR	Frank Baker, Phi.	12	Gavvy Cravath, Phi.	19
RBI	Frank Baker, Phi.	126	Gavvy Cravath, Phi.	128
SB	Clyde Milan, Wash.	75	Max Carey, Pit.	61
W-L Pct.	Walter Johnson, Wash.	36-7, .837	Bert Humphries, Chi.	16-4, .800
ERA	Walter Johnson, Wash.	1.09	Christy Mathewson, N.Y.	2.06
SO	Walter Johnson, Wash.	243	Tom Seaton, Phi.	168

★1914★

JANUARY-DECEMBER

WORLD SERIES REPORT

THE MIRACLE BRAVES

When the Boston Braves clinched the National League pennant September 29 with a 3-2 victory over the Chicago Cubs, they punctuated the greatest closing rush in baseball history. From an N.L.-worst 26-40 record on July 4, the Miracle Braves rose to a final 94-59 ledger, 10½ games clear of the New York Giants.

George Stallings' group of castoffs and misfits were 15 games behind the front-running Giants after losing both games of their Independence Day doubleheader and prospects for anything but a miserable season appeared dim. But a 10-3 spurt capped by a 3-2, July 19 victory over Cincinnati cut the Giants' margin to 10½ games and moved the Braves past Pittsburgh into seventh place.

Boston, building its charge around the 69-victory pitching of Dick Rudolph, Bill James and George (Lefty) Tyler, finally reached .500 for the first time on August 1 and moved into second place nine days later. The Braves caught New York on August 23 and the teams wrestled for the lead over the ensuing two weeks. The Braves took sole possession of first place September 8 and then left the Giants in their pennant dust.

By the time that dust had cleared, Boston had gained 25½ games from July 4 while compiling a 68-19 record. Miracle No. 1 was complete. Next up: a Series date with the powerful Philadelphia Athletics.

No contest. With Rudolph, James and Tyler outpitching Connie Mack's aging mound corps, the Braves pulled off a stunning four-game sweep. Catcher Hank Gowdy batted .545, second baseman Johnny Evers .438 and sparkplug shortstop Rabbit Maranville .308 as Boston ripped off 7-1, 1-0, 5-4 and 3-1 victories to claim its first championship.

Game 1	Boston	7	Philadelphia	1
Game 2	Boston	1	Philadelphia	0
Game 3	Boston	5	Philadelphia	4
Game 4	Boston	3	Philadelphia	1

Miracle workers (left to right): Hank Gowdy, Dick Rudolph, Lefty Tyler and Joe Connolly helped the Boston Braves to a shocking baseball championship.

CAUGHT ON THE FLY

MAY
Chicago righthander Jim Scott pitched a nine-inning no-hitter against Washington at Griffith Stadium, but lost 1-0 in the 10th when the Senators scored on two hits.

JULY
Babe Ruth made his major league debut with Boston, pitching the Red Sox to a 4-3 win over Cleveland.

SEPTEMBER
Cleveland's Nap Lajoie collected career hit No. 3,000 in the Indians' 5-3 victory over the New York Yankees.

SEASON LEADERS

	American League		National League	
Avg.	Ty Cobb, Det.	.368	Jake Daubert, Bkn.	.329
HR	Frank Baker, Phi.	9	Gavvy Cravath, Phi.	19
RBI	Sam Crawford, Det.	104	Sherry Magee, Phi.	103
SB	Fred Maisel, N.Y.	74	George Burns, N.Y.	62
W-L Pct.	Chief Bender, Phi.	17-3, .850	Bill James, Bos.	26-7, .788
ERA	Dutch Leonard, Bos.	1.01	Bill Doak, St.L.	1.72
SO	Walter Johnson, Wash.	225	Grover Alexander, Phi.	214

Mack cleans house

Philadelphia Owner and Manager Connie Mack, upset over his team's showing in the World Series and fearful that he would lose his top players to Federal League overtures, began cleaning house November 1 with the sale of righthanded pitcher Jack Coombs to Brooklyn.

Eddie Plank and Chief Bender, two veterans who had combined for a 32-10 record in Philadelphia's pennant-winning campaign, were the next to go, jumping to the Federal League. But the bottom dropped out for Philadelphia fans on December 8 when Mack announced that he had sold second baseman Eddie Collins, the game's best position player, to the Chicago White Sox for $50,000.

Suddenly what had appeared to be a purge of aging veterans became a total retrenchment. Collins was the 27-year-old heart and soul of the Philadelphia dynasty. As part of the A's famed "$100,000 infield" with third baseman Home Run Baker, shortstop Jack Barry and first baseman Stuffy McInnis, he had topped the .300 mark for six straight seasons and led the A's to World Series victories in 1910, '11 and '13.

With the departure of Collins, other key players also became vulnerable.

Connie Mack cut out the heart of his Philadelphia machine when he sold star second baseman Eddie Collins to Chicago.

★1915★

Cobb breaks loose

Like him or not, Detroit star Ty Cobb is in a class by himself on a baseball field. He proved that again this season by setting two records that are not likely to be broken for many years.

Cobb's final .369 batting average was good enough to lead the American League for a record ninth consecutive year. Included in that string are two .400 seasons (.420 in 1911 and .410 in 1912) and his Triple Crown campaign of 1909.

Cobb's second record was set on the basepaths, where he ran wild and stole 96 bases. That mark did not come easily, however. The Georgia Peach also was caught stealing a record 38 times.

At age 32, Cobb already is closing in on the magic 3,000-hit barrier and he has shown no sign of slowing down.

Detroit's Ty Cobb complemented his booming bat with a daring, aggressive baserunning style.

Feds end 2-year war

After waging a costly two-year battle against the Federal League, American League and National League owners broke down December 22 and signed a peace settlement with the outlaw circuit.

Plagued by player raids and intra-city squabbling for the baseball dollar, major league owners agreed to pay $600,000 for distribution to the eight Federal League owners and to allow two to purchase major league franchises. Charles Weeghman, owner of the Federal League's Chicago Whales, will purchase the N.L.'s Cubs while Phil Ball, owner of the Federal League's St. Louis team, will buy the A.L.'s St. Louis Browns.

The Federal League's Baltimore team refused to accept the terms of surrender and filed an unsuccessful suit against major league baseball under the Sherman Antitrust Act.

Indianapolis and Chicago captured Federal League pennants in the circuit's two seasons.

New Chicago Cubs Owner Charles Weeghman.

CAUGHT ON THE FLY

APRIL
Rube Marquard, a 22-game loser for the New York Giants last year, pitched a no-hitter and defeated Brooklyn, 2-0, at the Polo Grounds in the Giants' second game of the season.

AUGUST
Boston rewarded 46,500 fans by beating the St. Louis Cardinals, 3-1, in the first game at new Braves Field.

OCTOBER
The Chicago Whales (86-66), a 1½-game runnerup to Indianapolis in 1914, finished .0009 percentage points ahead of St. Louis (87-67) and captured the second Federal League pennant.

SEASON LEADERS

	American League		National League	
Avg.	Ty Cobb, Det.	.369	Larry Doyle, N.Y.	.320
HR	Braggo Roth, Chi.-Cle.	7	Gavvy Cravath, Phi.	24
RBI	Sam Crawford, Det.	112	Gavvy Cravath, Phi.	115
SB	Ty Cobb, Det.	96	Max Carey, Pit.	36
W-L Pct.	Joe Wood, Bos.	15-5, .750	Grover Alexander, Phi.	31-10, .756
ERA	Joe Wood, Bos.	1.49	Grover Alexander, Phi.	1.22
SO	Walter Johnson, Wash.	203	Grover Alexander, Phi.	241

WORLD SERIES REPORT

RED SOX WIN IN FIVE

Duffy Lewis hit a game-tying home run in the eighth inning and Harry Hooper belted his second homer of the game in the ninth to give the Boston Red Sox a 5-4 victory over the Philadelphia Phillies and their third World Series championship.

Hooper's Game 5 blast at Shibe Park handed righthander Rube Foster his second Series victory and gave the Red Sox their fourth straight win after dropping the Series opener to Phillies ace Grover Cleveland Alexander. The talented righthander, a 31-game winner and author of four one-hitters during the regular season, outdueled Boston's Ernie Shore, 3-1.

But it was all Red Sox the rest of the way. Foster and Dutch Leonard both pitched three-hit, 2-1 victories and Shore followed with another 2-1 verdict, allowing seven hits. That set the stage for the offensive heroics of Hooper and Lewis in the Game 5 clincher.

Lewis finished the fall classic with a .444 average and Hooper batted .350. First baseman Fred Luderus led Philadelphia with a .438 mark.

Game 1	Philadelphia	3	Boston	1
Game 2	Boston	2	Philadelphia	1
Game 3	Boston	2	Philadelphia	1
Game 4	Boston	2	Philadelphia	1
Game 5	Boston	5	Philadelphia	4

★ 1916 ★

CAUGHT ON THE FLY

APRIL

Innovative Cubs Owner Charles Weeghman began allowing Chicago fans to keep foul balls hit into the stands.

JUNE

Cleveland officials conducted an experiment by having Indians players wear numbers on their sleeves corresponding to those on the scorecards.

JULY/SEPTEMBER

The New York Giants ended an era when they traded pitching great Christy Mathewson to Cincinnati so the Big Six could become the Reds' manager. In his only appearance not in a Giants uniform, he beat Chicago and old foe Mordecai (Three Finger) Brown, 10-8.

SEASON LEADERS

	American League		National League	
Avg.	Tris Speaker, Cle.	.386	Hal Chase, Cin.	.339
HR	Wally Pipp, N.Y.	12	Dave Robertson, N.Y.	12
			Cy Williams, Chi.	12
RBI	Del Pratt, St.L.	103	Heinie Zimmerman, Chi.-N.Y.	83
SB	Ty Cobb, Det.	68	Max Carey, Pit.	63
W-L Pct.	Ed Cicotte, Chi.	15-7, .682	Tom Hughes, Bos.	16-3, .842
ERA	Babe Ruth, Bos.	1.75	Grover Alexander, Phi.	1.55
SO	Walter Johnson, Wash.	228	Grover Alexander, Phi.	167

Streak ends at 26

The New York Giants' amazing 26-game winning streak came to an end September 30 when the Boston Braves scored five seventh-inning runs in the second game of a doubleheader and held on for an 8-3 victory before 38,000 fans at the Polo Grounds.

Rube Benton gave no indication of a letdown in the opener when he handcuffed the Braves on one hit in a 4-0 win. But in the nightcap, Boston broke a 2-2 tie with its seventh-inning explosion that featured back-to-back home runs by Red Smith and Sherry Magee. Lefty Tyler was credited with the streak-snapping victory.

The defeat ended more than three weeks of near-perfect baseball that had lifted the Giants from the depths of the National League standings to fourth place. The streak, which began September 7 with a win over Brooklyn, included four victories over Philadelphia, four over Cincinnati, five over Pittsburgh, three over Chicago, six over St. Louis and three over Boston. The only interruption was a 1-1 September 18 tie against Pittsburgh. Jeff Tesreau won seven of the 26 games, Ferdie Schupp six and Benton five.

The streak surpassed Chicago's record of 21 straight in 1880.

Alexander zeroes in

Grover Cleveland Alexander pitched a three-hitter for his modern major league-record 16th shutout October 2 as Philadelphia stopped the Boston Braves, 2-0, in the first game of a doubleheader. But the Phillies fell, 4-1, in the nightcap and lost twice to the Braves the next day, ending their hopes of winning the National League pennant.

Alexander's league-best 33rd win pulled the Phillies to within a half-game of first-place Brooklyn. Making his third start in six days, he cruised through the Boston lineup without incident.

The victory lifted his final record to 33-12 and he finished with an N.L.-leading 390 innings, 38 complete games and 1.55 earned-run average. Alexander's 16-shutout effort matched the 1876 performance of St. Louis' George Washington Bradley.

The Phillies' Grover Cleveland Alexander: 33 wins and a record 16 shutouts.

WORLD SERIES REPORT

RED SOX WIN AGAIN

Ernie Shore fired a three-hitter and defeated Brooklyn, 4-1, giving the Boston Red Sox their second straight World Series championship and fourth overall.

Shore, in picking up his second win, allowed only a second-inning run in the Game 5 finale. The righthander also had won the October 7 opener, pitching 8⅔ innings in Boston's 6-5 victory at Braves Field, home of the National League's Boston franchise but the Red Sox's home field for the Series.

Game 2 was easily the most exciting. With Boston's Babe Ruth matched against Brooklyn's Sherry Smith, the Dodgers jumped to a 1-0 lead in the first inning on Hy Myers' inside-the-park home run. After Ruth's run-scoring grounder tied the game in the third, the pitchers matched zeroes for the next 10 innings. Boston broke through for a 2-1 victory in the bottom of the 14th on pinch-hitter Del Gainor's RBI single.

When the action moved to Ebbets Field, the Dodgers captured their first Series victory — a 4-3 conquest fueled by Jake Daubert's three hits and Ivy Olson's two RBIs. But Boston won 6-2 the next day on the pitching of Dutch Leonard and Larry Gardner's three-run homer.

Boston's World Series pitching hero Ernie Shore.

Game 1	Boston	6	Brooklyn	5
Game 2	Boston	2	Brooklyn	1
Game 3	Brooklyn	4	Boston	3
Game 4	Boston	6	Brooklyn	2
Game 5	Boston	4	Brooklyn	1

★ 1917 ★

WORLD SERIES REPORT

SOX CHASE THE GIANTS

New York baseball fans watched in horror October 15 when John McGraw's team blundered its way to another World Series loss, this time to the Chicago White Sox.

With the Giants trailing three games to two and locked in a scoreless Game 6 battle, Chicago's Eddie Collins led off the fourth inning with a grounder to third baseman Heinie Zimmerman, who made a two-base throwing error. When right fielder Dave Robertson dropped Joe Jackson's fly ball, the White Sox had runners on first and third.

On the next play, Happy Felsch grounded to pitcher Rube Benton. The lefthander saw Collins break from third and fired to Zimmerman, who ran him toward home plate. But Collins bounded past catcher Bill Rariden, who was inexplicably up the line, and with nobody covering the plate it became a race — the slow-footed Zimmerman chasing the swift Collins, who scored easily. Two more runs scored and Chicago closed out the Series with a 4-2 victory.

The Giants, who had lost the 1908 National League pennant on Fred Merkle's baserunning blunder and the 1912 Series on two 10th-inning misplays in the final game, had rebounded in this classic from a two-game deficit on the pitching of Benton and Ferdie Schupp.

Game 1	Chicago	2	New York	1
Game 2	Chicago	7	New York	2
Game 3	New York	2	Chicago	0
Game 4	New York	5	Chicago	0
Game 5	Chicago	8	New York	5
Game 6	Chicago	4	New York	2

Chicago's Eddie Collins slides across the plate as New York third baseman Heinie Zimmerman pursues and catcher Bill Rariden watches.

A double no-hitter

The 3,500 Chicago fans who braved miserable conditions to attend a May 2 game between the Cubs and Cincinnati Reds at Weeghman Park were rewarded with a baseball masterpiece. The artists, Reds' righthander Fred Toney and Cubs' lefty Jim (Hippo) Vaughn, were nearly flawless.

Toney sailed through the first nine innings, mowing down Chicago hitters while allowing only two walks to Cy Williams. But Vaughn allowed only three Reds to reach base through regulation — two walks and an infield error.

It was baseball's first double no-hitter and purists would have ended the game right there, as a 0-0 tie. But somebody's career moment had to end on a negative note and it was Vaughn who stumbled first.

Cincinnati shortstop Larry Kopf led off the 10th with the game's first hit — a single to right. Kopf came around to score on two errors and a swinging bunt.

Toney then retired the Cubs in order, finishing his no-hitter.

Chicago's Hippo Vaughn was a tough-luck loser after no-hitting Cincinnati for nine innings.

CAUGHT ON THE FLY

MAY

St. Louis Browns Ernie Koob and Bob Groom pitched no-hitters on consecutive days against the Chicago White Sox. Groom's came in the second game of a doubleheader.

JUNE

Boston righthander Ernie Shore, who came on to pitch when starter Babe Ruth was ejected after walking the first batter of the game, retired 27 straight Senators in a perfect 4-0 Boston victory at Fenway Park.

SEASON LEADERS

	American League		National League	
Avg.	Ty Cobb, Det.	.383	Edd Roush, Cin.	.341
HR	Wally Pipp, N.Y.	9	Dave Robertson, N.Y.	12
			Gavvy Cravath, Phi.	12
RBI	Bobby Veach, Det.	103	Heinie Zimmerman, N.Y.	102
SB	Ty Cobb, Det.	55	Max Carey, Pit.	46
W-L Pct.	Reb Russell, Chi.	15-5, .750	Ferdie Schupp, N.Y.	21-7, .750
ERA	Ed Cicotte, Chi.	1.53	Grover Alexander, Phi.	1.86
SO	Walter Johnson, Wash.	188	Grover Alexander, Phi.	201

★1918★

JANUARY-DECEMBER

A world goes to war

As the United States became more deeply involved in World War I, an air of uncertainty floated over ballparks around the country. But major league officials, ignoring warning signs that should have prompted a more common-sense approach, followed a dangerous business-as-usual course into the new season.

They were shocked in mid-July when U.S. Secretary of War Newton Baker and General Enoch Crowder, director of the military draft, issued a "Work or Fight" order forcing all able-bodied Americans of draft age out of non-essential employment and into the Army or jobs considered essential to the war. Baseball, they said, was a non-essential occupation.

Baker rejected baseball's appeal and gave all players until September 1 to comply. Both leagues voted to end their seasons by Labor Day (September 2) and to play the World Series immediately after. Baker granted players involved in the fall classic a 15-day grace period.

Even before the "Work or Fight" rule, baseball faced a serious manpower drain. The military claimed 56 percent of the American League work force, 63 percent of the National League. Many big names (Grover Cleveland Alexander, Christy Mathewson, Rabbit Maranville, Rube Marquard, Casey Stengel, Dutch Ruether) were missing from

major league lineups, and several major leaguers (Eddie Grant, Bun Troy, Alex Burr and Larry Chappell) had suffered war-related deaths.

Attendance was down at the start of the campaign but picked up in mid-May and held until the end. The minor leagues were virtually shut down by the war.

With the early November collapse of the Central Powers and the armistice agreement that ended the fighting, baseball's future brightened.

Grover Cleveland Alexander donned a different kind of uniform while serving in World War 1.

Those players who did not serve in the war spent plenty of time drilling, like this group of St. Louis Browns.

CAUGHT ON THE FLY

JUNE
Boston's Dutch Leonard pitched his second no-hitter, stopping the Tigers, 5-0, in a game at Detroit.

SEPTEMBER
Boston lefthander Babe Ruth finished the season with a 13-7 record, but he also crashed 11 home runs while playing 95 games in the Red Sox outfield.

DECEMBER
National League officials elected John Heydler to replace John K. Tener as the circuit's president.

SEASON LEADERS

	American League		National League	
Avg.	Ty Cobb, Det.	.382	Zack Wheat, Bkn.	.335
HR	Babe Ruth, Bos.	11	Gavvy Cravath, Phi.	8
	Tilly Walker, Phi.	11		
RBI	Bobby Veach, Det.	78	Sherry Magee, Cin.	76
SB	George Sisler, St.L.	45	Max Carey, Pit.	58
W-L Pct.	Sam Jones, Bos.	16-5, .762	Claude Hendrix, Chi.	19-7, .731
ERA	Walter Johnson, Wash.	1.27	Hippo Vaughn, Chi.	1.74
SO	Walter Johnson, Wash.	162	Hippo Vaughn, Chi.	148

WORLD SERIES REPORT

RUTH LIFTS RED SOX

Carl Mays pitched a three-hitter and Boston scored two unearned runs in the third inning to give the Red Sox a 2-1 victory over the Chicago Cubs and their third World Series victory in the last four years.

Pitchers dominated as the Red Sox rolled to their fifth World Series championship in as many tries. Boston pitchers combined for a 1.70 earned-run average while Red Sox hitters batted a paltry .186. Conversely, Chicago pitchers posted a sparkling 1.04 ERA while Cubs hitters

struggled to a .210 mark. There were no home runs and neither team scored more than three runs in one game.

Boston's top performer was Babe Ruth, who won twice and drove in two key Game 4 runs with a triple. Ruth pitched a 1-0 Game 1 shutout over Chicago's Hippo Vaughn and extended his World Series scoreless-innings streak to a record 29 before surrendering two runs in a 3-2 Game 4 victory. Mays also posted two victories and a 1.00 ERA.

Game 1	Boston	1	Chicago	0
Game 2	Chicago	3	Boston	1
Game 3	Boston	2	Chicago	1
Game 4	Boston	3	Chicago	2
Game 5	Chicago	3	Boston	0
Game 6	Boston	2	Chicago	1

★1919★

SEASON LEADERS

	American League		National League	
Avg.	Ty Cobb, Det.	.384	Edd Roush, Cin.	.321
HR	Babe Ruth, Bos.	29	Gavvy Cravath, Phi.	12
RBI	Babe Ruth, Bos.	114	Hy Myers, Bkn.	73
SB	Eddie Collins, Chi.	33	George Burns, N.Y.	40
W-L Pct.	Ed Cicotte, Chi.	29-7, .806	Dutch Ruether, Cin.	19-6, .760
ERA	Walter Johnson, Wash.	1.49	Grover Alexander, Chi.	1.72
SO	Walter Johnson, Wash.	147	Hippo Vaughn, Chi.	141

CAUGHT ON THE FLY

AUGUST

Joe Wilhoit, an outfielder for Wichita of the Western League, compiled a 69-game hitting streak, a record for organized baseball.

SEPTEMBER

Boston's Babe Ruth finished the season with a record 29 home runs in 139 games.

A two-day marathon

When the New York Yankees and Washington Senators ended their May 12 game deadlocked 4-4 after 15 innings, players from both teams and thousands of fans were afflicted with a serious case of frustration. But it was a fitting conclusion to the "series that never happened."

First, the scheduled May 9 and 10 games at New York's Polo Grounds were washed away by rain. Then the teams treated 3,000 shivering spectators to a scoreless 12-inning tie that was stopped because of a Sunday curfew. When the 15-inning marathon brought the no-decision total to 27 innings, the teams faced the prospect of playing 10 games in six days in July.

The scoreless tie was a pitching masterpiece. Washington's Walter Johnson was brilliant, allowing only two singles and one walk while retiring 28 consecutive batters at one point. New York's Jack Quinn allowed nine hits, but pitched his way out of three jams.

The Yankees led the May 12 contest, 3-1, after eight innings. But Joe Judge led off with a home run and a two-out throwing error by second baseman Del Pratt allowed the Senators to tie. Catcher Patsy Gharrity's daring steal of home gave Washington a 4-3 lead, but the Yankees tied the game in the bottom of the frame and forced extra innings.

WORLD SERIES REPORT

REDS PULL SHOCKER

The Cincinnati Reds, heavy underdogs to the Chicago White Sox, blasted Lefty Williams for four first-inning runs and cruised to a 10-5 Game 8 victory that concluded a shocking World Series upset and left many fans and officials wondering if everything was above board.

Suspicions that something might be amiss were aroused by a sharp shift in the betting odds shortly before the Series opened and the sloppy performances of several Chicago players. In the opener, the Reds battered 29-game winner Eddie Cicotte while Dutch Ruether pitched a six-hitter in a 9-1 victory. In Game 2, 23-game winner Williams walked six batters and the Reds took advantage for a 4-2 triumph.

Chicago rookie Dickie Kerr pitched a three-hit, 3-0 shutout in the third game, but Cincinnati's Jimmy Ring and Hod Eller matched that effort in 2-0 and 5-0 wins. The loser in Game 4 was Cicotte, who committed a pair of fifth-inning errors that led to both Cincinnati runs.

The only consolation for Chicago fans was that the Series had been expanded to a best-of-nine format and the Reds still needed another victory for the championship.

Kerr pitched Chicago to a 5-4 win and Cicotte posted a 4-1 triumph to make things respectable, but the Reds closed out the Series behind Eller in Game 8. It was Eller's second victory and Edd Roush and Pat Duncan combined for seven runs batted in.

Chicago's Shoeless Joe Jackson, a .351 hitter during the regular season, batted .375 with a home run and six RBIs in the Series.

Edd Roush's bat helped the Reds post their Series-clinching victory over Chicago.

A cloud of suspicion surrounded Chicago White Sox pitcher Eddie Cicotte after he lost two World Series games to Cincinnati.

Game 1	Cincinnati	9	Chicago	1
Game 2	Cincinnati	4	Chicago	2
Game 3	Chicago	3	Cincinnati	0
Game 4	Cincinnati	2	Chicago	0
Game 5	Cincinnati	5	Chicago	1
Game 6	Chicago	5	Cincinnati	4
Game 7	Chicago	4	Cincinnati	1
Game 8	Cincinnati	10	Chicago	5

The 1920s

The popularity bonanza of "The Roaring Twenties" was but a distant dream when the decade opened under a dark cloud.

Grand jury indictments against eight members of the Chicago White Sox for conspiring to fix the 1919 World Series had come as a slap in the face to Americans who still were trying to cope with the aftershocks of World War I. As baseball's reputation, not to mention its image as America's National Pastime, stood on the gallows, its officials searched desperately for a reprieve.

The first step toward forgiveness was an unqualified admission of guilt, which baseball took with the hiring of Kenesaw Mountain Landis as its first commissioner. Landis, a crusty, iron-fisted federal judge, used his powers to issue a lifetime ban against the eight "Black Sox," thus cleansing the game's conscience while restoring integrity.

But officials had no miracle cure for the loss of popularity that surely would follow such a sordid experience. Only an extraordinary stroke of luck could speed up what figured to be a lengthy healing process.

Babe Ruth was indeed extraordinary, although there was nothing

NATIONAL LEAGUE

League Batting Leaders

Average

Year	Player-Team	Avg.
1920	Rogers Hornsby, St. L.	.370
1921	Rogers Hornsby, St. L.	.397
1922	Rogers Hornsby, St. L.	.401
1923	Rogers Hornsby, St. L.	.384
1924	Rogers Hornsby, St. L.	.424
1925	Rogers Hornsby, St. L.	.403
1926	Bubbles Hargrave, Cin.	.353
1927	Paul Waner, Pit.	.380
1928	Rogers Hornsby, Bos.	.387
1929	Lefty O'Doul, Phil.	.398

Home Runs

Year	Player-Team	HR
1920	Cy Williams, Phil.	15
1921	George Kelly, N.Y.	23
1922	Rogers Hornsby, St. L.	42
1923	Cy Williams, Phil.	41
1924	Jack Fournier, Bkn.	27
1925	Rogers Hornsby, St. L.	39
1926	Hack Wilson, Chi.	21
1927	Cy Williams, Phil.	30
	Hack Wilson, Chi.	30
1928	Jim Bottomley, St. L.	31
	Hack Wilson, Chi.	31
1929	Chuck Klein, Phil.	43

RBIs

Year	Player-Team	RBI
1920	George Kelly, N.Y.	94
	Rogers Hornsby, St. L.	94
1921	Rogers Hornsby, St. L.	126
1922	Rogers Hornsby, St. L.	152
1923	Irish Meusel, N.Y.	125
1924	George Kelly, N.Y.	136
1925	Rogers Hornsby, St. L.	143
1926	Jim Bottomley, St. L.	120
1927	Paul Waner, Pit.	131
1928	Jim Bottomley, St. L.	136
1929	Hack Wilson, Chi.	159

Most Valuable Players

Presented by N.L.

Year	Player-Team	Pos.
1924	Dazzy Vance, Bkn.	P
1925	Rogers Hornsby, St. L.	2B
1926	Bob O'Farrell, St. L.	C
1927	Paul Waner, Pit.	OF
1928	Jim Bottomley, St. L.	1B
1929	Rogers Hornsby, Chi.	2B

League Pitching Leaders

Winning Percentage

Year	Pitcher-Team	W-L	Pct.
1920	Burleigh Grimes, Bkn.	23-11	.676
1921	Bill Doak, St. L.	15-6	.714
1922	Pete Donohue, Cin.	18-9	.667
1923	Dolf Luque, Cin.	27-8	.771
1924	Emil Yde, Pit.	16-3	.842
1925	Bill Sherdel, St. L.	15-6	.714
1926	Ray Kremer, Pitt.	20-6	.769
1927	Larry Benton, Bos.-N.Y.	17-7	.708
1928	Larry Benton, N.Y.	25-9	.735
1929	Charlie Root, Chi.	19-6	.760

Earned-Run Average

Year	Pitcher-Team	ERA
1920	Grover Alexander, Chi.	1.91
1921	Bill Doak, St. L.	2.59
1922	Rosy Ryan, N.Y.	3.01
1923	Dolf Luque, Cin.	1.93
1924	Dazzy Vance, Bkn.	2.16
1925	Dolf Luque, Cin.	2.63
1926	Ray Kremer, Pit.	2.61
1927	Ray Kremer, Pit.	2.47
1928	Dazzy Vance, Bkn.	2.09
1929	Bill Walker, N.Y.	3.08

Strikeouts

Year	Pitcher-Team	SO
1920	Grover Alexander, Chi.	173
1921	Burleigh Grimes, Bkn.	136
1922	Dazzy Vance, Bkn.	134
1923	Dazzy Vance, Bkn.	197
1924	Dazzy Vance, Bkn.	262
1925	Dazzy Vance, Bkn.	221
1926	Dazzy Vance, Bkn.	140
1927	Dazzy Vance, Bkn.	184
1928	Dazzy Vance, Bkn.	200
1929	Pat Malone, Chi.	166

WORLD SERIES

Year	Winner	Pennant Winner	Games
1920	Cleveland Indians	Brooklyn Dodgers	5-2
1921	New York Giants	New York Yankees	5-3
1922	New York Giants	New York Yankees	4-0-1
1923	New York Yankees	New York Giants	4-2
1924	Washington Senators	New York Giants	4-3
1925	Pittsburgh Pirates	Washington Senators	4-3
1926	St. Louis Cardinals	New York Yankees	4-3
1927	New York Yankees	Pittsburgh Pirates	4-0
1928	New York Yankees	St. Louis Cardinals	4-0
1929	Philadelphia Athletics	Chicago Cubs	4-1

Brooklyn righthander Dazzy Vance.

Final Standings

1920

	W	L	PCT.	GB
Brooklyn	93	61	.604	- -
New York	86	68	.558	7
Cincinnati	82	71	.536	10.5
Pittsburgh	79	75	.513	14
Chicago	75	79	.487	18
St. Louis	75	79	.487	18
Boston	62	90	.408	30
Philadelphia	62	91	.405	30.5

1921

	W	L	Pct.	GB
New York	94	59	.614	- -
Pittsburgh	90	63	.588	4
St. Louis	87	66	.569	7
Boston	79	74	.516	15
Brooklyn	77	75	.507	16.5
Cincinnati	70	83	.458	24
Chicago	64	89	.418	30
Philadelphia	51	103	.331	43.5

1922

	W	L	Pct.	GB
New York	93	61	.604	- -
Cincinnati	86	68	.558	7
Pittsburgh	85	69	.552	8
St. Louis	85	69	.552	8
Chicago	80	74	.519	13
Brooklyn	76	78	.494	17
Philadelphia	57	96	.373	35.5
Boston	53	100	.346	39.5

1923

	W	L	Pct.	GB
New York	95	58	.621	- -
Cincinnati	91	63	.591	4.5
Pittsburgh	87	67	.565	8.5
Chicago	83	71	.539	12.5
St. Louis	79	74	.516	16
Brooklyn	76	78	.494	19.5
Boston	54	100	.351	41.5
Philadelphia	50	104	.325	45.5

1924

	W	L	Pct.	GB
New York	93	60	.608	- -
Brooklyn	92	62	.597	1.5
Pittsburgh	90	63	.588	3
Cincinnati	83	70	.542	10
Chicago	81	72	.529	12
St. Louis	65	89	.422	28.5
Philadelphia	55	96	.364	37
Boston	53	100	.346	40

1925

	W	L	Pct.	GB
Pittsburgh	95	58	.621	- -
New York	86	66	.566	8.5
Cincinnati	80	73	.523	15
St. Louis	77	76	.503	18
Boston	70	83	.458	25
Brooklyn	68	85	.444	27
Philadelphia	68	85	.444	27
Chicago	68	86	.442	27.5

1926

	W	L	Pct.	GB
St. Louis	89	65	.578	- -
Cincinnati	87	67	.565	2
Pittsburgh	84	69	.549	4.5
Chicago	82	72	.532	7
New York	74	77	.490	13.5
Brooklyn	71	82	.464	17.5
Boston	66	86	.434	22
Philadelphia	58	93	.384	29.5

1927

	W	L	Pct.	GB
Pittsburgh	94	60	.610	- -
St. Louis	92	61	.601	1.5
New York	92	62	.597	2
Chicago	85	68	.556	8.5
Cincinnati	75	78	.490	18.5
Brooklyn	65	88	.425	28.5
Boston	60	94	.390	34
Philadelphia	51	103	.331	43

1928

	W	L	Pct.	GB
St. Louis	95	59	.617	- -
New York	93	61	.604	2
Chicago	91	63	.591	4
Pittsburgh	85	67	.559	9
Cincinnati	78	74	.513	16
Brooklyn	77	76	.503	17.5
Boston	50	103	.327	44.5
Philadelphia	43	109	.283	51

1929

	W	L	Pct.	GB
Chicago	98	54	.645	- -
Pittsburgh	88	65	.575	10.5
New York	84	67	.556	13.5
St. Louis	78	74	.513	20
Philadelphia	71	82	.464	27.5
Brooklyn	70	83	.458	28.5
Cincinnati	66	88	.429	33
Boston	56	98	.364	43

Detroit's Harry Heilmann

lucky about the stroke he used to send balls soaring into oblivion. Ruth was exciting and magnetic. The colorful New York Yankee outfielder ushered in an era of prosperity with his uncanny ability to hit home runs, and adoring fans flocked to see him play. Ruth arrived in New York in 1920 and began dominating the game like nobody before him, treating fans to daily power shows while posting unbelievable numbers: 54 home runs in 1920, 59 in 1921 and 60 in 1927 for what many considered the greatest team in history.

The Babe changed the style of the game from speed and finesse to instant offense. In the wake of his long-ball exploits, other teams began looking for muscular hitters who could win a game with one swing of the bat. And with fans clamoring for excitement, officials began changing rules that previously had favored pitchers.

But other seeds of change took longer to germinate. When the first radio broadcast of a game took place in 1921, the idea was chastised by the press. Sunday baseball was condemned in some quarters as unholy and sinful. And when Branch Rickey set up the first farm system for the St. Louis Cardinals, New York Giants Manager John McGraw branded it a "stupid idea."

Ruth was king of this decade, but Ty Cobb, Walter Johnson and Grover Cleveland Alexander were close behind. And a whole new galaxy of stars gave baseball renewed luster. Rogers Hornsby, Lou Gehrig, Jimmie Foxx, Al Simmons, Carl Hubbell, Mel Ott, Bill Terry and George Sisler were legitimate attractions. So were McGraw's Giants, who won a record four straight National League pennants and two World Series, and Miller Huggins' Yankees, who captured three Series while establishing the foundation for a baseball dynasty.

Ironically, this "Golden Age" closed with Ruth trying to become the first six-figure athlete in team-sports history. As he haggled with the Yankees in 1929, the country was plunging into the Great Depression.

AMERICAN LEAGUE

League Batting Leaders

Average

Year	Player-Team	Avg.
1920	George Sisler, St. L.	.407
1921	Harry Heilmann, Det.	.394
1922	George Sisler, St. L.	.420
1923	Harry Heilmann, Det.	.403
1924	Babe Ruth, N.Y.	.378
1925	Harry Heilmann, Det.	.393
1926	Heinie Manush, Det.	.378
1927	Harry Heilmann, Det.	.398
1928	Goose Goslin, Wash.	.379
1929	Lew Fonseca, Cle.	.369

Home Runs

Year	Player-Team	HR
1920	Babe Ruth, N.Y.	54
1921	Babe Ruth, N.Y.	59
1922	Ken Williams, St. L.	39
1923	Babe Ruth, N.Y.	41
1924	Babe Ruth, N.Y.	46
1925	Bob Meusel, N.Y.	33
1926	Babe Ruth, N.Y.	47
1927	Babe Ruth, N.Y.	60
1928	Babe Ruth, N.Y.	54
1929	Babe Ruth, N.Y.	46

RBIs

Year	Player-Team	RBI
1920	Babe Ruth, N.Y.	137
1921	Babe Ruth, N.Y.	171
1922	Ken Williams, St. L.	155
1923	Babe Ruth, N.Y.	131
1924	Goose Goslin, Wash.	129
1925	Bob Meusel, N.Y.	138
1926	Babe Ruth, N.Y.	145
1927	Lou Gehrig, N.Y.	175
1928	Lou Gehrig, N.Y.	142
	Babe Ruth, N.Y.	142
1929	Al Simmons, Phil.	157

Most Valuable Players

Presented by A.L.

Year	Player-Team	Pos.
1922	George Sisler, St. L.	1B
1923	Babe Ruth, N.Y.	OF
1924	Walter Johnson, Wash.	P
1925	Roger Peckinpaugh, Wash.	SS
1926	George Burns, Cle.	1B
1927	Lou Gehrig, N.Y.	1B
1928	Mickey Cochrane, Phil.	C

League Pitching Leaders

Winning Percentage

Year	Pitcher-Team	W-L	Pct.
1920	Jim Bagby, Cle.	31-12	.721
1921	Carl Mays, N.Y.	27-9	.750
1922	Joe Bush, N.Y.	26-7	.788
1923	Herb Pennock, N.Y.	19-6	.760
1924	Walter Johnson, Wash.	23-7	.767
1925	Stan Coveleski, Wash.	20-5	.800
1926	George Uhle, Cle.	27-11	.711
1927	Waite Hoyt, N.Y.	22-7	.759
1928	General Crowder, St. L.	21-5	.808
1929	Lefty Grove, Phil.	20-6	.769

Earned-Run Average

Year	Pitcher-Team	ERA
1920	Bob Shawkey, N.Y.	2.45
1921	Red Faber, Chi.	2.48
1922	Red Faber, Chi.	2.80
1923	Stan Coveleski, Cle.	2.76
1924	Walter Johnson, Wash.	2.72
1925	Stan Coveleski, Wash.	2.84
1926	Lefty Grove, Phil.	2.51
1927	Wilcy Moore, N.Y.	2.28
1928	Garland Braxton, Wash.	2.51
1929	Lefty Grove, Phil.	2.81

Strikeouts

Year	Pitcher-Team	SO
1920	Stan Coveleski, Cle.	133
1921	Walter Johnson, Wash.	143
1922	Urban Shocker, St. L.	149
1923	Walter Johnson, Wash.	130
1924	Walter Johnson, Wash.	158
1925	Lefty Grove, Phil.	116
1926	Lefty Grove, Phil.	194
1927	Lefty Grove, Phil.	174
1928	Lefty Grove, Phil.	183
1929	Lefty Grove, Phil.	170

Final Standings

1920

	W	L	PCT.	GB
Cleveland	98	56	.636	--
Chicago	96	58	.623	2
New York	95	59	.617	3
St. Louis	76	77	.497	21.5
Boston	72	81	.471	25.5
Washington	68	84	.447	29
Detroit	61	93	.396	37
Philadelphia	48	106	.312	50

1921

	W	L	Pct.	GB
New York	98	55	.641	--
Cleveland	94	60	.610	4.5
St. Louis	81	73	.526	17.5
Washington	80	73	.523	18
Boston	75	79	.487	23.5
Detroit	71	82	.464	27
Chicago	62	92	.403	36.5
Philadelphia	53	100	.346	45

1922

	W	L	Pct.	GB
New York	94	60	.610	--
St. Louis	93	61	.604	1
Detroit	79	75	.513	15
Cleveland	78	76	.506	16
Chicago	77	77	.500	17
Washington	69	85	.448	25
Philadelphia	65	89	.422	29
Boston	61	93	.396	33

1923

	W	L	Pct.	GB
New York	98	54	.645	--
Detroit	83	71	.539	16
Cleveland	82	71	.536	16.5
Washington	75	78	.490	23.5
St. Louis	74	78	.487	24
Philadelphia	69	83	.454	29
Chicago	69	85	.448	30
Boston	61	91	.401	37

1924

	W	L	Pct.	GB
Washington	92	62	.597	--
New York	89	63	.586	2
Detroit	86	68	.558	6
St. Louis	74	78	.487	17
Philadelphia	71	81	.467	20
Cleveland	67	86	.438	24.5
Boston	67	87	.435	25
Chicago	66	87	.431	25.5

1925

	W	L	Pct.	GB
Washington	96	55	.636	--
Philadelphia	88	64	.579	8.5
St. Louis	82	71	.536	15
Detroit	81	73	.526	16.5
Chicago	79	75	.513	18.5
Cleveland	70	84	.455	27.5
New York	69	85	.448	28.5
Boston	47	105	.309	49.5

1926

	W	L	Pct.	GB
New York	91	63	.591	--
Cleveland	88	66	.571	3
Philadelphia	83	67	.553	6
Washington	81	69	.540	8
Chicago	81	72	.529	9.5
Detroit	79	75	.513	12
St. Louis	62	92	.403	29
Boston	46	107	.301	44.5

1927

	W	L	Pct.	GB
New York	110	44	.714	--
Philadelphia	91	63	.591	19
Washington	85	69	.552	25
Detroit	82	71	.536	27.5
Chicago	70	83	.458	39.5
Cleveland	66	87	.431	43.5
St. Louis	59	94	.386	50.5
Boston	51	103	.331	59

1928

	W	L	Pct.	GB
New York	101	53	.656	--
Philadelphia	98	55	.641	2.5
St. Louis	82	72	.532	19
Washington	75	79	.487	26
Chicago	72	82	.468	29
Detroit	68	86	.442	33
Cleveland	62	92	.403	39
Boston	57	96	.373	43.5

1929

	W	L	Pct.	GB
Philadelphia	104	46	.693	--
New York	88	66	.571	18
Cleveland	81	71	.533	24
St. Louis	79	73	.520	26
Washington	71	81	.467	34
Detroit	70	84	.455	36
Chicago	59	93	.388	46
Boston	58	96	.377	48

★1920★

JANUARY - DECEMBER

The longest game

Boston's Joe Oeschger and Brooklyn's Leon Cadore waged the most Herculean pitching duel in baseball history on May 1, but both finished the day with a bad case of frustration.

For a major league-record 26 innings, the righthanders traded pitches. And for 3 hours and 50 minutes, their teammates could score only one run. Finally, with darkness enveloping Braves Field, umpire Bill McCormick halted the 1-1 game.

The marathon broke the previous major league record of 24 innings, set in 1906 when the Philadelphia Athletics beat the Red Sox, 4-1, in an American League contest at Boston. Oeschger allowed only nine hits and three walks while striking out four. Cadore surrendered 15 hits and five walks while striking out eight.

Brooklyn scored in the fifth inning on Ivy Olson's single and Boston tied in the sixth on Walt Cruise's triple and Tony Boeckel's single. Neither team could score over the next 20 innings.

Each team loaded the bases once with one out, but both rallies were snuffed out by double plays.

Brooklyn's Leon Cadore worked an exhausting 26 innings in a game against Boston, but had to settle for a 1-1 tie.

CAUGHT ON THE FLY

FEBRUARY
The National Association of Colored Professional Baseball Clubs, a new league providing blacks a chance to display their skills, was organized in Kansas City.

MAY
Washington ace Walter Johnson joined an elite club when he beat Detroit, 9-8, for his 300th career victory.

JULY
Cleveland's Tris Speaker set a big-league record by banging out 11 consecutive hits.

OCTOBER
The Pittsburgh Pirates salvaged a 6-0 victory against Cincinnati after losing the first two games of the century's first tripleheader, 13-4 and 7-3.

St. Louis first baseman George Sisler set a major league record when he collected his 257th hit in the Browns' 16-7 season-closing win over Chicago.

Spitballs outlawed

Baseball's joint rules committee made life a little easier for major league hitters February 9 when it banned the use of all foreign substances and ball-doctoring methods employed by many American and National league pitchers.

The rule will keep big-league hurlers from using resin, saliva, talcum powder, paraffin or any other substance that makes the ball do unusual tricks. It also prohibits pitchers from rubbing the ball on gloves or clothing and using any tool that scuffs the ball. Anybody caught breaking the rule will be ejected from the game

and suspended for 10 days.

There will, however, be exceptions for the 1920 season only. Not wanting to jeopardize the careers of some established pitchers, the committee certified a number of legal "spitballers." A.L. teams will be allowed to designate two spitball pitchers while N.L. teams can exempt all of their spitballers for one more year.

The committee also decided to ban the intentional walk, give umpires control over rainouts once the game has started and give hitters credit for game-ending home runs, even when the run is not needed to win the game.

Yanks get the Babe

The New York Yankees paid the incredible price of $125,000 January 5 for flamboyant Boston pitcher-outfielder Babe Ruth.

Yankee co-Owner Jacob Ruppert immediately announced that the 26-year-old will become an everyday right fielder in New York. The Yankees, badly in need of some punch in their outfield, are anxious to see what the lefthanded hitter can do as a full-time player.

Ruth set a record last season by hitting 29 home runs, even though he played only 130 games and got

432 official at-bats. He has been an outstanding pitcher in Boston, compiling an 89-46 record and helping the Red Sox to two World Series championships.

Boston Owner Harry Frazee said he made the deal because the Red Sox are becoming a one-man team. But it is more likely he parted with his top player and gate attraction because of Ruth's demands for more money and his own sagging financial fortunes.

The sale price more than doubled any previous major league transaction.

Yankee co-Owner Jacob Ruppert, the man who brought Babe Ruth to New York.

Mays beans Chapman

Cleveland shortstop Ray Chapman, hit on the head by a pitch from Yankee submarine right-hander Carl Mays during an August 16 game at the Polo Grounds, died the next day at New York's St. Lawrence Hospital after two unsuccessful operations.

The 29-year-old Chapman, a nine-year veteran and .278 career hitter, suffered massive head trauma when he was struck by a Mays fastball and became the first major league player ever to die as a result of injuries suffered during a game. He was leading off the fifth inning with the Indians ahead, 3-0, when the tragedy occurred.

Mays, who likes to dust off aggressive hitters, is a two-time 20-game winner. Chapman was a righthanded hitter who liked to crouch over the plate. When Mays' pitch rose toward Chapman's head, the batter simply froze.

Mays, thinking at first that the ball had struck Chapman's bat, fielded it and made the throw to first base.

Cleveland shortstop Ray Chapman died after being struck on the head by a pitch from New York Yankee Carl Mays.

SEASON LEADERS

	American League		National League	
Avg.	George Sisler, St.L.	.407	Rogers Hornsby, St.L.	.370
HR	Babe Ruth, N.Y.	54	Cy Williams, Phi.	15
RBI	Babe Ruth, N.Y.	137	George Kelly, N.Y.	94
			Rogers Hornsby, St.L.	94
SB	Sam Rice, Wash.	63	Max Carey, Pit.	52
W-L Pct.	Jim Bagby, Cle.	31-12, .721	Burleigh Grimes, Bkn.	23-11, .676
ERA	Bob Shawkey, N.Y.	2.45	Grover Alexander, Chi.	1.91
SO	Stan Coveleski, Cle.	133	Grover Alexander, Chi.	173

Cleveland hangs on

The Cleveland Indians clinched their first American League pennant October 2 when Jim Bagby recorded his 31st victory, a 10-1 decision over Detroit. The Indians finished with a 98-56 record, two games in front of Chicago and three games ahead of the New York Yankees.

The Indians were aided by the Chicago grand jury indictment that implicated eight members of the White Sox in a conspiracy to "fix" the 1919 World Series against the Cincinnati Reds. The eight players were suspended with the White Sox trailing Cleveland by 1½ games and five days left in the season. Chicago lost two of its last three games.

The Yankees fell short in a bid for their first A.L. pennant, but New York fans were amazed by the incredible performance of newcomer Babe Ruth. Ruth hit 54 home runs and beat his one-season major league record by 25. He also set a modern record with 158 runs scored while batting .376 and driving in 137 runs.

AN 'INDIAN' UPRISING

When the Cleveland Indians and Brooklyn Dodgers squared off October 10 in Game 5 of the World Series at Cleveland, there was no hint that anything unusual was about to unfold. The Series was tied at two games apiece and the Indians seemed to have an edge with 31-game winner Jim Bagby on the mound.

But the fireworks started in the first inning when Cleveland outfielder Elmer Smith smashed a Burleigh Grimes pitch for the first grand slam home run in Series history. In the fourth, Bagby connected off Grimes for a three-run shot — the first Series home run ever by a pitcher.

This historic game was capped in the fifth when Brooklyn's Pete Kilduff singled and moved to second on Otto Miller's hit. But Clarence Mitchell lined a ball to second baseman Bill Wambsganss, who caught it, stepped on second to double off Kilduff and wheeled around to tag out Miller. The first triple play in World Series history was *unassisted*.

The Indians won, 8-1, and then went on to beat the Dodgers, 1-0 and 3-0 in Games 6 and 7. Stan Coveleski, also a winner in Games 1 and 4, stopped Brooklyn on five hits in the clincher.

Game 1	Cleveland	3	Brooklyn	1
Game 2	Brooklyn	3	Cleveland	0
Game 3	Brooklyn	2	Cleveland	1
Game 4	Cleveland	5	Brooklyn	1
Game 5	Cleveland	8	Brooklyn	1
Game 6	Cleveland	1	Brooklyn	0
Game 7	Cleveland	3	Brooklyn	0

Cleveland second baseman Bill Wambsganss completes his unassisted World Series triple play by tagging out Brooklyn's Otto Miller.

SHOELESS JOE AND THE BLACK SOX SCANDAL

"I used my brain to become a great hitter. I studied the art scientifically. Jackson just swung. If he had my knowledge, his averages would have been phenomenal."

Ty Cobb

He has been vilified as a traitor, portrayed as a tragic victim and praised as a Hall of Fame-worthy superstar. In truth Shoeless Joe Jackson was all of the above. And even today, more than 70 years after the sordid Black Sox scandal that soiled his reputation, more than four decades after his death in Greenville, S.C., the very mention of his name triggers feelings ranging from contempt to sympathy.

He has been the subject of books as well as scores of magazine and newspaper articles. He has been glorified and chastised on the movie screen, and groups have been formed to plead for his reinstatement into baseball's good graces. "Say it ain't so, Joe," the alleged plea of a dirty-faced youngster to Jackson outside a Chicago courthouse in 1920, has become the symbolic battlecry of his growing legion of supporters.

Guilty or innocent? The question does not have a simple answer. Jackson probably was both, a statement that requires examination.

Joe Jackson was a South Carolina farmboy, an uneducated and illiterate hillbilly. The 6-foot-1, 175-pounder was jovial and good natured, a prime target for practical jokers when he arrived on the major league scene in 1910 with Cleveland after two brief stints with the Philadelphia Athletics.

But what Jackson lacked in social graces, he made up for with superior athletic abilities. His bat was lethal, his sweet swing the talk of envious American League hitters.

"I used my brain to become a great hitter," Detroit immortal Ty Cobb once said. "I studied the art scientifically. Jackson just swung. If he had my knowledge, his averages would have been phenomenal."

Perhaps Cobb should have said "more phenomenal." In his first full season with the Indians (1911), Jackson batted a whopping .408 but lost in the A.L. batting race to Cobb, who finished at .420. The lefthanded-hitting Jackson followed with .395, .373 and .338 campaigns before being dealt by the financially strapped Indians to Chicago in 1915. He continued his assault on A.L. pitchers as a member of the White Sox for the next 5½ seasons and finished his career with a .356 mark, third highest in history.

Jackson played in the dead-ball era and never hit more than 12 home runs in a season, but Cobb claimed the immortal Babe Ruth copied his swing. Another Jackson supporter was former White Sox teammate Shano Collins.

"If Joe had been faster, he would have hit over .400 every year," Collins said. "Cobb got plenty of hits on plays that Joe would be thrown out on. With the lively ball that is in use now, Joe would have killed a few infielders. He hit line drives mostly, savage shots that whistled. Everyone feared him."

Jackson also was a classy outfielder with a cannon arm.

And "you could tell he loved playing baseball by just watching him," Cobb said.

Jackson, who earned his nickname as a minor leaguer when he played a game in his stocking feet because of a blister, naturally became the centerpiece of a White Sox team that won a World Series championship in 1917 and captured another A.L. pennant in 1919. Many considered the Chicago team that would meet Cincinnati in a best-of-nine World Series one of the best ever assembled.

Among its stars were Jackson, second baseman Eddie Collins, third baseman Buck Weaver, shortstop Swede Risberg, first baseman Chick Gandil and outfielder Happy Felsch. Pitchers Eddie Cicotte and Lefty Williams had combined for 52 victories during the regular season. Unfortunately, nobody would ever find out just how good this Chicago team really was. The White Sox would lose the Series, five games to three, and Jackson, Weaver, Risberg, Gandil, Felsch, Cicotte, Williams and reserve Fred McMullin later would be implicated in a plot to fix its outcome.

The first clue of conspiracy actually surfaced before the classic even opened. The White Sox had been established as heavy favorites in gambling circles and early money supported the odds. But

Chicago's 1919 infield featured (left to right): third baseman Buck Weaver, shortstop Swede Risberg, second baseman Eddie Collins and first baseman Chick Gandil. All but Collins were banned from baseball.

suddenly, as the teams prepared for the October 1 opener, the odds shifted drastically. Some high rollers were pumping in serious money on Cincinnati.

The details of how the eight White Sox went about their dark duties are sketchy. But there is no denying that their Series play left plenty of room for suspicion — with the exception of Jackson and Weaver. Game 1 opened with Cicotte hitting Reds leadoff man Morrie Rath with a pitch, supposedly the signal to bettors that the fix was on. Cicotte, a 29-game winner during the regular season, would go on to lose two games while performing erratically and 23-game winner Williams would lose all three Series starts while compiling a horrendous 6.61 earned-run average.

For the record, Jackson batted a Series-leading .375, hit one home run and fielded flawlessly. Weaver contributed a .324 mark and Gandil supplied winning hits in the third and sixth games. But Gandil hit only .233, Felsch and Risberg batted .192 and McMullin got one hit in two pinch-hitting appearances.

While most of the nation accepted the outcome as a simple case of David knocking off Goliath, those closer to the game suspected otherwise. Rumors of a fix before the Series, the strange shift in betting odds and the suspicious performances of several players prompted White Sox Owner Charles A. Comiskey to launch an exhaustive investigation.

Comiskey wasn't alone. American League President Ban Johnson initiated an investigation of his own and, as the 1920 season was drawing to a close with the White Sox, Cleveland and New York locked in a torrid pennant race, a bombshell was dropped. Cicotte, Jackson and Williams had confessed their roles in the Series fix and implicated the other five conspirators. On September 28, with Chicago one game behind Cleveland with three games left to play, a Cook County grand

Shoeless Joe Jackson

jury returned indictments and all eight were suspended. The player-depleted Sox lost two of their last three games and the Indians captured the pennant.

The eight players eventually were found innocent of criminal charges by a Chicago jury, primarily because the prosecution's case had been destroyed by the mysterious disappearance of all paperwork concerning the fix, including the signed confessions of Cicotte, Jackson and Williams. But Judge Kenesaw Mountain Landis, exercising the dictatorial powers given to him as baseball's first commissioner, banned the players from

baseball for life because of their undeniable link to gamblers.

Cicotte reportedly received a $10,000 payoff, but it remains unclear whether anybody else received a dime. Jackson and Weaver maintained innocence to their death. It would appear that both had prior knowledge of the fix, but did not help carry it through.

"The record of the Series alone vindicated Joe," said Eddie Collins, who always maintained Jackson was an unfortunate victim. "He was our leading hitter and he fielded perfectly."

Weaver continued to petition for reinstatement every year right up to his death in 1958. Jackson supporters, pointing out that Shoeless Joe was uneducated and incapable of understanding the complicity with which he was unwittingly involved, have carried on his cause, hoping to clear him for inclusion in baseball's Hall of Fame. All pleas have been denied.

"Joe was a nice, quiet fellow," Shano Collins said. "He was handicapped. He couldn't read or write, but I guess there was nothing else to be done but bar him along with the others. Baseball couldn't forgive him just because he wasn't smart.

"I never saw him make a mistake on the field, though. He knew what to do with the ball when he got his hands on it and he never made a mistake with that bat."

Hard-hitting Joe Jackson began his career with the Cleveland Indians.

★1921★
JANUARY - DECEMBER

Landis takes reins as first commissioner

Federal Judge Kenesaw Mountain Landis, guaranteed dictatorial powers over both players and owners, officially began his seven-year reign as baseball's first Commissioner January 21.

Landis, elected to the newly created post November 12, is being asked to bring integrity and order into a game that has fast been losing the public's confidence. The biggest blow was the 1919 scandal that led to the indictment of eight Chicago White Sox, who were accused of accepting money to intentionally lose the World Series to Cincinnati.

Landis replaces the three-man National Commission that had ruled baseball since 1903, when the American and National leagues reached a merger agreement. The Commission had often bowed to special interests, a problem that no longer should exist with Landis in control.

The move severely restricts the power of A.L. President Ban Johnson, baseball's primary moving force since 1903.

A distinguished group of owners and officials gather around Judge Kenesaw Mountain Landis as he signs a contract to become commissioner.

Babe goes on binge

A week in the colorful life of New York's Babe Ruth:

On June 8, the Bambino was arrested for speeding in New York, drawing a $100 fine and a short stay in jail. Ruth was released after the start of a Yankee game against Cleveland and rushed to the Polo Grounds, changing into his uniform in the car. Ruth arrived in the sixth inning and batted twice, walking and grounding out in a 4-3 victory.

Two days later, Ruth connected for his 120th career home run in a game against the Indians and became the all-time leader, passing former star Gavvy Cra-

vath. That was the beginning of one of Ruth's patented home run binges that produced seven in five games.

Fittingly, they were not all *ordinary* home runs. On June 13 against Detroit, Ruth hit two, the second an historic shot into the center-field bleachers at the Polo Grounds. The seventh-inning blow, the first ever hit over the park's center-field fence, traveled an incredible 460 feet.

The next day Ruth blasted two more moon shots. The second, his 23rd of the season, became the second ever to settle into the Polo Grounds' center-field bleachers.

CAUGHT ON THE FLY

AUGUST
Detroit's 34-year-old Ty Cobb became the youngest player to reach the 3,000-hit plateau when he connected against Boston righthander Elmer Myers.

OCTOBER
New York slugger Babe Ruth closed his record-setting home run campaign by hitting No. 59 off Curt Fullerton in the Yankees' 7-6 victory over the Boston Red Sox.

DECEMBER
Eight N.L. spitball pitchers and nine from the A.L. were given official permission to use the now-illegal pitch for the remainder of their careers.

Fans flock to openers

Major league officials, still reeling from the effects of World War I and the negative publicity generated by the infamous "Black Sox" scandal, hailed April 13 as the "comeback of baseball" after seven Opening Day games attracted more than 160,000 fans.

Records were set at Chicago's Wrigley Field (nearly 25,000) and at New York's Polo Grounds, where 37,000 watched Babe Ruth garner five hits in an 11-1 Yankee victory over Philadelphia. The Chicago-Detroit opener was postponed because of rain.

The most ceremonial opener was staged in Washington, where numerous dignitaries were on hand to watch the Senators play host to Boston. President Warren Harding threw out the first ball for a game attended by Vice President Calvin Coolidge, former President Woodrow Wilson, General John Pershing, members of the Cabinet and Congress and A.L. President Ban Johnson.

Washington ace Walter Johnson, who had never failed to complete an Opening Day start, lasted only four innings in a 6-3 loss.

U.S. President Warren Harding throwing out the ceremonial first pitch at Washington's season-opening game.

Landis suspends Ruth

Commissioner Kenesaw Mountain Landis, displaying his authority over major league baseball, suspended New York Yankee slugger Babe Ruth and two teammates for the first six weeks of the 1922 season because of their illegal postseason barnstorming tour.

Ruth, Bob Meusel and pitcher Bill Piercy also were fined $3,362, the loser's share in the World Series the Yankees had just dropped to the New York Giants. The punishment comes in the wake of the players' refusal to heed Landis' warning that they would be violating a 1912 rule that prohibits players from participating in postseason exhibitions.

Ruth literally thumbed his nose at the first-year commissioner and played New York exhibitions in Buffalo, Jamestown and Elmira beginning October 16. When the tour reached Scranton, Pa., Ruth backed down and issued an apology to Landis. But with Yankee ownership backing his move, Landis made it clear who is running the show.

Ruth, baseball's most popular player and top gate attraction, is coming off a monster season in which he batted .378, crashed a record 59 home runs, drove in 171 runs and scored 177. Meusel had 24 homers and 135 RBIs.

Commissioner Kenesaw Mountain Landis suspended Yankees Babe Ruth (left) and Bob Meusel (right) in 1921 for their rule-breaking postseason barnstorming tour.

Baseball on radio

Harold Arlin, a Westinghouse Company foreman, made radio history August 5 when he described a baseball game over the KDKA airwaves from Pittsburgh's Forbes Field.

The Pittsburgh station, owned by Westinghouse, selected a Pirates-Philadelphia game for its broadcast and asked the 26-year-old Arlin to handle play-by-play. Using a converted telephone as his microphone, he described a one-hour, 57-minute contest that produced 21 hits and seven walks. The Pirates won, 8-5.

Arlin, working from a ground-level box seat, used a faulty transmitter, never knowing for sure whether he was being heard. Sometimes the crowd noise drowned out his words.

But he persevered and the station broadcast tennis, World Series and college football games later in the year.

SEASON LEADERS

	American League		National League	
Avg.	Harry Heilmann, Det.	.394	Rogers Hornsby, St.L.	.397
HR	Babe Ruth, N.Y.	59	George Kelly, N.Y.	23
RBI	Babe Ruth, N.Y.	171	Rogers Hornsby, St.L.	126
SB	George Sisler, St.L.	35	Frank Frisch, N.Y.	49
W-L Pct.	Carl Mays, N.Y.	27-9, .750	Bill Doak, St.L.	15-6, .714
ERA	Red Faber, Chi.	2.48	Bill Doak, St.L.	2.59
SO	Walter Johnson, Wash.	143	Burleigh Grimes, Bkn.	136

WORLD SERIES REPORT

BATTLE OF NEW YORK

Lefthander Art Nehf pitched a four-hitter October 13 and made an unearned first-inning run stand up for a 1-0 victory over the Yankees, giving the Giants their first World Series championship since 1905.

The Game 8 triumph concluded an emotional all-New York, all-Polo Grounds battle. The Yankees, featuring the long-ball exploits of Babe Ruth, were making their first postseason appearance while the Giants were trying to avenge four straight fall classic losses.

The Series opened with Yankee starters Carl Mays and Waite Hoyt pitching consecutive 3-0 shutouts. Mays allowed five hits, Hoyt two. Things looked bleak for John McGraw's troops when they fell behind the Yankees, 4-0, after 2½ innings of Game 3.

But the Giants, getting four runs batted in from Ross Youngs and three from Irish Meusel and Johnny Rawlings, roared back for a 13-5 victory and evened the Series with a 4-2 triumph in Game 4.

Hoyt was masterful again in Game 5 as the Yankees scored a 3-1 victory, but the Giants closed out the Series with 8-5, 2-1 and 1-0 wins. Hoyt, who did not allow an earned run in 27 innings, was the tough-luck loser in Game 8.

Pittsburgh radio station KDKA aired the Series opener with sportswriter Grantland Rice handling play-by-play.

Waite Hoyt did not allow an earned run in 27 innings, but the Giants still prevailed in the all-New York World Series.

Game 1	Yankees	3	Giants	0
Game 2	Yankees	3	Giants	0
Game 3	Giants	13	Yankees	5
Game 4	Giants	4	Yankees	2
Game 5	Yankees	3	Giants	1
Game 6	Giants	8	Yankees	5
Game 7	Giants	2	Yankees	1
Game 8	Giants	1	Yankees	0

★1922★

SEASON LEADERS

	American League		National League	
Avg.	George Sisler, St.L.	.420	Rogers Hornsby, St.L.	.401
HR	Ken Williams, St.L.	39	Rogers Hornsby, St.L.	42
RBI	Ken Williams, St.L.	155	Rogers Hornsby, St.L.	152
SB	George Sisler, St.L.	51	Max Carey, Pit.	51
W-L Pct.	Joe Bush, N.Y.	26-7, .788	Pete Donohue, Cin.18-9, .667	
ERA	Red Faber, Chi.	2.80	Rosy Ryan, N.Y.	3.01
SO	Urban Shocker, St.L.	149	Dazzy Vance, Bkn.	134

Robertson is perfect

Chicago's Charlie Robertson, a rookie righthander with pinpoint control, withstood the taunts of 25,000 howling Detroit fans April 30 and pitched baseball's third modern-era perfect game, beating the Tigers 2-0 at Navin Field.

The 26-year-old Texan was untouchable, retiring all 27 Tigers and striking out six. He ignored the hostile Detroit fans and the psychological ploys of Tiger stars Harry Heilmann and Ty Cobb, who protested that Robertson was doctoring the ball. The umpires failed to detect any wrongdoing and by the latter stages of the game, even the fans changed their tune.

When Robertson retired Danny Clark, Clyde Manion and Johnny Bassler in the ninth inning, the Detroit faithful broke through the roped-off outfield barrier and carried him off the field in triumph.

The victory was only the second for Robertson since the White Sox purchased his contract from Minneapolis of the American Association. He joins the Boston Red Sox's Cy Young (1904) and Cleveland's Addie Joss (1908) as the only pitchers since 1900 to pitch perfect games. Boston's Ernie Shore retired all 27 batters

he faced in a 1917 contest against Washington, but he was pitching in relief of Babe Ruth, who was ejected after walking the game's first batter.

Chicago scored both runs in the second inning on Earl Sheely's single.

Chicago's Mr. Perfect, Charlie Robertson.

Walter Johnson adds to shutout record

Washington's Walter Johnson outdueled New York ace Waite Hoyt June 28 and won his third straight shutout and the 95th of his spectacular career as the Senators edged the Yankees, 1-0, at Griffith Stadium.

Johnson, pitching in his 16th big-league season and already a 300-game winner, allowed seven hits and struck out nine. He was especially tough when the

Yankees put men on base.

But Hoyt allowed only two hits through eight innings before tiring in the ninth. Howard Shanks led off the crucial inning with a single, moved to second on a sacrifice bunt and scored the game's winning run on Earl Smith's double.

Babe Ruth collected a pair of singles off Johnson and Everett Scott had a single and double.

Ruth gets 'the call'

New York Yankee slugger Babe Ruth became the highest-paid player in baseball history March 5 when he agreed to a three-year contract that will pay him in excess of $50,000 per season. Final terms of the deal were decided by a *coin flip* in the Hot Springs, Ark., hotel room of Colonel Tillinghast Huston, co-owner of the Yankees.

Ruth, who hit 59 home runs last season and 54 in 1920, made the coin-flip offer when the two parties reached an impasse during negotiations. Huston contacted Jacob Ruppert in New York and

his partner agreed. When Huston flipped a half dollar, Ruth correctly called "tails."

The contract, which dwarfs anything previously paid in baseball history, also calls for Ruth to receive $500 for every home run he hits and gives the Yankees a two-year option. Ruth is believed to have made $40,000 in salary and bonuses last year. Huston said Ruth's new contract is "worthy of a railroad president."

Ruth, who took part in an unauthorized barnstorming tour last year, is under suspension for the first six weeks of the 1922 season.

New York Yankee co-Owner Jacob Ruppert with Babe Ruth after the Bambino had signed his "coin flip" contract.

GIANTS STEP ON YANKEES

Lefthander Art Nehf allowed five hits October 8 and the Giants staged a three-run eighth-inning rally that gave them a 5-3 victory over the Yankees and their second straight World Series triumph.

The Game 5 victory gave the Giants a four-game sweep and officially ended the Yankees' 10-year co-tenancy in the Polo Grounds. The Yankees, who managed only a 3-3 Game 2 tie, will move into a spacious new stadium in 1923.

The Giants also used a three-run eighth inning to win Game 1. Irish Meusel's two-run single and Ross Youngs' sacrifice fly wiped out a 2-0 Yankee advantage and ruined Joe Bush's nice pitching effort. After darkness forced postponement of Game 2, the Giants, who held Babe Ruth to a meager .118 average, roared to 3-0 and 4-3 wins, setting up their Series-clinching victory.

It marked the first year since 1919 that the fall classic was played with a best-of-seven format and the first time ever that an entire Series was broadcast over the radio.

New York Giants lefty Art Nehf pitched the World Series clincher for the second year in a row.

Game 1	Giants	3	Yankees	2
Game 2	Giants	3	Yankees	3
Game 3	Giants	3	Yankees	0
Game 4	Giants	4	Yankees	3
Game 5	Giants	5	Yankees	3

JANUARY

Ben Shibe, half owner and president of the Philadelphia Athletics since their A.L. debut, died at age 84.

MAY

A fifth-inning walk was the only blemish against New York Giants righthander Jesse Barnes as he pitched a 6-0 no-hitter against the Philadelphia Phillies at the Polo Grounds.

SEPTEMBER

The New York Yankees rewarded an overflow crowd of 40,000 with a doubleheader sweep of the Philadelphia Athletics in their farewell home appearance at the Polo Grounds.

The A.L., having reinstated the MVP award last presented in 1914, selected St. Louis Browns first baseman George Sisler in voting by one writer from each league city.

Cubs win, 26-23

It wasn't pretty, but the August 25 game between the Chicago Cubs and Philadelphia Phillies will be long remembered. The Cubs' 26-23 victory at Chicago's Wrigley Field left a big imprint on baseball's record books.

The teams combined for an unprecedented 49 runs and 51 hits in the three-hour, one-minute slugfest. They also combined for nine errors and 21 walks while stranding 16 runners. The Cubs, who had scored 10 runs in a big second inning, tied a major league record by scoring 14 times and sending 19 batters to the plate in a wild fourth, at which point they boasted a 25-6 lead.

But the Phillies stormed back with three runs in the fifth, eight in the eighth and six more in the ninth. They had the bases loaded when Tiny Osborne, Chicago's fifth pitcher, struck out Bevo LeBourveau to end the game.

Philadelphia pitchers Jimmy Ring and Lefty Weinert allowed 25 hits, including five by Cliff Heathcote and four apiece by Hack Miller and Marty Krug. Miller hit two home runs.

St. Louisans sizzle

While two New York teams dominated the final standings, a pair of St. Louis players ran off with National and American league batting honors.

Cardinals second baseman Rogers Hornsby became the N.L.'s first .400 hitter in the post-1900 era and its second Triple Crown winner. Hornsby captured his third straight batting title with a .401 average, thanks to a final-day 3-for-5 push. He also led the N.L. in home runs (42), runs batted in (152), hits (250), runs scored (141), extra-base hits (102) and doubles (46). His hit total was an N.L. record and he punctuated his season with a 33-game hitting streak.

Browns first baseman George Sisler was equally hard on A.L. pitchers. The lefthander batted .420 and also led the league in hits (246), triples (18), runs scored (134) and stolen bases (51). Sisler, who led the A.L. with a .407 mark in 1920, also collected 105 RBIs while striking out only 14 times.

Sisler also compiled a 41-game hitting streak, baseball's longest since 1900. His average tied for second highest in modern major league history.

St. Louis Browns first baseman and .420 hitter George Sisler.

★1923★

SEASON LEADERS

	American League		National League	
Avg.	Harry Heilmann, Det.	.403	Rogers Hornsby, St.L.	.384
HR	Babe Ruth, N.Y.	41	Cy Williams, Phi.	41
RBI	Babe Ruth, N.Y.	131	Irish Meusel, N.Y.	125
SB	Eddie Collins, Chi.	49	Max Carey, Pit.	51
W-L Pct.	Herb Pennock, N.Y.	19-6, .760	Dolf Luque, Cin.	27-8, .771
ERA	Stan Coveleski, Cle.	2.76	Dolf Luque, Cin.	1.93
SO	Walter Johnson, Wash.	130	Dazzy Vance, Bkn.	197

Ruth christens grand new Yankee Stadium

Governors, generals, colonels, politicians and baseball officials were on hand April 18 when the New York Yankees unveiled the grandest ballpark ever constructed. Fittingly, Babe Ruth christened the new structure with a three-run homer that helped the Yankees post a 4-1 victory over the Boston Red Sox.

More than 74,200 fans, by far the largest crowd ever to attend a major league game, jammed into new Yankee Stadium while another 25,000 had to be turned away. What they saw was a beautiful $2.5 million, three-tier facility with all the modern conveniences. The stadium, which took 11 months to construct and is located just across the Harlem River from the Polo Grounds, has irregular field dimensions with an inviting right-field fence.

That's where Ruth stroked his fourth-inning home run off a 2-2 pitch from Boston's Howard Ehmke. The Yankees scored all their runs in the inning and Bob Shawkey went on to stop the Red Sox on three hits.

The record crowd was treated to Opening Day festivities that included New York Governor Al Smith throwing out the first ball and Yankee officials raising their 1922 American League championship pennant.

Part of the record throng that packed into beautiful new Yankee Stadium watching Opening Day action against Boston.

Cardinals, Phillies stage power display

Baker Bowl fans got a special treat May 11 when the hometown Phillies and St. Louis Cardinals put on the most awesome power display in baseball history, belting a major league single-game record 10 home runs in a 20-14 Philadelphia victory.

Phillies center fielder Cy Williams blasted three, lifting his major league-leading total to 12. He joined a host of players who managed three-homer games, but fell one short of the one-game record set by Boston's Bobby Lowe in 1894 and matched two years later by Philadelphia's Ed Delahanty.

Also getting in on the act were Phillies Johnny Mokan, who hit two three-run blasts, and Frank Parkinson. Les Mann homered twice for the Cardinals and Eddie Dyer and pitcher Bill Sherdel added one apiece.

The Cardinals collected 22 hits off three pitchers and the Phillies managed 18 off five. The Cardinals, who enjoyed a 3-0 lead after 2½ innings, finished their series in Philadelphia with a four-game major league record of 70 hits.

Philadelphia's Cy Williams accounted for three of the single-game record 10 home runs hit by the Phillies and St. Louis Cardinals in a contest at cozy Baker Bowl.

A.L. honors Scott

New York shortstop Everett Scott was the center of attention before the Yankees' May 2 game at Washington. But once the action started, 35-year-old Senators righthander Walter Johnson stole the spotlight.

Johnson set the Yankees down on three hits and outdueled Bob Shawkey, 3-0. The New Yorkers came close to scoring once, but Johnson pitched around Whitey Witt's leadoff sixth-inning triple. The Senators scored one run on a Goose Goslin single and two more on Rip Wade's double.

Scott, who went 0 for 3 against Johnson, was honored in pregame ceremonies for his major league-record streak of 1,000 straight games. With players from both teams lining the field, Scott and American League President Ban Johnson were paraded to home plate, where U.S. Secretary of the Navy, Edwin C. Denby, presented Scott with a gold medal.

Scott started his streak on June 20, 1916, while playing with the Boston Red Sox. The previous modern record had been held by Fred Luderus of the Philadelphia Phillies, who played in 533 consecutive contests.

Chicago fans riot

Commissioner Kenesaw Mountain Landis and National League President John A. Heydler saw first hand September 16 that rowdy fans still present a problem for the National Pastime. They watched angry fans at Chicago's Wrigley Field pelt umpire Charles Moran and New York Giants players with pop bottles after a disputed call at second base.

The trouble started when Moran called out Chicago's Sparky Adams on a close play at second to end the eighth inning. The crowd, remembering a similar call in the fourth that led to the ejection of Cliff Heathcote, began throwing bottles and other objects, holding the game up for 10 minutes. Landis stood up and shook his cane at the angry mob, but nobody paid heed.

When play resumed, the Giants closed out their 10-6 victory and were hustled off the field by police. Moran also was escorted away by policemen who had to repel a mob moving menacingly toward the umpire. It took a large force to clear the park.

Nobody was seriously hurt, but Giants Irish Meusel and Barney Friberg were struck by bottles.

A's go hitless — again

Boston's Howard Ehmke emulated New York Yankee righthander Sam Jones, becoming the second pitcher in four days to throw a no-hitter in Philadelphia against the struggling Athletics.

Ehmke's 4-0 September 7 no-hitter was aided by a baserunning gaffe by opposing pitcher Slim Harriss and an official scorer's change. Harriss drove an apparent double to the fence in the seventh inning, but was signaled out on appeal for missing first base. In the eighth, Philadelphia's Frank Welch reached first when Boston left fielder Mike Menosky dropped his low line drive. The play was first ruled a hit, then changed to an error. Ehmke faced only 28 batters.

Jones had faced only 29 in his 2-0 September 4 no-hitter. Chick Galloway drew a walk in the first inning and Welch reached on Everett Scott's eighth-inning error.

New York Yankee no-hit man Sam Jones.

CAUGHT ON THE FLY

MAY

Detroit's Ty Cobb became baseball's all-time leader in runs scored when he notched his 1,741st in a game against Chicago, passing former Pittsburgh great Honus Wagner.

JULY

Washington righthander Walter Johnson became the first pitcher to record 3,000 career strikeouts when he fanned five in a 3-1 victory over Cleveland.

OCTOBER

St. Louis Cardinals slugger Rogers Hornsby captured his fourth straight National League batting championship with a .384 mark.

YANKS BREAK THROUGH

The New York Yankees, trying to wipe out the stain of World Series losses to the New York Giants in 1921 and 1922, spotted the National League champs a two games to one lead and then roared back with three straight victories to claim their first-ever fall classic.

The clincher came October 15 at the Polo Grounds, the park the Yankees had shared for 10 seasons with the Giants. The 6-4 triumph featured Babe Ruth's third home run of the Series and the second win by pitcher Herb Pennock.

The Series got off to a sobering start for Yankee fans, thanks to the heroics of veteran Casey Stengel. The Giants outfielder christened Yankee Stadium with its first World Series home run in the opener, a ninth-inning inside-the-park clout that broke a 4-4 tie. He hit the stadium's second Series homer in Game 3 to give Art Nehf and the Giants a 1-0 victory.

But the rest of the Series belonged to the Yankees, who rolled off 8-4, 8-1 and 6-4 victories. Ruth, who had hit two solo homers in the Yankees' 4-2 Game 2 win, ignited the clinching triumph with a first-inning blast off Nehf. Bob Meusel got the big hit, however, when he singled home two teammates in a five-run eighth-inning rally.

Game 1	Giants	5	Yankees	4
Game 2	Yankees	4	Giants	2
Game 3	Giants	1	Yankees	0
Game 4	Yankees	8	Giants	4
Game 5	Yankees	8	Giants	1
Game 6	Yankees	6	Giants	4

Herb Pennock posted two victories in the New York Yankees' first-ever World Series championship.

Johnson regains form

Walter Johnson, Washington's 36-year-old pitching machine, fired a one-hitter and struck out 14 White Sox May 23 in a 4-0 victory over Chicago at Griffith Stadium.

Johnson, who had struggled through four mediocre seasons after winning 20 games in 1919, looked like the Walter of old. His effort was marred only by Harry Hooper's fourth-inning single and one walk. He struck out the side twice and fanned six straight Chicago batters from the second to fourth innings.

Johnson, the career strikeout record-holder with more than 3,000 and a 350-game winner, was aided by an offense that scored single runs in the first three innings and another in the fifth. Nemo Leibold contributed two hits and scored three runs.

Washington veteran Walter Johnson.

SEASON LEADERS

	American League		National League	
Avg.	Babe Ruth, N.Y.	.378	Rogers Hornsby, St.L.	.424
HR	Babe Ruth, N.Y.	46	Jack Fournier, Bkn.	27
RBI	Goose Goslin, Wash.	129	George Kelly, N.Y.	136
SB	Eddie Collins, Chi.	42	Max Carey, Pit.	49
W-L Pct.	Walter Johnson, Wash.	23-7, .767	Emil Yde, Pit.	16-3, .842
ERA	Walter Johnson, Wash.	2.72	Dazzy Vance, Bkn.	2.16
SO	Walter Johnson, Wash.	158	Dazzy Vance, Bkn.	262

Reds manager dies

Pat Moran, manager of the Cincinnati Reds for the last five seasons, died March 7 of Bright's disease at a hospital in Orlando, Fla., the team's spring training home. The former catcher was 48 years old.

Moran, known as a great handler of pitchers and an excellent field strategist, had struggled with his health during the winter, but chose to accompany the team to Florida anyway. He entered the hospital on Monday and died four days later when poison filled his lungs and made breathing impossible. He had lapsed into a coma and was not aware that his wife and two sons were at his bedside.

Moran is best known as the "Miracle Man" who guided the Reds to their 1919 World Series upset of the Chicago White Sox. He previously had managed Philadelphia, guiding the Phillies to their first National League pennant in 1915. They lost in the World Series to Boston.

Moran, who compiled a 748-586 managerial record, played 14 years as a backup catcher for the Boston Braves, Chicago Cubs and Phillies, batting .235.

Detroit fans riot

Bad blood between the New York Yankees and Detroit Tigers boiled over June 13 and led to a full-scale riot at Navin Field, resulting in a forfeit and a life-threatening situation for players, umpires and police.

The Yankees led the final game of the intense series, 10-6, in the ninth inning when a pitch from lefthander Bert Cole struck New York right fielder Bob Meusel in the back. Meusel dropped his bat, rushed the mound and swung wildly at Cole, missing his mark.

Meusel was restrained by umpire Emmett Ormsby, but Detroit Manager Ty Cobb ran onto the field and began arguing with Yankee slugger Babe Ruth, who had barely avoided a Cole pitch earlier in the inning. Ruth was restrained and both Meusel and the Bambino were ejected. As the two Yankees passed through the Detroit dugout on their way to the dressing room, they began arguing and shoving with Tiger players.

That's when fans spilled onto the field. Police managed to usher the Yankee players and umpires to safety, but could not restore peace. Policemen had to threaten the crowd with clubs and guns to protect themselves. At one point, the field was a mass of bobbing straw hats and flying fists.

Umpire Bill Evans awarded the Yankees a 9-0 forfeit, allowing the Bronx Bombers to remain tied for first place with Boston.

New York Yankee Bob Meusel rushed the mound and started a major league riot in Detroit.

Bottomley goes wild

Jim Bottomley, a 24-year-old first baseman with a perpetual smile, collected six hits, including two home runs, and drove in a major league-record 12 runs September 16 in the St. Louis Cardinals' 17-3 victory over the Brooklyn Dodgers at Ebbets Field.

Sunny Jim's 12-RBI explosion bettered the record of 11 set in 1892 by Baltimore's Wilbert Robinson. Uncle Robbie, ironically, sat in the opposing dugout watching Bottomley's performance — as Dodgers manager.

Bottomley drove in two runs with a first-inning single, doubled home another run in the second, hit a grand slam off Art Decatur in the fourth, hit a two-run homer in the sixth, singled home a pair of runs in the seventh and drove home his final run with a ninth-inning single.

The beneficiary of Bottomley's outburst was lefthander Willie Sherdel, who surrendered eight hits and two runs in eight innings.

St. Louis' Sunny Jim Bottomley exploded for 12 RBIs in a game against Brooklyn.

CAUGHT ON THE FLY

JULY

New York Giants first baseman George Kelly, who belted three homers and drove in eight runs during a June game against Cincinnati, set a major league record by hitting home runs in six consecutive contests.

SEPTEMBER

Dazzy Vance's N.L.-leading numbers for the Brooklyn Dodgers: 28 wins, 2.16 ERA, 30 complete games and 262 strikeouts.

DECEMBER

A new format for World Series play: The first two games at one team's park, the next three at the other's and the final two, if necessary, at the first team's field. Series openers will be alternated between leagues on an annual basis.

Hornsby bats .424

Rogers Hornsby reinforced his claim as the best righthanded hitter in the history of baseball when he finished the 1924 campaign with a record-high .424 average. The St Louis Cardinals' second baseman topped the previous high of .422 set by the Philadelphia Athletics' Nap Lajoie in 1901.

Hornsby, who won a National League Triple Crown in 1922 when he batted .401 with 42 home runs and 152 runs batted in, was the model of consistency as he rolled to his fifth consecutive N.L. batting title. He played in 143 games and was shut out only 24 times. He collected one hit in 44 contests, two in 46, three in 25 and four in four. He also led the N.L. in hits (227) and doubles (43) while tying for the lead with 121 runs scored.

Hornsby, who had 25 homers and 94 RBIs, missed three games in May because of a dislocated thumb and eight late-season contests because of back trouble.

WORLD SERIES REPORT

SENATORIAL PRIDE

Fate has not always been kind to the New York Giants and Washington Senators, so when the teams hooked up in Game 7 of the World Series October 10 at Griffith Stadium, something had to give.

With President Calvin Coolidge among the 31,667 spectators, the Giants led 3-1 in the eighth inning. But Lady Luck smiled on the Senators when player-manager Bucky Harris drove a bases-loaded, two-out grounder toward third baseman Fred Lindstrom. As the 18-year-old braced to make the play, the ball took a bad hop over his head, driving in two runs and tying the game.

Harris turned to veteran Walter Johnson — 0-2 in the Series — and he shut down the Giants for four innings, despite allowing three hits and three walks. Lady Luck smiled on the Senators again in the 12th.

With one out, Muddy Ruel lifted a pop foul behind the plate. But Giants catcher Hank Gowdy tripped over his own mask and failed to make the catch. Reprieved, Ruel doubled and then held second when Johnson reached on an error by shortstop Travis Jackson.

The next batter, Earl McNeely, drove another routine grounder toward Lindstrom. Again he braced and again the ball inexplicably bounded high over his head. Ruel scored and Washington had its first championship.

Game 1	New York	4	Washington	3
Game 2	Washington	4	New York	3
Game 3	New York	6	Washington	4
Game 4	Washington	7	New York	4
Game 5	New York	6	Washington	2
Game 6	Washington	2	New York	1
Game 7	Washington	4	New York	3

U.S. President Calvin Coolidge and Washington Manager Bucky Harris before Game 7 of the World Series.

★1925★

JANUARY-DECEMBER

Cobb goes on a tear

Ty Cobb, Detroit's 38-year-old player-manager, tied a pair of modern major league records May 5 when he belted three home runs and collected 16 total bases in the Tigers' 14-8 victory over the Browns in a game at St. Louis.

The 12-time American League batting champion hit home runs in the first, second and eighth innings and added two singles and a double in his 6-for-6 performance. He drove in five runs and scored four while breaking the 6-year-old A.L. record of 13 total bases set by Washington catcher Patsy Gharrity.

The major league mark of 17 total bases was set in 1894 by Boston's Bobby Lowe and tied two years later by Philadelphia's Ed Delahanty. Both players hit four home runs and a single.

Cobb came back the next day with two more home runs and six RBIs against the Browns, setting another modern record — five homers in two games.

Detroit's Ty Cobb (right) did his best Babe Ruth impression on May 5 when he homered three times and collected 16 total bases in a game at St. Louis.

Scott's streak ends

New York Yankee Manager Miller Huggins, looking for a way to shake up his struggling 5-11 team, shocked a Yankee Stadium crowd May 6 when he benched shortstop Everett Scott and ended his record consecutive-game streak at 1,307.

When the Yankee lineup was introduced before a game against Philadelphia, Scott's name was conspicuously absent. Pee Wee Wanninger was penciled in at shortstop and word was received that Scott "was not feeling well."

But after the Athletics' 6-2 victory, Scott told reporters he was feeling fine and expressed unhappiness over his sudden demotion.

"It seems funny that it should happen the day after we win and I make two hits," Scott said. "Not that I care about the record. When I passed the 1,000 mark, I lost interest in the matter."

Scott's streak started June 20, 1916, and endured through all or parts of 10 seasons. He broke the major league record held by Brooklyn's George B. Pinckney (1885-90) when he played in his 578th straight game. He batted .254 with 18 homers and 53 stolen bases during the streak.

Shortstop Pee Wee Wanninger, the man who replaced Everett Scott in the New York Yankee lineup and ended his iron man streak at 1,307 games.

SEASON LEADERS

	American League		National League	
Avg.	Harry Heilmann, Det.	.393	Rogers Hornsby, St.L.	.403
HR	Bob Meusel, N.Y.	33	Rogers Hornsby, St.L.	39
RBI	Bob Meusel, N.Y.	138	Rogers Hornsby, St.L.	143
SB	John Mostil, Chi.	43	Max Carey, Pit.	46
W-L Pct.	Stan Coveleski, Wash.	20-5, .800	Bill Sherdel, St.L.	15-6, .714
ERA	Stan Coveleski, Wash.	2.84	Dolf Luque, Cin.	2.63
SO	Lefty Grove, Phi.	116	Dazzy Vance, Bkn.	221

Ruth gets operation

Babe Ruth returned to the New York lineup June 1 after missing the first two months of the season with a stomach disorder that required surgery and kept him confined to bed until late May.

Ruth's problems actually began April 5 in Atlanta when he complained of chills and fever as the Yankees and Brooklyn were barnstorming their way north before opening the season. Ruth insisted on making the journey to Chattanooga, Tenn., for an exhibition game and delighted an overflow crowd with two gargantuan home runs.

After hitting another homer the next day at Knoxville, Ruth collapsed April 7 as he stepped off the train at Asheville, N.C. He was taken unconscious to the Park Hotel where he was diagnosed as having influenza. Yankee officials decided to send him on to New York but he collapsed again on the train and hit his head on a wash basin. He arrived unconscious and was hospitalized.

Ruth's problem finally was diagnosed as an intestinal abscess and surgery was performed April 17. He remained in bed until May 26 with what the media dubbed "the stomach ache heard 'round the world."

A's stage wild rally

The Philadelphia Athletics staged one of the great comebacks of baseball history June 15 and defeated Cleveland, 17-15.

The American League-leading A's trailed 15-4 when they came to bat in the eighth inning. Many fans already had departed and those who remained held out little hope for victory. But walks to Chick Galloway and Max Bishop sandwiched around pitcher Tom Glass' fly out triggered an offensive explosion that would feature two more walks and nine hits against four Cleveland pitchers.

Jimmie Dykes delivered a two-run triple and Bill Lamar, Frank Welch and Charlie Berry produced RBI singles ahead of Galloway's two-run hit. Pinch-hitter Sammy Hale got in on the act with a run-scoring single and Bishop drove in two more with another

single. A walk to Lamar set the stage for the biggest hit of all — a three-run homer by Al Simmons that wiped out a 15-14 Philadelphia deficit.

The beneficiary of this 13-run outburst was Glass, who picked up his first major league victory.

Philadelphia Athletics slugger Al Simmons.

CAUGHT ON THE FLY

APRIL

A Chicago first: Radio station WGN aired a broadcast of a regular-season Cubs game against Pittsburgh.

The Cleveland Indians scored 12 eighth-inning runs to defeat the St. Louis Browns, 21-14.

Brooklyn Owner Charles Ebbets died on the morning of the Dodgers' Opening Day game against the New York Giants at Ebbets Field.

MAY-JUNE

Two new members of baseball's 3,000-hit club: Cleveland's Tris Speaker and Chicago White Sox Manager Eddie Collins.

Mathewson dies

Christy Mathewson, considered by many the greatest pitcher in history, died October 7 in Saranac, N.Y., after a five-year bout with tuberculosis. He was 45.

The Big Six as he was known, began his professional career in 1901 with New York and pitched 17 seasons, compiling a 373-188 record while leading the Giants to four National League pennants. His best campaign came in 1908 when he finished 37-11 with a league-leading 12 shutouts. Mathewson topped 30 victories four times and

20 a record 13 times.

Mathewson, a football and baseball star at Bucknell College before joining the Giants, is best remembered for his performance in the 1905 World Series against Philadelphia. He pitched three shutouts and allowed only 14 hits over a six-day span in the Giants' five-game victory.

Mathewson also managed Cincinnati for 2½ years, coached briefly for the Giants and became part owner of the Boston Braves until his death.

PIRATES WHIP SENATORS

Kiki Cuyler belted a tie-breaking two-run double in the eighth inning off Washington ace Walter Johnson October 15, giving Pittsburgh a 9-7 victory and its first World Series championship since 1909.

The Game 7 defeat at Forbes Field was tough for Johnson, the 37-year-old righthander who had won 20 games while lifting his career victory total to 396 during the regular season. Washington's Big Train had been overpowering in two previous starts as the Senators built a three games to one advantage, but he could not hold 4-0 and 6-3 leads in the finale.

Johnson had pitched a five-hitter in the opener and a six-hitter in Game 4

to lift Washington to within one win of its second straight fall classic title. But the Pirates fought back for 6-3 and 3-2 victories and completed the first three-games-to-one comeback in Series history.

Pittsburgh's Max Carey batted .458 while pitchers Vic Aldridge and Ray Kremer both won two games. For the Senators, Goose Goslin enjoyed his second straight three-homer Series, Joe Harris batted a lofty .440 and belted three homers and Sam Rice batted .364 and made a game-saving catch in Game 3. On the other side of the coin, Washington shortstop Roger Peckinpaugh committed a World Series-record eight errors.

Game 1	Washington	4	Pittsburgh	1
Game 2	Pittsburgh	3	Washington	2
Game 3	Washington	4	Pittsburgh	3
Game 4	Washington	4	Pittsburgh	0
Game 5	Pittsburgh	6	Washington	3
Game 6	Pittsburgh	3	Washington	2
Game 7	Pittsburgh	9	Washington	7

World Series Managers Bucky Harris of Washington and Bill McKechnie of Pittsburgh get a festive World Series greeting.

★1926★

SEASON LEADERS

	American League		National League	
Avg.	Heinie Manush, Det.	.378	Bubbles Hargrave, Cin.	.353
HR	Babe Ruth, N.Y.	47	Hack Wilson, Chi.	21
RBI	Babe Ruth, N.Y.	145	Jim Bottomley, St.L.	120
SB	John Mostil, Chi.	35	Kiki Cuyler, Pit.	35
W-L Pct.	George Uhle, Cle.	27-11, .711	Ray Kremer, Pit.	20-6, .769
ERA	Lefty Grove, Phi.	2.51	Ray Kremer, Pit.	2.61
SO	Lefty Grove, Phi.	194	Dazzy Vance, Bkn.	140

Braves get decision in basebrawl game

The July 25 game at Cincinnati between the Reds and Boston Braves was far from an artistic masterpiece. But the Braves' 8-4 victory is sure to be remembered as one of the hardest hitting games in history — literally.

The excitement started in the third inning when Cincinnati third baseman Babe Pinelli and Boston third base coach Art Devlin exchanged words and suddenly started swinging. Players from both teams joined in. The melee got so out of hand that city policemen were called onto the field to restore order.

When the fracas ended, Devlin sported a split cheek and badly bruised eye, Pinelli was ejected and Boston reserve outfielder Frank Wilson was carted off to jail for striking a police inspector. But that was only Round 1. Hostilities resumed in the fourth inning when Boston's Jimmy Welsh belted Reds catcher Val Picinich in a home plate collision and Picinich retaliated.

Again police intervened and again order was restored, this time with Picinich getting ejected. The remainder of the game was played in peace.

Giants get Hornsby

St. Louis and New York officials completed what insiders are calling the biggest trade in baseball history December 21, a deal that sends Cardinals Manager and six-time National League batting champion Rogers Hornsby to the Giants for infielder Frank Frisch and pitcher Jimmy Ring.

The trade came only two months after Hornsby had led St. Louis to its first World Series championship. Hornsby had recently demanded a three-year contract from Cardinals Owner Sam Breadon, who chose instead to listen to the overtures of Giants

Manager John McGraw and Owner Charles A. Stoneham.

The 30-year-old second baseman won six consecutive batting titles from 1920 to '25 and recorded the highest one-season average in baseball history in 1924, when he batted .424. He was a Triple Crown winner in both 1922 and '25.

The 28-year-old Frisch is a steady veteran and regular .300 hitter. He will take over at second base. Ring, a 31-year-old right-hander, was 11-10 with a 4.57 earned-run average for the Giants last year.

Sheely ties record

Chicago's Earl Sheely made history May 21 when he collected three doubles and a home run against Boston, giving the first baseman a record-tying seven straight extra-base hits.

Sheely had doubled in each of his last three at-bats the previous day in Chicago's 13-4 victory over the Red Sox at Fenway Park. His home run stretched his extra-base hit streak to seven and allowed him to tie the major league record

set in 1921 by Cleveland's Elmer Smith. Smith collected three doubles, four home runs and a pair of walks in three games.

Sheely, who drove in four runs in the May 20 game, added three RBIs the next day while taking the White Sox to a 7-5 lead after 7½ innings. But the seventh-place Red Sox rallied for three ninth-inning runs to win 8-7.

Sheely flied out in his final at-bat.

Chicago's Earl Sheely stroked seven straight extra-base hits.

CAUGHT ON THE FLY

JANUARY
The major league Rules Committee agreed to allow pitchers use of a resin bag at any time during a game.

SEPTEMBER
Babe Ruth compiled a .372 average with A.L.-leading totals in home runs (47), RBIs (145) and runs scored (139), but Cleveland's George Burns won the MVP award after hitting .358 with a major league-record 64 doubles.

DECEMBER
Kenesaw Mountain Landis was given a new seven-year term as baseball commissioner with a raise to $65,000.

Cobb-Speaker scandal

Ty Cobb and Tris Speaker, two of the greatest players in baseball history, were on the hotseat December 22 when they denied charges by former Detroit pitcher Dutch Leonard that they conspired to throw a 1919 Tigers-Cleveland Indians game and to profit by betting on its outcome.

Leonard testified to Commissioner Kenesaw Mountain Landis that he met under the grandstand of Navin Field in Detroit on September 24, 1919, with Cobb and Cleveland players Speaker and Joe Wood. All agreed the Tigers should win their game the next day to give them a chance to finish third in the American League race and gain extra money. Leonard also said the four planned to place money on the game.

Leonard produced two letters, one from Wood and another from Cobb, that alluded to betting on major league games. Cobb acknowledged the letter, but said the betting reference was to an entirely different matter. He said it was customary for players to bet on games in the other league and added that he had never bet a cent on an A.L. contest.

Cobb and Speaker both resigned their managerial posts after the season. Both said they had attempted to get Leonard to face them, but he refused. Landis, who confirmed that Leonard refused to appear at a hearing, traveled to California to get his testimony.

The accused eventually were cleared for lack of evidence.

Baseball greats Ty Cobb (left) and Tris Speaker (right) angrily denied scandalous accusations by former Detroit pitcher Dutch Leonard.

WORLD SERIES REPORT

PETE TO THE RESCUE

Aging Grover Cleveland Alexander, called out of the Yankee Stadium bullpen October 10 to face young New York slugger Tony Lazzeri with the bases loaded, recorded a crucial seventh-inning strikeout and then retired the New Yorkers without incident the rest of the way to preserve a 3-2 Cardinal victory and the Redbirds' first-ever World Series championship.

In one of the most tension-filled moments in Series history, Ol' Pete reached back to see if there was anything left in his tired right arm. He had pitched a complete-game 10-2 victory the day before to even the fall classic at three games apiece and figured he would not be pitching again for several months. But when St. Louis starter Jesse Haines ran into trouble, Cardinals Manager Rogers Hornsby called on his 39-year-old veteran.

The 22-year-old Lazzeri, coming off a 114-RBI rookie campaign, worked the count to 1-1 before drilling Alexander's third pitch into the left-field seats, just foul. As the noise level increased significantly, Alexander delivered his next pitch. Lazzeri swung and missed and the Cardinals had escaped serious trouble.

Alexander retired the Yanks in order in the eighth and got the first two outs of the ninth before walking Babe Ruth. Ruth shocked everybody by getting thrown out on a Series-ending steal attempt.

Ruth had homered earlier in the game, bringing his Series total to four. Three came in one game — a 10-5 New York victory in Game 4 at St. Louis' Sportsman's Park.

Alexander and Haines accounted for all four St. Louis victories. Haines was a 4-0 Game 3 winner, Alexander a 6-2 victor in Game 2. Light-hitting shortstop Tommy Thevenow provided a big spark with a Series-leading .417 average while Jim Bottomley and Billy Southworth both batted .345.

Game 1	New York	2	St. Louis	1
Game 2	St. Louis	6	New York	2
Game 3	St. Louis	4	New York	0
Game 4	New York	10	St. Louis	5
Game 5	New York	3	St. Louis	2
Game 6	St. Louis	10	New York	2
Game 7	St. Louis	3	New York	2

Yankee star Babe Ruth brought the Series to a surprising conclusion when he was thrown out (above) trying to steal second base.

Left: New York Yankee Babe Ruth and St. Louis player-Manager Rogers Hornsby exchange greetings before Game 1 of the World Series.

★1927★

Babe hits 60th homer

Babe Ruth added another feather of immortality to his cap September 30 when he blasted home run No. 60 off Washington lefthander Tom Zachary, giving the New York Yankees a 4-2 victory over the Senators and breaking his own one-season home run mark of 59.

The Bambino, who had logged homers 58 and 59 the day before to tie the record he set in 1921 during his second New York season, stepped to the plate in the eighth inning of a 2-2 game at Yankee Stadium. Mark Koenig was standing on third when Ruth stroked a 1-1 pitch into the right-field bleachers. As the crowd of 10,000 roared its approval, the Babe slowly circled the bases.

Hats flew through the air, confetti rained over the field and New York players beat their bats against the wooden floor of the dugout. Fans greeted Ruth with another deafening ovation when he returned to right field and he responded with a brisk military march that sent the crowd into another frenzy.

The home run, his third hit, was Ruth's record 17th in September and came in his second-to-last regular-season game. The Babe homered 12 times in May and nine times in June, July and August.

Yankee Babe Ruth watches the flight of his record 60th home run.

Cobb gets 4,000th hit

Philadelphia's Ty Cobb blazed a new trail into the record books July 18 when he collected his 4,000th career hit, a double off Sam Gibson at Detroit — the city where he played for 22 seasons.

The 40-year-old Cobb, who signed with the Athletics in February after getting his release from Detroit, reached his milestone during a 5-3 loss to the Tigers. He entered the season with 3,902 hits, far ahead of former Pittsburgh great Honus Wagner, who ranks second on the all-time charts with 3,430.

Cobb, a 12-time American League batting champion who won nine consecutive titles from 1907 to 1915, is a three-time .400 hitter who has topped 200 hits in a season nine times. Cobb, always controversial because of his surly, never-give-an-inch attitude, batted a whopping .420 in 1911 and won a Triple Crown in 1909, when he batted .377 with nine homers and 107 RBIs.

SEASON LEADERS

	American League		National League	
Avg.	Harry Heilmann, Det.	.398	Paul Waner, Pit.	.380
HR	Babe Ruth, N.Y.	60	Cy Williams, Phi.	30
			Hack Wilson, Chi.	30
RBI	Lou Gehrig, N.Y.	175	Paul Waner, Pit.	131
SB	George Sisler, St.L.	27	Frank Frisch, St.L.	48
W-L Pct.	Waite Hoyt, N.Y.	22-7, .759	Larry Benton, Bos.-N.Y.	17-7, .708
ERA	Wilcy Moore, N.Y.	2.28	Ray Kremer, Pit.	2.47
SO	Lefty Grove, Phi.	174	Dazzy Vance, Bkn.	184

Triple play mania

Detroit's Rip Collins had sailed through eight innings of a May 31 game against Cleveland, allowing only three hits and clinging to the Tigers' 1-0 lead. But the right-hander walked pinch-hitter Glenn Myatt to lead off the ninth and Charlie Jamieson dropped a perfect bunt for a base hit.

Collins suddenly appeared vulnerable and Cleveland's Homer Summa increased the tension level at Navin Field when he lashed a wicked liner — right at Detroit first baseman Johnny Neun. Neun grabbed the drive, tagged Jamieson before he could return to first and raced to second to force Myatt. Unassisted triple play. Game over.

But that's only part of the story. The unassisted triple killing, one of baseball's rarest occurrences, was the second in two days. Chicago Cubs shortstop Jimmy Cooney had pulled one off the day before in the first game of a doubleheader at Pittsburgh.

A record Forbes Field crowd of more than 60,000 watched Cooney catch Glenn Wright's line drive, step on second to force Paul Waner and tag George Grantham dashing into second. The play helped the Cubs post a 7-6, 10-inning victory that snapped the Pirates' 11-game winning streak.

Detroit first baseman Johnny Neun thwarted a Cleveland rally with an unassisted triple play.

Johnsons step aside

Two eras passed in late October when baseball's most famous Johnsons, Washington pitcher Walter and American League President Ban, announced their retirements from the game they have served so well.

Ban Johnson, fighting health problems, gave up the post he had held for 28 years after founding the A.L. in 1900 and declaring it a second major league in 1901. An iron-fisted manager and one of the prime ruling forces of baseball through most of the 20th century, he will be succeeded by Frank Navin, owner of Detroit Tigers and A.L. vice president.

Walter Johnson, the premier pitcher in baseball since his arrival in 1907, leaves with 416 career victories and a major league-record 110 shutouts. The 39-year-old righthander has agreed to manage the Newark club of the International League next season.

The Big Train slumped to a 5-6 record in his final campaign.

A.L. President Ban Johnson shortly before retirement.

CAUGHT ON THE FLY

MARCH

The New York Yankees made Babe Ruth the highest paid player in baseball history when they signed him for three years at a reported $70,000.

JULY

The Chicago Cubs spoiled John McGraw Day at the Polo Grounds with an 8-5 victory. The celebration honored McGraw's 25 years as manager of the New York Giants.

OCTOBER

Ross Youngs, a .322 hitter in 10 outstanding seasons with the New York Giants, died of Bright's disease at age 30.

DECEMBER

Washington received permission to host the annual A.L. opener and the league installed E. S. Barnard as its president.

WORLD SERIES REPORT

THE GREAT YANKEES

When Earle Combs danced across the plate on John Miljus' World Series-ending wild pitch October 8, a Yankee Stadium crowd of 57,909 began a delirious celebration that officially cemented this New York team's place in baseball history. If the 1927 Yankees were not the best team ever assembled, they were close.

The two-out, ninth-inning run gave the Yankees a 4-3 victory and completed their sweep of the National League-champion Pittsburgh Pirates. The finale featured Babe Ruth's second home run of the Series and a solid pitching effort by Wilcy Moore.

To say the Pirates were unworthy opponents would be unfair. *Any team* would have fallen quickly to this Yankee machine. The Bronx Bombers of Manager Miller Huggins had rolled to an American League-record 110 victories and had won the pennant by a staggering 19 games with a lineup that plundered its opposition.

Ruth and his record-setting 60 home runs drew most of the attention, but first baseman Lou Gehrig was equally devastating. The two combined for 107 homers and 339 runs batted in, Gehrig's 175 RBIs setting a major league record. Joining Ruth and Gehrig on the Yankees' "Murderer's Row" were Bob Meusel (103 RBIs) and Tony Lazzeri (102).

The Yankees were not all power. Gehrig batted .373 and the three outfielders combined for 597 hits and a .350 average. Ruth and Combs batted .356, Meusel .337. Meusel finished second in the league with 24 stolen bases and Lazzeri tied for third with 22.

Offense is nice, but pitching wins games. Well, the Yankees had Waite Hoyt, who tied for the A.L. lead with 22 victories and tied for second with a 2.63 earned-run average — right behind teammate Moore (2.28). Moore tied Herb Pennock with 19 victories, Urban Shocker won 18 games and Dutch Ruether and George Pipgras combined to record a 23-9 mark.

It was no wonder the Yankees dismissed the Pirates quickly in the fall classic. They won the opener, 5-4, at Pittsburgh's Forbes Field and the second game, 6-2. They returned home to record an 8-1 triumph and then finished off their championship stampede in fitting style.

Game 1	New York	5	Pittsburgh	4
Game 2	New York	6	Pittsburgh	2
Game 3	New York	8	Pittsburgh	1
Game 4	New York	4	Pittsburgh	3

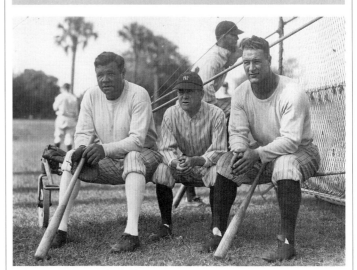

Diminutive New York Yankee Manager Miller Huggins with stars Babe Ruth (left) and Lou Gehrig (right).

RUTH AND GEHRIG

The Yankee Bash Brothers

"I'm just the guy who's in there every day, the fellow who follows Babe in the batting order. When Babe's turn at bat is over, whether he strikes out or belts a home run, the fans are still talking about him when I come up. If I stood on my head at the plate, nobody would pay any attention."

Lou Gehrig on Babe Ruth

"When that guy came to bat, all you could do was hold your breath. When you consider everything, the number of games he played, the way he hit, his reliability and his drive, he was, for me, the greatest first baseman of all time."

Bucky Harris on Lou Gehrig

Watching Babe Ruth play baseball was like having a marching band parade through your living room. There was nothing subtle about the man. He was loud, gaudy, entertaining, endearing and magnetic. He was the happy-go-lucky Sultan of Swat.

Following Lou Gehrig, however, was a little like watching grass grow. Everything about the man was subtle. He was quiet, shy, down to earth, simple and genuine. He was unspectacular, the blue-collar superstar.

Ruth has withstood the test of time as baseball's greatest slugger. But Gehrig's vast accomplishments will forever be overshadowed by those of the Bambino, just as he was as a player from 1925 (Gehrig's first full season with the New York

Yankees) to 1934 (Ruth's last campaign with the Bronx Bombers). While fans were understandably attracted to the showmanship of Ruth, embattled American League pitchers feared Gehrig as the enforcer of baseball's original Bash Brothers, the greatest 1-2 punch the sport has ever known.

"I'm not a headline guy and we may as well face it," Gehrig once said about his perceived role as Ruth's caddy. "I'm just the guy who's in there every day, the fellow who follows Babe in the batting order. When Babe's turn at bat is over, whether he strikes out or belts a home run, the fans are still talking about him when I come up. If I stood on my head at the plate, nobody would pay any attention."

Indeed, the 6-foot-1, 212-pound rock did play every day,

Far left: Babe Ruth, New York's Sultan of Swat.

Left: Gehrig kept a low profile, preferring the simpler pleasures of life.

amassing 2,130 straight games over 14-plus seasons. He performed his amazing iron man feat without fanfare, and he protected Ruth in the batting order, forcing pitchers to throw strikes. With Ruth batting third and Gehrig fourth, the Yankees tore through the American League like a herd of elephants through a straw hut.

The Ruth-Gehrig rampage started in 1926, when both were healthy and playing full time. With Ruth batting .372 and the young Gehrig .313, the duo combined for 63 home runs and 252 RBIs, leading the Yankees to an A.L. pennant and a seven-game loss to St. Louis in the World Series. But that was just the appetizer.

With a Murderer's Row lineup of Ruth, Gehrig, Tony Lazzeri and Bob Meusel combining for 544 RBIs and an outstanding pitching staff of Waite Hoyt, Wilcy Moore, Herb Pennock and Urban Shocker totaling 78 wins, the 1927 Yankees, a.k.a. the greatest team in baseball history, rolled to 110 victories and won the A.L. pennant by a whopping 19 games. They capped their onslaught by sweeping Pittsburgh in the World Series.

But the season's highlight was Ruth's 60-home run barrage, the standard by which future generations of power hitters would be judged. The Babe also batted .356 and drove in 164 runs. Lost in his massive shadow was Gehrig: .373, 47 homers and a major league-record 175 RBIs.

And so it continued. The duo combined for 81 homers and 284 RBIs in 1928 as the Yankees swept to another championship, 81 and 280 in 1929, 90 and 327 in 1930, 92 and 347 in 1931, 75 and 288 in 1932, 66 and 242 in 1933 and 71 and 249 in 1934. For nine seasons, they averaged 81 homers and 290 RBIs.

Through those years, Ruth captured five home run titles and tied for another. Gehrig was an RBI machine, winning four league titles and tying for one.

The teacher and the pupil — young Lou Gehrig (left) and Babe Ruth.

He set the current single-season A.L. record in 1931 when he drove in 184. Ruth also won one RBI crown outright while Gehrig claimed the 1934 home run title.

It is fascinating that two such different personalities should be linked so tightly by the bonds of time. Ruth, the troubled street kid who grew up in a Baltimore orphanage. Gehrig, the native New Yorker who spent most of his life under the spell of an overprotective mother. Ruth, the gregarious, friendly, oft-suspended night owl. Gehrig, the withdrawn, modest, trouble-free homebody. Ruth, the father of the long, majestic home run. Gehrig, the prototype slasher who drove line drives all over the park.

But in reality, these two bashers were perfect complements.

"They were very different, you know," said former Yankee pitcher George Pipgras. "Babe was outgoing and friendly — he loved people, he loved giving autographs. Lou was the quiet one. . . .

"I remember one time we were coming into some town in the South to play an exhibition game. When the bus pulled up to the ballpark there was a great crowd of people outside waiting for autographs. Lou sort of froze up. He didn't like a lot of people around him. I could see he didn't want to get off the bus. Finally, I said to him, 'Lou, just wait until

Babe gets off. He'll draw them away and then you can sneak off.' And that's just what happened."

Ruth, of course, has been hailed as the savior of the game, the man who ushered in baseball's long-ball era. His 29 homers in 1919 set a major league record and he soared to mind-boggling totals of 54 in 1920 and 59 in 1921, his first two seasons in New York. He drew massive crowds, earned headlines all over the country and helped erase the stigma of the 1919 Black Sox scandal. He was the perfect man for the job, a magnetic personality who coveted the spotlight.

"Babe was no ordinary man," said Hoyt. "He was not alone the idol of the fans, he was a superman to the ballplayers. Ruth possessed a magnetism that was positively infectious. When

he entered a clubhouse or a room, when he appeared on a field, it was as if he was the whole parade. There seemed to be flags waving, bands playing constantly."

Such powerful personalities need a buffer, and Gehrig provided that. The Yankees' Iron Horse never seemed to mind playing second fiddle to the great Ruth, viewing his teammate with fascination and awe. Ruth was everything he was not and his spellbinding effect on people amazed Gehrig. Both players appeared content with their roles.

And no matter what Gehrig did, he seemed doomed to be upstaged anyway. Such as in 1927, when Lou's incredible numbers were shoved into the

Ruth was always the center of attention, whether performing on the baseball field or getting off a train.

background by Ruth's home run rampage. Such as the 1928 World Series, when Gehrig batted a whopping .545 and hit four home runs but Ruth batted .625 with three homers — all in the decisive fourth game. Such as the 1932 Series, when Gehrig batted .529

with three home runs but Ruth called his shot in a Game 3 victory over Chicago. Such as 1932, when Gehrig set a modern record with four homers in one game but was pushed off the front page when 30-year New York Giants Manager John McGraw suddenly retired.

Still, while Gehrig was taken for granted by the New York fans and media, he was not underestimated by his contemporaries.

"Listen," said former Washington player-Manager Bucky Harris, "when that guy came to bat, all you could do was hold your breath. When you consider everything, the number of games he played, the way he hit, his reliability and his drive, he was, for me, the greatest first baseman of all time."

Gehrig eventually did get his due, but only because of a fatal disease that tugged at the nation's heart strings and brought a premature conclusion to his career in 1939. Ruth retired as a living legend in 1935 and then took on a mystical aura after his death in 1948.

Ironically, Gehrig's final years also were played in the shadows, even though Ruth was retired from the New York baseball scene. The new headliner: Joseph Paul DiMaggio.

Gehrig was a slasher who drove line drives to all sections of the ballpark.

★1928★

McGraw hit by car

New York Giants Manager John McGraw was struck down by an automobile May 14 as he tried to cross a street outside Chicago's Wrigley Field, sentencing him to six weeks on the sideline while Roger Bresnahan called the shots as interim boss.

McGraw, who has guided the Giants to three World Series championships and nine National League pennants since taking over as manager midway through the 1902 campaign, was leaving the ballpark after watching the Cubs post an 8-2 victory over his fourth-place New Yorkers.

Accompanied by coaches Bresnahan and Hans Lobert, McGraw threaded his way through moving traffic toward a waiting taxi cab. As he emerged from behind a car, he was struck on the right leg by a roadster and sent sprawling into the street. Shaken badly, McGraw was helped to his feet, but refused to even take the name of the driver, saying the accident was entirely his fault.

The leg injury was first diagnosed as a bad sprain and doctors said McGraw would be able to rejoin the team in a few days. But when swelling persisted, X-rays showed the leg was broken and McGraw was restricted to crutches.

New York Giants Manager John McGraw.

CAUGHT ON THE FLY

JUNE
Eddie Brown's streak of 618 consecutive games came to an unceremonious halt when the Boston Braves outfielder was benched.

SEPTEMBER
Urban Shocker, a righthander who won 187 games over 13 seasons with the New York Yankees and St. Louis Browns, died of pneumonia at age 38.

NOVEMBER
Voters in Massachusetts allowed the two Boston franchises to play Sunday baseball, leaving Pennsylvania as the only state still outlawing the sport on the Sabbath.

Ty Cobb ends career

Ty Cobb, the greatest pure hitter baseball has ever produced, retired September 30 after his 24th major league season. The Georgia Peach spent 22 years with the Detroit Tigers and finished his unparalleled career with the Philadelphia Athletics.

Cobb, limited at age 41 to pinch-hitting and some spot duty, goes out as the holder of many important baseball records. The 12-time American League batting champion holds career marks for games (3,033), average (.367), runs scored (2,245), hits (4,191), 200-hit seasons (nine), runs batted in (1,960) and consecutive batting titles (nine). He ranks second in doubles (724) to Tris Speaker, in triples (298) to Sam Crawford and stolen bases (892) to Billy Hamilton.

Among the milestones Cobb reached in his final campaign were 3,000 games (June 28) and 700 doubles (May 3). He collected his final hit, a double, on September 3 and popped out in his final big-league at-bat September 17. The lefthanded hitting outfielder, who managed the Tigers from 1921 through '26, says he will not return to the game in any capacity.

Foxx steals the show

Veteran sluggers Al Simmons, Joe Hauser and Jimmie Dykes all hit home runs keying Philadelphia's 8-2 and 7-3 doubleheader sweep of the St. Louis Browns July 21, but one swing from muscular 20-year-old first baseman Jimmie Foxx stole the spotlight.

Foxx, batting in the fifth inning of the opener with Simmons on base, smashed a Johnny Ogden pitch over the double-deck left-field stands and out of Shibe Park. The drive, the first ever to leave the stadium without bouncing on the roof, was measured at 450 feet and left everyone gasping.

But the Athletics' bombardment was just beginning. Simmons connected in the eighth inning of the opener and drove a ball into the upper-deck right-field bleachers off Walter (Boom-Boom) Beck, and Dykes and Hauser both homered in the nightcap. The A's collected 27 hits in the doubleheader and every player in the Philadelphia lineup hit safely in both games.

The double win completed a five-game sweep of the Browns and moved the second-place A's to within 11 games of the New York Yankees.

Powerful young Philadelphia slugger Jimmie Foxx.

DH idea voted down

An interesting proposal by National League President John Heydler to adopt a rule placing a 10th player in lineups to hit for the pitcher was voted down December 13 at the major league meetings in Chicago.

A.L. owners listened to Heydler's idea for a "designated hitter" who would not play in the field but would bat every time the pitcher's spot in the order came around. Heydler, contending fans are tired of watching weak-hitting pitchers attempt to hit, claimed the move would speed up the game.

Heydler was supported by New York Giants Manager John McGraw and other officials, but most American Leaguers favored keeping the game in its traditional form without unnecessary tampering.

National League President John Heydler was an early designated hitter proponent.

SEASON LEADERS

	American League		National League	
Avg.	Goose Goslin, Wash.	.379	Rogers Hornsby, Bos.	.387
HR	Babe Ruth, N.Y.	54	Jim Bottomley, St.L.	31
			Hack Wilson, Chi.	31
RBI	Lou Gehrig, N.Y.	142	Jim Bottomley, St.L.	136
	Babe Ruth, N.Y.	142		
SB	Buddy Myer, Bos.	30	Kiki Cuyler, Chi.	37
W-L Pct.	General Crowder, St.L.	21-5, .808	Larry Benton, N.Y.	25-9, .735
ERA	Garland Braxton, Wash.	2.51	Dazzy Vance, Bkn.	2.09
SO	Lefty Grove, Phi.	183	Dazzy Vance, Bkn.	200

Yankees hold off A's

The New York Yankees held off Philadelphia in the American League and the St. Louis Cardinals outlasted New York in the National League as baseball fans enjoyed the most thrilling double pennant races since 1908.

The Yankees, coming off 110 victories and a four-game World Series sweep of Pittsburgh in 1927, appeared to have A.L. matters well in hand as they darted to a 13½-game lead on July 1. But just as the A's heated up, the Yankees stumbled, primarily because of injuries.

The Mackmen caught the Yanks on September 7 and took a half-game lead the next day. But the Bronx Bombers regained control September 9 when a record baseball crowd of 85,265 turned out for a doubleheader at Yankee Stadium and watched the New Yorkers post 5-0 and 7-3 victories over the A's. The Yankees held on the rest of the way and clinched their second straight pennant September 28, posting a final 2½-game margin.

The Cardinals took the N.L. lead on June 16 and never fell out of first, although they were challenged by the Giants and Chicago Cubs. By September 26, only a half-game separated St. Louis from New York. But the Cubs, having fallen out of contention, knocked off the Giants in a crucial season-closing series and the Cardinals clinched on September 29, finally winning by two games.

YANKS SWEEP AGAIN

Babe Ruth and Lou Gehrig, the New York Yankees' two-man wrecking machine, dropped their lethal hammer on the St. Louis Cardinals and carried the Bronx Bombers to their second straight World Series sweep.

Ruth, playing on a bad ankle, collected 10 hits in 16 at-bats for a whopping .625 Series average. His best work came October 9 in Game 4, when he belted solo home runs in the fourth, seventh and eighth innings of New York's 7-3 victory at Sportsman's Park. It must have seemed like deja vu for Cardinal fans, who had watched the Bambino perform the same three-homer trick against the Redbirds in the 1926 World Series.

But Ruth shared the spotlight with Gehrig, who blasted four homers while driving in nine runs and batting .545. Gehrig drove in two runs in the Yankees' 4-1 opening-game victory, hit a three-run homer to key a 9-3 Game 2 win and drilled two more home runs in a 7-3 third-game triumph. He capped his effort with a seventh-inning homer in Game 4.

Lost in the shadow of the seven-homer, 13-RBI Ruth-Gehrig explosion was the solid pitching of Waite Hoyt (two wins), George Pipgras and Tom Zachary, who combined for four complete-game efforts.

Game 1	New York	4	St. Louis	1
Game 2	New York	9	St. Louis	3
Game 3	New York	7	St. Louis	3
Game 4	New York	7	St. Louis	3

Yankees Lou Gehrig (left) and Babe Ruth combined for seven home runs and 13 RBIs in New York's World Series sweep of St. Louis.

★1929★

Alexander ties Matty

Grover Cleveland Alexander held Philadelphia scoreless for four innings and St. Louis rallied in the second game of an August 10 doubleheader to defeat the Phillies 11-9 in 11 innings, giving the veteran righthander his National League record-tying 373rd career victory.

Pitching in the city where he spent the first seven seasons of his 19-year career, Old Pete took over in the eighth inning with the Cardinals trailing, 9-8. St. Louis rallied to tie in the ninth and scored two runs in the top of the 11th. Alexander pitched his fourth shutout inning to earn his ninth victory of the season and tie Christy Mathewson, who won 373 games in 17 years with the New York Giants.

The 42-year-old Alexander has posted three 30-win seasons and nine campaigns of 20 or more victories in an outstanding career that began with the Phillies in 1911. Alexander and Mathewson are tied for third on the all-time major league win list behind Cy Young (511 wins in 22 seasons) and Walter Johnson (416 in 21).

Cardinals score 28

Jim Bottomley and Chick Hafey hit grand slam homers July 6 and the St. Louis Cardinals snapped their 11-game losing streak with a vengeance, exploding for two 10-run innings and pounding out a 28-6 victory over Philadelphia in the second game of a double-header at the Baker Bowl.

The 28 runs — a one-game modern record — allowed the defending National League champions to break out of a losing funk that had stretched almost two weeks. The Cardinals collected 28 hits in their second-game onslaught and 15 in their 10-6 opening-game loss, with Bottomley collecting seven hits in 10 at-bats, hitting three homers and driving in 10 runs.

Bottomley had four hits and six RBIs in the nightcap while Hafey contributed five hits and five RBIs. Taylor Douthit also had five hits, pitcher Fred Frankhouse had four and every member of the lineup had at least one. Eight players collected two or more hits.

The Cardinals scored 10 in the first, 10 more in the fifth and five in the eighth. The outburst broke the single-game record of 27 runs set by Cleveland in 1923 against Boston.

St. Louis' Chick Hafey contributed his fair share to the Cardinals' 28-run explosion against Philadelphia.

SEASON LEADERS

	American League		National League	
Avg.	Lew Fonseca, Cle.	.369	Lefty O'Doul, Phi.	.398
HR	Babe Ruth, N.Y.	46	Chuck Klein, Phi.	43
RBI	Al Simmons, Phi.	157	Hack Wilson, Chi.	159
SB	Charley Gehringer, Det.	27	Kiki Cuyler, Chi.	43
W-L Pct.	Lefty Grove, Phi. 20-6, .769		Charlie Root, Chi. 19-6, .760	
ERA	Lefty Grove, Phi.	2.81	Bill Walker, N.Y.	3.08
SO	Lefty Grove, Phi.	170	Pat Malone, Chi.	166

CAUGHT ON THE FLY

JANUARY
The New York Yankees announced they will put permanent numbers on the backs of their uniforms, corresponding to a player's spot in the batting order.

JULY
The New York Giants unveiled a baseball innovation — the use of a public address system at the Polo Grounds.

OCTOBER
Cleveland third baseman Joe Sewell, the ultimate contact hitter, finished the season with an amazing four strikeouts in 578 official at-bats.

Grover Cleveland Alexander recorded career win No. 373 when St. Louis rallied for an 11-9 victory over Philadelphia.

Ruth connects for 500th homer

The incomparable Babe Ruth reached another career milestone August 11 when he hit a towering drive out of Cleveland's League Park for his 500th home run.

The New York Yankee slugger muscled up and drove Willis Hudlin's first pitch of the second inning over the right-field fence near the foul line, much to the delight of an overflow crowd of Cleveland fans. The home run, Ruth's sixth in his last seven games and 30th of the season, gave the second-place Yankees a 1-0 lead in a game they eventually lost to the third-place Indians, 6-5. The ball was retrieved by a passerby outside the park on Lexington Avenue and returned to the Bambino.

Ruth's 500 total is more than twice the number hit by second-place slugger Cy Williams, the Philadelphia Phillies' veteran outfielder. Williams, playing in his 18th big-league season, has connected 237 times. Ruth belted 227 homers in his four biggest seasons: 54 in 1920 and 1928, 59 in 1921 and 60 in 1927. The 15-year veteran also has hit 13 World Series homers.

Klein sets record

Philadelphia slugger Chuck Klein set a National League one-season home run record and teammate Frank O'Doul broke the N.L. season hit mark in an eventful October 5 doubleheader against the New York Giants at the Baker Bowl.

Klein and the Giants' Mel Ott both had tied the 1922 N.L. home run record of Rogers Hornsby and entered the day with 42 apiece. Klein connected for No. 43 in the Phillies' 5-4 opening-game victory while Ott went 1 for 3 with a walk. Klein went 0 for 5 in the nightcap (the Phillies' final game of the season) while Philadelphia pitchers walked Ott five times in New York's 12-3 triumph. Ott failed to homer in his final game at Boston.

O'Doul collected six hits in the doubleheader and lifted his final season total to 254, four more than Hornsby's 1922 N.L. record and three behind George Sisler's 1920 major league record total for the St. Louis Browns. O'Doul led the league with a .398 average.

Philadelphia teammates Chuck Klein (left) and Frank O'Doul completed record-setting seasons in the Phillies' final-day doubleheader split with New York.

Miller Huggins dies

Miller Huggins, the diminutive 49-year-old manager who led the New York Yankees to six pennants and three World Series championships in 12 seasons at the helm, died September 25 of blood poisoning, sending shockwaves through major league baseball.

The 5-foot-4 Huggins, a second baseman through a 13-year big-league career with Cincinnati and the St. Louis Cardinals, fought a week-long battle after falling ill with an infection below his left eye. Thought to be a minor problem at first, Huggins grew progressively sicker and died after lapsing into unconsciousness.

Yankee players were informed of Huggins' death midway through their game at Boston's Fenway Park. Both teams lined up at home plate after the fifth inning and paid tribute. The Yankees went on to record an 11-inning, 11-10 victory that clinched second place in the American League. All A.L. games were canceled the next day.

Huggins managed the Cardinals from 1913 through 1917 before taking over the last-place Yankees in 1918. He was both praised and hated for the battles he waged to discipline high-living star outfielder Babe Ruth.

A'S SHOCK THE CUBS

The Philadelphia Athletics' October 14 World Series-deciding fifth-game victory over the Chicago Cubs was merely a formality. The fall classic actually had been decided two days earlier, in the seventh inning of an amazing fourth game.

After dropping the first two games at Chicago's Wrigley Field, the Cubs had rebounded for a 3-1 triumph in Game 3 at Philadelphia's Shibe Park. They appeared on the verge of squaring things at two games apiece when they carried an 8-0 lead into the seventh inning of Game 4 with starter Charlie Root working on a three-hitter. Nobody was prepared for what happened next.

Al Simmons' leadoff home run looked like too little too late. But Jimmie Foxx, Bing Miller, Jimmie Dykes and Joe Boley all singled and before the dust could clear, the Athletics had plated 10 runs. The key hit was a Mule Haas drive that the Cubs' Hack Wilson lost in the sun. Haas circled the bases with a three-run inside-the-park home run.

The A's were back in control. They won Game 4, 10-8, and Howard Ehmke and Rube Walberg pitched the Series-clinching 3-2 victory.

Game 1	Philadelphia	3	Chicago	1
Game 2	Philadelphia	9	Chicago	3
Game 3	Chicago	3	Philadelphia	1
Game 4	Philadelphia	10	Chicago	8
Game 5	Philadelphia	3	Chicago	2

World Series Managers Connie Mack of Philadelphia and Joe McCarthy of the Chicago Cubs.

The 1930s

Baseball had survived talent raids, riotous fans, rowdy players, a rival league, a world war, scandal and its own ineptitude while negotiating the American minefields of growth and progress.

Nothing, it seemed, could keep it from collecting on the promise of prosperity and great riches, and the economic indicators of the late 1920s suggested that the next decade would be just as affluent as the "Golden Age" baseball was now enjoying.

But just as the curtain was ready to fall on "The Roaring Twenties," the game's growing notion of invincibility turned into fear and depression. Depression as in the great stock market crash of 1929 that plunged the continent into economic chaos. Sports growth would take a backseat for the next 10 years as the nation struggled to keep its head above water.

That baseball was able to survive yet another crisis was a tribute to its impressive resiliency and determination as well as to the patience, dedication and creativity of those who called the shots. With the national income cut in half from 1929 to '32, profit ledgers suffered and gate receipts fell more than $6 million. Americans were fighting for their very

NATIONAL LEAGUE

League Batting Leaders

Average

Year	Player-Team	Avg.
1930	Bill Terry, N.Y.	.401
1931	Chick Hafey, St. L.	.349
1932	Lefty O'Doul, Bkn.	.368
1933	Chuck Klein, Phil.	.368
1934	Paul Waner, Pit.	.362
1935	Arky Vaughan, Pit.	.385
1936	Paul Waner, Pit.	.373
1937	Joe Medwick, St. L.	.374
1938	Ernie Lombardi, Cin.	.342
1939	Johnny Mize, St. L.	.349

Home Runs

Year	Player-Team	HR
1930	Hack Wilson, Chi.	56
1931	Chuck Klein, Phil.	31
1932	Chuck Klein, Phil.	38
	Mel Ott, N.Y.	38
1933	Chuck Klein, Phil.	28
1934	Rip Collins, St. L.	35
	Mel Ott, N.Y.	35
1935	Wally Berger, Bos.	34
1936	Mel Ott, N.Y.	33
1937	Joe Medwick, St. L.	31
	Mel Ott, N.Y.	31
1938	Mel Ott, N.Y.	36
1939	Johnny Mize, St. L.	28

RBIs

Year	Player-Team	RBI
1930	Hack Wilson, Chi.	190
1931	Chuck Klein, Phil.	121
1932	Don Hurst, Phil.	143
1933	Chuck Klein, Phil.	120
1934	Mel Ott, N.Y.	135
1935	Wally Berger, Bos.	130
1936	Joe Medwick, St. L.	138
1937	Joe Medwick, St. L.	154
1938	Joe Medwick, St. L.	122
1939	Frank McCormick, Cin.	128

Most Valuable Players

Selected by BBWAA

Year	Player-Team	Pos.
1931	Frank Frisch, St. L.	2B
1932	Chuck Klein, Phil.	OF
1933	Carl Hubbell, N.Y.	P
1934	Dizzy Dean, St. L.	P
1935	Gabby Hartnett, Chi.	C
1936	Carl Hubbell, N.Y.	P
1937	Joe Medwick, St. L.	OF
1938	Ernie Lombardi, Cin.	C
1939	Bucky Walters, Cin.	P

League Pitching Leaders

Winning Percentage

Year	Pitcher-Team	W-L	Pct.
1930	Freddie Fitzsimmons, N.Y.		
		19-7	.731
1931	Paul Derringer, St. L.	18-8	.692
1932	Lon Warneke, Chi.	22-6	.786
1933	Ben Cantwell, Bos.	20-10	.667
1934	Dizzy Dean, St. L.	30-7	.811
1935	Bill Lee, Chi.	20-6	.769
1936	Carl Hubbell, N.Y.	26-6	.813
1937	Carl Hubbell, N.Y.	22-8	.733
1938	Bill Lee, Chi.	22-9	.710
1939	Paul Derringer, Cin.	25-7	.781

Earned-Run Average

Year	Pitcher-Team	ERA
1930	Dazzy Vance, Bkn.	2.61
1931	Bill Walker, N.Y.	2.26
1932	Lon Warneke, Chi.	2.37
1933	Carl Hubbell, N.Y.	1.66
1934	Carl Hubbell, N.Y.	2.30
1935	Cy Blanton, Pit.	2.59
1936	Carl Hubbell, N.Y.	2.31
1937	Jim Turner, Bos.	2.38
1938	Bill Lee, Chi.	2.66
1939	Bucky Walters, Cin.	2.29

Strikeouts

Year	Pitcher-Team	SO
1930	Bill Hallahan, St. L.	177
1931	Bill Hallahan, St. L.	159
1932	Dizzy Dean, St. L.	191
1933	Dizzy Dean, St. L.	199
1934	Dizzy Dean, St. L.	195
1935	Dizzy Dean, St. L.	182
1936	Van Lingle Mungo, Bkn.	238
1937	Carl Hubbell, N.Y.	159
1938	Clay Bryant, Chi.	135
1939	Claude Passeau, Phil.-Chi.	137
	Bucky Walters, Cin.	137

WORLD SERIES

Year	Winner	Pennant Winner	Games
1930	Philadelphia Athletics	St. Louis Cardinals	4-2
1931	St. Louis Cardinals	Philadelphia Athletics	4-3
1932	New York Yankees	Chicago Cubs	4-0
1933	New York Giants	Washington Senators	4-1
1934	St. Louis Cardinals	Detroit Tigers	4-3
1935	Detroit Tigers	Chicago Cubs	4-2
1936	New York Yankees	New York Giants	4-2
1937	New York Yankees	New York Giants	4-1
1938	New York Yankees	Chicago Cubs	4-0
1939	New York Yankees	Cincinnati Reds	4-0

HALL OF FAME   Electees and Additions

1936 Ty Cobb, Honus Wagner, Babe Ruth, Christy Mathewson, Walter Johnson.

1937 Napoleon Lajoie, Tris Speaker, Cy Young, George Wright, Morgan G. Bulkeley, Ban Johnson, John McGraw, Connie Mack.

1938 Grover Cleveland Alexander, Henry Chadwick, Alexander Cartwright.

1939 George Sisler, Eddie Collins, Willie Keeler, Lou Gehrig, Albert G. Spalding, Cap Anson, Charles A. Comiskey, Buck Ewing, Charles Radbourn, Candy Cummings.

Final Standings

1930

	W	L	PCT.	GB
St. Louis	92	62	.597	--
Chicago	90	64	.584	2
New York	87	67	.565	5
Brooklyn	86	68	.558	6
Pittsburgh	80	74	.519	12
Boston	70	84	.455	22
Cincinnati	59	95	.383	33
Philadelphia	52	102	.338	40

1931

	W	L	Pct.	GB
St. Louis	101	53	.656	--
New York	87	65	.572	13
Chicago	84	70	.545	17
Brooklyn	79	73	.520	21
Pittsburgh	75	79	.487	26
Philadelphia	66	88	.429	35
Boston	64	90	.416	37
Cincinnati	58	96	.377	43

1932

	W	L	Pct.	GB
Chicago	90	64	.584	--
Pittsburgh	86	68	.558	4
Brooklyn	81	73	.526	9
Philadelphia	78	76	.506	12
Boston	77	77	.500	13
New York	72	82	.468	18
St. Louis	72	82	.468	18
Cincinnati	60	94	.390	30

1933

	W	L	Pct.	GB
New York	91	61	.599	--
Pittsburgh	87	67	.565	5
Chicago	86	68	.558	6
Boston	83	71	.539	9
St. Louis	82	71	.536	9.5
Brooklyn	65	88	.425	26.5
Philadelphia	60	92	.395	31
Cincinnati	58	94	.382	33

1934

	W	L	Pct.	GB
St. Louis	95	58	.621	--
New York	93	60	.608	2
Chicago	86	65	.570	8
Boston	78	73	.517	16
Pittsburgh	74	76	.493	19.5
Brooklyn	71	81	.467	23.5
Philadelphia	56	93	.376	37
Cincinnati	52	99	.344	42

1935

	W	L	Pct.	GB
Chicago	100	54	.649	--
St. Louis	96	58	.623	4
New York	91	62	.595	8.5
Pittsburgh	86	67	.562	13.5
Brooklyn	70	83	.458	29.5
Cincinnati	68	85	.444	31.5
Philadelphia	64	89	.418	35.5
Boston	38	115	.248	61.5

1936

	W	L	Pct.	GB
New York	92	62	.597	--
Chicago	87	67	.565	5
St. Louis	87	67	.565	5
Pittsburgh	84	70	.545	8
Cincinnati	74	80	.481	18
Boston	71	83	.461	21
Brooklyn	67	87	.435	25
Philadelphia	54	100	.351	38

1937

	W	L	Pct.	GB
New York	95	57	.625	--
Chicago	93	61	.604	3
Pittsburgh	86	68	.558	10
St. Louis	81	73	.526	15
Boston	79	73	.520	16
Brooklyn	62	91	.405	33.5
Philadelphia	61	92	.399	34.5
Cincinnati	56	98	.364	40

1938

	W	L	Pct.	GB
Chicago	89	63	.586	--
Pittsburgh	86	64	.573	2
New York	83	67	.553	5
Cincinnati	82	68	.547	6
Boston	77	75	.507	12
St. Louis	71	80	.470	17.5
Brooklyn	69	80	.463	18.5
Philadelphia	45	105	.300	43

1939

	W	L	Pct.	GB
Cincinnati	97	57	.630	--
St. Louis	92	61	.601	4.5
Brooklyn	84	69	.549	12.5
Chicago	84	70	.545	13
New York	77	74	.510	18.5
Pittsburgh	68	85	.444	28.5
Boston	63	88	.417	32.5
Philadelphia	45	106	.298	50.5

Cubs righthander Bill Lee.

survival and recreational pursuits were an unaffordable luxury. But baseball teams also were under the financial gun. Philadelphia's Connie Mack, who had just watched his two-time defending World Series-champion Athletics lose to St. Louis in the 1931 fall classic, broke up his outstanding team by auctioning off his best talent.

There was little anyone could do except tighten the belt, make prudent economic decisions and wait for the worst to pass. After the Depression hit rock bottom in the early '30s, baseball owners looked for creative ways to bring fans back to their parks.

The sport's first All-Star Game was played in 1933 before a full house at Chicago's Comiskey Park, Sunday baseball finally received unanimous support and, in 1935, innovative Cincinnati General Manager Larry MacPhail introduced night baseball to the major leagues after watching it flourish in the minors.

The game's Depression-era losses were not confined to the pocket-

book. Babe Ruth announced his retirement in 1935 and four years later, New York iron man Lou Gehrig, stricken with an incurable debilitating disease, bid a tear-jerking farewell to a packed house at Yankee Stadium. But three shiny new stars arrived to take their place — colorful right-hander Dizzy Dean, unofficial leader of St. Louis' Gashouse Gang, Yankee Clipper Joe DiMaggio, one of the best center fielders ever to play the game, and temperamental Ted Williams, the Boston Red Sox's hitting machine. And Cincinnati pitcher Johnny Vander Meer created history by throwing no-hitters in two consecutive appearances.

DiMaggio's 1936 arrival served as a beacon for better economic times and a warning for Yankee opponents. With DiMaggio providing the spark, Joe McCarthy's Ruth-less and talent-rich Bronx Bombers closed out the decade by capturing a record four straight World Series championships while setting the stage for the greatest dynastic run in sports history.

AMERICAN LEAGUE

League Batting Leaders

Average

Year	Player-Team	Avg.
1930	Al Simmons, Phil.	.381
1931	Al Simmons, Phil.	.390
1932	Dale Alexander, Det.-Bos.	.367
1933	Jimmie Foxx, Phil.	.356
1934	Lou Gehrig, N.Y.	.363
1935	Buddy Myer, Wash.	.349
1936	Luke Appling, Chi.	.388
1937	Charley Gehringer, Det.	.371
1938	Jimmie Foxx, Bos.	.349
1939	Joe DiMaggio, N.Y.	.381

Home Runs

Year	Player-Team	HR
1930	Babe Ruth, N.Y.	49
1931	Lou Gehrig, N.Y.	46
	Babe Ruth, N.Y.	46
1932	Jimmie Foxx, Phil.	58
1933	Jimmie Foxx, Phil.	48
1934	Lou Gehrig, N.Y.	49
1935	Jimmie Foxx, Phil.	36
	Hank Greenberg, Det.	36
1936	Lou Gehrig, N.Y.	49
1937	Joe DiMaggio, N.Y.	46
1938	Hank Greenberg, Det.	58
1939	Jimmie Foxx, Bos.	35

RBIs

Year	Player-Team	RBI
1930	Lou Gehrig, N.Y.	174
1931	Lou Gehrig, N.Y.	184
1932	Jimmie Foxx, Phil.	169
1933	Jimmie Foxx, Phil.	163
1934	Lou Gehrig, N.Y.	165
1935	Hank Greenberg, Det.	170
1936	Hal Trosky, Cle.	162
1937	Hank Greenberg, Det.	183
1938	Jimmie Foxx, Bos.	175
1939	Ted Williams, Bos.	145

Most Valuable Players

Selected by BBWAA

Year	Player-Team	Pos.
1931	Lefty Grove, Phil.	P
1932	Jimmie Foxx, Phil.	1B
1933	Jimmie Foxx, Phil.	1B
1934	Mickey Cochrane, Det.	C
1935	Hank Greenberg, Det.	1B
1936	Lou Gehrig, N.Y.	1B
1937	Charley Gehringer, Det.	2B
1938	Jimmie Foxx, Bos.	1B
1939	Joe DiMaggio, N.Y.	OF

League Pitching Leaders

Winning Percentage

Year	Pitcher-Team	W-L	Pct.
1930	Lefty Grove, Phil.	28-5	.848
1931	Lefty Grove, Phil.	31-4	.886
1932	Johnny Allen, N.Y.	17-4	.810
1933	Lefty Grove, Phil.	24-8	.750
1934	Lefty Gomez, N.Y.	26-5	.839
1935	Eldon Auker, Det.	18-7	.720
1936	Monte Pearson, N.Y.	19-7	.731
1937	Johnny Allen, Cle.	15-1	.938
1938	Red Ruffing, N.Y.	21-7	.750
1939	Lefty Grove, Bos.	15-4	.789

Earned-Run Average

Year	Pitcher-Team	ERA
1930	Lefty Grove, Phil.	2.54
1931	Lefty Grove, Phil.	2.06
1932	Lefty Grove, Phil.	2.84
1933	Monte Pearson, Cle.	2.33
1934	Lefty Gomez, N.Y.	2.33
1935	Lefty Grove, Bos.	2.70
1936	Lefty Grove, Bos.	2.81
1937	Lefty Gomez, N.Y.	2.33
1938	Lefty Grove, Bos.	3.07
1939	Lefty Grove, Bos.	2.54

Strikeouts

Year	Pitcher-Team	SO
1930	Lefty Grove, Phil.	209
1931	Lefty Grove, Phil.	175
1932	Red Ruffing, N.Y.	190
1933	Lefty Gomez, N.Y.	163
1934	Lefty Gomez, N.Y.	158
1935	Tommy Bridges, Det.	163
1936	Tommy Bridges, Det.	175
1937	Lefty Gomez, N.Y.	194
1938	Bob Feller, Cle.	240
1939	Bob Feller, Cle.	246

Philadelphia Athletics slugger Al Simmons.

Final Standings

1930

	W	L	PCT.	GB
Philadelphia	102	52	.662	--
Washington	94	60	.610	8
New York	86	68	.558	16
Cleveland	81	73	.526	21
Detroit	75	79	.487	27
St. Louis	64	90	.416	38
Chicago	62	92	.403	40
Boston	52	102	.338	50

1931

	W	L	Pct.	GB
Philadelphia	107	45	.704	--
New York	94	59	.614	13.5
Washington	92	62	.597	16
Cleveland	78	76	.506	30
St. Louis	63	91	.409	45
Boston	62	90	.408	45
Detroit	61	93	.396	47
Chicago	56	97	.366	51.5

1932

	W	L	Pct.	GB
New York	107	47	.695	--
Philadelphia	94	60	.610	13
Washington	93	61	.604	14
Cleveland	87	65	.572	19
Detroit	76	75	.503	29.5
St. Louis	63	91	.409	44
Chicago	49	102	.325	56.5
Boston	43	111	.279	64

1933

	W	L	Pct.	GB
Washington	99	53	.651	--
New York	91	59	.607	7
Philadelphia	79	72	.523	19.5
Cleveland	75	76	.497	23.5
Detroit	75	79	.487	25
Chicago	67	83	.447	31
Boston	63	86	.423	34.5
St. Louis	55	96	.364	43.5

1934

	W	L	Pct.	GB
Detroit	101	53	.656	--
New York	94	60	.610	7
Cleveland	85	69	.552	16
Boston	76	76	.500	24
Philadelphia	68	82	.453	31
St. Louis	67	85	.441	33
Washington	66	86	.434	34
Chicago	53	99	.349	47

1935

	W	L	Pct.	GB
Detroit	93	58	.616	--
New York	89	60	.597	3
Cleveland	82	71	.536	12
Boston	78	75	.510	16
Chicago	74	78	.487	19.5
Washington	67	86	.438	27
St. Louis	65	87	.428	28.5
Philadelphia	58	91	.389	34

1936

	W	L	Pct.	GB
New York	102	51	.667	--
Detroit	83	71	.539	19.5
Chicago	81	70	.536	20
Washington	82	71	.536	20
Cleveland	80	74	.519	22.5
Boston	74	80	.481	28.5
St. Louis	57	95	.375	44.5
Philadelphia	53	100	.346	49

1937

	W	L	Pct.	GB
New York	102	52	.662	--
Detroit	89	65	.578	13
Chicago	86	68	.558	16
Cleveland	83	71	.539	19
Boston	80	72	.526	21
Washington	73	80	.477	28.5
Philadelphia	54	97	.358	46.5
St. Louis	46	108	.299	56

1938

	W	L	Pct.	GB
New York	99	53	.651	--
Boston	88	61	.591	9.5
Cleveland	86	66	.566	13
Detroit	84	70	.545	16
Washington	75	76	.497	23.5
Chicago	65	83	.439	32
St. Louis	55	97	.362	44
Philadelphia	53	99	.349	46

1939

	W	L	Pct.	GB
New York	106	45	.702	--
Boston	89	62	.589	17
Cleveland	87	67	.565	20.5
Chicago	85	69	.552	22.5
Detroit	81	73	.526	26.5
Washington	65	87	.428	41.5
Philadelphia	55	97	.362	51.5
St. Louis	43	111	.279	64.5

★1930★

Des Moines lights up

Commissioner Kenesaw Mountain Landis, American League President E. S. Barnard and numerous other curious officials were on hand May 2 when Des Moines (Iowa) of the Western League played host to Wichita in the first game ever played under permanently installed lights in organized baseball.

The game was attended by 12,000 fans who watched Des Moines post a 13-6 victory. There did not appear to be any problems with visibility or judgment under the artificial lights, either on the field or at the plate. Four errors were committed, all on infield plays. Many minor league owners were immediately sold on the idea of night baseball as the solution to their financial problems.

There were two previous known attempts to play night baseball, but both games were played under temporary lights with about half the power of those installed at Des Moines.

Vital stats

Offense was the name of the game in 1930 as National League hitters conducted an incredible assault on the record books. In a league that amazingly batted a composite .303, the chief antagonist was Chicago outfielder Hack Wilson.

Wilson shattered Chuck Klein's 1-year-old N.L. home run record by smashing 56 and set a one-season major league mark for runs batted in with 190, 15 more than New York Yankee Lou Gehrig managed in 1927. Only Babe Ruth has hit more homers in a single season — 59 in 1921 and 60 in 1927. The Cubs finished with a team-record 171 round-trippers.

Other notable performances: The Boston Braves' Wally Berger belted a rookie-record 38 homers, New York Giant Bill Terry tied the N.L. hit record (254) en route to a league-leading .401 average, and Philadelphia's Chuck Klein set N.L. marks for doubles (59) and runs (158).

Six N.L. teams topped the .300 mark, with the Giants batting a modern record .319, the Phillies .315 and the pennant-winning Cardinals .314. Every Cardinal regular batted .300 or above.

Chicago Cubs slugger Hack Wilson exploded for 56 home runs and an incredible 190 RBIs.

Right: New York Giants star Bill Terry topped the N.L. charts with a .401 batting average.

Rhem disappears, but Cardinals still prevail

St. Louis won 39 of its final 49 games and outlasted Chicago, New York and Brooklyn in one of the hottest National League pennant races in years. The Cubs finished two games back, the Giants five and the Dodgers six.

The Redbirds were 53-52 and 12 games behind the first-place Dodgers on August 9 when they began their winning surge. They moved into serious contention September 1 when they swept a doubleheader from Pittsburgh and then jockeyed for position over the next two weeks with the other contenders. In one three-day mid-September stretch, three different teams held the lead.

The Cardinals appeared to suffer a setback September 15, on the eve of a crucial three-game series in Brooklyn. Pitcher Flint Rhem, a notorious bad boy and winner of six straight games, disappeared. After the Cardinals won the opener to move one game ahead of the Dodgers and 1½ ahead of the Cubs, the right-hander, scheduled to pitch the next day, showed up in a condition "unbecoming a major league player." Rhem claimed he had been kidnapped by several men who warned him not to pitch against Brooklyn and forced him to drink bootlegged whiskey. He was put to bed and was closely monitored the rest of the trip.

But the incident did not seem to affect the Cardinals. They went on to sweep the Dodgers, won their next two from Philadelphia and clinched the pennant September 26 with a 10-5 victory over Pittsburgh. Rhem beat the Phillies, 9-3, in his September 19 return outing.

Flint Rhem's mysterious disappearance did not derail the St. Louis Cardinals' pennant express.

Ruth bombs Athletics

New York slugger Babe Ruth muscled up May 21, 22 and 24 to stage another of his power displays, bombing the defending-American League champion Philadelphia Athletics for eight home runs and 18 runs batted in over a three-day, six-game stretch.

In the first game of a May 21 doubleheader at Philadelphia's Shibe Park, Ruth belted home runs in the first, third and eighth innings and drove in six runs — in a losing cause. Ruth's first three-homer regular-season game (he had performed the feat twice in World Series play) came in a 15-7 loss and the A's also won the nightcap, 4-1.

The tide turned the next day as the Yankees swept the A's, 10-1 and 20-13. Ruth homered twice in the opener and connected for his 12th home run of the season in the second game, giving him a record-tying six in four games. Teammate Lou Gehrig smashed three homers in the second game and tied his own A.L. record with eight RBIs. The teams combined for a record-tying 10 homers in the nightcap.

After a day off, the Yankees met the A's in another doubleheader — this time at Yankee Stadium. Ruth hit homer 13 in the Yankees' 10-6 first-game win and added his 14th in an 11-1 nightcap victory. His eight in six games was a major league record.

ATHLETICS SHOW CHAMPIONSHIP FORM

Jimmie Dykes and Al Simmons crashed home runs October 8 to back the five-hit pitching of George Earnshaw, giving the Philadelphia Athletics a 7-1 victory over St. Louis and their second straight World Series championship.

The Game 6 triumph at Philadelphia's Shibe Park ended a fall classic that produced an unexpected pitching duel in what had been the Year of the Hitter. The Cardinals, featuring an all-.300 hitting lineup, were held to a .197 average while the A's managed only a .200 mark. But 18 of the A's 35 hits were for extra bases.

After the Athletics won the first two contests behind Lefty Grove and Earnshaw, the Cardinals took the next two. Game 5 at St. Louis was a masterpiece, with Earnshaw and Grove combining to match eight scoreless innings with veteran Burleigh Grimes. But the A's broke through in the ninth when slugger Jimmie Foxx slammed a two-run, game-winning homer into the left-field stands.

Grove won that contest in relief and Earnshaw won his second victory two days later in the Series finale.

Game 1	Philadelphia	5	St. Louis	2
Game 2	Philadelphia	6	St. Louis	1
Game 3	St. Louis	5	Philadelphia	0
Game 4	St. Louis	3	Philadelphia	1
Game 5	Philadelphia	2	St. Louis	0
Game 6	Philadelphia	7	St. Louis	1

Committee eliminates sacrifice fly rule

Baseball's Rules Committee eliminated the sacrifice fly December 12 at the major league meetings in New York.

The rule, which gave hitters a free at-bat any time they advanced a baserunner with a fly ball out, had been stricken from the books once before, only to be reinstated in 1920. Then the rule covered only fly balls that scored runners from third base, but it was revised in 1926 to cover fly outs that advanced any runner.

The committee also decided that balls bouncing into the stands will be treated as ground-rule doubles, rather than home runs.

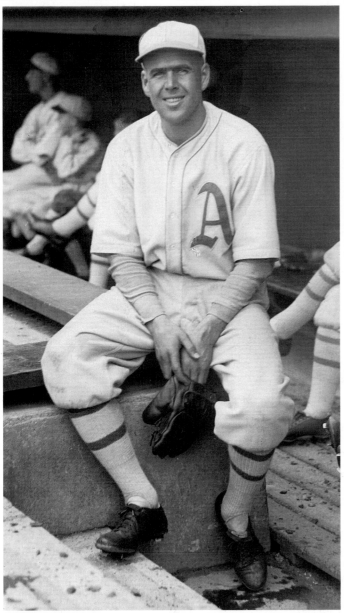

George Earnshaw's five-hit pitching stopped St. Louis and wrapped up the Philadelphia Athletics' second straight World Series championship.

CAUGHT ON THE FLY

JUNE
The Philadelphia Phillies released Grover Cleveland Alexander, ending the 20-year, 373-win career of the talented righthander.

OCTOBER
Joe McCarthy, who resigned as Chicago Cubs manager two weeks earlier, signed a four-year contract to manage the New York Yankees.

DECEMBER
Major league officials granted the Baseball Writers' Association of America permission to conduct future Most Valuable Player balloting in both leagues.

SEASON LEADERS

	American League		National League	
Avg.	Al Simmons, Phi.	.381	Bill Terry, N.Y.	.401
HR	Babe Ruth, N.Y.	49	Hack Wilson, Chi.	56
RBI	Lou Gehrig, N.Y.	174	Hack Wilson, Chi.	190
SB	Martin McManus, Det.	23	Kiki Cuyler, Chi.	37
W-L Pct.	Lefty Grove, Phi.	28-5, .848	Fred Fitzsimmons, N.Y.	19-7, .731
ERA	Lefty Grove, Phi.	2.54	Dazzy Vance, Bkn.	2.61
SO	Lefty Grove, Phi.	209	Bill Hallahan, St.L.	177

★ 1931 ★

SEASON LEADERS

	American League		National League	
Avg.	Al Simmons, Phi.	.390	Chick Hafey, St.L.	.349
HR	Lou Gehrig, N.Y.	46	Chuck Klein, Phi.	31
	Babe Ruth, N.Y.	46		
RBI	Lou Gehrig, N.Y.	184	Chuck Klein, Phi.	121
SB	Ben Chapman, N.Y.	61	Frank Frisch, St.L.	28
W-L Pct.	Lefty Grove, Phi.	31-4, .886	Paul Derringer, St.L.	18-8, .692
ERA	Lefty Grove, Phi.	2.06	Bill Walker, N.Y.	2.26
SO	Lefty Grove, Phi.	175	Bill Hallahan, St.L.	159

A's streak hits 17

The Philadelphia Athletics stretched their winning streak to 17 games on May 25 with an emotional and emphatic doubleheader sweep of the New York Yankees.

Playing before a packed house at Shibe Park, the defending A.L. champs carried a 4-2 lead into the seventh inning of the opener with dependable Lefty Grove on the mound. When the first two Yankees reached base, Grove reached back and retired the next three batters, including Babe Ruth and Lou Gehrig. But that was just a warmup for a ninth-inning pitching exhibition that threw the 32,000 A's fans into a delirious state.

With one out in the final frame, Earle Combs singled and Red Ruffing doubled for the New Yorkers, again bringing Ruth to the plate. Grove struck him out as the crowd roared its approval and then ended the game by fanning Gehrig. The A's 16th straight victory was secure.

Emotions still were high when the second game started and the Athletics really dropped the hammer, roaring out of the gate with nine first-inning runs, three scoring on Mickey Cochrane's triple. They added two in the fourth and five more in the fifth en route to a 16-4 victory that dropped the Yankees into third place, 5½ games behind the A's.

Philadelphia Athletics ace Lefty Grove.

Barnard, Johnson die

Byron Bancroft Johnson, the founder of the American League and its dictatorial president for more than a quarter of a century, died March 28 at age 67, 16 hours after the death of E. S. Barnard, the man who had succeeded him.

Johnson's health had deteriorated rapidly after his 1927 retirement and he had lapsed into a coma several days earlier at St. John's Hospital in St. Louis. The end came quietly for the man who once was considered the most powerful force in the game.

Barnard's death was sudden. While touring the spring training camps in Florida, the 56-year-old former football coach had suffered what he thought was indigestion. He traveled to the Mayo Clinic in Rochester, Minn., and underwent tests. While under observation, he died of a heart attack.

The careers of these men were uncannily parallel. Both were former sports editors of Ohio newspapers, both cut their baseball teeth in the minor leagues and both became president of the A.L. Johnson held the post from 1901 to '27 and Barnard from 1927 to his death.

Former A.L. President E. S. Barnard.

Ruth blasts 600th

New York Yankee slugger Babe Ruth hit his historic 600th home run and teammate Lou Gehrig followed with another blast as the Bronx Bombers lived up to their nickname and belted the St. Louis Browns, 11-7, in an August 21 game at St. Louis.

Ruth connected for his 35th home run of the season off St. Louis righthander George Blaeholder in the third inning with the Yankees already holding a 1-0 lead. Gehrig followed with his 34th homer and the Yankees scored five times in the inning to break the game open.

The ball hit by the Bambino was retrieved by a youngster after it bounced off a car outside Sportsman's Park, the site of several historic Ruth home runs over the years. He brought it to the Babe after the game and was rewarded with a new autographed ball and a crisp $10 bill.

Grove's streak ends

Dick Coffman pitched a three-hitter and second baseman Oscar Melillo drove in the game's only run with a fly ball double, as the St. Louis Browns overcame Philadelphia August 23, ruining Lefty Grove's bid to secure his American League-record 17th straight victory.

Grove, who had tied the A.L. record of 16 consecutive wins shared by Smokey Joe Wood and Walter Johnson with a run that began in early June, gave a solid effort, allowing seven hits and striking out six without issuing a walk. But Coffman was better.

The 25-year-old righthander thrilled the St. Louis fans by allowing only three harmless singles and one walk while controlling the Athletics' powerful lineup.

The Browns scored in the third inning when Fred Schulte singled and came around to score on Melillo's double. Melillo's routine fly ball was misjudged by backup left fielder Jimmy Moore, who was filling in for regular Al Simmons.

The heart-breaking loss dropped Grove's phenomenal record to 27-3.

Gehrig's homer binge

New York Yankee slugger Lou Gehrig continued his home run assault September 1 when he connected in each game of a doubleheader against Boston at Yankee Stadium and stretched his consecutive-game homer streak to a record-tying six.

The Iron Horse matched the record shared by George Kelly (New York Giants, 1924) and Ken Williams (St. Louis Browns, 1922). But Gehrig added a little spice to his streak — three grand slams in five days.

Gehrig's 39th homer of the season came in the seventh inning off Milt Gaston and capped the Yankees' 11-3 first-game victory over the Red Sox. No. 40 was hit off Ed Morris with the bases loaded in the third inning of the nightcap, sparking a 5-1 triumph. His seven runs batted in for the day brought his streak-long RBI count to 21.

Gehrig's binge began on August 28 and he has hit a single homer in every game since. Williams also hit six home runs in his streak, but Kelly managed seven.

CAUGHT ON THE FLY

AUGUST
New York Yankees first baseman Lou Gehrig became the second man in major league history to play in 1,000 consecutive games.

SEPTEMBER
Boston Red Sox outfielder Earl Webb set a major league one-season record by belting 67 doubles.

An American League record: Yankee Lou Gehrig finished the season with 184 RBIs.

OCTOBER
The first Baseball Writers' Association of America MVPs: St. Louis' Frank Frisch in the N.L. and Philadelphia's Lefty Grove in the A.L.

NOVEMBER
Charles Comiskey, owner of the Chicago White Sox since the founding of the American League in 1901, died at age 72.

CARDINALS GET REVENGE

George Watkins hit a two-run homer and Wild Bill Hallahan provided last-out relief for Burleigh Grimes October 10 as the St. Louis Cardinals defeated Philadelphia, 4-2, and denied the Athletics' bid for a record third straight World Series championship.

The Game 7 finale at Sportsman's Park featured three hits by the Cardinals' Andy High, Watkins' timely home run and the seven-hit pitching of the 38-year-old Grimes, the last of baseball's legal spitballers. But the rest of the Series belonged to 27-year-old Cardinal rookie center fielder Pepper Martin, the Wild Horse of the Osage.

Martin was simply unstoppable through the first five games of the fall classic, collecting 12 hits in 18 at-bats, four doubles, one home run, five runs batted in, four stolen bases and five runs scored. St. Louis built a three games to two lead with Hallahan winning Games 2 and 5 (2-0 and 5-1) and Grimes triumphing in Game 3 (5-2).

But the Philadelphia machine did not roll over and die. Lefty Grove, who had pitched the A's to a 6-2 Game 1 victory, knotted the Series at three games apiece with an 8-1 decision in Game 6.

Game 1	Philadelphia	6	St. Louis	2
Game 2	St. Louis	2	Philadelphia	0
Game 3	St. Louis	5	Philadelphia	2
Game 4	Philadelphia	3	St. Louis	0
Game 5	St. Louis	5	Philadelphia	1
Game 6	Philadelphia	8	St. Louis	1
Game 7	St. Louis	4	Philadelphia	2

Pepper Martin, St. Louis' sparkplug center fielder, put on an incredible offensive show in the first six games of the World Series.

Spitballer Burleigh Grimes closed the door on Philadelphia's championship hopes in Game 7 of the fall classic.

★1932★

A's capture marathon

Everybody should have known something was up when the Philadelphia Athletics scored two runs in the first inning of their July 10 game at Cleveland and the Indians responded with three of their own. That's the way it went for 18 innings in one of the craziest games in history — a contest finally won by the A's 18-17.

Cleveland collected a modern-record 33 hits and the teams combined for a record 58, easily surpassing the 1922 mark (51) set by the Philadelphia Phillies and Chicago Cubs. Indians' shortstop Johnny Burnett set a one-game record with nine hits in 11 at-bats.

Jimmie Foxx provided the A's firepower, counting his 31st, 32nd and 33rd home runs among his six hits and eight runs batted in. Foxx, who kept the A's alive in the top of the ninth with a two-out, two-run single that forged a 15-14 lead, also scored the winning run in the 18th.

A's Manager Connie Mack,

cutting costs on a single-date trip, brought only two pitchers and starter Lew Krausse left after allowing four hits in the first inning. Ed Rommel pitched the rest of the way, allowing 14 runs on 29 hits and nine walks but collected the win. Cleveland used three pitchers.

Philadelphia pitcher Ed Rommel surrendered 14 runs and 29 hits in an 18-17 victory over Cleveland.

Gehrig hits 4 homers

New York Yankee first baseman Lou Gehrig smashed his way into baseball's record books June 3, drilling four home runs and narrowly missing a fifth in the Bronx Bombers' 20-13 victory over Philadelphia at Shibe Park.

Gehrig connected for a two-run homer off George Earnshaw in the first inning and added solo shots in the fourth, fifth and seventh to become the first modern-era major leaguer to hit four homers in one game. He tied the all-time mark set by Boston's Bobby Lowe in 1894 and matched two years later by Philadelphia's Ed Delahanty. Both Lowe and Delahanty added a single for a record 17 total bases.

Gehrig had two chances to tie that mark. He grounded out in the eighth and hit a ninth-inning shot that was caught at the fence. He finished with six runs batted in and the Yankees finished with seven homers, tying a one-game team record.

Tony Lazzeri hit for the cycle and finished off the Athletics with a ninth-inning grand slam. Babe Ruth also homered.

SEASON LEADERS

		American League		National League	
Avg.		Dale Alexander, Det.-Bos.		Lefty O'Doul, Bkn.	.368
			.367		
HR		Jimmie Foxx, Phi.	58	Chuck Klein, Phi.	38
				Mel Ott, N.Y.	38
RBI		Jimmie Foxx, Phi.	169	Don Hurst, Phi.	143
SB		Ben Chapman, N.Y.	38	Chuck Klein, Phi.	20
W-L Pct.		Johnny Allen, N.Y.	17-4, .810	Lon Warneke, Chi.	22-6, .786
ERA		Lefty Grove, Phi.	2.84	Lon Warneke, Chi.	2.37
SO		Red Ruffing, N.Y.	190	Dizzy Dean, St.L.	191

McGraw steps down

New York fans were shocked June 3 when John McGraw, the key figure in Giants baseball for more than a quarter century, resigned as manager and turned his duties over to star first baseman Bill Terry.

McGraw, citing ill health, made his unexpected announcement shortly after a scheduled doubleheader against Philadelphia at the Polo Grounds had been postponed because of rain. Although McGraw will remain active as a team vice president and stockholder, he promised that Terry will be left alone to run the team.

McGraw's managerial record includes 2,836 wins, 10 pennants and three World Series championships in 33 seasons, all but two with the Giants. A former star player with the pre-1900 Baltimore Orioles, he is the only manager to direct a team to four consecutive pennants (1921-24).

Bill Terry took over as New York Giants Manager when John McGraw resigned after more than a quarter century on the job.

CAUGHT ON THE FLY

MAY

A monument honoring the late Miller Huggins, former manager of the New York Yankees, was dedicated during ceremonies at Yankee Stadium.

JULY

New York Yankee catcher Bill Dickey was fined $1,000 and suspended 30 days for breaking the jaw of Washington outfielder Carl Reynolds in a one-punch fight after a collision at home plate.

With a paid crowd of 76,979 looking on, Philadelphia's Lefty Grove outdueled the Indians' Mel Harder in a 1-0 thriller that dedicated Cleveland's new Municipal Stadium.

SEPTEMBER

Philadelphia's Connie Mack began dismantling his Athletics powerhouse with the sale of Al Simmons, Jimmie Dykes and Mule Haas to the Chicago White Sox for $100,000.

Foxx blasts 58th, falls two short of record

Jimmie Foxx's bid to match Babe Ruth's one-season home run record fell two short September 25 when the Philadelphia slugger finished the campaign with one solo shot in the Athletics' 2-1 loss to the Washington Senators at Griffith Stadium.

The 24-year-old Foxx, who also collected two singles and finished the season with a .364 batting average, connected in the ninth inning to cut Washington's lead in half. The home run was his 58th of the season, a record for somebody not named Ruth, and the run batted in was his American League-leading 169th.

Alvin Crowder dominated the A's in securing his A.L.-best 26th victory of the season and his 15th straight, one below the A.L. record. Besides Foxx, the right-hander allowed only two runners to reach second base.

The Athletics, after three consecutive A.L. pennants and two World Series, finished in second place, 13 games behind the New York Yankees. Washington finished a game further back in third.

WORLD SERIES REPORT

YANKS SWEEP CUBS

Game 1	New York	12	Chicago	6
Game 2	New York	5	Chicago	2
Game 3	New York	7	Chicago	5
Game 4	New York	13	Chicago	6

Tony Lazzeri hit a pair of two-run homers and Earle Combs added a solo shot October 2 as the New York Yankees completed their World Series sweep of the Chicago Cubs with a 13-6 victory at Chicago's Wrigley Field.

Lazzeri shared the Game 4 spotlight with reliever Wilcy Moore, who pitched 5⅓ innings of two-hit ball to pick up the victory. But the real Series hero was Babe Ruth, who put on a third-game show that will be talked about for years to come.

Ruth, who had hit a three-run homer off Chicago pitcher Charlie Root in the first inning, strode to the plate to face the righthander again in the fifth with one out, nobody on base and the score tied, 4-4.

Tension and emotions were especially high at this point in the Series because of the Yankee players' criticism of the Cubs and their division of the World Series pot, which afforded former Yankee Mark Koenig only half a share. Insults had been traded on the field and Ruth, representing all the power and glory of the mighty Yankees, was a prime target for the hostile Cubs' faithful.

With the noise level increasing and Chicago players firing their best verbal shots, Ruth took a called strike, which he acknowledged with a raised hand. Root threw two balls and then got another called strike, which the Babe again acknowledged. This only sparked more taunting, which in turn prompted Ruth to make a sweeping gesture, seemingly toward center field.

What the gesture meant is anybody's guess. Some players and fans insisted Ruth was calling his shot, others claimed he was motioning toward the Chicago bench. But Ruth deposited Root's next pitch over the center-field fence, a towering drive that landed near the base of the Wrigley Field flagpole. The blast put the Yankees ahead, 5-4, and Lou Gehrig followed with his second home run of the game. The New Yorkers won the contest, 7-5.

When the Series came to a merciful end, Joe McCarthy's Yankees had manhandled his former team, totaling 37 runs and 45 hits in the four games.

Above: Cubs pitcher Charlie Root, Babe Ruth's "called shot" victim.

Left: Yankee Babe Ruth gets a handshake from Lou Gehrig after hitting his "called shot" homer in Game 3 of the World Series at Chicago's Wrigley Field.

★1933★

JANUARY-DECEMBER

Giants dazzle Cards

A Polo Grounds crowd of 50,000 fans watched in amazement July 2 as New York Giants hurlers Carl Hubbell and Roy Parmelee put on a dazzling exhibition in a doubleheader sweep of St. Louis.

The Giants, who stretched their National League lead over the Cardinals to 5½ games, took the opener 1-0 in 18 innings and won the nightcap by the same score in regulation. Hubbell was phenomenal, allowing six hits in his iron man first-game effort and Parmelee stopped the frustrated Cardinals on four hits.

King Carl dueled the Cardinals' Tex Carleton and reliever Jess Haines in a tension-filled opener.

The tall lefthander retired the Redbirds 1-2-3 in 12 of the 18 innings and never allowed more than one baserunner. Four of St. Louis' hits were infield singles. Hubbell, who struck out 12, neither issued a walk nor allowed a runner past second base.

Carleton permitted eight hits in 16 innings. The Giants only broke through when they faced Haines in the 18th. Joe Moore led off with a walk and eventually scored on a Hughie Critz single.

Parmelee, opposing Dizzy Dean, allowed only four runners and struck out 13 in a game decided by Johnny Vergez' fourth-inning home run.

Dean strikes out 17

Dizzy Dean, the colorful ace of the St. Louis Cardinals' pitching staff, struck out a modern major league-record 17 Cubs July 30 as the Redbirds defeated Chicago, 8-2, in the first game of a Sportsman's Park doubleheader.

Dean's effort broke by one the previous modern single-game strikeout record shared by Cincinnati's Frank Hahn, the New York Giants' Christy Mathewson, the

St. Louis Browns' Rube Waddell and Brooklyn's Nap Rucker. Dean fell two short of the all-time record, set by Charlie Sweeney of Providence in 1884.

Dean allowed six hits and one walk. Cardinal catcher Jimmie Wilson benefited from Dean's effort and set a modern record with 18 putouts.

The third-place Cardinals also won the nightcap, 6-5.

CAUGHT ON THE FLY

JANUARY

Commissioner Kenesaw Mountain Landis, setting an example for baseball during the Depression, took a 40 percent cut in salary.

APRIL

Pennsylvania fell into line with the rest of America and permitted Sunday baseball games in the state.

AUGUST

New York Giants ace Carl Hubbell ran his N.L.-record scoreless-innings streak to 45⅓ in a game against the Boston Braves.

After 308 games without suffering a shutout, the New York Yankees were stopped by Philadelphia ace Lefty Grove, 7-0.

Ruth steals spotlight in 'Game of Century'

It came as no big surprise when, with 47,595 fans gathered at Chicago's Comiskey Park for baseball's July 6 "Game of the Century," New York Yankee slugger Babe Ruth took center stage and propelled his American League All-Star team to a 4-2 victory over a squad of National League stars.

The Bambino pounded a two-run homer into the right-field stands off Cardinals' lefthander Wild Bill Hallahan in the third inning with the A.L. already holding a 1-0 advantage. That first run had come unexpectedly in the second inning, when starting A.L. pitcher Lefty Gomez, a notoriously weak hitter, singled home Chicago's Jimmie Dykes.

The National Leaguers scored their runs in the sixth off Washington pitcher Alvin Crowder (one on a home run by St. Louis' Frank Frisch), but Philadelphia's Lefty Grove halted the N.L. over the final three innings to preserve the victory.

Based on fan reaction to the All-Star exhibition, baseball executives are considering turning the game into an annual event. The atmosphere was electric as excited fans saluted the greatest gathering of baseball talent ever assembled on one field. Most of the credit has to go to Arch Ward, the *Chicago Tribune* sportswriter who conceived the idea in conjunction with Chicago's Century of Progress Exposition.

Fans line up at the Comiskey Park ticket windows before the "Game of the Century" All-Star battle.

A Who's Who of American League stars pose with Manager Connie Mack at Chicago's Comiskey Park before baseball's first All-Star Game.

Gehrig sets record

Lou Gehrig, the New York Yankees' Iron Horse, topped Everett Scott's endurance record August 17 when he played in his 1,308th consecutive game — a 10-inning, 7-6 loss to the St. Louis Browns at Sportsman's Park.

Gehrig's streak began on June 1, 1925, when he was sent to the plate to pinch-hit for Pee Wee Wanninger. The inconspicuous move by Yankee Manager Miller Huggins came 25 days after he had benched shortstop Scott, ending his streak at 1,307 games. Since replacing Wally Pipp at first base the next day, Gehrig has not

missed a Yankee game — spring training, exhibition, regular season or World Series.

After completing the first full inning of the historic contest, Yankee and Brown players gathered around home plate, where Gehrig was presented with a silver statuette by American League President Will Harridge. The Yankees went on to lose when Rogers Hornsby tied the score with a ninth-inning pinch-hit homer and Jim Levey provided the game-winner with a 10th-inning double. Gehrig was 2 for 5 with one RBI.

New York Yankee Iron Horse Lou Gehrig.

SEASON LEADERS

	American League			National League	
Avg.	Jimmie Foxx, Phi.	.356		Chuck Klein, Phi.	.368
HR	Jimmie Foxx, Phi.	48		Chuck Klein, Phi.	28
RBI	Jimmie Foxx, Phi.	163		Chuck Klein, Phi.	120
SB	Ben Chapman, N.Y.	27		Pepper Martin, St.L.	26
W-L Pct.	Lefty Grove, Phi.	24-8, .750		Ben Cantwell, Bos.	20-10, .667
ERA	Monte Pearson, Cle.	2.33		Carl Hubbell, N.Y.	1.66
SO	Lefty Gomez, N.Y.	163		Dizzy Dean, St.L.	199

Two Triple Crowns

For the first time, baseball produced two Triple Crown winners in the same season — and both played for Philadelphia teams.

Jimmie Foxx enjoyed a monstrous campaign for the Athletics, dominating the American League with a .356 average, 48 home runs and 163 runs batted in. His cross-city rival, the Phillies' Chuck Klein, swept National League honors by batting .368 with 28 homers and 120 RBIs.

Foxx was rewarded with the

A.L. Most Valuable Player award, but Klein was defeated in the N.L. voting by New York Giants' ace lefthander Carl Hubbell, who led the league with 23 victories, 10 shutouts and a 1.66 earned-run average.

Klein was shut out again on November 21 when the financially struggling Phillies, who finished 31 lengths behind the first-place Giants, sold his contract to the Chicago Cubs for $125,000 and three young players.

GIANTS STAND TALL

New York slugger Mel Ott drilled a 10th-inning pitch from Washington reliever Jack Russell into the center-field bleachers at Griffith Stadium October 7, giving the Giants a 4-3 victory and bringing down the curtain on their first World Series championship in 11 years.

Ott's Game 5 blast, his second of the Series, made a winner of reliever Dolf Luque, who replaced starter Hal Schumacher with two out in the sixth. Schumacher had surrendered a game-tying three-run homer to Fred Schulte, giving Washington a new life. But Joe Cronin's Senators couldn't solve Luque, who allowed only two hits in his sterling stint.

That was pretty much the story of the Series. The Giants, playing their first full season under player-manager Bill Terry, jumped off to a quick two games to none lead behind the pitching of Carl Hubbell, a 4-2 Game 1 victor, and Schumacher, who allowed five hits in a 6-1 second-game victory.

After Washington won Game 3, 4-0, behind the five-hit pitching of Earl Whitehill, Hubbell went all 11 innings in a thrilling fourth game that was decided, 2-1, on Blondy Ryan's single. King Carl nailed down the victory when he induced Cliff Bolton to hit into a bases-loaded, game-ending double play.

Game 1	New York	4	Washington	2
Game 2	New York	6	Washington	1
Game 3	Washington	4	New York	0
Game 4	New York	2	Washington	1
Game 5	New York	4	Washington	3

New York Giants slugger Mel Ott crosses the plate after drilling his World Series-winning home run against Washington.

CAUGHT ON THE FLY

FEBRUARY
Brooklyn coach Casey Stengel signed a two-year contract to manage the Dodgers, replacing Max Carey.

AUGUST
Detroit rookie Schoolboy Rowe's 4-2 victory over Washington was his 16th in a row, tying the one-season A.L. record shared by Walter Johnson, Joe Wood and Lefty Grove.

OCTOBER
Burleigh Grimes, last of baseball's legalized spitball pitchers and a 270-game career winner, was released by Pittsburgh.

NOVEMBER
Ford Frick was named to replace John Heydler as National League president. Heydler resigned because of poor health.

Ruth blasts 700th

The incomparable Babe Ruth hit his 700th career home run July 13, establishing a power-hitting milestone that may never again be approached. The historic blow, off Detroit righthander Tommy Bridges, helped the New York Yankees regain first place in the American League with a 4-2 victory at Navin Field.

Ruth's 14th homer of the season came on a 3-2 pitch with Earle Combs stationed on first base in the third inning of a scoreless battle. The ball sailed high over the right-field wall and was retrieved by a youngster, who traded it to Ruth for a $20 bill and an autographed replacement.

The 39-year-old Ruth, a 21-year veteran playing in what could be his farewell season with the Yankees, has more than doubled the career home run output of his nearest competitor — teammate Lou Gehrig, who has 314.

John McGraw dies

All of New York went into mourning February 25 when John McGraw, considered by most baseball followers the greatest manager of all time, died in New Rochelle, N.Y., of prostate cancer at age 60.

McGraw, a star for the pre-1900 Baltimore Orioles of the National League and manager of the American League's 1901 Baltimore entry, took over the Giants' reins during the 1902 season and proceeded to manage the team to 10 pennants and three World Series championships in 29 full campaigns and parts of two others. His 1921-24 Giants won a record four straight pennants and he retired in June 1932 with 2,836 victories and a .589 winning percentage.

McGraw was an astute judge of talent and a master motivator. He managed many great players, but his prize pupil was Christy Mathewson, a 373-game winner who pitched three shutouts in the Giants' 1905 World Series victory over the Philadelphia A's. McGraw's Giants also won championships in 1921 and '22.

McGraw's last baseball-related appearance was in July 1933 when he managed the N.L. in baseball's first All-Star Game.

Hubbell's star shines

The American League, spotting the National League an early 4-0 lead July 10 in baseball's second All-Star Game, roared back for a 9-7 victory. But the real showstopper in this "offensive battle" was a pitcher — New York Giants' lefthander Carl Hubbell.

Starting before his home fans at New York's Polo Grounds, Hubbell surrendered a leadoff single to Detroit's Charley Gehringer and walked Washington's Heinie Manush. But he used his devastating screwball to strike out Yankees Babe Ruth and Lou Gehrig and Philadelphia slugger Jimmie Foxx.

In the second, Chicago's Al Simmons and Washington's Joe Cronin went down on strikes. After Yankee catcher Bill Dickey singled to end the strikeout streak at five, Hubbell fanned opposing pitcher Lefty Gomez.

Hubbell completed three scoreless innings with six strikeouts and could have been the winning pitcher, but Lon Warneke, Van Lingle Mungo and Dizzy Dean couldn't hold a 4-0 lead and the A.L., with Cleveland's Earl Averill collecting three RBIs, stormed back to win.

New York Giant Carl Hubbell greets American League starter Lefty Gomez of the Yankees before the All-Star Game.

Four of Carl Hubbell's five consecutive All-Star strikeout victims (left to right): Chicago's Al Simmons, Yankees Lou Gehrig and Babe Ruth, and Philadelphia's Jimmie Foxx.

SEASON LEADERS

	American League		National League	
Avg.	Lou Gehrig, N.Y.	.363	Paul Waner, Pit.	.362
HR	Lou Gehrig, N.Y.	49	Rip Collins, St.L.	35
			Mel Ott, N.Y.	35
RBI	Lou Gehrig, N.Y.	165	Mel Ott, N.Y.	135
SB	Bill Werber, Bos.	40	Pepper Martin, St.L.	23
W-L Pct.	Lefty Gomez, N.Y. 26-5, .839		Dizzy Dean, St.L. 30-7, .811	
ERA	Lefty Gomez, N.Y.	2.33	Carl Hubbell, N.Y.	2.30
SO	Lefty Gomez, N.Y.	158	Dizzy Dean, St.L.	195

THE 'GARBAGE' SERIES

Game 1	St. Louis	8	Detroit	3
Game 2	Detroit	3	St. Louis	2
Game 3	St. Louis	4	Detroit	1
Game 4	Detroit	10	St. Louis	4
Game 5	Detroit	3	St. Louis	1
Game 6	St. Louis	4	Detroit	3
Game 7	St. Louis	11	Detroit	0

The raucous, brawling, hellbent-for-leather St. Louis Cardinals, known as the Gas House Gang, clawed their way to the top of the baseball world October 9 when they blew away Detroit, 11-0, in the seventh game of the World Series, surviving a near sixth-inning riot by irate and frustrated Tiger fans at Navin Field.

The Cardinals had taken control in the third inning with a seven-run outburst keyed by Manager Frank Frisch's three-run double. When St. Louis slugger Joe Medwick tripled home a sixth-inning run and slid hard into Detroit third baseman Marv Owen, the mood of the 40,902 fans turned ugly.

When Medwick returned to his left-field position, Tiger fans could no longer contain themselves. Bottles flew in Medwick's direction, as did fruit, vegetables and every other kind of debris and garbage imaginable. With the Cardinals safely ahead 9-0, Commissioner Kenesaw Mountain Landis, watching from his box seat, interceded and ordered Medwick re-moved from the game.

Landis' action quelled the uprising and Cardinal starter Dizzy Dean finished off the six-hit shutout that crowned the Cardinals as world champions, a prospect that had looked bleak only two days earlier.

That's because the Tigers, on the strength of Tommy Bridges' 3-1 victory in Game 5, held a three games to two advantage with the Series moving back to Detroit. But Paul Dean rescued the Cardinals in a 4-3 Game 6 thriller, pitching a seven-hitter and singling in the seventh-inning winning run.

While Medwick (.379, five RBIs), Frisch, Pepper Martin and Leo Durocher provided their usual offensive spark, the colorful Dean brothers captured the Series spotlight, each winning two games while posting 1.00 (Paul) and 1.73 (Dizzy) earned-run averages. Dizzy's only Series loss was a reasonable Game 5 effort the day after he had been hit on the head by a thrown ball while pinch-running. He had to be carried from the field.

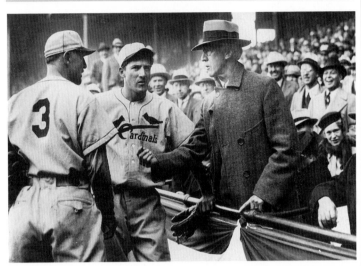

Commissioner Kenesaw Mountain Landis confers with St. Louis Manager Frank Frisch (3) and Joe Medwick, the target of the Detroit fans' outburst.

St. Louis players and the umpires inspect damage done by garbage-throwing Detroit fans in Game 7 of the World Series.

Dean brothers star as Cards win pennant

The St. Louis Cardinals, seven games behind the New York Giants on September 5, clinched the National League pennant September 30 on the final day of the season as Dizzy Dean defeated the Cincinnati Reds, 9-0, for his 30th victory and seventh shutout.

The colorful Dean, who com-bined with brother Paul to win 49 games and spark the Gas House Gang's incredible pennant charge, became the first N.L. 30-game winner since Philadelphia's Grover Cleveland Alexander in 1917. Lefty Grove was the last American Leaguer to turn the trick, winning 31 for the Philadelphia Athletics in 1931.

The Cardinals finished two games ahead of the Giants, who closed with five straight losses. The highlight of the Cardinals' stretch run was a September 21 doubleheader sweep of Brooklyn.

In the first game, Dizzy pitched a three-hit, 13-0 shutout for his 27th victory. But Paul, a rookie righthander, stole the spotlight in the nightcap when he pitched a no-hit, one-walk 3-0 gem for his 18th win. This unprecedented brother act gave the N.L. pennant race an air of inevitability.

After Paul's no-hitter, Dizzy only half-jokingly drawled, "If'n Paul had told me he was gonna pitch a no-hitter, I'd of throwed one, too."

DIZZY DEAN AND THE GASHOUSE GANG

"Dizzy had everything. Fastball, curve and, later, control. He gave it to them sidearm, overhand, three-quarters. The ball was always alive . . . He could tell the batters what was coming and strike them out."

Leo Durocher, former Cardinals shortstop

During the formative years of his career, Dizzy Dean was a walking, talking, fireballing contradiction, a writer's wildest dream *and* his worst nightmare. History has untangled most of the mysteries about the former St. Louis Cardinals righthander who baffled National League hitters with his blazing fastballs and biographers with his well-meaning curves.

Such as his real name: Dizzy was born Jay Hanna Dean, not Jerome Herman Dean as he identified himself originally and signed his early contracts. Jerome Herman was a childhood playmate who had died, prompting Dean to use his name because he felt sorry for the boy's father.

Such as his place of birth: Dean was born in Lucas, Ark., as opposed to Holdenville, Okla., and Bond, Miss., as he told different writers. "I wanted to give each of them fellas a scoop," he explained.

Whatever the specifics, there was no denying that Jay Hanna Jerome Herman (Dizzy) Dean was not your run-of-the-mill baseball star. From the moment he appeared on the professional scene with St. Joseph (Mo.) of the Western League in 1930 until his death in 1974 in Reno, Nev., he captivated writers, fans and television audiences with his cornpone expressions, fractured syntax and, oh yes, his pitching feats.

Dizzy Dean was colorful. He was fun. He was outlandish. He was amusing. He was, in baseball parlance, a flake and a character, the perfect centerpiece for St. Louis' rollicking, fun-loving Gashouse Gang.

"Going anywhere with him was like going with a brass band," Chicago Cubs Owner Phil Wrigley once said.

Dean was one of five children born to sharecropping parents who moved from cotton field to cotton field in Arkansas, Oklahoma and Texas. The family was too poor to even buy shoes and Jay Hanna, at age 10, was picking as much as 400 pounds of cotton per day. There was little time for pursuits such as baseball and most of the youngster's throwing skills were developed with well-aimed rocks that provided squirrels for the Deans' dinner table.

At age 16, Dizzy enlisted in the Army, got his first pair of shoes and pitched for his company team, attracting the attention of Cardinal scouts. He was signed and sent to St. Joseph, a quiet riverbank town that never had encountered anybody quite like him. Dizzy quickly attracted attention with his boasts, I.O.U.s, pranks, missed curfews, late arrivals for games and bizarre behavior. He also recorded 17 wins, earning a trip to Houston of the Texas League and a late-season look with the Cardinals.

General Manager Branch Rickey and crusty field Manager Gabby Street got more than they had bargained for. Dean swaggered into town and practically took credit for the Cardinals being in first place. The 6-foot-3, 200-pounder backed up his swagger with a three-hit victory over Pittsburgh in his major league debut.

"When this punk first came up from Texas to the Cardinals, we knew he was a great pitcher, but he was too fresh for any six managers to handle," said former Cardinals catcher Jimmie Wilson. "He had landed with one toothbrush and the one shirt he had on. I had several silk shirts that had cost me plenty and I guarded them carefully. But I missed a couple of them and couldn't figure out what had happened until one day I caught Dean wearing one. After calling him all the names I could think of, I asked Diz about it. Here's what he said.

" 'Listen, Jimmie, you wouldn't want the greatest pitcher that baseball has ever seen, or ever will see, going around a whole month in one shirt, would you?' "

Ol' Diz, as he liked to call himself, was too much for Street to fathom and thus spent the 1931 season winning 26 games for Houston. But the boastful youngster arrived in St. Louis to stay in 1932 and proceeded to win 120 games over the next five years, leading the N.L. in strikeouts in four of them.

"Dizzy had everything," said Leo Durocher, the Gashouse Gang's sometimes-zany shortstop. "Fastball, curve and, later, control. He gave it to them sidearm, overhand, three-quarters. The ball was always alive. . . . He could tell the batters what was coming and strike them out."

That was a favorite Dean ploy, usually in games the Cardinals had well in hand. Still, it frustrated Manager and second baseman Frank Frisch to no end, as did the always-colorful antics of fellow Gashousers Pepper Martin, Rip Collins, Joe (Ducky) Medwick, Durocher and Dean's brother Paul.

Paul arrived in St. Louis in 1934, after Dizzy had promoted him endlessly to Cardinal management. Paul was signed right off a cotton field, after Dizzy already had turned in 18-15 and 20-18 performances as a starter. "Why, I'm just a

A young and ambitious Dizzy Dean.

busher compared to Paul," Dizzy would say. "If you think I'm fast, wait'll you see my brother Paul."

Propaganda yes. But it also was great publicity for the Cardinals. In one of the zaniest seasons in history, Paul lived up to his brother's boasts and the Deans combined for 49 regular-season victories and all four of the Redbirds' World Series triumphs over Detroit.

"Me and Paul will win 45 games in 1934," Dizzy had been quoted as saying. And the Deans easily fulfilled that prophecy, Dizzy recording a 30-7 record and Paul a 19-11 mark despite a midsummer sitdown that cost them seven days' pay and another $100 apiece. Dizzy had decided Paul should get a raise and the brothers jumped ship, causing an angry Frisch to hand them a fine and suspension. They were reinstated after a week.

The summer highlight came on September 21 when Dizzy shut out Brooklyn

on three hits in the first game of a doubleheader and Paul came back in the nightcap to fire a no-hitter. "If'n Paul had told me he was gonna pitch a no-hitter, I'd of throwed one, too," Dizzy said.

After 1934, Paul enjoyed one more 19-win campaign before an arm injury sidetracked his career. Dizzy followed with 28- and 24-win seasons and was sailing along at the All-Star break in 1937 when fate intervened. Dean was struck on the foot by an Earl Averill line drive in the All-Star Game, suffering a broken toe. He tried to return too quickly and changed his pitching motion, resulting in an arm injury. He was traded the next season to Chicago where, relying on guile rather than his once-feared fastball, he compiled a 7-1 record. Three years later, with the exception of a brief 1947 appearance with the St. Louis

Ol' Diz found a new career behind the microphone after hanging up his uniform for the last time.

Browns, Dean's pitching career was over.

Fortunately for baseball, the death of Dizzy the ballplayer was the birth of Dizzy the announcer. Those who had delighted at his antics as a young, naive kid from the cotton fields were mesmerized all over again by his fractured grammar, malapropisms and colorful expressions from the broadcast booth. And he was discovered by a whole new generation.

Some teachers and mothers objected to pronunciations such as "slud" and "threwed" while shuddering at this fracturing of player names. But Dean was unruffled. "Thems that don't say ain't sometimes ain't eatin'," he replied. Dean, sometimes warbling "The Wabash Cannonball" on air between innings and always entertaining audiences with off-the-wall observations and anecdotes, became a 1950s institution on the CBS-TV *Game of the Week*.

Long after his retirement and election to baseball's Hall of Fame, Dean was asked the secret of his success. The aging 260-pounder with the trademark cowboy hat and big smile hit the nail right on the head when he replied, "I guess there'll never be another like me."

In 1938, sore-armed Dizzy was traded to the Chicago Cubs.

Dean was on his way to stardom as the colorful leader of St. Louis' Gashouse Gang by 1932.

★1935★

SEASON LEADERS

	American League		National League	
Avg.	Buddy Myer, Wash.	.349	Arky Vaughan, Pit.	.385
HR	Jimmie Foxx, Phi.	36	Wally Berger, Bos.	34
	Hank Greenberg, Det.	36		
RBI	Hank Greenberg, Det.	170	Wally Berger, Bos.	130
SB	Bill Werber, Bos.	29	Augie Galan, Chi.	22
W-L Pct.	Eldon Auker, Det.	18-7, .720	Bill Lee, Chi.	20-6, .769
ERA	Lefty Grove, Bos.	2.70	Cy Blanton, Pit.	2.59
SO	Tommy Bridges, Det.	163	Dizzy Dean, St. L.	182

Cincinnati General Manager Larry MacPhail, the man who lit the way for major league baseball.

Working overtime

The Cleveland Indians were more than happy to play a little overtime in their April 16 Opening Day victory at St. Louis. And they did not mind going a few extra innings in their second-game triumph at Detroit. But when the Tigers dumped the Tribe in another extra-inning contest the next day, it began to sink in that a season played at this pace could be a long, long nightmare.

Cleveland won its Opening Day game, 2-1, before 3,500 shivering fans at cold and damp Sportsman's Park in the 14th inning when Glenn Myatt doubled home Boze Berger, who had walked.

For the next three days, weather kept the Browns and Indians on the sideline. So Cleveland moved on to Detroit and engaged the Tigers in another 2-1 marathon, decided by Earl Averill's 14th-inning single. It was more of the same the next day — with a different result. Tied 2-2 after regulation, the Indians and Tigers battled until the bottom of the 13th inning, when Charley Gehringer scored from third base on Marv Owen's ground ball.

The toll for three games: an American League-record 41 innings with two victories and a loss. The Indians' three starters, Mel Harder, Oral Hildebrand and Monte Pearson, all turned in complete-game performances.

Baseball lights up

When U.S. President Franklin D. Roosevelt pressed a button hundreds of miles away in the White House May 24, he transformed Cincinnati's Crosley Field into a glittering wonderland, bringing night baseball to the major leagues and signaling the dawning of a new era.

With American League President Will Harridge, National League boss Ford Frick, a host of other baseball notables and 20,422 fans on hand for the noble experiment, Cincinnati General Manager Lee MacPhail spiced his innovative first with a heavy dose of pomp and circumstance. Ever the showman, he entertained the topcoat-clad fans on a chilly night with four drum and bugle corps and a fireworks display.

When the preliminaries had ended, President Roosevelt, through the magic of electronics, lit the field and Frick, subbing for Commissioner Kenesaw Mountain Landis, who was ill, threw out the historic first ball. Reds and Philadelphia Phillies players were given a six-minute warmup to get used to the lights.

When play got underway, the Reds scored single runs in the first and fourth innings off Phillies starter Joe Bowman and Cincinnati righthander Paul Derringer made them stand up for a 2-1 victory. The contest was errorless,

Curious Cincinnati fans were the first to turn on to baseball under the lights at Crosley Field.

players said that they had no problem picking up the ball and the experiment was generally heralded as a mechanical success. Still, tradition-minded major league officials decried the idea of night baseball becoming anything more than a novelty that would pass with time.

That's the same kind of resistance MacPhail had encountered when he first proposed staging the event. Armed with the knowledge that artificial lights and night baseball already had spelled

profits for, and in some cases the salvation of, numerous minor league clubs during the height of the Depression in the early 1930s, MacPhail lobbied long and hard to convince big-league owners that such an experiment was a worthy pursuit at the major league level.

They finally acceded — to a point. MacPhail was granted permission to stage no more than seven night games in 1935 — and only with permission from Reds' opponents.

Babe calls it quits

Babe Ruth, 40 years old, overweight and batting an embarrassing .181 in his first season with the Boston Braves, announced his retirement on June 2, three days after making a cameo final appearance in the first game of a doubleheader against Philadelphia at the Baker Bowl. Ruth, who hit 714 career home runs, retires as holder of virtually every slugging record conceivable.

The Bambino was released by the New York Yankees in February after 21 glorious seasons. He immediately signed with the Braves and his final campaign was not without its moments.

In his first National League game in the city where he began his career in 1914, Ruth homered and singled off New York Giants ace Carl Hubbell in the Braves' 4-2 victory. But the Sultan of Swat saved his best effort for a May 25 loss (11-7) at Pittsburgh's Forbes Field.

Ruth hit two-run homers in the first and third innings, a run-scoring single in the fifth and a solo home run, the last of his career, in the seventh. His final homer was a mammoth 600-foot blow over the right-field grandstand.

An overweight, 40-year-old Babe Ruth did his final clouting in a Boston Braves uniform.

CAUGHT ON THE FLY

MAY

Boston Braves star Rabbit Maranville set a National League service record by appearing in his 23rd season.

JUNE

Chicago White Sox rookie Johnny Whitehead lost his first major league game after eight straight victories, falling 2-0 to the St. Louis Browns.

Cleveland's Earl Averill, injured in a fireworks accident, saw his consecutive-games streak end at 673.

JULY

Detroit outfielder Pete Fox compiled a 29-game hitting streak.

" DUGOUT CHATTER "

"They may call that fellow Dizzy, but I am telling you there is nothing dizzy about him once he gets on that mound."

Frank Frisch

St. Louis Cardinals manager and second baseman, on pitching ace Dizzy Dean

A farce in Cincinnati

In a bizarre, farcical event that looked more like a county fair sideshow than a baseball game, an overflow crowd spilled out of the Crosley Field stands, ringed the diamond and intimidated everybody involved in Cincinnati's 10-inning 4-3 victory over the St. Louis Cardinals.

The July 31 night game was oversold and that led to problems. The Cardinals were batting in the fourth inning when the contest had to be halted so unruly fans could be removed from the outfield. When play resumed, part of the 30,000 crowd packed along both sidelines and behind the plate, making it difficult for players to make their ways to and from the dugouts. Both teams had to protect their equipment from souvenir-hungry fans, who wandered around, chatting with players throughout the game.

When play was delayed briefly in the eighth inning, a young lady grabbed a bat, broke through the crowd and stepped to the plate. St. Louis hurler Paul Dean lobbed a pitch and she grounded out, bringing a massive cheer. After the game, Cardinal officials charged — with justification — that the umpires were too intimidated to make impartial calls.

A.L. does Foxx trot

Philadelphia Athletics slugger Jimmie Foxx drove in three runs with a homer and single and American League pitchers Lefty Gomez and Mel Harder held the National League to four hits July 8 in a 4-1 All-Star Game victory before 69,831 fans at Cleveland.

The A.L.'s third victory in as many midsummer classics was decided early, when Foxx connected for a two-run first-inning blast off St. Louis Cardinal left-hander Bill Walker. Walker allowed a second-inning run on a triple by St. Louis Browns catcher Rollie Hemsley and a sacrifice fly by Boston player-manager Joe Cronin, and Foxx drove in the A.L.'s final run with a fifth-inning single off the New York Giants' Hal Schumacher.

New York Yankee ace Gomez pitched six strong innings, allowing only a fourth-inning run when Pittsburgh shortstop Arky Vaughan doubled and scored on a single by Giants manager and first baseman Bill Terry. Gomez has started all three All-Star Games, winning in 1933 and '35.

Harder, playing before his home fans, allowed only one hit over the final three innings.

Philadelphia's Jimmie Foxx crossing the plate after hitting a first-inning home run in the All-Star Game at Cleveland Stadium.

★1935★

Cubs streak to title

The Chicago Cubs, mired in fourth place and 10½ games behind the New York Giants just before the All-Star break, completed their incredible run to the National League pennant September 27 when they recorded their 20th straight victory, a 6-2 triumph over Dizzy Dean and the St. Louis Cardinals at Sportsman's Park.

The rampaging Cubs collected 15 hits off Dean, and Bill Lee won his 20th game, securing Chicago's first flag since 1932 and baseball's second-longest winning streak in history. The Cubs went on to win the nightcap, 5-3, for their 21st consecutive win, but lost the next day to the Cardinals. The 1916 New York Giants won 26 straight games, a streak broken only by one tie.

With losses in their final two games, Chicago finished with a 100-54 record, four games better than St. Louis and 8½ ahead of New York. No one would have predicted such a finish in early July, when the Giants were on fire and the Cubs were struggling with a 40-32 record. But as the Giants

began to falter the Chicago express began to roll.

Charley Grimm's Cubs reeled off 20 victories in 23 games to jump back into contention heading into August. In pulling to within two games of the Giants, Chicago beat Boston and Brooklyn five times each, New York and Cincinnati four times and Philadelphia twice. They lost two games to the Phillies and one to the Dodgers.

But that streak was nothing compared to what unfolded beginning September 4 with an 8-2 victory over the Phillies. Trailing St. Louis by 2½ games at that point, the Cubs became invincible for 24 days, winning 18 straight home contests and three in St. Louis. They rolled over everybody and won going away.

During the 21-game streak, six regulars batted .341 or higher, with Billy Herman at .400, Augie Galan .384, Fred Lindstrom .354, Gabby Hartnett .351, Stan Hack .343 and Frank Demaree .341. Lee and Larry French both won five games and Lon Warneke and Charlie Root four apiece.

Braves lose 115 times

The Boston Braves ended their season September 29 as they started it — with a victory over the New York Giants. Between those two wins, however, the Braves compiled the most inept and futile record in the history of baseball.

Boston finished the season with a 38-115 record, easily the most losses ever suffered by a team in a single campaign. That doomed them to last place in the National League, a whopping 61½ games behind first-place Chicago.

It was a team effort all the way. The Braves batted .263, last among N.L. teams, and finished sixth in fielding. Fred Frankhouse was their leading winner at 11-15 while Ben Cantwell, Ed Brandt and Bob Smith combined for a 17-62 record. No pitcher finished .500 or better.

The Braves were a miserable 25-50 at home, an even more miserable 13-65 on the road. They were a combined 14-73 against the N.L.'s top four teams.

" DUGOUT CHATTER "

"He wants to pitch all the time. If he isn't working he gives me the fidgets in a tight game. He wanders from one end of the dugout to the other. I remember one game last year our pitcher had filled the bases and Lefty got right in front of me, chinning himself on the dugout roof, so help me."

Joe McCarthy

Yankee manager, on Lefty Gomez, his young pitching star

Three key figures in Chicago's pennant drive (left to right): Shortstop Billy Jurges, 20-game winner Bill Lee and second baseman Billy Herman.

The brains behind Chicago's pennant-winning rampage: Manager Charley Grimm.

As easy as MVP

Team success meant everything to Most Valuable Player voters, who handed the annual awards to Detroit first baseman Hank Greenberg in the American League and Chicago Cubs catcher Gabby Hartnett in the National.

Greenberg enjoyed an outstanding season, batting .328 with 36 homers and 170 runs batted in — 100 of those RBIs coming before the All-Star break. The big slugger also belted a Game 2 World Series home run before fracturing his wrist and missing the remainder of the fall classic.

Hartnett was a key figure in the Cubs' pennant-clinching 21-game winning streak and finished with a .344 average, 13 homers and 91 RBIs. Hartnett also helped squeeze great results out of a patchwork pitching staff.

The most interesting statistical battle was for the A.L. batting title. Washington second baseman Buddy Myer went 4 for 5 on the final day of the season to edge out Cleveland's Joe Vosmik, .349 to .348.

Detroit slugger Hank Greenberg receiving his A.L. Most Valuable Player award from Commissioner Kenesaw Mountain Landis.

CAUGHT ON THE FLY

AUGUST
Chicago's Vern Kennedy hit a bases-loaded triple and pitched the first no-hitter in Comiskey Park history, beating Cleveland, 5-0.

DECEMBER
Ford Frick was given a new two-year term as N.L. president and A.L. executives voted against introducing night baseball during business at baseball's winter meetings.

WORLD SERIES REPORT

TIGERS FINALLY ROAR

Goose Goslin singled home Mickey Cochrane with two out in the bottom of the ninth inning October 7 to give the Detroit Tigers a 4-3 victory over the Chicago Cubs and the franchise's first World Series victory in five tries.

Cochrane had singled to open the final inning of the Game 6 thriller at Detroit and moved to second on an infield out. When he scored, the Navin Field faithful began a long-awaited victory celebration. The Tigers had escaped a potential Series-tying rally in the top of the frame when Tommy Bridges, a 21-game winner during the regular season and a two-time victor in the fall classic, allowed a leadoff triple by Stan Hack, but struck out Billy Jurges, induced pitcher Larry French to ground out and retired Augie Galan on a fly ball.

Bridges was an 8-3 winner in Game 2, after the Cubs had won the opener, 3-0, behind Lon Warneke. Detroit took the next two games with an 11-inning 6-5 win in Game 3 and a 2-1 triumph in the fourth game. Warneke's second win in Game 5 staved off early defeat for the Cubs.

Detroit was hampered by the loss of slugger Hank Greenberg, who broke his wrist in Game 2. But Pete Fox (.385) and Charley Gehringer (.375) provided the offensive spark the Tigers needed.

The Tigers had lost World Series in 1907, 1908, 1909 and 1934.

Game 1	Chicago	3	Detroit	0
Game 2	Detroit	8	Chicago	3
Game 3	Detroit	6	Chicago	5
Game 4	Detroit	2	Chicago	1
Game 5	Chicago	3	Detroit	1
Game 6	Detroit	4	Chicago	3

Former Dodger dies

Outfielder Len Koenecke, evidently despondent after being dropped by the Brooklyn Dodgers, was killed September 17 during a brawl with the two-man crew of a chartered airplane high above Toronto in one of baseball's more bizarre stories.

The 31-year-old Koenecke, a .297 hitter in three seasons with the New York Giants and Dodgers, chartered the small plane to fly from Detroit to Buffalo. The plane's pilot, William Mulqueeney, said Koenecke appeared to be under a lot of stress and had been drinking.

Everything was quiet at first. But when the plane reached the halfway point of its journey, Mulqueeney said Koenecke suddenly became belligerent and provoked a fight with him and his helper, Irwin Davis. Words turned into fisticuffs and the battle waged for 10 to 15 minutes with the pilots trying to subdue Koenecke as the plane rocked dangerously.

Mulqueeney finally hit Koenecke over the head with a fire extinguisher, regained control of the aircraft and made an emergency landing. Koenecke died from the blow.

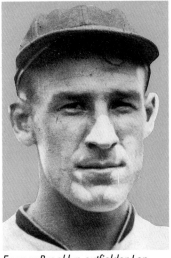

Former Brooklyn outfielder Len Koenecke.

★1936★

Lazzeri slams A's

New York Yankee second baseman Tony Lazzeri hammered three home runs, two with the bases loaded, and drove in an American League-record 11 runs May 24 as the Bronx Bombers buried the Philadelphia Athletics, 25-2, in a brutal massacre at Shibe Park.

Lazzeri, the first major leaguer to hit two grand slams in one game, connected with the bases filled in the second and fifth innings, hit a solo shot in the seventh and belted a two-run eighth-inning triple that barely missed going out of the park. The outburst gave Lazzeri major league records of seven homers in four games and six in three games and left him one RBI short of Jim Bottomley's single-game record of 12 (1924 for the Cardinals). Philadelphia's Jimmie Foxx had held the A.L. mark of nine.

The 32-year-old sparked a 19-hit, six-homer Yankee attack that came up three runs short of the modern record for one game. The beneficiary of the outburst was Monte Pearson, who stopped the A's on seven hits.

Tony Lazzeri, New York's two-grand slam, 11-RBI man.

" DUGOUT CHATTER "

"I have been very fortunate as a ballplayer. I have played with the greatest batter of all time — none other than Babe Ruth. My home runs are fouls in comparison with the Babe's drives."

Lou Gehrig

New York Yankee first baseman

SEASON LEADERS

	American League		National League	
Avg.	Luke Appling, Chi.	.388	Paul Waner, Pit.	.373
HR	Lou Gehrig, N.Y.	49	Mel Ott, N.Y.	33
RBI	Hal Trosky, Cle.	162	Joe Medwick, St. L.	138
SB	Lyn Lary, St. L.	37	Pepper Martin, St. L.	23
W-L Pct.	Monte Pearson, N.Y.	19-7, .731	Carl Hubbell, N.Y.	26-6, .813
ERA	Lefty Grove, Bos.	2.81	Carl Hubbell, N.Y.	2.31
SO	Tommy Bridges, Det.	175	Van Lingle Mungo, Bkn.	238

Cobb leads 'Hall' vote

Ty Cobb, Babe Ruth, Honus Wagner, Christy Mathewson and Walter Johnson were named charter members of baseball's new Hall of Fame February 2 by a nationwide panel of players and sportswriters.

This elite group will be enshrined at a new Hall of Fame museum in Cooperstown, N.Y., home of the first recorded game. Ceremonies to dedicate the building are planned for 1939 in conjunction with baseball's centennial celebration.

The voting, conducted by the Baseball Writers' Association of America, stipulated that a player must be named on 75 percent of the ballots to qualify for induction. Separate polls were taken for pre-1900 and post-1900 players and other individuals who have contributed greatly to the game. But nobody in the pre-1900 group received the required percentage.

Cobb was the leading vote-getter, being named on 222 of the 226 ballots. Ruth and Wagner were named on 215, Mathewson on 205 and Johnson on 189. Napoleon Lajoie, Tris Speaker, Cy Young and Rogers Hornsby all fell short of election.

DiMaggio impressive

New York Yankee phenom Joe DiMaggio made his long-awaited major league debut May 3, signaling his arrival with a triple, two singles, three runs scored and a run batted in as the Bronx Bombers routed the St. Louis Browns, 14-5, before 25,530 fans at Yankee Stadium.

The 21-year-old's debut was made under the pressure of great expectations heaped upon his young shoulders from the moment he arrived at the Yankee spring training camp in St. Petersburg, Fla. As an 18-year-old playing for the San Francisco Seals of the Pacific Coast League in 1933, DiMaggio had caught national attention when he compiled a 61-game hitting streak. Last year with the Seals, DiMaggio batted .398, hit 34 home runs and drove in 154 runs while registering 32 assists as a gazelle-like center fielder.

Baseball-hungry New Yorkers, further teased by DiMaggio's 12-for-20 spring training takeoff, couldn't wait to get their first look at the prodigy. But that's exactly what they had to do — wait. After bruising his foot in a spring game, DiMaggio suffered severe burns when he was left unattended with his foot in a diathermy machine. The Yankees opened the season and played 17 games without their prize rookie, who was hobbling on crutches.

Young Yankee star Joe DiMaggio with New York Owner Jacob Ruppert.

N.L. records first All-Star win

Dizzy Dean, Carl Hubbell and Lon Warneke combined for 8⅓ shutout innings and Chicago Cubs Augie Galan and Gabby Hartnett each drove in a run July 7 to help the National League post its first All-Star Game victory, a 4-3 decision over the American League at Braves Field in Boston.

A loser in each of the first three All-Star contests, the N.L. touched Boston's Lefty Grove for two second-inning runs on Hartnett's triple and a sacrifice fly. The senior circuit doubled its lead in the fifth when Galan hit a solo home run off Detroit's Schoolboy Rowe and St. Louis' Joe Medwick singled home Chicago's Billy Herman.

The lead was entrusted first to St. Louis Cardinals ace Dean, who responded with three hitless innings, and then to New York Giants ace Hubbell, who surrendered two harmless hits over his three-inning stint. The American Leaguers scored three runs off Chicago righthander Curt Davis in the seventh, but the Cubs' Warneke came in to retire New York Yankee rookie Joe DiMaggio with the bases loaded.

Billy Herman of the Chicago Cubs slides safely into second as Luke Appling of the Chicago White Sox applies the late tag during All-Star Game action at Boston's Braves Field.

Klein hits 4 homers

Philadelphia outfielder Chuck Klein joined one of baseball's select circles July 10 when he belted four home runs in a 10-inning, 9-6 victory over Pittsburgh at Forbes Field.

Klein became the fourth player in baseball history and the second modern-era blaster to accomplish the feat, driving pitches into the right-field stands in the first, fifth, seventh and 10th innings. New York Yankee Lou Gehrig (1932) is the only other post-1900 player to homer four times in the same game. Bobby Lowe (Boston, 1894) and Ed Delahanty (Phillies, 1896) did it before the turn of the century.

Klein's first homer came with two men on and his other three were solo shots, giving him six RBIs. He also hit a second-inning drive that Pittsburgh's Paul Waner caught against the wall.

Klein was fortunate to get his final at-bat. Trailing by two runs in the ninth, Pittsburgh tied the score when Philadelphia shortstop Leo Norris booted a grounder that could have ended the game. Klein led off the extra inning with his record-tying blow.

CAUGHT ON THE FLY

JANUARY
After polling Boston fans, new ownership of the National League "Braves" franchise changed the team nickname to "Bees."

JUNE
Brooklyn righthander Van Lingle Mungo tied a major league record when he struck out seven straight Reds during a 5-4 loss to Cincinnati.

JULY
St. Louis Cardinals slugger Joe Medwick tied a long-standing National League record when he collected 10 straight hits over three games.

The Boston Red Sox became the first major league team to be transported by airplane when they flew from St. Louis to Chicago, accompanied by A.L. President Will Harridge.

'Nervous' Cochrane sidelined

Detroit catcher and manager Mickey Cochrane, fretting over his slumping Tigers, spent much of the summer fighting a nervous breakdown that kept him away from baseball for two months and threatened his outstanding playing career.

The two-time American League Most Valuable Player had watched helplessly as a succession of injuries turned his defending World Series champions into also-rans. Admitting to sleepless nights and frazzled nerves, the 33-year-old Cochrane collapsed in the dugout during a June game at Philadelphia's Shibe Park.

A doctor recommended that Cochrane take himself out of the lineup and undergo tests. He heeded the first piece of advice, but ignored the second. When he suffered another dizzy spell a week later in Boston, he was sent to Detroit, where he checked into Henry Ford Hospital and underwent tests that revealed a nervous condition called hyper-thyroidism. Complete rest was ordered, Cochrane was sent to a Wyoming ranch and he returned to the Tiger bench in mid-July.

But Cochrane again suffered dizzy spells and returned to the hospital July 20. He finally was given the okay to return and spent the remainder of the season as a dugout-restricted manager.

Detroit catcher and manager Mickey Cochrane.

★1936★
SEPTEMBER-DECEMBER

Yankees bomb A.L.

The newest Yankee offensive machine completed its season September 27 with 102 victories and a whopping 19½-game lead over second-place Detroit. The New Yorkers of Joe McCarthy, second-place finishers in each of the previous three campaigns, took great satisfaction in their American League runaway and earliest clinching date (September 9) in baseball history.

The Yankees took over first place on May 10 and never looked back. The Bronx Bombers emphatically lived up to that nickname, with six of the eight regulars batting over .300 and five driving in more than 100 runs.

First baseman Lou Gehrig led the charge, batting .354 with 49 homers and 152 RBIs. But third baseman Red Rolfe (.319), right fielder George Selkirk (.308, 107 RBIs), center fielder Jake Powell (.306), left fielder Joe DiMaggio (.323, 29 homers, 125 RBIs), catcher Bill Dickey (.362, 22 homers, 107 RBIs) and second baseman Tony Lazzeri (109 RBIs) all were key figures. So, too, were shortstop Frank Crosetti, who played flawless defense while batting .287, and a pitching staff led by 20-game winner Red Ruffing and 19-game victor Monte Pearson.

New York Yankee Manager Joe McCarthy (right) and 20-game winner Red Ruffing.

Hubbell: 16 straight

New York lefthander Carl Hubbell, surviving a rocky finish September 23, posted his 16th straight victory and reduced the Giants' magic number for clinching the National League pennant to one.

With their 5-4 triumph over Philadelphia, the Giants need only one win in their final five games or one St. Louis loss to wrap up their 12th N.L. championship. That means Hubbell, with a chance to rest before the World Series, most likely will not get a chance to stretch his win streak to 17.

The major league record for consecutive wins in one season is 19, compiled by the Giants' Rube Marquard in 1912. The American League mark is 16, shared by Walter Johnson (1912), Joe Wood (1912), Lefty Grove (1931) and Schoolboy Rowe (1934).

Hubbell led 5-0 after seven innings, but the Phillies scored three runs on an infield out and Pinky Whitney's single. Things got tight when Dolf Camilli led off the ninth with a long home run, but King Carl settled down and closed out his 26th victory of the season. Jimmy Ripple drove in three runs for the Giants.

CAUGHT ON THE FLY

SEPTEMBER

St. Louis left fielder Joe Medwick rapped his N.L.-record 64th double of the season in the third inning of a 3-2 Cardinal loss to Cincinnati.

Philadelphia righthander Hod Lisenbee surrendered 26 hits to Chicago batters in a 17-2 loss to the White Sox at Comiskey Park. It tied the modern major league record for most hits allowed by one pitcher in a game.

DECEMBER

The American League adopted a new rule stating that no player can win a batting championship with less than 400 at-bats.

The St. Louis Browns received permission from A.L. officials to play night baseball in the 1937 campaign.

"DUGOUT CHATTER"

"Greenberg hits the ball harder than Babe Ruth, Jimmie Foxx or Lou Gehrig."

Harry Heilmann

Hall of Famer and four-time Detroit batting champion on Tiger first baseman Hank Greenberg

Feller strikes out 17

Cleveland righthander Bob Feller, the 17-year-old farm boy with a blazing fastball, tied the major league record for strikeouts in a game September 13 when he gunned down 17 Philadelphia Athletics en route to a two-hit, 5-2 victory at Cleveland Stadium.

Pitching in the first game of a doubleheader, Feller enhanced his growing reputation as the hardest thrower in baseball. He also kept A's hitters off balance, walking nine, hitting one and throwing a wild pitch.

After walking the first batter he faced, Feller struck out the side in the first inning. He also fanned three batters in the sixth and at least two in every other inning except the fourth and ninth. He struck out every batter in the Philadelphia lineup except pinch-hitter Charlie Moss, who walked.

Feller's performance tied the big-league record set by St. Louis Cardinal Dizzy Dean in 1933 and broke Rube Waddell's 28-year-old American League mark. The youngster had fanned 15 St. Louis Browns three weeks earlier in his first major league start.

Young Cleveland fireballer Bob Feller.

New Yorkers Gehrig, Hubbell sweep MVPs

When baseball's first Subway Series since 1923 was completed, it came as no great surprise that two New York players were chosen as American League and National League Most Valuable Players — and both won the coveted honor for a second time.

Yankee slugger Lou Gehrig, a winner in 1927, walked away with A.L. honors after batting .354 with 49 homers, 152 runs batted in and 167 runs scored. The home run and runs scored totals were the best in both leagues.

Giants lefty Carl Hubbell, who won in 1933, earned the N.L. award based on his 26-6 record, league-best 2.31 earned-run average and season-closing 16-game winning streak.

Pittsburgh's Paul Waner (.373) and the Chicago White Sox's Luke Appling (.388) won batting titles, the Giants' Mel Ott took N.L. home run honors (33) and St. Louis Cardinal Joe Medwick (138) and Cleveland's Hal Trosky (162) led their leagues in RBIs. Detroit righthander Tommy Bridges led the A.L. with 23 victories.

Pitchers Carl Hubbell of the Giants and Lefty Gomez of the Yankees, the media favorites on the eve of another all-New York World Series.

WORLD SERIES REPORT

YANKS BOMB GIANTS

The Yankees, living up to their nickname of Bronx Bombers, scored seven runs in the ninth inning and recorded an emphatic 13-5 victory over the Giants October 6, dropping the curtain on the first all-New York World Series since 1923.

The championship-clinching triumph at the Polo Grounds climaxed a typical Yankee offensive that produced a .302 team average and seven home runs in six games. The Yankees outscored the Giants, 43-23, and Giants pitchers finished with an embarrassing 6.79 earned-run average. Giants lefthander Carl Hubbell was his usual reliable self, but the rest of the staff felt the Yankees' offensive wrath.

Much of the damage occurred in a wild second game won by the Yankees, 18-4. Every member of the Yankee lineup produced at least one hit, everybody scored at least one run and Tony Lazzeri hit a grand slam homer, only the second in World Series history. The 18 runs, a fall classic record, made life easy for Lefty Gomez, who coasted to a six-hit victory.

Hubbell had outdueled Red Ruffing in the opener, a 6-1 decision at the Polo Grounds. When the Series moved to Yankee Stadium for Game 3, the Yankees temporarily set aside the heavy artillery and forged out a 2-1 victory on the pitching of Bump Hadley and Pat Malone. Lou Gehrig hit a solo home run and Frank Crosetti delivered the tie-breaking hit in the eighth inning.

Gehrig homered again the next day off Hubbell and the Bombers escaped with a 5-2 victory behind the pitching of Monte Pearson. But the Giants, on the edge of elimination, responded with a 10-inning 5-4 verdict decided on a fly ball single by Manager Bill Terry.

The Yankees brought matters to a close, however, behind the Game 6 pitching of Gomez and the four-RBI performance of Jake Powell. Joining Powell in the final-game onslaught were Lazzeri, DiMaggio and Red Rolfe, all of whom collected three hits. Gomez, the beneficiary of the two Yankee offensive explosions, won two games despite recording an unsightly 4.70 ERA.

Game 1	Giants	6	Yankees	1
Game 2	Yankees	18	Giants	4
Game 3	Yankees	2	Giants	1
Game 4	Yankees	5	Giants	2
Game 5	Giants	5	Yankees	4
Game 6	Yankees	13	Giants	5

Yankee George Selkirk heads for the dugout after hitting a Game 5 World Series home run.

SEASON LEADERS

	American League		National League	
Avg.	Charley Gehringer, Det.	.371	Joe Medwick, St. L.	.374
HR	Joe DiMaggio, N.Y.	46	Joe Medwick, St. L.	31
			Mel Ott, N.Y.	31
RBI	Hank Greenberg, Det.	183	Joe Medwick, St. L.	154
SB	Bill Werber, Phi.	35	Augie Galan, Chi.	23
	Ben Chapman, Wash-Bos.	35		
W-L Pct.	Johnny Allen, Cle. 15-1, .938		Carl Hubbell, N.Y. 22-8, .733	
ERA	Lefty Gomez, N.Y.	2.33	Jim Turner, Bos.	2.38
SO	Lefty Gomez, N.Y.	194	Carl Hubbell, N.Y.	159

Beaning threatens Cochrane's career

Mickey Cochrane, the outstanding catcher and manager of the Detroit Tigers, suffered a fractured skull May 25 when he was struck in the right temple by a pitch from New York righthander Bump Hadley during a game at Yankee Stadium. The 34-year-old Cochrane was rushed to the hospital, where he spent the night in critical condition.

Cochrane, who had hit his second home run of the season in the third inning, worked the count full in a fifth-inning at-bat with a runner on first and two out. Hadley's next pitch, a fastball, sailed high and inside. Cochrane froze, was hit and crumpled to the ground, unconscious.

Players from both teams gathered around as Yankee doctor Robert E. Walsh called for a stretcher. Hospital X-rays later revealed Cochrane's skull had been broken in three places. The Yankees went on to record a somber 4-3 victory.

The incident brought to mind the tragic 1920 beaning of Cleveland shortstop Ray Chapman by Yankee pitcher Carl Mays at the Polo Grounds. Chapman died from the head injury sustained in that accident.

Cochrane, however, improved dramatically and doctors predicted full recovery, although his career remained in jeopardy.

A pitch from New York righthander Bump Hadley sent Detroit catcher and manager Mickey Cochrane to the hospital.

Hall of Fame adds 3

Napoleon Lajoie, Tris Speaker and Cy Young became the sixth, seventh and eighth members of baseball's Hall of Fame January 19 when they received the required 75 percent of votes cast by members of the Baseball Writers' Association of America.

Lajoie, a career .339 hitter in 21 seasons, led the way by garnering 168 of a possible 201 votes. Speaker, a .345 career hitter and outstanding center fielder in 22 campaigns, earned 165 votes while Young, a record 511-game winner in 22 seasons, picked up 153. Ironically, Lajoie's best years were spent in Cleveland, Speaker thrived in Cleveland after starting with the Boston Red Sox and Young, who pitched three no-hitters, began his career in 1890 with Cleveland before going to the Red Sox.

That trio joins first-year electees Ty Cobb, Babe Ruth, Honus Wagner, Christy Mathewson and Walter Johnson, whose plaques already hang in the Hall of Fame museum at Cooperstown, N.Y. The museum will officially be dedicated in 1939 during baseball's centennial celebration.

Pitching great Grover Cleveland Alexander fell 26 votes shy of election.

Streak reaches 24

New York Giants ace Carl Hubbell, asked to make an unusual relief appearance, pitched two scoreless innings May 27 and was rewarded with a 3-2 victory — his record 24th straight over two seasons.

The lefthander, who finished the 1936 campaign with a 16-game winning streak and rolled off victories in his first seven starts this year, came on to face the Cincinnati Reds in the eighth inning of a 2-2 game at Crosley Field. He retired the side on three grounders and then watched from the dugout as roommate Mel Ott belted a 400-foot ninth-inning home run into the right-field bleachers.

Hubbell took the mound and again retired the side in order, this time on three pop flies. The victory, the sixth straight for the Giants, allowed King Carl to further distance himself from the 1911-12 record of Rube Marquard, who won 21 straight games.

This was Hubbell's second relief victory during the streak.

New York's Carl Hubbell showing the form that enabled him to win 24 straight games over two seasons.

Tigers get offensive

The Detroit Tigers, desperately trying to close a 10-game gap on the first-place New York Yankees in the American League pennant race, overpowered the St. Louis Browns August 14 in the most offensive doubleheader explosion of this century.

Playing before a home crowd at Navin Field, the Tigers flexed their muscles and pounded five St. Louis pitchers for 40 hits and eight home runs in 16-1 and 20-7 routs that set a modern major league record for most runs in a doubleheader.

Lanky sidearmer Eldon Auker got Detroit off to a good start, holding the Browns to four hits in the opener while blasting two homers and driving in five runs. Veteran second baseman Charley Gehringer was chief executioner in the nightcap, homering twice, collecting five hits and driving in six runs in support of Cletus Poffenberger.

Other Detroit home runs were hit by Rudy York, Gee Walker, Pete Fox and Goose Goslin. Poffenberger held the Browns to six hits through eight innings of the second game before being hammered for two homers and six runs in the ninth.

Second baseman Charley Gehringer was chief executioner in Detroit's 20-7 second-game victory over St. Louis.

CAUGHT ON THE FLY

APRIL

Veteran Detroit outfielder Gee Walker became the first player in history to hit for the cycle on Opening Day, collecting a single, double, triple and home run in the Tigers' 4-3 victory over Cleveland.

New York Giants lefthander Cliff Melton struck out 13 batters in his first major league game, but dropped a 3-1 decision to the Boston Bees.

MAY

Commissioner Kenesaw Mountain Landis announced that A.L. Manager Joe McCarthy (Yankees) and N.L. Manager Bill Terry (Giants) will select the players for the upcoming All-Star Game at Washington.

JUNE

The N.L.-record consecutive-games streak of Pittsburgh's Gus Suhr, which started in 1931, ended at 822 when the first baseman had to take leave to attend his mother's funeral.

Yankees star for A.L.

New York Yankee first baseman Lou Gehrig drove in four runs with a homer and double and the American League survived the four-hit barrage of St. Louis Cardinal left fielder Joe Medwick to record an 8-3 victory over the National League July 7 in the fifth annual All-Star Game at Washington's Griffith Stadium.

Gehrig, with President Franklin D. Roosevelt among the 31,391 fans in attendance on a sweltering day, blasted a third-inning pitch from St. Louis righthander Dizzy Dean over the right-field wall for a two-run homer and then doubled in a pair of sixth-inning runs to close out the scoring.

But Gehrig was not the only Yankee contributor on this day. Manager Joe McCarthy watched with satisfaction as five members of his first-place New York machine put on an All-Star show. Four Yankee regulars were a combined 7 for 15 with five runs scored and seven RBIs. Third baseman Red Rolfe singled, tripled and drove in two runs, right fielder Joe DiMaggio singled and catcher Bill Dickey singled, doubled and drove in a run.

Yankee pitcher Lefty Gomez, starting for the fourth time in All-Star Game competition, pitched three innings of one-hit ball and was rewarded with his third victory in the midsummer classic. Gomez was followed to the mound by Detroit curveballer Tommy Bridges, who allowed all three N.L. runs, and Cleveland's Mel Harder, who ran his All-Star scoreless innings streak to 13.

The biggest thorn for A.L. pitching was Medwick, who stroked two singles and a pair of doubles in becoming the first All-Star to collect four hits in a single game. Six N.L. pitchers were roughed up for 13 hits.

Dean, who pitched the first three innings and allowed four hits, recorded his final out the hard way. With two out in the third, Cleveland's Earl Averill hit a vicious line drive that struck Ol' Diz on the foot and bounded to second baseman Billy Herman, who threw to first for the out. When Dean retired to the clubhouse, it was determined he had suffered a broken toe.

The A.L. now holds a 4-1 edge in All-Star Game competition.

U.S. President Franklin D. Roosevelt doing the first-ball honors for baseball's fifth All-Star Game.

THE NEGRO LEAGUES

"It's too bad baseball couldn't have integrated 15 years sooner because the fans really would have seen the cream of the crop . . . many of them were awesome."

Monte Irvin, former Negro League and Major League star

The stories will have to spread from generation to generation by word of mouth. Some will be exaggerated beyond belief, others will lose their luster for lack of detail. There were no cameras filming their exploits, no statisticians chronicling their records, no reporters glorifying their feats, so the great Negro League stars of yesteryear are at the mercy of memories growing fuzzy with age.

Stories about the great Satchel Paige and Josh Gibson will endure. But what about Cool Papa Bell, Judy Johnson, Oscar Charleston, Buck Leonard and Smoky Joe Williams? What about Bullet Joe Rogan, Biz Mackey, Fats Jenkins, Mule Suttles and John Henry Lloyd? What about Willie Wells, Ray Dandridge, Martin Dihigo, Chino Smith and Jelly Gardner?

Of that group, only Paige saw action in a major league uniform — and not until age 42, well past his pitching prime. The others were outstanding players denied a place in big league baseball because of the color of their skin.

"Oh my, there were some players!" said Monte Irvin, a

former Negro League star who did see eight years of major league service with the New York Giants and Chicago Cubs after Brooklyn's Jackie Robinson had broken baseball's color barrier in 1947. "We had 12 teams, each team had 14 to 17 players and I'd say half of them could have made the major leagues. Fifty of them could have been Hall of Famers.

"It's too bad baseball couldn't have integrated 15 years sooner because the fans really would have seen the cream of the crop . . . many of them were awesome."

But unwelcome in the segregated fraternity of the major leagues. As a result, those talented blacks who could have been impacting baseball's record books as far back as the 1880s were left to showcase their abilities on shabby fields before small crowds in out-of-the-way cities for little money. Their meager paychecks were augmented by the satisfaction they gained from playing the sport they loved.

"Both playing and living conditions were pretty bad then," said Ted Page. "So were

Homestead Grays catcher Josh Gibson, the Negro League's Babe Ruth.

our equipment and playing fields. My salary from the Brooklyn Royal Giants in the mid-'20s was $150 a month and my first eating money was $1 a day. There weren't many hotels other than fifth or sixth class we could stay in so we boarded mostly in rooming houses.

"A lot of times we had no bed at all. We'd just drive from one town to the next and play the next day."

Blacks actually played with whites during the Civil War and into the 1880s, when Chicago White Stockings Manager and star Cap Anson refused to let his team play against them. White owners followed his lead, an injustice that would continue for six decades.

So Negro teams of the early century, unorganized and without alternatives, barnstormed through the rural cities of the East and Midwest, competing against local semipro and amateur teams as well as other black squads. Life became more organized, if not higher in quality, in 1919, when Rube Foster met with a group of black promoters in a Kansas City YMCA and organized the first Negro National League.

That league, which included Midwest powerhouse teams like the Kansas City Monarchs and Foster's Chicago American Giants, soon was joined by another "National League" in the East. The original league changed its name to "American" and in 1924 the Monarchs won the first Colored World Series against the rival Eastern League.

Negro baseball thrived through the 1920s, but both leagues were wiped out in 1930 by the Great Depression. The Monarchs survived through the genius of owner J. L. Wilkinson, who devised a portable lighting system and transported it from town to town for night games. But most other teams disbanded. A new and improved Negro League was formed in 1933 with two divisions, East and West. The famed Pittsburgh Crawfords featured Gibson (the black Babe Ruth), Bell (the so-called fastest player who ever lived), Johnson, Paige and Charleston. In 1937, most of the Crawfords jumped to the Homestead Grays and that team went on to win nine straight Negro League championships (1937-45).

But Negro League baseball was more than pennants and championships. It was a lifestyle, a difficult and demanding one. Most teams would play 200 games a year before the players dispersed to the Caribbean for winter seasons. A number of teams had two home cities. The Grays, for instance, would play half their games in Pittsburgh and the other half at Washington's Griffith Stadium, often outdrawing the Senators. Teams would play as many as three games per day and eight on weekends, sometimes in different cities. Their rickety buses were overloaded and players sometimes had to stand on long trips.

Former catcher Quincy Troupe recalled staying in places where bed bugs "would bite us so bad we couldn't sleep. We'd just have to get out of bed and sit up all night." The teams would stop at roadside restaurants and players with the

The West all-stars before the 1947 East-West game at Chicago's Comiskey Park.

Homestead Grays first baseman Buck Leonard in action against the New York Cubans.

Negro stars Monte Irvin (left) and Sam Jethroe (right) with teammate Al Gionfriddo while playing in Cuba.

lightest skin would be sent in to buy sandwiches.

But the great Negro stars never failed to put on a show. Famous for their flashy play, pitchers would use exaggerated windups, jack-rabbit bunters would leave their bats suspended in mid-air as they high-tailed it down the line and outfielders would perform amazing athletic feats. Center fielder Oscar Charleston would play shallow and charge apparent base hits so hard that he sometimes could throw out a runner at first.

The good Negro League teams often would draw 15,000 fans, both black and white, and the Negro League all-star game, first played in Chicago's Comiskey Park in 1933, would fill the stadium. Some credit that annual contest as the driving force to integration. The players were able to showcase their talents and eyes were opened to the potentials of improved gate revenues. Major league players had known about their Negro League counterparts for a long time. White and black all-star teams had barnstormed over the years, playing more than 400

games. Records uncovered by historian John Holway showed an interesting result: the blacks won 268, the whites 168.

In one 1910 game, Detroit's Ty Cobb, the American League batting and stolen base champion, was outhit by Lloyd and thrown out on three straight steal attempts. He stomped off the field and vowed never to play against blacks again. In 1931, a year after batting .401 for the Giants, Bill Terry struck out three times in an exhibition against a black team in St. Louis. He blamed the lighting.

Paige used his "beebee" ball and hesitation pitch to win four straight celebrated pitching duels against St. Louis' Dizzy Dean, Smoky Joe Williams, a 6-foot-5 fireballer, recorded a 22-7-1 record against white teams and Charleston earned former Giants Manager John McGraw's praise as the greatest player of all time, black or white. Black stars often insisted that honor really belonged to Dihigo, the classy Cuban pitcher-outfielder.

When Robinson broke the color barrier, the Negro League's days were numbered. Losing its top stars, the league played its final World Series in 1948 and consolidated into one circuit, the Negro American League. That lasted through the mid-1950s.

In recent years, baseball has taken steps to correct its longtime slight against the Negro Leaguers, electing 10 former black stars plus organizer Rube Foster to the Hall of Fame. Those getting consideration by a special committee were Paige, Gibson, Bell, Charleston, Dihigo, Irvin, Johnson, Lloyd, Leonard and Dandridge.

"They say good things come to those who wait," said former Negro League second baseman Clarence Bruce. "We waited. And we waited. And we waited. . . . Now the good times are coming. We haven't been forgotten."

Kansas City Monarchs great Satchel Paige in 1945 with Cleveland ace Bob Feller.

★1937★

AUGUST-DECEMBER

York goes on a binge

Detroit rookie Rudy York capped the biggest home run-hitting month in baseball history August 31 when he connected two times and drove in seven runs during a 12-3 victory over Washington.

The muscular 24-year-old catcher drove two balls over the Navin Field scoreboard to bring his August home run total to 18, one more than New York Yankee great Babe Ruth belted in September 1927 — his record 60-homer season. York, who also singled twice against the Senators, now has hit 30 in his first full big-league campaign.

York hit a three-run homer in the first off Washington starter Pete Appleton and connected off Appleton again in the sixth with two more teammates on base.

Detroit's Charley Gehringer also enjoyed a perfect day, collecting a double and two singles.

Detroit's record-setting Rudy York.

"DUGOUT CHATTER"

"He is the meanest, roughest guy you could imagine. He just stands up there and whales everything within reach. Doubles, triples, home runs . . . he sprays them all over every park and if he has a weakness, it is a ball over the plate."

Leo Durocher

St. Louis Cardinals shortstop, on Gashouse Gang teammate
Joe (Ducky) Medwick

The rookie rage

When Grover Cleveland Alexander won 28 games for the Philadelphia Phillies in 1911, he did so without any previous major league experience. For the next 26 years, no pitcher was able to win 20 games as a "true" rookie. But that changed in 1937 as three pitchers performed the feat — and they all did it in a space of four days against the Phillies.

New York Giants' lefthander Cliff Melton was the first. The 25-year-old's 20th victory came in the first game of a September 29 doubleheader at the Baker Bowl, a win that reduced the Giants' magic number for clinching the National League pennant to one.

The Phillies rebounded to win the nightcap, 6-5, but the Giants clinched the next day behind ace Carl Hubbell.

Then, on consecutive days, Boston Bees' rookie roommates Jim Turner and Lou Fette joined Melton in the 20-win circle.

Turner, at age 34, lifted his record to 20-11 October 2 with a nine-hit, 7-1 victory at Boston. The husky 6-footer helped his own cause with two hits and a run batted in. Fette, a 30-year-old righthander, improved his mark to 20-10 the next day when he stopped the Phillies, 6-0.

Turner and Fette combined for 40 of Boston's 79 total victories.

Allen win streak stopped in season finale

Johnny Allen's bid to make baseball history ended in frustration on the final day of the season at Navin Field as the Cleveland righthander came up on the short end of a 1-0 loss to Whistling Jake Wade and the Detroit Tigers after 15 straight victories.

Allen, 15-0 and one win away from tying the American League record for consecutive triumphs, allowed only five hits in the October 3 contest. But two of them, a double by Pete Fox and a single by Hank Greenberg, produced a first-inning run that Wade protected brilliantly.

The rookie lefthander, 6-10 going into the game, held the Indians hitless until Hal Trosky singled over second with two out in the seventh inning and then pitched the final two innings in completing his one-hit masterpiece. The game ended when Wade struck out Trosky with Lyn

Cleveland's Johnny Allen, 15-1 with a .938 winning percentage, is honored as the top A.L. pitcher of 1937.

Lary on second after a walk and sacrifice.

Allen already had set the A.L. record for most consecutive wins to open a season. He was trying to

match the A.L. mark of 16 straight triumphs shared by Walter Johnson, Joe Wood, Lefty Grove and Schoolboy Rowe. Former New York Giant Rube

Marquard holds the major league one-season record of 19 consecutive victories.

The RBI was Greenberg's A.L.-leading 183rd.

St. Louis' Medwick wins Triple Crown

St. Louis Cardinals slugger Joe Medwick, the National League's second Triple Crown winner in 13 years, was named the circuit's Most Valuable Player November 9 in voting by the Baseball Writers' Association of America.

Medwick led N.L. hitters with a .374 average and 154 runs batted in while tying New York Giants slugger Mel Ott for home run honors with 31. He also topped the league in at-bats (633), runs (111), hits (237) and doubles (56). Despite his gigantic contribution, the Cardinals finished in fourth place, 15 games behind the first-place Giants.

Medwick's Triple Crown is the N.L.'s first since Philadelphia's Chuck Klein turned the trick in 1933 and the league's second since Rogers Hornsby did it in 1925 for the Cardinals. New York Yankee first baseman Lou Gehrig was the last Triple Crown winner in 1934.

American League MVP honors went to Detroit second baseman Charley Gehringer, who finished with a .371 average. At age 34, the 14-year veteran is the oldest A.L. player to win a batting title.

N.L. Triple Crown winner Joe Medwick of the St. Louis Cardinals.

CAUGHT ON THE FLY

AUGUST
Roy Johnson and Rabbit Warstler of the Boston Bees made major league history when they became the first modern-era players to lead off a game with back-to-back home runs, victimizing Chicago's Tex Carleton.

SEPTEMBER
Paul Waner, Pittsburgh's three-time batting champion, set a modern N.L. record when he reached the 200-hit plateau for the eighth time.

DECEMBER
Five additions to the Hall of Fame: Pioneers Connie Mack, John McGraw, Morgan Bulkeley, Ban Johnson and George Wright.

WORLD SERIES REPORT

YANKS TOPPLE GIANTS

Lefty Gomez scattered 10 hits and singled home the winning run in a two-run fifth inning October 10 as the powerful New York Yankees recorded a 4-2 victory that wrapped up their second straight World Series rout of the cross-town New York Giants.

The Bronx Bombers needed only five games to dispatch the Giants. Outscoring their National League rivals 28-12 and outhomering them 4-1, the Yankees rolled behind the pitching of Gomez, Red Ruffing, Johnny Murphy, Monte Pearson and Kemp Wicker, who combined to allow the Giants only five earned runs in 37 innings.

The heart of the Yankee batting order — Joe DiMaggio, Lou Gehrig and Bill Dickey — had combined for 112 home runs and a whopping 459 runs batted in during the regular season, and all were prominent in the Series. So were 20-game winners Gomez and Ruffing, who produced three victories in the fall classic.

Gomez got the Yankees off to a fast start in the Yankee Stadium opener when he pitched a six-hitter and rode a seven-run sixth inning to an 8-1 victory. Giants ace Carl Hubbell was the victim of that uprising, during which DiMaggio and George Selkirk both stroked bases-loaded singles.

Selkirk and Ruffing both drove in three runs the next day as the Yankees matched their first-day effort with another 8-1 victory, during which they scored all their runs in the fifth, sixth and seventh innings.

Dickey tripled home a run and third baseman Red Rolfe collected a pair of doubles to back the pitching of Pearson in Game 3. Pearson needed last-out relief from Murphy to record his 5-1 victory after the Giants loaded the bases in the ninth.

Hubbell saved the Giants from extinction in Game 4 with a six-hit effort that resulted in a 7-3 victory, but Gomez, backed by DiMaggio and Myril Hoag home runs, slammed the door the next day at the Polo Grounds. The win was Gomez' fifth without a loss in World Series play.

The championship was the record sixth for the Yankees, who had been tied for top honors with the Philadelphia Athletics.

Game 1	Yankees	8	Giants	1
Game 2	Yankees	8	Giants	1
Game 3	Yankees	5	Giants	1
Game 4	Giants	7	Yankees	3
Game 5	Yankees	4	Giants	2

World Series pitching opponents Cliff Melton (left) of the New York Giants and Red Ruffing of the New York Yankees.

★1938★
JANUARY-AUGUST

Gehrig reaches 2,000

The iron man streak of New York Yankee first baseman Lou Gehrig reached another milestone May 31 when the 34-year-old slugger played in his 2,000th consecutive game, a 12-5 victory over Boston at Yankee Stadium.

Gehrig began his streak on June 1, 1925, when Manager Miller Huggins sent him to the plate as a pinch-hitter for Pee Wee Wanninger. For the next 1,999 games, Gehrig played in every Yankee contest, persevering whenever it appeared injury or illness might force him to the sideline. He passed former Yankee shortstop Everett Scott's major league record of 1,307 straight games in 1933.

Over the 2,000 games, Gehrig batted .343, collected 2,559 hits, belted 468 homers, drove in 1,897 runs and scored 1,785. He earned American League Most Valuable Player honors in 1927 and '36.

Gehrig celebrated the historic occasion by contributing a run-scoring single to the Yankee victory.

Cardinals trade Dean

The St. Louis Cardinals, apparently unhappy with the performance of righthander Dizzy Dean over the second half of the 1937 campaign after he had suffered a broken toe in the All-Star Game, sent shockwaves through the baseball world April 16 when they traded the colorful superstar to the Chicago Cubs for two pitchers and an outfielder.

Dean, a 30-game winner in 1934 and a winner of 102 games in four seasons from 1933 through '36, had his toe broken by an Earl Averill line drive in last year's All-Star Game at Washington. He tried to come back too quickly from the injury and struggled to a final 13-10 record.

St. Louis officials believe Dean will no longer be a major force in N.L. pitching circles. They sent him packing for pitchers Curt Davis and Clyde Shoun and outfielder Tuck Stainback. Davis and Shoun were a combined 17-12 last season while Stainback hit .231.

Dizzy Dean became a Chicago Cub in a shocking April trade.

Reds' Vander Meer doubles his pleasure

An excited throng of 40,000 Brooklyn fans gathered at Ebbets Field June 15 to witness the first major league night game outside of Cincinnati. But Brooklyn's spotlight was stolen by Reds lefthander Johnny Vander Meer, who fired his second consecutive no-hitter en route to a 6-0 victory.

The fireballing 22-year-old had no-hit the Boston Bees (3-0) five days earlier in the daylight of Cincinnati. And as the fans settled in under the bright lights of Ebbets Field, it quickly became apparent that Vander Meer would be tough to hit on this occasion, too. Presented with a 4-0 lead in the third inning, he mowed down the Dodgers with mechanical consistency, only his wildness presenting anything resembling a hurdle.

Vander Meer made it unscathed through six innings and the crowd became his ally. He walked two batters in the seventh and really pitched himself into a jam when he walked the bases loaded in the ninth with one out. But he got Ernie Koy to bounce into a force at the plate and capped his big night by retiring Leo Durocher on a fly ball.

It was a magnificent feat that may never be duplicated. Seven pitchers had thrown more than one career no-hitter, but nobody had ever pitched two in one season. Vander Meer, who struck out seven Dodgers, has pitched 18⅓ straight hitless innings and 26 consecutive scoreless frames.

Cincinnati's Johnny Vander Meer working on his second straight no-hitter while pitching in the first night game at Brooklyn's Ebbets Field.

CAUGHT ON THE FLY

JUNE
Babe Ruth was signed as a coach by the Brooklyn Dodgers.

The Philadelphia Phillies, slated to join the Athletics as co-tenants of Shibe Park, played their final game at the Baker Bowl, losing 14-1 to the New York Giants.

AUGUST
Yankee slugger Lou Gehrig hit his major league-record 23rd grand slam homer in an 11-3 victory over the Philadelphia Athletics.

Monte Pearson pitched a no-hitter and won his 10th straight game for first-place New York, beating Cleveland, 13-0, in the second game of a doubleheader at Yankee Stadium.

Stars shine for N.L.

Cincinnati's Johnny Vander Meer, Chicago's Bill Lee and Pittsburgh's Mace Brown combined on a seven-hitter and the National League took advantage of some sloppy fielding by the American League to post a 4-1 All-Star Game victory July 6 at Cincinnati's Crosley Field.

The tone for the game was set in the bottom of the first inning when an error by Boston Red Sox shortstop Joe Cronin resulted in an unearned run for the N.L. After doubling its lead with a fourth-inning run, the N.L. scored twice in the seventh on the most unusual play in the midsummer classic's history.

With Cincinnati's Frank McCormick already on first base Brooklyn's Leo Durocher dropped down a sacrifice bunt. A.L. third baseman Jimmie Foxx charged and threw wildly, the ball sailing down the right-field line where it was retrieved by Joe DiMaggio. The New York Yankee star fired home — well over the head of catcher Bill Dickey as McCormick and the hustling Durocher both came in to score. A home run on a bunt!

The A.L. managed only two hits through six innings against Vander Meer and Lee, but touched Brown for five hits and a ninth-inning run on Cronin's double. Yankee pitcher Lefty Gomez, a three-time All-Star Game winner, took the loss as a result of the N.L.'s unearned first-inning run.

Lefty Gomez of the New York Yankees suffered his first All-Star Game loss after winning three of the first five played.

" DUGOUT CHATTER "

"Pitching in Fenway is like playing baseball in this room. You can't throw sidearm without bruising your knuckles."

Lefty Gomez

Yankee pitching ace

Baseball goes yellow

Brooklyn General Manager Larry MacPhail unveiled another of his baseball innovations August 2 when the Dodgers and St. Louis Cardinals used yellow baseballs in the first game of a doubleheader at Ebbets Field.

MacPhail, the man who introduced night baseball to the major leagues in 1935 while working for the Cincinnati Reds, secured permission to use the canary-colored balls from National League President Ford Frick, who ordered a special batch, signed each one and sent them to Brooklyn with his blessing. The experiment was conducted to see if the "stitched lemons" provide better visibility to players, as MacPhail claims.

The Dodgers won the game, 6-2, but the Cardinals enjoyed the consolation of watching first baseman Johnny Mize hit one of Freddie Fitzsimmons' yellow knuckleballs for a monster home run.

SEASON LEADERS

	American League		National League	
Avg.	Jimmie Foxx, Bos.	.349	Ernie Lombardi, Cin.	.342
HR	Hank Greenberg, Det.	58	Mel Ott, N.Y.	36
RBI	Jimmie Foxx, Bos.	175	Joe Medwick, St. L.	122
SB	Frank Crosetti, N.Y.	27	Stan Hack, Chi.	16
W-L Pct.	Red Ruffing, N.Y.	21-7, .750	Bill Lee, Chi.	22-9, .710
ERA	Lefty Grove, Bos.	3.07	Bill Lee, Chi.	2.66
SO	Bob Feller, Cle.	240	Clay Bryant, Chi.	135

Pinky's hit parade

Boston third baseman Pinky Higgins took a giant step into the baseball record book June 21 when he drove a single over Detroit second baseman Charley Gehringer for his eighth hit of a doubleheader against the Tigers and a record-setting 12th hit in a row over a two-day, four-game period.

Higgins, who started his streak with four hits in his last four official at-bats of a June 19 doubleheader at Chicago, collected a double and three singles in Boston's 8-3 first-game victory over the Tigers at Navin Field. With his third single in the nightcap, a 5-4 Boston loss, he tied the record of 11 straight hits set by Cleveland's Tris Speaker in 1920.

His record-breaker came in the eighth inning with 26,400 tense fans on the edge of their seats. Higgins lined a pitch toward right field that Gehringer just missed snagging with a leap.

Higgins, who struck out in his first at-bat the next day to end the streak, overshadowed the two-homer performance of Detroit's Rudy York, who moved into a tie for the A.L. lead with Boston's Jimmie Foxx. Both have 19.

Boston's Pinky Higgins collected a major league-record 12 straight hits over three games against Chicago and Detroit.

★1938★

Feller fans 18 Tigers

Young fireballer Bob Feller won a battle but lost the war October 2 when he struck out a major league-record 18 Detroit hitters while dropping a 4-1 decision to the Tigers in the opener of a doubleheader at Cleveland Stadium.

The 19-year-old righthander topped the modern record he shared with Dizzy Dean. Feller had struck out 17 Philadelphia Athletics as a 17-year-old rookie in 1936, three years after Dean set the mark during a game against the Chicago Cubs.

Feller's 18th victim was Chet Laabs, who went down for the fifth time in the ninth inning. The youngster fanned Mark Christman and opposing pitcher Harry Eisenstat three times and Pete Fox, Benny McCoy and Hank Greenberg two times each.

But Feller also allowed seven hits and walked seven while Eisenstat was quietly pitching a four-hitter. The Indians also bowed in the nightcap, 10-8.

While Cleveland's Bob Feller was striking out a record 18 Tigers, Detroit's Harry Eisenstat was quietly pitching a four-hitter against the Indians.

CAUGHT ON THE FLY

SEPTEMBER

Two special Hall of Fame additions: Pioneers Alexander Cartwright and Henry Chadwick, the first baseball writer and inventor of the box score.

DECEMBER

The Cincinnati Reds received N.L. permission to play future season openers a day ahead of the rest of the league in recognition of the 1869 Red Stockings being the first professional team.

American League officials elected Will Harridge to a 10-year term as the circuit's president.

Hartnett lifts Cubs

Gabby Hartnett, the red-faced, chatty catcher and manager of the Chicago Cubs, stroked a two-strike, two-out, ninth-inning home run into the thickening gloom of Wrigley Field September 28 to give his team a 6-5 victory over Pittsburgh and a half-game lead in the tense National League pennant race.

With 34,465 fans straining to see through the fast-settling Chicago darkness, Hartnett connected with a Mace Brown curveball and sent it sailing toward the left-field bleachers. Everybody knew by the crack of the bat where the ball was headed, but not many saw it land. Ecstatic fans stormed onto the field and Hartnett had to fight his way through the hysterical mob to touch the bases.

Hartnett's home run capped a pair of gritty Chicago comebacks from two-run deficits and came as umpires were preparing to declare the game a tie. That would have necessitated a next-day doubleheader, presenting serious problems for the Cubs' overextended pitching staff.

Chicago broke on top in the second inning with an unearned run, but Pittsburgh broke through for three in the sixth, one coming on a home run by Johnny Rizzo. The Cubs tied in the bottom of the sixth, the Pirates took a 5-3 lead in the eighth and Chicago answered again in the bottom of the inning, scoring twice to knot the score at 5-5.

With darkness now posing a serious threat, Charlie Root retired the Pirates in the top of the ninth. Brown disposed of the first two Cubs in the bottom of the inning and quickly fired two strikes past Hartnett, who sent the next pitch sailing into the night.

The home run officially wiped out a Pittsburgh lead that had stood at seven games on September 1. The Pirates had moved into first place on July 12 and were in full control until the Cubs mounted their late charge. When the Pirates came to Chicago for a three-game series beginning September 27, only 1½ games separated the contenders.

Hartnett made a surprise choice in the series opener when he tabbed sore-armed Dizzy Dean as his starting pitcher. But Dean responded with a gutty performance, firing eight shutout innings before Bill Lee rescued him in the ninth for a 2-1 victory.

After Hartnett's homer in Game 2, the Cubs pounded out a 10-1 victory over the demoralized Pirates in the third game and went on to clinch the pennant two days later.

Gabby Hartnett's homer in the thickening gloom at Wrigley Field swung the N.L. pennant race in Chicago's favor.

Stratton loses his leg in a hunting accident

Monty Stratton, the outstanding young pitcher of the Chicago White Sox, saw his promising career come to an end November 28 when his right leg was amputated at the knee after a hunting accident in Greenville, Tex.

The 26-year-old righthander had shot himself while hunting rabbits on his mother's farm.

Doctors operated to check the spread of gangrene, which threatened Stratton's life.

The youngster had won 15 games in each of the last two major league seasons after short stints with the White Sox in 1934, '35 and '36. He figured to be the ace of Chicago's staff entering the 1939 campaign.

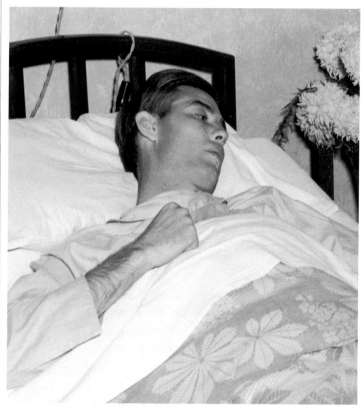

Chicago White Sox pitcher Monty Stratton recuperating in the hospital after losing his right leg in a hunting accident.

Foxx steals the show

Slugging Detroit first baseman Hank Greenberg captured national attention with his run at Babe Ruth's one-season home run record, but Boston's Jimmie Foxx quietly posted an outstanding campaign that resulted in him winning a record third American League Most Valuable Player award.

Greenberg recorded 11 multiple-homer games, the last of which came September 27 in the nightcap of a doubleheader against the St. Louis Browns. He blasted two in that contest, giving him 58 for the season — two short of Ruth's 1927 60-homer record with five games left to play. But Greenberg failed to hit another the rest of the way.

Foxx, who belted 58 homers in 1932 while playing for the Philadelphia Athletics, finished with A.L.-leading totals in average (.349), runs batted in (175) and slugging (.704). He finished second to Greenberg in home runs (50) while becoming the only man other than Ruth to hit 50-plus homers in a season more than once. Foxx also earned MVP citations in 1932 and '33.

Cincinnati catcher Ernie Lombardi won National League MVP honors.

" DUGOUT CHATTER "

"It's just a breeze to catch (Red) Ruffing, (Lefty) Gomez, (Monte) Pearson and the rest. I could almost receive Red with my eyes shut, his control is so good."

Bill Dickey

Yankee catcher, on the talented pitching staff he works with every day

WORLD SERIES REPORT

YANKS SWEEP CUBS

Frank Crosetti, the lightest hitting regular in New York's vaunted power lineup, drove in four runs October 9 with a triple and a double to lead the Yankees to an 8-3 victory over the Chicago Cubs and their record third straight World Series championship.

Crosetti provided more than enough firepower in the Yankee Stadium clincher, making it easy for Red Ruffing to post his second Series victory. The 21-game regular-season winner allowed eight hits after stopping the Cubs, 3-1, in the fall classic opener at Wrigley Field.

That victory, featuring a 4-for-4 performance from Yankee catcher Bill Dickey, set the tone for the Series. The teams dueled through seven innings of the second game with Chicago's Dizzy Dean holding a 3-2 edge over veteran Lefty Gomez. But Dean, no longer the hard thrower he was a few years earlier when he pitched for St. Louis, ran short of guile and finesse in the eighth and ninth innings when Crosetti and Joe DiMaggio belted two-run homers for a 6-3 Yankee victory.

Monte Pearson's five-hit pitching and second baseman Joe Gordon's three-RBI performance led the New Yorkers to a 5-2 third-game win and the Yankees closed the door the next day on their fourth sweep in their last six Series appearances. The Cubs, conversely, dropped their sixth straight fall classic since beating Detroit in 1908.

Game 1	New York	3	Chicago	1
Game 2	New York	6	Chicago	3
Game 3	New York	5	Chicago	2
Game 4	New York	8	Chicago	3

Tommy Henrich completes his Game 4 home run trot and the New York Yankees complete their four-game World Series sweep of Chicago.

★1939★

" DUGOUT CHATTER "

"I was neither surprised nor shocked. It had to happen. Lou could hardly defend himself anymore."

Charlie Keller

Yankee rookie, on teammate Lou Gehrig's decision to bench himself after a record 2,130 straight games

CAUGHT ON THE FLY

JANUARY
Colonel Jacob Ruppert, owner of the New York Yankees for 25 years, died in his New York home at age 72. General Manager Ed Barrow succeeds him as president of the Yankees.

New Hall of Fame electees: George Sisler, Eddie Collins and Wee Willie Keeler.

APRIL
A good-looking rookie outfielder: Boston's Ted Williams doubled in his major league debut against Red Ruffing in a 2-0 New York victory at Yankee Stadium.

MAY
In a Chicago benefit for White Sox pitcher Monty Stratton, who lost his leg in a November hunting accident, the Sox beat the Cubs, 4-1, and raised between $25,000 and $30,000.

Shibe Park lights up in 1st A.L. night game

The American League was introduced to the magic of night baseball May 16 when the Philadelphia Athletics played host to the Cleveland Indians under the newly installed lights at Shibe Park.

The Indians spoiled the occasion by scoring five runs in the 10th inning and defeating the A's, 8-3. But they could not spoil Shibe Park's spot in the history books as the first A.L. stadium to host night baseball and the third in the major leagues. Cincinnati's Crosley Field was the first in 1935 and Brooklyn hosted its inaugural game under the lights in 1938.

Cleveland's Hal Trosky and Philadelphia's Frankie Hayes hit home runs and John Humphries pitched three innings of scoreless, one-hit relief to pick up the victory in the historic contest. Indians outfielder Jeff Heath picked up the big 10th-inning hit, a two-run, bases-loaded double that disappointed 15,109 fans.

Gehrig sits down

Lou Gehrig, the great Iron Horse of the New York Yankees, voluntarily withdrew himself from the lineup May 2 "for the good of the team" after playing in a major league-record 2,130 consecutive games.

Gehrig's streak, which started on June 1, 1925, came to a sudden halt when he approached Manager Joe McCarthy and informed him of his difficult decision.

"Lou just told me he felt it would be best for the club if he took himself out of the lineup," McCarthy said. "I asked him if he really felt that way. He told me he was serious. He feels blue. He is dejected."

What has happened to the 35-year-old superstar remains a mystery. After batting .295, hitting 29 homers and driving in 114 runs last season while helping the Yankees win their third straight World Series championship, Gehrig arrived at New York's St. Petersburg, Fla., spring training camp feeling weak and out of shape. No matter how hard he worked, he couldn't shake the sluggishness from his body and it was reflected in his play, both at the plate and on the field.

All eyes were on Gehrig as the Yankees opened their season against Boston. He grounded into two double plays in that game and made an error, setting the tone for the days to come. Batting only .143 after eight games and suddenly a liability with his glove, it was painfully apparent something was seriously wrong — and Gehrig made the inevitable decision.

"I haven't been a bit of good to the team since the season started," he explained. "It would not be fair to the boys, to Joe or to the baseball public for me to try going on. In fact, it would not be fair to myself, and I'm the last consideration."

Continuing in his role as team captain, Gehrig carried the lineup to the plate at Detroit's Briggs Stadium for the May 2 game, and then retired to a dugout bench for the first time in 15 years. Detroit fans gave him a rousing ovation and his emotional teammates went out and mauled the Tigers, 22-2. Gehrig's replacement, Babe Dahlgren, drove in three runs with a homer and a double.

Gehrig completed his incredible streak with a .340 average, 493 home runs, 1,976 RBIs and 2,704 hits.

Babe Dahlgren, the Yankee who replaced Iron Horse Lou Gehrig in the lineup.

New York great Lou Gehrig, sitting out after 2,130 consecutive games, gets a few words of encouragement from Yankee Manager Joe McCarthy.

Yankees muscle up

The New York Yankees put on the greatest fireworks display in the history of major league baseball June 28, rocketing 13 home runs out of Shibe Park in a 23-2 and 10-0 doubleheader bombardment of the Philadelphia Athletics.

The first-place Yankees connected for a single-game record eight round-trippers in the opener, breaking the previous mark of seven set in 1886 and matched five times. They belted five more in the nightcap, setting a record for most home runs in consecutive games.

The biggest perpetrators of destruction were Joe DiMaggio, Joe Gordon and Babe Dahlgren, who blasted three home runs apiece. Bill Dickey, George Selkirk, Tommy Henrich and Frank Crosetti all connected once.

Ironically, the New York Giants had tied the one-game home run record only 22 days earlier. Joe Moore hit two homers and Mel Ott, Harry Danning, Frank Demaree, Burgess Whitehead and pitcher Manny Salvo one apiece in a 17-3 victory over Cincinnati. Five of those blasts came in one record-setting inning.

Marathon ends in tie

The Brooklyn Dodgers and Boston Bees, rekindling memories of their 26-inning, 1-1 marathon at Boston 19 years ago, battled for 23 innings June 27 at Braves Field in a frustrating game that was called because of darkness with the score tied 2-2.

The five-hour, 15-minute contest was the third longest in baseball history, ranking only behind their 1920 game and a 24-inning contest between the Philadelphia Athletics and Boston in 1906.

Brooklyn scored in the third and eighth innings before being held scoreless for 15 frames. Boston tallied both of its runs in the second before hitting a 21-inning drought. Both teams had plenty of chances, but neither cashed in. Boston seemingly had the game in hand in the 13th inning when pinch-runner Otto Huber rounded third but stumbled, falling flat on his face. Forced to retreat, the embarrassed Huber was stranded at third as Dodger pitcher Whit Wyatt struck out Stan Andrews and retired Debs Garms.

Wyatt pitched 16 innings, allowing both Boston runs and 15 hits. Both teams used four hurlers in the 33-hit, 12-walk struggle.

Baseball celebrates birthday at Cooperstown

Baseball officially began its second century June 12 as the game's top dignitaries gathered with some of its greatest stars and about 11,000 fans in Cooperstown, N.Y., for a centennial party at the site where the sport was invented by Abner Doubleday.

Parades, dedications and speeches were the order of the day before everyone moved to Doubleday Field to watch a game between two groups of current major league stars. With Kenesaw Mountain Landis, baseball's commissioner, serving as master of ceremonies, the Hall of Fame's museum and Doubleday Field were dedicated, all previously selected Hall of Famers were inducted and speeches were delivered extolling the virtues of the great sport of baseball.

Ty Cobb was unable to attend because of illness, but the other 10 living Hall of Famers were present. As Landis dedicated the Hall of Fame "to all America," such former greats as Babe Ruth, Connie Mack, Honus Wagner, Nap Lajoie, Walter Johnson, George Sisler, Tris Speaker, Grover Cleveland Alexander, Cy Young and Eddie Collins sat proudly on the platform leading the cheers.

After the formalities, a team managed by Wagner topped another directed by Collins, 4-2.

The first Hall of Fame induction class (sitting, left to right): Eddie Collins, Babe Ruth, Connie Mack and Cy Young; (standing) Honus Wagner, Grover Alexander, Tris Speaker, Nap Lajoie, George Sisler and Walter Johnson.

Players and fans mill around the streets of Cooperstown, N.Y., after the Hall of Fame exhibition game at historic Doubleday Field.

★1939★

Yankees spark A.L.

A Yankee-studded American League team, playing before 62,892 fans in Yankee Stadium, carved out an easy 3-1 victory over the National League July 11, giving the junior circuit its fifth win in seven midsummer classics.

A.L. Manager Joe McCarthy had plenty of weapons from his vaunted New York Yankee machine and made good use of them. Red Rolfe (third base), Joe DiMaggio (center field), George Selkirk (left field), Joe Gordon (second base) and Bill Dickey (catcher) played all the way for the A.L., with Red Ruffing getting the call as starting pitcher.

The N.L. touched Ruffing for a third-inning run on Lonny Frey's double, but the A.L. took the lead in the fourth when Selkirk singled across a run and another scored on Pittsburgh shortstop Arky Vaughan's error. The A.L.'s final run came in the fifth on a long home run by DiMaggio.

The victory went to Detroit righthander Tommy Bridges, but the veteran needed sixth-inning help from Bob Feller, the 20-year-old fireballer from Cleveland. Feller entered the game with one out and the bases loaded and got Vaughan to hit into a first-pitch double play. He then pitched three more innings of one-hit relief.

CAUGHT ON THE FLY

JULY

Boston slugger Jim Tabor hit four homers, drove in 11 runs and totaled 19 bases as the Red Sox swept a doubleheader from Philadelphia, 17-7 and 18-12. Two of his home runs were second-game grand slams.

SEPTEMBER

Cleveland's 20-year-old Bob Feller became the youngest modern-era pitcher to win 20 games in a season when he beat the St. Louis Browns, 12-1.

DECEMBER

New York Yankee great Lou Gehrig, forced into retirement by ill health earlier in the year, was elected to the Hall of Fame in a special vote.

" DUGOUT CHATTER "

"So far as being a problem child or a tough player to handle, that is ridiculous. He probably is the most enthusiastic, most eager to win and attentive to business, always-hustling player on our squad."

Joe Cronin

Boston Red Sox manager, on young star Ted Williams

A touching moment during "Lou Gehrig Day" ceremonies.

A farewell to Gehrig

In one of the most dramatic tributes ever delivered on a baseball field, 61,808 roaring fans bid an emotional farewell to Lou Gehrig between games of a July 4 doubleheader at Yankee Stadium.

The two games between the Yankees and Washington Senators were merely background for the festivities honoring Gehrig, the great Iron Horse who two months earlier had been tragically forced by ill health to retire after playing in a major league-record 2,130 consecutive games. Gehrig's outstanding career ended when he was diagnosed as having amyotrophic lateral sclerosis, a form of infantile paralysis.

Joining in the ceremony were political dignitaries, assorted celebrities and members of the 1927 Yankees, the record-setting championship team of which Gehrig was a vital cog. Babe Ruth, Bob Meusel, Tony Lazzeri and other former stars were escorted onto the field by the Seventh Regiment Band. The current Yankees joined the activities along with the Senators and various other baseball officials. A human rectangle was formed around home plate and Gehrig, obviously weak and fraught with emotion, emerged from the dugout to a thunderous ovation.

Tributes were delivered, gifts were presented and tears flowed freely. Finally Gehrig moved to the microphone, choked back his emotion and began speaking in a slow, even manner.

"What young man wouldn't give anything to mingle with such men for a single day as I have for all these years?" he told the crowd. "You've been reading about my bad break for weeks now. But today I think I'm the luckiest man alive. I now feel more than ever that I have much to live for."

As Gehrig finished his speech, the robust Ruth was nudged toward the microphone. He offered his opinion that the 1927 Yankees were greater than the Yanks of today and then threw his massive arms around Lou's neck in a public display of affection that brought a long roar of approval.

Babe Ruth (right) and Lou Gehrig: a tear-jerking reunion.

Baseball on the air

Major league baseball made its television debut August 26 when New York experimental station W2XBS aired the first game of a doubleheader between the Cincinnati Reds and Dodgers at Brooklyn's Ebbets Field.

With Red Barber handling play-by-play duties for the National Broadcasting Company affiliate, two cameras brought the action to approximately 400 television sets in the New York area. One camera was stationed at ground level near home plate, the other in the upper deck near third base. Reception was fuzzy, but viewers could witness the action from as far away as 50 miles.

After the Reds' 5-2 victory, Barber left his upper-deck perch and hurried to the field for interviews. Rival Managers Bill McKechnie of Cincinnati and Brooklyn's Leo Durocher were guests on television's first postgame show.

This was the second attempt of W2XBS to televise a baseball game. On May 17, the station had aired a Princeton-Columbia college contest from Columbia's Baker Field. Princeton won, 2-1, in 10 innings.

Red Barber interviewing Brooklyn Manager Leo Durocher after handling play-by-play for the first televised major league game.

Rookie ties record

New York righthander Atley Donald stopped the St. Louis Browns, 5-1, on five hits July 25 and won his 12th consecutive game, tying the major league record for most wins at the beginning of a season by a rookie.

The 28-year-old held the Browns hitless for 5⅔ innings as 6,076 fans looked on at Yankee Stadium. Consecutive singles by Billy Sullivan and George McQuinn broke that streak, but Donald held tough, allowing only a seventh-inning run on Chet Laabs' sacrifice fly. Home runs by Joe DiMaggio and Red Rolfe gave the youngster all the support he needed to raise his record to 12-0 and tie the record set by New York Giants lefthander Hooks Wiltse in 1904.

DiMaggio's homer was a titanic 450-foot blast into Yankee Stadium's center-field bleachers. Only Detroit's Hank Greenberg previously had managed to hit a home run into that area.

SEASON LEADERS

	American League		National League	
Avg.	Joe DiMaggio, N.Y.	.381	Johnny Mize, St. L.	.349
HR	Jimmie Foxx, Bos.	35	Johnny Mize, St. L.	28
RBI	Ted Williams, Bos.	145	Frank McCormick, Cin.	128
SB	George Case, Wash.	51	Stan Hack, Chi.	17
			Lee Handley, Pit.	17
W-L Pct.	Lefty Grove, Bos.	15-4, .789	Paul Derringer, Cin.	25-7, .781
ERA	Lefty Grove, Bos.	2.54	Bucky Walters, Cin.	2.29
SO	Bob Feller, Cle.	246	Claude Passeau, Phi.-Chi.	137
			Bucky Walters, Cin.	137

WORLD SERIES REPORT

YANKS 'STUN' REDS

Joe DiMaggio singled home the tie-breaking run in the 10th inning and then circled the bases as Cincinnati catcher Ernie Lombardi lay stunned after a collision at home plate, giving the New York Yankees a 7-4 victory over the Reds and their record fourth straight World Series championship.

The clinching triumph at Crosley Field October 8 gave the Yankees their second straight fall classic sweep and their 13th victory in 14 Series games dating back to 1936.

Red Ruffing throttled Cincinnati on four hits in a 2-1 New York opening-game win at Yankee Stadium. Then fellow righthander Monte Pearson no-hit the Reds for 8⅓ innings en route to a two-hit, 4-0 triumph.

The Yankees unloaded their heavy artillery in Game 3. Outhit 10-5 in the contest, the Bronx Bombers got a pair of two-run homers from Charlie Keller, a two-run blast from Joe DiMaggio and a solo shot from Bill Dickey en route to a 7-3 victory.

The finale, tied 4-4 after nine innings, was decided by a DiMaggio single with runners at the corners and one out in the 10th. When right fielder Ival Goodman misplayed the ball, Keller tried to score from first and bowled over Lombardi. DiMaggio circled the bases as the catcher "snoozed" near the plate and slid home safely.

Game 1	New York	2	Cincinnati	1
Game 2	New York	4	Cincinnati	0
Game 3	New York	7	Cincinnati	3
Game 4	New York	7	Cincinnati	4

New York's Joe DiMaggio slides past Cincinnati catcher Ernie Lombardi, who lay stunned after a Game 4 collision with Yankee Charlie Keller.

The 1940s

The Decade of Hope opened with a financial bang and ended with an economic explosion.

In between, Americans once again were forced to tighten their belts and persevere through hard times that threatened the deepest fibers of baseball's up-and-down existence.

The future looked bright in 1940 with predictions of great riches setting the stage for an unprecedented sports boom. But, after shedding the austerity of the Great Depression and embracing their recreational diversions with open arms and pocketbooks, sports loving Americans were shocked back to reality on December 7, 1941, when Japanese planes unleashed their fury on Pearl Harbor, pushing the United States head-first into World War II. Sports booms and other non-essential activities would have to be shoved into the background.

Baseball, as it had during World War I, dug in and prepared to ride out the storm while doing its part for war relief. But unlike World War I when events were cancelled and schedules reduced, Americans refused to give up their sports diversions. President Franklin D. Roosevelt

NATIONAL LEAGUE

League Batting Leaders

Average

Year	Player-Team	Avg.
1940	Debs Garms, Pit.	.355
1941	Pete Reiser, Bkn.	.343
1942	Ernie Lombardi, Bos.	.330
1943	Stan Musial, St. L.	.357
1944	Dixie Walker, Bkn.	.357
1945	Phil Cavarretta, Chi.	.355
1946	Stan Musial, St. L.	.365
1947	Harry Walker, St. L.-Phil.	.363
1948	Stan Musial.St. L.	.376
1949	Jackie Robinson, Bkn.	.342

Home Runs

Year	Player-Team	HR
1940	Johnny Mize, St. L.	43
1941	Dolph Camilli, Bkn.	34
1942	Mel Ott, N.Y.	30
1943	Bill Nicholson, Chi.	29
1944	Bill Nicholson, Chi.	33
1945	Tommy Holmes, Bos.	28
1946	Ralph Kiner, Pit.	23
1947	Ralph Kiner, Pit.	51
	Johnny Mize, N.Y.	51
1948	Ralph Kiner, Pit.	40
	Johnny Mize, N.Y.	40
1949	Ralph Kiner, Pit.	54

RBIs

Year	Player-Team	RBI
1940	Johnny Mize, St. L.	137
1941	Dolph Camilli, Bkn.	120
1942	Johnny Mize, N.Y.	110
1943	Bill Nicholson, Chi.	128
1944	Bill Nicholson, Chi.	122
1945	Dixie Walker, Bkn.	124
1946	Enos Slaughter, St. L.	130
1947	Johnny Mize, N.Y.	138
1948	Stan Musial, St. L.	131
1949	Ralph Kiner, Pit.	127

Most Valuable Players

Selected by BBWAA

Year	Player-Team	Pos.
1940	Frank McCormick, Cin.	1B
1941	Dolph Camilli, Bkn.	1B
1942	Mort Cooper, St. L.	P
1943	Stan Musial, St. L.	OF
1944	Marty Marion, St. L.	SS
1945	Phil Cavarretta, Chi.	1B
1946	Stan Musial, St. L.	OF
1947	Bob Elliott, Bos.	3B
1948	Stan Musial, St. L.	OF
1949	Jackie Robinson, Bkn.	2B

League Pitching Leaders

Winning Percentage

Year	Pitcher-Team	W-L	Pct.
1940	F. Fitzsimmons, Bkn.	16-2	.889
1941	Elmer Riddle, Cin.	19-4	.826
1942	Larry French, Bkn.	15-4	.789
1943	Mort Cooper, St. L.	21-8	.724
1944	Ted Wilks, St. L.	17-4	.810
1945	Harry Brecheen, St. L.	15-4	.789
1946	Murry Dickson, St. L.	15-6	.714
1947	Larry Jansen, N.Y.	21-5	.808
1948	Harry Brecheen, St. L.	20-7	.741
1949	Preacher Roe, Bkn.	15-6	.714

Earned-Run Average

Year	Pitcher-Team	ERA
1940	Bucky Walters, Cin.	2.48
1941	Elmer Riddle, Cin.	2.24
1942	Mort Cooper, St. L.	1.77
1943	Howie Pollet, St. L.	1.75
1944	Ed Heusser, Cin.	2.38
1945	Hank Borowy, Chi.	2.14
1946	Howie Pollet, St. L.	2.10
1947	Warren Spahn, Bos.	2.33
1948	Harry Brecheen, St. L.	2.24
1949	Dave Koslo, N.Y.	2.50

Strikeouts

Year	Pitcher-Team	SO
1940	Kirby Higbe, Phil.	137
1941	J. Vander Meer, Cin.	202
1942	J. Vander Meer, Cin.	186
1943	J. Vander Meer, Cin.	174
1944	Bill Voiselle, N.Y.	161
1945	Preacher Roe, Pit.	148
1946	Johnny Schmitz, Chi.	135
1947	Ewell Blackwell, Cin.	193
1948	Harry Brecheen, St. L.	149
1949	Warren Spahn, Bos.	151

WORLD SERIES

Year	Winner	Pennant Winner	Games
1940	Cincinnati Reds	Detroit Tigers	4-3
1941	New York Yankees	Brooklyn Dodgers	4-1
1942	St. Louis Cardinals	New York Yankees	4-1
1943	New York Yankees	St. Louis Cardinals	4-1
1944	St. Louis Cardinals	St. Louis Browns	4-2
1945	Detroit Tigers	Chicago Cubs	4-3
1946	St. Louis Cardinals	Boston Red Sox	4-3
1947	New York Yankees	Brooklyn Dodgers	4-3
1948	Cleveland Indians	Boston Braves	4-2
1949	New York Yankees	Brooklyn Dodgers	4-1

HALL OF FAME   Electees and Additions

1942 Rogers Hornsby.

1944 Kenesaw Mountain Landis.

1945 Hugh Duffy, Jimmy Collins, Hugh Jennings, Ed Delahanty, Fred Clarke, Mike Kelly, Wilbert Robinson, Jim O'Rourke, Dan Brouthers, Roger Bresnahan.

1946 Jesse Burkett, Frank Chance, Jack Chesbro, Johnny Evers, Clark Griffith, Tom McCarthy, Joe McGinnity, Eddie Plank, Joe Tinker, Rube Waddell, Ed Walsh.

1947 Carl Hubbell, Frank Frisch, Mickey Cochrane, Lefty Grove.

1948 Herb Pennock, Pie Traynor.

1949 Charley Gehringer, Kid Nichols, Mordecai Brown.

Final Standings

1940

	W	L	PCT.	GB
Cincinnati	100	53	.654	--
Brooklyn	88	65	.575	12
St. Louis	84	69	.549	16
Pittsburgh	78	76	.506	22.5
Chicago	75	79	.487	25.5
New York	72	80	.474	27.5
Boston	65	87	.428	34.5
Philadelphia	50	103	.327	50

1941

	W	L	Pct.	GB
Brooklyn	100	54	.649	--
St. Louis	97	56	.634	2.5
Cincinnati	88	66	.571	12
Pittsburgh	81	73	.526	19
New York	74	79	.484	25.5
Chicago	70	84	.455	30
Boston	62	92	.403	38
Philadelphia	43	111	.279	57

1942

	W	L	Pct.	GB
St. Louis	106	48	.688	--
Brooklyn	104	50	.675	2
New York	85	67	.559	20
Cincinnati	76	76	.500	29
Pittsburgh	66	81	.449	36.5
Chicago	68	86	.442	38
Boston	59	89	.399	44
Philadelphia	42	109	.278	62.5

1943

	W	L	Pct.	GB
St. Louis	105	49	.682	--
Cincinnati	87	67	.565	18
Brooklyn	81	72	.529	23.5
Pittsburgh	80	74	.519	25
Chicago	74	79	.484	30.5
Boston	68	85	.444	36.5
Philadelphia	64	90	.416	41
New York	55	98	.359	49.5

1944

	W	L	Pct.	GB
St. Louis	105	49	.682	--
Pittsburgh	90	63	.588	14.5
Cincinnati	89	65	.578	16
Chicago	75	79	.487	30
New York	67	87	.435	38
Boston	65	89	.422	40
Brooklyn	63	91	.409	42
Philadelphia	61	92	.399	43.5

1945

	W	L	Pct.	GB
Chicago	98	56	.636	--
St. Louis	95	59	.617	3
Brooklyn	87	67	.565	11
Pittsburgh	82	72	.532	16
New York	78	74	.513	19
Boston	67	85	.441	30
Cincinnati	61	93	.396	37
Philadelphia	46	108	.299	52

1946

	W	L	Pct.	GB
*St. Louis	98	58	.628	--
Brooklyn	96	60	.615	2
Chicago	82	71	.536	14.5
Boston	81	72	.529	15.5
Philadelphia	69	85	.448	28
Cincinnati	67	87	.435	30
Pittsburgh	63	91	.409	34
New York	61	93	.396	36

*Defeated Brooklyn 2-0 in pennant playoff

1947

	W	L	Pct.	GB
Brooklyn	94	60	.610	--
St. Louis	89	65	.578	5
Boston	86	68	.558	8
New York	81	73	.526	13
Cincinnati	73	81	.474	21
Chicago	69	85	.448	25
Philadelphia	62	92	.403	32
Pittsburgh	62	92	.403	32

1948

	W	L	Pct.	GB
Boston	91	62	.595	--
St. Louis	85	69	.552	6.5
Brooklyn	84	70	.545	7.5
Pittsburgh	83	71	.539	8.5
New York	78	76	.506	13.5
Philadelphia	66	88	.429	25.5
Cincinnati	64	89	.418	27
Chicago	64	90	.416	27.5

1949

	W	L	Pct.	GB
Brooklyn	97	57	.630	--
St. Louis	96	58	.623	1
Philadelphia	81	73	.526	16
Boston	75	79	.487	22
New York	73	81	.474	24
Pittsburgh	71	83	.461	26
Cincinnati	62	92	.403	35
Chicago	61	93	.396	36

Brooklyn's Pete Reiser.

issued his "Green Light Letter" saying that baseball should continue and fans who remained on the home front supported their teams.

Stars like Hank Greenberg, Bob Feller, Joe DiMaggio and Ted Williams heeded Uncle Sam's call, as did many players from all the sports. There were cancellations of some major individual events and several unstable pro football franchises went under, but for the most part college and professional team sports muddled through.

As it turned out, the world crisis merely stimulated interest and whetted the sports appetite. When the fighting ceased, it quickly became evident that new seeds of growth were taking root — a growth that would exceed even the wildest of expectations.

Improved air service would trigger a wild rush of expansion. NBC, CBS and ABC soon would become the most important initials in athletics as television looked to expand its own horizons. Organized labor soon would beckon to the baseball community. And blacks who

had fought alongside whites for freedom against Germany and Japan soon would be fighting for justice in their own country — a fight that drew attention with Jackie Robinson's 1947 arrival in the major leagues.

Through all the difficulty and despite the watered-down talent base of the war years, baseball produced some magic moments.

DiMaggio hit in a record 56 straight games; Boston's Williams became baseball's first .400 hitter in 11 years; the lowly St. Louis Browns won the first pennant of their long history and employed a one-armed outfielder; the St. Louis Cardinals and Cleveland Indians won baseball's first-ever pennant playoffs; the Cardinals' Enos Slaughter decided a World Series with a mad dash around the bases, and the Yankees and Cardinals combined for seven Series championships.

The Yankees, who closed the decade with their first title under new manager Casey Stengel, were just getting started. As Casey warned his American League opponents at the time, "You ain't seen nuttin yet."

Detroit lefthander Hal Newhouser.

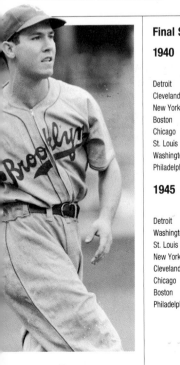

AMERICAN LEAGUE

League Batting Leaders

Average

Year	Player-Team	Avg.
1940	Joe DiMaggio, N.Y.	.352
1941	Ted Williams, Bos.	.406
1942	Ted Williams, Bos.	.356
1943	Luke Appling, Chi.	.328
1944	Lou Boudreau, Cle.	.327
1945	Snuffy Stirnweiss, N.Y.	.309
1946	Mickey Vernon, Wash.	.353
1947	Ted Williams, Bos.	.343
1948	Ted Williams, Bos.	.369
1949	George Kell, Det.	.343

Home Runs

Year	Player-Team	HR
1940	Hank Greenberg, Det.	41
1941	Ted Williams, Bos.	37
1942	Ted Williams, Bos.	36
1943	Rudy York, Det.	34
1944	Nick Etten, N.Y.	22
1945	Vern Stephens, St. L.	24
1946	Hank Greenberg, Det.	44
1947	Ted Williams, Bos.	32
1948	Joe DiMaggio, N.Y.	39
1949	Ted Williams, Bos.	43

RBIs

Year	Player-Team	RBI
1940	Hank Greenberg, Det.	150
1941	Joe DiMaggio, N.Y.	125
1942	Ted Williams, Bos.	137
1943	Rudy York, Det.	118
1944	Vern Stephens, St. L.	109
1945	Nick Etten, N.Y.	111
1946	Hank Greenberg, Det.	127
1947	Ted Williams, Bos.	114
1948	Joe DiMaggio, N.Y.	155
1949	Ted Williams, Bos.	159
	Vern Stephens, Bos.	159

Most Valuable Players

Selected by BBWAA

Year	Player-Team	Pos.
1940	Hank Greenberg, Det.	OF
1941	Joe DiMaggio, N.Y.	OF
1942	Joe Gordon, N.Y.	2B
1943	Spud Chandler, N.Y.	P
1944	Hal Newhouser, Det.	P
1945	Hal Newhouser, Det.	P
1946	Ted Williams, Bos.	OF
1947	Joe DiMaggio, N.Y.	OF
1948	Lou Boudreau, Cle.	SS
1949	Ted Williams, Bos.	OF

League Pitching Leaders

Winning Percentage

Year	Pitcher-Team	W-L	Pct.
1940	Schoolboy Rowe, Det.	16-3	.842
1941	Lefty Gomez, N.Y.	15-5	.750
1942	Ernie Bonham, N.Y.	21-5	.808
1943	Spud Chandler, N.Y.	20-4	.833
1944	Tex Hughson, Bos.	18-5	.783
1945	Hal Newhouser, Det.	25-9	.735
1946	Boo Ferriss, Bos.	25-6	.806
1947	Allie Reynolds, N.Y.	19-8	.704
1948	Jack Kramer, Bos.	18-5	.783
1949	Ellis Kinder, Bos.	23-6	.793

Earned-Run Average

Year	Pitcher-Team	ERA
1940	Bob Feller, Cle.	2.62
1941	Thornton Lee, Chi.	2.37
1942	Ted Lyons, Chi.	2.10
1943	Spud Chandler, N.Y.	1.64
1944	Dizzy Trout, Det.	2.12
1945	Hal Newhouser, Det.	1.81
1946	Hal Newhouser, Det.	1.94
1947	Spud Chandler, N.Y.	2.46
1948	Gene Bearden, Cle.	2.43
1949	Mel Parnell, Bos.	2.77

Strikeouts

Year	Pitcher-Team	SO
1940	Bob Feller, Cle.	261
1941	Bob Feller, Cle.	260
1942	Tex Hughson, Bos.	113
	Bobo Newsom, Wash.	113
1943	Allie Reynolds, N.Y.	151
1944	Hal Newhouser, Det.	187
1945	Hal Newhouser, Det.	212
1946	Bob Feller, Cle.	348
1947	Bob Feller, Cle.	196
1948	Bob Feller, Cle.	164
1949	Virgil Trucks, Det.	153

Final Standings

*Defeated Boston in one-game pennant playoff

1940

	W	L	PCT.	GB
Detroit	90	64	.584	--
Cleveland	89	65	.578	1
New York	88	66	.571	2
Boston	82	72	.532	8
Chicago	82	72	.532	8
St. Louis	67	87	.435	23
Washington	64	90	.416	26
Philadelphia	54	100	.351	36

1941

	W	L	Pct.	GB
New York	101	53	.656	--
Boston	84	70	.545	17
Chicago	77	77	.500	24
Cleveland	75	79	.487	26
Detroit	75	79	.487	26
St. Louis	70	84	.455	31
Washington	70	84	.455	31
Philadelphia	64	90	.416	37

1942

	W	L	Pct.	GB
New York	103	51	.669	--
Boston	93	59	.612	9
St. Louis	82	69	.543	19.5
Cleveland	75	79	.487	28
Detroit	73	81	.474	30
Chicago	66	82	.446	34
Washington	62	89	.411	39.5
Philadelphia	55	99	.357	48

1943

	W	L	Pct.	GB
New York	98	56	.636	--
Washington	84	69	.549	13.5
Cleveland	82	71	.536	15.5
Chicago	82	72	.532	16
Detroit	78	76	.506	20
St. Louis	72	80	.474	25
Boston	68	84	.447	29
Philadelphia	49	105	.318	49

1944

	W	L	Pct.	GB
St. Louis	89	65	.578	--
Detroit	88	66	.571	1
New York	83	71	.539	6
Boston	77	77	.500	12
Cleveland	72	82	.468	17
Philadelphia	72	82	.468	17
Chicago	71	83	.461	18
Washington	64	90	.416	25

1945

	W	L	Pct.	GB
Detroit	88	65	.575	--
Washington	87	67	.565	1.5
St. Louis	81	70	.536	6
New York	81	71	.533	6.5
Cleveland	73	72	.503	11
Chicago	71	78	.477	15
Boston	71	83	.461	17.5
Philadelphia	52	98	.347	34.5

1946

	W	L	Pct.	GB
Boston	104	50	.675	--
Detroit	92	62	.597	12
New York	87	67	.565	17
Washington	76	78	.494	28
Chicago	74	80	.481	30
Cleveland	68	86	.442	36
St. Louis	66	88	.429	38
Philadelphia	49	105	.318	55

1947

	W	L	Pct.	GB
New York	97	57	.630	--
Detroit	85	69	.552	12
Boston	83	71	.539	14
Cleveland	80	74	.519	17
Philadelphia	78	76	.506	19
Chicago	70	84	.455	27
Washington	64	90	.416	33
St. Louis	59	95	.383	38

1948

	W	L	Pct.	GB
*Cleveland	97	58	.626	--
Boston	96	59	.619	1
New York	94	60	.610	2.5
Philadelphia	84	70	.545	12.5
Detroit	78	76	.506	18.5
St. Louis	59	94	.386	37
Washington	56	97	.366	40
Chicago	51	101	.336	44.5

1949

	W	L	Pct.	GB
New York	97	57	.630	--
Boston	96	58	.623	1
Cleveland	89	65	.578	8
Detroit	87	67	.565	10
Philadelphia	81	73	.526	16
Chicago	63	91	.409	34
St. Louis	53	101	.344	44
Washington	50	104	.325	47

★ 1940 ★

SEASON LEADERS

	American League		National League	
Avg.	Joe DiMaggio, N.Y.	.352	Debs Garms, Pit.	.355
HR	Hank Greenberg, Det.	41	Johnny Mize, St. L.	43
RBI	Hank Greenberg, Det.	150	Johnny Mize, St. L.	137
SB	George Case, Wash.	35	Lonny Frey, Cin.	22
W-L Pct.	Schoolboy Rowe, Det.	16-3, .842	Freddie Fitzsimmons, Bkn.	16-2, .889
ERA	Bob Feller, Cle.	2.62	Bucky Walters, Cin.	2.48
SO	Bob Feller, Cle.	261	Kirby Higbe, Phi.	137

" DUGOUT CHATTER "

"I don't know whether I signed him or he signed me."

Alva Bradley

Cleveland President, referring to Bob Feller's 1940 contract for a reported $32,500

Feller opens in style

Cleveland's Bob Feller, trying to show that his 24-win 1939 season was no fluke, opened the 1940 campaign with a bang April 16 when he fired his first no-hitter and defeated the White Sox, 1-0, at Chicago's Comiskey Park.

Working in 47-degree weather, the fireballer struck out eight and walked five in posting the first Opening Day no-hit victory in modern major league history. The New York Giants' Red Ames pitched 9⅓ hitless innings on Opening Day in 1909, but he ended up losing, 3-0, in 13 innings.

It was not all clear sailing for the husky righthander, who was given a 1-0 lead in the fourth on Rollie Hemsley's run-scoring triple. The White Sox loaded the bases on three second-inning walks, but Feller threw a blazing fastball past rookie Bob Kennedy. In the ninth, Luke Appling came close to hits with four foul smashes before drawing a two-out walk. The final batter, Taft Wright, then smashed a grounder that second baseman Ray Mack knocked down, picked up and threw to first for the out.

Feller, who had thrown three one-hitters in his brief big-league career, outdueled Chicago loser Edgar Smith, who allowed only six hits.

Cleveland's Bob Feller (left) gets a pat on the back from Hal Trosky after pitching the first Opening Day no-hitter in modern major league history.

Reds 'flooded out'

Cincinnati team officials, watching helplessly as home plate at Crosley Field vanished under the backwaters of the Ohio River, postponed their April 23 and 24 games against St. Louis and became the third team in major league history to call off a contest on account of flood.

Players would have needed boats or hipboots to negotiate the waters dumped on Crosley by a river seven feet above flood stage and still climbing. Only the park's outfield terraces were still dry at game time and even they were expected to be covered by the time the river crested April 24 at a predicted eight feet.

Once the water begins to recede, a giant siphon fashioned out of firehose will be used to speed the drying process. Five inches of sand was dumped on the diamond to protect the field's surface.

The Reds held a brief throw-and-catch practice on the few remaining dry areas of the field.

Cincinnati's Crosley Field under siege from the Ohio River.

Landis stuns Tigers

Baseball Commissioner Kenesaw Mountain Landis, citing Detroit for covering up the movement of its players, awarded free agency to 91 members of the Tigers organization January 14, cutting adrift talent valued in excess of $500,000.

In what is considered the biggest free agency ruling of its kind in baseball history, Landis cut the ties between the Tigers and 87 minor leaguers while freeing four players from the team's parent roster — second baseman Benny McCoy, outfielder Roy Cullenbine and pitchers Lloyd Dietz and Steve Rachunok. McCoy had recently been traded to the Philadelphia Athletics for outfielder Wally Moses, a deal nullified by the ruling.

Detroit officials were understandably stunned and said it will take years to repair the damage it does to the Tiger farm system. The Tigers also were ordered to pay nearly $50,000 in compensation to 14 players.

The covering up of players within the farm system is a pet peeve of the commissioner. Two years ago, he freed 74 members of the St. Louis Cardinals organization, but most of the players came from lower classifications.

Carleton unhittable

Tex Carleton, a 33-year-old right-hander who spent the 1939 season in the minor leagues, fired a no-hit 3-0 shutout at the Cincinnati Reds April 30 as the undefeated Brooklyn Dodgers tied the modern record for most victories to open a season.

Brooklyn's ninth straight win was fashioned spectacularly before 10,544 fans at Crosley Field. Carleton walked the first batter he faced and then embarked on a nine-inning journey during which the Reds managed only three more baserunners — two on errors and one on another walk. In winning his second game in a Brooklyn uniform, the former St. Louis Cardinal and Chicago Cub struck out four and set down the last 17 Reds he faced.

Young second baseman Pete Coscarart provided all the offense

Carleton needed with a fifth-inning home run that drove home Herman Franks and Dixie Walker ahead of him.

The no-hitter was the second of this young season after a 1939 campaign in which nobody accomplished the feat.

Brooklyn righthander Tex Carleton.

CAUGHT ON THE FLY

MAY/JUNE
The first night games were played at New York's Polo Grounds, St. Louis' Sportsman's Park and Pittsburgh's Forbes Field.

MAY
The Brooklyn Dodgers became the first N.L. team to travel by airplane when they flew from St. Louis to Chicago and from Chicago to Brooklyn two days later.

JUNE
The Chicago Cubs, hoping that the warmer weather in the Class AA Texas League would help his sore arm, sent former St. Louis pitching great Dizzy Dean to Tulsa.

Boston first baseman Buddy Hassett tied an N.L. record when he got four hits during a 4-2 victory over Chicago at Braves Field, giving him 10 straight over a three-game period.

N.L. stars zero in

Boston Bees outfielder Max West clubbed a three-run, first-inning homer and five National League pitchers combined for the first shutout in All-Star Game history as the senior circuit posted a 4-0 victory over the American League July 9 at St. Louis' Sportsman's Park.

West connected with a delivery from New York's Red Ruffing after Pittsburgh's Arky Vaughan and Chicago's Billy Herman had led off the bottom of the first with singles. An inning later, West connected with the outfield wall while chasing a Luke Appling

smash and had to leave the game.

But his home run stood up the rest of the way, thanks to the sturdy three-hit pitching of Cincinnati's Paul Derringer and Bucky Walters, Brooklyn's Whitlow Wyatt, Cubs lefty Larry French and New York's Carl Hubbell. Derringer, Wyatt and French allowed one hit apiece in their two-inning stints and two American Leaguers reached base on walks.

Detroit's Bobo Newsom followed Ruffing for the A.L. and Cleveland's Bob Feller finished up, allowing an eighth-inning run.

National League players rush to the aid of Boston's Max West, who had to leave the All-Star Game after colliding with the outfield wall.

Dodgers cry foul after Medwick beaning

Brooklyn left fielder Joe Medwick, the 1937 National League Most Valuable Player acquired from St. Louis six days earlier, was hit on the head June 18 by a fastball from Cardinal right-hander Bob Bowman and had to be carried from Ebbets Field on a stretcher.

The beaning, the second involving Brooklyn and part of a

growing epidemic around the major leagues, drew hostile reactions from several Dodgers and team President Larry MacPhail. As Medwick lay unconscious near home plate, several players had to be restrained from going after Bowman and MacPhail walked over to the St. Louis dugout and exchanged harsh words with the Cardinals.

MacPhail, who had watched the beaning of shortstop Pee Wee Reese during a game in Chicago, accused Bowman of throwing at his former teammate and demanded that the pitcher be disciplined. St. Louis Manager Billy Southworth, fearing fan hostility, removed Bowman after the incident and police escorted him from the park.

Medwick, who suffered only a concussion, was to remain under observation for a week. He is expected to make a full recovery.

Ill feelings have existed between Cardinal and Dodger players for more than a year and Bowman reportedly exchanged heated words with fiery Brooklyn Manager Leo Durocher shortly before the Cardinals' 7-5 victory.

Giebell whips Feller in pennant clincher

Floyd Giebell, a 30-year-old rookie with nerves of steel, ignored riotous Cleveland fans September 27 while outdueling Bob Feller and posting a 2-0 victory that clinched the American League pennant for the Detroit Tigers.

Giebell, a righthander who was 1-10 for Toledo (American Association) in 1939 and 15-17 for Buffalo (International League) before joining Detroit this season, was the surprise starter for Del Baker's Tigers in the opening contest of the crucial season-closing three-game series against the second-place Indians. Detroit led Cleveland by two games and needed only one more victory to claim its first pennant since 1935.

So Floyd Giebell against Bob Feller?

With that thought in everybody's mind and garbage and other debris raining down on helpless Detroit players courtesy of 45,553 hyped-up fans at Cleveland Stadium, the game began. Giebell struggled, but every time the Indians mounted a threat, he cut it off with clutch pitching. Feller, on the other hand, was in top form — until Rudy York caught hold of a fourth-inning fastball and sent it into the left-field seats for a two-run homer. The Tigers managed only one hit the rest of the way, but Giebell made the runs stand up.

The game had to be held up several times while debris was removed from the field, prompting the umpires to warn fans that any future disturbances could result in a forfeit. The most serious incident occurred when a spectator in the second deck dropped a bushel basket filled with tomatoes and empty beer bottles into the bullpen, hitting catcher Birdie Tebbetts on the head. Tebbetts was knocked unconscious and the severity of the incident had a fortunate calming effect on the crowd.

The Detroit victory capped a frantic pennant chase that also included the New York Yankees. The highlight of the long race was an early season revolt by Cleveland players against Manager Oscar Vitt.

Upset by Vitt's dugout demeanor, criticism and disparaging conduct, 11 Indian veterans met with Owner Alva Bradley on the morning of June 13, airing their grievances and demanding that the manager be dismissed. When Bradley refused after careful consideration and a meeting with Vitt, the players backed down.

Reds' Hershberger commits suicide

Cincinnati catcher Willard Hershberger, batting .309 and doing a good job as a replacement for the injured Ernie Lombardi, committed suicide August 3 in his Boston hotel room.

Hershberger, depressed over what he considered inadequate play and blaming himself for calling wrong pitches during a July 31 loss to the New York Giants, cut his throat with a razor blade in the hotel suite's bathroom. His body was discovered by Cincinnati businessman Sam Cohen, a close friend who went to investigate when Hershberger did not show for a game at Braves Field.

Hershberger was in his third season with the Reds and carried a .316 career average in 160 games. Reds Manager Bill McKechnie said he had noticed Hershberger's "depressed mental condition" following a recent game and had talked to him for some time. He said the 30-year-old catcher appeared to be in much better spirits after the talk and joined with other players in the normal clubhouse horseplay.

Cincinnati catcher Willard Hershberger.

Detroit's pennant-clinching heroes (left to right): First baseman Rudy York, pitcher Floyd Giebell and catcher Billy Sullivan.

Foxx matches Ruth

Jimmie Foxx's 500th career home run was the feature blast of a four-homer sixth-inning salvo fired by the Boston Red Sox September 24 during a 16-8 victory over the Philadelphia Athletics in the first game of a doubleheader at Shibe Park. The Red Sox also won the nightcap, 4-3.

Foxx, who joins former New York Yankee star Babe Ruth as the only players to reach the 500 barrier, connected off right-hander George Caster. Ted Williams hit the first home run of the sixth off Caster, Foxx followed with his and Joe Cronin made it three in a row. The next batter, Bobby Doerr, belted a long drive to center but was held up at third. Jim Tabor followed with the fourth home run of the inning, one short of the major league record set by the New York Giants in 1939.

The 32-year-old Foxx now trails Ruth by 214 home runs on the all-time list. It was only fitting that the milestone blast should come in Philadelphia, the city where he began his career in 1925. The three-time American League Most Valuable Player hit 58 homers for the Athletics in 1932.

Boston's Jimmie Foxx: Baseball's second 500-homer man.

CAUGHT ON THE FLY

SEPTEMBER

The Detroit Tigers set a major league record when they hit at least one home run in 17 successive games. The Tigers belted 26 during the streak, 13 coming from the big bat of Hank Greenberg.

DECEMBER

Connie Mack paid the Shibe family $42,000 for controlling interest in the Philadelphia Athletics.

" DUGOUT CHATTER "

"I don't know any girls in New York. Some of those female fans in Kansas City send me letters signed with lipsticked kisses, but I don't mind them. I showed 'em to my sisters and how they giggle over them."

Phil Rizzuto

Yankee shortstop-of-the-future, who played the 1940 season with Kansas City in the American Association

REDS TAME TIGERS

Paul Derringer pitched a gritty seven-hitter and Billy Myers drove in the winning run with a seventh-inning sacrifice fly October 8 as the Cincinnati Reds defeated the Detroit Tigers, 2-1, and captured their first World Series championship since their scandal-marred victory of 1919.

Derringer's Game 7 triumph at Cincinnati's Crosley Field ended an alternating victory pattern that started with Detroit's opening-game win and continued through six contests. He outdueled Tiger ace Bobo Newsom, who made an unearned third-inning run stand up through six frames before running into trouble in the seventh.

Frank McCormick and Jimmy Ripple led off the inning with consecutive doubles to tie the score and Ripple was sacrificed to third. After pinch-hitter Ernie Lombardi was walked intentionally, Myers drove a Newsom pitch deep to center field, scoring Ripple. Derringer, a four-time 20-game winner, made the lead stand up the rest of the way.

Derringer was not so fortunate in his Series-opening matchup against Newsom, a three-time 20-game winner. The Tigers exploded for five runs in the second inning, sending Derringer to the showers, and added two more in the fifth en route to a 7-2 victory.

Ripple's two-run homer and the three-hit pitching of Bucky Walters enabled the Reds to even the count the next day with a 5-3 victory, but the Tigers regained the upper hand in Game 3 as Rudy York and Pinky Higgins belted two-run, seventh-inning homers that resulted in a 7-4 Detroit win. Derringer's five-hit, 5-2 victory in the fourth game deadlocked the fall classic again.

Newsom fired a three-hitter and Hank Greenberg homered and drove in four runs as the Tigers regained the advantage with an 8-0 victory, but Walters' homer and five-hit pitching produced a 4-0 win that forced a seventh game.

Game 1	Detroit	7	Cincinnati	2
Game 2	Cincinnati	5	Detroit	3
Game 3	Detroit	7	Cincinnati	4
Game 4	Cincinnati	5	Detroit	2
Game 5	Detroit	8	Cincinnati	0
Game 6	Cincinnati	4	Detroit	0
Game 7	Cincinnati	2	Detroit	1

The World Series-champion Cincinnati Reds boasted a Big Six of (left to right): Eddie Joost, Ival Goodman, Frank McCormick, Ernie Lombardi, Bill Werber and Mike McCormick.

★1941★
JANUARY-JULY

Batting helmets

Greenberg enlists

Lou Gehrig dies

The well-decorated grave of former Yankee star Lou Gehrig, who died on June 2.

Lou Gehrig, the great Iron Horse of the New York Yankees, died June 2 at age 37 from the incurable disease that had forced his retirement from baseball in 1939 after 14-plus brilliant campaigns that helped produce seven American League pennants and six World Series championships.

Gehrig, who set an incredible major league record by playing in 2,130 consecutive games, passed away at his New York home after a two-year battle with amyotrophic lateral sclerosis, a disease that hardens the spinal cord and causes muscles to shrivel. Gehrig wasted away quickly in the final weeks and reportedly was 25 pounds underweight and barely able to speak.

Gehrig leaves behind a legacy of baseball excellence and quiet efficiency that long will be remembered by Yankee fans. Always overshadowed by colorful teammate Babe Ruth, Gehrig nevertheless forged an outstanding career that produced a .340 average, 493 home runs (third on the all-time list), 2,721 hits, 1,990 runs batted in and 1,888 runs.

He spent his final year and a half as a member of the New York City parole commission and visited his office regularly until about a month ago.

Brooklyn President Larry MacPhail announced May 1 that he had submitted an application for patent on the "Brooklyn Safety Cap," the team hat lined with plastic to protect Dodger players from beanballs thrown by wild or angry pitchers.

The Dodgers began wearing the innovative caps April 20 and the move paid a quick dividend when outfielder Pete Reiser ducked away from an errant pitch by Philadelphia's Ike Pearson and was hit on the side of his skull. The cap took the brunt of the punishment and doctors said Reiser, who was knocked unconscious, was spared a potentially serious injury.

The protective headgear, a takeoff of the skull caps worn by jockeys under their silk hats, was designed in response to the beanball wars of 1940. The perfected cap, with molded plastic shields sewn permanently into the lining, evolved from 25 experimental models.

MacPhail said the Dodgers have no intention of profiting from the invention and added that he will extend permission to any club or individual for use of the cap and license to manufacture.

Slugging Detroit first baseman Hank Greenberg gave Tiger fans a May 6 farewell present as he prepared to report to Fort Custer, Mich., for basic training as a private in the U.S. Army.

The 1940 American League Most Valuable Player said goodbye with a two-homer barrage that buried the New York Yankees, 7-4, at Briggs Stadium and lifted the Tigers into second place in the A.L., four games behind Cleveland. Greenberg's first and last homers of the season drove in three runs and gave his teammates a needed lift.

Greenberg, notified after the game that his local draft board had authorized his appearance at the May 7 A.L. pennant raising ceremonies in Detroit, said he would report at 6:30 a.m. as scheduled for induction into the Army. "I've asked no favors and I'll accept none now," he said.

Greenberg, an enlistee, will be giving up a reported $50,000 yearly baseball salary for $21 per month Army pay. He batted .340, hit 41 homers and drove in 150 runs last year in leading Detroit to the A.L. pennant.

The first major leaguer to be drafted was Philadelphia Phillies righthander Hugh Mulcahy.

SEASON LEADERS

	American League			National League	
Avg.	Ted Williams, Bos.	.406		Pete Reiser, Bkn.	.343
HR	Ted Williams, Bos.	37		Dolph Camilli, Bkn.	34
RBI	Joe DiMaggio, N.Y.	125		Dolph Camilli, Bkn.	120
SB	George Case, Wash.	33		Danny Murtaugh, Phi.	18
W-L Pct.	Lefty Gomez, N.Y. 15-5, .750			Elmer Riddle, Cin. 19-4, .826	
ERA	Thornton Lee, Chi.	2.37		Elmer Riddle, Cin.	2.24
SO	Bob Feller, Cle.	260		Johnny Vander Meer, Cin.	
					202

"DUGOUT CHATTER"

"He dresses like Joe Broadway when things are going right, but when he gets the collar he wears dark clothes and a face as long as a doubleheader with the Phillies."

Pete Reiser

Dodger outfielder, on teammate Pee Wee Reese

Detroit's Hank Greenberg gave up his reported $50,000-per-year salary for a $21 monthly check from the Army.

Williams blasts N.L. in dramatic fashion

Boston slugger Ted Williams, getting a chance to bat when National League second baseman Billy Herman made a poor relay throw to first on what should have been a game-ending double play, belted a two-out, three-run, ninth-inning homer July 8 to give the American League a dramatic 7-5 All-Star Game victory at Detroit's Briggs Stadium.

Williams, who entered the midsummer classic batting .405, drove a fastball from Chicago Cubs righthander Claude Passeau off the upper parapet of the right-field stands to cap a four-run rally and end the most exciting contest in All-Star Game history. The N.L. appeared to have the victory in hand when Yankee Joe DiMaggio, batting right before Williams, hit a bases-loaded grounder to Boston Braves shortstop Eddie Miller. Miller fielded cleanly and tossed to Herman, but the Dodger second sacker's throw pulled first baseman Frank McCormick off the bag.

The N.L. had built its lead on a pair of two-run homers by Pittsburgh's Arky Vaughan, a man not known for his power. Brooklyn's Whitlow Wyatt and Reds Paul Derringer and Bucky Walters held the A.L. to a pair of runs through seven innings before turning matters over to Passeau.

American League President Will Harridge congratulates Boston's Ted Williams after his All-Star Game-winning home run.

" DUGOUT CHATTER "

"I just shut my eyes and swung with all I had. Then, when I looked up, I heard the yell of the crowd and saw the ball headed for the stands."

Ted Williams

Boston slugger, describing his dramatic ninth-inning All-Star Game-winning home run

CAUGHT ON THE FLY

MAY

The city of Philadelphia declared a legal holiday to honor Connie Mack, the venerable grand old man of the Athletics who was feted during ceremonies at Shibe Park.

The New York Yankees spoiled the first night game in the history of Griffith Stadium by defeating the Senators, 6-5.

JUNE

New York slugger Mel Ott collected his 400th career homer and 1,500th RBI during a 3-2 Giants' victory over the Cincinnati Reds.

DiMaggio streak ends

Performing under the intense pressure of a national spotlight and the curious eyes of 67,468 fans July 17 at Cleveland Stadium, New York Yankee center fielder Joe DiMaggio failed to get a hit against two Indians pitchers and ended his phenomenal hitting streak at 56 games.

Lefthander Al Smith and righthander Jim Bagby Jr. were the hurlers credited with ending one of the greatest record runs in baseball history. But the glove of third baseman Ken Keltner was the real culprit. Facing Smith in the first inning, DiMaggio smashed a ball down the third-base line. Keltner made an outstanding backhand stop, turned and threw out the Yankee Clipper on a close play at first.

DiMaggio faced Smith again in the fourth and drew a full-count walk. With the score tied 1-1 in the seventh, DiMaggio hit another smash, this time right at Keltner. He fielded it cleanly and threw to first for the out.

DiMaggio's fourth at-bat came with the bases loaded in the eighth inning and the Yankees now on top, 3-1. Facing Bagby, the son of Cleveland's 31-game winner of 1920, DiMaggio hit a grounder up the middle. Shortstop Lou Boudreau grabbed the ball, stepped on second and threw to first for a double play. The Indians fought back to 4-3 in the ninth inning, but Yankee reliever Johnny Murphy ended the uprising. The streak that began innocently enough May 15 with a single off Chicago lefty Edgar Smith was over.

In the glorious two-month run, DiMaggio passed former St. Louis Browns star George Sisler (41 games in 1922) to set the modern major league record and former Baltimore Oriole Willie Keeler (44 in 1897) to set the all-time mark. Over the course of the streak, DiMaggio batted .408 in 223 at-bats with 91 hits, 16 doubles, four triples, 15 homers and 55 RBIs.

When the streak started, the Yankees were in fourth place, 5½ games behind the Indians. When it ended, they were in first place, six games ahead of Cleveland. The Yanks were 41-13 with two ties in the 56 games.

When Yankee Joe DiMaggio hit safely in his 44th straight game, he equaled the all-time record set by turn-of-the-century star Willie Keeler.

Grove wins 300th

Boston's Lefty Grove, newest member of pitching's "300 club."

He stumbled, staggered and held on for dear life, but Boston's Lefty Grove stuck it out and finally won his milestone 300th career victory, beating Cleveland, 10-6, in a July 25 battle at Fenway Park.

The 41-year-old veteran fell behind 4-0 and 6-4, but showed dogged determination in his third attempt for the magic victory. His teammates rewarded him with two rallies and Jimmie Foxx, Grove's teammate in both Philadelphia and Boston, provided the go-ahead punch with a two-run triple during the Red Sox's four-run eighth inning.

Grove, who also received support from Jim Tabor — a home run and four RBIs — in winning for the seventh time this season, became the 12th pitcher to achieve 300 victories. He won in nine years 195 with the Athletics, 105 in eight years with Boston.

Brooklyn fans party

In a zany and happy conclusion to the 1941 regular season, Brooklyn fans and players partied at Ebbets Field September 28 as the World Series-bound Bums recorded their record 100th victory.

Leo Durocher's Dodgers, who had clinched their first National League pennant in 21 years September 25 after a torrid battle with St. Louis, were in good spirits during the finale, a 5-1 victory over Philadelphia. So were 12,870 fans, who were entertained by Brooklyn's rag-tag band and an appearance by actress Betty Grable while entertaining themselves with between-inning dashes onto the field for player autographs. It was that kind of day and that kind of season.

The Dodgers' final 2½-game victory over the Cardinals prompted a celebration parade that drew more than a million fans to downtown Brooklyn. In winning their first N.L. pennant since 1920 and third overall, the Dodgers drew a record 1,215,253 fans to Ebbets Field.

Brooklyn's wild jubilation stood in contrast to the mechanical, ho-hum American League victory of the New York Yankees. The Yanks, winners of five pennants in the last six years and eight World Series, recorded the earliest clinching date in big-league history when they defeated Boston, 6-3, on September 4.

Feisty Brooklyn Manager Leo Durocher hard at work during the 1941 N.L. pennant race.

CAUGHT ON THE FLY

AUGUST
New York Yankee ace Lefty Gomez allowed five hits and walked 11 batters — and still threw a 9-0 shutout of the St. Louis Browns. The losers stranded 15 runners in the game at Yankee Stadium.

SEPTEMBER
Brooklyn's 22-year-old Pete Reiser became the youngest N.L. batting champion in history when he finished at .343.

NOVEMBER
The Cleveland Indians tabbed 24-year-old shortstop Lou Boudreau to succeed Roger Peckinpaugh as player-manager.

Williams bats .406

Ted Williams, Boston's 23-year-old Splendid Splinter, capped his season in spectacular fashion September 28, collecting six hits in eight at-bats during a doubleheader split with Philadelphia to raise his major league-leading batting mark to .406.

Williams became baseball's first .400 hitter since the New York Giants' Bill Terry (.401) in 1930 and the first in the American League since Detroit's Harry Heilmann (.403) in 1923.

Williams started the day with a .39955 average, which rounded off to .400. Boston Manager Joe Cronin offered to let his star sit out and insure his .400 finish, but Williams refused, saying, "I don't care to be known as a .400 hitter with a lousy average of .39955. If I'm going to be a .400 hitter, I want to have more than my toenails on the line."

Williams proceeded to go 4 for 5 with a homer in the opener, a 12-11 Red Sox victory, and 2 for 3 in the nightcap, a 7-1 Boston loss. He also finished with league-leading totals in homers (37), runs scored (135) and walks (145) and drove in 120 runs while leading Boston to a second-place finish.

DiMaggio wins MVP

The Baseball Writers' Association of America, obviously more impressed by Joe DiMaggio's 56-game hitting streak than Ted Williams' final .406 average, rewarded the Yankee Clipper with his second Most Valuable Player citation in the closest vote since the organization took control of the award in 1931.

DiMaggio, American League MVP in 1939, finished the season with a .357 average, 30 homers and a league-leading 125 runs batted in and then helped New York dispatch Brooklyn in a five-game World Series. But the record hitting streak and a sub-sequent 16-game streak that started the day after the record-setter ended were the deciding factors. Hitting in 72 of 73 games was the most remarkable exhibition of sustained offense ever seen in the major leagues and DiMaggio garnered 291 points in the balloting, 37 more than Williams.

Boston's left fielder, the first .400 hitter in the big leagues since 1930 and the A.L. home run leader with 37, fell five RBIs short of becoming the league's fifth Triple Crown winner.

DiMaggio received 15 first-place votes, seven more than Williams.

Yankee Clipper Joe DiMaggio (left) edged out Boston slugger Ted Williams in a close vote for A.L. Most Valuable Player honors.

" DUGOUT CHATTER "

"Playing those Dodgers is like shooting quail on the ground. But I'm glad there's no law against it."

Charlie Keller

Yankee star, after his team's five-game win over Brooklyn in the World Series

---

WORLD SERIES REPORT

OWEN'S PASSED BALL

Ernie Bonham stopped Brooklyn on four hits October 6 and Tommy Henrich hit a home run, giving the New York Yankees a 3-1 victory over the Dodgers and their fifth World Series championship in six years.

The Game 5 clincher at Ebbets Field was the inevitable conclusion to a fall classic that was actually decided the day before. That's when the Yankees, leading the Series two games to one, staged one of the most improbable rallies in baseball history and handed the Dodgers a bitter 7-4 setback.

Brooklyn had rallied from an early 3-0 deficit in the fourth game to grab a 4-3 lead on a two-run double by Jimmy Wasdell and a two-run homer by Pete Reiser. Reliever Hugh Casey, who had come on to end a bases-loaded Yankee threat in the top of the fifth inning, was in control over the next three innings and quickly retired the first two Yankees in the ninth.

That's when disaster struck. Casey got two strikes on Henrich and 33,813 Dodger fans moved to the edge of their seats, ready to let out a victory roar. They got their wish when Henrich fanned on a sharp-breaking curve, but the roar became muffled when Dodger catcher Mickey Owen jumped out of his crouch to chase down the pitch he failed to catch. Henrich, representing the tying run, sprinted to first base.

The game that should have been over was just getting started. Joe DiMaggio followed with a single and Charlie Keller stunned the Dodger faithful by ripping a two-run double. The Yankees now led, 5-4. After a walk to catcher Bill Dickey, Joe Gordon belted another two-run double and Yankee reliever Johnny Murphy closed out the Yankees' miracle win.

The teams had traded 3-2 victories in the first two games, the Yankees winning the opener at Yankee Stadium behind Red Ruffing and the Dodgers winning Game 2 behind Whitlow Wyatt. New York's Marius Russo allowed Brooklyn only four hits in a 2-1 Game 3 win.

The Bronx Bombers managed only a .247 average and two home runs, but the Dodgers batted only .182 and hit one homer.

Game 1	New York	3	Brooklyn	2
Game 2	Brooklyn	3	New York	2
Game 3	New York	2	Brooklyn	1
Game 4	New York	7	Brooklyn	4
Game 5	New York	3	Brooklyn	1

New York's Tommy Henrich heads for first base as strike three eludes Brooklyn catcher Mickey Owen in Game 4 of the World Series.

★1942★

JANUARY-JULY

Let there be lights

Major league owners, the same men who had greeted the advent of night baseball with much skepticism and disdain a few years earlier, opened up the floodlights February 3 in response to U.S. President Franklin D. Roosevelt's request for more nocturnal games as a war-time concession.

Meeting, appropriately, at New York's Hotel Roosevelt, owners voted to permit the 11 teams with lighting systems in place to play 14 night contests per year, double what they had been allowed in the past. Washington received special approval to host 21, meaning that as many as 161 contests could be played under lights.

The rule is not compulsory and

several owners were undecided about how many night games their teams will play. Others indicated they will take full advantage of the rule and Washington Owner Clark Griffith even lobbied for 28 dates.

The other major decision was to play two All-Star Games, the proceeds of which will benefit war-related funds. The first contest, a normal midsummer classic, will be played at New York's Polo Grounds. The second, matching the winner of that game against an Armed Forces All-Star team, will be played in Cleveland.

Owners also established a night curfew for games with no inning to start after 12:50 a.m.

Feller enlists in Navy

Cleveland fireballer Bob Feller, a 76-game winner over the last three seasons, became the second high-magnitude big-league star to report for duty in the armed forces January 6 when he arrived at the Naval training camp in Norfolk, Va.

Following Detroit slugger Hank Greenberg, who reported for Army duty last May, the 22-year-old Feller embarked on his new career with the hope that "I can throw a few strikes for Uncle Sam."

Appearing in the uniform of a

chief boatswain's mate, Feller said, "I've always wanted to be on the winning side and this time I know I'm with a winner." The talented righthander asked to be treated like one of the fellows and brushed aside questions about himself and baseball.

With the U.S. involvement in World War II, Greenberg and Feller are merely the cream of a growing crop of enlistees and draftees from the baseball ranks. Many players already have reported for duty and more are being called every day.

Cleveland's Bob Feller (left), taking the oath to "throw a few strikes for Uncle Sam."

The green light letter

U.S. President Franklin D. Roosevelt delivered an emphatic "play ball" message to major and minor league teams January 16 in a "green light" letter addressed to Commissioner Kenesaw Mountain Landis.

Responding to a letter from Landis asking if baseball should continue play during the war, Roosevelt said, "I honestly feel that it would be best for the country to keep baseball going," and added that he would like to see more night games that hard-working people could attend.

Roosevelt, emphasizing that he

was expressing a personal opinion and leaving final decisions up to baseball club owners, said fewer people would be unemployed during the war and American workers would be putting in longer hours. Baseball could provide a needed diversion to take their minds off jobs and other troubles.

He added that the 6,000 players employed by 300 or so teams could provide invaluable entertainment for at least 20 million people. Roosevelt added, however, that players subject to draft should not be deferred.

THE WHITE HOUSE
WASHINGTON

January 15, 1942.

My dear Judge:-

Thank you for yours of January fourteenth. As you will, of course, realize the final decision about the baseball season must rest with you and the Baseball Club owners -- so what I am going to say is solely a personal and not an official point of view.

I honestly feel that it would be best for the country to keep baseball going. There will be fewer people unemployed and everybody will work longer hours and harder than ever before.

And that means that they ought to have a chance for recreation and for taking their minds off their work even more than before.

Baseball provides a recreation which does not last over two hours or two hours and a half, and which can be got for very little cost. And, incidentally, I hope that night games can be extended because it gives an opportunity to the day shift to see a game occasionally.

As to the players themselves, I know you agree with me that individual players who are of active military or naval age should go, without question, into the services. Even if the actual quality of the teams is lowered by the greater use of older players, this will not dampen the popularity of the sport. Of course, if any individual has some particular aptitude in a trade or profession, he ought to serve the Government. That, however, is a matter which I know you can handle with complete justice.

Here is another way of looking at it -- if 300 teams use 5,000 or 6,000 players, these players are a definite recreational asset to at least 20,000,000 of their fellow citizens -- and that in my judgment is thoroughly worthwhile.

With every best wish,

Very sincerely yours,

Franklin D. Roosevelt

Hon. Kenesaw M. Landis,
333 North Michigan Avenue,
Chicago,
Illinois.

U.S. President Franklin D. Roosevelt's green light letter to Commissioner Kenesaw Mountain Landis.

" DUGOUT CHATTER "

"My losing streak is over for the duration . . . I am on a winning team now."

Hugh Mulcahy

A hard-luck righthander for the Philadelphia Phillies who was the first regular drafted by the Army for war duty

York overpowers N.L.

Detroit's Rudy York capped a three-run first inning with an opposite-field homer and two American League pitchers combined on a six-hitter as the junior circuit handed the National League its seventh loss in 10 All-Star Games with a 3-1 rainy-day decision July 6 before 34, 178 fans at New York's Polo Grounds.

With another All-Star contest scheduled for the next day between the winning team and an Armed Service team in Cleveland, the rule limiting pitchers to three innings was removed. As a result, A.L. Manager Joe McCarthy used the ace from his own New York Yankee pitching staff, Spud Chandler, for four innings and Detroit's Al Benton for the other five. McCarthy, in fact, used only 11 players in the game while N.L. Manager Leo Durocher (Brooklyn) employed 22 in his losing effort.

After Cleveland's Lou Boudreau had led off the game with a home run off St. Louis' Mort Cooper, York sliced a two-run drive down the right-field line that settled into the short seats just inside the foul pole. Cooper, Cincinnati's Johnny Vander Meer, Chicago's Claude Passeau and the Reds' Bucky Walters held the A.L. scoreless the rest of the way, but the damage already had been done.

The only N.L. run came on an eighth-inning homer by Brooklyn catcher Mickey Owen.

Detroit slugger Rudy York steps on the plate after giving the American League a quick jump with a first-inning All-Star Game home run.

CAUGHT ON THE FLY

JUNE

Boston's Paul Waner became the seventh major leaguer and third N.L. player to record 3,000 career hits.

Young Boston star Ted Williams has enlisted in the Navy as an aviator, but he remains on the Red Sox roster awaiting the call to active duty.

Tobin turns slugger

Boston righthander Jim Tobin set a major league record May 13 when he crashed three consecutive home runs to support his own five-hit pitching and gave the Braves a 6-5 victory over the Chicago Cubs at Braves Field.

Tobin, plagued by poor run support in his previous seven starts, took matters into his own hands, homering to lead off the fifth and seventh innings and belting a two-run shot in the eighth after Paul Waner had singled. The final homer gave him a 6-4 lead he protected the rest of the way.

Amazingly, Tobin had homered in a pinch-hitting role the day before against the Cubs. That means he now has four home runs in his last five at-bats and a season average of .407.

Also supporting Tobin with home runs were catcher Ernie Lombardi and shortstop Eddie Miller, while Bill Nicholson crashed a two-run shot for Chicago.

" DUGOUT CHATTER "

"A ballplayer has only two hours of concentrated work every day, with occasional days off. If he cannot attend to business with the pay high and the working hours so pleasant, something is wrong with him and he ought to move on."

Joe McCarthy

Yankee manager

A.L. triumphs again

One day after defeating the National League in the annual All-Star Game at New York, the American League team traveled to Cleveland July 7 and overpowered Mickey Cochrane's Armed Service All-Stars, 5-0.

But the result was incidental to the cause it supported and the pregame military show staged for 62,094 fans and 2,000 additional soldiers and sailors. The two All-Star Games raised nearly $200,000 for war-related funds and focused national interest on the U.S. war effort.

Rumbling tanks, jumping Jeeps, drilling Marines, bands and the parading of colors provided impressive entertainment that filled massive Cleveland Stadium with patriotic fervor. When the game got underway, the A.L. jumped on Chief Boatswain's Mate Bob Feller for four hits and three runs in one inning.

The service team was made up of big-league stars and other players who are fulfilling their military commitment.

Mickey Cochrane's Service All-Stars, who donned baseball uniforms long enough to drop a 5-0 decision to the A.L. All-Star team at Cleveland.

☆1942☆

AUGUST-DECEMBER

" DUGOUT CHATTER "

"He could hit me at midnight with the lights out."

Lefty Grove

Yankee veteran, on the problems he encountered pitching to Jimmie Foxx

Cardinals rush home

Ernie White pitched a five-hitter and St. Louis broke the game open with a four-run fifth inning September 27 en route to a 9-2 final-day victory over the Chicago Cubs that clinched the National League pennant and capped an amazing closing rush past the stunned Brooklyn Dodgers.

By winning that game and the nightcap of their doubleheader against the Cubs, 4-1, the Cardinals concluded their season with an impressive 106-48 record. The Dodgers won 104 times, but still finished two games back.

The Cardinals' task appeared impossible on the morning of August 5, when they boasted an excellent 63-40 record but still trailed the sizzling Dodgers by 10 games. Things were not much brighter nine days later when the Redbirds had managed to chip only a half game off the deficit.

But Brooklyn suddenly slowed down and St. Louis really put on the pressure. Day after day the Cardinals hammered away and soon the panic-stricken Dodgers were looking over their shoulders. On September 12, Mort Cooper claimed his 20th victory and Max Lanier stopped Brooklyn, 2-1, in a doubleheader to pull the Cardinals even. St. Louis pulled ahead the next day when it split a doubleheader with Philadelphia while the Dodgers were losing twice to Cincinnati. The Cardinals were never headed, even though Brooklyn won its final eight contests.

St. Louis was an amazing 43-8 from August 5. The 104 Dodger victories were the most for a runnerup since the 1909 Cubs posted as many. The pennant is St. Louis' sixth in 17 years but its first since 1934.

The Cardinals' pennant express was fueled by the hard-hitting outfield of (left to right): Enos Slaughter, Terry Moore and Stan Musial.

Ruth puts on a show

Befitting their status as champions of the baseball world, the New York Yankees, with a major assist from immortal slugger Babe Ruth, put on a gaudy, glorious show for 69,136 fans at Yankee Stadium August 23 and raised more than $80,000 for the Army-Navy relief fund.

The Washington Senators defeated the New Yorkers, 7-6, in the first game of a doubleheader and the Yankees won the nightcap, 3-0 — a contest shortened to 5½ innings by darkness. But the results were incidental to the between-games show put on by Ruth and former Washington pitching great Walter Johnson.

Many fans were attracted by the Johnson-pitching-to-Ruth promotion, and nobody was disappointed. With the 55-year-old Big Train delivering his no-so-fast pitches with the same effortless delivery of yesteryear and the portly, 48-year-old Bambino swinging with the same Ruthian luster, the crowd watched breathlessly.

On Johnson's fifth pitch, Babe crashed a drive into the lower right-field stands, the site of many of his record 714 major league home runs. The crowd thundered its approval and the Babe smiled. The show culminated when Ruth hit a towering upper-deck shot just foul and circled the bases, doffing his cap and saluting the roaring crowd with every step. Ruth and Johnson left the field together to a thunderous ovation.

Of the numerous games played for war relief, none could match the money raised by the Yankees on this day. Or what the fans got for their money.

Former greats Walter Johnson (left) and Babe Ruth (right) put on a pitching-hitting show in front of 69,136 cheering fans between games of a doubleheader at Yankee Stadium that helped raise more than $80,000 for the Army-Navy relief fund.

SEASON LEADERS

	American League		National League	
Avg.	Ted Williams, Bos.	.356	Ernie Lombardi, Bos.	.330
HR	Ted Williams, Bos.	36	Mel Ott, N.Y.	30
RBI	Ted Williams, Bos.	137	Johnny Mize, N.Y.	110
SB	George Case, Wash.	44	Pete Reiser, Bkn.	20
W-L Pct.	Ernie Bonham, N.Y.21-5, .808		Larry French, Bkn. 15-4, .789	
ERA	Ted Lyons, Chi.	2.10	Mort Cooper, St. L.	1.77
SO	Tex Hughson, Bos.	113	Johnny Vander Meer, Cin.	
	Bobo Newsom, Wash.	113		186

Gordon nips Williams in close MVP vote

Boston left fielder Ted Williams, who finished second in last year's American League Most Valuable Player voting despite batting .406, came up second-best again November 4 when a 24-member committee of the Baseball Writers' Association of America surprisingly gave the prestigious award to New York Yankee second baseman Joe Gordon.

All Williams did was become the A.L.'s fifth Triple Crown winner. The Splendid Splinter batted .356, hit 36 homers and drove in 137 runs, all major league-leading figures, as were his slugging average (.648), runs scored (141), walks (145) and total bases (338).

But those numbers evidently were downplayed by voters who gave Gordon 12 first-place citations and 270 total points. Williams was named first on nine ballots and received 249 points.

Gordon batted .322, hit 18 home runs and collected 103 RBIs while playing sparkling defense for the pennant-bound Yankees. Voters might have been influenced by Gordon's prominence on a championship team and the moody Williams' penchant for antagonizing fans and writers.

New York Yankee second baseman Joe Gordon receiving his 1942 A.L. Most Valuable Player award.

CAUGHT ON THE FLY

SEPTEMBER

Danny Litwhiler of the Philadelphia Phillies became the first major league outfield regular to survive an entire season without making an error. Litwhiler had 308 putouts and nine assists in 151 games.

NOVEMBER

Branch Rickey resigned his job as vice-president of the St. Louis Cardinals and was named president of the Brooklyn Dodgers, succeeding Larry MacPhail, who had enlisted.

Of the 31 minor leagues that started the season, 26 finished. The 1941 campaign had started with 41.

WORLD SERIES REPORT

CARDS DECK YANKS

Whitey Kurowski's two-run ninth-inning home run supported the seven-hit pitching of Johnny Beazley October 5 giving the St. Louis Cardinals a 4-2 victory over New York and capping their surprising World Series thrashing of the proud Yankees.

Kurowski's Game 5 homer at Yankee Stadium provided a shocking conclusion to a shocking fall classic. The young Cardinals, making their first Series appearance since 1934, were pitted against the mighty Yankees, competing in their sixth Series in seven years. It figured to be a mismatch. And the forecast looked ominous for the Cardinals as the Yankees and Red Ruffing carried a 7-0 lead into the ninth inning of the Series opener at Sportsman's Park.

But suddenly the momentum shifted dramatically. After 21-year-old Stan Musial fouled out to open the inning, Walker Cooper singled and Johnny Hopp flied out. Pinch-hitter Ray Sanders walked and the next five Cardinals collected hits that produced four runs. Musial came to the plate with the bases loaded but grounded out against reliever Spud Chandler. The Yankees escaped with a 7-4 victory, but the Cardinals had given them something to think about.

Rookie Beazley, a 21-game winner, carried a 3-0 lead into the eighth inning of Game 2. But Joe DiMaggio singled home a run and Charlie Keller's two-run homer tied the score, setting the stage for St. Louis right fielder Enos Slaughter. Slaughter doubled in the bottom of the inning, scored on Musial's single and then made a great throw in the ninth to cut down runner Tuck Stainback and preserve a 4-3 victory.

It was off to the races for the Cardinals. Ernie White pitched a six-hitter and blanked the Yankees, 2-0, in the third game and St. Louis posted a wild 9-6 Game 4 victory for a two-game advantage.

New York took a 1-0 lead in the clincher on Phil Rizzuto's first-inning home run, but Slaughter tied the game in the fourth with a homer. DiMaggio's run-scoring single in the bottom of the fourth made it 2-1, but St. Louis tied again in the sixth on Walker Cooper's sacrifice fly. Then came Kurowski's game-deciding home run off Ruffing just inside the left-field foul pole.

Game 1	New York	7	St. Louis	4
Game 2	St. Louis	4	New York	3
Game 3	St. Louis	2	New York	0
Game 4	St. Louis	9	New York	6
Game 5	St. Louis	4	New York	2

St. Louis World Series celebrants (standing, left to right): Enos Slaughter, Stan Musial, Johnny Beazley and Whitey Kurowski with (front row) Manager Billy Southworth and Harry Walker.

★1943★
JANUARY-JUNE

War takes a big toll

The major league season opened April 21, eight days behind schedule and with a depleted work force. But the absence of such luminaries as Joe DiMaggio, Ted Williams, Enos Slaughter and Johnny Mize was dismissed as a minor inconvenience and a concession to the much more important battles being fought throughout Europe and other parts of the world.

Baseball was dedicated to staying alive through these difficult times and doing its part to entertain a war-frenzied public while helping to raise money for relief efforts. Difficult decisions were being made daily by Commissioner Kenesaw Mountain Landis and team owners who considered cost-cutting measures while trying to operate under war-time restrictions and guidelines.

At an emergency meeting in Chicago January 5, Landis and team owners decided to move the opening of the season back and extend its closing one week to October 3 while retaining the 154-game schedule. They also agreed to move spring training from the warm-weather areas of Florida and California to sites north of the Potomac and Ohio Rivers and east of the Mississippi, with the exception of the two St. Louis teams, which would be allowed to train in Missouri. Other means of holding transportation to a minimum were considered, such as taking fewer players on road trips and playing longer series in each city, but decisions were delayed on those ideas.

An announcement that would have an immediate impact on the field came March 13 when both leagues approved and adopted a new official ball. The interior of the new ball will be made from reclaimed cork and balata not needed for the war effort and officials insist it will have the resiliency of the 1939 model.

The most serious problem facing major league teams is a manpower shortage created by the draft and voluntary enlistment of players. The American League reported March 17 that 144 of its players had reported to the armed forces and that more are leaving daily. Detroit and Chicago are the biggest A.L. losers with 23 apiece, while the New York Yankees have lost only 14.

Although figures were not made available, National League losses figure to be similar.

Joe DiMaggio giving batting tips to his new teammates — members of the U.S. Army.

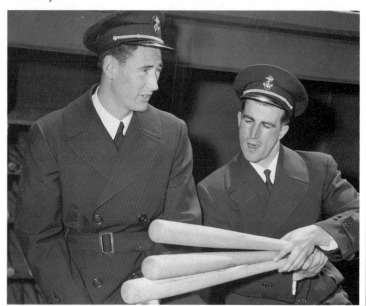

Navy men Ted Williams and Johnny Pesky during a visit to their old baseball home at Boston's Fenway Park.

Some minor problems

With the February 28 announcement that the Texas League will suspend operations for the duration of the war, the ranks of minor league baseball dwindled to nine circuits with manpower and transportation problems continuing to present serious obstacles.

The International League, American Association, Pacific Coast League, Southern Association, Eastern League, Piedmont League, Interstate League, Appalachian League and Pony League will continue to fly the minor league banner. From a peak of 41 circuits operating in 1941, the National Association membership dropped to 31 at the start of the 1942 campaign and shrunk to 26 when five leagues folded last summer. Those 26 leagues fielded 184 teams with 2,912 players on their active rosters.

Overall, minor league baseball has lost 2,431 players to national defense and voluntary retirement lists since October 1, 1940. The hardest hit organization has been St. Louis. The Cardinals have lost 265 players and reduced their farm system from 22 to six teams.

The Cardinals even placed an unprecedented advertisement in *The Sporting News* for free-agent players "with previous professional experience."

CAUGHT ON THE FLY

APRIL
Braves Manager Casey Stengel was sidelined when he suffered a fractured leg after being struck by a Boston taxi cab.

MAY
Lefty Gomez, sold by the New York Yankees to Boston in January, was released by the Braves and signed by the Washington Senators.

JUNE
Boston player-manager Joe Cronin set a major league record when he crashed three-run pinch-hit homers in each end of a doubleheader against Philadelphia at Fenway Park.

Dead ball is buried

Offense became fashionable again in major league baseball after more than two weeks of low-hit, low-run, pitching-dominated games that were the result of the new ball introduced by manufacturer A.G. Spalding.

The balls, made from materials not essential to the war effort, were tested before the season by Spalding and pronounced as resilient as the 1939 model. These contained balata and cork compounds rather than the normal rubber and cork centers of past years.

But when the season opened, it quickly became apparent Spalding's lively ball claims were unfounded. In the first 29 contests played, 11 were shutouts and most of the rest were low-scoring affairs. Pitchers' earned-run averages sparkled at the expense of big-league hitters, who could not drive the ball with authority.

Cincinnati General Manager Warren C. Giles, who had campaigned all winter for a livelier ball, watched with dismay as his Reds opened at Crosley Field with a four-game series against World Series-champion St. Louis. Three of the contests ended 1-0, the other 2-1. Both teams scored three runs in the four games, both managed four extra base hits. Giles fired off a telegram to National League President Ford

Frick demanding something be done about the "dead ball" and threatening to have a new ball made at his own expense and use it at the risk of becoming an "outlaw" team.

The threat received quick response. Officials at Spalding, who had insisted the new ball had not received a fair test because of cold and inclement weather, finally admitted on April 23 that the balls did not measure up. They blamed the rubber cement they were forced to use for a 25 percent drop in resiliency and promised to replace the inferior balls "in about two weeks."

When the "new" new balls were introduced May 8 and 9, the results were convincing. In four May 9 doubleheaders in the American League, six home runs were hit — three less than had been hit in the season up to that point. In the first two days of N.L. play, three games featured 16 total hits and others had 15, 13 and 12, prompting Philadelphia Manager Bucky Harris to remark, "Some of the pitchers will have to duck fast or get hit by line drives."

SEASON LEADERS

	American League		National League	
Avg.	Luke Appling, Chi.	.328	Stan Musial, St. L.	.357
HR	Rudy York, Det.	34	Bill Nicholson, Chi.	29
RBI	Rudy York, Det.	118	Bill Nicholson, Chi.	128
SB	George Case, Wash.	61	Arky Vaughan, Bkn.	20
W-L Pct.	Spud Chandler, N.Y.	20-4, .833	Mort Cooper, St. L. 21-8, .724	
ERA	Spud Chandler, N.Y.	1.64	Howie Pollet, St. L.	1.75
SO	Allie Reynolds, Cle.	151	Johnny Vander Meer, Cin.	174

"DUGOUT CHATTER"

"I am young and I thought I was in great shape when I got into the Army. But I cannot tell you what all that marching and drilling has done for my legs. Boy, I'm toughened up."

Pete Reiser

Dodgers star, on the joys of Army life during World War II

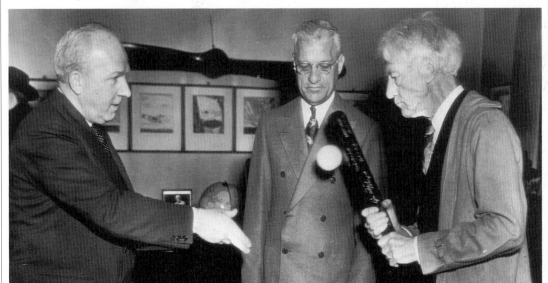

Cincinnati General Manager Warren Giles (left), A.L. President Will Harridge (center) and Commissioner Kenesaw Mountain Landis play a little pepper with the new wartime baseball introduced by manufacturer A.G. Spalding.

Cooper is super

St. Louis ace Mort Cooper was super during consecutive one-hit performances in late May and early June.

Mort Cooper, the 30-year-old ace of the St. Louis staff, showed why June 4 when he pitched his second straight one-hit shutout and led the Cardinals to a 5-0 victory over Philadelphia at Sportsman's Park.

The fireballing righthander was perfect through five innings before his error allowed Pinky May to reach first base leading off the sixth. May was wiped out on a double play and Cooper coasted through the seventh having faced the minimum of 21 batters. But his hopes for a no-hitter vanished in the eighth when Jimmy Wasdell led off with a single to left field.

Cooper retired the final six batters to record his sixth victory in nine decisions. He got all the support he needed from Harry Walker and Stan Musial, who singled home third-inning runs, and Ken O'Dea, who belted a two-run homer in the eighth.

Cooper's one-hitter came four days after he had stopped Brooklyn on one hit in a 7-0 victory at Sportsman's Park. The only Dodger hit was a fly ball double down the right-field line by second baseman Billy Herman in the fifth inning.

★ 1943 ★

" DUGOUT CHATTER "

"You hardly can blame the kids nowadays for passing up catching. When I was a youngster, everybody wanted to pitch. Then came Ruth and everybody wanted to be an outfielder and hit."

Bill Dickey

Yankee catcher

A Yankeeless victory

New York Manager Joe McCarthy, thumbing his nose at critics who claimed he had shown flagrant partiality to his Yankee players in All-Star Game competition, guided his American League team through the July 13 midsummer classic without using a single Yankee — and produced a 5-3 victory over the National League.

The game at Philadelphia's Shibe Park drew 31,938 fans who watched the A.L. jump on St. Louis Cardinal righthander Mort Cooper for four early runs. Three came on a second-inning home run by Boston's Bobby Doerr and the A.L. added single tallies in the third and fifth.

After scoring a first-inning run on a double by St. Louis' Stan Musial, the N.L. was held in check through six innings by Washington's Dutch Leonard and Detroit's Hal Newhouser. Pittsburgh's Vince DiMaggio, Joe's older brother, accounted for two late runs when he tripled and scored in the seventh off Boston's Tex Hughson and hit a long homer off Hughson in the ninth.

Five members of the powerful Yankees — pitchers Spud Chandler and Ernie Bonham, catcher Bill Dickey, outfielder Johnny Lindell and second baseman Joe Gordon — were held out.

The big blow of the A.L.'s 5-3 All-Star Game victory was a three-run second-inning homer by Boston's Bobby Doerr (above).

Ruth's All-Stars win

A service all-star team managed by Babe Ruth pounded out a 9-8 exhibition victory over the Braves July 12 as part of Boston Mayor Maurice J. Tobin's annual charity field day program.

Playing at Fenway Park, Ruth's old stomping grounds when he played for the Red Sox, the stars put on a good show for 12,000 fans who came to watch Ruth and Boston favorites Ted Williams and Dom DiMaggio battle the Braves. Williams hit a three-run seventh-inning home run and DiMaggio belted a two-run triple in the third to key the all-star victory.

Before the game, Williams, and the 48-year-old Ruth squared off in a home run-hitting contest that never really got off the ground. Williams parked three balls in the right-field bleachers but Ruth, bothered by an aching knee, could not come close to the fences.

The Bambino did give in to the pleas of fans, however, and pinch-hit in the eighth inning. He flew out to right field.

Babe Ruth (left) was manager and Naval officer Ted Williams (right) was the featured star of a Service All-Star team that beat the Boston Braves, 9-8.

A's end losing streak

Roger Wolff allowed eight hits and his Philadelphia teammates scored eight third-inning runs in the second game of an August 24 doubleheader at Chicago's Comiskey Park, giving the Athletics an 8-1 victory over the White Sox and snapping their American League record-tying losing streak at 20 games.

It appeared the A's would fall short of the record as they carried a 5-4 lead into the ninth inning of the opening game. But the White Sox scored two runs off Luman Harris, continuing the A's futility. The 20-game streak matched the skeins compiled by the 1906 Boston Red Sox and 1916 Athletics.

The eight-run outburst against Chicago's Bill Dietrich provided Wolff with the cushion he needed. Jimmy Ripple keyed the explosion with a three-run double. Ironically, Wolff had been the last Philadelphia pitcher to win a game — on August 6 against the New York Yankees, the team the last-place A's now trail by 32 games.

Cardinal pitchers, Musial dominate statistics

A young hitter named Stan Musial and a stingy pitching staff headed by righthander Mort Cooper were the primary reasons behind the National League pennant-winning success story of the St. Louis Cardinals.

Musial fueled the Cardinal express, which ran up 105 victories and an 18-game margin of victory over Cincinnati. The 22-year-old led the N.L. with a .357 average, a .562 slugging percentage, 347 total bases, 220 hits, 48 doubles and 20 triples. Musial also scored 108 runs and drove in 81.

Cooper finished 21-8 for a .724 winning percentage and compiled a 2.30 earned-run average, ranking third in the N.L. in that category behind teammates Howie Pollet (1.75) and Max Lanier (1.90). Al Brazle (1.53) and Harry Brecheen (2.26) fell a few innings short of giving the Cardinals a 1-through-5 ERA sweep.

Chicago's Bill Nicholson led the N.L. with 29 homers and 128 RBIs and Cincinnati's Elmer Riddle and Pittsburgh's Rip Sewell joined Cooper as 21-game winners.

Chicago's Luke Appling won the American League batting title with a .328 mark while Detroit's Rudy York took home run and RBI honors with 34 and 118. New York's Spud Chandler and Detroit's Dizzy Trout were 20-game winners.

American League batting champion Luke Appling of Chicago.

CAUGHT ON THE FLY

JULY

Boston Red Sox second baseman Bobby Doerr dropped a pop fly, ending his two-month errorless streak after handling 349 chances.

JULY/AUGUST

Guy Curtwright, a Chicago White Sox outfielder, had a 26-game hitting streak and St. Louis Cardinal Harry (The Hat) Walker had one of 29 games.

NOVEMBER

The Carpenter family of Delaware purchased the Philadelphia Phillies and installed 28-year-old Bob Carpenter as team president.

WORLD SERIES REPORT

YANKS GET REVENGE

Game 1	New York	4	St. Louis	2
Game 2	St. Louis	4	New York	3
Game 3	New York	6	St. Louis	2
Game 4	New York	2	St. Louis	1
Game 5	New York	2	St. Louis	0

Bill Dickey crashed a two-run homer and righthander Spud Chandler persevered through a 10-hit, two-walk shutout October 11 as the New York Yankees defeated the St. Louis Cardinals, 2-0, and captured their sixth World Series championship in eight years.

The Game 5 victory at Sportsman's Park avenged the Yankees' surprising five-game fall classic loss to St. Louis in 1942. It also returned them to the top of a baseball pedestal they now have occupied 10 times.

After splitting the first two games at Yankee Stadium, the Bronx Bombers took control of the Series. Chandler opened the proceedings October 5 with a seven-hit, 4-2 victory that was decided by a run-scoring wild pitch and Dickey's RBI single in the eighth inning. Second baseman Joe Gordon had hit a solo home run earlier in the contest.

But St. Louis fought back for a 4-3 second-game win on the strength of home runs by Marty Marion and Ray Sanders. Mort Cooper pitched eight strong innings and brother Walker

caught despite the death of their father earlier in the day. Mort, a 20-game winner in each of the last two seasons, was credited with his first World Series victory.

It would be the last for both him and the Cardinals in this fall classic. Rookie Al Brazle carried a 2-1 lead into the eighth inning of Game 3, but the roof suddenly caved in. A single, two errors and a walk loaded the bases and Yankee third baseman Billy Johnson delivered a three-run triple. A walk and three more hits gave the Yankees the final run in their 6-2 victory.

Marius Russo gave the Yanks a three games to one advantage October 10 when he pitched a 2-1 victory, scoring the winning run himself in the eighth inning after hitting a double.

That set up the clincher and the 36-year-old Chandler responded with one of the shakiest shutouts in World Series history. Shaky, but effective. And with Dickey delivering his game-winning homer in the sixth inning, the Yankees were champions once more.

New York Yankee World Series hero Marius Russo.

★1944★
JANUARY-JULY

" DUGOUT CHATTER "

"The important thing right now — and for some time to come — is the war. Nothing else matters."

Hank Greenberg

Detroit slugger's response when asked about his baseball future after the war

Baseball stops play as invasion begins

Baseball and other sports throughout the United States cancelled their June 6 schedules as American forces began their crucial invasion of Europe on the beaches of Normandy, France.

U.S. President Franklin D. Roosevelt called for American citizens to spend June 6 at their homes and churches as Allied Forces began the D-day invasion that could be the pivotal point of World War II. In deference to D-day, the two scheduled major league games were cancelled, as were the schedules of the International League, American Association, Eastern League and other minor circuits.

Baseball and other sports will resume their activities June 7 and enter into a critical stage of their war-time survival battles. With casualties figuring to be high and the future of the world hinging on what happens in Europe in the coming weeks, sports news suddenly seems inconsequential.

Giants score 30 runs, but split doubleheader

New York exploded for 30 runs in an April 30 doubleheader against Brooklyn, but all it got out of its major offensive was a split. The Giants delighted 58,068 fans at the Polo Grounds by pounding the Dodgers, 26-8, in the opener but fell, 5-4, in the nightcap.

First baseman Phil Weintraub was the big gun in New York's 26-run barrage, which fell two short of the single-game record. Weintraub hit a homer, triple and two doubles to drive in 11 runs, one short of the big-league RBI mark. Catcher Ernie Lombardi chipped in with three hits and seven RBIs and Manager Mel Ott collected two hits, walked five times and scored six runs.

Five Dodgers pitchers contributed to their own downfall by walking a record-tying 17 batters and Brooklyn first baseman Howie Schultz hit two solo homers in a losing cause.

Hal Gregg picked up his first big-league victory in the nightcap, a game shortened to seven innings because of darkness.

New York's Phil Weintraub fell one RBI short of the single-game record in the Giants' 26-8 pasting of Brooklyn.

" DUGOUT CHATTER "

"Boudreau doesn't like me and I don't care a hell of a lot for him. We never can get along on the same ball club . . . the best thing Cleveland can do is trade me. Where? Anywhere."

Jim Bagby

Veteran Indians pitcher, who had been feuding with shortstop and boy-Manager Lou Boudreau

Tobins fires no-hitter

Knuckleballer Jim Tobin pitched the first Boston Braves' no-hitter in 28 years and iced his 2-0 victory over Brooklyn with a long home run April 27 in a game before 1,984 fans at Braves Field.

The 31-year-old Tobin walked Paul Waner, the Dodgers' 3,000-hit man, to lead off the game and then proceeded to retire 26 straight batters before walking Waner again in the ninth. But he ended the contest by retiring Dixie Walker on a ground ball to second.

The Dodgers twice came close to hits. In the second inning, Bill Hart dumped a near-perfect bunt down the third-base line that rolled just foul and Waner hit a smash up the middle in the third, but Tobin knocked the ball down and recovered to throw the veteran out at first.

Connie Ryan produced Boston's first run when he hit a third-inning double, moved to third on a fly ball and scored on Chuck Workman's single. Tobin belted his long drive over the left-field wall leading off the eighth inning against Fritz Ostermueller.

The no-hitter is the first in the major leagues since Lon Warneke turned the trick on August 30, 1941, for the St. Louis Cardinals.

Boston Braves no-hit man Jim Tobin (right) with brother John, a third baseman for the cross-city Red Sox.

Reds use Nuxhall, 15

Mort Cooper pitched a five-hitter and St. Louis pounded out the most lopsided National League shutout victory in 38 years, but the biggest news in the Cardinals' 18-0 June 10 victory over Cincinnati was the inauspicious debut of a baby-faced lefthander named Joe Nuxhall.

Nuxhall pitched only ⅔ of an inning and allowed five runs, on five walks, two singles and a wild pitch before Reds Manager Bill McKechnie removed him from the game. Nuxhall's performance was noteworthy because at age 15 years and 10 months, he became the youngest player ever to compete in the majors. A week earlier, the youngster was pitching for his high school team.

Every player in the St. Louis lineup contributed at least one hit and nine of the 11 Cardinals drove in at least one run. Oddly, only two Redbirds managed extra-base hits in the 21-hit assault.

The most one-sided shutout in N.L. history occurred in 1906 when Chicago beat New York, 19-0.

Cincinnati Manager Bill McKechnie (left) with 15-year-old pitching prodigy Joe Nuxhall.

Big inning lifts N.L. to the stars

National League hitters exploded for the biggest inning in All-Star Game history and four pitchers combined on a six-hitter July 11 as the senior circuit captured the midsummer classic with a 7-1 victory at Pittsburgh's Forbes Field.

Cincinnati's Bucky Walters, Philadelphia's Ken Raffensberger, Pittsburgh's Rip Sewell and Boston's Jim Tobin held the American League in check while their teammates got untracked in a four-run fifth inning that wiped out a 1-0 deficit. Chicago's Bill Nicholson doubled home one run and the other three scored on singles by St. Louis' Walker Cooper and Dodgers Augie Galan and Dixie Walker.

Cardinal Whitey Kurowski doubled home two seventh-inning runs and St. Louis' Stan Musial drove in the final tally in the ninth. The Cubs' Phil Cavarretta reached base five times on a triple, a single and three walks.

The highlight, however, was Sewell's demonstration of his famed "ephus pitch," a high-arcing lob that catches batters off stride and tempts them to take wild swings. Sewell, who unveiled the pitch last year in a 21-win campaign, floated two rainbows to St. Louis' George McQuinn in the eighth inning, much to the delight of his hometown fans. McQuinn took the first for a strike and bunted the other for an out.

Nicholson explodes

Chicago outfielder Bill Nicholson capped a 48-hour home run spree with four in a July 23 doubleheader against the New York Giants at the Polo Grounds, tying him for the major league lead with Mel Ott and matching two big-league slugging records.

Nicholson hammered out three homers in the Cubs' first-game 7-4 victory and connected again in the nightcap, a 12-10 New York win. The four home runs tied the record for most in a doubleheader and his three straight in the opener, combined with the homer he hit in his final at-bat July 22, tied a National League mark for consecutive home runs that had stood since 1894.

Nicholson, who also had homered July 21, brought his season total to 21, six of which were hit in a 48-hour period. Ott hit his 21st in the fourth inning of the opening game.

Nicholson drove in seven runs for the day, three in the wild nightcap that featured a major league–record 14 pitchers.

St. Louis Manager Billy Southworth (center) with N.L. All-Star heroes Rip Sewell (left) and Phil Cavarretta (right).

CAUGHT ON THE FLY

MAY

Cincinnati lefthander Clyde Shoun pitched a 1-0 no-hitter against Boston, missing a perfect game when he issued a third-inning walk to opposing pitcher Jim Tobin.

JUNE

Boston's Jim Tobin, who had no-hit Brooklyn in April, pitched a five-inning no-hitter against Philadelphia in the second game of a doubleheader at Braves Field. The 7-0 contest was called on account of darkness.

JULY

The Brooklyn Dodgers ended their club-record 15-game losing streak with an 8-5 victory over Boston at Braves Field.

Oriole Park, home of the International League's Baltimore club, was burned to the ground in a Fourth of July blaze. The wooden structure was erected in 1914 by the Baltimore entry in the outlaw Federal League.

SEASON LEADERS

	American League		National League	
Avg.	Lou Boudreau, Cle.	.327	Dixie Walker, Bkn.	.357
HR	Nick Etten, N.Y.	22	Bill Nicholson, Chi.	33
RBI	Vern Stephens, St. L.	109	Bill Nicholson, Chi.	122
SB	Snuffy Stirnweiss, N.Y.	55	John Barrett, Pit.	28
W-L Pct.	Tex Hughson, Bos.	18-5, .783	Ted Wilks, St. L.	17-4, .810
ERA	Dizzy Trout, Det.	2.12	Ed Heusser, Cin.	2.38
SO	Hal Newhouser, Det.	187	Bill Voiselle, N.Y.	161

★1944★

" DUGOUT CHATTER "

"I just shut my eyes and swing. I think my power comes from my wrists and forearms."

Rudy York

Detroit slugging first baseman

Chet Laabs (left) belted two final-day home runs to give the St. Louis Browns their pennant-clinching victory over the Yankees.

War Relief games

Major league baseball raised $329,555 for the National War Fund Inc. and the American Red Cross through its 16 war relief games, according to figures released by the commissioner's office.

The 16 games, one hosted by each major league team, were sponsored by the War Relief and Service Fund Inc. and even the players, umpires and club presidents had to pay admission into the ballpark. American League teams turned over $205,740 in gate receipts and the National League chipped in with $122,270.

The biggest individual gate, $34,587, was turned over by the New York Yankees with Detroit close behind at $33,287. The biggest N.L. contributor was St. Louis, which produced $25,832 for the war effort.

Browns end 43 years of pennant frustration

Forty-three years of frustration came to a grinding halt October 1 when the St. Louis Browns, long the doormat of the American League, defeated the New York Yankees, 5-2, and captured the first pennant of their bleak history.

The final-day victory at Sportsman's Park was executed before the Browns' first sellout crowd in 20 years and it snapped a tie atop the A.L. standings with Detroit. The Tigers and 27-game winner Dizzy Trout suffered a simultaneous 4-1 season-ending loss to Washington and Dutch Leonard at Briggs Stadium.

The Browns needed all the grit they could muster to finish off their surprising pennant drive and qualify for a World Series date with their St. Louis rivals and Sportsman's Park co-tenants, the Cardinals. The Browns trailed the Yankees 2-0 after 3½ innings and were tied 2-2 after 4½ as the 37,815 hometown faithful fidgeted nervously in their seats. But, thanks to Chet Laabs and Sig Jakucki, 43 years of perseverance paid off.

Laabs hit his fourth home run of the season, a two-run shot, off Yankee starter Mel Queen to tie the game in the bottom of the fourth inning. In the fifth, Laabs hit his fifth homer, another two-run blast, off Queen to give the Browns a 4-2 lead. Shortstop Vern Stephens added a solo shot in the eighth for insurance, but the 32-year-old Jakucki did not really need it in pitching a six-hitter and gaining his 13th win.

The victory, the Browns' 89th, was their fourth straight against the Yankees to close the campaign. The Tigers, who entered their final series against Washington with a one-game lead, managed only two victories in four games against the Senators. It seemed only fitting that the Browns, long a symbol of ineptitude, should clinch their first pennant at the expense of the Yankees, long the symbol of baseball excellence.

St. Louis thus becomes the third city to have two same-season qualifiers for the World Series. Chicago was the first in 1906 and the two New York teams have met five times in the fall classic.

The St. Louis Browns pitching staff that helped end 43 years of frustration (left to right): Denny Galehouse, George Caster, Sam Zoldak, Bob Muncrief, Al Hollingsworth, Jack Kramer and Nelson Potter.

Judge Landis dies

Kenesaw Mountain Landis, the man who restored dignity and integrity to baseball after the infamous "Black Sox" scandal, died of a heart attack November 25 at St. Luke's Hospital in Chicago. He was 78.

The former federal judge took over as baseball's first commissioner in November 1920 and ruled the sport with an iron fist through thick and thin. Operating with dictatorial powers, the gruff-speaking, craggy-faced man with shaggy white hair forced his will on baseball and lifted its status to new heights. He was known for his dedication to honesty and fair play and his decisions always reflected that dedication.

Landis, who had just observed his birthday, entered the hospital October 2 for a rest after battling what doctors described as fatigue and a severe cold. He suffered his heart attack while in the hospital and had several relapses before his condition grew serious.

Landis will always be remembered for his lifetime ban against eight members of the Chicago White Sox who conspired to fix the 1919 World Series against Cincinnati. The players were cleared in court, but baseball's new commissioner barred them anyway and set the tone for an exemplary 24-year reign over baseball.

Commissioner Kenesaw Mountain Landis (right), shortly before his death.

CAUGHT ON THE FLY

AUGUST
In a 1-hour, 15-minute masterpiece, Boston Braves righthander Red Barrett shut out Cincinnati, 2-0, while throwing a major league-record low 58 pitches.

SEPTEMBER
Boston outfielder George Metkovich ended his Red Sox club-record 25-game hitting streak when he failed to connect off Washington lefthander Mickey Haefner in a game at Griffith Stadium.

OCTOBER
The major leagues reported attendances totaling 8,976,902, the highest since 10,250,208 watched games in the last peace-time year of 1941. Detroit attracted the most fans in 1944 — 923,000.

NOVEMBER
Detroit lefthander Hal Newhouser was rewarded for his 29-win season with selection as the A.L. Most Valuable Player.

WORLD SERIES REPORT

A ST. LOUIS AFFAIR

Max Lanier and Ted Wilks combined on a three-hitter October 9 and the Cardinals coasted to a 3-1 victory over the Cinderella Browns in the first all-St. Louis World Series.

The Cardinals, making their third straight Series appearance and winning for the fifth time, scored all of their Game 6 runs in the fourth inning, one coming on a throwing error by Browns' shortstop Vern Stephens and the others on singles by Emil Verban and Lanier. Lanier allowed all three hits in 5⅓ innings and Wilks retired all 11 batters he faced in closing out the Cardinal victory.

While the Cardinals entered the all-Sportsman's Park classic as World Series veterans, the Browns were making their first postseason appearance — ever. Long a symbol of baseball ineptitude, the Browns took advantage of the war-caused talent drain to make their big breakthrough in the American League standings.

It did not take long for them to show they had no intention of rolling over for their powerful rivals. Denny Galehouse allowed seven hits in the opener while Cardinals Mort Cooper and Blix Donnelly combined on a two-hitter. But one of those hits was a two-run fourth-inning home run by George McQuinn that resulted in a 2-1 victory.

The Cardinals rebounded the next day behind the pitching of Lanier and Donnelly for a 3-2 triumph, but the Browns reclaimed the lead in Game 3 as Jack Kramer pitched a seven-hitter and McQuinn drove in two runs in a 6-2 win.

It was all downhill the rest of the way for the Browns. The Cardinals reeled off 5-1 and 2-0 victories to take the Series lead and they put the Browns away in Game 6. The Cardinals outhit the Browns, .240 to .183, but both pitching staffs compiled sub-2.00 earned-run averages. Browns' pitchers finished with a stingy 1.49 ERA, but 10 errors handed the Cardinals seven unearned runs. That was the difference.

Game 1	Browns	2	Cardinals	1
Game 2	Cardinals	3	Browns	2
Game 3	Browns	6	Cardinals	2
Game 4	Cardinals	5	Browns	1
Game 5	Cardinals	2	Browns	0
Game 6	Cardinals	3	Browns	1

A jubilant group of St. Louis Cardinals celebrate their six-game World Series victory over the Browns.

★1945★

One arm, a big heart

Pete Gray, the St. Louis Browns' 30-year-old rookie outfielder, made his major league debut April 18 at Sportsman's Park, collecting a single in four at-bats during a 7-1 victory over Detroit.

So, what's so special about Pete Gray? Simple. He plays the game with one arm.

Gray, who lost his right arm at age 6 when he fell off a grocer's truck, drew the Opening Day starting assignment in left field for the defending American League champions. His first big-league at-bat came against Hal Newhouser, a 29-game winner in 1944, and he grounded out.

In his next two times up against the talented lefty, Gray was called out on strikes and hit a wicked drive into right-center field. Doc Cramer made a diving catch of the liner, robbing Gray of extra bases. In his final at-bat against reliever Les Mueller, Gray managed an infield single.

On his only outfield chance, Gray slipped and fell while chasing down a hit by Eddie Mayo but held him to a double.

Gray takes his one-armed swing from the left side of the plate and plays defense by catching the ball, flipping it in the air as he drops his glove, catching it with his bare hand and throwing it back to the infield.

Chandler selected

Baseball ended its search for a new commissioner April 24 when Kentucky Senator Albert B. (Happy) Chandler was elected on a unanimous first-ballot vote by the 16 major league clubs.

The surprisingly easy decision ended baseball's quest to replace Kenesaw Mountain Landis, who died last November after 24 years as the game's first commissioner. The 46-year-old Chandler, a graduate of the University of Kentucky and Harvard Law School, was elected for a seven-year team at an annual salary of $50,000 after an amicable four-hour discussion.

It was not expected to be that easy. Some owners had wanted to hire a baseball man. Others had expressed interest in retaining the three-man commission that had ruled since Landis' death. But when news surfaced that the former Kentucky governor would be available, heavy pressure swung in his direction. A favorable report by baseball's four-man steering committee sealed the verdict.

" DUGOUT CHATTER "

"So much fuss has been made over Gray that he'd have to be as good as Babe Ruth to live up to what people expect of him. He's a fine ballplayer, fast, courageous and he can hit. We use him when he can help us win, the same as any two-armed player."

Luke Sewell

St. Louis Browns manager, on one-armed outfielder Pete Gray

CAUGHT ON THE FLY

JANUARY
The triumvirate of Lee MacPhail, Dan Topping and Del Webb paid $2.8 million to purchase the vast baseball empire of the New York Yankees from the heirs of the late Colonel Jacob Ruppert.

MAY
Mort Cooper, a 20-game winner for St. Louis in each of his last three seasons, was traded to the Boston Braves for Red Barrett and $60,000 after threatening to leave the Cardinals for a third time over a salary dispute.

JULY
With Les Mueller pitching 19⅔ innings for Detroit, the Tigers battled the Philadelphia Athletics to a 24-inning 1-1 tie in a game called because of darkness at Shibe Park.

AUGUST
New York Giants Manager Mel Ott became the third member of baseball's 500-homer club when he connected off Boston's Johnny Hutchings in a game at the Polo Grounds.

St. Louis Browns outfielder Pete Gray, the one-armed wonder.

Newly elected Commissioner A.B. (Happy) Chandler.

Vet Borowy says Boo to rookie

What happens when the two hottest pitchers in baseball match their talents? Someone has to lose. And in the June 10 case of New York's Hank Borowy versus Boston's Dave (Boo) Ferriss, the 23-year-old rookie came out on the short end of a 3-2 score.

That rookie would be Ferriss, who had taken the major leagues by storm in his debut season. The big righthander had started his first campaign with a record 22 scoreless innings (opening a career) and had won his first eight decisions entering the game at Yankee Stadium. Borowy, a 46-game winner in three Yankee seasons, came in with a 7-1 record.

The Yanks scored in the first on Herschel Martin's single, in the third when Borowy doubled and eventually came home on a double-play grounder and in the sixth on another Martin single. Boston's runs came on an error and a mental lapse by Borowy in the ninth inning that resulted in Manager Joe McCarthy calling in reliever Jim Turner.

Cubs stop Holmes

The first-place Chicago Cubs accomplished July 12 what no team had been able to do for more than five weeks — keep Boston's Tommy Holmes from getting a hit. In the first game of a double-header at Wrigley Field, the Cubs defeated the Braves, 6-1, and stopped Holmes' modern-era National League-record consecutive-game hitting streak at 37.

With his hometown Chicago fans cheering lustily for Holmes, righthander Hank Wyse, who allowed only three hits in the game, stopped the Boston outfielder in four at-bats, letting him hit only one ball out of the infield. Thus ended the sixth-longest streak in major league history, 19 games short of Joe DiMaggio's 1941 mark of 56. The St. Louis Browns' George Sisler hit in 41 straight in 1922 and Detroit's Ty Cobb reached 40 games in 1911. Two pre-1900 N.L. players, Baltimore's Willie Keeler (44 in 1897) and Chicago's Bill Dahlen (42 in 1894), also compiled longer streaks.

Holmes got some consolation in the nightcap when he singled in the ninth inning and scored ahead of Carden Gillenwater's game-winning two-run homer off Claude Passeau. The Braves' 3-1 victory snapped the Cubs' winning streak at 11.

Holmes had started his streak on June 4, a day after he went hitless in a game at Wrigley Field. The lefthanded hitting three-year veteran batted .433 during the 37 games.

Boston's Tommy Holmes saw his N.L.-record hitting streak end after 37 games.

SEASON LEADERS

	American League		National League	
Avg.	Snuffy Stirnweiss, N.Y.	.309	Phil Cavarretta, Chi.	.355
HR	Vern Stephens, St. L.	24	Tommy Holmes, Bos.	28
RBI	Nick Etten, N.Y.	111	Dixie Walker, Bkn.	124
SB	Snuffy Stirnweiss, N.Y.	33	Red Schoendienst, St. L.	26
W-L Pct.	Hal Newhouser, Det.	25-9, .735	Harry Brecheen, St. L.	15-4, .789
ERA	Hal Newhouser, Det.	1.81	Hank Borowy, Chi.	2.14
SO	Hal Newhouser, Det.	212	Preacher Roe, Pit.	148

Star game cancelled

Baseball's All-Star Game became a war casualty when it was cancelled because of travel restrictions. In its place, seven interleague games were played over the two-day All-Star break to raise money for war relief.

On July 10, the Cubs and White Sox battled in Chicago, the Yankees and Giants faced off in New York and the Cincinnati Reds battled the in-state rival Indians at Cleveland. On July 11, the Braves played the Red Sox in Boston, the Browns and Cardinals squared off in St. Louis, the Phillies and Athletics met in Philadelphia and Brooklyn faced the Senators in Washington.

Pittsburgh and Detroit did not meet because of the travel problems.

" DUGOUT CHATTER "

"I'm not worried about my arm — it's my legs and how they may lose their drive that makes me reach for the aspirin when I consider my baseball future."

Bob Feller

Cleveland ace, upon his return from Navy duty during World War II

A triumphant return

Cleveland's Bob Feller, making his first major league appearance in almost four years, struck out 12 Detroit Tigers and rewarded 46,477 ecstatic fans with a four-hit, 4-2 victory at Cleveland's Municipal Stadium August 24.

The fireballing righthander returned from Navy war duty and outdueled Detroit ace Hal Newhouser, who fell to a 20-8 record. Feller pitched hitless ball over the final $6\frac{2}{3}$ innings after allowing both Tiger runs on three hits in the third.

The big crowd, on hand to see Rapid Robert more than the fifth-place Indians, roared its approval throughout his return engagement. Pat Seerey's two-run homer in the first inning and single runs in the third and fifth provided Feller all the support he needed.

Feller is one of the big-name stars who are slipping back onto major league rosters with the fighting in Germany now over. One of the first star returnees was Detroit first baseman Hank Greenberg, who punctuated a four-year absence with a first-game homer on July 1.

Other star-quality players back in uniform after stints in the armed forces are New York Yankees Red Ruffing and Charlie Keller, Detroit righthander Virgil Trucks and Washington outfielder Buddy Lewis.

Bob Feller returned from his four-year Navy stint and rewarded Cleveland fans with a four-hit, 4-2 victory over Detroit.

★1945★

A no-hit comeback

Dick Fowler, a 24-year-old right-hander recently discharged from the Canadian Army, made his first return start for the Philadelphia Athletics a memorable one, pitching a 1-0 no-hitter against St. Louis in the second game of a September 9 doubleheader at Shibe Park.

Fowler, released from his military commitment only nine days earlier, walked four and received flawless defensive support in recording the first no-hitter by an Athletic since 1916 and the first by an American Leaguer since Bob Feller's Opening Day gem for Cleveland in 1940.

But his teammates kept him in suspense until the very end, pushing across the game's only run after Fowler had completed nine innings of no-hit pitching. Hal Peck's triple and Irv Hall's single in the bottom of the ninth made a tough-luck loser of the Browns' John Miller, who allowed five hits.

Fowler, a seven-game winner in his pre-war career, had made three relief appearances since his return with no decisions.

Philadelphia Athletics Manager Connie Mack with Dick Fowler, who pitched a no-hitter in his first start after being discharged from the Canadian Army.

" DUGOUT CHATTER "

"I learned that I don't want to be a manager. It's a lot easier to hit home runs than to handle 17 guys who think they are home run hitters."

Jimmie Foxx

The veteran Phillies slugger, after trying his hand at managing in the Piedmont League

Tigers clinch pennant

Hank Greenberg belted a ninth-inning grand slam through the St. Louis mist and the Detroit Tigers clinched the American League pennant with a dramatic 6-3 final-day victory over the Browns in the first game of a scheduled double-header at Sportsman's Park.

Greenberg, the two-time Most Valuable Player who had returned to baseball July 1 after four years of military service, connected off St. Louis righthander Nelson Potter to give the Tigers their first A.L. flag since 1940. Potter had scattered seven hits and carried a 3-2 lead into the final frame, but pinch-hitter Hub Walker led off with a single, Skeeter Webb reached on a fielder's choice and both runners advanced on a sacrifice. Doc Cramer was walked intentionally, bringing up Greenberg.

The big first baseman, who had hit 12 homers since his return, buried the hopes of second-place Washington with his drive just inside the left-field foul pole. The Senators, who had finished their season a week earlier, needed a St. Louis sweep to force a first-place tie. Bad weather forced the cancellation of the nightcap, giving the Tigers a final 1½-game pennant cushion.

The Senators were victimized by their owner's bad judgment. Washington had finished the 1944 season in eighth place and did not figure to challenge for anything in 1945. Accordingly, Clark Griffith made arrangements to lease Griffith Stadium to the National Football League's Washington Redskins for the final week of the baseball season and conclude his team's schedule early by piling up doubleheaders.

Griffith's reasoning appeared sound on June 12 when the Senators rested in seventh place, but a month later they had climbed to second, 4½ games behind the Tigers. They remained in the thick of the race the rest of the way and concluded their schedule on September 23 by splitting a doubleheader with Philadelphia. At 87-67, the Senators were one game behind 86-64 Detroit. The Tigers would have to lose three of their final four to produce a tie.

Detroit split a doubleheader with Cleveland and then sat for three days before meeting St. Louis in the final-day twin-bill. Greenberg's blast gave Hal Newhouser, pitching in relief of Virgil Trucks, his 25th victory.

Hank Greenberg, recently returned from the Army, hit a final-day grand slam against St. Louis that clinched the A.L. pennant for Detroit.

Star-depleted A.L. has inoffensive year

The most inoffensive American League season since the first decade of the century ended with three players topping the .300 level, one hitting more than 20 home runs, one collecting more than 100 runs batted in and one scoring more than 100 runs.

With many star-quality players still fighting in World War II, A.L. hitters appeared to take the year off. New York second baseman George (Snuffy) Stirnweiss led the league with a .309 average, St. Louis' Vern Stephens topped the circuit with 24 home runs, Yankee Nick Etten won the RBI race with 111 and Stirnweiss scored a league-leading 107 runs.

Stirnweiss needed three final-day hits and a doubleheader rainout in Chicago to win his first batting title. The White Sox's Tony Cuccinello, who finished at .308, was denied a chance to win the championship on the final day by the inclement weather and teammate Johnny Dickshot (.302) was the only other hitter to top the .300 mark. Only Cleveland's Elmer Flick (.306) had ever won an A.L. batting title with a lower average.

The home run runnerup managed only 18, the RBI runnerup 93 and the runs scored runnerup 90. Pete Gray, St. Louis' one-armed outfielder, finished his first big-league season with a .218 average in 234 at-bats.

Dodgers' Rickey signs black star Robinson

Brooklyn President Branch Rickey made baseball history October 23 when he announced the signing of infielder Jackie Robinson, the first black player in Organized Baseball since the turn of the century, to a contract with the Dodgers' International League farm team in Montreal.

Robinson, a former four-sport star at UCLA, was Rickey's choice to break baseball's color barrier after an exhaustive three-year search for a black player who could meet the tough talent and temperament requirements he had set down. Robinson, a former U.S. Army lieutenant, will begin testing the sociological waters next season in the uniform of the Class AAA Royals.

Robinson, who played last year for the Kansas City Monarchs of the Negro League, has been well drilled on what is expected of him and detailed rules have been laid out for his conduct, both on the field and off. He is being groomed for the bigger experiment that lies ahead — the major leagues.

CAUGHT ON THE FLY

SEPTEMBER
Brooklyn's Eddie Stanky set a one-season major league record when he drew his 148th walk from Philadelphia's Hugh Mulcahy to break Jimmy Sheckard's 34-year-old mark of 147.

OCTOBER
With the country still at war, baseball set a record by drawing 10,951,502 fans to its ballparks.

NOVEMBER
Detroit's Hal Newhouser captured his second straight MVP citation after compiling a 25-9 record and leading the A.L. in ERA (1.81), strikeouts (212), shutouts (8) and innings pitched (313).

WORLD SERIES REPORT

TIGERS CLAW CUBS

Catcher Paul Richards drove in four runs with a pair of doubles and Hal Newhouser scattered 10 hits as Detroit captured its second World Series championship with a 9-3 Game 7 victory over the Chicago Cubs October 10 at Wrigley Field.

The big blow was Richards' first-inning three-run double off Hank Borowy, who was appearing in his third straight game. He did not make it through the first inning as the Tigers scored five times.

Borowy had opened the Series with a six-hit 9-0 shutout, pitched five innings of an 8-4 Game 5 loss and worked the final four innings of an 8-7, 12-inning victory in Game 6. Chicago's other win came on a one-hit 3-0 effort by Claude Passeau, who allowed only a second-inning single to Rudy York.

Detroit won both Games 2 and 4, 4-1, behind the pitching of Virgil Trucks and Dizzy Trout, while first baseman Hank Greenberg contributed a pair of homers and seven RBIs.

Game 1	Chicago	9	Detroit	0
Game 2	Detroit	4	Chicago	1
Game 3	Chicago	3	Detroit	0
Game 4	Detroit	4	Chicago	1
Game 5	Detroit	8	Chicago	4
Game 6	Chicago	8	Detroit	7
Game 7	Detroit	9	Chicago	3

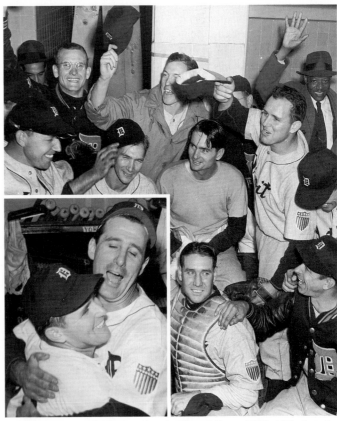

A jubilant Detroit clubhouse after the Tigers' Game 7 World Series win over Chicago.
Inset: Detroit slugger Hank Greenberg (right) hit a three-run homer to help Virgil Trucks (left) record a 4-1 Game 2 victory over the Cubs at Briggs Stadium.

Feller answers critics

Cleveland's Bob Feller, answering critics who had suggested that four years in the Navy had taken a toll on his powerful arm, fired his second career no-hitter April 30, stopping the Yankees, 1-0, before 38,112 fans at Yankee Stadium.

Feller struck out 11 and walked five in outdueling Floyd Bevens. The righthander had allowed only six hits through 8⅓ innings when Cleveland catcher Frankie Hayes belted a home run, giving Feller all the cushion he needed.

But the end was not without excitement. Snuffy Stirnweiss led off the New York ninth by reaching base on an error by first baseman Les Fleming. Stirnweiss moved to second on a sacrifice, to third on Joe DiMaggio's ground out and was stranded as Charlie Keller grounded to second.

The effort matched Feller's Opening Day no-hitter of 1940, a 1-0 victory over Chicago. The righthander also has thrown six career one-hitters.

Robinson makes debut

Jackie Robinson, battling the pressure of becoming Organized Baseball's first black player of the century, put on a brilliant opening day show April 18 when he collected four hits, including a home run, to led the Montreal Royals to a 14-1 International League victory over the Jersey City Giants before a packed house of 25,000 at Jersey City's Roosevelt Stadium.

The 26-year-old Robinson, a four-sport star during his days at UCLA, hit three singles and a three-run homer in five at-bats, drove in four runs, scored four and stole two bases. The crowd

greeted him warmly but without much enthusiasm as he stepped to the plate for the first time. When the game ended, the ecstatic crowd mobbed the history-making second baseman.

Robinson, signed last October by Brooklyn President Branch Rickey and assigned to the Dodgers' Montreal farm team, reached base on two infield singles and a sharp single to right field. His home run traveled 335 feet.

The only negative was a fifth-inning throwing error as the middle man in a double play attempt.

Black pioneers John Wright (center left) and Jackie Robinson get pointers from their new Montreal teammates.

Cardinal stars defect to Mexican League

Three prominent St. Louis Cardinals — pitchers Max Lanier and Fred Martin and second baseman Lou Klein — became the latest major leaguers to be lured south by the big-money inducements of the outlaw Mexican League May 23, automatically blacklisting their return for at least five years. But other Cardinals — including Stan Musial, Enos Slaughter, Whitey Kurowski and Terry Moore — resisted lucrative offers and remained in St. Louis.

Commissioner A.B. (Happy) Chandler had announced April 16 that any players who jump their American contracts to play baseball in foreign leagues would be suspended for at least five years. Player raids reminiscent of the 1914-15 Federal League war have been carried out by the wealthy Pasquel brothers of Mexico — Jorge, Alfonso, Bernardo, Mario and Gerardo.

Other players who had succumbed to offers were St. Louis Browns shortstop Vern Stephens, Brooklyn catcher Mickey Owen, New York Giants outfielder Danny Gardella and Chicago White Sox pitcher Alex Carrasquel.

Three Giants, Sal Maglie,

George Hausmann and Roy Zimmerman, didn't get the chance to say no. They were fired by Owner Horace Stoneham for dickering with the Pasquels.

Chandler gave all jumpers a grace period, saying no action would be taken against those who returned to their teams by Opening Day. Only Stephens came home.

Brooklyn catcher Mickey Owen gave up his Dodger uniform for the Mexican League colors of the Vera Cruz team.

CAUGHT ON THE FLY

APRIL
New York Giants Manager Mel Ott hit his 511th and final major league home run in an Opening Day 8-4 victory over Philadelphia.

MAY
The New York Giants played spoiler when they defeated Boston, 5-1, in the first night game at Braves Field, and Washington did the same at Yankee Stadium, beating New York, 2-1, in its first home game under the lights.

Joe McCarthy, who guided the New York Yankees to seven World Series championships, resigned because of bad health and was replaced by catcher Bill Dickey.

JULY
Boston's Rudy York became the third player in big-league history to hit two grand slams in the same game and finished his big day with 10 RBIs in the Red Sox's 13-6 win over St. Louis.

Ted's All-Star show

Boston slugger Ted Williams rewarded his home fans at Fenway Park with a four-hit, two-homer, five-RBI performance as the American League belted the Nationals, 12-0, in the July 9 All-Star Game.

After a one-year cancellation of the midsummer classic because of World War II travel restrictions, most of baseball's big names were back in uniform and ready for action. Unfortunately for the National Leaguers, most of the action occurred when the A.L. players were batting.

Cleveland's Bob Feller, Detroit's Hal Newhouser and St. Louis' Jack Kramer held the N.L. stars to three hits and Yankee Charlie Keller and Williams pro-vided all the support they really needed with early home runs.

But the highlight of the game was an eighth-inning matchup of Williams against Pittsburgh pitcher Rip Sewell, the man known for his slow, high-arcing "ephus pitch." With the score out of reach at 9-0 and two runners on base, 34,906 fans wondered what would happen if . . .

They didn't have to wonder long. Sewell wound up like he was going to throw a fastball and delivered his "ephus." Williams swung mightily and just tipped the ball. Everybody broke up laughing. Sewell threw another "ephus" for a ball and a third, which Williams belted for his second homer of the game.

All-Star Game starters Bob Feller (left) and Claude Passeau.

" DUGOUT CHATTER "

"There are three big leagues now. The American, the National and Ted Williams."

Mickey Harris

Boston pitcher, after teammate Williams had belted two homers and driven in five runs in a 12-0 A.L. All-Star rout

---

SEASON LEADERS

	American League		National League	
Avg.	Mickey Vernon, Wash.	.353	Stan Musial, St. L.	.365
HR	Hank Greenberg, Det.	44	Ralph Kiner, Pit.	23
RBI	Hank Greenberg, Det.	127	Enos Slaughter, St. L.	130
SB	George Case, Cle.	28	Pete Reiser, Bkn.	34
W-L Pct.	Boo Ferriss, Bos.	25-6, .806	Murry Dickson, St. L.	15-6, .714
ERA	Hal Newhouser, Det.	1.94	Howie Pollet, St. L.	2.10
SO	Bob Feller, Cle.	348	Johnny Schmitz, Chi.	135

19 innings of futility

The Brooklyn Dodgers, chasing the St. Louis Cardinals in the hot National League pennant race, battled Cincinnati to the longest scoreless tie in baseball history September 11, a 19-inning contest at Ebbets Field that was finally called because of darkness.

It took a dramatic one-out throw in the 19th inning from Brooklyn right fielder Dixie Walker to preserve the tie and move the Dodgers to within 1½ games of the Cardinals. Walker fielded a sharp single by Cincinna-ti's Bert Haas and fired a one-hop strike to catcher Bruce Edwards, nailing speedy Dain Clay trying to score from second base. Earlier in the game, Dodger outfielder Pete Reiser had thrown out another Cincinnati runner at the plate.

Cincinnati's Johnny Vander Meer worked 15 innings, allowed seven hits and struck out 14 while Harry Gumbert permitted only one hit over the final four frames.

Brooklyn used four pitchers — Hal Gregg, Hugh Casey, Art Herring and Hank Behrman.

Boudreau, Williams match wits, RBIs

It was supposed to be Cleveland versus Boston in a July 14 double-header at Fenway Park, but what fans watched was Lou Boudreau versus Ted Williams in a day-long battle of both hitting skills and wits.

Boudreau, the Indians' short-stop-manager, was unstoppable in the opener, collecting a homer, four doubles and four runs batted in. But his five-hit performance played second fiddle to Williams, who blasted three home runs, stroked a single and drove in eight runs in Boston's 11-10 victory. He also scored four times, one more than Boudreau.

After digesting that double dose of offense, Red Sox fans watched Boston score a second-game 6-4 win that pushed its American League lead to 11 games over New York. But the highlight of this one was Boudreau's strategy when Williams came to bat.

The Indians positioned six defenders on the right side of the field, literally daring Williams to go the opposite way. Williams lined a double down the right-field line, grounded out and walked twice against the unprecedented shift.

The Ted Williams shift, instigated by Cleveland Manager Lou Boudreau, placed three infielders and two outfielders on the right side and dared the Boston slugger to hit the opposite way.

★1946★

SEPTEMBER - DECEMBER

" DUGOUT CHATTER "

"I've had kids try to take my job before. Some guys say I break their spirit the first day of spring training by starting to run and never quitting. If that's so, then they don't belong. You've got to bear down in baseball — day and night, sick or well, win or lose."

Enos Slaughter

Veteran Cardinal outfielder and World Series hero

Players win benefits

Major league baseball's policy committee agreed to virtually every concession requested by the players September 16 and granted them unprecedented benefits at a historic meeting in New York. An executive council — comprised of the Commissioner, the two league presidents and one owner and player representative from each league — will replace the committee and see that the new policies are carried out.

Some of the major concessions: a minimum major league salary of $5,000; no player will be asked to take a salary cut in excess of 25 percent; incidental spring training expenses of $25 per week; a spring training schedule that cannot start before February 15 next year and

March 1 in 1948; injured players will get their full-season salary plus hospital and medical expenses, and all player contracts must be mailed by February 1.

The generosity of the game's hierarchy was a direct result of the attempt by Boston attorney Robert Murphy to unionize baseball. Murphy, who formed the American Baseball Guild in April, directed most of his attacks at baseball's reserve clause, which prohibits players under contract from bartering for their services. The owners, not wanting to test the legality of the reserve clause in the courts, headed off the union by forming the policy committee to ascertain what the players wanted in a new contract.

Boston attorney Robert Murphy, the man who tried to unionize baseball.

Cardinals win playoff

Happy St. Louisans celebrate the Cardinals' pennant playoff victory over Brooklyn.

The St. Louis Cardinals used a 13-hit attack and a fine pitching effort by righthander Murry Dickson October 3 to throttle the Brooklyn Dodgers, 8-4, and win baseball's first pennant playoff.

The victory at Ebbets Field gave the Cardinals a two-game playoff sweep and their ninth National League title in the last 20 years. It capped a seesaw pennant race that ended with both teams sporting 96-58 records.

The best-of-three playoff opened in St. Louis with Games 2 and 3 scheduled for Brooklyn. Workhorse lefthander Howie Pollet, a 20-game winner who fought a sore arm down the stretch of the regular season, got the call for the Cardinals and responded with an eight-hit effort. The Redbirds' 4-2 triumph brought them to within one win of a World Series date with the American League's Boston Red Sox.

Brooklyn scored a first-inning run against Dickson in the second

game, but the Dodgers did not manage another hit until the ninth as the Cardinals forged an 8-1 lead. Marty Marion, Enos Slaughter and Whitey Kurowski drove in two runs apiece for St. Louis.

The Dodgers, however, fought back in the ninth to score three times and had the bases loaded with only one out. But reliever Harry Brecheen struck out Eddie Stanky and Howie Schultz to give the Cardinals their fourth pennant in the last five years.

The victory culminated a season-long struggle. Both teams had leads at various times, but neither could put the other away. The Cardinals had the best chance to win in regulation. They moved into first place alone on August 28 and held the lead until September 27, when they lost to Chicago and dropped into a tie with the Dodgers. Both teams won on September 28 and both lost the next day as the regular season ended.

SLAUGHTER'S MAD DASH

Enos (Country) Slaughter's mad dash around the bases produced the winning run and Harry Brecheen's clutch pitching sealed the verdict as the St. Louis Cardinals defeated the Boston Red Sox, 4-3, October 15 in a dramatic Game 7 conclusion to the World Series.

After Boston had rallied to tie the game on Dom DiMaggio's two-run, eighth-inning double, Slaughter led off the bottom of the inning with a single off Bob Klinger. But he could not advance as Whitey Kurowski and Del Rice were retired. Now it was up to Harry Walker.

The Cardinal left fielder came through, lining a shot toward the left-center-field gap. Boston center fielder Leon Culberson made an outstanding play, cutting the ball off and firing it back to the infield — quickly enough that Slaughter would have to remain at third.

Wrong. Slaughter never slowed down as he rounded the bag and headed home. Red Sox shortstop Johnny Pesky took the relay and hesitated, obviously surprised by Slaughter's bold move. His hurried throw was up the third-base line and the Cardinals had a 4-3 lead.

Brecheen, who had relieved Murry Dickson in the eighth, added to the excitement in the ninth when he allowed the first two Red Sox, Rudy York and Bobby Doerr, to reach base with singles. But with 36,143 fans at St. Louis' Sportsman's Park sitting on the edge of their seats, he induced Pinky Higgins to hit into a forceout, retired Roy Partee on a foul pop and insured the Cardinals' sixth World Series victory by getting Tom McBride to ground into another force.

Boston had opened the Series with a 3-2, 10-inning victory that was decided on a Rudy York home run. But St. Louis answered with a 3-0 win on a Brecheen four-hitter. That was the pattern the fall classic would follow as Boo Ferriss pitched the Red Sox to a 4-0 victory and the Cardinals squared matters with a 12-3 pounding at Fenway Park. Boston's 6-3 Game 5 victory was followed by another Brecheen win — a 4-1 seven-hitter.

The team's two stars, Boston's Ted Williams and St. Louis' Stan Musial, struggled through the Series with .200 and .222 averages, respectively.

St. Louis' Enos Slaughter slides safely across the plate with the World Series-winning run after his Game 7 "mad dash" around the bases.

Seventh-game World Series hero Enos Slaughter (left) clowns with teammates (left to right): George Munger, Whitey Kurowski and Joe Garagiola.

Game 1	Boston	3	St. Louis	2
Game 2	St. Louis	3	Boston	0
Game 3	Boston	4	St. Louis	0
Game 4	St. Louis	12	Boston	3
Game 5	Boston	6	St. Louis	3
Game 6	St. Louis	4	Boston	1
Game 7	St. Louis	4	Boston	3

An impressive debut

Jackie Robinson finished his first season in Organized Baseball in style, winning the International League batting title, leading the circuit's second basemen in fielding percentage and starring in the Montreal Royals' Junior World Series conquest of Louisville.

After the Royals had defeated the American Association champions in the final game of the Series, Robinson and Manager Clay Hopper were carried off the field by exuberant spectators in Montreal.

Robinson finished with a .349 average, topping Newark's Bobby Brown by five points. He also collected 25 doubles, eight triples, three home runs, 65 RBIs and scored 113 runs while stealing 40 bases. But his presence did more than insure a postseason championship for the Royals.

With Robinson in the lineup, Montreal drew a record 412,744 fans at home and played before 399,047 on the road.

CAUGHT ON THE FLY

OCTOBER

Cleveland's Bob Feller finished the season with 348 strikeouts, one more than Rube Waddell fanned for the Philadelphia Athletics in his record-setting 1904 campaign.

The New York Yankees set a major league attendance record by drawing 2,265,512 fans, almost 800,000 more than the previous best figure turned in by the 1929 Chicago Cubs. Total major league attendance was a record 18,534,444.

DECEMBER

Major league officials decided to return the All-Star Game vote to the fans, with managers reserving the right to select pitchers.

Former Washington pitching great Walter Johnson died after a six-month illness resulting from a brain tumor at age 59.

Durocher suspended

Commissioner A.B. (Happy) Chandler shocked the baseball world April 9 when he suspended Brooklyn Manager Leo Durocher for the 1947 season — less than a week before Opening Day. Chandler's action, the most drastic ever taken against a major league manager, reprimands Durocher for conduct "detrimental to baseball."

Chandler said the suspension was the "result of the accumulation of unpleasant incidents in which he (Durocher) has been involved," but the final straw was a spring training tirade against New York Yankee President Larry MacPhail. Durocher charged his former Brooklyn boss with entertaining alleged gamblers in his box during a Yankee-Dodger spring game at Havana, Cuba. An irate MacPhail reacted by filing defamation charges against both Durocher and Dodger President Branch Rickey with the commissioner's office.

Chandler opened an investigation and listened to testimony from numerous players and officials before announcing Durocher's punishment and clearing both Rickey and MacPhail. Durocher, known affectionately to Dodger fans as "The Lip," has a checkered history of on and off-field indiscretions and recently was cleared in court of charges that he fractured a fan's jaw during a fracas last July at Ebbets Field.

Durocher, who was involved in a meeting mapping the strategy for breaking baseball's color barrier by bringing Jackie Robinson to the major leagues, will be replaced on an interim basis by coach Clyde Sukeforth. Rickey said a full-time manager will be in place by Opening Day.

Chandler also fined the Dodger and Yankee teams "because their officials engaged in a public controversy damaging to baseball."

Color barrier tumbles

Jackie Robinson, breaking a color barrier that had existed for more than 60 years, became the first black player in major league baseball since Moses Fleetwood Walker in 1884 when he put on a Brooklyn Dodgers uniform and played first base in the team's April 15 opener at Ebbets Field against the Boston Braves.

With 25,623 fans on hand to witness the beginning of the great sociological experiment, Robinson went hitless in three official at-bats but scored the winning run in a 5-3 Dodger victory after reaching base on a seventh-inning error. He played flawlessly at first base, a new position, and received a warm reception from Brooklyn fans.

The 28-year-old Robinson, picked by Dodger President Branch Rickey as the man to integrate the National Pastime, prepared for this historic day by playing the 1946 season for Brooklyn's Class AAA farm team at Montreal. Robinson won the International League batting title, led the Royals to the Junior World Series championship and won over the Montreal fans with his aggressive and hustling style of play. He was rewarded April 10 when the Dodgers purchased his contract.

In his first at-bat, Robinson grounded out to third base. He followed that by grounding out to shortstop and flying to left field. But in the seventh inning, with the Dodgers trailing 3-2 and a man on first, Robinson laid down a perfect sacrifice bunt and Boston first baseman Earl Torgeson made a wild throw. Robinson later scored on Pete Reiser's two-run double.

Robinson got his first major league hit, a bunt single, April 17 in the Dodgers' second game against Boston and hit his first home run the next day against the New York Giants.

Jackie Robinson was easy to spot in the Brooklyn dugout when the historic 1947 campaign opened.

Brooklyn Manager Leo Durocher (right), suspended for the 1947 season, with Dodger President Branch Rickey.

SEASON LEADERS

	American League		National League	
Avg.	Ted Williams, Bos.	.343	Harry Walker, St. L.-Phi.	.363
HR	Ted Williams, Bos.	32	Ralph Kiner, Pit.	51
			Johnny Mize, N.Y.	51
RBI	Ted Williams, Bos.	114	Johnny Mize, N.Y.	138
SB	Robert Dillinger, St. L.	34	Jackie Robinson, Bkn.	29
W-L Pct.	Allie Reynolds, N.Y.	19-8, .704	Larry Jansen, N.Y.	21-5, .808
ERA	Spud Chandler, N.Y.	2.46	Warren Spahn, Bos.	2.33
SO	Bob Feller, Cle.	196	Ewell Blackwell, Cin.	193

Ruth has his day

April 27 was "Babe Ruth Day" throughout the baseball world and players, managers, officials and fans everywhere took time out to honor the game's most cherished superstar. But nowhere was the tribute more poignant than at Yankee Stadium, where 58,339 fans gathered to say a loving farewell before a scheduled game between the Yankees and Washington.

After being presented with many awards and gifts, Ruth enjoyed a thunderous greeting as he stepped to the microphone. He looked thin and weak from a series of operations to combat throat cancer and his voice was raspy and subdued. But he still flashed the same Ruthian smile and he spoke straight from the heart. His closing words, piped in to ballparks around the major leagues, were simple and elegant.

"The only real game in the world, I think, is baseball," he said. "There's been so many lovely things said about me, I'm just glad I had the opportunity to thank everybody."

With that, the 53-year-old Ruth flashed his patented smile, waved to the crowd and walked into the Yankee dugout.

Babe Ruth, his voice raspy because of throat cancer, speaks to adoring fans at Yankee Stadium on a day in his honor.

CAUGHT ON THE FLY

JANUARY
In a shocking transaction, Detroit sold slugger Hank Greenberg, the 1946 A.L. home run (44) and RBI (127) leader, to Pittsburgh for $75,000.

Negro League great Josh Gibson, one of the great sluggers in baseball history, died of a brain tumor at age 35.

JUNE
The Boston Red Sox celebrated the first night game ever played at Fenway Park by defeating the Chicago White Sox, 5-3.

New York Giants catcher Walker Cooper matched the record of former Giant George Kelly when he homered in his sixth consecutive game, a 14-6 victory over Philadelphia.

JULY
The New York Giants pushed across a 10th-inning run for a 5-4 victory over Cincinnati, ending the 16-game winning streak of Reds righthander Ewell Blackwell.

"DUGOUT CHATTER"

"Now there is a guy who is really skinny. He reminds me of Ted Williams in 1937."

Ted Williams

Boston slugger, on getting his first look at stringbean Cincinnati righthander Ewell Blackwell

A.L. gets first black

Cleveland's Larry Doby, a 22-year-old former Negro League star, became the first black player in the 47-year history of the American League July 5 when he struck out as a pinch-hitter during a 6-5 Indians loss to the White Sox at Chicago's Comiskey Park.

Doby, the century's second black major leaguer, pinch-hit for pitcher Bryan Stephens with one out in the seventh inning and runners on first and third base. As he stepped to the plate, he received a big hand from an enthusiastic Comiskey Park crowd of more than 18,000. The 6-foot-1, 185-pound lefthanded hitter took a lusty but futile cut at Earl Harrist's first offering, drove the second pitch foul and took two balls before going down swinging.

The youngster made his big-league debut less than three hours after signing a contract. He had been purchased last week from the Newark Eagles of the Negro League, where he was batting .415. Doby was greeted cordially by his new teammates after being escorted to the park by Cleveland Owner Bill Veeck.

Blackwell just misses no-hit feat

Cincinnati's Ewell Blackwell, two outs away from duplicating Johnny Vander Meer's 1938 double no-hitter feat, surrendered a one-out single to Eddie Stanky in the ninth inning June 22 and settled for a two-hit 4-0 victory over Brooklyn in the first game of a doubleheader at Crosley Field.

Blackwell had pitched the season's first no-hitter four days earlier at Cincinnati, beating the Boston Braves 6-0 behind Babe Young's two three-run homers. With 31,204 fans on hand to see the Dodgers, Blackwell carried another no-hitter into the ninth, having faced only 28 batters.

But Stanky spoiled Blackwell's bid by hitting a ground ball through the lanky 24-year-old righthander's legs and into center field. Blackwell retired the next batter, Al Gionfriddo, on a fly ball, but yielded a bloop single to Jackie Robinson before getting the final out.

Ironically, Vander Meer, also a Cincinnati pitcher, had thrown his consecutive no-hitters against the same two teams Blackwell faced.

Blackwell's ninth straight victory was his 11th of the season and his fourth shutout.

Brooklyn won the nightcap, 9-8, as Carl Furillo drove in seven runs with a grand slam homer and two singles.

Cincinnati's Ewell Blackwell (center) was the toast of the Reds locker room after pitching a no-hitter against Boston.

JACKIE ROBINSON BREAKS THE COLOR BARRIER

Robinson fit all of Rickey's criteria. He did not smoke, drink or swear. He was intelligent, patient and proud. A former Army lieutenant, he understood the problems faced by his race and realized that equality — in sports or otherwise — was a battle that would not be won overnight.

Never in his wildest dreams had Jackie Robinson ever envisioned himself as a pioneer. Yet there he was in that fateful summer of '47, dodging beanballs, flying spikes and racial epithets as the centerpiece of Branch Rickey's Great Sociological Experiment. "Wear an armor of humility," Rickey had warned his 28-year-old rookie, adding that endurance, patience, pride and heart were the tools he would need to tear down baseball's long-enduring color barrier.

This barrier, rooted in place since the 1880s, would not crumble easily. Rickey, the visionary president of the Brooklyn Dodgers, understood that and had spent several years looking for just the right player, both in character and athletic ability, to shoulder the overwhelming burden. After an arduous search, Rickey's scouts came up with Jackie Roosevelt Robinson, an unassuming Negro League player and former four-

sport star at UCLA.

Robinson fit all of Rickey's criteria. He did not smoke, drink or swear. He was intelligent, patient and proud. A former Army lieutenant, he understood the problems faced by his race and realized that equality — in sports or otherwise — was a battle that would not be won overnight. But when Dodger coach Clyde Sukeforth first outlined the plan and asked him to meet with Rickey, Robinson was taken by surprise.

"I was thunderstruck," he said. "I had always believed that eventually Negroes would play in the majors, but I didn't think it would happen in my time. And I certainly never dreamed the first real chance would come my way."

Robinson was even more incredulous when Rickey explained what he expected.

No responding to the inevitable racial slurs. No fighting back when spiked or hit by pitches. No arguing with

umpires. No endorsements. No signing his name to newspaper or magazine articles. He would leave the park every day by a secret exit and he would not accept any social invitations — either from blacks or whites. With Dodger games sure to attract throngs of black fans wanting to see their hero in action, it would be paramount that he avoid adulation as well as retaliation.

"Don't you want a player with guts enough to fight back?" Robinson asked.

"I want a player with guts enough *not* to fight back," Rickey responded.

The Pasadena, Calif., product agreed to the conditions and the great experiment was underway. Rickey signed Robinson and five other blacks to Dodger contracts in 1945 and assigned them to Montreal. He at least would have help breaking the Class AAA International League color barrier before coming under microscopic scrutiny with the Dodgers in 1947.

What Montreal fans saw was a muscular 6-foot, 195-pound pigeontoed former football star with deceptive speed and amazing quickness. He swung the bat with authority, fielded his second base position with sure-handed grace and ran the bases with reckless abandon. The real measure of Robinson's

Jackie Robinson in 1946.

Robinson signs as Dodger boss Branch Rickey looks on.

greatness was on the basepaths, where he showed fire and instinct that rekindled memories of the great Ty Cobb. "Daring," was the way Robinson described himself, and his aggressiveness sent opposing infields into panic.

Whether beating out bunts, taking the extra base or stealing, Jackie was disruptive. He also was one or two steps ahead of everybody strategically, and he used the element of surprise to great advantage. He would go from first to third on bunts, score from first on a single or steal a base. He was especially adept at swiping home, which to him was a simple case of timing.

His timing was great in 1946 as he quickly won over skeptical Montreal fans. Rickey's intentions, clear enough already, were strengthened when Robinson batted a league-leading .349, stole 40 bases and led second basemen in fielding while helping the Royals capture the Junior League World Series. When Robinson batted .625 in seven 1947 exhibition games against Brooklyn, baseball stood on the brink of a breakthrough.

Rickey kept everybody in suspense until April 10, five days before the season was to begin. His announcement that Robinson was being called up to play first base for the Dodgers was greeted by character assassinations and threats of boycott from officials, players and fans around the major leagues. Some Dodger players took a wait-and-see attitude while other reactions ranged from stand-offishness to outright hostility. Before Robinson arrived in Brooklyn, southern players on the Dodgers circulated a petition demanding that he not be promoted to the majors. The move dried up when shortstop Pee Wee Reese, a southerner, the team captain and later Robinson's close friend, refused to sign and Rickey agreed to trade any unhappy players.

Robinson's April 15 Ebbets Field debut was unspectacular. Batting second and playing his new position, he succumbed to a steady diet of curveballs from Boston's Johnny Sain and went 0 for 3. He got his first big-league hit, a bunt single, in his second game, hit his first home run in

Robinson, a daring baserunner, raises the dirt as he steals home against the Cubs in 1948.

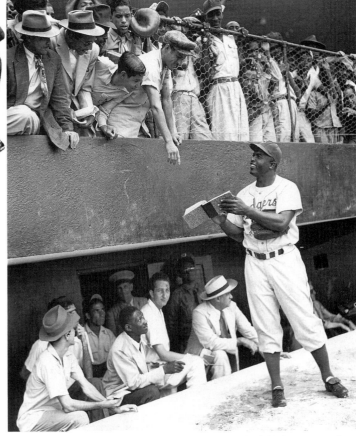

Robinson became a hero and cult figure for the black community.

his third contest and stole his first base in the fifth game. He went on to finish his rookie season with a .297 average, 12 homers and a National League-leading 29 steals. Considering the pressure and abuse he endured, it was a marvelous effort.

Robinson spent the campaign ducking pitches aimed at his skull, sidestepping spikes directed at his legs and other body parts and ignoring racial invectives pointed at his heart. Fans in cities such as St. Louis, Cincinnati and Philadelphia were ruthless, but the most difficult task was swallowing his pride while cruel bench jockeys fired away. The worst was Philadelphia Manager Ben Chapman, a southern loudmouth and the accepted master of vile verbal abuse.

The first time Brooklyn traveled to St. Louis, the Cardinals threatened a boycott that was cut short by N.L. President Ford Frick's warning that those who take part "will be suspended and I don't care if it wrecks the National League for five years." There also were celebrated spiking incidents involving St. Louis stars Enos Slaughter and Joe Garagiola and countless meals eaten on the bus while his teammates dined in segregated roadside restaurants. As programmed by Rickey, Robinson accepted his torment quietly, answering only with his daring, combative play.

Acceptance in the Dodger clubhouse came grudgingly, but it did come. First several of Robinson's teammates began saying "hello." Soon he was being invited to participate in clubhouse card games. By the end of the Dodgers' pennant-winning season, Jackie was being hailed by teammates as one of the team's key performers.

But all was not smooth inside the Dodger clubhouse. "It isn't too tough on me," Robinson wrote to his high school baseball coach during the season. "I have played with white boys all my life. But they haven't played with a Negro before, and it sure is rough on some of them."

Robinson remained aloof and withdrawn through much of that first season, forcing his teammates to make the first move. As he explained in his 1972 autobiography, he was not trying to win favor in the white man's world, he was trying to earn it.

"I had to fight hard against loneliness, abuse and the knowledge that any mistake I made would be magnified because I was the only black man out there," Robinson wrote. "Many people resented my impatience and honesty, but I never cared about acceptance as much as I cared about respect."

Respect came unexpectedly in August, when a group of Brooklyn players approached Robinson after the Slaughter incident and said, "If they give you the works, give it back to them — and the team will be behind you 100 percent."

That was the day Jackie Robinson won his first major battle, a victory that would inspire him through an outstanding 10-year career as one of baseball's noblest trailblazers.

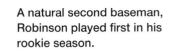

A natural second baseman, Robinson played first in his rookie season.

★1947★

The American way

Boston's Bobby Doerr slides into second with a stolen base during seventh-inning All-Star Game action at Chicago's Wrigley Field.

Washington pinch-hitter Stan Spence singled home Boston's Bobby Doerr with the go-ahead run in the seventh inning July 8 and the American League captured its 10th All-Star victory in 14 games with a 2-1 decision over the National League at Chicago's Wrigley Field.

Pitchers dominated, and the A.L.'s Hal Newhouser (Detroit), Frank Shea (New York), Walt Masterson (Washington) and reliever Joe Page (New York) allowed only five hits in outdueling the N.L.'s Ewell Blackwell (Cincinnati), Harry Brecheen (St. Louis), Johnny Sain (Boston) and Warren Spahn (Boston). The only N.L. run was scored in the fourth inning on a long homer by the New York Giants' Johnny Mize.

The Americans tied in the sixth against Brecheen on singles by Chicago's Luke Appling and Boston's Ted Williams and a double-play grounder by New York's Joe DiMaggio. Doerr singled in the seventh, stole second, went to third on Sain's errant pickoff throw and scored on Spence's single.

Yankees tie record

Detroit righthander Fred Hutchinson pulled the plug on New York's offensive machine July 18 with a brilliant two-hit, 8-0 victory that snapped the Yankees' American League record-tying winning streak at 19 games.

The Yankees had swept a doubleheader behind Bobo Newsom and Vic Raschi the day before at Cleveland to match the A.L.-record string set back in 1906 by the Chicago White Sox. The major league mark of 26 games was set by the New York Giants in 1916.

But Hutchinson carved up the Yankees with pinpoint control and a sharp curveball. He faced 28 batters and allowed a second-inning single to Joe DiMaggio and a seventh-inning bunt single to Snuffy Stirnweiss. The second-place Tigers, 10½ games behind the Yankees, backed Hutchinson with an 18-hit assault.

The Yankees had started their streak on June 29.

2 in N.L. blast 51

The greatest home run duel in the history of major league baseball ended on a quiet note September 28 with neither Ralph Kiner nor Johnny Mize adding to their National League-leading totals of 51. Kiner, who plays for last-place Pittsburgh, belted his final homer September 23 off St. Louis' Jim Hearn and Mize, the New York Giants' slugger, tied him two days later when he connected off Boston's Johnny Sain.

But both were shut down over the final three days and they finished as only the second and third National Leaguers (Chicago's Hack Wilson hit 56 in 1930) to break the 50-homer barrier. It was an intense battle all the way with neither player able to break away from the other.

Mize held the lead through early September until Kiner, taking advantage of the shortened left-field fence at Forbes Field, went on an amazing home run spree. The Pittsburgh strong man blasted a major league-record eight in four games to pass Mize and break the previous mark (seven in four games) set in 1936 by Yankee Tony Lazzeri. Four of the home runs came in a September 11 doubleheader and the final two, his 48th and 49th, came in a September 12 victory over Boston.

Mize captured N.L. RBI honors with 138, 11 more than Kiner.

" DUGOUT CHATTER "

"I don't dare show my nose out of this dugout. Autographs here, autographs there. I don't like to turn down any of the kids, but man, my hand is sore. No foolin'."

Johnny Mize

New York Giants first baseman, before a game at Brooklyn's Ebbets Field

---

CAUGHT ON THE FLY

AUGUST

The Maynard Midgets captured the first Little League World Series tournament in their hometown of Williamsport, Pa.

Brooklyn's Dan Bankhead became the first black pitcher in major league history when he worked 3⅓ innings of relief against Pittsburgh, giving up 10 hits. Bankhead made history by homering in his first big-league at-bat.

OCTOBER

Commissioner A.B. (Happy) Chandler sold World Series radio rights for $475,000 over three years.

N.L. home run co-champion Johnny Mize of the New York Giants.

YANKEES WIN THRILLER

New York relief ace Joe Page pitched five innings of one-hit relief and the Yankees closed out one of the most exciting World Series in history October 6 with a 5-2 victory over Brooklyn before 71,548 fans at Yankee Stadium.

The Game 7 clincher was almost anticlimactic in comparison to the Game 4 and 6 thrillers that kept Brooklyn's hopes for a first World Series championship alive. After the Dodgers broke on top against Yankee starter Frank Shea with a two-run second inning, Floyd Bevens and Page closed the door while the Yankees chipped away against five Brooklyn pitchers.

The Yankees had threatened to make short work of the Dodgers as they opened the fall classic with 5-3 and 10-3 victories. But the fireworks started in Game 3 when the Dodgers scored six runs in the second inning and owned a 9-4 advantage after four. A two-run homer by Joe DiMaggio and a pinch-hit home run by Yogi Berra, the first in Series history, struck fear into 33,098 Ebbets Field fans before reliever Hugh Casey came on to preserve a 9-8 Dodger win.

Game 4 was a classic. Yankee starter Bevens entered the ninth inning with a 2-1 lead — and a no-hitter. The Dodgers had scored in the fifth on two walks, a sacrifice and a ground out. When Bevens sandwiched two outs around a walk in the ninth, he stepped to the brink of World Series history. But pinch-runner Al Gionfriddo heightened the tension by stealing second and prompting Bevens to walk Pete Reiser intentionally — his 10th free pass of the game.

Pinch-hitter Cookie Lavagetto spoiled the no-hitter and shocked Yankee fans by walloping a two-run game-winning double off the right-field wall.

After the Yankees rebounded for a 2-1 win behind Shea, Brooklyn responded with a hair-raising 8-6 victory in Game 6. The Dodgers had jumped to a 4-0 lead, fallen behind 5-4 and regained the advantage with a four-run sixth. But with two on and two out in the bottom of the sixth, DiMaggio smashed a Joe Hatten pitch toward the left-field bullpen.

Just as it was about to drop over the fence for a game-tying homer, Gionfriddo, inserted as a defensive replacement, made a tremendous twisting glove-hand catch near the 415-foot mark. The Dodgers were alive — for one more day.

Cookie Lavagetto is escorted from the field by police and a Dodger teammate after breaking up Floyd Bevens' no-hit attempt with a two-run ninth-inning double in Game 4 of the World Series.

Game 1	New York	5	Brooklyn	3
Game 2	New York	10	Brooklyn	3
Game 3	Brooklyn	9	New York	8
Game 4	Brooklyn	3	New York	2
Game 5	New York	2	Brooklyn	1
Game 6	Brooklyn	8	New York	6
Game 7	New York	5	Brooklyn	2

Ecstatic New York Yankees and their fans rush onto the field to celebrate their seventh-game World Series victory over Brooklyn.

Triple Crown winner Williams loses MVP

For the second time in six years, Boston's Ted Williams won an American League Triple Crown but did not win the circuit's Most Valuable Player award.

Williams won his third batting title with a .343 average, hit 32 homers and drove in 114 runs to become the second player in history to win two Triple Crowns. The Splendid Splinter repeated his 1942 feat, when he lost out in MVP voting to New York's Joe Gordon.

This time Williams lost to Yankee Joe DiMaggio by one point in voting by the Baseball Writers' Association of America. DiMaggio, who hit .315 with 20 homers and 97 RBIs while leading the Yankees to the A.L. pennant, garnered eight first-place votes and 202 points in winning the award for a third time. The unpopular Williams, who won the citation in 1946, received only three first-place votes, earned 201 points and was left off one writer's ballot. A 10th-place vote would have given Williams a victory.

The Baseball Writers' first Rookie of the Year award was given to Brooklyn's Jackie Robinson, who broke the big-league color barrier and finished his historic season with a .297 average.

★1948★

" DUGOUT CHATTER "

"Let that be a lesson to you other pitchers. If you pitch the way Lemon did tonight, you'll very seldom lose."

Joe Gordon

Cleveland second baseman, after teammate Bob Lemon had no-hit the Detroit Tigers

"I've pitched with a lot of different teams in a lot of different countries, but this is it. In the big leagues at last."

Satchel Paige

The long-time Negro League star, on being signed by the Cleveland Indians

Tigers finally light up

The Detroit Tigers, the last American League team to host a night baseball game, christened their new $400,000 lighting system June 15 with a 4-1 victory over Philadelphia before 54,480 fans at Briggs Stadium.

Lefthander Hal Newhouser, a three-time 20-game winner, was accorded the pitching honor and he didn't disappoint, allowing only two hits while winning his seventh straight decision. Newhouser walked six and allowed two doubles — a run-scoring two-bagger to Hank Majeski in the first inning and another to Eddie Joost in the eighth.

Newhouser got all the support he needed in the third when Hoot Evers hit a two-run single, but Dick Wakefield and Pat Mullin provided eighth-inning insurance with home runs. Philadelphia's Barney McCosky crashed into the left-field wall chasing Wakefield's drive and had to be carried from the field on a stretcher.

Briggs Stadium lights up for the first time as Detroit becomes the last American League team to host a night baseball game.

Yankee fans take trip down memory lane

The New York Yankees, as proficient at celebrating special occasions as they are at winning American League pennants and World Series championships, took 49,641 fans on a trip down memory lane June 13 in honor of Yankee Stadium's 25th anniversary.

On a rainy afternoon designated as Silver Anniversary Day, Yankee Stadium literally dripped with nostalgia as master of ceremonies Mel Allen introduced players from the New York teams of yesteryear — beginning with the members of the 1923 team that christened the new facility in a victory over Boston and went on to capture the first of the franchise's 11 World Series titles. The biggest ovation was reserved for Babe Ruth, the man who revolution-ized baseball with his mighty home runs and hit the first in the Stadium that later would be known as "the House That Ruth Built."

The Bambino, attired in his old uniform No. 3 and carrying a bat, strolled to the home plate area as the crowd vigorously saluted their hero. In a brief ceremony, A.L. President Will Harridge officially retired Ruth's number and presented the uniform to the Hall of Fame for display at the Cooperstown, N.Y., museum. After speeches and presentations, members of the 1923 Yankee team played a two-inning exhibition against the members of later Yankee squads.

In a rousing conclusion to the festivities, the current Yankees defeated Cleveland, 5-3.

This Who's Who of New York Yankee baseball was photographed during Yankee Stadium's 25th anniversary celebration.

14 runs in one inning

The Boston Red Sox, locked in a 5-5 battle with Philadelphia, celebrated the Fourth of July by exploding for a modern major league record-tying 14 runs in the seventh inning and coasted to a 19-5 victory before 24,363 fans at Fenway Park.

The victim of the outburst was 22-year-old A's reliever Charlie Harris, who retired only one of the 14 batters he faced in the inning and allowed 12 runs. Harris, who had recorded the last out of the sixth in relief of starter Carl Scheib, allowed five walks and six hits to the first 11 batters in the seventh and then surrendered another single and walk after retiring Stan Spence on a fly ball.

Bill McCahan relieved Harris and allowed two inherited runners and two of his own to score before Ted Williams mercifully grounded out to end the massacre. It was the third at-bat of the inning for Williams, who had walked twice against Harris.

The Red Sox matched the record set in 1920 by the New York Yankees and equaled two years later by the Chicago Cubs. The 1883 Cubs set the all-time mark of 18 runs in one inning

A.L. stars shoot down N.L. again

New York Yankee righthander Vic Raschi singled home two fourth-inning runs to break a 2-2 tie and pitched three scoreless innings as the American League added to the National League's growing frustration with a 5-2 All-Star Game victory July 13 at St. Louis' Sportsman's Park.

The A.L.'s win was cemented by a three-run fourth-inning rally that capped a comeback from a 2-0 first-inning deficit. Hometown Cardinal hero Stan Musial had given the Nationals a promising start with a two-run homer off A.L. starter Walt Masterson.

But it was all A.L. after that as Washington's Masterson settled down and was followed to the mound for scoreless three-inning stints by Raschi and Philadelphia's Joe Coleman.

Detroit's Hoot Evers got the A.L. on track with a second-inning homer and Cleveland shortstop Lou Boudreau's third-inning

An A.L. Murderer's Row of (left to right): Ted Williams, Joe DiMaggio, George Kell and Lou Boudreau before the 1948 All-Star Game.

sacrifice fly tied the game. Raschi's bases-loaded single put the A.L. in front and Yankee Joe DiMaggio, pinch-hitting because of an injury, capped the scoring with a run-producing fly ball.

Ruth dies of cancer

New York Yankee slugger Babe Ruth, king of the baseball world during his home run-hitting heyday in the 1920s and early '30s, died August 16 at New York's Memorial Hospital after a long battle with throat cancer. A saddened nation stopped to mourn the passing of one of its greatest heroes.

The 53-year-old Ruth, who set an incredible 54 major league records and 10 additional American League marks during his 22-year big-league career, had been battling the cancer for two years. He died at 8 p.m. with his family at his bedside, including wife Claire and his two adopted daughters.

Condolences began pouring in immediately, from statesmen like President Harry Truman and former President Herbert Hoover to baseball officials and former friends and teammates.

Ruth's two most famous records were the 60 home runs he hit in 1927 and his career total of 714 homers. Both of those marks should stand for a long time.

CAUGHT ON THE FLY

JANUARY
Commissioner A.B. (Happy) Chandler fined the New York Yankees, Chicago White Sox and Philadelphia Phillies $500 each for signing players still attending high school.

JUNE
Philadelphia's Richie Ashburn hit safely in his 23rd consecutive game, a major league rookie record. The Phillies defeated the Cubs at Chicago, 6-5.

JULY
Three managerial changes in one day: Leo Durocher left Brooklyn to take over for the New York Giants' Mel Ott, Burt Shotton took control of the Dodgers and Eddie Sawyer replaced the Phillies' Ben Chapman.

SEASON LEADERS

	American League		National League	
Avg.	Ted Williams, Bos.	.369	Stan Musial, St. L.	.376
HR	Joe DiMaggio, N.Y.	39	Ralph Kiner, Pit.	40
			Johnny Mize, N.Y.	40
RBI	Joe DiMaggio, N.Y.	155	Stan Musial, St. L.	131
SB	Robert Dillinger, St. L.	28	Richie Ashburn, Phi.	32
W-L Pct.	Jack Kramer, Bos.	18-5, .783	Harry Brecheen, St. L.	20-7, .741
ERA	Gene Bearden, Cle.	2.43	Harry Brecheen, St. L.	2.24
SO	Bob Feller, Cle.	164	Harry Brecheen, St. L.	149

Seerey goes wild

Pat Seerey's 11th-inning home run, his record-tying fourth of the game, gave the Chicago White Sox a wild 12-11 victory over the Philadelphia Athletics July 18 in the first game of a doubleheader at Shibe Park. The A's came back to win the curfew-shortened nightcap in five innings, 6-1.

Seerey, acquired from Cleveland earlier in the season, became only the fifth major league player to turn the four-homer trick. Bobby Lowe of Boston and Ed Delahanty of Philadelphia accomplished the feat in the pre-1900 era while New York Yankee Lou Gehrig (1932) and Philadelphia Phillie Chuck Klein (1936) enjoyed four-homer games in more recent times. Klein needed 10 innings to match the record.

The A's jumped on Chicago for five early runs and appeared well on their way to victory. But with Seerey connecting in the fourth, fifth and sixth innings and driving home six runs, Chicago turned the game around and gained an 11-7 advantage. A three-run homer by Philadelphia's Eddie Joost in the seventh forced extra innings.

Seerey, a five-year veteran who hit 26 homers in 1946 for the Indians, belted his game-winner and collected his seventh RBI in the 11th.

Chicago's Pat Seerey kisses the bat he used to belt four home runs in a game against Philadelphia.

★1948★

AUGUST-DECEMBER

Shutout streak ends

Ninth-inning homers by Aaron Robinson and Dave Philley gave last-place Chicago a 3-2 win over first-place Cleveland August 20 and snapped three streaks — the Indians had won eight straight games and their pitchers had thrown 47 straight scoreless innings and four consecutive shutouts.

Bob Lemon — who had pitched a no-hitter against Detroit on June 30 — entered the ninth with a 2-0 lead and appeared well on his way to Cleveland's American League-record fifth straight shutout. But the righthander walked Pat Seerey and surrendered a game-tying homer to Robinson, snapping the Indians' A.L.-record scoreless innings streak that had started in the first game of an August 15 doubleheader at Chicago. Philley followed with his blast and Chicago's Randy Gumpert retired the Indians in the bot-

tom of the inning, cutting Cleveland's lead over second-place Boston to two games.

The highlight of the scoreless streak had occurred the night before, when a record night-game crowd of 78,382 at Cleveland Stadium watched 42-year-old former Negro League star Satchel Paige perform his magic. The ageless righthander blanked the White Sox, 1-0, on three hits while recording his second straight shutout.

Paige, who had blanked the White Sox, 5-0, on August 13, was nearly flawless as he retired Chicago in order six times and walked only one. Larry Doby singled home the game's only run in the fourth inning.

The colorful Paige has drawn 201,829 fans to watch his three major league starts, all victories. He is 5-1 since signing in July — a move viewed at the time as a Bill Veeck publicity stunt.

Indians claim pennant

Cleveland Manager Lou Boudreau hit two solo home runs, Ken Keltner added a three-run blast and Gene Bearden pitched a five-hitter October 4 as the Indians captured their first American League championship in 28 years with an 8-3 victory over Boston in their one-game pennant playoff.

A four-run fourth inning, keyed by Keltner's homer, broke a 1-1 deadlock, knocked out Red Sox starter Denny Galehouse and silenced a Fenway Park crowd of 33,957 fans who watched the rest of the game in silence. They saw Boudreau collect four hits (two singles in addition to his home runs) and lead his team to victory in the first playoff in American League history.

The game was the culmination of an exciting three-team sprint that resulted in a photo finish be-

tween Cleveland and Boston (96-58) with New York two games back. The Yankees and Red Sox were one game behind the Indians as they prepared to butt heads on the final two days of the season.

Boston kept its hopes alive October 2 as Ted Williams keyed a 5-1 victory over the Yankees with a two-run homer while Bearden was blanking Detroit, 8-0. But Detroit's Hal Newhouser pitched the Tigers to a 7-1 finalday triumph that, coupled with Boston's 10-5 win over New York, forced the playoff.

The A.L. race had been a four-team affair. After games of August 8, Cleveland (60-39) and Philadelphia (63-42) were tied for first with the Yankees (59-42) two games back and Boston (60-44) 2½ behind. An eight-game losing streak in late August ruined the A's.

Cleveland players had reason to celebrate after the Indians defeated Boston in a one-game pennant playoff.

" DUGOUT CHATTER "

"Hustle makes a poor ballplayer into a fair ballplayer, a fair ballplayer into a good ballplayer, a good ballplayer into an excellent player and an excellent player into . . . well, that's the guy I want on my club."

Eddie Sawyer

The new Phillies manager

A key figure in Cleveland's four-shutout streak was 42-year-old Satchel Paige, who is pictured with teammate Larry Doby.

INDIANS SCALP BRAVES

Bob Lemon and Gene Bearden combined on a nine-hitter October 11 and Cleveland completed its Boston Massacre with a 4-3 victory over the Braves that clinched the Indians' second World Series championship.

The Game 6 triumph at Braves Field gave the Indians their first Series title since 1920 and dashed the hopes of Bostonians for the city's first fall classic championship since 1918. To get to the Series, Cleveland had to defeat the Red Sox in a one-game American League pennant playoff and the Indians then disposed of the Braves after a tough opening-game loss.

That first game, played October 6 at Boston, matched a pair of outstanding righthanders — Cleveland's 19-game winner Bob Feller and Boston's Johnny Sain, a 24-game victor. Both were in top form and the game was scoreless entering the last of the eighth inning.

Boston catcher Bill Salkeld walked to open the inning, pinch-runner Phil Masi was sacrificed to second and Eddie Stanky was walked intentionally. Feller and shortstop Lou Bou-

dreau worked a pickoff play at second as Masi was caught off guard, sliding back on a bang-bang play. But umpire Bill Stewart signaled safe.

After Feller retired Sain, Tommy Holmes singled home Masi. Sain completed his four-hit shutout and Feller was a tough-luck loser, having yielded only two hits.

Lemon pitched an eight-hitter and Boudreau and Larry Doby led the offensive charge as Cleveland evened matters the next day with a 4-1 victory. Bearden's five-hit 2-0 win in the first contest at Cleveland and Steve Gromek's 2-1 triumph in Game 4 gave the Indians a three games to one advantage. Bob Elliott's two-homer, four-RBI performance gave the Braves a reprieve in Game 5, an 11-5 victory over Feller, but the Indians closed out the Series when the scene shifted back to Boston.

Joe Gordon hit a solo homer and Boudreau, Eddie Robinson and Jim Hegan drove in runs to lift Lemon to his second victory of the fall classic.

Game 1	Boston	1	Cleveland	0
Game 2	Cleveland	4	Boston	1
Game 3	Cleveland	2	Boston	0
Game 4	Cleveland	2	Boston	1
Game 5	Boston	11	Cleveland	5
Game 6	Cleveland	4	Boston	3

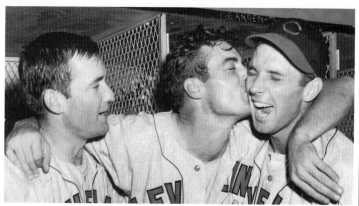

Gene Bearden kisses catcher Jim Hegan as Bob Lemon looks on after Cleveland's Game 6 World Series victory over the Boston Braves.

CAUGHT ON THE FLY

SEPTEMBER
Some heady numbers for Bob Crues, who played for Amarillo of the Class C West Texas-New Mexico League: a .404 batting average, 228 hits, 69 home runs and 254 RBIs — in a 140-game schedule.

OCTOBER
The Homestead Grays captured the final Negro League World Series with a five-game triumph over the Birmingham Black Barons.

The Cleveland Indians set a one-season attendance record with 2,620,627 fans. The Indians drew a one-day record crowd of 82,781 for a June doubleheader.

NOVEMBER
Hall of Famer Hack Wilson, who set the one-season major league RBI record (190) for the Chicago Cubs in 1930, died in Baltimore at age 48.

Indians Manager Lou Boudreau waves to the crowd as his wife and Owner Bill Veeck enjoy Cleveland's World Series victory parade.

Yankees hire Stengel

Colorful Casey Stengel, regarded by many Brooklyn and Boston fans as a managerial buffoon, landed one of the most prestigious jobs in baseball October 12 when he was named to manage the New York Yankees.

Stengel was signed to a two-year contract by Yankee President Dan Topping after guiding the Class AAA Oakland Oaks to the 1948 Pacific Coast League championship. He will take over a proud and experienced New York team that finished third in the American League last season after winning the A.L. pennant

and World Series championship in 1947 under Bucky Harris.

Stengel was a surprise selection after Harris was released. The colorful Casey, a player for 14 seasons with five major league teams and a manager for nine years with Brooklyn and the Boston Braves, brings in a reputation as a lovable clown. He was entertaining at first with both the Dodgers and Braves, but fans became surly when his teams never finished above fifth place.

That will not be good enough in New York, where only winning will be tolerated.

Mexican ban is lifted

Baseball Commissioner A.B. (Happy) Chandler announced June 5 that he was forwarding by mail an offer to reinstate the 18 players who were handed five-year suspensions in 1946 for breaking their contracts and jumping to the outlaw Mexican League.

Chandler said all the jumpers have to do is apply in writing to their league president and reinstatement will be automatic. He told reporters they are being welcomed back now because the gravity of their actions has been driven home to all players and court action has removed the threat of compulsory reinstatement.

Two lawsuits had been filed, one by former New York Giants outfielder Danny Gardella and another by St. Louis Cardinal pitchers Max Lanier and Fred Martin, seeking forced reinstatement on the grounds that baseball's contracts and its entire structure was an illegal violation of anti-trust laws.

A District Court judge ruled in favor of baseball, saying the players had violated their contracts and in effect resigned from their positions voluntarily, and the decision was later affirmed by the Circuit Court of Appeals in New York.

DiMaggios pace A.L.

Two of the DiMaggio brothers, Boston's Dom and the New York Yankees' Joe, combined for four hits and four RBIs to lead the American League to a sloppy 11-7 victory over the National League in the July 12 All-Star Game at Brooklyn's Ebbets Field.

But the result, the A.L.'s 12th victory in 16 midsummer classics, was overshadowed by a more significant occurrence — the first appearance of black players in All-Star Game competition. Brooklyn's Jackie Robinson, Roy Campanella and Don Newcombe played for the Nationals while Cleveland's Larry Doby competed for the A.L. Robinson, who broke the color barrier two years ago, was the only black to get a hit (a first-inning double) while Newcombe allowed two runs in 2⅔ innings and took the loss.

Five N.L. errors, two of which led to four unearned runs in the first inning, contributed greatly to the A.L. victory. So did the one-hit pitching of Yankee Vic Raschi, who set down the N.L. over the last three innings. St. Louis Cardinal Stan Musial and Pittsburgh's Ralph Kiner hit home runs in a losing cause.

Brooklyn's Jackie Robinson, posing with Yankees Joe Gordon (center) and Joe DiMaggio (right), was one of four blacks who broke the All-Star Game color barrier.

Phillies' star shot

Philadelphia Phillies first baseman Eddie Waitkus was shot and seriously wounded in a Chicago hotel room June 15 by an obsessive 19-year-old woman with a secret crush on him.

The bizarre incident occurred at the fashionable Edgewater Beach Hotel, where the Phillies were staying during a series with the Cubs. Ruth Steinhagen, a typist, lured the 28-year-old former Chicago star to her room with an urgent note. When Waitkus entered and sat down, Steinhagen pulled a rifle from the closet and shot him near the heart.

Waitkus, a four-year veteran who hit .295 last year for Chicago, was rushed to Illinois Masonic Hospital. His doctor described his condition as serious, but said the bleeding was under control and he expected Waitkus to recover barring unusual complications.

Steinhagen told police she wanted "to do something exciting in my life" and admitted she had considered killing somebody for two years. Steinhagen's mother and friends said she had a major crush on Waitkus and wrote him lots of letters. When he was traded to Philadelphia, she threatened to move there to be near him. Steinhagen had visited two psychiatrists about her obsessive behavior.

Philadelphia's Eddie Waitkus, still recuperating after being shot by a feminine admirer in Chicago, visits with teammates Robin Roberts (left) and Russ Meyer (right) at Shibe Park.

CAUGHT ON THE FLY

FEBRUARY
Yankee great Joe DiMaggio signed a contract for $100,000, the first six-figure pact in baseball history.

APRIL
During pregame ceremonies before the Yankee Stadium home opener, a granite monument honoring Babe Ruth and plaques honoring Lou Gehrig and Miller Huggins were unveiled.

JUNE
The Philadelphia Phillies exploded for a major league record-tying five home runs in the eighth inning of a 12-3 victory over Cincinnati at Shibe Park. Andy Seminick hit two during the 10-run onslaught while Del Ennis, Willie Jones and pitcher Schoolboy Rowe hit one apiece.

AUGUST
New York Yankees righthander Vic Raschi stopped the Boston-record 34-game hitting streak of Red Sox center fielder Dom DiMaggio.

Kiner hits 54 homers

Pittsburgh slugger Ralph Kiner captured his fourth home run title and became the first National Leaguer to reach the 50-homer plateau twice when he finished the campaign with 54, three more than he hit in 1947.

Kiner's final blast came during a 3-2 September 30 victory over Cincinnati when he drove a pitch over the Forbes Field scoreboard clock in left field. That gave him an N.L.-record 16 home runs in one month, one more than Cy Williams managed for Philadelphia in May 1923. Detroit's Rudy York set the major league mark of 18 in August 1937.

Kiner's total was two behind the N.L.-record 56 hit by Chicago's Hack Wilson in 1930 and six behind former New York Yankee great Babe Ruth's all-time mark of 60 (1927). Kiner belted his 51st and 52nd home runs against Boston with nine days remaining in the season.

Of Kiner's 29 blasts at Forbes Field, 14 went into the bullpen enclosure known affectionately as "Greenberg Gardens." The left-

Pittsburgh slugger Ralph Kiner, a two-time 50-home run man.

field fence was shortened in 1947 when the Pirates acquired veteran Detroit slugger Hank Greenberg, but the area has more accurately been dubbed "Kiner's Korner."

" DUGOUT CHATTER "

"The man is tremendous. When you think of the things he has accomplished in Cleveland, you have to rate him No. 1. If I had the money to invest in a ball club, he's the fellow I'd want running it. He's the greatest in the business."

Lou Boudreau

Cleveland manager, on team Owner Bill Veeck

Indians bury pennant

In a late-season promotion that only Bill Veeck could have dreamed up, the Cleveland Indians buried their 1949 American League pennant hopes in a "grave" behind the center-field fence at Municipal Stadium.

As 35,000 fans looked on before a September 23 game against Detroit, Veeck, wearing a top hat and wiping his eyes in mock sadness, drove a horse-drawn hearse at the head of a funeral procession to the grave-site. A casket was removed from the hearse by Indians Manager Lou Boudreau and his coaches, who served as pallbearers, and last rites were read over the grave by business manager Rudie Schaffer from *The Sporting News*, "the bible of baseball."

When the ceremony concluded, a tombstone was set in place bearing the inscription "1948 champs" in honor of Cleveland's 1948 World Series championship. Fans were allowed to pay their last respects.

The Tigers, obviously not moved by the occasion, recorded a 5-0 victory.

SEASON LEADERS

	American League		National League	
Avg.	George Kell, Det.	.343	Jackie Robinson, Bkn.	.342
HR	Ted Williams, Bos.	43	Ralph Kiner, Pit.	54
RBI	Ted Williams, Bos.	159	Ralph Kiner, Pit.	127
	Vern Stephens, Bos.	159		
SB	Robert Dillinger, St. L.	20	Jackie Robinson, Bkn.	37
W-L Pct.	Ellis Kinder, Bos.	23-6, .793	Preacher Roe, Bkn. 15-6, .714	
ERA	Mel Parnell, Bos.	2.77	Dave Koslo, N.Y.	2.50
SO	Virgil Trucks, Det.	153	Warren Spahn, Bos.	151

Tiny Bonham dies

Ernie (Tiny) Bonham, a 103-game winner in 10 major league seasons, died September 15 at a Pittsburgh hospital when complications arose from an appendectomy. The 36-year-old Bonham had recorded an 8-2 victory over Philadelphia in his final big-league pitching appearance 18 days earlier.

Bonham, who was 7-4 and a winner of six straight decisions for the Pirates when he entered the hospital for his emergency appendicitis operation, was a 10-year veteran who had spent his best seasons with the New York Yankees. A 21-game winner for the Bronx Bombers in 1942, Bonham helped pitch Joe McCarthy's New Yorkers to three pennants and worked the Yankees' World Series clincher against the Brooklyn Dodgers in 1941.

Hampered by a chronic bad back, Bonham was sold to the Pirates in 1946 and worked mostly as a spot starter.

Bonham was listed as 6-foot-2, 210 pounds by major league rosters, but those numbers were conservative, especially in his later years. Hence the nickname "Tiny."

Coaches, players officials and Cleveland Owner Bill Veeck (holding handkerchief) listen to business manager Rudie Schaffer read last rites from The Sporting News, *"the bible of baseball," over the Indians' lost pennant hopes.*

★1949★

Dodgers clinch late

The Brooklyn Dodgers pushed across two 10th-inning runs against Philadelphia lefthander Ken Heintzelman October 2 for a 9-7 season-ending victory that clinched the Flatbushers' third National League pennant of the decade.

The Cardinals already had snapped their untimely four-game losing streak with a 13-5 final-day win at Chicago that put them in position to force a pennant playoff should the Dodgers lose at Shibe Park. And Brooklyn showed signs of faltering when rookie 17-game winner Don Newcombe squandered a 5-0 advantage and allowed the Phillies to rally for a 7-7 tie. But the Dodgers broke through in the 10th to end one of the most exciting pennant races in N.L. history.

The Cardinals had struggled early in the campaign, but battled back. They moved into first place on July 24 and, except for three days in mid-August, remained there until September 29. The Dodgers, however, doggedly shadowed their rivals.

When the Cardinals won their final home contest on September 25, they held a 1½-game lead with five to play. But two losses to Pittsburgh combined with a pair of Brooklyn wins put the Dodgers on top by a half-game. St. Louis missed its chance to tie the idle Dodgers when it lost to the Cubs, 6-5, on September 30, and the Cardinals' skid continued the next day when they lost to Chicago, 3-1. But Brooklyn missed its chance to clinch, falling to the Phillies, 6-4.

Sporting a one-game lead going into the final day, Burt Shotton's Dodgers ended the drama by recording their 97th win.

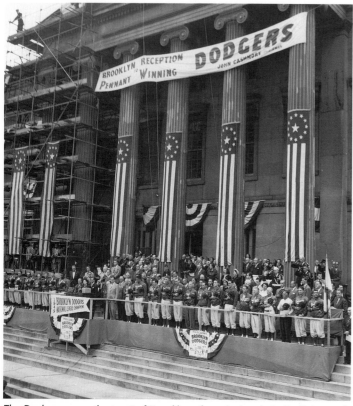

The Dodgers were the toast of Brooklyn after winning their third National League pennant of the decade.

Yanks hold off Boston

A solo home run by Tommy Henrich and Jerry Coleman's bases-loaded bloop double scored four eighth-inning runs October 2 and provided Vic Raschi the cushion he needed to wrap up a 5-3 New York victory over Boston and the Yankees' 16th American League pennant.

The final-day triumph, Raschi's 21st of the season, broke a first-place deadlock between the Yankees and Red Sox and ended another outstanding pennant race. Boston had lost in a one-game playoff last year to Cleveland after the teams finished with identical 96-58 records.

The Red Sox, managed by former Yankee boss Joe McCarthy, came agonizingly close again, needing only one victory in their final two games to win their second pennant in 31 years. But Boston squandered a 4-0 lead October 1 and lost, 5-4, on Johnny Lindell's eighth-inning homer. The Yankees led the finale, 1-0, when they broke through in the eighth. Raschi survived a ninth-inning Boston rally as the Yanks recorded their 97th victory.

The defeat spoiled a gallant Boston comeback from a 12-game deficit. After the All-Star Game the Red Sox sizzled, winning 19 of 23 games in one stretch and 24 of 32 in August. By Labor Day, they trailed by only 1½ games and they caught the Yankees September 25 when Mel Parnell shut down the Bombers, 4-1. When Boston rallied the next day for a 7-6 victory, the Yankees dropped out of the lead for the first time in the 161-day-old season.

Boston clung to that slim one-game margin, setting the stage for the tense two-game showdown that would decide the pennant.

Righthander Vic Raschi pitched the New York Yankees to a final-day pennant-clinching victory over Boston.

" DUGOUT CHATTER "

"Sure I'm ugly, but what about it? In this racket, all you have to do is hit the ball and I ain't never seen anybody hit it with his face."

Yogi Berra

Yankee catcher

Robinson wins MVP

When Brooklyn second baseman Jackie Robinson walked away with the National League Most Valuable Player award and teammate Don Newcombe, a 17-game winner, was named N.L. Rookie of the Year, baseball officially received notice that black players figure to play a major role in the sport for years to come.

Robinson was listed first on 12 of the 24 ballots turned in by the Baseball Writers' Association of America committee. The man who broke baseball's color barrier outdistanced St. Louis' Stan Musial after winning the N.L. batting title with a .342 mark.

Newcombe, 17-8 with 19 complete games, and St. Louis Browns outfielder Roy Sievers, a .306 hitter with 16 homers and 91 RBIs, were the leagues' top rookies. It was the first time the BBWAA had honored first-year players from both circuits.

American League MVP honors went to Boston's Ted Williams, who won the award for the second time. Williams barely missed what would have been a record third Triple Crown when he was edged in the race for his fifth batting title on the last day of the season by Detroit's George Kell.

Williams, who led the league with 43 homers and tied with teammate Vern Stephens for RBI honors with 159, went hitless in two final-day at-bats to finish at .3427. Kell went 2-for-3 and finished at .3429.

N.L. batting champion Jackie Robinson of Brooklyn receives his 1949 Most Valuable Player award from Commissioner Ford Frick.

CAUGHT ON THE FLY

NOVEMBER

A group headed by insurance executive Ellis W. Ryan purchased controlling interest of the Cleveland Indians from Bill Veeck for $2.2 million.

DECEMBER

The major league Rules Committee shortened the strike zone, redefining it as the area over home plate between the batter's armpits and the top of his knees.

WORLD SERIES REPORT

YANKEES BELT DODGERS

Jerry Coleman drove in three runs as New York built a 10-2 lead and reliever Joe Page shut down Brooklyn's Game 5 comeback attempt with 2⅓ scoreless innings as the Yankees closed out their 12th World Series championship October 9 with a 10-6 victory over the Dodgers at Ebbets Field.

Coleman doubled and singled in support of starter Vic Raschi, who was cruising until Gil Hodges belted a three-run seventh-inning homer that cut the Yankee lead to four. Page came in to close the door on the Yankees' first title under Manager Casey Stengel.

The teams, both of which ended the campaign with 97-57 records, appeared to be evenly matched. And the first two games did nothing to dispel that notion.

For eight innings in the opener at Yankee Stadium, Brooklyn's Don Newcombe and New York's Allie Reynolds staged an outstanding pitching duel. Newcombe yielded four hits and no walks while striking out 11. Reynolds permitted only two hits while walking four and striking out nine. Reynolds retired the Dodgers in order in the ninth to keep the game scoreless, but Tommy Henrich spoiled Newcombe's effort in the bottom of the inning with a solo homer.

The Dodgers secured a 1-0 victory of their own the next day, with Preacher Roe outpitching Raschi and Hodges singling home the game's only run in the second inning. But that would be Brooklyn's last hurrah in this fall classic.

Three ninth-inning runs gave the Yankees a 4-3 third-game win and the New Yorkers went ahead by two games with a 6-4 win in Game 4. When the Dodgers lost the finale, they went down in World Series competition for the fifth time in as many tries and the third time to the Yankees.

Game 1	New York	1	Brooklyn	0
Game 2	Brooklyn	1	New York	0
Game 3	New York	4	Brooklyn	3
Game 4	New York	6	Brooklyn	4
Game 5	New York	10	Brooklyn	6

New York's Tommy Henrich heads for home after belting a game-deciding ninth-inning home run off Brooklyn's Don Newcombe in Game 1 of the World Series.

The 1950s

As Casey Stengel's New York Yankee machine marched relentlessly into the 1950s, a fuse was quietly burning its way toward a powder keg.

Not even the Bronx Bombers' unprecedented five straight World Series championships could muffle the coming technological explosion that would open the door to revolutionary change while redefining the boundaries and values of a sport in transition.

Transition as in more efficient automobiles that would carry a society to the suburbs. Transition as in improved air travel that would help trigger a population shift west. The two coasts and everything between would be linked by more sophisticated communication methods.

The most important method was television and those with foresight began to grasp the innovative little tube's power potential. Its equipment and techniques were crude and it was lacking in direction, but that soon would change. Enterprising major league officials courted the new medium at the expense of their minor league brethren, a courtship that eventually would lead to marriage.

That marriage would mean money — lots of money. And with that

NATIONAL LEAGUE

League Batting Leaders

Average

Year	Player-Team	Avg.
1950	Stan Musial, St. L.	.346
1951	Stan Musial, St. L.	.355
1952	Stan Musial, St. L.	.336
1953	Carl Furillo, Bkn.	.344
1954	Willie Mays, N.Y.	.345
1955	Richie Ashburn, Phil.	.338
1956	Hank Aaron, Mil.	.328
1957	Stan Musial, St. L.	.351
1958	Richie Ashburn, Phil.	.350
1959	Hank Aaron, Mil.	.355

Home Runs

Year	Player-Team	HR
1950	Ralph Kiner, Pit.	47
1951	Ralph Kiner, Pit.	42
1952	Ralph Kiner, Pit.	37
	Hank Sauer, Chi.	37
1953	Eddie Mathews, Mil.	47
1954	Ted Kluszewski, Cin.	49
1955	Willie Mays, N.Y.	51
1956	Duke Snider, Bkn.	43
1957	Hank Aaron, Mil.	44
1958	Ernie Banks, Chi.	47
1959	Eddie Mathews, Mil.	46

RBIs

Year	Player-Team	RBI
1950	Del Ennis, Phil.	126
1951	Monte Irvin, N.Y.	121
1952	Hank Sauer, Chi.	121
1953	Roy Campanella, Bkn.	142
1954	Ted Kluszewski, Cin.	141
1955	Duke Snider, Bkn.	136
1956	Stan Musial, St. L.	109
1957	Hank Aaron, Mil.	132
1958	Ernie Banks, Chi.	129
1959	Ernie Banks, Chi.	143

Most Valuable Players

Selected by BBWAA

Year	Player-Team	Pos.
1950	Jim Konstanty, Phil.	P
1951	Roy Campanella, Bkn.	C
1952	Hank Sauer, Chi.	OF
1953	Roy Campanella, Bkn.	C
1954	Willie Mays, N.Y.	OF
1955	Roy Campanella, Bkn.	C
1956	Don Newcombe, Bkn.	P
1957	Hank Aaron, Mil.	OF
1958	Ernie Banks, Chi.	SS
1959	Ernie Banks, Chi.	SS

League Pitching Leaders

Winning Percentage

Year	Pitcher-Team	W-L	Pct.
1950	Sal Maglie, N.Y.	18-4	.818
1951	Preacher Roe, Bkn.	22-3	.880
1952	Hoyt Wilhelm, N.Y.	15-3	.833
1953	Carl Erskine, Bkn.	20-6	.769
1954	Johnny Antonelli, N.Y.		
		21-7	.750
1955	Don Newcombe, Bkn.		
		20-5	.800
1956	Don Newcombe, Bkn.		
		27-7	.794
1957	Bob Buhl, Mil.	18-7	.720
1958	Warren Spahn, Mil.	22-11	.667
	Lew Burdette, Mil.	20-10	.667
1959	Roy Face, Pit.	18-1	.947

Earned-Run Average

Year	Pitcher-Team	ERA
1950	Jim Hearn, St. L.-N.Y.	2.49
1951	Chet Nichols, Bos.	2.88
1952	Hoyt Wilhelm, N.Y.	2.43
1953	Warren Spahn, Mil.	2.10
1954	Johnny Antonelli, N.Y.	2.29
1955	Bob Friend, Pit.	2.84
1956	Lew Burdette, Mil.	2.71
1957	Johnny Podres, Bkn.	2.66
1958	Stu Miller, S.F.	2.47
1959	Sam Jones, S.F.	2.82

Strikeouts

Year	Pitcher-Team	SO
1950	Warren Spahn, Bos.	191
1951	Don Newcombe, Bkn.	164
	Warren Spahn, Bos.	164
1952	Warren Spahn, Bos.	183
1953	Robin Roberts, Phil.	198
1954	Robin Roberts, Phil.	185
1955	Sam Jones, Chi.	198
1956	Sam Jones, Chi.	176
1957	Jack Sanford, Phil.	188
1958	Sam Jones, St. L.	225
1959	Don Drysdale, L.A.	242

Cy Young Winners

A.L. and N.L. combined

Year	Pitcher-Team	Thr.
1956	Don Newcombe, Bkn.	R
1957	Warren Spahn, Mil.	L
1958	Bob Turley, N.Y.	R
1959	Early Wynn, Chi. (A.L.)	R

WORLD SERIES

Year	Winner	Pennant Winner	Games
1950	New York Yankees	Philadelphia Phillies	4-0
1951	New York Yankees	New York Giants	4-2
1952	New York Yankees	Brooklyn Dodgers	4-3
1953	New York Yankees	Brooklyn Dodgers	4-2
1954	New York Giants	Cleveland Indians	4-0
1955	Brooklyn Dodgers	New York Yankees	4-3
1956	New York Yankees	Brooklyn Dodgers	4-3
1957	Milwaukee Braves	New York Yankees	4-3
1958	New York Yankees	Milwaukee Braves	4-3
1959	Los Angeles Dodgers	Chicago White Sox	4-2

HALL OF FAME   Electees and Additions

1951	Mel Ott, Jimmie Foxx.
1952	Harry Heilmann, Paul Waner.
1953	Dizzy Dean, Al Simmons, Chief Bender, Bobby Wallace, Bill Klem, Tom Connolly, Edward G. Barrow, Harry Wright.
1954	Rabbit Maranville, Bill Dickey, Bill Terry.
1955	Joe DiMaggio, Ted Lyons, Dazzy Vance, Gabby Hartnett, Frank (Home Run) Baker, Ray Schalk.
1956	Hank Greenberg, Joe Cronin.
1957	Joe McCarthy, Sam Crawford.
1959	Zack Wheat.

Final Standings

*Defeated Brooklyn 2-1 in pennant playoff   †Defeated Milwaukee 2-0 in pennant playoff

1950

	W	L	PCT.	GB
Philadelphia	91	63	.591	--
Brooklyn	89	65	.578	2
New York	86	68	.558	5
Boston	83	71	.539	8
St. Louis	78	75	.510	12.5
Cincinnati	66	87	.431	24.5
Chicago	64	89	.418	26.5
Pittsburgh	57	96	.373	33.5

1951

	W	L	Pct.	GB
*New York	98	59	.624	--
Brooklyn	97	60	.618	1
St. Louis	81	73	.526	15.5
Boston	76	78	.494	20.5
Philadelphia	73	81	.474	23.5
Cincinnati	68	86	.442	28.5
Pittsburgh	64	90	.416	32.5
Chicago	62	92	.403	34.5

1952

	W	L	Pct.	GB
Brooklyn	96	57	.627	--
New York	92	62	.597	4.5
St. Louis	88	66	.571	8.5
Philadelphia	87	67	.565	9.5
Chicago	77	77	.500	19.5
Cincinnati	69	85	.448	27.5
Boston	64	89	.418	32
Pittsburgh	42	112	.273	54.5

1953

	W	L	Pct.	GB
Brooklyn	105	49	.682	--
Milwaukee	92	62	.597	13
Philadelphia	83	71	.539	22
St. Louis	83	71	.539	22
New York	70	84	.455	35
Cincinnati	68	86	.442	37
Chicago	65	89	.422	40
Pittsburgh	50	104	.325	55

1954

	W	L	Pct.	GB
New York	97	57	.630	--
Brooklyn	92	62	.597	5
Milwaukee	89	65	.578	8
Philadelphia	75	79	.487	22
Cincinnati	74	80	.481	23
St. Louis	72	82	.468	25
Chicago	64	90	.416	33
Pittsburgh	53	101	.344	44

1955

	W	L	Pct.	GB
Brooklyn	98	55	.641	--
Milwaukee	85	69	.552	13.5
New York	80	74	.519	18.5
Philadelphia	77	77	.500	21.5
Cincinnati	75	79	.487	23.5
Chicago	72	81	.471	26
St. Louis	68	86	.442	30.5
Pittsburgh	60	94	.390	38.5

1956

	W	L	Pct.	GB
Brooklyn	93	61	.604	--
Milwaukee	92	62	.597	1
Cincinnati	91	63	.591	2
St. Louis	76	78	.494	17
Philadelphia	71	83	.461	22
New York	67	87	.435	26
Pittsburgh	66	88	.429	27
Chicago	60	94	.390	33

1957

	W	L	Pct.	GB
Milwaukee	95	59	.617	--
St. Louis	87	67	.565	8
Brooklyn	84	70	.545	11
Cincinnati	80	74	.519	15
Philadelphia	77	77	.500	18
New York	69	85	.448	26
Chicago	62	92	.403	33
Pittsburgh	62	92	.403	33

1958

	W	L	Pct.	GB
Milwaukee	92	62	.597	--
Pittsburgh	84	70	.545	8
S.F.	80	74	.519	12
Cincinnati	76	78	.494	16
Chicago	72	82	.468	20
St. Louis	72	82	.468	20
Los Angeles	71	83	.461	21
Philadelphia	69	85	.448	23

1959

	W	L	Pct.	GB
†Los Angeles	88	68	.564	--
Milwaukee	86	70	.551	2
S.F.	83	71	.539	4
Pittsburgh	78	76	.506	9
Chicago	74	80	.481	13
Cincinnati	74	80	.481	13
St. Louis	71	83	.461	16
Philadelphia	64	90	.416	23

Brooklyn slugger Duke Snider.

prospect just around the corner, officials began jockeying for position. The new infatuation with television exposed some distasteful realities.

With the exodus to the suburbs and the growth of major metropolises, sports officials began looking to the previously ignored but more fertile markets. *Fertile* as in *big*. The result was a rash of franchise shifts in search of that all-important bottom line.

The official linking of sports to big business was made in 1957, when the New York Giants and Brooklyn Dodgers, two of baseball's most glamorous and beloved franchises, jolted their fans with the announcements they were moving to the West Coast. Those shifts followed on the heels of the Boston Braves moving to Milwaukee, the St. Louis Browns to Baltimore and the Philadelphia Athletics to Kansas City. Before Milwaukee, baseball had not seen a franchise shift in 50 years.

As the owners jockeyed for position, so did the players, whose financial status strengthened with the formation of the Major League Players Association and periodic challenges to baseball's reserve system.

The Yankees dominated the decade by winning six World Series, but the most dramatic moment was supplied by Giants outfielder Bobby Thomson, who won the National League pennant with his "Shot Heard 'Round the World." Other magical moments were provided by Yankee pitcher Don Larsen, who pitched a World Series perfect game; Pittsburgh's Dale Long, who hit home runs in eight consecutive games; St. Louis' Stan Musial, who hit five homers in a doubleheader, and Pittsburgh's Harvey Haddix, who pitched 12 perfect innings against Milwaukee — only to lose in the 13th.

On a sad note, the outstanding career of Dodger catcher Roy Campanella was ended by a paralyzing car accident, and on a positive note, the Boston Red Sox became the last team to break the color barrier. As the decade closed, the new Continental League provided a threat to baseball's establishment. Expansion was just ahead.

Cleveland strongman Al Rosen.

AMERICAN LEAGUE

League Batting Leaders

Average

Year	Player-Team	Avg.
1950	Billy Goodman, Bos.	.354
1951	Ferris Fain, Phil.	.344
1952	Ferris Fain, Phil.	.327
1953	Mickey Vernon, Wash.	.337
1954	Bobby Avila, Cle.	.341
1955	Al Kaline, Det.	.340
1956	Mickey Mantle, N.Y.	.353
1957	Ted Williams, Bos.	.388
1958	Ted Williams, Bos.	.328
1959	Harvey Kuenn, Det.	.353

Home Runs

Year	Player-Team	HR
1950	Al Rosen, Cle.	37
1951	Gus Zernial, Chi.-Phil.	33
1952	Larry Doby, Cle.	32
1953	Al Rosen, Cle.	43
1954	Larry Doby, Cle.	32
1955	Mickey Mantle, N.Y.	37
1956	Mickey Mantle, N.Y.	52
1957	Roy Sievers, Wash.	42
1958	Mickey Mantle, N.Y.	42
1959	Harmon Killebrew, Wash.	42
	Rocky Colavito, Cle.	42

RBIs

Year	Player-Team	RBI
1950	Walt Dropo, Bos.	144
	Vern Stephens, Bos.	144
1951	Gus Zernial, Chi.-Phil.	129
1952	Al Rosen, Cle.	105
1953	Al Rosen, Cle.	145
1954	Larry Doby, Cle.	126
1955	Ray Boone, Det.	116
	Jackie Jensen, Bos.	116
1956	Mickey Mantle, N.Y.	130
1957	Roy Sievers, Wash.	114
1958	Jackie Jensen, Bos.	122
1959	Jackie Jensen, Bos.	112

Most Valuable Players

Selected by BBWAA

Year	Player-Team	Pos.
1950	Phil Rizzuto, N.Y.	SS
1951	Yogi Berra, N.Y.	C
1952	Bobby Shantz, Phil.	P
1953	Al Rosen, Cle.	3B
1954	Yogi Berra, N.Y.	C
1955	Yogi Berra, N.Y.	C
1956	Mickey Mantle, N.Y.	OF
1957	Mickey Mantle, N.Y.	OF
1958	Jackie Jensen, Bos.	OF
1959	Nellie Fox, Chi.	2B

League Pitching Leaders

Winning Percentage

Year	Pitcher-Team	W-L	Pct.
1950	Vic Raschi, N.Y.	21-8	.724
1951	Bob Feller, Cle.	22-8	.733
1952	Bobby Shantz, Phil.	24-7	.774
1953	Ed Lopat, N.Y.	16-4	.800
1954	Sandy Consuegra, Chi.	16-3	.842
1955	Tommy Byrne, N.Y.	16-5	.762
1956	Whitey Ford, N.Y.	19-6	.760
1957	Dick Donovan, Chi.	16-6	.727
	Tom Sturdivant, N.Y.	16-6	.727
1958	Bob Turley, N.Y.	21-7	.750
1959	Bob Shaw, Chi.	18-6	.750

Earned-Run Average

Year	Pitcher-Team	ERA
1950	Early Wynn, Cle.	3.20
1951	Saul Rogovin, Det.-Chi.	2.78
1952	Allie Reynolds, N.Y.	2.06
1953	Ed Lopat, N.Y.	2.42
1954	Mike Garcia, Cle.	2.64
1955	Billy Pierce, Chi.	1.97
1956	Whitey Ford, N.Y.	2.47
1957	Bobby Shantz, N.Y.	2.45
1958	Whitey Ford, N.Y.	2.01
1959	Hoyt Wilhelm, Bal.	2.19

Strikeouts

Year	Pitcher-Team	SO
1950	Bob Lemon, Cle.	170
1951	Vic Raschi, N.Y.	164
1952	Allie Reynolds, N.Y.	160
1953	Billy Pierce, Chi.	186
1954	Bob Turley, Bal.	185
1955	Herb Score, Cle.	245
1956	Herb Score, Cle.	263
1957	Early Wynn, Cle.	184
1958	Early Wynn, Chi.	179
1959	Jim Bunning, Det.	201

Cy Young Winners

A.L. and N.L. combined

Year	Pitcher-Team	Thr.
1956	Don Newcombe, Bkn.	R
1957	Warren Spahn, Mil.	L
1958	Bob Turley, N.Y.	R
1959	Early Wynn, Chi. (A.L.)	R

Final Standings

1950

	W	L	PCT.	GB
New York	98	56	.636	--
Detroit	95	59	.617	3
Boston	94	60	.610	4
Cleveland	92	62	.597	6
Washington	67	87	.435	31
Chicago	60	94	.390	38
St. Louis	58	96	.377	40
Philadelphia	52	102	.338	46

1951

	W	L	Pct.	GB
New York	98	56	.636	--
Cleveland	93	61	.604	5
Boston	87	67	.565	11
Chicago	81	73	.526	17
Detroit	73	81	.474	25
Philadelphia	70	84	.455	28
Washington	62	92	.403	36
St. Louis	52	102	.338	46

1952

	W	L	Pct.	GB
New York	95	59	.617	--
Cleveland	93	61	.604	2
Chicago	81	73	.526	14
Philadelphia	79	75	.513	16
Washington	78	76	.506	17
Boston	76	78	.494	19
St. Louis	64	90	.416	31
Detroit	50	104	.325	45

1953

	W	L	Pct.	GB
New York	99	52	.656	--
Cleveland	92	62	.597	8.5
Chicago	89	65	.578	11.5
Boston	84	69	.549	16
Washington	76	76	.500	23.5
Detroit	60	94	.390	40.5
Philadelphia	59	95	.383	41.5
St. Louis	54	100	.351	46.5

1954

	W	L	Pct.	GB
Cleveland	111	43	.721	--
New York	103	51	.669	8
Chicago	94	60	.610	17
Boston	69	85	.448	42
Detroit	68	86	.442	43
Washington	66	88	.429	45
Baltimore	54	100	.351	57
Philadelphia	51	103	.331	60

1955

	W	L	Pct.	GB
New York	96	58	.623	--
Cleveland	93	61	.604	3
Chicago	91	63	.591	5
Boston	84	70	.545	12
Detroit	79	75	.513	17
Kansas City	63	91	.409	33
Baltimore	57	97	.370	39
Washington	53	101	.344	43

1956

	W	L	Pct.	GB
New York	97	57	.630	--
Cleveland	88	66	.571	9
Chicago	85	69	.552	12
Boston	84	70	.545	13
Detroit	82	72	.532	15
Baltimore	69	85	.448	28
Washington	59	95	.383	38
Kansas City	52	102	.338	45

1957

	W	L	Pct.	GB
New York	98	56	.636	--
Chicago	90	64	.584	8
Boston	82	72	.532	16
Detroit	78	76	.506	20
Baltimore	76	76	.500	21
Cleveland	76	77	.497	21.5
Kansas City	59	94	.386	38.5
Washington	55	99	.357	43

1958

	W	L	Pct.	GB
New York	92	62	.597	--
Chicago	82	72	.532	10
Boston	79	75	.513	13
Cleveland	77	76	.503	14.5
Detroit	77	77	.500	15
Baltimore	74	79	.484	17.5
Kansas City	73	81	.474	19
Washington	61	93	.396	31

1959

	W	L	Pct.	GB
Chicago	94	60	.610	--
Cleveland	89	65	.578	5
New York	79	75	.513	15
Detroit	76	78	.494	18
Boston	75	79	.487	19
Baltimore	74	80	.481	20
Kansas City	66	88	.429	28
Washington	63	91	.409	31

★1950★

Stars go Hollywood

It was no April Fools' Day gag when the Hollywood Stars of the Class AAA Pacific Coast League trotted onto the field for their April 1 game against Portland clad in T-shirt-style uniform tops and pin-striped shorts.

The innovative garb was greeted by catcalls from amused Hollywood fans and Portland Manager Bill Sweeney joined in the fun by presenting Hollywood Manager Fred Haney with a bouquet of pansies at the home plate lineup exchange while wearing a long, curly wig and an apron.

"This isn't a gag, nor are we going Hollywood," Haney said of the shorts, which are expected to provide welcome relief for the players on those soon-to-come hot and steamy summer days. "It stands to reason that players should be faster wearing them — and that half step down to first wins or loses many games."

Hollywood Stars Manager Fred Haney, modeling his team's innovative new attire.

CAUGHT ON THE FLY

JANUARY
Pittsburgh gave 18-year-old pitcher Paul Pettit a record $100,000 bonus to sign with the Pirates.

JUNE
The Cleveland Indians erupted for 14 runs in the first inning against the Philadelphia Athletics, tying a modern major league record for most runs in one inning and setting the mark for most runs in a first frame.

JULY
Stan Musial, trying to extend his 30-game streak, was the only St. Louis regular who failed to get a hit off five Brooklyn pitchers in a 13-3 Cardinal victory.

AUGUST
Boston righthander Vern Bickford pitched the first major league no-hitter in nearly two years, stopping Brooklyn, 7-0, at Braves Field.

"DUGOUT CHATTER"

"Leo never takes it out on me when he comes home to dinner after a losing game. He takes it out on the players before he leaves the park."

Laraine Day

The actress, on husband Leo Durocher, the temperamental manager of the Giants

A home run derby

The Detroit Tigers won an unprecedented home run duel from the New York Yankees June 23 and escaped with a 10-9 victory that gave them a two-game lead over the Bronx Bombers.

Before 51,400 screaming fans at Briggs Stadium, the teams combined for a one-game record 11 home runs in a contest that was decided in the ninth inning by Hoot Evers' two-run inside-the-park blast off New York reliever Joe Page.

Every run in the exciting contest was driven in by a home run. Evers connected twice for the Tigers, pitcher Dizzy Trout added a grand slam, Vic Wertz belted a two-run shot and Gerry Priddy a solo job. Hank Bauer hit two homers for New York while Yogi Berra, Jerry Coleman, Joe DiMaggio and Tommy Henrich hit one apiece. Henrich's pinch-hit two-run shot in the eighth-inning had given the Yankees a 9-8 advantage.

Ironically, except for Evers' game-winner, all of Detroit's home runs were hit during an eight-run fourth-inning explosion against pitchers Tommy Byrne and Fred Sanford.

Detroit's Hoot Evers connected twice as the Tigers and New York Yankees combined for a one-game record 11 home runs.

Red Sox demolish Browns, 29-4

The Boston Red Sox, fresh off a 20-4 thrashing of St. Louis a day earlier, humiliated the Browns June 8 with an unprecedented offensive explosion that smashed four major league records and amazed a small crowd at Fenway Park.

Boston's 29-4 victory set records for most runs by one team, most total bases in a game (60), most runs by one team in consecutive games (49) and most hits by a team in two straight contests (51). Johnny Pesky and Al Zarilla accounted for 10 of Boston's 28 hits and three players combined for seven home runs and 20 RBIs.

Bobby Doerr drove in eight runs with three homers, Walt Dropo homered twice and drove in seven and Ted Williams bashed a pair of round-trippers while driving in five. Winning pitcher Chuck Stobbs collected two hits and walked four consecutive times.

Boston exploded for eight runs in the second inning, five in the third, seven in the fourth, two in the fifth, two in the seventh and five in the eighth while posting its sixth win in seven games on the current homestand. During those games, the Red Sox have outscored their opposition, 104-37. Boston's June 7 win featured 23 hits, six home runs and 42 total bases.

Schoendienst homer wins All-Star Game

St. Louis Cardinals second baseman Red Schoendienst, who had watched the first 10 innings of the July 11 All-Star Game from the bench, belted a dramatic 14th-inning home run off Detroit lefthander Ted Gray to give the National League a 4-3 victory that snapped the American League's winning streak at four games. The A.L. still leads the series, 12-5.

Schoendienst, who had replaced Brooklyn's Jackie Robinson defensively in the 11th inning, made his first All-Star at-bat a memorable one by driving Gray's pitch into the left-field seats at Chicago's Comiskey Park. The blast ended the first extra-inning All-Star contest.

Burt Shotton's National Leaguers had tied the score in the ninth when Pittsburgh slugger Ralph Kiner homered off Detroit's Art Houtteman. Giants curveballer Larry Jansen and Cincinnati's Ewell Blackwell were outstanding over the last eight innings for the N.L., while the Americans got good efforts from Cleveland's Bob Lemon and Yankee Allie Reynolds.

Brooklyn Manager Burt Shotton (center) with N.L. All-Star Game home run hitters Ralph Kiner of Pittsburgh and Red Schoendienst of St. Louis.

	American League		**National League**	
		SEASON LEADERS		
Avg.	Billy Goodman, Bos.	.354	Stan Musial, St. L.	.346
HR	Al Rosen, Cle.	37	Ralph Kiner, Pit.	47
RBI	Walt Dropo. Bos.	144	Del Ennis, Phi.	126
	Vern Stephens, Bos.	144		
SB	Dom DiMaggio, Bos.	15	Sam Jethroe, Bos.	35
W-L Pct.	Vic Raschi, N.Y.	21-8, .724	Sal Maglie, N.Y.	18-4, .818
ERA	Early Wynn, Cle.	3.20	Jim Hearn, St. L.-N.Y.	2.49
SO	Bob Lemon, Cle.	170	Warren Spahn, Bos.	191

Hodges blasts four

Big Brooklyn first baseman Gil Hodges joined an exclusive fraternity August 31 when he became the fourth modern player and sixth of all time to hit four home runs in a single game. Hodges' four blasts and nine runs batted in sparked a 19-3 Dodger rout of Boston at Ebbets Field.

Hodges connected off four different pitchers in the second, third, sixth and eighth innings. Carl Furillo was on base for each blow and Jackie Robinson also was aboard in the third. Hodges' homer blitz was interrupted by a ground out in the fourth and a single in the seventh.

The 17 total bases tied the major league record shared by Bobby Lowe and Ed Delahanty, players who competed in the 1890s. Both hit four homers and a single.

Former New York Yankee Lou Gehrig is the only other modern player to have homered four times in a nine-inning game. Philadelphia Phillie Chuck Klein (1936) and the Chicago White Sox's Pat Seerey (1948) both hit their fourth homers in extra-inning contests.

Duke Snider also homered and winning pitcher Carl Erskine collected four hits.

Gil Hodges (left), Brooklyn's four-homer man, with shortstop Pee Wee Reese.

Williams' tough year

Boston's Ted Williams, four-time American League batting champion and two-time Most Valuable Player, underwent a 75-minute operation July 13 to remove seven bone fragments from the left elbow he fractured two days earlier in the first inning of the All-Star Game at Chicago's Comiskey Park.

Williams broke the elbow while making a leaping catch of a Ralph Kiner drive against the left-field wall. He remained in the game for eight innings and contributed a run-scoring single, but the arm began to swell and X-rays were taken the next day. Dr. Joseph Shortell, the orthopedic specialist who performed the surgery, said Williams could see action by the end of the season.

It has not been the best of years for the temperamental star. He missed 10 games early with a viral infection and he incurred the wrath of fans May 11 with angry tirades in both games of a doubleheader against Detroit at Fenway Park. Williams made errors in each contest, including a second-game muff that allowed the Tigers to score the winning run. Fans showered their superstar with boos and Williams responded with a series of "insulting gestures."

After a next-day conference with Boston Owner Tom Yawkey, Williams issued a public apology for his "impulsive actions."

Sisler's homer ends Phillies' frustration

Center fielder Richie Ashburn threw out the potential winning run at home plate in the bottom of the ninth inning and Dick Sisler hit a dramatic three-run homer in the 10th to give the Philadelphia Phillies a 4-1 victory over Brooklyn and their first National League pennant in 35 years.

The October 1 game at Ebbets Field concluded an outstanding pennant race that had the Whiz Kids leading the Dodgers by one game with one to play. The Phillies' Robin Roberts, making his third start in five days, and Brooklyn's Don Newcombe both were looking for their 20th victories and a crowd of 35,073 was on hand to witness the proceedings. Nobody was disappointed.

Philadelphia broke on top in the first on Puddin' Head Jones' single and Brooklyn tied in the sixth on a freak home run by shortstop Pee Wee Reese — a towering fly to right that wedged between the scoreboard and the top of the fence.

Prospects looked bad for the Phillies in the bottom of the ninth as Cal Abrams walked and Reese singled him to second. When Duke Snider followed with a line shot to center, visions of a pennant-deciding playoff danced through everybody's mind. But Ashburn raced in and fired a bullet to catcher Stan Lopata, who was waiting with the ball when Abrams arrived. Roberts escaped further trouble by walking Jackie Robinson intentionally, retiring Carl Furillo on a foul pop and getting Gil Hodges on a fly ball.

Newcombe was not so fortunate in the 10th. After Roberts and Eddie Waitkus led off with singles, Sisler drove a 1-2 pitch into the left-field stands.

The Phillies' first pennant since 1915 did not come easily. Leading Boston by 7½ games and Brooklyn by nine on September 19, they lost nine of 12 while the Dodgers were winning 13 of 16 to make the race close. Brooklyn beat Philadelphia, 7-3, on the second-to-last day of the season to set the stage for the dramatic finale.

Philadelphia's Dick Sisler is welcomed home on his pennant-winning 10th-inning home run against Brooklyn.

YANKEES PULL SWEEP

Yogi Berra drove in two runs with a homer and a single and rookie Whitey Ford did not allow an earned run in 8⅔ innings as the New York Yankees completed their four-game World Series sweep of Philadelphia with a 5-2 victory October 7 at Yankee Stadium.

The Yankees, in nailing down their 13th Series title, scored two first-inning runs and added three more in the sixth. Ford, who was 9-1 during the regular season, took care of the rest. The lefthander was one out away from a shutout when left fielder Gene Woodling dropped a fly ball that let the Phillies score their only runs.

The Whiz Kids were stymied by Yankee pitching the entire Series.

They managed only five runs while batting .203 and Yankee pitchers finished with a sparkling 0.73 ERA.

Vic Raschi got New York off to a fast start in the October 4 opener at Philadelphia when he outdueled veteran Jim Konstanty in a 1-0 thriller, allowing only two hits.

Allie Reynolds pitched a 10-inning 2-1 victory in the second game and Eddie Lopat and Tom Ferrick combined for a 3-2 Game 3 victory that was decided in the ninth by Jerry Coleman's single.

The Yankees did not show their typical offensive punch, but it did not matter. Woodling batted .429 and paced an attack that featured only two home runs.

Game 1	New York	1	Philadelphia	0
Game 2	New York	2	Philadelphia	1
Game 3	New York	3	Philadelphia	2
Game 4	New York	5	Philadelphia	2

New York Manager Casey Stengel celebrates the Yankees' World Series sweep of Philadelphia with team co-Owners Dan Topping and Del Webb.

Chandler voted out

In a shocking development, 16 major league owners voted December 11 not to renew the seven-year contract of Commissioner A.B. (Happy) Chandler.

The decision was made during baseball's winter meetings in St. Petersburg, Fla. The matter of Chandler's re-election, generally considered to be a formality, was to be discussed in a December 12 meeting and many baseball people were unaware of the undercurrent that swept the game's second commissioner out of office.

At a preliminary conference, a trial vote came out 9-7 in favor of re-electing Chandler. The Commissioner needed 12 votes to retain his job. The owners decided to go ahead with a formal vote and this one came out 8-8, at which time Chandler was notified of the result. He asked for one more ballot, which produced a 9-7 count.

St. Louis Cardinals Owner Fred Saigh, a long-time Chandler critic, led opposition that included the Phillies, Cubs and Yankees ownerships. Chandler, a former governor of Kentucky and the man who replaced Kenesaw Mountain Landis in 1945, was blamed for jeopardizing baseball's reserve clause and for making bad financial deals involving radio and television rights. His term officially expires April 30, 1952.

A.B. (Happy) Chandler, baseball's ousted commissioner.

Connie Mack ends 50-year reign

Connie Mack, the grand old man of baseball, retired October 18 after 50 years as owner-manager of the Philadelphia Athletics, the team he founded in 1901 when he helped Ban Johnson organize the American League.

The 87-year-old patriarch of the National Pastime told newspapermen and sportscasters that he was turning over the managerial reins to Jimmie Dykes and giving responsibility for all business decisions to General Manager Arthur Ehlers. Although he will retain his title as team president, Mack said he will remove himself from day-to-day decisions.

In his long career, Mack built, tore down and rebuilt teams that would win nine pennants and five World Series championships as well as finish last in the A.L. 17 times. His 1910 and 1911 A's won consecutive Series titles, as did his 1929 and 1930 squads. Mack began his professional career as a catcher for Washington in 1886 and later managed the National League's Pittsburgh club before

Philadelphia's grand old man, Connie Mack, with his wife shortly before his retirement as Athletics manager.

founding the A's.

The fatherly, soft-spoken Mack always will be remembered for the way he stood in the dugout, waving his scorecard to signal players on the field. He was one of baseball's original Hall of Fame pioneer electees in 1937.

" DUGOUT CHATTER "

"If Kiner had cut that drive up into small pieces, he would have had enough singles to last him for a month."

Luke Sewell

Cincinnati manager, after watching Pirates slugger Ralph Kiner hit a titanic smash over the Forbes Field scoreboard

CAUGHT ON THE FLY

OCTOBER
New York Giants infielder Eddie Stanky finished the season with eight home runs, one more than he had hit in his first seven major league campaigns combined.

Branch Rickey resigned as Brooklyn President after surrendering his Dodger stock to former partner Walter O'Malley.

NOVEMBER
Grover Cleveland Alexander, who shares the all-time N.L. record for victories (373) with Christy Mathewson, died in St. Paul, Neb., at age 63.

A TV windfall

Baseball Commissioner A.B. (Happy) Chandler announced December 26 that the Gillette Safety Razor Company had agreed to pay $6 million over six years for television rights to the World Series and All-Star Game.

Gillette already had agreed to pay $1.37 million for the radio rights to the same events through 1956. Chandler said that a large portion of that $7.37 million would be committed to the players' annuity and pension plan.

Although no network agreement has been made for television, a hookup is expected to include Mutual Broadcasting System affiliates in New York, Chicago and Boston. Mutual already has agreed to pay Gillette for radio broadcasts.

Since 1946, all television rights to World Series have been sold on a year-to-year basis. Gillette paid an all-time high of $800,000 for the 1950 package.

★1951★

Bill Veeck's midget

Bill Veeck, the maverick showman who purchased the St. Louis Browns in July, pulled off the greatest promotional stunt in baseball history August 19 when he sent a midget to the plate during a game at Sportsman's Park.

Veeck had promised an extravagant show as St. Louis' contribution to the American League's 50th anniversary celebration and more than 20,000 curious fans turned out to watch the lowly Browns engage Detroit in a doubleheader. The mood was festive, even after the Tigers had dispatched the hometowners, 5-2, in the opening contest.

True to his word, Veeck unveiled a wild between-games birthday party. Performers streamed onto the field and a three-ring circus of hand balancers, jugglers and a trampoline troupe entertained at each base. Old bicycles and classic cars paraded, aerial bombs released miniature American flags and a Brownie band featuring pitcher Satchel Paige performed at home plate. At the height of the festivities, a 7-foot papier-mache cake was wheeled out and a midget dressed in a Browns uniform popped out and scurried into the St. Louis dugout. Everybody

applauded and sat back to watch the second game.

But after St. Louis retired Detroit in order in the top of the first, Veeck unleashed his coup de grace. Suddenly the announcer's voice echoed through the park: "Batting for Frank Saucier, number one-eighth, Eddie Gaedel."

Everyone was stunned as the 65-pound cake-popping midget approached the plate, swinging three toy bats. Umpire Ed Hurley called St. Louis Manager Zack Taylor to a conference and was presented with an official A.L. contract. Seeing that everything was in order, Hurley ordered the game to continue.

As the 3-foot-7 Gaedel crouched into his stance, Detroit lefthander Bob Cain tried, unsuccessfully, to distinguish a strike zone, walking baseball's first midget on four pitches. Gaedel waddled to first and was replaced by pinch-runner Jim Delsing. The game then continued with the Tigers recording a 6-2 victory.

Gaedel was released the next day when A.L. President Will Harridge, saying the use of a midget was not in the best interests of baseball, refused to approve the contract. But Veeck already had his victory.

St. Louis Browns midget Eddie Gaedel takes a ball from Detroit pitcher Bob Cain during Bill Veeck's master promotional caper in the second game of a doubleheader at Sportsman's Park.

Feller does it again

Cleveland's Bob Feller, bypassed by American League Manager Casey Stengel for the upcoming All-Star Game, fired his modern record third career no-hitter July 1 and ran his record to 11-2 as he pitched the Indians to a 2-1 victory over Detroit in the first game of a doubleheader at Cleveland Stadium.

The 32-year-old Feller rewarded 42,891 hysterical fans with a three-walk, five-strikeout effort. Johnny Lipon reached base on shortstop Ray Boone's fourth-inning error, stole second, moved to third on a wild pickoff throw and scored Detroit's only run on a fly ball. Luke Easter drove in both Cleveland runs off lefthander Bob Cain.

Feller, who pitched his first no-hitter on Opening Day in 1940 and

his second in 1946, joins Cy Young and Lawrence Corcoran as pitchers who have thrown three no-hitters. All of Corcoran's came in the 1880s for Chicago while Young pitched his first in 1897 and added two more in 1904 and 1907.

Bob Feller, a happy Indian, after his record third career no-hitter.

SEASON LEADERS

	American League		National League	
Avg.	Ferris Fain, Phi.	.344	Stan Musial, St. L.	.355
HR	Gus Zernial, Chi.-Phi.	33	Ralph Kiner, Pit.	42
RBI	Gus Zernial, Chi.-Phi.	129	Monte Irvin, N.Y.	121
SB	Minnie Minoso, Cle.-Chi.	31	Sam Jethroe, Bos.	35
W-L Pct.	Bob Feller, Cle. 22-8, .733		Preacher Roe, Bkn. 22-3, .880	
ERA	Saul Rogovin, Det.-Chi.	2.78	Chet Nichols, Bos.	2.88
SO	Vic Raschi, N.Y.	164	Don Newcombe, Bkn.	164
			Warren Spahn, Bos.	164

CAUGHT ON THE FLY

MARCH

Eddie Collins, a Hall of Fame second baseman for the Philadelphia Athletics and Chicago White Sox and a member of baseball's exclusive 3,000-hit club, died in Boston at age 63. Collins had been vice-president of the Boston Red Sox since 1933.

JUNE

Cleveland fireballer Bob Feller brought an end to Boston star Dom DiMaggio's 27-game hitting streak.

JULY

Chicago and Boston set records on successive nights when they staged 17-inning and 19-inning thrillers at Comiskey Park — the two longest A.L. games ever played under lights. Boston won the first contest, 5-4, and the White Sox won the next night by the same score.

AUGUST

Pittsburgh lefthander Howie Pollet halted New York's 16-game winning streak when he blanked the Giants, 2-0, on three hits.

" DUGOUT CHATTER "

"I like to get 'em hopping mad. When they get mad, they can't concentrate on the game. They make mistakes. Some people say, 'Let sleeping dogs lie,' but I say to hell with that."

Chuck Dressen

Dodger manager, on his penchant for getting opposing teams riled up over his cocky remarks

N.L. flexes muscle

Four National Leaguers belted home runs and Brooklyn's Don Newcombe and Cincinnati's Ewell Blackwell combined to shut down the American League over the final four innings in an 8-3 All-Star Game victory July 10 at Detroit's Briggs Stadium.

The victory marked the first time the N.L. had won consecutive All-Star contests and cut the A.L.'s advantage to 12-6. The four-homer barrage was an All-Star Game record, as was the six-home run two-team total.

After the N.L. had scored an unearned first-inning run off St. Louis Browns righthander Ned Garver, the A.L. tied the score in the second on a run-scoring triple by Philadelphia's Ferris Fain. When New York Yankee lefthander Eddie Lopat replaced Garver to start the fourth, the N.L. broke out its heavy artillery.

St. Louis' Stan Musial and Boston's Bob Elliott connected in a three-run fourth, Brooklyn's Gil Hodges hit one in the sixth and Pittsburgh's Ralph Kiner homered in his third straight All-Star Game in the eighth. Hometown favorites Vic Wertz and George Kell hit A.L. home runs.

Gil Hodges' sixth-inning home run was one of four hit by National Leaguers in an 8-3 All-Star Game victory at Detroit.

Nieman sets record

St. Louis Browns outfielder Bob Nieman made baseball history September 14 when he hit home runs in his first two major league at-bats, both coming off Red Sox lefthander Mickey McDermott at Boston's Fenway Park.

Nieman, who was leading the Texas League in hitting (.325) when his contract was purchased by the Browns, belted his first homer over Fenway's famed "Green Monster" in left field on a 2-1 pitch in the second inning with one man aboard. He followed an inning later with another two-run shot over the left-field wall, this one on a 3-1 delivery. The home runs were hit on Nieman's first two big-league swings.

The 24-year-old rookie also bunted for a hit in the ninth off reliever Ellis Kinder, completing his 3-for-5 debut performance. But despite Nieman's heroics, the last-place Browns dropped a 9-6 decision to the Red Sox. Seven of Boston's runs scored on homers by Walt Dropo, Ted Williams and Dom DiMaggio.

St. Louis Browns youngster Bob Nieman had a real blast in his record-setting big-league debut.

Cardinals double up

When the New York Giants, fighting to catch Brooklyn in the National League pennant race, were rained out in their series-closing game at St. Louis September 12, only one date was available for a makeup contest. Available, that is, for the Giants.

So the New Yorkers, given the blessing of N.L. President Ford Frick, stayed over on their off day and met the Cardinals in a September 13 afternoon contest at Sportsman's Park. That night, the Redbirds played host to Boston, completing the first two-opponent major league doubleheader since 1883.

The double matchup pitted the Cardinals against the two best pitchers in the N.L. — New York's Sal Maglie, a 20-game winner, and Boston 19-game victor Warren Spahn. Maglie had won five consecutive starts for the hottest team in baseball and figured to make short work of the Cardinals.

But St. Louis exploded for six runs in a six-hit second inning that carried it to a 6-4 victory, dropping New York six games behind Brooklyn with 13 to play.

The Cardinals, however, were no match for Spahn, who fired a one-hit 2-0 shutout and faced only 29 batters for his 20th win. The only Cardinal hit was a sixth-inning single by pitcher Al Brazle.

BILL VEECK

The Barnum of Baseball

"All sports entrepreneurs, whether baseball, horse racing, football or whatever, should keep in mind one thing. They should strive to create an atmosphere of fun. This is the entertainment business, not religion."

Bill Veeck

He was like a salmon swimming upstream, a colorful piece of confetti fluttering through a maze of corporate predictability. Bill Veeck (as in wreck) was both a thorn in the side of baseball's establishment and the game's foremost ambassador. He rankled his fellow owners, tested the patience of the game's hierarchy and delighted fans as the sport's master showman.

Veeck actually was more than a showman. He was a promoter extraordinaire who injected large doses of fun and excitement into the staid and conservative game he had grown to love. Baseball, he believed, needed a facelift, and casual fans needed an incentive to come to the ballpark.

"I believe that a ball game is not conducted for a few devout fans," said Veeck during his early years. "I believe that without distracting from the game, you can do a lot of things that make going a lot of fun for everyone. I like for people to have the feeling of being relaxed and friendly while they're at the ball game — to promote the kind of atmosphere that will get

them talking and laughing together."

Veeck, a World War I baby and the product of a Chicago Cubs franchise run by his father, Bill Sr., developed those ideas as a young workaholic who bulled his way from the bottom of the organization as a stockboy to a front-office position. By age 27, some of his theories bordered on radical and he longed for a laboratory to test them out.

He found his laboratory in 1941, using his meager savings to buy the nearly bankrupt Milwaukee Brewers of the American Association. When he examined his holdings, Veeck discovered a hopelessly inept team ("the worst club I had ever seen"), a dirty, unpainted stadium and abysmal attendance figures. The night he took over, there were 24 people in the grandstand.

His first order of business was to repair the park and provide a nice atmosphere to watch baseball. Then he offered a string of giveaways and incentives. His promotions were unusual, creative and well received — and baseball fever

Average, everyday fan Joe Earley and his wife accept Veeck's gifts during a 1948 promotion in his honor at Cleveland's Municipal Stadium.

returned to Milwaukee.

Fans were seldom disappointed. There were breakfast games, offering orange juice and cereal, for the night-time war workers, fireworks displays, clowns performing in the stands, free orchids for women and hilarious concerts — by makeshift bands made up of players and fans on such instruments as washboards, bull fiddles and slide whistles.

Veeck loved handing out gag gifts, such as a swayback horse, a flock of pigeons or a 200-pound block of ice. The fan would receive his prize and then spend the rest of the night trying to figure out what to do with it during the game or how to get it home. The other fans would delight at his discomfort and Veeck inevitably would come to the rescue by repurchasing the gift at a generous price.

The Brewers finished in last place in 1941, but Veeck turned that around, too, with some astute buying, selling and trading. The team finished second in 1942 and then won three straight pennants. Veeck became an instant folk hero.

Veeck spent much of the 1943 and '44 campaigns in the South

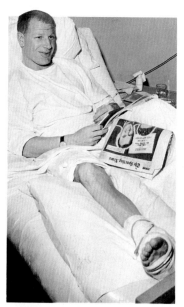

Bill Veeck had a smile for the camera prior to the 1946 operation to amputate his foot because of a war injury.

Pacific with the U.S. Marine Corps during World War II. While at Bougainville, his foot was crushed by a recoiling artillery piece, an injury that later would result in amputation of his right leg and assorted other health problems. But if life with a peg leg bothered him, Veeck never let on.

It was business as usual in 1945 for the energetic entrepreneur, who sold his Brewers and headed a syndicate that purchased the struggling Cleveland Indians. He arrived on the major league scene with the reputation as a maverick and quickly began working his promotional magic on the woeful American League team. As Veeck ran afoul of baseball norms, Cleveland doubled its attendance in 1947 and won a World Series the next season. En route to their first fall classic appearance since 1920, the Indians attracted 2,620,677 fans, still a franchise record.

Veeck sold his Cleveland interests in 1949 and returned to baseball in 1951 for another challenge — the lowly St. Louis Browns. But unlike his previous franchise salvage attempts, Veeck could not beat the Cardinals in the battle of St. Louis. With Veeck in financial trouble in 1953, his fellow owners saw their chance and forced him to sell. Baltimore interests purchased the team, which left St. Louis and became the Orioles.

Veeck, the lovable, tie-hating, chain-smoking man of the people, was out of baseball, but tales of his promotional genius already had become part of baseball lore. In Cleveland, Veeck had:
- Signed outfielder Larry Doby in 1947, breaking the A.L. color barrier.
- Established a combination playground-nursery with well-trained attendants at the ballpark so mothers could attend games.
- Staged Good Old Joe Earley Night, honoring an average fan in a special promotion. Earley, a night guard at an auto plant, was presented a new car, clothes, luggage, books and numerous appliances while livestock, poultry and other gifts were given to some of the 60,405 fans

Indians fan Charley Lupica atop the flagpole that was moved to Municipal Stadium, where he dismounted on the 117th day of his fruitless pennant vigil.

New Chicago White Sox Owner Veeck (right) with top man Hank Greenberg in 1959.

who attended the game.
•Moved a flagpole bearing Cleveland fan Charley Lupica to Municipal Stadium. Lupica had taken up residence atop the pole in 1949, saying he would not come down until the Indians moved into first place. The fruitless vigil ended after 117 days.
•Buried the Indians' 1949 pennant hopes in a pregame ceremony complete with a horse-drawn hearse, a casket, a gravesite behind the center-field fence and a solemn funeral procession that included Manager Lou Boudreau and his coaches.

Veeck worked overtime in St. Louis trying to revive the hopeless Browns, but nothing worked. One gimmick featured 1,115 "grandstand managers," who called the shots during a game against Philadelphia with "yes" and "no" cards that flashed answers to coaches' strategy questions.

But Veeck's coup de grace occurred in 1951, when he lured more than 18,000 fans to Sportsman's Park with the promise of something big to celebrate the A.L.'s 50th birthday. "Something big" was a midget named Eddie Gaedel who, wearing a Browns uniform

Veeck's 'grandstand managers' call the shots for the Browns during a 1951 game.

bearing No. ⅛, popped out of a huge cardboard cake between games of a doubleheader against Detroit. Everybody applauded and sat back to watch the nightcap. But in the bottom of the first inning, Gaedel suddenly popped out of the St. Louis dugout, approached the plate swinging three toy bats and was announced as a pinch-hitter. When Manager Zack Taylor produced a signed contract, Gaedel was allowed to bat. He walked on four pitches, trotted to first and left for a pinch-runner.

The stunt shocked everybody and A.L. President Will Harridge ruled the next day that a midget was not in the best interests of baseball. Veeck was chastised by critics for making a mockery of the game and praised by supporters for his creative genius. Veeck viewed it as a million dollars' worth of publicity.

Veeck resurfaced in 1959 as owner of the Chicago White Sox and watched his team capture an A.L. pennant. Before he retired again in 1961 because of health problems, he made one of his most lasting contributions to the game — baseball's first exploding scoreboard.

He came back again in 1975 to purchase the White Sox, but soon discovered he did not have the resources to compete in the skyrocketing free-agent market. He sold the team in 1980 and retired again. He died in 1986, leaving a legacy that many of his stuffed-shirt contemporaries never were able to comprehend.

"All sports entrepreneurs, whether baseball, horse racing, football or whatever, should keep in mind one thing," he often said. "They should strive to create an atmosphere of fun. This is the entertainment business, not religion."

Veeck's master stunt occurred in 1951 when midget Eddie Gaedel donned a Browns uniform and batted in a game against Detroit. St. Louis Manager Zack Taylor is tying Gaedel's shoe.

★1951★
SEPTEMBER-DECEMBER

DiMaggio ends career

Joe DiMaggio, New York's great Yankee Clipper, announced his retirement from baseball after 13 seasons, 10 of which were spent playing for Yankee teams that captured American League pennants. The three-time A.L. Most Valuable Player leaves the game with a .325 career average, 2,214 hits and 361 home runs.

Those numbers could have been better, but DiMaggio missed a lot of time with injuries and he spent three full seasons in the service during World War II.

While not surprising, the announcement still sent shock waves throughout baseball. One of the game's most beloved superstars since his 1936 debut, DiMaggio has entertained fans around the country with his outstanding hitting and defensive play in center field. His 56-game hitting streak in 1941 is one of baseball's most cherished records.

Ford Frick elected

Ford Frick, president of the National League since 1934, was elected to a seven-year term as baseball's third commissioner September 20 during a marathon meeting at the Palmer House in Chicago.

The decision was reached late at night after morning and afternoon sessions had failed to produce a result. In a battle between Frick and Cincinnati Reds General Manager Warren Giles, stalemated representatives of the 16 major league teams voted "at least 50 times" before Giles withdrew his name from consideration. With Giles out of the running, Frick quickly received the three-fourths majority vote he needed.

Frick, a former teacher, sportswriter and radio commentator, became the first baseball man elected to the game's highest post. Kenesaw Mountain Landis, the first commissioner, was a former federal judge and second commissioner A.B. (Happy) Chandler was a former governor of Kentucky and a U.S. Senator. After a tempestuous reign, Chandler fell three votes short of re-election last December and stepped down in July.

Giles was named to replace Frick as N.L. president September 27.

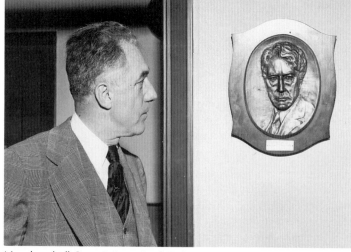

New baseball Commissioner Ford Frick.

Yanks clinch pennant

New York's Allie Reynolds pitched his record-tying second no-hitter of the season to clinch at least a tie for the American League pennant and Vic Raschi stopped Boston in the second game of a September 28 doubleheader to give the Yankees their third flag in a row and 18th in 30 years.

The 8-0 and 11-3 sweep of the Red Sox before 39,038 fans at Yankee Stadium gave New York a 3½-game lead over Cleveland with two to play. It also gave Casey Stengel his third A.L. pennant in as many seasons at the Yankee helm.

Reynolds struck out nine and walked four to join Cincinnati's Johnny Vander Meer (1938) as the only pitchers to throw two no-hitters in the same season. Vander Meer fired his gems on successive starts. Reynolds' first came July 12 when he outdueled Cleveland ace Bob Feller in a 1-0 classic.

This no-hitter was punctuated dramatically when catcher Yogi Berra caught a foul pop by Boston slugger Ted Williams for the final out. Seconds earlier, Berra had dropped Williams' foul behind the plate, forcing Reynolds to deal with the A.L.'s most dangerous hitter again. He did and preserved his 17th victory.

Raschi won his 21st game in the nightcap with Joe DiMaggio contributing a three-run homer.

New York's Allie Reynolds (right) celebrates his record-tying second no-hitter of the season with Gene Woodling between games of a doubleheader victory that clinched the Yankees' third straight A.L. pennant.

CAUGHT ON THE FLY

SEPTEMBER
New York's Don Mueller tied a major league record when he blasted five home runs in two consecutive games against the Brooklyn Dodgers.

New York Giants Sal Maglie and Larry Jansen won 23 games apiece and headed a list of 13 20-game winners — seven in the N.L. and six in the A.L.. It was the biggest group of 20-game winners in 31 years.

NOVEMBER
A pair of New York catchers, Brooklyn's Roy Campanella and Yankee Yogi Berra, captured their first MVP awards.

Thomson's home run crushes Dodgers

New York Giant Bobby Thomson gets a well-deserved victory ride after ending Brooklyn's pennant hopes with "The Shot Heard 'Round the World."

"The Giants win the pennant! The Giants win the pennant! . . . The Giants win the pennant, and they're going crazy!"

So went the dramatic call of radio announcer Russ Hodges October 3 as New York's Bobby Thomson danced around the bases after hitting "The Shot Heard 'Round the World." Pandemonium reigned at the Polo Grounds. Giants' players celebrated. Excited fans stormed the field.

Only the stunned Brooklyn Dodgers seemed immune to the delirious frenzy that had engulfed Flatbush. They hurried toward their center-field clubhouse with the heart-sickening realization that, for the second year in a row, their National League pennant hopes had been dashed by a last-game, final-inning three-run homer.

Only this was an especially bitter pill to swallow. The Dodgers had controlled the 1951 pennant race and appeared uncatchable when their lead reached a whopping 13½ games over the second-place Giants August 11. But New York won 37 times in 44 games and a 13-1 stretch run forced a

first-place tie and the second three-game pennant playoff in N.L. history.

The Giants gained the upper hand in the playoff October 1 when they beat the Dodgers, 3-1, on the strength of Thomson's two-run homer at Ebbets Field. But Clem Labine pitched a six-hitter the next day and the Dodgers squared the series with a 10-0 victory at the Polo Grounds.

Things looked bleak for the Giants as 20-game winner Don Newcombe carried a 4-1 lead into the bottom of the ninth of Game 3. But Alvin Dark and Don Mueller singled and, after Monte Irvin had fouled out, Whitey Lockman slapped a double down the left-field line. Dodger Manager Chuck Dressen, his team now leading 4-2, called in Ralph Branca to pitch to Thomson.

On the third pitch from the righthander, Thomson stroked a line drive toward left field. A full house of shocked fans sat silently as Dodger left fielder Andy Pafko watched the ball disappear. Giants win, 5-4. Pandemonium!

The most dramatic pennant-winning comeback in history was complete.

WORLD SERIES REPORT

BAUER TRIPS GIANTS

New York Yankee right fielder Hank Bauer, a .132 career World Series hitter, belted a bases-loaded triple in the sixth inning and then made a sensational game-saving catch in the ninth to preserve a 4-3 victory over the New York Giants and the Yankees' third straight World Series championship.

The October 10 Game 6 clincher belonged to Bauer, who had managed only five singles in 38 career Series at-bats. Bauer's game-winning triple came off Giants starter Dave Koslo and his game-ending catch came on a line drive by pinch-hitter Sal Yvars with the potential tying run in scoring position.

The Giants, aided by Alvin Dark's three-run homer, opened the Series October 4 with a 5-1 victory behind Koslo. After the Yankees had squared matters, 3-1, on Eddie Lopat's five-hitter, the Giants regained the advantage with a 6-2 win at the Polo Grounds.

But the rest of this Subway Series belonged to the Yankees. Allie Reynolds claimed a 6-2 fourth-game win as Joe DiMaggio hit a two-run homer and the Bronx Bombers stormed to a 13-1 Game 5 win behind Lopat. The offensive hero of that game was rookie infielder Gil McDougald, who hit the third grand slam in Series history.

Game 1	Giants	5	Yankees	1
Game 2	Yankees	3	Giants	1
Game 3	Giants	6	Yankees	2
Game 4	Yankees	6	Giants	2
Game 5	Yankees	13	Giants	1
Game 6	Yankees	4	Giants	3

Joe DiMaggio gets a warm welcome in the New York Yankee dugout after hitting a Game 4 World Series home run against the Giants.

" DUGOUT CHATTER "

"I had Erskine and Branca both warming up and I asked Sukey (bullpen coach Clyde Sukeforth) which one was throwing better and he told me Branca."

Chuck Dressen

Dodger manager, after watching New York's Bobby Thomson win the N.L. pennant with his "Shot Heard 'Round the World" off Ralph Branca

★ 1952 ★
JANUARY-JULY

SEASON LEADERS

	American League		National League	
Avg.	Ferris Fain, Phi.	.327	Stan Musial, St. L.	.336
HR	Larry Doby, Cle.	32	Ralph Kiner, Pit.	37
			Hank Sauer, Chi.	37
RBI	Al Rosen, Cle.	105	Hank Sauer, Chi.	121
SB	Minnie Minoso, Chi.	22	Pee Wee Reese, Bkn.	30
W-L Pct.	Bobby Shantz, Phi. 24-7, .774		Hoyt Wilhelm, N.Y. 15-3, .833	
ERA	Allie Reynolds, N.Y.	2.06	Hoyt Wilhelm, N.Y.	2.43
SO	Allie Reynolds, N.Y.	160	Warren Spahn, Bos.	183

A Dodger rampage

The Brooklyn Dodgers went on a record rampage in the first inning of a May 21 game against Cincinnati at Ebbets Field, scoring 15 times en route to a 19-1 victory that moved them into first place in the National League.

The 59-minute first-inning massacre, perpetrated against four Reds pitchers, was fueled by 10 hits, seven walks and two hit batsmen. Everybody in the lineup got in on the act and a modern record 19 batters in a row reached base safely. Ironically, the inning opened with an out — Cincinnati third baseman Bobby Adams robbing leadoff man Billy Cox of a hit.

Six modern one-inning records were set: 15 runs; 15 runs in a first inning; 12 runs scoring after two were out; 21 batters coming to the plate; 15 runs batted in, and 19 straight batters reaching base.

Duke Snider, who hit a two-run homer during the onslaught, struck out against Frank Smith to end the carnage. Smith was working in relief of Ewell Blackwell, Bud Byerly and Herm Wehmeier.

Amazingly, only one Dodger collected more than two hits in the contest — pitcher Chris Van Cuyk, who managed four. A pair of two-run homers by Bobby Morgan accounted for the final four Brooklyn runs.

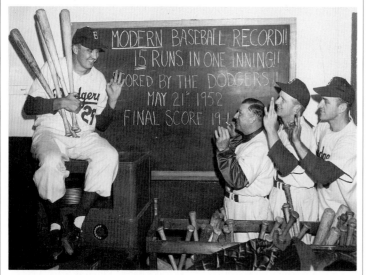

Winning Brooklyn pitcher Chris Van Cuyk (left) celebrates with (left to right) Manager Chuck Dressen, Bobby Morgan and George Shuba after the Dodgers' record run-scoring binge.

Feller loses 1-hit duel

St. Louis Browns lefthander Bob Cain outdueled Cleveland ace Bob Feller April 23 in a battle of one-hitters that tied the major league record and set an American League mark for fewest hits in a game.

St. Louis' 1-0 victory at Sportsman's Park was decided early when Bobby Young hit a first-inning triple and scored on an error by Indians third baseman Al Rosen. The 33-year-old Feller allowed only two baserunners (both walks) the rest of the way.

Cain lost his no-hit bid in the fifth on Luke Easter's harmless single. The 27-year-old struck out seven and walked three in picking up his second victory. Ironically, Cain was Feller's victim last July when the fireballer pitched his third career no-hitter. The game marked Feller's 11th one-hitter and his first in a losing cause.

The low-hit record originally was set in a 1906 Chicago-Pittsburgh game and tied in 1917 during the famous Hippo Vaughn-Fred Toney double no-hitter that was decided on two 10th-inning hits. The A.L. low-hit record was three.

St. Louis' Bob Cain outdueled Cleveland ace Bob Feller in a record-tying battle of one-hitters.

Ted says farewell

Ted Williams, who lost three seasons to military service during World War II, said another farewell to Boston fans April 30 at Fenway Park as he prepared to report to the U.S. Marine Corps for a 17-month tour of duty as a fighter pilot in Korea. The Splendid Splinter rose to the occasion by hitting a game-winning homer against Detroit.

As 24,764 fans roared their approval, Williams was showered with praise and gifts during pregame ceremonies. He then collected two hits and keyed a 5-3 Red Sox victory that gave the American League leaders a two-game bulge over St. Louis.

Tiger Vic Wertz set the stage for Williams when he blasted a two-run homer off Boston starter Mel Parnell in the top of the seventh, knotting the score at 3-3. In the bottom of the inning, Williams answered with a two-run blow off Tiger hurler Dizzy Trout.

Williams, who was starting his first game since pulling a muscle on Opening Day, reported to the Marine camp in Willow Grove, Pa., on May 2.

CAUGHT ON THE FLY

APRIL
New York Giants rookie reliever Hoyt Wilhelm was a 9-5 winner in his first major league game and he spiced his five-inning effort with a first at-bat home run off Boston rookie Dick Hoover.

MAY
Ron Necciai, a pitcher for Pittsburgh's Bristol team in the Class D Appalachian League, brought new meaning to perfection when he struck out 27 batters in a nine-inning no-hitter against Welch.

JUNE
Boston lefthander Warren Spahn struck out 18 Cubs but dropped a 15-inning 3-1 decision to Chicago at Braves Field.

> **" DUGOUT CHATTER "**
>
> *"It was a tremendous thrill. I felt as if I were flying on air as I circled the bases."*
>
> **Hank Sauer**
>
> Chicago slugger, after hitting the game-winning homer in a 3-2 N.L. All-Star Game win

That rainy day feeling

Chicago's Hank Sauer drove a pitch from Cleveland's Bob Lemon onto the left-field roof of Philadelphia's Shibe Park for a two-run homer, giving the National League a 3-2 fourth-inning lead that held up in a rain-shortened All-Star Game victory July 8 over the American League.

The N.L.'s third straight All-Star win was decided by Sauer's long shot, which also drove in St. Louis' Stan Musial. Sauer's homer made a winner of teammate Bob Rush, who pitched two innings and surrendered both A.L. runs.

The Americans had taken a 2-1 lead in the top of the inning on run-scoring singles by the Chicago White Sox's Eddie Robinson and Cleveland's Bobby Avila. Philadelphia's Curt Simmons had held them scoreless for the first three frames, protecting a 1-0 lead produced by Brooklyn's Jackie Robinson with a first-inning homer off Yankee Vic Raschi.

The game started 20 minutes late because of the rain and was delayed for 56 minutes in the top of the sixth before it was called. The highlight for Philadelphia fans was the performance of Simmons and the fifth-inning three-strikeout effort of Athletics' lefthander Bobby Shantz.

New York Yankee Manager Casey Stengel (left) with Philadelphia All-Star Bobby Shantz.

Korean war takes toll

As the war in Korea continues, major and minor league baseball can expect to lose players to military service. A significant number already have been called to duty, including several of the game's top names.

The United States Army grabbed Brooklyn pitching star Don Newcombe in February and young New York Giants outfielder Willie Mays in May. Boston's four-time American League batting champion Ted Williams, New York Yankee second baseman Jerry Coleman and Cleveland outfielder Bob Kennedy all were called to service by the U.S. Marine Corps in May.

Two more Yankees — third baseman Bobby Brown and pitcher Tom Morgan — were called away in July.

Among players who already have returned from military commitments are Philadelphia lefty Curt Simmons and Detroit righthander Art Houtteman.

Brooklyn ace Don Newcombe (center) in his new role as coach for his Army battalion baseball team.

A Cardinal comeback

The St. Louis Cardinals, down 11-0 to one of the best pitchers in baseball after four innings, pulled off one of the greatest comebacks in history June 15 when they rallied for a 14-12 victory over the New York Giants in the first game of a doubleheader at the Polo Grounds.

The Giants jumped on the Redbirds for five runs in the second inning and six more in the third and appeared to be headed for an easy victory with nine-game winner Sal Maglie on the hill. But The Barber surrendered seven runs in the fifth and then watched helplessly from the dugout as four more Giants pitchers were battered mercilessly by the now-inspired Cardinals.

Tommy Glaviano got St. Louis started in the big fifth with a solo homer and Enos Slaughter capped the rally with a three-run blast. After the Cardinals scored three more runs in the seventh to cut the New York lead to one, Solly Hemus tied the score in the eighth with a solo homer and Slaughter put St. Louis ahead with a run-scoring single. Hemus connected again in the ninth with a man aboard to cap the Cardinal scoring.

Despite the stunning setback, the Giants won the nightcap, 3-0, behind Dave Koslo's five-hit pitching and Wes Westrum's three-run homer.

★1952★

Dropo hits jackpot

Detroit first baseman Walt Dropo tied a major league record July 15 when he doubled during the second game of a doubleheader against Washington for his 12th consecutive hit.

Dropo, who had collected five singles in the previous day's game against the New York Yankees, singled in four straight at-bats in the doubleheader opener at Griffith Stadium. In the nightcap, Dropo tripled home three runs in the first inning, singled in the third and doubled in the fifth to match the 1938 mark of 12 straight hits by Boston's Pinky Higgins.

Dropo's streak ended in the seventh when he fouled out to catcher Mickey Grasso, but he came back in the ninth to single home two runs. Despite Dropo's efforts, Washington swept the last-place Tigers, 8-2 and 9-8.

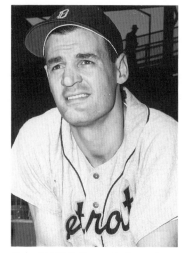

Detroit's Walt Dropo tied a major league record with his 12-hit binge in mid-July.

Since July 4, Dropo has collected 22 hits in 42 at-bats for a .524 average.

" DUGOUT CHATTER "

"I just stood there and prayed the ball would drop into the stands."

Walt Dropo

Detroit first baseman, as he watched his record-tying streak of 12 straight hits end on a foul pop to Washington catcher Mickey Grasso

---

CAUGHT ON THE FLY

SEPTEMBER
The Brooklyn Dodgers clinched a tie for the N.L. pennant when they defeated Boston, 8-2, in the final game at Braves Field.

Philadelphia Phillies righthander Robin Roberts won 17 of his final 18 decisions and finished with 28 victories — the highest N.L. total since St. Louis' Dizzy Dean won that many in 1935.

NOVEMBER
Major league attendance dropped for the fourth straight year, with the N.L. down 904,854 and the A.L. off 588,788.

Russian magazine denounces baseball

In a vicious Cold War attack on an American institution, the Russian magazine *Smena* denounced baseball as a "beastly battle, a bloody fight with mayhem and murder" and claimed that the United States stole its national game from the Soviet Union and perverted it beyond repair.

In a story under the title "Beizbol," *Smena* described the game for its readers and said that both players and spectators frequently suffer terrible wounds and even death. The article claimed that American businessmen implant this bloody sport among its 14 and 15-year-old adolescents who "supplement their lack of technique by a surplus of rough play." The story added that these businessmen reap huge profits and treat their athletes as slaves, throwing them out the door when they become too old or so disabled they can no longer compete.

Smena claimed that baseball is an imitation of the Russian village sport of lapta, which was being played "when the United States was not even marked on the maps."

The U.S. State Department dismissed the article as part of the Soviet Union's "Hate America" campaign.

Trucks matches feat

Detroit righthander Virgil (Fire) Trucks became the third major league pitcher to throw two no-hitters in the same season August 25 when he stymied New York, 1-0, in a game at Yankee Stadium.

The 33-year-old Trucks, who had pitched a 1-0 no-hit gem against Washington on May 15, retired the last 20 batters he faced, benefiting from a controversial call in the third inning. Yankee Phil Rizzuto hit a grounder to Detroit shortstop Johnny Pesky, who appeared to have trouble getting the ball out of his glove and threw late to first.

The play was called an error, then changed to a hit because a number of writers argued that the ball had stuck in Pesky's glove. It was changed back to an error after consulting with Pesky in the dugout. That announcement came shortly after the last-place Tigers had scored the game's only run in the seventh inning.

Ironically, the victory was only the fifth of the year against 15 losses for Trucks. Among his five wins are two no-hitters, a one-hitter and a two-hitter. Only Cincinnati's Johnny Vander Meer (1938) and Yankee Allie Reynolds (1951) had accomplished the feat of two no-hitters in the same season.

Detroit's Virgil Trucks, an unsightly 5-15 for the year, celebrates his record-tying second no-hitter of the season.

MARTIN TO THE RESCUE

The ever-raucous fans of Brooklyn, packed into the friendly bleachers of cozy Ebbets Field, were more vocal and euphoric than ever. The Dodgers had a three games to two World Series lead over the New York Yankees and there was justifiable anticipation that Brooklyn soon would have its first championship flag to fly with all those National League pennants.

But euphoria turned to discomfort October 6 when home runs by Yogi Berra and Mickey Mantle offset two homers by Brooklyn's Duke Snider and the Yankees rallied for a Series-tying 3-2 victory. The discomfort heightened the next day when Mantle homered again and the Yanks carried a 4-2 lead into the bottom of the seventh inning.

The Dodgers, however, refused to die, loading the bases on two walks and a single against Vic Raschi with one out. As the tension mounted, Yankee Manager Casey Stengel called Bob Kuzava from the bullpen and the lefthander induced Snider to pop out. Jackie Robinson worked the count full before hitting another popup near the mound.

But as Kuzava stood transfixed and the runners circled the bases at full speed, first baseman Joe Collins searched frantically for a ball he could not find. Recognizing the dilemma, second baseman Billy Martin sprinted in and made a miraculous knee-high catch.

Kuzava set down the Dodgers the rest of the way and the Yankees had their record-matching fourth consecutive World Series victory. The Dodgers were denied a Series championship for the sixth time in as many tries.

Brooklyn had opened the Series with a three-homer barrage (Snider, Robinson and Pee Wee Reese) that produced a 4-2 victory. But the Yankees fought back in Game 2 behind Martin's three-run homer and Raschi's three-hit pitching for a 7-1 victory.

The teams traded wins in the next two games, Brooklyn triumphing 5-3 and New York squaring matters again on a four-hit, 2-0 shutout by Allie Reynolds. Snider, who tied the Series record with four homers, hit his second in Game 5 and drove in four runs.

New York second baseman Billy Martin makes his World Series-saving catch of a bases-loaded popup as Brooklyn's Jackie Robinson heads for first base.

World Series Yankee celebrants Mickey Mantle (left) and Phil Rizzuto.

Game 1	Brooklyn	4	New York	2
Game 2	New York	7	Brooklyn	1
Game 3	Brooklyn	5	New York	3
Game 4	New York	2	Brooklyn	0
Game 5	Brooklyn	6	New York	5
Game 6	New York	3	Brooklyn	2
Game 7	New York	4	Brooklyn	2

Dodger Robinson calls Yankees prejudiced

Jackie Robinson, Brooklyn's star second baseman who broke baseball's color barrier in 1947, charged November 30 that the New York Yankees are prejudiced toward members of his race.

Robinson, appearing on an NBC-TV program "Youth Wants to Know," was asked by a young boy whether he thought there was prejudice in the Yankee organization, which has yet to field a black player. "Yes," he replied, adding that "there isn't a single Negro on the team now and there are very few in the entire Yankee farm system." Robinson pointed out that the problem lies with the club's executives, not its players.

Robinson expanded on his comments. "It seems to me the Yankee front office has used racial prejudice in its dealings with Negro ballplayers. I may be wrong, but the Yankees will have to prove it to me."

Yankee General Manager George Weiss took issue, saying the club has numerous blacks in its farm system. "It has always been our hope that one of these shall prove good enough to make it with the Yankees," he said. "But we do not intend under any circumstances to bring up one just for exploitation."

★1953★

SEASON LEADERS

	American League			National League		
Avg.	Mickey Vernon, Wash.		.337	Carl Furillo, Bkn.		.344
HR	Al Rosen, Cle.		43	Eddie Mathews, Mil.		47
RBI	Al Rosen, Cle.		145	Roy Campanella, Bkn.		142
SB	Minnie Minoso, Chi.		25	Bill Bruton, Mil.		26
W-L Pct.	Ed Lopat, N.Y.	16-4,	.800	Carl Erskine, Bkn.	20-6,	.769
ERA	Ed Lopat, N.Y.		2.42	Warren Spahn, Mil.		2.10
SO	Billy Pierce, Chi.		186	Robin Roberts, Phi.		198

Braves leave Boston, head for Milwaukee

The Braves, charter members of the National League and fixtures in Boston for 77 years, will open the 1953 season in a new home — County Stadium in Milwaukee. The franchise shift is the first in baseball since 1903, when Baltimore moved to New York.

The move is a result of sagging attendance and lost revenue. The Braves drew only 281,000 fans last season and Owner Lou Perini reported a loss of $700,000. Perini, who claims Boston has become a one-team city since the arrival of television, petitioned National League owners to okay the move and received unanimous approval on March 18.

The short notice move created minor problems in scheduling and travel arrangements, but the biggest obstacle was getting a go-ahead from the Milwaukee Brewers of the Class AAA American Association. The Brewers accepted a cash payment for their territorial rights and agreed to move to Toledo.

The Braves will play in County Stadium, a new $5 million facility still under construction.

Mantle has a blast

In an amazing display of raw power, 21-year-old New York Yankee slugger Mickey Mantle blasted a home run April 17 that cleared the 50-foot outer wall of Washington's Griffith Stadium and came to rest in the back yard of a house 565 feet away from home plate.

If it wasn't the longest ball ever hit, it had to be close. Batting righthanded against Senators lefthander Chuck Stobbs with two out and Yogi Berra on first base in the top of the fifth inning, the switch-hitting youngster sent a shot toward left-center field. Mantle's blast cleared the bleacher fence, 391 feet from the plate, glanced off a football scoreboard that sits atop the 50-foot outer barrier and bounded out of sight.

The ball traveled 460 feet in the air and there's no telling how much farther it might have gone had it cleared the scoreboard. It marked the first time a ball had ever been hit completely out of Griffith Stadium on the fly to left field. The Yankees went on to defeat the Senators, 7-3.

Young New York Yankee slugger Mickey Mantle admires the display put together in honor of his 565-foot home run.

Wisconsin Governor Walter Kohler makes a curtain-raising pitch for Milwaukee baseball as Commissioner Ford Frick (left) and N.L. President Warren Giles look on.

Braves start over

A 10th-inning home run by rookie center fielder Bill Bruton, his first in the big leagues, gave the Braves a 3-2 victory over St. Louis as Milwaukee welcomed back major league baseball after more than a half-century absence.

Bruton's drive off Gerry Staley glanced off the glove of Cardinal right fielder Enos Slaughter and caromed over the four-foot wire fence at Milwaukee's new County Stadium, giving Warren Spahn his first win of the season.

Bruton played last year for the American Association's Brewers, the team that had entertained Milwaukee fans since 1902. That was the year the major league Brewers, one of the original American League franchises in 1901, moved to St. Louis to become the Browns.

In pregame ceremonies, Commissioner Ford Frick welcomed Milwaukee into the National League and various civic officials welcomed the Braves to Milwaukee. Then, braving damp, 45-degree weather, 34,357 fans were treated to an excellent game. Bruton tripled and scored in the eighth to give the Braves a 2-1 lead, but the Cardinals tied in the ninth on Peanuts Lowrey's pinch-hit double. That set the stage for Bruton's 10th-inning heroics.

Milwaukee had opened its season the day before with a 2-0 victory at Cincinnati.

Bobo has fast start

St. Louis Browns righthander Bobo Holloman carved his niche in the record books May 6 when he celebrated his first major league start by throwing a no-hitter at the Philadelphia Athletics.

Holloman's 6-0 victory at Sportsman's Park was witnessed by only 2,473 fans. In becoming the first pitcher in modern times to record a no-hitter in his initial big-league starting assignment, Holloman faced 31 batters, striking out three and walking five. Three of the walks, sandwiched around a double play, were issued in the ninth inning.

As if his pitching heroics were not enough, the 28-year-old rookie also collected two hits and drove in three runs. He owned a 2-0 lead after three innings and was never really in danger through eight frames.

But in the ninth, the rookie walked the first two A's he faced. After Dave Philley bounced into a double play, Holloman walked Loren Babe before retiring Eddie Robinson on a fly ball.

Holloman had made four relief appearances earlier in the season.

St. Louis Browns rookie Bobo Holloman and family enjoy the fanfare after the youngster's first-start no-hitter.

CAUGHT ON THE FLY

FEBRUARY

As a tribute to their venerable owner and manager, the Philadelphia Athletics changed the name of Shibe Park to Connie Mack Stadium.

August A. Busch Jr. took control of the St. Louis Cardinals when Anheuser-Busch Inc., a St. Louis-based brewery, bought out Fred Saigh.

APRIL

Kid Nichols, a turn-of-the-century 300-game major league winner and Hall of Famer, died in Kansas City at age 83.

MAY

Milwaukee's Max Surkont struck out a modern major league-record eight straight Reds while pitching the Braves to a 10-3 rout of Cincinnati in the second game of a County Stadium doubleheader.

JUNE

Duane Pillette and Satchel Paige combined on a six-hitter and St. Louis snapped the New York Yankees' 18-game winning streak one short of the A.L. record. The Browns' 3-1 win also ended their 14-game losing streak.

A Red Sox explosion

The Boston Red Sox administered an unmerciful beating on last-place Detroit June 18, breaking four modern major league records in a 17-run seventh-inning explosion that keyed a 23-3 victory at Fenway Park.

The Red Sox sent 23 batters to the plate during the 47-minute massacre against three Detroit pitchers, collecting 14 hits and six walks. Dick Gernert's home run and doubles by Gene Stephens and George Kell were the only extra-base hits of the inning and the Tigers, who committed five errors in the game, were not guilty of any miscues in that frame.

The 17 runs, two more than Brooklyn scored in the first inning of a 1952 contest, and the 14 hits were modern major league records. Stephens set a record with three hits in the inning and Sammy White made history by scoring three times. The 1883 Chicago Cubs hold the all-time one-inning record of 18 runs.

The Red Sox, who collected 27 hits, led 5-3 going into the seventh. Steve Gromek allowed nine seventh-inning runs, Dick Weik and Earl Harrist four apiece. Boston had belted out 20 hits the day before in beating the Tigers, 17-1.

" DUGOUT CHATTER "

"Funny, ain't it, how I was such a bum when I had the Dodgers and the Braves and how now I'm a genius. I never had players like this before."

Casey Stengel

New York Yankee manager, after his team had won its fifth straight A.L. pennant

War hero Williams returns to States

The Boston Red Sox received good news in June when it was learned that slugging outfielder Ted Williams is being ordered back to the United States to get treatment for an ear and nose ailment. That's good because it means Williams is alive and well after flying 38 missions as a Marine Corps captain in Korea.

Most of those missions went off routinely, but Williams did receive a major scare on February 19 when his F-9 Panther jet was hit by small-arms fire. He perilously flew his burning plane back over enemy lines and somehow crash landed it on an allied airfield. Soon after Williams escaped from the cockpit, the plane exploded into flames.

There have been rumors that the 35-year-old Williams, who has been overseas for 5½ months, will be released from his military commitment soon, but nobody knows when he will be free to rejoin the Red Sox. The four-time American League batting champion and two-time Most Valuable Player also lost three years to military service during World War II.

Marine Corps Captain Ted Williams: Man on a mission.

★1953★

N.L. streak hits four

Brooklyn shortstop Pee Wee Reese had two hits and a pair of runs batted in July 14 as the National League recorded its fourth straight All-Star Game victory, 5-1, over the American League at Cincinnati's Crosley Field.

Reese, who had been 0-for-15 in All-Star competition, singled home a fifth-inning run and doubled home another in the seventh. Philadelphia's Richie Ashburn, St. Louis' Enos Slaughter and Pittsburgh pitcher Murry Dickson also singled in runs and four N.L. hurlers throttled the Americans on five hits.

The Phillies' Robin Roberts pitched three shutout innings, Milwaukee's Warren Spahn picked up the win with two scoreless frames and Phillies lefthander Curt Simmons and Dickson finished up.

After Chicago's Billy Pierce worked three scoreless innings for the A.L., New York's Allie Reynolds, Cleveland's Mike Garcia and St. Louis' Satchel Paige surrendered nine hits and all five N.L. runs. The 47-year-old Paige, far from his Negro League prime, became the oldest man ever to play in an All-Star Game.

Browns move east

After 50 years of stability, the major league baseball map changed for the second time in six months September 29 when Bill Veeck sold his controlling interest in the St. Louis Browns to a syndicate that received quick American League approval to move the franchise to Baltimore.

The first A.L. franchise shift since 1903, when the Baltimore Orioles were dropped in favor of the New York Highlanders, was approved in a quick meeting in New York. This was in stark contrast to the marathon sessions

held the previous two days when Veeck was still in the picture as an administrative officer.

A checkered past and hopeless future doomed the Browns in St. Louis, but Veeck's year-long efforts to move the team to Baltimore had been blocked by A.L. executives who wanted the maverick owner out of the league.

In their 52 seasons in St. Louis, the Browns captured one A.L. pennant (1944).

The move followed the Boston Braves' shift to Milwaukee earlier this year.

CAUGHT ON THE FLY

SEPTEMBER

Chicago's Johnny Klippstein held Brooklyn's Duke Snider hitless in four at-bats and ended his 27-game hitting streak.

NOVEMBER

The major league Rules Committee restored the sacrifice fly rule, erasing official at-bats from a player's record any time he advances a runner with a fly ball out.

Little-known Walter Alston was tabbed to replace Chuck Dressen as Brooklyn manager after Dressen demanded a contract in excess of one year.

Indian Rosen misses in Triple Crown bid

Washington first baseman Mickey Vernon collected two hits in his final four season at-bats against Philadelphia September 27 to hold off a late charge by Cleveland's Al Rosen and win his second American League batting championship.

Vernon, who had captured his first title in 1946, finished with a .33717 mark, .00161 ahead of Rosen. The Cleveland third baseman, trying to complete the final leg of his Triple Crown, made a valiant final-day rush with a 3-for-5 effort. Rosen led the A.L. with 43 home runs and 145 RBIs.

Brooklyn outfielder Carl Furillo was sidelined on September 6 by a broken finger, but Cardinals Red Schoendienst and Stan Musial fell short of his .344 average. Schoendienst, 2-for-5 in his finale against Chicago, finished at .342. Musial, six-time N.L. champion, closed at .337.

Milwaukee's Eddie Mathews captured his first N.L. home run title with 47 and Brooklyn's Roy Campanella set the RBI pace with 142.

N.L. batting champion Carl Furillo of Brooklyn.

Cleveland's Al Rosen (right) won the A.L. home run and RBI titles, but fell short in his bid for a Triple Crown.

YANKEES AGAIN

Billy Martin's ninth-inning single, his record-tying 12th hit of the 1953 World Series, drove in Hank Bauer with the winning run October 5 in a 4-3 New York victory that gave the Yankees their record fifth straight baseball championship and doomed the Brooklyn Dodgers to their seventh straight fall classic defeat.

The New Yorkers' Game 6 triumph at Yankee Stadium did not come easily. The Dodgers, with their backs planted firmly against the wall, had tied the game in dramatic fashion in the top of the ninth when Carl Furillo bashed a one-out two-run homer off Allie Reynolds, who was pitching in relief of Whitey Ford.

But the Yankees fought back in the bottom of the inning. Bauer led off with a walk and, one out later, Mickey Mantle beat out a slow roller to the left side of the infield. Martin followed with his Series-winning hit, a line drive over second base that gave him a six-game record and tied the seven-game mark.

Martin, a .257 regular-season hit-ter, was clearly the hero of this Series. He got the Bronx Bombers off to a flying start in the opener with a bases-loaded first-inning triple off Carl Erskine that keyed a 9-5 triumph and he homered in New York's 4-2 second-game win. He added an-other round-tripper in an 11-7 Game 5 victory that also included a grand slam by Mantle and other Yankee homers by Gene Woodling and Gil McDougald.

The peppery second baseman, whose mad-dash seventh-game catch of Jackie Robinson's popup had saved the 1952 Series for the Yankees, finished with a .500 aver-age and eight runs batted in. Mantle batted only .208, but belted a pair of homers and drove in seven runs.

The Dodgers, winless in World Series competition and five-time vic-tims of the Yankees, managed only 3-2 and 7-3 victories in Games 3 and 4. Those wins were keyed by homers from National League Most Valu-able Player Roy Campanella and Duke Snider.

Mickey Mantle arrives home with a big smile and four RBIs after hitting a grand slam in Game 5 of the World Series.

Yankee World Series Game 6 heroes (left to right): Hank Bauer, Yogi Berra, Billy Martin and Joe Collins.

Game 1	New York	9	Brooklyn	5
Game 2	New York	4	Brooklyn	2
Game 3	Brooklyn	3	New York	2
Game 4	Brooklyn	7	New York	3
Game 5	New York	11	Brooklyn	7
Game 6	New York	4	Brooklyn	3

" DUGOUT CHATTER "

"The biggest mistake since they invented buttermilk."

Preacher Roe

Dodger lefthander, on the curveball Billy Martin hit for a home run in the seventh inning of the Yankees' 4-2 Game 2 World Series victory

Court clears baseball in antitrust challenge

In a major victory for baseball's controversial reserve system, the United States Supreme Court ruled November 9 that the National Pastime is a sport, not an interstate business, and as such is not subject to the nation's anti-trust laws.

In a 7-2 opinion read by Chief Justice Earl Warren, the court decided there was no reason to overturn the Supreme Court ruling of 1922. The reserve clause, which binds a player to his team and denies him the opportunity to negotiate with other clubs, has been the target of litigation and Congressional hearings for a number of years.

The ruling means that baseball cannot be challenged in the courts as an illegal monopoly and that the reserve clause will stay on the books unless Congress decides to do something about it. Congress' monopoly subcommittee looked extensively at baseball two years ago, but decided not to act.

★ 1954 ★

JANUARY - SEPTEMBER

" DUGOUT CHATTER "

"Do you think they would dare pull a Mathews or a Williams or a Sauer shift on Stan Musial? No one would be that crazy. Stan would rap one into left and clear the bases. Musial is the greatest team hitter I ever saw."

Paul Waner

Former Pittsburgh star and Hall of Famer

Musial muscles up

Stan (The Man) Musial, a six-time National League batting champion and three-time Most Valuable Player, muscled his way into the record books May 2 with a five-home run doubleheader barrage against the New York Giants at St. Louis' Busch Stadium. Despite Musial's heroics, the Cardinals could manage only a split, winning the first game, 10-6, and losing the nightcap, 9-7.

Musial connected three times in the opener, twice off lefthander Johnny Antonelli and once off righthander Jim Hearn. He then hit a pair of second-game homers against knuckleballer Hoyt Wilhelm, giving him eight for the season and tying Chicago's Hank Sauer for the major league lead.

Musial's five home runs accounted for nine runs batted in, three coming on his eighth-inning opening-game blast that broke a 6-6 tie and sent the Cardinals on their way to victory. He also had a single in his 6-for-8 two-game performance.

The previous record for home runs by one player in a doubleheader was four. The teams combined for 12 round-trippers in the twin bill.

Stan Musial, a man of many bats, rifled a record five home runs in a doubleheader against the New York Giants.

O's get big welcome

The new Orioles, mired in an ocean of indifference for years as the St. Louis Browns, were welcomed by baseball-hungry Baltimore fans as conquering heroes April 15 and then acted out the role with a 3-1 victory over Chicago at reconstructed Memorial Stadium.

Baltimore, without major league baseball since 1901, was in a party mood as more than 500,000 people crowded along a 3½-mile parade route to greet the team that had struggled to a 54-100 record last season in St. Louis. The uniformed Orioles, who had split their two season-opening games at Detroit, arrived at the train station and were whisked into top-down convertibles that carried them on the colorful 1½-hour procession.

As they passed, delirious fans sprinkled them with orchids and confetti. The players and Manager Jimmie Dykes responded by throwing plastic balls to the crowd. More than 20 bands and 32 elaborate floats gave the parade a Mardi Gras feel.

After the celebration, 46,354 fans packed into the new stadium and Vice President Richard Nixon threw out the first ball. Bob Turley punctuated the day with a seven-hit, nine-strikeout performance that was aided by Clint Courtney and Vern Stephens home runs.

More than a half million Baltimore fans turned out to give their new Orioles a rousing reception.

Players organize

Big-league players, beginning to look and act more and more like a union, formally organized into a group called the Major League Baseball Players Association July 12 and hired J. Norman Lewis to represent them in negotiations with team owners.

The 16 player representatives from the American and National leagues, meeting for 3½ hours, adopted by-laws and a constitution. Lewis will be paid a reported $30,000 a year, the money to come out of baseball's central fund. The fund consists of money derived from All-Star Game gate receipts and the television and radio receipts obtained from the All-Star Game and World Series.

Lewis denied that the player action resulted in a union, pointing out that no dues would be paid to the association. The player representative group had organized informally in 1946 as the "players' fraternity."

New player representatives from each of the 16 teams will be elected in July 1955 and this group will in turn elect one representative from each league.

CAUGHT ON THE FLY

MARCH

Chicago Manager Phil Cavarretta, having told Owner Philip K. Wrigley that his Cubs were a second-division team, was fired during spring training and replaced by Stan Hack.

JUNE

The Brooklyn Dodgers held St. Louis outfielder Rip Repulski to one single during a game at Ebbets Field, snapping an incredible 10-game streak in which he had collected two or more hits in each contest.

JULY

Chicago righthander Bob Rush retired St. Louis' Red Schoendienst four times in a game at Busch Stadium, ending the second baseman's 28-game hitting streak.

Indians' trio stages All-Star power show

Indians stars Al Rosen, Bobby Avila and Larry Doby delighted their hometown fans July 13 with a combined 7-for-8, three-homer, eight-RBI performance that lifted the American League to a wild 11-9 victory over the National League at Cleveland's Municipal Stadium.

Rosen led the charge with two home runs and five RBIs in a three-hit effort. Avila drove in two runs with his three hits and Doby smashed a game-tying eighth-inning homer in a pinch-hitting role. The teams combined for six home runs in a game that produced numerous offensive All-Star records.

The Nationals, boasting a four-year winning streak, opened with Philadelphia ace Robin Roberts, who surrendered a three-run blast to Rosen and four A.L. tallies in the third inning. The N.L. struck back for five runs in the fourth, two coming on a double by Brooklyn's Jackie Robinson.

The lead see-sawed back and forth the rest of the way with Chicago's Nellie Fox finally providing the deciding eighth-inning blow — a looping two-run single off Brooklyn's Carl Erskine.

American League conquering heroes (left to right): Larry Doby, Ray Boone, Al Rosen, Bobby Avila and Nellie Fox.

Adcock goes wild

Milwaukee first baseman Joe Adcock set a record for one-game slugging July 31 when he belted home runs off four different Brooklyn pitchers and added a double in a 15-7 victory over the Dodgers at Ebbets Field.

Adcock became the seventh player to hit four homers in one game and the fifth to do it in nine innings. His 18 total bases were the most in one contest, bettering the four-homer, one-single efforts (17 total bases) of Boston's Bobby Lowe in 1894, Philadelphia's Ed Delahanty in 1896 and Brooklyn's Gil Hodges in 1950.

Adcock hit a solo homer off Don Newcombe in the second inning, a double off Erv Palica in the third, a three-run blast off Palica in the fifth, a two-run shot off Pete Wojey in the seventh and another solo drive off Johnny Podres in the ninth. He finished with seven runs batted in.

The Braves also got two homers from Eddie Mathews and one from Andy Pafko. Adcock, who had homered the day before, tied the record for most homers in two games.

Milwaukee's Joe Adcock (9) was a popular guy during his four-home run rampage against Brooklyn.

Yankee hopes fizzle

The Cleveland Indians did not officially clinch the American League pennant September 12 when they thrilled the biggest crowd in history with a doubleheader sweep of the New York Yankees, but for all intents and purposes they put the five-time defending champs out of their misery.

With 86,563 fans at Municipal Stadium cheering their every move, the Indians recorded 4-1 and 3-2 victories and stretched their A.L. lead over New York to 8½ games. Cleveland needs only three more wins to clinch its first pennant since 1948.

Bob Lemon pitched a six-hitter in the opener to record his 22nd victory and Early Wynn came back with a three-hit, 12-strikeout performance in the nightcap for his 21st win. Al Rosen's two-run seventh-inning double was the Indians' key hit in the first game and Wally Westlake's fifth-inning double drove home the tying and lead runs in Game 2 after Yogi Berra had given the Yankees a 2-0 lead with a first-inning homer.

The crowds surpassed the record set October 10, 1948, when 86,288 turned out at Municipal Stadium for a World Series game.

★ 1954 ★

SEPTEMBER-DECEMBER

WORLD SERIES REPORT

A GIANT UPSET

Monte Irvin and Wes Westrum drove in two runs apiece October 2 and the New York Giants held off a desperate Cleveland rally for a 7-4 victory that completed an astonishing four-game World Series sweep.

The Giants, heavy underdogs to the team that had set an A.L. record with 111 victories, built a 7-0 advantage through 4½ innings of the finale at Cleveland's Municipal Stadium. The Indians got three back in the fifth when Hank Majeski slammed a three-run pinch-hit homer off starter Don Liddle and added another in the seventh, but Hoyt Wilhelm and Johnny Antonelli pitched 2⅓ innings of scoreless relief to seal the Series-clinching verdict.

Giants center fielder Willie Mays and pinch-hit specialist Dusty Rhodes stole the spotlight in this Series. Their heroics got the New Yorkers off to a rousing start in the September 29 opener at the Polo Grounds.

The Indians looked like winners when, with two runners on base and the score tied 2-2 in the eighth inning, Vic Wertz belted a drive that appeared to be well beyond Mays' reach. Mays pursued the ball and, with his back to the infield, made an incredible over-the-shoulder catch 460 feet from home plate — possibly the greatest defensive play in Series history. The Giants won the game in the 10th when Rhodes, pinch-hitting for Irvin, dropped a fly ball into the short right-field stands for a 260-foot three-run homer off Cleveland starter Bob Lemon.

The next day, Rhodes pinch-hit a run-scoring single and added a solo homer in a 3-1 Giants victory, and they followed that with a 6-2 win at Cleveland, Rhodes getting a two-run pinch-hit single.

Rhodes finished with four hits in six at-bats (a .667 average), two homers and seven RBIs.

Game 1	New York	5	Cleveland	2
Game 2	New York	3	Cleveland	1
Game 3	New York	6	Cleveland	2
Game 4	New York	7	Cleveland	4

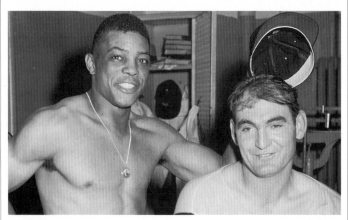

Two World Series Giants in New York's clubhouse: Willie Mays (left) and Dusty Rhodes.

Indians win 111 games

Early Wynn lost his no-hit bid and shutout in the ninth inning September 25, but that did not spoil the festive mood in Cleveland as the Indians defeated Detroit, 11-1, for their American League-record 111th victory on the second-to-last day of the season.

Wynn, looking for his 23rd win, carried a no-hitter into the ninth, but Detroit's Fred Hatfield ruined that prospect with a leadoff single, and Steve Souchock tripled one out later.

The Indians, who collected 14 hits, pulled steadily away en route to their record-setting triumph. The 111 wins broke the league mark of 110 set by the 1927 New York Yankees. The 1906 Chicago Cubs hold the major league record of 116.

An 8-7 final-day loss to the Tigers left Cleveland with a 111-43 record. Amazingly, the Yankees, looking for their sixth straight A.L. pennant, won 103 times and finished eight games back.

Pitching was the key to Cleveland's success. Wynn and Bob Lemon tied for the A.L. lead with 23 wins and Mike Garcia, a 19-game victor, led the A.L. with a 2.64 earned-run average. Lemon (2.72) and Wynn (2.73) finished third and fourth.

Second baseman Bobby Avila led the league with a .341 mark and Larry Doby led the A.L. in home runs (32) and RBIs (126).

Pitching coach Mel Harder (second from right) with the Big Three of Cleveland's staff (left to right): Mike Garcia, Early Wynn and Bob Lemon.

SEASON LEADERS

	American League		National League	
Avg.	Bobby Avila, Cle.	.341	Willie Mays, N.Y.	.345
HR	Larry Doby, Cle.	32	Ted Kluszewski, Cin.	49
RBI	Larry Doby, Cle.	126	Ted Kluszewski, Cin.	141
SB	Jackie Jensen, Bos.	22	Bill Bruton, Mil.	34
W-L Pct.	Sandy Consuegra, Chi.	16-3, .842	Johnny Antonelli, N.Y.	21-7, .750
ERA	Mike Garcia, Cle.	2.64	Johnny Antonelli, N.Y.	2.29
SO	Bob Turley, Bal.	185	Robin Roberts, Phi.	185

" DUGOUT CHATTER "

"I went to St. Louis to watch the Browns and the Red Sox. I went to see Ted Williams hit."

Willie Mays

The young Giants star, telling about the only major league game he had ever seen before reaching the big time as a player

THE trade

The Baltimore Orioles and New York Yankees completed the biggest trade in baseball history December 1 when the final eight names of a 17-player deal were announced.

The trade was completed in two stages. On November 18, Baltimore sent pitchers Bob Turley and Don Larsen and shortstop Billy Hunter to the Yankees for six players — pitchers Harry Byrd and Jim McDonald, outfielder Gene Woodling, shortstop Willie Miranda and catchers Hal Smith and Gus Triandos.

When the deal was concluded 13 days later after the major league draft, Baltimore received pitcher Bill Miller and infielders Kal Segrist and Don Leppert while giving up five players — pitcher Mike Blyzka, catcher Darrell Johnson, first baseman Dick Kryhoski and outfielders Jim Fridley and Ted Del Guercio.

When the dust finally cleared, Baltimore had received nine players from the Yankees, who got eight in return.

New York Yankee-turned-Baltimore Oriole Gus Triandos.

Athletics move to Kansas City

Arnold Johnson, the 47-year-old Chicago industrialist who recently bought the Athletics from the Mack family, received a double dose of good news November 8. Both the sale and the transfer of the team to Kansas City was approved by American League owners at a meeting in New York.

The news ended weeks of haggling and speculation concerning the future of the downtrodden A's franchise, which was a charter member of the A.L. under the direction of Connie Mack. The Athletics, winners of nine pennants and five World Series in their history, had fallen on hard times and were losing the battle of Philadelphia to the National League's Phillies.

There had been some A.L. opposition to Johnson because of his close association with New York Yankees co-Owner Dan Topping and his ownership of Yankee Stadium, which Johnson has agreed to sell.

The A's will open next season in Kansas City's Municipal Stadium, which will be expanded from 17,000 seats to 36,000. The stadium has been the home of the Kansas City Blues, a Yankee farm team that Topping plans to relocate. The franchise transfer is baseball's third in 20 months.

CAUGHT ON THE FLY

SEPTEMBER

For the second straight season, the Milwaukee Braves set an N.L. attendance mark, attracting 2,131,388 fans.

Brooklyn rookie lefthander Karl Spooner's impressive debut: Two shutouts and a major league two-game record 27 strikeouts.

NOVEMBER

Seven-time National League home run champion Ralph Kiner, traded by Pittsburgh to Chicago last year, was sent by the Cubs to Cleveland for two players and cash.

Mays wins bat title on final day

Willie Mays, the outstanding 23-year-old center fielder of the New York Giants, celebrated his return from military service by capturing the 1954 National League batting championship with a final-day three-hit flurry that buried the hopes of teammate Don Mueller and Brooklyn's Duke Snider.

Mays trailed his two competitors by percentage points as the N.L.-champion Giants prepared for the September 26 finale against Philadelphia and the Dodgers encountered Pittsburgh. Mueller started the day at .3426, Snider at .3425 and Mays at .3422.

Both Mueller and Mays singled in their first at-bats against Phillies ace Robin Roberts and both made outs in their next plate appearances. But Mays went on to collect a triple, a double and a walk in the Giants' 3-2, 11-inning victory while Mueller managed only one more hit in his 2-for-6 performance. The Pirates held Snider hitless.

Final averages: Mays .345, Mueller .342 and Snider, who had led most of the season, .341. Mays became the first Giant to win a batting title since Bill Terry batted .401 in 1930.

Willie also finished with 41 home runs and 110 RBIs.

N.L. batting champion Willie Mays (right) of New York and one of the men he beat out, Brooklyn's Duke Snider.

Athletics win debut

After a festive civic parade that drew more than 200,000 persons, the Athletics gave Kansas City its first-ever taste of major league baseball April 12 when they defeated the Detroit Tigers, 6-2, before 32,844 enthusiastic fans at Municipal Stadium.

The team that had played more than half a century as the Philadelphia Athletics put on a good show for an Opening Day throng that included such dignitaries as former President Harry S Truman, Commissioner Ford Frick, American League President Will Harridge, 92-year-old former Philadelphia A's owner and manager Connie Mack and numerous other baseball notables and politicians.

The Athletics, a team that finished 51-103 and 60 games behind first-place Cleveland in its final Philadelphia campaign, took control of the contest in the sixth inning. Elmer Valo broke a 2-2 deadlock when he walked with the bases loaded and Don Bollweg's pinch-hit single drove in two more. Bill Wilson stroked the A's first Kansas City home run in the eighth.

Alex Kellner got credit for the victory, thanks to excellent relief from veteran Ewell Blackwell.

The arrival of the Athletics in Kansas City was greeted with appropriate fanfare and a festive Opening Day parade.

Yanks cross barrier

The New York Yankees became the 13th major league team to break the color barrier April 14 when Elston Howard singled in his first big-league at-bat and played three innings in Boston's 8-4 victory at Fenway Park.

The Yankees, criticized by Brooklyn's Jackie Robinson in 1952 as prejudiced toward blacks and an inviting target for other racial snipers because of their long winning tradition and national image, took the big plunge when left fielder Irv Noren was ejected from the game against Boston for arguing an out call at home plate. Howard replaced him and delivered a run-scoring single in his only plate appearance.

Howard's pinstripe debut came eight years after Robinson broke the color barrier in 1947 for the Dodgers. Only three teams — the Philadelphia Phillies, Detroit Tigers and Boston Red Sox — have yet to employ a black player on the major league level.

New York Manager Casey Stengel with Eddie Andrews (center) and Elston Howard, the man who broke the Yankee color barrier.

" DUGOUT CHATTER "

"When I saw him at his peak, he came as close to being a perfect ballplayer as I've ever seen."

Chuck Dressen

Washington manager, on Jackie Robinson, whom he formerly managed at Brooklyn

Chisox bury A's, 29-6

Aided by a gusty wind, the Chicago White Sox belted seven home runs out of Kansas City's Municipal Stadium April 23, tying the modern major league run-scoring record in a 29-6 bombing of the Athletics.

The Kansas City massacre began in the first inning when Chicago's Bob Nieman hit a three-run homer off Bobby Shantz and continued in the second when the White Sox scored seven times off Shantz and reliever Leroy Wheat. Chicago matched the 1950 record of the Boston Red Sox while collecting 29 hits, one short of the modern record set by the 1953 Yankees.

Nieman and Sherm Lollar both hit a pair of homers while Walt Dropo, Minnie Minoso and pitcher Jack Harshman hit one apiece. Nieman drove in seven runs, Lollar and Minoso five each. Lollar and Chico Carrasquel both collected five hits. Lollar set a major league record by stroking two hits in both the second and sixth innings — the first time that feat had been accomplished twice in the same game.

Ford's 1-hitters

Whitey Ford, doing his part as the New York Yankees try to keep pace with first-place Cleveland, fired his second straight one-hitter September 7 and defeated Kansas City, 2-1, for his 17th win of the season.

Working at Yankee Stadium, Ford held the A's hitless for 6⅔ innings before surrendering a walk to Hector Lopez and a ground-rule double down the right-field line to Jim Finigan. Lopez scored the tying run on Ford's wild pitch.

The score remained tied until the ninth, when A's righthander Arnie Portocarrero yielded a one-out double to Hank Bauer, an infield single to Yogi Berra and an intentional walk to Mickey Mantle. Irv Noren walked on four pitches to force in the winning run and keep the Yankees one-half game behind the Indians in the American League standings.

Ford, the fifth pitcher in history to throw consecutive one-hitters, had stopped Washington, 4-2, in his previous start, yielding only a seventh-inning single to Carlos Paula. Mickey Vernon, who had walked, scored when Paula's hit bounced away from left fielder Noren and Paula came home on a grounder. Mantle belted a three-run homer for the Yanks.

New York Yankee lefty Whitey Ford fired consecutive one-hitters.

Musial's homer in 12th lifts N.L.

St. Louis slugger Stan Musial belted the first pitch he saw in the bottom of the 12th inning from Boston's Frank Sullivan for a game-winning home run as the National League posted a come-from-behind 6-5 All-Star Game victory over the American League July 12 at Milwaukee's County Stadium.

Musial's record fourth All-Star homer ended the second-longest contest in All-Star history. The stage was set by a furious N.L. rally from a seventh-inning 5-0 deficit. The Americans had scored four runs in the first inning, three on a home run by New York Yankee Mickey Mantle, and added a solo tally in the sixth. But the N.L. tied with two runs in the seventh and three in the eighth.

Milwaukee's Gene Conley delighted his home fans by striking out the side in the top of the 12th and earning the victory after relieving Joe Nuxhall, the Cincinnati lefty who had pitched 3⅓ innings of two-hit relief.

The game was played on the same day that funeral services were held for Arch Ward, the former *Chicago Tribune* sports editor who founded the midsummer classic in 1933.

N.L. All-Star heroes (left to right): Milwaukee's Gene Conley, Cincinnati's Joe Nuxhall and St. Louis' Stan Musial.

CAUGHT ON THE FLY

APRIL
The Brooklyn Dodgers set a modern major league record when they won their first 10 games of the season, breaking the previous mark of nine shared by three teams.

MAY
The Boston Red Sox got a double dose of heat when Cleveland's Bob Feller pitched his 12th career one-hitter for a 2-0 victory in the first game of a doubleheader and Herb Score struck out 16 in a 2-1 nightcap win.

Chicago righthander Sam (Toothpick) Jones fired the first no-hitter at Wrigley Field in 37 years, beating Pittsburgh, 4-0.

JUNE
The Boston Red Sox were stunned when 25-year-old first baseman Harry Agganis, a second-year major leaguer, died of complications resulting from pneumonia.

AUGUST
St. Louis star Stan Musial became the ninth player in major league history to collect 1,000 career exta-base hits when he doubled off Lew Burdette during the first inning of a game at Milwaukee.

Mays hits 50 homers

Willie Mays became the seventh player in major league history to hit 50 home runs in a single season September 20 when he connected for two-run shots in each game of the New York Giants' 11-1 and 14-8 doubleheader sweep of Pittsburgh at the Polo Grounds.

Mays drove homer No. 49 off the left-field roof in the first inning of the opener, sending the Giants on their way to an easy victory behind lefthander Johnny Antonelli. The young center fielder hit his 50th in the fifth inning of the nightcap and joined Babe Ruth, Ralph Kiner, Jimmie Foxx, Hank Greenberg, Hack Wilson and Johnny Mize in the select circle of 50-homer bashers. Ruth accomplished the feat four times, Kiner and Foxx twice each. Mize set the Giants record with 51 in 1947.

Mays' 50th blast also allowed him to tie a major league record shared by former Giants George Kelly (1924) and Walker Cooper (1947) — seven home runs in six games.

BROOKLYN'S WACKY DODGERS

Baseball at Ebbets Field

While pennants, World Series championships and victories over the more affluent New York Giants and Yankees were the ultimate Dodger goals, baseball played with a Brooklyn accent carried a much deeper meaning. It was a crusade for respect, a religious experience. It was serious in theory but raucous and amusing in practice.

She was classy, charming and warm. Subtle, unusual curves added to her distinctive air. Gorgeous, no, but she had personality and a fun-loving mystique that invited wild, daffy and wacky behavior. On one hand, Ebbets Field stood as baseball's monument to comedy and compassion. On the other, she stood as a stately cathedral in the Borough of Churches.

To the zany, protective, loving and passionate Brooklyn fans who knew Ebbets Field as the home of the Dodgers for 45 seasons, she was baseball's Mount Olympus, where the Gods of Flatbush lived in perfect harmony with their worshipers. Well, maybe not perfect. These sometimes stumbling and bumbling deities were idolized with equal doses of love and disapproval, but indiscretions always were forgiven and no disappointment was so great that Brooklyn fans couldn't "wait till

next year."

Their heroes were lovingly referred to as "Dem Bums," a name coined by New York cartoonist Willard Mullin, and they carried such colorful monickers as Leo, Zack, Skoonj, Dazzy, Dixie, Campy, Jackie, Casey, Pee Wee, Newk, Uncle Robbie and, of course, Oisk and the Dook. "Oisk" was pitcher Carl Erskine and "the Dook" was center fielder Duke Snider, both products of a Brooklyn dialect that made such transformations as "murder" to "moider" and "girl" to "goil." Dodger fans, from the 1913 opening of Ebbets Field to the team's final Brooklyn season in 1957, were always loud, knowledgeable and ready to heap their colorful abuse on opposing teams.

"There was a feeling in that ballpark that probably will never be recaptured again," said Dixie Walker, "The People's Cherce"

Left: The Dodgers' self-declared team orchestra, the rag-tag Sym-phony Band, stayed out of tune for two glorious decades.

Hilda Chester (right), the cowbell-ringing queen of the left-centerfield bleacherites.

who played outfield for Brooklyn from 1940 to '47. "I'll always be fond of my years in Brooklyn, even though I didn't know what I was getting into when I went there. The people loved the Dodgers as if they were a part of them."

The Brooklyn fans were part of the Dodgers and Ebbets Field promoted that feeling, perhaps as no ballpark before or after. It was cozy and inviting with a seating capacity of 34,219. "You were so close to the field sitting anywhere in that old park that you could hear the players talking to each other," said former Dodger vice president Red Patterson.

The right-field wall was only 297 feet from home plate at the foul line, and what a right-field wall it was. It stood 20 feet high and was topped by a 20-foot high screen to protect windows on Bedford Avenue. The wall was concave, which produced strange bounces that only a few outfielders ever learned to negotiate with any consistency.

A giant scoreboard jutted out from the wall and its base was

The roly-poly Wilbert Robinson (right) managed the Dodgers for 18 zany seasons.

covered by an Abe Stark sign that offered a free suit to anybody who hit it on the fly with a batted ball. Numerous other trademark signs added to the park's distinct character, as did a number of wild and crazy fans who became permanent fixtures in its lore.

The most famous was Hilda Chester, the cowbell-ringing queen of the left-center field bleacherites. Hilda was there every day, leading the serenade of cheers and epithets that rained down on the field from the first pitch of the game to its final out. Another regular was known simply as Carrie, the first in line at the bleacher gate for every Dodger home game. And who could forget the infamous Sym-phony band, which stayed out of tune for two decades as the self-declared team orchestra. The Sym-phonies liked to irritate opponents by banging on instruments to celebrate a strikeout or other such failure.

In deference to the band, Dodger Owner Walter O'Malley once promoted a game at Ebbets as Music Depreciation Night and offered free admission to any fan bearing a musical instrument. The 2,426 who accepted the challenge were seated in the upper left-field bleachers and serenaded the remainder of the 24,560 in noisy confusion throughout the game. It was pure Brooklynese.

Such confusion was not uncommon and the Dodgers themselves added to the wacky mystique. The inept Daffiness Boys of Wilbert Robinson and Casey Stengel ruled at Ebbets Field in the 1920s and '30s and Leo Durocher's Bums battled to a National League pennant in 1941, setting the stage for the pennant-winning machines of Burt Shotton, Chuck Dressen and Walter Alston in the late 1940s and '50s. The boys of Uncle Robbie and Casey tormented Brooklyn with a string of sub-.500 seasons. The pennant-winners of later years tortured their fans in a different way — with a string of World Series losses to the New York Yankees, their hated American League cousins from across the East River.

While pennants, World Series championships and victories over the more affluent New York

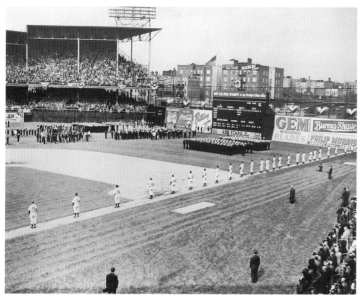

Always-colorful Ebbets Field, with its distinctive look and cozy atmosphere, was the home of baseball's beloved Brooklyn Dodgers.

Giants and Yankees were the ultimate Dodger goals, baseball played with a Brooklyn accent carried much deeper meaning. It was a crusade for respect, a religious experience. It was serious in theory, but raucous and amusing in practice. Even when the Boys of Summer — Pee Wee Reese, Jackie Robinson, Roy Campanella, Carl Furillo, Gil Hodges, Snider, Don Newcombe, Erskine, et al — were winning six N.L.

pennants in 10 years (1947-56) and losing two others on final-day home runs, they never lost perspective. They were as colorful and fun to watch in victory as their predecessors had been in defeat.

Predecessors such as the roly-poly Uncle Robbie, who managed for 18 zany years (1914-31), producing two pennants and many happy memories. Stengel, who as a Pittsburgh player once doffed his cap to a screaming Brooklyn crowd as a sparrow

flew out. Pitcher Billy Loes, who complained during the 1952 World Series that he had lost a ground ball in the sun. Babe Herman, a talented hitter and brutal defensive outfielder who once doubled into a double play. Herman, dressing next to Fresco Thompson in 1931, announced to his teammates, "I'm pretty embarrassed dressing next to a .250 hitter." To which Thompson replied, "No more embarrassed than I am dressing next to a .250 fielder."

The stories are endless. So were the magical moments that gave Ebbets Field a special place in history. Such as Cincinnati's Johnny Vander Meer firing his second straight no-hitter in 1938 to punctuate the first night game in Brooklyn. Catcher Mickey Owen committing the infamous passed ball that cost the Dodgers a victory in the 1941 World Series. Durocher drawing a year's suspension from Commissioner Happy Chandler and Jackie Robinson breaking baseball's color barrier in 1947. Dodger Cookie Lavagetto breaking up Yankee pitcher Bill Bevens' 1947 World Series no-hit bid with a two-out, two-run, game-winning double in the ninth inning. Four-homer games by Hodges and Milwaukee's Joe Adcock. A World Series-saving shoetop catch by Yankee second

baseman Billy Martin in 1952.

But the most wonderful and enduring moment was reserved for 1955, when Johnny Podres completed his 2-0 Game 7 shutout of the Yankees, giving Brooklyn its long-awaited first World Series championship. After seven failures in the fall classic, Dem Bums ruled the baseball world. Brooklyn celebrated as only Brooklyn could.

Little did anybody know that Brooklyn's first championship also would be its last. The Dodgers gave Flatbush one more pennant and two more seasons before O'Malley, in search of greener pastures, carted Dem Bums off to Los Angeles, 3,000 miles from their roots. It was like cutting the heart out of the city, and its soul was removed in 1960, when Ebbets Field was torn down.

Umpteen years later, Brooklyn fans remained emotional about the Dodgers, although the bitterness had given way to nostalgia. O'Malley might have wiped away their reason to smile, but he could not take away their memories.

Part of Brooklyn's 'Boys of Summer' lineup (left to right): Duke Snider, Jackie Robinson, Roy Campanella, Gil Hodges and Carl Furillo.

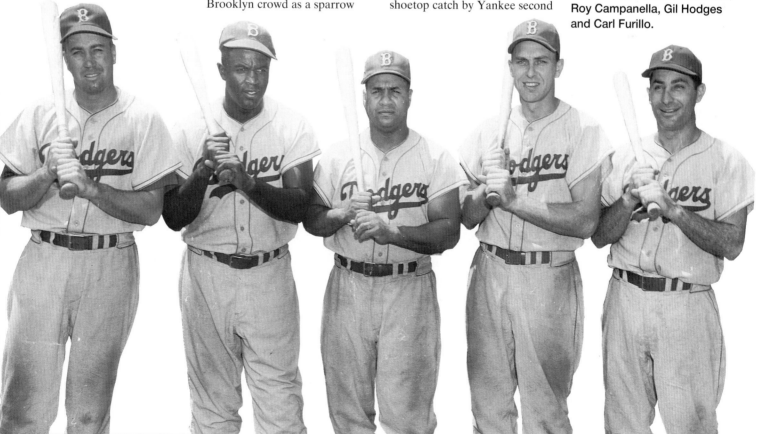

WORLD SERIES REPORT

DODGERS FINALLY WIN

Lefthander Johnny Podres pitched an eight-hit shutout and Sandy Amoros, a sixth-inning defensive replacement in left field, made an incredible game-saving catch as the Brooklyn Dodgers defeated New York, 2-0, in the October 4 seventh game of the World Series at Yankee Stadium.

The victory ended more than a half century of Brooklyn frustration and snapped the Dodgers' World Series losing streak at seven. They had won pennants in 1916, 1920, 1941, 1947, 1949, 1952 and 1953, but had lost the Series on each occasion, the last five to the hated Yankees.

When the 1955 fall classic opened, it didn't appear that this one would be any different. The Yanks won the first two games at Yankee Stadium, 6-5 and 4-2. Joe Collins hit two homers and Elston Howard one for the Yankees in the opener while Carl Furillo and Duke Snider connected for the Dodgers in a losing cause. Tommy Byrne pitched a five-hitter in the second game and helped his own cause with two RBIs.

But Podres, working on his 23rd birthday, got Brooklyn back on track in the third game with an 8-3 win at Ebbets Field and the Dodgers won the next day, 8-5, as Roy Campa-

nella, Gil Hodges and Snider hit home runs. Two more blasts by Snider, giving him a record-tying four for the Series, keyed a 5-3 Game 5 victory that put Brooklyn in command.

With two shots to win the Series at Yankee Stadium, the Dodgers faced off against Yankee ace lefthander Whitey Ford in Game 6. But Ford was outstanding, pitching a four-hitter, and Bill Skowron contributed a three-run homer to the Yankees' 5-1 Series-squaring victory.

The Dodgers were leading 2-0 in Game 7 when the critical play occurred in the sixth. Shaded toward center with two Yankees on base and a lefthanded power hitter at the plate, the fleet Amoros raced to the left-field foul line and lunged to snare Yogi Berra's fly ball. He quickly wheeled to relay the ball back to the infield and the Dodgers turned what appeared to be a sure two-run double into a rally-killing double play.

Podres worked out of an eighth-inning jam and retired the Yankees in order in the ninth to give Dodger fans their long-awaited championship. Brooklyn's Bums were kings of the baseball world and "next year" was finally "this year" in Flatbush.

Kaline captures title

Al Kaline, Detroit's outstanding 20-year-old right fielder, became the youngest batting champion in major league history September 25 when he finished the season with an American League-best .340 average.

Hitless in one at-bat in his final game against Cleveland, Kaline nevertheless outdistanced the field in becoming Detroit's 20th batting champion and first since George Kell in 1949. He finished the season with 27 home runs, 102 RBIs and a league-leading 200 hits.

Kaline, born December 19, 1934, was one day younger than former Detroit great Ty Cobb was when he won the first of his 12 A.L. batting titles in 1907.

The National League also produced a wunderkind in 1955 — Chicago's Ernie Banks. The 24-year-old set two major league records — home runs by a shortstop (44) and grand slams in one season (5). Banks batted .295 and drove in 117 runs.

Detroit's 20-year-old Al Kaline, the youngest batting champion in big-league history.

Game 1	New York	6	Brooklyn	5
Game 2	New York	4	Brooklyn	2
Game 3	Brooklyn	8	New York	3
Game 4	Brooklyn	8	New York	5
Game 5	Brooklyn	5	New York	3
Game 6	New York	5	Brooklyn	1
Game 7	Brooklyn	2	New York	0

Above: Game 7 winning pitcher Johnny Podres gets a lift from catcher Roy Campanella as Don Hoak joins the celebration of Brooklyn's first World Series triumph. Left: Winners at last: Dodger Owner Walter O'Malley (left) and Manager Walter Alston.

3 former greats die

Clark Griffith, Cy Young and Honus Wagner, three Hall of Famers who helped usher in the modern era of baseball, died within a six-week period, leaving behind legacies that will live forever

Griffith, baseball's "Old Fox," died in his sleep October 27 at age 85. A long-time pitcher, manager, executive and owner of the Washington Senators, Griffith compiled 240 big-league victories in 21 seasons and served as one of Ban Johnson's top guns when the American League was organized in 1901. Griffith, who began his big-league career in 1893, won 24 games for Chicago in the A.L.'s first season and later pitched for New York, Cincinnati and Washington before retiring. He was president of the Senators from 1920 until his death.

Young, the oldest of the three at age 88, died of natural causes November 4 at his home in Newcomerstown, O. In a career that spanned 22 seasons beginning in 1890 with Cleveland of the National League, the talented righthander won 511 games, a record that may never be broken, and pitched three no-hitters, one a perfect game. From 1891 to 1904, when he pitched for Cleveland, St. Louis and the Boston Red Sox, he never won fewer than 20 games and topped the 30-win plateau five times.

The 81-year-old Wagner died in his sleep December 6 at Pittsburgh. One of the game's all-time great hitters, the bandy-legged shortstop compiled a career average of .329 for the Pirates and won eight National League batting titles in 21 seasons. Wagner's career hit total of 3,430 ranks third on the all-time list behind Ty Cobb and Tris Speaker. From 1900 to 1912, Wagner never hit below .320.

Wagner was elected to the Hall of Fame in 1936, Young in 1937 and Griffith in 1946.

Brooklyn catcher Roy Campanella receiving the N.L. Most Valuable Player award from League President Warren Giles.

Catchers win MVPs

Roy Campanella and Yogi Berra completed their second New York sweep in Most Valuable Player voting when both earned the honor for a record-tying third time and enhanced their reputations as the best catchers in baseball.

Campanella, who led the Brooklyn Dodgers to their eighth National League pennant and first World Series championship, outdistanced teammate Duke Snider by five points in balloting by the 24-man committee of the Baseball Writers Association of America. Berra, who helped the New York Yankees win their unprecedented 21st American League pennant, outpolled Detroit batting champion Al Kaline by 17 points.

In 1951, the two stocky catchers swept the coveted award, with Campanella winning again in 1953 and Berra in 1954. Only Stan Musial, Joe DiMaggio and Jimmie Foxx had previously won MVP citations three times.

The 30-year-old Berra, who received seven first-place votes, batted .272 with 27 home runs and 108 RBIs. The seven-time All-Star is considered a near-flawless receiver and one of baseball's most dangerous clutch hitters. He has hit 208 homers and driven in 898 runs in his 10-year Yankee career.

The 34-year-old Campanella, who had an injury-plagued 1954 campaign, rebounded to hit .318 with 32 homers and 107 RBIs. He barely beat out Snider, who batted .309 with 42 home runs and 136 RBIs. Both were named first by eight voters, but Campanella benefited when Snider was not named on one writer's ballot.

" DUGOUT CHATTER "

"I caught him without a sponge, and boy am I sorry. My hand's as sore as it has ever been."

Roy Campanella

Dodger catcher, after Johnny Podres had shut out the Yankees in Game 7 of the World Series

SEASON LEADERS

	American League		National League	
Avg.	Al Kaline, Det.	.340	Richie Ashburn, Phi.	.338
HR	Mickey Mantle, N.Y.	37	Willie Mays, N.Y.	51
RBI	Ray Boone, Det.	116	Duke Snider, Bkn.	136
	Jackie Jensen, Bos.	116		
SB	Jim Rivera, Chi.	25	Bill Bruton, Mil.	35
W-L Pct.	Tommy Byrne, N.Y. 16-5, .762		Don Newcombe, Bkn.	20-5, .800
ERA	Billy Pierce, Chi.	1.97	Bob Friend, Pit.	2.84
SO	Herb Score, Cle.	245	Sam Jones, Chi.	198

CAUGHT ON THE FLY

SEPTEMBER

An American League first: The circuit finished its season without a single 20-game winner.

Cleveland's Herb Score led the A.L. with a rookie-record 245 strikeouts and Pittsburgh's Bob Friend became the first pitcher to lead his league in ERA (2.83) while pitching for a last-place team.

★1956★
JANUARY-AUGUST

Long makes history

Pittsburgh's Dale Long continued his amazing slugging streak May 28 when he belted his record eighth home run in eight consecutive games to key a 3-2 Pirate victory over Brooklyn's Carl Erskine at Forbes Field.

With 32,221 fans roaring their approval, Long circled the bases after his fourth-inning, game-tying shot into the right-center field stands. The big first baseman listened to the cheering for several minutes before stepping out of the dugout to doff his cap. Bob Skinner's run-scoring single in the fifth gave the Pirates a lead that stood up behind the two-hit pitching of Bob Friend, who had been touched for a two-run, first-inning homer by Duke Snider.

Long, who had spent most of his 11-year career in the minor leagues, began his streak May 19 against Jim Davis of the Chicago Cubs and continued it with blasts off Ray Crone and Warren Spahn of Milwaukee, Herman Wehmeier and Lindy McDaniel of St. Louis and Curt Simmons and Ben Flowers of Philadelphia. The seventh homer, against Flowers, broke the previous major league record.

Brooklyn's Don Newcombe held Long hitless May 29 to end the streak.

Jersey City Dodgers — for a day

The Bums from Brooklyn, defending their first World Series championship, became the Jersey City Dodgers for an April 19 game against Philadelphia and 12,214 fans watched them post a 10-inning 5-4 comeback victory in the first regular-season major league game ever played at Roosevelt Stadium.

It was the first of seven home-away-from-home contests that Walter O'Malley's Dodgers will play in Jersey City this season as a way of demonstrating to Brooklyn officials a growing dissatisfaction with the cramped facilities at Ebbets Field. A biting wind from Newark Bay kept the crowd at about half capacity.

After a ceremonial pregame for the Dodgers' second "home" opener, the teams battled evenly for nine innings. The Phillies took their first lead in the 10th when Granny Hamner doubled home a run, but the Dodgers struck back in the bottom of the frame. Roy Campanella doubled home one

run and the winner scored on pinch-hitter Rube Walker's sacrifice fly.

Brooklyn Dodger officials inspect Roosevelt Stadium in Jersey City.

Reds lose no-hit bid

Hank Aaron tripled in the 11th inning and scored on Frank Torre's one-out single, giving first-place Milwaukee a zany 2-1 victory over Cincinnati May 26 after the Braves had been no-hit by three Reds pitchers for 9⅔ innings.

The Braves came within one out of winning the County Stadium contest in regulation, even though Cincinnati righthanders Johnny Klippstein, Hersh Freeman and Joe Black were on their way to becoming the first pitchers in modern major league history to combine on a nine-inning no-hitter. Milwaukee had taken advantage of Klippstein's wildness to

" DUGOUT CHATTER "

"For anticipation, nervousness and excitement, it beats the All-Star Game or pitching in a World Series game. The only exception I might make would be the seventh game of the World Series."

Bob Feller

Cleveland Indians veteran righthander, on what it is like to pitch on Opening Day

manufacture a second-inning run on a hit batsman, two walks and Torre's sacrifice fly and carried that lead into the ninth behind the pitching of Ray Crone.

But with two out, Crone surrendered his fifth hit, a Ted Kluszewski single, and Wally Post tied the score with a double off the left-field fence. Milwaukee finally

managed its first hit, a double by Jack Dittmer, with two out in the 10th.

Klippstein pitched seven hitless innings, but allowed seven walks before being lifted for a pinch-hitter. Freeman pitched a hitless eighth before giving way to Black, who allowed three hits over 2⅓ innings.

Pittsburgh's Dale Long: Home runs in a record eight consecutive games.

Another Mantle blast

Young Mickey Mantle, fast becoming known for his tape-measure home runs, hit another of legendary proportions May 30 at Yankee Stadium in the first game of New York's 4-3 and 12-5 doubleheader sweep of Washington.

With two men on base and the Yankees trailing righthander Pedro Ramos 1-0 in the fifth inning of the opener, Mantle connected with a 2-2 pitch and sent a skyscraper shot soaring toward the right-field roof high above Yankee Stadium's third deck. The ball hit a cornice and bounced all the way back onto the field. It missed leaving the ballpark by 18 incredible inches.

The ball struck a point about 370 feet from home plate some 117 feet above the ground. Yankee officials estimated the ball would have traveled more than 600 feet unimpeded. It was the switch-hitting Mantle's 19th homer and he added No. 20 in the second-game rout off Camilo Pascual.

With 16 homers in May, Mantle finds himself 11 games ahead of the pace Babe Ruth set in 1927 when he belted a record-setting 60. The 24-year-old center fielder is batting a torrid .425 with 50 RBIs.

Red Sox fine Williams

Temperamental Boston slugger Ted Williams was handed a $5,000 fine August 7 for his spitting gestures toward fans and sportswriters during the Red Sox's thrilling 11-inning, 1-0 victory over New York at Fenway Park.

Williams, who has a checkered history of on-field temper tantrums and off-field feuds with the press, muffed a fly ball in the 11th inning and quickly became the target of catcalls from Boston fans. He responded by making an outstanding inning-ending catch and then showed his contempt by spitting toward the crowd and the press box as he neared the Red Sox dugout.

In the bottom of the 11th, Williams drew a bases-loaded walk that forced in the winning run and threw his bat about 40 feet in the air as he trotted toward first. After the game, Boston General Manager Joe Cronin announced the fine.

The fine matches the largest ever levied against a major league player. In 1925, the New York Yankees fined Babe Ruth $5,000 for insubordination and breaking training rules.

Boston's Ted Williams directing his $5,000 spit toward the press box at Fenway Park.

Boyer, Mays, Musial star for Nationals

Willie Mays and Stan Musial hit home runs and third baseman Ken Boyer starred with both his bat and glove, lifting the National League to a 7-3 All-Star Game victory over the American League in a July 10 battle at Washington's Griffith Stadium.

In winning for the sixth time in seven years and cutting the A.L.'s All-Star lead to 13-10, the Nationals exhibited superior firepower and the solid pitching of Pittsburgh's Bob Friend, Milwaukee's Warren Spahn and New York's Johnny Antonelli.

St. Louis' Boyer drew rave reviews after singling three times, driving in one run and making three outstanding defensive plays. Mays contributed a pinch-hit two-run homer off New York's Whitey Ford in the fourth inning and Musial hit his record fifth All-Star Game home run off Boston's Tom Brewer in the seventh, when the N.L. also scored on a double by Cincinnati's Ted Kluszewski.

The A.L. broke through against Spahn in the sixth when Boston's Ted Williams hit a two-run homer and New York's Mickey Mantle followed with a solo shot.

All-Star Game celebrants (left to right): N.L. President Warren Giles, Manager Walter Alston, Ken Boyer, Stan Musial and Willie Mays.

CAUGHT ON THE FLY

FEBRUARY
Connie Mack, the founder, owner and manager of the Philadelphia Athletics for 50 years, died in Germantown, Pa., at age 93.

MAY
Brooklyn veteran Carl Erskine pitched the second no-hitter of his career, stopping the New York Giants, 3-0, at Ebbets Field.

Hall of Famer Al Simmons, a .334 lifetime hitter over 21 major league seasons, died in Milwaukee at age 53.

JULY
Commissioner Ford Frick announced a new five-year, $16.25 million contract with NBC for television rights to baseball's All-Star Game and World Series.

★1956★

"DUGOUT CHATTER"

"You can catch him with a pair of pliers."

Art Fowler

Cincinnati pitcher on Phillies junkball pitcher Saul Rogovin

Brooklyn wins again

Duke Snider and Sandy Amoros belted two home runs apiece and Brooklyn held off Pittsburgh in an 8-6 final-day thriller that gave the Dodgers their second straight National League pennant and fourth in the last five years.

As 31,963 delirious fans watched the September 30 clincher at Ebbets Field, Milwaukee was defeating the Cardinals, 4-2, at St. Louis. The final-day results gave Brooklyn a one-game edge over the Braves, who had spent 126 days atop the N.L. standings. Cincinnati finished a game behind Milwaukee.

The homers by Snider and Amoros and another by Jackie Robinson dropped the curtain on one of the most exciting pennant races in history. The Braves boasted a one-game lead over Brooklyn as both teams entered their final series and appeared to be in the driver's seat.

But the Cardinals had other ideas, posting a 5-4 September 28 win over Milwaukee as the Brooklyn game against Pittsburgh was being rained out, and a 12-inning 2-1 decision the next day as Brooklyn swept a doubleheader from the Pirates. The Dodgers, suddenly a game ahead, were primed for the kill.

The biggest lead held by any of the contenders was a 5½-game bulge by Milwaukee on July 26. The Dodgers, never more than six games off the pace, were tied with the Reds, 3½ games behind, at the close of Labor Day doubleheaders. But the Braves finished 11-12 while Brooklyn was going 15-7.

A key win for the Dodgers, both physically and emotionally, occurred September 25 when veteran Sal Maglie pitched his first career no-hitter, a 5-0 victory over Philadelphia that kept Brooklyn a half-game behind.

Pee Wee Reese takes a pennant-winning beer bath, courtesy of Brooklyn teammates (left to right): Carl Erskine, Don Bessent and Don Newcombe.

1st Cy Young Award

Brooklyn righthander Don Newcombe, already cited as the National League's Most Valuable Player, captured the first Cy Young Memorial Award, an honor that will be given annually to the top pitcher in baseball.

Newcombe, who finished 27-7 and helped the Dodgers win their fourth N.L. pennant in five years, was awarded 10 of the 16 first-place votes by a special committee of the Baseball Writers' Association of America. Brooklyn teammate Sal Maglie finished second in the voting ahead of Milwaukee's Warren Spahn and New York Yankee Whitey Ford.

The award is in honor of Cy Young, the career 511-game winner and Hall of Famer who died last November.

Brooklyn ace Don Newcombe, holding his Cy Young and Most Valuable Player plaques, with young Dodger pitcher Don Drysdale.

SEASON LEADERS

	American League		National League	
Avg.	Mickey Mantle, N.Y.	.353	Hank Aaron, Mil.	.328
HR	Mickey Mantle, N.Y.	52	Duke Snider, Bkn.	43
RBI	Mickey Mantle, N.Y.	130	Stan Musial, St. L.	109
SB	Luis Aparicio, Chi.	21	Willie Mays, N.Y.	40
W-L Pct.	Whitey Ford, N.Y.	19-6, .760	Don Newcombe, Bkn.	27-7, .794
ERA	Whitey Ford, N.Y.	2.47	Lew Burdette, Mil.	2.71
SO	Herb Score, Cle.	263	Sam Jones, Chi.	176

Mantle pulls sweep

New York Yankee Mickey Mantle drove in a run as a pinch-hitter in his final plate appearance of the season September 30, completing his journey to an American League Triple Crown. His .353 average, 52 home runs and 130 RBIs all were top figures in the A.L. this season, marking him as the 10th modern-era player to lead his circuit in all three categories.

Mantle, who grounded out in the ninth inning of a season-ending 7-4 loss to Boston, joins the Red Sox's Ted Williams as the only active players who have performed the trick. Williams, who did it in both 1942 and '47, was the only Triple Crown winner of the 1940s.

Mantle also became the eighth major leaguer to top the 50-homer plateau and the first in the A.L. since 1938, when Detroit's Hank Greenberg belted 58. New York's Willie Mays led the National League with 51 last year.

PERFECTO

Johnny Kucks pitched a three-hit shutout and Yogi Berra and Bill Skowron combined for eight runs batted in October 10 as the New York Yankees avenged their 1955 World Series loss to Brooklyn with a 9-0 seventh-game triumph at Ebbets Field.

Kucks' victory wrapped up a fall classic that included the most incredible pitching performance in Series history. With the count deadlocked at two games apiece, New York's Don Larsen squared off against Brooklyn's Sal Maglie in a memorable Game 5 battle at Yankee Stadium.

The 39-year-old Maglie got off to a great start, retiring the first 11 Yankees he faced. But New York's Mickey Mantle emphatically ended that streak with a fourth-inning home run into the right-field stands. Hank Bauer's run-scoring single in the sixth was the only other run The Barber would allow on this historic afternoon.

But Maglie's effort was not good enough. The 27-year-old Larsen matched Maglie pitch for pitch and completed the fourth inning unscathed. The Dodgers went 1-2-3 in the fifth . . . and the sixth . . . and the seventh . . . and the eighth as 64,519

fans roared their approval. Not only was the journeyman righthander on the verge of throwing the first no-hitter in World Series history, he was closing in on baseball's first perfect game in 34 years.

Larsen opened the ninth by getting Carl Furillo on a fly ball. Roy Campanella followed by grounding out. When pinch-hitter Dale Mitchell took a called third strike on Larsen's 97th pitch, catcher Berra went leaping into his arms and pandemonium broke out in the House That Ruth Built.

Larsen, who had failed to get through the second inning in Brooklyn's 13-8 Game 2 victory, was in the record books with his seven-strikeout masterpiece. And the Yankees, despite Bob Turley's tough 10-inning 1-0 loss to Brooklyn's Clem Labine in Game 6, were on their way to their 17th World Series title. Kucks pitched the clincher, Berra hit two home runs and Skowron clubbed a seventh-inning grand slam.

The Yankees, who had used 11 pitchers in dropping the first two contests, received complete-game performances in the next five by five different pitchers who combined to allow only six runs and 21 hits over 45⅔ innings.

Game 1	Brooklyn	6	New York	3
Game 2	Brooklyn	13	New York	8
Game 3	New York	5	Brooklyn	3
Game 4	New York	6	Brooklyn	2
Game 5	New York	2	Brooklyn	0
Game 6	Brooklyn	1	New York	0
Game 7	New York	9	Brooklyn	0

World Series perfect game principals (left to right): Yankee pitcher Don Larsen, umpire Babe Pinelli and New York catcher Yogi Berra.

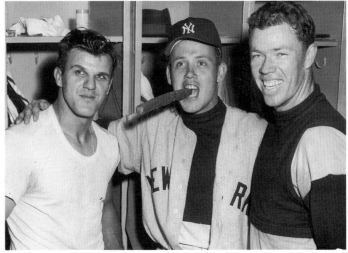

A happy threesome of (left to right): Moose Skowron, Billy Hunter and Gil McDougald celebrate New York's return to the victory circle.

SEPTEMBER

New York Yankee Yogi Berra became the all-time home run leader among catchers when he blasted No. 237 off Detroit righthander Jim Bunning, breaking the mark held by former Chicago Cub Gabby Hartnett.

Frank Robinson tied a major league rookie home run record when he belted 38 first-year shots for the Cincinnati Reds.

Artful Dodger Jackie Robinson retires

Jackie Robinson, traded December 13 by the Brooklyn Dodgers to the rival New York Giants, announced his retirement from major league baseball in a copyrighted story written for *Look* magazine.

Robinson, the outstanding second baseman who broke baseball's color barrier as a first baseman in 1947, said he was retiring because "I have to think of the future and the security of my family." The former four-sport UCLA star added that he had made his decision before the trade was announced and kept it quiet only because he had made an exclusive deal a long time ago with *Look* magazine to write his "retirement story."

The 38-year-old Robinson leaves baseball with a .311 career average and 1,518 hits in 10 big-league seasons. He was the National League batting champion (.342) and Most Valuable Player in 1949 and he led N.L. second basemen in fielding percentage three times. The two-time stolen base leader appeared in six World Series and six All-Star Games.

Robinson will become an executive with a New York restaurant chain.

Copacabana incident

New York second baseman Billy Martin, one of the principals in the May 16 Copacabana night club incident that involved six Yankees, was sent to Kansas City June 15 as part of a seven-player trade.

Martin, rumored to be on the trading block because of his "negative influence" over teammate Mickey Mantle, was dealt to the Athletics with shortstop Woody Held and outfielder Bob Martyn for pitcher Ryne Duren, second baseman Milt Graff and outfielders Harry Simpson and Jim Pisoni. The 29-year-old Martin has been involved in numerous scrapes and fights during his 6½-year Yankee career.

Martin's most recent transgression might have been his most innocent. It was during his birthday celebration at the Copacabana that an alleged "fight" took place between Yankee outfielder Hank Bauer and Edwin Jones of Manhattan. Jones claimed he was struck by Bauer, who denied the charge.

Bauer and Martin were at a table that also included Yankee players Mantle, Whitey Ford, Yogi Berra and Johnny Kucks as well as several wives. Jones approached the party and tried to make conservation. The attack allegedly took place later, in the club's basement.

Bauer, Martin, Mantle, Ford and Berra were fined $1,000, Kucks $500.

Two innings in a fog

The Brooklyn Dodgers, leading Chicago 1-0 with one out in the second inning, were defeated June 6 by Mother Nature, who dropped a foggy shroud over Ebbets Field and forced one of the stranger postponements in baseball history.

A light fog that engulfed the ballpark as the game began drew steadily thicker as the Dodgers broke on top in the first inning, play becoming more treacherous with every pitch. It became apparent by the top of the second that anything hit in the air would

be a problem. Brooklyn's Don Zimmer made a last-second lunging catch of a Dale Long popup that nobody else could even see.

When Charlie Neal's routine fly ball to left dropped for a double in the bottom of the inning, the Cubs appealed to the umpires and the arbiters halted play. The game was called after one hour and 26 minutes.

The same two teams were victimized by another strange postponement at Ebbets Field in 1947. That game was called on account of swarming gnats.

" DUGOUT CHATTER "

"He was the closest to perfection I ever saw. And I never saw a perfect ballplayer. Joe could do everything and do it well. He was a team star and an individual star — that's a rare combination."

Tommy Henrich

Detroit coach, on former New York Yankee teammate Joe DiMaggio

Line drive fells Score

The Cleveland Indians won their May 7 game against New York, but lost, maybe permanently, their best pitcher — 23-year-old lefthander Herb Score.

With the game only about three minutes old, 18,386 fans at Cleveland's Municipal Stadium watched in horror as Gil McDougald, the Yankees' second batter, smashed a line drive toward the pitcher. Score, unable to get his glove up in time, was hit on the right eye and crumpled to the ground as the ball caromed to third baseman Al Smith.

Players from both teams rushed to the fallen pitcher, who was

bleeding from both his broken nose and his mouth with his eye closed and swollen. He was taken to Lakeside Hospital, where he was examined by Dr. C. W. Thomas, an eye specialist. The physician reported hemorrhaging in the eye so severe that the exact nature of the injury could not be determined for several days.

Score, a 16-game winner in his 1955 rookie season and a 20-game winner last year, never lost consciousness. The fireballer, regarded by many as the best young pitcher in baseball, was replaced by Bob Lemon, who went on to record a 2-1 victory.

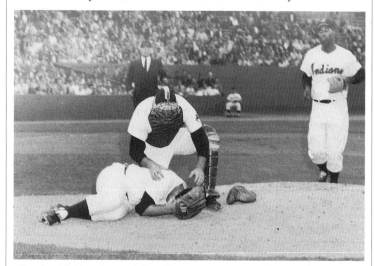

Cleveland lefthander Herb Score goes down after getting hit in the eye by a line drive off the bat of New York's Gil McDougald.

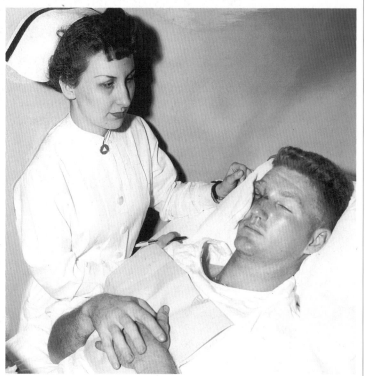

Indians ace Herb Score resting in the hospital the morning after.

Mini-Mexicans win

A pint-sized contingent of youngsters from Monterrey, Mexico, wrote the perfect ending to a baseball fairy tale August 23 when it captured the Little League World Series with a 4-0 victory over an American team from La Mesa, Calif. And the Mexicans did it in style. Angel Macias, a 5-foot, 88-pound 12-year-old, retired every batter he faced.

In a classic David-versus-Goliath battle at Williamsport, Pa., the La Mesa team, averaging 5-4 and 127 pounds per player, was matched in the final against the midgets from Monterrey, averaging a mere 4-11 and 92 pounds. It was raw power versus finesse —

and the little guys won.

Macias recorded 11 strikeouts and La Mesa did not hit a ball out of the infield. Monterrey scored all four of its runs in the fifth inning on two walks, two hits, two fielders' choices and two very costly errors.

The greatest success story in the 11-year history of the Little League World Series, the unheralded Mexicans started the long road to Williamsport with a 150-mile trip to McAllen, Tex., for a playoff game and then made stops at Corpus Christi, Tex., Fort Worth, Tex., and Louisville, Ky., that resulted in 11 straight victories.

Angel Macias, a 12-year-old Mexican pitcher, was perfect in the final game of the Little League World Series.

CAUGHT ON THE FLY

APRIL
When John Kennedy was sent into a game against Brooklyn as a pinch-runner, the Philadelphia Phillies became the last N.L. team to break the color barrier.

JULY
Commissioner Ford Frick received a vote of confidence from the major league owners in the form of a seven-year contract extension.

AUGUST
Stan Musial's N.L.-record consecutive-games streak ended at 895 when the St. Louis star was forced to the bench with a shoulder injury.

Reds fans see stars

Commissioner Ford Frick headed off the ballot-stuffing antics of Cincinnati fans June 28 by naming three replacements for Reds in the National League starting lineup for the July 9 All-Star Game at St. Louis.

Cardinal first baseman Stan Musial, New York outfielder Willie Mays and Milwaukee outfielder Hank Aaron were named to replace George Crowe (first base), Gus Bell (center field) and Wally Post (right field). That threesome, plus five other Cincinnati players, appeared to be

headed for starting berths after an avalanche of votes had been received from the Cincinnati area. More than 500,000 poured in last week, lifting Bell from third place to first and Post from second to first. Crowe was not even among the leaders in the early count.

Other Redleg starters: Johnny Temple (second base), Don Hoak (third base), Roy McMillan (shortstop), Frank Robinson (left field) and Ed Bailey (catcher).

As it turned out, final tabulations gave Musial a slight final edge over Crowe anyway.

Minoso rescues A.L.

Chicago left fielder Minnie Minoso, who had delivered a run-scoring double in the top of the ninth inning, threw one runner out at third base and made an outstanding game-ending catch to preserve the American League's 6-5 victory over the National League in the July 9 All-Star Game at St. Louis' Busch Stadium.

The Americans appeared in control when they scored three ninth-inning runs to stretch their lead to 6-2. But St. Louis' Stan Musial drew a walk and New York's Willie Mays tripled him

home. After Mays scored on a wild pitch, Pittsburgh's Hank Foiles singled and Cincinnati's Gus Bell walked.

Milwaukee's Eddie Mathews struck out, but Chicago's Ernie Banks singled home another run. Minoso eased some of the tension when he cut down Bell trying to go to third. With the tying run on second, Minoso ended the contest with an excellent running catch of Gil Hodges' drive to left-center.

The A.L. had built an early 3-0 lead that the N.L. cut to one on Bell's two-run pinch-hit double in the seventh.

All-Star Game hero Minnie Minoso of Chicago.

MILWAUKEE WINS FIRST TITLE

Aaron decks Cards

Hank Aaron gave Milwaukee its first National League pennant September 23 when he smashed an 11th-inning two-run homer to give the Braves a clinching 4-2 victory over second-place St. Louis at County Stadium.

Aaron's blow, his league-leading 43rd, ended the frustration of three second-place finishes in the Braves' four seasons at Milwaukee and broke a 10-year stranglehold of eastern clubs on the N.L. pennant. The victory gave the Braves a six-game lead over the Cardinals with five to play and insured that hungry Milwaukee fans will get their first taste of World Series play. The Braves, who drew 2,215,404 fans this year, have topped the 2-million attendance mark in each of their four Milwaukee seasons.

The Braves were locked in a five-team struggle when July came to a close, but one by one the other contenders fell as Milwaukee put together a 10-game winning streak. Philadelphia lost 20 of 27 games beginning July 31, Brooklyn dropped 11 of 18 starting August 2, Cincinnati lost 18 of 23 starting August 3 and St. Louis lost nine straight beginning August 6.

Two keys to Milwaukee's success were the June acquisition of second baseman Red Schoendienst from New York and the July 28 purchase of Bob Hazle from Wichita. "Hurricane," as Hazle came to be known, was a .279 hitter in the Class AAA American Association who proceeded to bat .403 in 41 games for Milwaukee while replacing injured Bill Bruton in the outfield.

Hank Aaron, the biggest bat in Milwaukee's pennant-winning arsenal.

Lew Burdette scattered seven hits and Eddie Mathews keyed a four-run third inning with a two-run double as the Braves toppled New York, 5-0, October 10 at Yankee Stadium to give Milwaukee its first World Series championship.

Burdette's third victory and second straight shutout came at the expense of Yankee starter Don Larsen, the hero of the 1956 fall classic. Larsen lasted only 2⅓ innings before giving way to Bobby Shantz. By then, the damage had been done and catcher Del Crandall provided eighth-inning insurance with a solo home run.

Burdette's first victory, a 4-2 decision in Game 2, had evened the Series at a game apiece and his 1-0 win in Game 5 gave the Braves a three games to two advantage. That game was decided by Joe Adcock's run-scoring single.

Game 4, a 10-inning 7-5 victory for Milwaukee and Warren Spahn, was easily the most exciting game of this fall classic. Spahn carried a 4-1 lead into the ninth and retired the first two Yankees. One strike away from victory, Spahn surrendered singles to Yogi Berra and Gil McDougald and a game-tying homer to Elston Howard.

When Hank Bauer tripled home Tony Kubek in the top of the 10th, it appeared the Braves were doomed. But Johnny Logan doubled home the tying run in the bottom of the 10th and Mathews brought an electrifying end to the contest with a home run.

The Series offensive star was Milwaukee's Hank Aaron, who batted .393 with three homers and seven RBIs.

Game 1	New York	3	Milwaukee	1
Game 2	Milwaukee	4	New York	2
Game 3	New York	12	Milwaukee	3
Game 4	Milwaukee	7	New York	5
Game 5	Milwaukee	1	New York	0
Game 6	New York	3	Milwaukee	2
Game 7	Milwaukee	5	New York	0

Milwaukee fans were eager to celebrate the Braves' seven-game World Series victory over the New York Yankees.

CAUGHT ON THE FLY

SEPTEMBER
Boston's Ted Williams reached base 16 straight times during a September streak that finally ended when he grounded out against Washington's Hal Griggs. Williams walked nine times and was hit by a pitch.

OCTOBER
World Series-champion Milwaukee set an N.L. record by drawing 2,215,404 fans to County Stadium.

NOVEMBER
Milwaukee's 21-game winner Warren Spahn was a landslide choice for the second Cy Young Award, earning 15 of the available 16 votes.

Mantle named MVP

Boston's 39-year-old left fielder, Ted Williams, the oldest batting champion in baseball history, was aced out in the American League Most Valuable Player voting for the third time in his career November 22 when New York's Mickey Mantle received the coveted award for the second straight year.

Mantle, who batted .365, hit 34 homers and drove in 94 runs while missing most of the final three weeks with severe shin splints, outpolled the veteran Williams, 233 points to 209. Boston's Splendid Splinter, who won his fifth A.L. batting title with a whopping .388 mark while belting 38 home runs, was considered the favorite. But one member of the 24-man Baseball Writers' Association of America committee voted Williams ninth on his ballot and another listed him 10th. Mantle's lowest vote was fourth.

"I do not think that anyone who lets personalities interfere with his judgment is qualified or competent to vote," said an irate Tom Yawkey, owner of the Red Sox.

Mantle was shocked. "I thought Williams would get it for sure," he said.

Williams, a two-time MVP, has carried on a running feud with the media and that could have been the deciding factor.

A.L. Most Valuable Player Mickey Mantle (right) and N.L. batting champion Stan Musial.

" DUGOUT CHATTER "

"Hank is so relaxed at the plate that he takes a nap between pitches."

Joe Garagiola

Cleveland broadcaster and former big-league catcher, referring to Milwaukee star Hank Aaron

---

SEASON LEADERS

	American League		National League	
Avg.	Ted Williams, Bos.	.388	Stan Musial, St. L.	.351
HR	Roy Sievers, Wash.	42	Hank Aaron, Mil.	44
RBI	Roy Sievers, Wash.	114	Hank Aaron, Mil.	132
SB	Luis Aparicio, Chi.	28	Willie Mays, N.Y.	38
W-L Pct.	Dick Donovan, Chi.	16-6, .727	Bob Buhl, Mil.	18-7, .720
	Tom Sturdivant, N.Y.	16-6, .727		
ERA	Bobby Shantz, N.Y.	2.45	Johnny Podres, Bkn.	2.66
SO	Early Wynn, Cle.	184	Jack Sanford, Phi.	188

Baseball heads west

It was widely accepted that baseball would someday follow professional football's example and expand to the booming population-rich West Coast. But the fall confirmations that the New York Giants are moving to San Francisco and the Brooklyn Dodgers to Los Angeles for the 1958 season still shocked the puzzled fans of New York City.

Those fans were not exactly blindsided. Rumors had been circulating for months. But still the official news was greeted with disbelief. How could two of baseball's most glamorous, tradition-steeped franchises run out on their faithful fans?

The answer, of course, is money. The old bottom line.

The Giants had a 52,000-seat stadium (the Polo Grounds), but they also had a parking problem and were feeling the pinch of a population shift to the suburbs. After drawing 1.15 million fans in their championship season of 1954, attendance skidded to 653,923 in 1957.

The Dodgers had a different kind of problem. They had the fan support and population, but they did not have an adequate facility. Aging Ebbets Field seats only 32,000 and that simply was not enough. The perennial pennant contenders regularly have drawn 1 million fans to their games, but that figure might easily have doubled in a more spacious stadium.

Dodger President Walter O'Malley had made no secret of his dissatisfaction and even transferred 15 of the Dodgers' 1956 and 1957 home games to Roosevelt Stadium in Jersey City. Civic officials explored the possibility of a new facility but found the costs too prohibitive.

The Giants have been promised a new stadium. Until then, they will play their games in 22,500-seat Seals Stadium, which had served as home of the Pacific Coast League Seals for 27 seasons.

The Dodgers have not yet decided on a stadium, although they are considering Wrigley Field, a minor league facility in Los Angeles, the Rose Bowl in Pasadena and the 90,000-seat Los Angeles Coliseum.

Dodger Owner Walter O'Malley (center) gets an official welcome to Los Angeles from County Supervisor Kenneth Hahn and city council member Rosalind Wyman.

★1958★

CAUGHT ON THE FLY

JANUARY

The New York Yankees signed a contract worth more than a million dollars to televise 140 of their 1958 games.

St. Louis' Stan Musial became the National League's first six-figure superstar when he signed a $100,000 contract. Only Boston's Ted Williams at a reported $125,000 is paid more.

MARCH

A new rule: All major leaguers must wear helmets when they step into the batter's box.

JUNE

Third baseman Ozzie Virgil, obtained in January from San Francisco, became the first black to play in a Detroit Tigers uniform when he collected one hit in an 11-2 win over Washington.

Fans lose Star vote

Commissioner Ford Frick, in an unspoken reaction to last year's ballot stuffing in Cincinnati, took the All-Star vote away from the fans January 30 and turned it over to the players, coaches and managers.

Frick, calling his new system a one-year experiment, will ask every player, coach and manager to fill out a form listing three opposing players at every position for their respective leagues. The top vote-getters will be starters, with the managers filling out the reserve lists and pitching staffs.

Frick's unhappiness with the fan selection process stemmed from last year's vote, when an avalanche of Cincinnati ballots threatened to give the National League an all-Redleg starting lineup. Frick named three replacement starters.

The fans have been selecting the All-Star starters since 1947. Prior to that, managers made all the picks.

Score comes back

Cleveland's Herb Score, hit in the eye by a career-threatening line drive last May, won his first game in almost a year April 18 when he pitched nine innings and defeated Detroit, 7-5, at Tiger Stadium.

The fireballing lefthander had fallen short in his first comeback attempt, losing April 15 to Kansas City and Ned Garver, 5-0. He pitched three innings in that game, surrendering three runs and four walks while striking out six.

He appeared to be facing an early exit against the Tigers, too. Detroit scored two first-inning runs and was threatening to get more in the third when Score dramatically struck out Harvey Kuenn on a 3-2 curveball. That seemed to be the turning point as he settled down and turned in a 169-pitch effort that resulted in his first win since April 28, 1957.

The 24-year-old had been hailed as baseball's next great pitcher before the accident. The line drive almost cost him the sight in his right eye.

Campanella injured

Catcher Roy Campanella, three-time Most Valuable Player of the Brooklyn Dodgers, suffered a broken neck and paralysis from his shoulders down when the car he was driving January 28 overturned on a slippery road in Glen Cove, N.Y.

Campanella was driving a rental car to his Glen Cove home at 3:34 a.m. after making a television appearance in New York. About a mile and a half from his home, the 1957 sedan skidded on wet pavement, turned on its right side and crashed into a telephone pole. Campanella was pinned in the car, his body twisted like a pretzel, for about 30 minutes as rescuers worked to pry open the doors.

The burly 5-foot-9, 225-pounder was rushed to Community Hospital where a seven-man team of surgeons performed a four-hour, 15-minute operation to repair two fractured vertebrae in his neck. Campanella had some movement in both arms after the surgery, but none in his fingers or the lower part of his body. Doctors questioned whether he would ever walk again, much less play baseball.

The 36-year-old Campanella joined the Dodgers in 1948 and proceeded to compile a .276 average with 242 home runs in his 10 major league seasons. He earned National League MVP citations in 1951, '53 and '55. He was scheduled to move with the Dodgers to Los Angeles for the 1958 campaign, but that move, along with everything else in Campy's life, now is on hold.

Former Brooklyn catcher Roy Campanella after his career-ending car accident.

Youngsters inspect the 1957 Chevrolet that Dodger Roy Campanella was driving the night of his crippling accident.

" DUGOUT CHATTER "

"When I heard the fans booing Joe DiMaggio in 1950, I made up my mind I'd never feel too bad if they booed me."

Carl Erskine

Dodger pitcher

Dodgers, Giants square off in Coast debut

It seemed only fitting that the Dodgers and Giants, newly arrived from Brooklyn and New York, should be opponents when West Coast fans got their first taste of major league baseball. And it seemed only right that both home teams should provide their new fans with rousing victories.

All eyes were on San Francisco April 15 as 23,448 fans turned out at Seals Stadium to watch their new home-town Giants play host to the first West Coast regular-season game in major league history. The mood was festive as the crowd listened to the usual welcoming speeches from politicians, baseball dignitaries and other notables, and the Giants got into the swing of things with an eight-hit attack that produced an 8-0 victory over Don Drysdale and the Los Angeles Dodgers.

With Ruben Gomez pitching a six-hitter, center fielder Willie Mays hitting a two-run single and shortstop Daryl Spencer and rookie first baseman Orlando Cepeda contributing home runs, the Giants made short work of the Dodgers. The Giants scored two third-inning runs and erupted for four in the fourth as they manhandled three Dodger hurlers.

After the Giants won two of

Players from the Dodgers and Giants line up on the field during the festive first-game ceremonies at the Los Angeles Coliseum.

three from the Dodgers, the scene shifted to the massive Los Angeles Coliseum for another festive first. The inaugural big-league contest in Los Angeles would be played before 78,672 baseball-hungry fans, the largest crowd in National League history.

Extensive alterations had been made on the field surface of the Coliseum, a horseshoe-shaped structure built for the 1932 Olympics but used more recently for football. Dugouts had been constructed, along with three new light towers, a backstop screen and a five-tier press box. Because the left-field fence loomed a cozy 251 feet from home plate, a 40-foot screen extending 140 feet from the foul line toward center field was erected to minimize chances for cheap home runs.

The record crowd watched the Dodgers jump to a 5-2 lead in the April 18 opener, then hold off the Giants for a 6-5 victory. The key play came in the San Francisco ninth when Jim Davenport was called out for missing third base after scoring an apparent run, short-circuiting what should have been a game-tying rally.

" DUGOUT CHATTER "

"If baseball players had to jump around for one season of a basketball schedule in our league, they'd never gripe about anything again."

Ben Kerner

Owner of the National Basketball Association's St. Louis Hawks

Musial reaches 3,000

St. Louis slugger Stan (The Man) Musial became the eighth member of baseball's 3,000-hit club May 13 when he delivered a ringing opposite-field double in a pinch-hitting role during a 5-3 Cardinal victory over the Chicago Cubs at Wrigley Field.

Musial, a seven-time National League batting champion and three-time Most Valuable Player, had been given the day off so that he could go after the historic hit in front of his home fans on May 15. But with the Cardinals trailing 3-1 and a man stationed at second in the sixth inning, Manager Fred Hutchinson hailed his star from the bullpen and sent him to the plate in place of pitcher Sam Jones. Musial hit Moe Drabowsky's sixth pitch off the left-field wall, driving in Gene Green and keying a four-run Cardinal rally.

The 37-year-old Musial, who got his first major league hit in

St. Louis' 3,000-hit man, Stan Musial, is escorted from Chicago's Wrigley Field (left) after collecting his historic double and giving way to a pinch-runner.

September 1941 against Jim Tobin of the Boston Braves, joins Ty Cobb, Tris Speaker, Honus Wagner, Eddie Collins, Nap Lajoie, Paul Waner and Cap Anson in the 3,000-hit fraternity. Cobb (4,191) is the only player to top 4,000 hits.

★1958★

SEASON LEADERS

	American League		National League	
Avg.	Ted Williams, Bos.	.328	Richie Ashburn, Phi.	.350
HR	Mickey Mantle, N.Y.	42	Ernie Banks, Chi.	47
RBI	Jackie Jensen, Bos.	122	Ernie Banks, Chi.	129
SB	Luis Aparicio, Chi.	29	Willie Mays, S.F.	31
W-L Pct.	Bob Turley, N.Y.	21-7, .750	Warren Spahn, Mil.	22-11, .667
			Lew Burdette, Mil.	20-10, .667
ERA	Whitey Ford, N.Y.	2.01	Stu Miller, S.F.	2.47
SO	Early Wynn, Chi.	179	Sam Jones, St. L.	225

" DUGOUT CHATTER "

"There are twice as many spitters being thrown today as when they were legal."

Waite Hoyt

Former major league pitcher

A.L. earns 4-3 win

New York Yankee Gil McDougald delivered a run-scoring pinch-hit single in the sixth inning and three American League pitchers combined for 7⅓ scoreless innings as the junior circuit scored a 4-3 victory over the National League in the July 8 All-Star Game at Baltimore's Memorial Stadium.

In winning for the 15th time in 25 midsummer classics, the Americans spotted the N.L. a 2-0 first-inning lead and a 3-1 second-inning margin before turning matters over to Cleveland's Ray Narleski, Chicago's Early Wynn and Baltimore's Billy O'Dell. That threesome surrendered only one hit.

The A.L. chipped away with single runs in the first, second, fifth and sixth innings, the final coming when McDougald drove home Boston's Frank Malzone.

The Americans collected nine hits, the Nationals four — and all 13 were singles. This was the first All-Star Game without an extra-base hit.

Pierce is 'perfect' for 8⅔

Chicago's Billy Pierce came within one out of perfection.

Chicago lefthander Billy Pierce, one out away from pitching baseball's first regular-season perfect game since 1922, surrendered a first-pitch double to pinch-hitter Ed Fitz Gerald June 27 before closing out his 3-0 victory over Washington at Comiskey Park.

With 11,300 White Sox fans on the edge of their seats, Fitz Gerald hit an opposite-field line drive just inside the right-field line, spoiling Pierce's bid to become the fifth modern-era pitcher to retire 27 straight batters. The 31-year-old completed his third career one-hitter by striking out Albie Pearson for his seventh victory in 12 decisions and third consecutive shutout.

Pierce, who struck out nine, allowed only six balls to be hit out of the infield and went to three-ball counts on two batters. A two-run eighth-inning single by catcher Sherm Lollar provided him with all the cushion he needed.

Former White Sox pitcher Charlie Robertson pitched the last regular-season perfect game in 1922, beating Detroit, 2-0. The last big-league pitcher to perform the feat was New York Yankee Don Larsen, who beat Brooklyn, 2-0, in Game 5 of the 1956 World Series.

Wilhelm unhittable

Hoyt Wilhelm, a six-year veteran who had never started a major league game before this season, pitched the second no-hitter of the campaign September 20, baffling the New York Yankees with a knuckleball that danced and darted like an elusive butterfly around the home plate area at Memorial Stadium.

The 35-year-old righthander made his third appearance for the Orioles a dramatic one. Wilhelm struck out eight and walked two in recording only his third victory in 13 decisions — a misleading record considering his 2.62 earned-run average.

Wilhelm, acquired from Cleveland on August 23, worked through a drizzling rain and had the Yankees swinging futilely. He outdueled Don Larsen and Bobby Shantz, who surrendered the 30th home run of the season to Balti-

Baltimore knuckleballer Hoyt Wilhelm (right) with catcher Gus Triandos after pitching a no-hitter against New York.

more catcher Gus Triandos for the game's only run.

Detroit's Jim Bunning had

recorded the season's first no-hitter July 20 when he defeated Boston, 3-0, at Fenway Park.

Williams closes fast

Aging Boston slugger Ted Williams belted a final-day home run and a double to complete a 7-for-11 surge that lifted him past teammate Pete Runnels in a race for the American League batting championship. Williams captured his sixth title with a .328 average while Runnels, 0-for-4 in the Red Sox's 6-4 victory over Washington, finished at .322.

The 40-year-old Williams, who had become the oldest batting champion in history last year when he hit a whopping .388, struggled through much of the 1958 campaign and was under .300 as late as June. He rallied to trail Runnels, .324 to .320, as the final four-game series against the Senators opened and he held a .327 to .324 advantage going into the September 28 finale.

As always, the three-time A.L. Most Valuable Player finished in style. His seventh-inning solo homer broke a 4-4 tie and lifted the Red Sox to victory.

The National League batting championship also was decided on the final day. Philadelphia's Richie Ashburn captured his second title with a 3-for-4 push during a 6-4 win over Pittsburgh that allowed him to edge out San Francisco's Willie Mays, .3495 to .3466. Mays was 3 for 5 in the Giants' 7-2 win over St. Louis.

In search of the A.L. batting title (left to right): Cleveland's Vic Power and Boston teammates Ted Williams and Pete Runnels in early September.

Philadelphia's Richie Ashburn (right) beat out San Francisco's Willie Mays for the N.L. batting title with a 3-for-4 final day.

YANKS CATCH BRAVES

First baseman Bill Skowron capped a four-run eighth-inning rally with a three-run homer October 9 as the New York Yankees defeated the Milwaukee Braves, 6-2, in Game 7 of the World Series at Milwaukee. The Yankees became only the second team to recover from a three games to one Series deficit.

Bob Turley, pitching 6⅔ innings of two-hit relief, picked up his second win, having shut out the Braves, 7-0, in Game 5. The big righthander, who replaced starter Don Larsen with one out in the third and the bases loaded, got out of that jam and then limited Milwaukee to a game-tying sixth-inning homer by Del Crandall.

The Yankees got to Braves starter Lew Burdette and broke the 2-2 tie in the eighth when Yogi Berra doubled and scored on Elston Howard's single. Andy Carey followed with another single and Skowron crashed a drive over the left-center field fence at County Stadium.

Skowron's homer capped a valiant comeback by the Yankees, who lost the first two games and played much of the Series with their backs planted firmly against the wall. Skowron and Hank Bauer homered in the October 1 opener at Milwaukee, but Warren Spahn still pitched the Braves to a 4-3 victory. A seven-run first inning and the pitching of Burdette were too much for the New Yorkers to overcome in a 13-5 second-game loss.

After the Yankees had recorded a 4-0 victory behind the combined six-hit pitching of Larsen and Ryne Duren, Spahn gave Milwaukee a commanding lead with a 3-0, two-hit whitewash.

But that would be the last hurrah for the defending champions. Gil McDougald homered and drove in three runs as the Yankees rolled in the fifth game, and he homered again in the 10th inning of Game 6 to break a 2-2 tie and spark a 4-3 triumph.

Bauer, McDougald and Skowron combined for eight homers and 19 RBIs for the Yankees, who won their sixth Series of the decade and 18th overall.

Game 1	Milwaukee	4	New York	3
Game 2	Milwaukee	13	New York	5
Game 3	New York	4	Milwaukee	0
Game 4	Milwaukee	3	New York	0
Game 5	New York	7	Milwaukee	0
Game 6	New York	4	Milwaukee	3
Game 7	New York	6	Milwaukee	2

CAUGHT ON THE FLY

AUGUST

Chicago first baseman Dale Long became baseball's first lefthanded catcher since 1902 when he went behind the plate in the ninth inning of a game against Pittsburgh at Wrigley Field.

NOVEMBER/DECEMBER

Two Hall of Famers died: Long-time New York Giant slugger Mel Ott of injuries suffered in a Mississippi automobile accident at age 49 and Tris Speaker of a heart attack at Lake Whitney, Tex., at age 70.

DECEMBER

Will Harridge, president of the American League for more than 27 years, announced his retirement at age of 72.

★1959★
JANUARY-JULY

SEASON LEADERS

	American League		National League	
Avg.	Harvey Kuenn, Det.	.353	Hank Aaron, Mil.	.355
HR	Harmon Killebrew, Wash.	42	Eddie Mathews, Mil.	46
	Rocky Colavito, Cle.	42		
RBI	Jackie Jensen, Bos.	112	Ernie Banks, Chi.	143
SB	Luis Aparicio, Chi.	56	Willie Mays, S.F.	27
W-L Pct.	Bob Shaw, Chi.	18-6, .750	Elroy Face, Pit.	18-1, .947
ERA	Hoyt Wilhelm, Bal.	2.19	Sam Jones, S.F.	2.82
SO	Jim Bunning, Det.	201	Don Drysdale, L.A.	242

Perfect for 12, but. . .

A disconsolate Harvey Haddix after pitching 12 perfect innings, only to lose in the 13th.

Pittsburgh's Harvey Haddix was unhittable May 26 against Milwaukee, but that was not good enough. In one of the most incredible performances in history, the little lefthander mesmerized the Braves and 19,194 fans at County Stadium for 12 perfect innings — and then lost, 1-0, in a 13th frame that ranked somewhere on the other side of perfect.

Combining his fastball and sharp-breaking curve with impeccable control, Haddix stuck out eight and mowed down the Braves with boring consistency. Thirty-six batters stepped to the plate, 36 went back to the dugout without a hit. He coasted through the Milwaukee batting order, becoming the sixth modern-era pitcher to throw nine perfect innings and the first ever to take a perfect game beyond regulation.

But his Pirate teammates were suffering a different kind of futility against Braves starter Lew Burdette. Plenty got on base (12 hits), but nobody could cross the plate. After nine innings, the game remained scoreless. After 10 . . . after 11 . . . after 12.

Haddix's bubble finally burst in a bizarre 13th, after Burdette had retired the Pirates in the top of the inning. Felix Mantilla broke Haddix's perfect string by reaching first base on a throwing error by Pittsburgh third baseman Don Hoak. Mantilla was sacrificed to second and Hank Aaron was walked intentionally. Haddix now had to face big first baseman Joe Adcock with the game on the line.

Adcock ended the suspense with a long drive that barely cleared the right-center field fence for an apparent game-winning home run. But Aaron threw the final moments into further confusion by leaving the basepaths to join the celebration, apparently thinking the ball had hit at the base of the fence and Mantilla had scored the winning run. Adcock was ruled out for having passed his teammate.

When the dust cleared, Milwaukee was declared a 1-0 winner and Adcock's hit was ruled a double, not a home run. But the cruel bottom line was still the same. Harvey Haddix had pitched the first extra-inning perfect game in baseball history — and lost.

Paralyzed Campy king for a night

A massive, roaring crowd of 93,103 at the Los Angeles Coliseum paid an emotional tribute to one of the greatest catchers in history May 7 before watching the New York Yankees beat the Dodgers, 6-2, in an exhibition on "Roy Campanella Night."

The largest crowd ever to fill a baseball stadium rose en masse and produced a thunderous ovation when Campanella, the paralyzed former Brooklyn catcher, was wheeled to the second base area. In a tear-jerking moment, the solitary wheel chair-confined figure sat with tears running down his face as he received a greeting fit for a king.

"This is something I'll never forget," said Campanella, who was paralyzed in a 1958 car accident that ended his outstanding 10-year career. "I thank God I'm here living to be able to see it. It's a wonderful thing."

The game, set up to raise money for the financially strapped former star, exceeded all expectations. Campanella, a three-time National League Most Valuable Player, received the Dodgers' entire share of the receipts, believed to be between $50,000 and $75,000. The Yankees pledged their take to other charities.

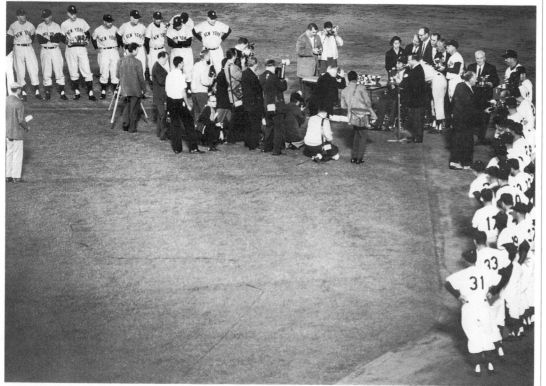

Former Brooklyn catcher Roy Campanella, confined to a wheel chair, is the center of attention on a night in his honor at the Los Angeles Coliseum.

Colavito belts four

Cleveland slugger Rocky Colavito became the eighth player in major league history to slug four home runs in one game June 10 when he drove in six runs and keyed the Indians' 11-8 victory over Baltimore at Memorial Stadium.

Colavito, who hit 41 homers last year and finished one behind American League leader Mickey Mantle of New York, walked in the first inning, connected off starter Jerry Walker with a man on base in the third, hit a solo shot in the fifth off Arnie Portocarrero, belted another two-run shot off Portocarrero in the sixth and capped his big day with a solo blast off Ernie Johnson in the ninth. Johnson, who had retired the first four Indians he faced, had not given up a homer this year.

Colavito is the third A.L. player to perform the feat and the third major leaguer to hit his four homers in consecutive at-bats. Milwaukee's Joe Adcock was baseball's last four-homer man, turning the trick in 1954.

Colavito now has 18 home runs for the season. The win moved the second-place Indians to within a half-game of the Orioles.

Cleveland's Rocky Colavito, baseball's eighth four-homer man.

CAUGHT ON THE FLY

JANUARY
Joe Cronin signed a seven-year contract as new American League president, replacing the retired Will Harridge.

FEBRUARY
Hall of Famer Napoleon Lajoie, a long-time Cleveland fixture at second base and one of the great hitters in baseball history, died in Daytona Beach, Fla., at age 83.

MARCH
Bill Veeck jumped back into the baseball spotlight when he purchased 54 percent of the Chicago White Sox's majority stock from Dorothy Comiskey-Rigney.

Another barrier falls

Pumpsie Green, the center of a spring controversy when he was sent back to the minor leagues, became the first black player in the long history of the Boston Red Sox July 21 when he served as a pinch-runner in a game at Chicago and played one inning at shortstop.

Green's promotion made him the first black player for the last major league team to break the color barrier. When Ozzie Virgil played his first game for Detroit on June 6 last year, Boston became the only team never to employ a black. And when Green was sent back to Minneapolis (American Association) just before the 1959 season opened, the National Association for the Advancement of Colored People (NAACP) cried discrimination and initiated an investigation into Red Sox policy.

Green got his big-league baptism on the same day he was recalled from Minneapolis. The next day against the White Sox, Green started at second base and went 0 for 3 with a walk and stolen base.

" DUGOUT CHATTER "

"I know what he can hit, but I'm still trying to find out what he can't hit."

Whitey Ford

Yankee lefty, after surrendering a key triple to San Francisco's Willie Mays in the All-Star Game

Mays settles issue

San Francisco center fielder Willie Mays belted an eighth-inning triple to right-center field, driving in Milwaukee's Hank Aaron with the lead run and giving the National League a 5-4 victory over the American League in the July 7 All-Star Game at Pittsburgh's Forbes Field.

Mays' clutch hit, his fourth straight in All-Star competition against New York lefthander Whitey Ford, capped the scoring in this midsummer classic, the first of two to be played this year.

The Nationals broke on top in the first inning when Milwaukee's Eddie Mathews hit a home run off Chicago's Early Wynn, but the A.L. answered in the fourth when Detroit's Al Kaline connected off Brave Lew Burdette. With Wynn and Yankee Ryne Duren pitching effectively for the A.L. and Los Angeles' Don Drysdale and Burdette for the N.L., the score remained tied through six innings.

But the Nationals broke through for a pair of seventh-inning runs and the A.L. struck for three in the top of the eighth. Aaron tied the score in the bottom of the inning with a single and scored the winner on Mays' shot.

All-Star headliners (left to right): Pittsburgh's Bill Mazeroski and a pair of Giants, pitcher Johnny Antonelli and Willie Mays.

FIELDS OF DREAMS

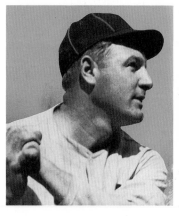 

The Minor Leagues

. . . Such quirks and surprises are what minor league baseball is all about. The players admittedly would rather be somewhere else, but they are giving their best effort with the hope it will lead to a promotion. Effort translates into performance and that means anything can happen at any time — and it usually does.

Nig Clarke was a 19-year-old catcher for Corsicana of the Class B Texas League in 1902 when he muscled up and hit eight home runs in a single game against Texarkana. Joe Bauman was a 32-year-old first baseman with Roswell of the Class C Longhorn League in 1954 when he exploded for an Organized Baseball-record 72 home runs. Ron Necciai was a 19-year-old fireballer with grand ideas of a successful major league career when he pitched a no-hitter for Bristol of the Class D Appalachian League in 1952 — striking out 27 Welch batters.

Necciai's dream fizzled after one short stay with Pittsburgh while Bauman never even tasted a major league cup of coffee. Clarke, who performed his eight-home run feat in a small park that was being used only because Sunday blue laws prohibited play in Corsicana, went on to play nine undistinguished major league seasons, hitting a total of six home runs for five teams. While all three fell short of the success they craved, no one could take away that one brief shining moment when they reigned as

the greatest slugger or best pitcher in the long history of the professional game. Hall of Famers, no, but the names of Clarke, Bauman and Necciai forever will be rooted in the colorful and wacky annals of minor league baseball, that wonderful world where no record is sacred and no dream beyond reach.

Minor league baseball as we know it today is a necessary and tolerable stop for most young players on the road to success — a no-guarantee apprenticeship that could pay big dividends. But it wasn't always so tolerable. The "bush leagues" of yesteryear, several of which date back to the 1880s, were a difficult life of long bus rides, second-class hotels, roadside diners, dusty fields, poor facilities and low pay. The minors were a baseball purgatory where players struggled to survive and prayed for recognition, which usually came in small doses. Most would-be stars never became more than a distant speck in the baseball universe.

But in their failure, all were contributors to a greater success.

Left: Baltimore's Buzz Arlett raised more than a few eyebrows in 1932 when he blasted four homers in a single game — twice.

Minneapolis' Joe Hauser fell short of Bauman when he blasted 69 home runs in 1933.

A big part of baseball's charm are the oddities and unexpected feats that balance its continuous flow of individual and team accomplishments. Many of those feats were performed by minor league nobodies who rose up briefly to become somebodies. The amazing accomplishments of Clarke, Bauman and Necciai are but a few of the many amazing occurrences that have taken place on minor league fields throughout the game's well-chronicled history.

If you like home runs, you have to appreciate such names as Joe Hauser, Bob Crues, Pete Schneider, Buzz Arlett and Bob Seeds. Hauser could not quite match Bauman's 72 homers, but he hit 63 in 1930 while playing for Baltimore of the International League and belted 69 in 1933 while playing for Minneapolis of the American Association. Both leagues were the equivalent of today's Triple-A circuits. Crues also blasted 69 for Amarillo of the Class C West Texas-New Mexico League in 1948, driving in an Organized Baseball-record 254 runs while batting .404. Bauman, Hauser and Crues are three of 10 minor leaguers who

Joe Bauman, Roswell's 72-home run phenom.

either matched or topped Babe Ruth's 1927 major league homer record of 60.

Schneider never hit 60 in a season, but he did blast five in a single game for Vernon of the Pacific Coast League in 1923. Three other players, Lou Frierson (1934), Cecil Dunn (1936) and Dick Lane (1948), matched Schneider while playing in the lower minors, and 71 players belted four homers, matching the major league record for round-trippers in a game. Of those 71, Arlett accomplished the feat twice for Baltimore in the *same season* (1932) and Seeds followed his 1938 four-homer rampage for Newark (International) with a three-homer performance and a two-day RBI total of 17.

If you prefer oddities, try these on for size. Gene Ryan, a left fielder for Waco (Texas) in 1930, belted three home runs — in one inning. John Cantley, a pitcher for Opelika (Georgia-Alabama) in 1914, hit three grand slams — in one game. In 1947, Las Vegas of the Sunset League hit three grand slams in one 16-run inning — two by Kenny Myers. But one of baseball's strangest records occurred in 1958, when Douglas of the Arizona-Mexico League hit nine homers in a game against Chihuahua — one by each player in the lineup.

On the other side of the coin, the Cordele team of the Georgia-Florida League hit only one home run in the entire 1952 season.

Joe Wilhoit was not known for his long-ball prowess, but the Wichita (Western) outfielder hit in 69 consecutive games during the 1919 season, 13 more than Joe DiMaggio's major league record. Lew Flick once collected nine straight hits for Little Rock (Southern Association) during a 19-inning game against Memphis. When Modesto's Kevin Stock performed a rare cycle (single, double, triple and home run in the same game) against Visalia in a 1985 California League contest, he had to share the spotlight with teammate Bob Loscalzo, who also hit for the cycle. Texas League fans were treated to an unprecedented explosion in 1983 when El Paso and Beaumont

Fireballer Ron Necciai struck out 27 batters during a 1952 no-hitter for Bristol.

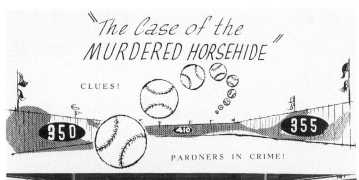

"The Case of the MURDERED HORSEHIDE"

CLUES!

PARDNERS IN CRIME!

RF - FILIPELLI — 2B - TORRES — 3B - McCALL — LF - WILKINS — P MGR - CLEAR — CF - PREVEDELLO — SS - PULFORD — C - BINFORD — 1B - VAN BURKLEO

GUILTY!

SET NEW ALL TIME ORGANIZED BASEBALL RECORD
NEVER ACCOMPLISHED BEFORE — LIKELY NEVER AGAIN

DOUGLAS, ARIZONA. POPULATION 12,000. SMALLEST SPORTS MINDED CITY IN CLASS C BASEBALL. WINNERS OF 1958 ARIZONA-MEXICO LEAGUE PENNANT. ON AUGUST 19th AT CHIHUAHUA, MEXICO EACH OF THE ABOVE NINE DOUGLAS PLAYERS HIT AN "OUT OF THE PARK" HOME RUN. THE DISTANCES GREATER THAN SEVERAL MAJOR LEAGUE PARKS.

This poster tells the story of Douglas' 1958 all-home run starting lineup.

combined for 89 runs while splitting consecutive games, 35-21 and 20-13.

Offense was not the name of the game on August 20, 1952, when Pony League fans watched a double no-hitter. A Batavia error allowed the game's only run and made a winner of Bradford's Frank Etchberger over tough-luck loser Jim Mitchell. There was nothing but good luck that same season for Bristol's Bill Bell, who matched Johnny Vander Meer's major league feat of consecutive no-hitters. Fourteen years later, teammates Dick Drago and Darrell Clark both pitched seven-inning no-hitters for Rocky Mount (Carolina) in a doubleheader sweep of Greensboro. Two of baseball's more dominating one-season performances were provided by Walter Justis, who pitched four no-hitters in 1908 for Lancaster (Ohio State), and Bob Riesener, who compiled a 20-0 mark for Alexandria (Evangeline) in 1957.

One of the oddest occurrences ever witnessed came in a 1911 contest when Vernon *center fielder* Walter Carlisle pulled off an unassisted triple play. Carlisle made a sensational shoe-top catch and then touched second base and first to force out overexuberant Los Angeles runners.

Several of the most notable team accomplishments occurred after 1980, drawing considerable national attention.

Perhaps the most publicized minor league game ever played took place in 1981 at Pawtucket, R.I., in the midst of the major league's 50-day players' strike. On April 18, Rochester and Paw-tucket (International) played 32 innings in the longest game in baseball history — without resolution. The game, tied 2-2, was resumed June 23 and ended when Pawtucket scored in the bottom of the 33rd.

Six years later, on July 27, 1987, Billings posted a 7-5 victory over Salt Lake City of the Pioneer League, ending the Trappers' baseball-record 29-game winning streak. But that mark did not last long. The 1992 Toronto East team of the Dominican Summer League (Rookie) opened its season with 38 consecutive victories and went on to post a phenomenal 68-2 record. Ironically, it lost in a best-of-three playoff to Oakland.

Such quirks and surprises are what minor league baseball is all about. The players admittedly would rather be somewhere else, but they are giving their best effort with the hope it will lead to a promotion. Effort translates into performance and that means anything can happen at any time — and it usually does.

"Outrageous" is a word often used to describe what does happen and it appropriately portrays baseball at its charming best. They may not be the game's superstars, but anybody who has watched minor league baseball can testify that they often are as much fun to watch.

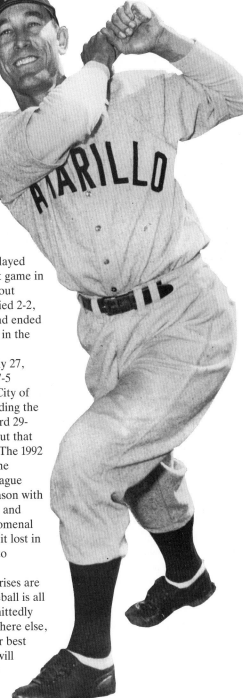

Amarillo slugger Bob Crues spiced his 69-homer 1948 season with an Organized Baseball-record 254 RBIs.

★1959★
AUGUST-DECEMBER

A.L. wins homer duel

Home runs by Boston's Frank Malzone, New York's Yogi Berra and Cleveland's Rocky Colavito accounted for four runs and lifted the American League to a 5-3 victory over the National League in the second All-Star Game of 1959, an August 3 contest at the Los Angeles Coliseum.

With 55,105 fans looking on, baseball broke tradition and played its second midsummer classic of the year — a game that will benefit the Players' Pension Fund, needy old-time players and youth baseball. Personnel was the same as the first game, but

Managers Casey Stengel (New York) and Fred Haney (Milwaukee) were not bound by voted-in starting lineups.

Malzone's solo homer off Dodger Don Drysdale in the second inning and Berra's two-run shot off Drysdale in the third jumped the Americans to a 3-1 lead and the N.L. never recovered. Twice it pulled within a run, but both times the A.L. answered, its final tally coming in the eighth on Colavito's blast. Five A.L. pitchers allowed six hits, including N.L. homers by Frank Robinson and Jim Gilliam.

New York catcher Yogi Berra completes his home run trot after connecting in the third inning of the year's second All-Star Game.

"DUGOUT CHATTER"

"I could almost see the bat bend. I was just lucky he didn't hit it through the box, because I might not have lived to see it."

Glen Hobbie

Chicago Cubs pitcher, after surrendering a 500-foot blast to Dick Stuart, reportedly the longest ball ever hit at Pittsburgh's Forbes Field

CAUGHT ON THE FLY

AUGUST
Getting 15 of his last 17 outs on strikes, Los Angeles lefty Sandy Koufax tied Bob Feller's major league record of 18 strikeouts during a 5-2 victory over San Francisco.

SEPTEMBER
Chicago righthander Glen Hobbie held St. Louis' Ken Boyer hitless in four at-bats during an 8-0 Cubs victory at Wrigley Field, snapping the third baseman's 29-game hitting streak.

NOVEMBER
The Los Angeles Dodgers broke the 2 million attendance barrier for the first time, drawing 2,071,045 to the massive Coliseum.

New league formed

The Continental League, a new circuit that hopes to exist as a third major league by 1961, announced July 27 that it will place franchises in New York City, Houston, Toronto, Denver and Minneapolis-St. Paul while considering at least 11 other sites.

The long-rumored new league expects to begin operation as an eight, 10 or 12-team circuit and the franchise owners of the founding teams have committed to spend from $2.5 to $3 million, exclusive of stadium construction costs. Each owner already has deposited $50,000 in the league treasury.

Lawyer William A. Shea, who headed a year-long effort to attract another team to New York after the Dodgers and Giants moved to California in 1957, organized the third league as an alternative. The effort received a boost from Tennessee Senator Estes Kefauver, the head of the Senate's Antitrust and Monopoly subcommittee who warned baseball executives that their attitudes toward the proposed league would be watched closely.

Big-league officials have discussed expansion as a third-league alternative.

Face finally loses

The amazing 22-game winning streak of Pittsburgh relief ace Elroy Face ended September 11 when Los Angeles nicked him for two ninth-inning runs in the first game of a doubleheader and squeezed out a 5-4 victory over the Pirates' righthander. The Dodgers also captured the second game at the Coliseum, 4-0.

Face, who had not lost in an incredible 98 appearances dating back to May 30, 1958, took over in the eighth inning with the Pirates holding a 4-3 lead and a runner at first base. He retired the Dodgers in that inning, but surrendered a single to Maury Wills, a triple to Jim Gilliam and a game-winning single to Charlie Neal in the ninth. The loss dropped his record to 17-1 and stopped his one-season streak two victories short of Giant Rube Marquard's major league-

record 19-game string of 1912.

Carl Hubbell set the two-season record of 24 straight wins in 1936 and 1937.

Pittsburgh reliever Elroy Face: 22 consecutive victories before a defeat at Los Angeles.

Dodgers bring first pennant to Los Angeles

Gil Hodges scored the winning run in the 12th inning on a wild throw by second baseman Felix Mantilla and Los Angeles defeated Milwaukee, 6-5, to sweep a two-game playoff for the National League pennant.

The September 29 victory at the Coliseum completed the Dodgers' exciting rise from seventh place in 1958 to their first pennant in Los Angeles. But nothing about that rise came easy.

First the Dodgers had to sweat out a three-way battle with San Francisco and Milwaukee, finally tying the Braves for first place with an 86-68 mark. Then they had to come from behind to win the opener of a best-of-three playoff series in Milwaukee, 3-2, on John Roseboro's sixth-inning home run. When the scene shifted to Los Angeles, the Braves carried a seemingly secure 5-2 lead into the bottom of the ninth with 21-game winner Lew Burdette on the mound.

But singles by Wally Moon, Duke Snider and Gil Hodges loaded the bases with nobody out and Norm Larker drove in two runs with a single off reliever Don McMahon. Pinch-hitter Carl Furillo's sacrifice fly off Warren Spahn tied the game. The Dodgers earned their seventh pennant in 13 years when Hodges walked with two out in the 12th, moved to second on Joe Pignatano's single and scored on Mantilla's bad throw.

That victory capped one of baseball's greatest races. Going into games of September 19, San Francisco owned a two-game lead over both Milwaukee and Los Angeles with eight contests remaining. But the Giants' lead quickly faded into a nightmarish five-game losing streak.

The Dodgers started the Giants on their slide by sweeping a day-night doubleheader at Seals Stadium while Milwaukee was beating Philadelphia. Through the end of the regular season, the Dodgers and Braves would exchange the lead seven times. The Giants still had a chance going into the September 27 finale, needing a doubleheader sweep against St. Louis combined with Dodger and Brave losses. But both of the co-leaders won, the Dodgers beating Chicago 7-1 and the Braves stopping the Phillies 5-2, while the Giants were dropping two to the Cardinals.

The resulting playoff was the third in N.L. history and the Dodgers' 88 wins were the fewest ever compiled by an N.L. pennant-winner.

The Los Angeles Dodgers' biggest guns (left to right): Gil Hodges, Duke Snider and Carl Furillo.

WORLD SERIES REPORT

L.A. PULLS DOWN SOX

Two-run homers by Duke Snider and Wally Moon helped Los Angeles build an 8-0 lead and Larry Sherry pitched 5⅔ innings of four-hit relief October 8, giving the Dodgers a 9-3 victory over the Chicago White Sox and their first World Series championship since moving to the West Coast.

The Dodgers' 13-hit Game 6 assault against Chicago pitchers Early Wynn and Dick Donovan at Comiskey Park also featured a Series-record second pinch-hit homer by Chuck Essegian. His Game 2 blast, combined with two homers by Charlie Neal, had given the Dodgers a 4-3 triumph.

The only bright spots for the "Go-Go" Sox were a bam-bam 11-0 first-game assault that featured two home runs and five RBIs by Ted Kluszewski and a 1-0 fifth-game victory. The Dodgers captured the third game, 3-1, behind Don Drysdale and the fourth game, 5-4, on Gil Hodges' eighth-inning home run.

The White Sox were buoyed by the record 10-RBI performance of Kluszewski.

Game 1	Chicago	11	Los Angeles	0
Game 2	Los Angeles	4	Chicago	3
Game 3	Los Angeles	3	Chicago	1
Game 4	Los Angeles	5	Chicago	4
Game 5	Chicago	1	Los Angeles	0
Game 6	Los Angeles	9	Chicago	3

Los Angeles center fielder Duke Snider after hitting his two-run Game 6 homer in the World Series.

The 1960s

While Americans protested, rebelled, cried, celebrated and adjusted to life in the technological fast lane, their National Pastime enjoyed the greatest period of growth and prosperity it had ever known.

Amid a backdrop of civil unrest fueled by the unpopular Vietnam war and three shocking political assassinations, baseball expanded its horizons and took its place in the corporate, bottom-line-oriented community.

The completed transformation from game to business was made possible by the tremendous infusion of television dollars by hungry executives who were reaping windfalls through increased sports programming. Baseball, like football and other sports, signed long-term, big-money TV contracts and the television networks provided coast-to-coast coverage of its events while acquiring a national viewer base that attracted advertising dollars. This simple formula was wildly successful and everybody clamored for more.

"More" translated into a decade dominated by franchise shifts and expansion. No longer heeding the passionate cries of jilted fans, sports officials began playing musical cities while searching for the ultimate

NATIONAL LEAGUE

League Batting Leaders

Average

Year	Player-Team	Avg.
1960	Dick Groat, Pit.	.325
1961	Roberto Clemente, Pit.	.351
1962	Tommy Davis, L.A.	.346
1963	Tommy Davis, L.A.	.326
1964	Roberto Clemente, Pit.	.339
1965	Roberto Clemente, Pit.	.329
1966	Matty Alou, Pit.	.342
1967	Roberto Clemente, Pit.	.357
1968	Pete Rose, Cin.	.335
1969	Pete Rose, Cin.	.348

Home Runs

Year	Player-Team	HR
1960	Ernie Banks, Chi.	41
1961	Orlando Cepeda, S.F.	46
1962	Willie Mays, S.F.	49
1963	Hank Aaron, Mil.	44
	Willie McCovey, S.F.	44
1964	Willie Mays, S.F.	47
1965	Willie Mays, S.F.	52
1966	Hank Aaron, Atl.	44
1967	Hank Aaron, Atl.	39
1968	Willie McCovey, S.F.	36
1969	Willie McCovey, S.F.	45

RBIs

Year	Player-Team	RBI
1960	Hank Aaron, Mil.	126
1961	Orlando Cepeda, S.F.	142
1962	Tommy Davis, L.A.	153
1963	Hank Aaron, Mil.	130
1964	Ken Boyer, St. L.	119
1965	Deron Johnson, Cin.	130
1966	Hank Aaron, Atl.	127
1967	Orlando Cepeda, St. L.	111
1968	Willie McCovey, S.F.	105
1969	Willie McCovey, S.F.	126

Most Valuable Players

Selected by BBWAA

Year	Player-Team	Pos.
1960	Dick Groat, Pit.	SS
1961	Frank Robinson, Cin.	OF
1962	Maury Wills, L.A.	SS
1963	Sandy Koufax, L.A.	P
1964	Ken Boyer, St. L.	3B
1965	Willie Mays, S.F.	OF
1966	Roberto Clemente, Pit.	OF
1967	Orlando Cepeda, St. L.	1B
1968	Bob Gibson, St. L.	P
1969	Willie McCovey, S.F.	1B

League Pitching Leaders

Winning Percentage

Year	Pitcher-Team	W-L	Pct.
1960	Ernie Broglio, St. L.	21-9	.700
1961	Johnny Podres, L.A.	18-5	.783
1962	Bob Purkey, Cin.	23-5	.821
1963	Ron Perranoski, L.A.	16-3	.842
1964	Sandy Koufax, L.A.	19-5	.792
1965	Sandy Koufax, L.A.	26-8	.765
1966	Juan Marichal, S.F.	25-6	.806
1967	Dick Hughes, St. L.	16-6	.727
1968	Steve Blass, Pit.	18-6	.750
1969	Tom Seaver, N.Y.	25-7	.781

Earned-Run Average

Year	Pitcher-Team	ERA
1960	Mike McCormick, S.F.	2.70
1961	Warren Spahn, Mil.	3.01
1962	Sandy Koufax, L.A.	2.54
1963	Sandy Koufax, L.A.	1.88
1964	Sandy Koufax, L.A.	1.74
1965	Sandy Koufax, L.A.	2.04
1966	Sandy Koufax, L.A.	1.73
1967	Phil Niekro, Atl.	1.87
1968	Bob Gibson, St. L.	1.12
1969	Juan Marichal, S.F.	2.10

Strikeouts

Year	Pitcher-Team	SO
1960	Don Drysdale, L.A.	246
1961	Sandy Koufax, L.A.	269
1962	Don Drysdale, L.A.	232
1963	Sandy Koufax, L.A.	306
1964	Bob Veale, Pit.	250
1965	Sandy Koufax, L.A.	382
1966	Sandy Koufax, L.A.	317
1967	Jim Bunning, Phil.	253
1968	Bob Gibson, St. L.	268
1969	Fergie Jenkins, Chi.	273

Cy Young Winners

A.L. and N.L. combined through 1966

Year	Pitcher-Team	Thr.
1960	Vernon Law, Pit.	R
1961	Whitey Ford, N.Y.	L
1962	Don Drysdale, L.A. (N.L.)	R
1963	Sandy Koufax, L.A. (N.L.)	L
1964	Dean Chance, L.A. (A.L.)	R
1965	Sandy Koufax, L.A. (N.L.)	L
1966	Sandy Koufax, L.A. (N.L.)	L
1967	Mike McCormick, S.F.	L
1968	Bob Gibson, St. L.	R
1969	Tom Seaver, N.Y.	R

LEAGUE CHAMPIONSHIP SERIES

National League

Year	Winner	Runnerup	Games
1969	New York Mets	Atlanta Braves	3-0

American League

Year	Winner	Runnerup	Games
1969	Baltimore Orioles	Minnesota Twins	3-0

Los Angeles run producer Tommy Davis.

Final Standings

*Defeated Los Angeles 2-1 in pennant playoff

1960

	W	L	PCT.	GB
Pittsburgh	95	59	.617	- -
Milwaukee	88	66	.571	7
St. Louis	86	68	.558	9
Los Angeles	82	72	.532	13
S.F.	79	75	.513	16
Cincinnati	67	87	.435	28
Chicago	60	94	.390	35
Philadelphia	59	95	.383	36

1961

	W	L	Pct.	GB
Cincinnati	93	61	.604	- -
Los Angeles	89	65	.578	4
S.F.	85	69	.552	8
Milwaukee	83	71	.539	10
St. Louis	80	74	.519	13
Pittsburgh	75	79	.487	18
Chicago	64	90	.416	29
Philadelphia	47	107	.305	46

1962

	W	L	Pct.	GB
*S.F.	103	62	.624	- -
Los Angeles	102	63	.618	1
Cincinnati	98	64	.605	3.5
Pittsburgh	93	68	.578	8
Milwaukee	86	76	.531	15.5
St. Louis	84	78	.519	17.5
Philadelphia	81	80	.503	20
Houston	64	96	.400	36.5
Chicago	59	103	.364	42.5
New York	40	120	.250	60.5

1963

	W	L	Pct.	GB
Los Angeles	99	63	.611	- -
St. Louis	93	69	.574	6
S.F.	88	74	.543	11
Philadelphia	87	75	.537	12
Cincinnati	86	76	.531	13
Milwaukee	84	78	.519	15
Chicago	82	80	.506	17
Pittsburgh	74	88	.457	25
Houston	66	96	.407	33
New York	51	111	.315	48

1964

	W	L	Pct.	GB
St. Louis	93	69	.574	- -
Cincinnati	92	70	.568	1
Philadelphia	92	70	.568	1
S.F.	90	72	.556	3
Milwaukee	88	74	.543	5
Los Angeles	80	82	.494	13
Pittsburgh	80	82	.494	13
Chicago	76	86	.469	17
Houston	66	96	.407	27
New York	53	109	.327	40

1965

	W	L	Pct.	GB
Los Angeles	97	65	.599	- -
S.F.	95	67	.586	2
Pittsburgh	90	72	.556	7
Cincinnati	89	73	.549	8
Milwaukee	86	76	.531	11
Philadelphia	85	76	.528	11.5
St. Louis	80	81	.497	16.5
Chicago	72	90	.444	25
Houston	65	97	.401	32
New York	50	112	.309	47

1966

	W	L	Pct.	GB
Los Angeles	95	67	.586	- -
S.F.	93	68	.578	1.5
Pittsburgh	92	70	.568	3
Philadelphia	87	75	.537	8
Atlanta	85	77	.525	10
St. Louis	83	79	.512	12
Cincinnati	76	84	.475	18
Houston	72	90	.444	23
New York	66	95	.410	28.5
Chicago	59	103	.364	36

1967

	W	L	Pct.	GB
St. Louis	101	60	.627	- -
S.F.	91	71	.562	10.5
Chicago	87	74	.540	14
Cincinnati	87	75	.537	14.5
Philadelphia	82	80	.506	19.5
Pittsburgh	81	81	.500	20.5
Atlanta	77	85	.475	24.5
Los Angeles	73	89	.451	28.5
Houston	69	93	.426	32.5
New York	61	101	.377	40.5

1968

	W	L	Pct.	GB
St. Louis	97	65	.599	- -
S.F.	88	74	.543	9
Chicago	84	78	.519	13
Cincinnati	83	79	.512	14
Atlanta	81	81	.500	16
Pittsburgh	80	82	.494	17
Los Angeles	76	86	.469	21
Philadelphia	76	86	.469	21
New York	73	89	.451	24
Houston	72	90	.444	25

1969

East

	W	L	Pct.	GB
New York	100	62	.617	- -
Chicago	92	70	.568	8
Pittsburgh	88	74	.543	12
St. Louis	87	75	.537	13
Philadelphia	63	99	.389	37
Montreal	52	110	.321	48

West

	W	L	Pct.	GB
Atlanta	93	69	.574	- -
S.F.	90	72	.556	3
Cincinnati	89	73	.549	4
Los Angeles	85	77	.525	8
Houston	81	81	.500	12
San Diego	52	110	.321	41

Minnesota slugger Harmon Killebr

television markets, and growing metropolises actively lobbied for their own teams. By the end of the decade, the sport that had existed 60 years with 16 clubs numbered 24, and its games were even being contested on the foreign soil of Canada under the flag of the expansion Montreal Expos.

A sports world in transition was not without its memorable moments. The decade opened with a dramatic World Series-winning home run by Pittsburgh's Bill Mazeroski and ended with New York's Amazing Mets blowing past the Atlanta Braves in the first Championship Series and powerful Baltimore in the World Series. Sandwiched between were the 61-home run season of Yankee Roger Maris, the 31-win campaign of Detroit's Denny McLain, the 1.12-ERA campaign of St. Louis right-hander Bob Gibson, perfect games by dominating Los Angeles left-hander Sandy Koufax, Philadelphia's Jim Bunning and Oakland's Catfish Hunter and the 104-steal effort of speedy Los Angeles

shortstop Maury Wills, who made the long-lost art of baserunning fashionable once again.

The game's greatest dynasty ended when the Yankees' star finally faded after 40 glorious years filled with American League pennants and World Series championships. And as man prepared for his first steps on the moon, baseball rushed head-first into the technological age with the introduction of Houston's wondrous Astrodome and new cookie-cutter stadiums, complete with artificial turf and flashing scoreboards, in New York, Philadelphia, Cincinnati and Pittsburgh.

This decade of prosperity ended on an ominous note — for baseball franchise owners. Former St. Louis Cardinal center fielder Curt Flood, upset over a trade to the Philadelphia Phillies, retired and filed a civil lawsuit challenging the game's reserve clause. "Slavery," as Flood described it, was about to end and the players' financial star was about to rise — dramatically.

WORLD SERIES

Year	Winner	Pennant Winner	Games
1960	Pittsburgh Pirates	New York Yankees	4-3
1961	New York Yankees	Cincinnati Reds	4-1
1962	New York Yankees	San Francisco Giants	4-3
1963	Los Angeles Dodgers	New York Yankees	4-0
1964	St. Louis Cardinals	New York Yankees	4-3
1965	Los Angeles Dodgers	Minnesota Twins	4-3
1966	Baltimore Orioles	Los Angeles Dodgers	4-0
1967	St. Louis Cardinals	Boston Red Sox	4-3
1968	Detroit Tigers	St. Louis Cardinals	4-3
1969	New York Mets	Baltimore Orioles	4-1

HALL OF FAME Electees and Additions

1961	Max Carey, Billy Hamilton.
1962	Bob Feller, Jackie Robinson, Bill McKechnie, Edd Roush.
1963	Eppa Rixey, Sam Rice, Elmer Flick, John Clarkson.
1964	Luke Appling, Red Faber, Burleigh Grimes, Tim Keefe, Heinie Manush, Miller Huggins, John Montgomery Ward.
1965	Pud Galvin.
1966	Ted Williams, Casey Stengel.
1967	Red Ruffing, Branch Rickey, Lloyd Waner.
1968	Joe Medwick, Goose Goslin, Kiki Cuyler.
1969	Stan Musial, Roy Campanella, Stan Coveleski, Waite Hoyt.

AMERICAN LEAGUE

League Batting Leaders

Average

Year	Player-Team	Avg.
1960	Pete Runnels, Bos.	.320
1961	Norm Cash, Det.	.361
1962	Pete Runnels, Bos.	.326
1963	Carl Yastrzemski, Bos.	.321
1964	Tony Oliva, Min.	.323
1965	Tony Oliva, Min.	.321
1966	Frank Robinson, Bal.	.316
1967	Carl Yastrzemski, Bos.	.326
1968	Carl Yastrzemski, Bos.	.301
1969	Rod Carew, Min.	.332

Home Runs

Year	Player-Team	HR
1960	Mickey Mantle, N.Y.	40
1961	Roger Maris, N.Y.	61
1962	Harmon Killebrew, Min.	48
1963	Harmon Killebrew, Min.	45
1964	Harmon Killebrew, Min.	49
1965	Tony Conigliaro, Bos.	32
1966	Frank Robinson, Bal.	49
1967	Harmon Killebrew, Min.	44
	Carl Yastrzemski, Bos.	44
1968	Frank Howard, Wash.	44
1969	Harmon Killebrew, Min.	49

RBIs

Year	Player-Team	RBI
1960	Roger Maris, N.Y.	112
1961	Roger Maris, N.Y.	142
1962	Harmon Killebrew, Min.	126
1963	Dick Stuart, Bos.	118
1964	Brooks Robinson, Bal.	118
1965	Rocky Colavito, Cle.	108
1966	Frank Robinson, Bal.	122
1967	Carl Yastrzemski, Bos.	121
1968	Ken Harrelson, Bos.	109
1969	Harmon Killebrew, Min.	140

Most Valuable Players

Selected by BBWAA

Year	Player-Team	Pos.
1960	Roger Maris, N.Y.	OF
1961	Roger Maris, N.Y.	OF
1962	Mickey Mantle, N.Y.	OF
1963	Elston Howard, N.Y.	C
1964	Brooks Robinson, Bal.	3B
1965	Zoilo Versalles, Min.	SS
1966	Frank Robinson, Bal.	OF
1967	Carl Yastrzemski, Bos.	OF
1968	Denny McLain, Det.	P
1969	Harmon Killebrew, Min.	3B

League Pitching Leaders

Winning Percentage

Year	Pitcher-Team	W-L	Pct.
1960	Jim Perry, Cle.	18-10	.643
1961	Whitey Ford, N.Y.	25-4	.862
1962	Ray Herbert, Chi.	20-9	.690
1963	Whitey Ford, N.Y.	24-7	.774
1964	Wally Bunker, Bal.	19-5	.792
1965	Mudcat Grant, Min.	21-7	.750
1966	Sonny Siebert, Cle.	16-8	.667
1967	Joe Horlen, Chi.	19-7	.731
1968	Denny McLain, Det.	31-6	.838
1969	Jim Palmer, Bal.	16-4	.800

Earned-Run Average

Year	Pitcher-Team	ERA
1960	Frank Baumann, Chi.	2.67
1961	Dick Donovan, Wash.	2.40
1962	Hank Aguirre, Det.	2.21
1963	Gary Peters, Chi.	2.33
1964	Dean Chance, L.A.	1.65
1965	Sam McDowell, Cle.	2.18
1966	Gary Peters, Chi.	1.98
1967	Joe Horlen, Chi.	2.06
1968	Luis Tiant, Cle.	1.60
1969	Dick Bosman, Wash.	2.19

Strikeouts

Year	Pitcher-Team	SO
1960	Jim Bunning, Det.	201
1961	Camilo Pascual, Min.	221
1962	Camilo Pascual, Min.	206
1963	Camilo Pascual, Min.	202
1964	Al Downing, N.Y.	217
1965	Sam McDowell, Cle.	325
1966	Sam McDowell, Cle.	225
1967	Jim Lonborg, Bos.	246
1968	Sam McDowell, Cle.	283
1969	Sam McDowell, Cle.	279

Cy Young Winners

A.L. and N.L. combined through 1966

Year	Pitcher-Team	Thr.
1960	Vernon Law, Pit.	R
1961	Whitey Ford, N.Y.	L
1962	Don Drysdale, L.A. (N.L.)	R
1963	Sandy Koufax, L.A. (N.L.)	L
1964	Dean Chance, L.A. (A.L.)	R
1965	Sandy Koufax, L.A. (N.L.)	L
1966	Sandy Koufax, L.A. (N.L.)	L
1967	Jim Lonborg, Bos.	R
1968	Denny McLain, Det.	R
1969	Denny McLain, Det.	R
	Mike Cuellar, Bal.	L

Final Standings

1960

	W	L	PCT.	GB
New York	97	57	.630	--
Baltimore	89	65	.578	8
Chicago	87	67	.565	10
Cleveland	76	78	.494	21
Washington	73	81	.474	24
Detroit	71	83	.461	26
Boston	65	89	.422	32
Kansas City	58	96	.377	39

1961

	W	L	Pct.	GB
New York	109	53	.673	--
Detroit	101	61	.623	8
Baltimore	95	67	.586	14
Chicago	86	76	.531	23
Cleveland	78	83	.484	30.5
Boston	76	86	.469	33
Minnesota	70	90	.438	38
Los Angeles	70	91	.435	38.5
Kansas City	61	100	.379	47.5
Washington	61	100	.379	47.5

1962

	W	L	Pct.	GB
New York	96	66	.593	--
Minnesota	91	71	.562	5
Los Angeles	86	76	.531	10
Detroit	85	76	.528	10.5
Chicago	85	77	.525	11
Cleveland	80	82	.494	16
Baltimore	77	85	.475	19
Boston	76	84	.475	19
Kansas City	72	90	.444	24
Washington	60	101	.373	35.5

1963

	W	L	Pct.	GB
New York	104	57	.646	--
Chicago	94	68	.580	10.5
Minnesota	91	70	.565	13
Baltimore	86	76	.531	18.5
Cleveland	79	83	.488	25.5
Detroit	79	83	.488	25.5
Boston	76	85	.472	28
Kansas City	73	89	.451	31.5
Los Angeles	70	91	.435	34
Washington	56	106	.346	48.5

1964

	W	L	Pct.	GB
New York	99	63	.611	--
Chicago	98	64	.605	1
Baltimore	97	65	.599	2
Detroit	85	77	.525	14
Los Angeles	82	80	.506	17
Cleveland	79	83	.488	20
Minnesota	79	83	.488	20
Boston	72	90	.444	27
Washington	62	100	.383	37
Kansas City	57	105	.352	42

1965

	W	L	Pct.	GB
Minnesota	102	60	.630	--
Chicago	95	67	.586	7
Baltimore	94	68	.580	8
Detroit	89	73	.549	13
Cleveland	87	75	.537	15
New York	77	85	.475	25
California	75	87	.463	27
Washington	70	92	.432	32
Boston	62	100	.383	40
Kansas City	59	103	.364	43

1966

	W	L	Pct.	GB
Baltimore	97	63	.606	--
Minnesota	89	73	.549	9
Detroit	88	74	.543	10
Chicago	83	79	.512	15
Cleveland	81	81	.500	17
California	80	82	.494	18
Kansas City	74	86	.463	23
Washington	71	88	.447	25.5
Boston	72	90	.444	26
New York	70	89	.440	26.5

1967

	W	L	Pct.	GB
Boston	92	70	.568	--
Detroit	91	71	.562	1
Minnesota	91	71	.562	1
Chicago	89	73	.549	3
California	84	77	.522	7.5
Baltimore	76	85	.472	15.5
Washington	76	85	.472	15.5
Cleveland	75	87	.463	17
New York	72	90	.444	20
Kansas City	62	99	.385	29.5

1968

	W	L	Pct.	GB
Detroit	103	59	.636	--
Baltimore	91	71	.562	12
Cleveland	86	75	.534	16.5
Boston	86	76	.531	17
New York	83	79	.512	20
Oakland	82	80	.506	21
Minnesota	79	83	.488	24
California	67	95	.414	36
Chicago	67	95	.414	36
Washington	65	96	.404	37.5

1969

East	W	L	Pct.	GB
Baltimore	109	53	.673	--
Detroit	90	72	.556	19
Boston	87	75	.537	22
Washington	86	76	.531	23
New York	80	81	.497	28.5
Cleveland	62	99	.385	46.5

West	W	L	Pct.	GB
Minnesota	97	65	.599	--
Oakland	88	74	.543	9
California	71	91	.438	26
Kansas City	69	93	.426	28
Chicago	68	94	.420	29
Seattle	64	98	.395	33

★1960★

N.L. pulls off sweep

In what could be classified as a three-day All-Star Game doubleheader, the National League rolled up two easy victories and narrowed the American League's once-commanding midsummer classic lead to 16-13. The N.L. jumped to a 5-0 lead in the July 11 contest at Kansas City and held on for a 5-3 triumph and then posted a 6-0 shutout two days later at Yankee Stadium.

A leadoff triple by San Francisco's Willie Mays, a single by Pittsburgh's Bob Skinner and a home run by Chicago's Ernie Banks got the Nationals off to a fast start in the 101-degree heat of Kansas City and they added a run in the second on Milwaukee catcher Del Crandall's homer and another in the third on a single by Pittsburgh's Bill Mazeroski.

The only highlight for the A.L. was a two-run eighth-inning homer by Detroit's Al Kaline.

It was bombs away in the second contest as the N.L. used homers by Mays, Milwaukee's Eddie Mathews and two St. Louisans, Stan Musial and Ken Boyer, to build its lead. Six pitchers scatted eight hits and six walks but still shut out the A.L.

St. Louis' Stan Musial connects for a home run in the season's second All-Star Game, a 6-0 N.L. victory.

" DUGOUT CHATTER "

"I just wrote down 'Monbo.' "

Al Lopez

Manager of the A.L. All-Star team, admitting he did not know how to spell Boston pitcher Bill Monbouquette's name

A fond farewell to Ebbets Field

It had been the home of Leo, Zack, Dazzy, Dixie, Campy, Jackie, Pee Wee, Duke and many other zany characters. It was where super-fan Hilda Chester clanged her cowbell and the Sym-Phony Band stayed out of tune for two decades. Pennants were won and lost there. Hopes were dashed and dreams were fulfilled. When Dem Bums fell short, Brooklyn fans always could "wait till next year."

Thousands of fond memories were violated February 23 when demolition began on Ebbets Field, home of the Brooklyn Dodgers for 44 daffy years. In a brief pre-demolition ceremony conducted at home plate, Lucy Monroe sang the national anthem and Al Helfer, former Dodger broadcaster, introduced guests that included former players Roy Campanella, Carl Erskine and Ralph Branca.

Campy, now confined to a wheelchair because of a 1958 auto accident, was presented with three treasures — his old No. 39 uniform, his locker and a pot of dirt from the area where he squatted for 10 seasons behind home plate.

When the ceremonies ended, the group retired to the park rotunda and watched sadly as the wrecking ball, painted white with stitches to resemble a baseball, smashed a hole in the roof of the visitors' dugout. So began the 10-week slaughter of a revered baseball shrine. The end of an era.

Williams hits 500th

Boston's Ted Williams made another entry into the baseball record books June 17 when he drove a pitch from Cleveland's Wynn Hawkins over the left-center field fence at Municipal Stadium, becoming only the fourth player in history to hit 500 career home runs.

The 41-year-old Williams, whose two-run shot keyed the Red Sox's 3-1 victory, joins Babe Ruth (714 homers), Jimmie Foxx (534) and Mel Ott (511) in the 500-homer club. And the three-time American League Most Valuable Player reached the 500 plateau despite missing more than four full seasons to military service.

Williams wore a wide grin as he circled the bases after his memorable clout and was greeted by his excited teammates. The six-time batting champion left the game for a pinch-runner after walking in the seventh.

Ebbets Field, once the pride of Brooklyn, under the spell of a wrecking ball.

A top-level trade

In the most bizarre baseball trade ever made, Cleveland and Detroit swapped managers August 3, the fourth-place Indians getting 63-year-old Jimmie Dykes and the sixth-place Tigers landing 45-year-old Joe Gordon.

"I've been around baseball a long time," said Dykes, "but I've never seen anything like this."

The deal was pulled off by Cleveland General Manager Frank Lane and Detroit counterpart Bill DeWitt after a telephone conversation during which DeWitt jokingly suggested, "We've been trading players, why don't we trade managers?" With both teams hopelessly behind the American League-leading New York Yankees, they did just that.

Gordon, who guided the Indians to a second-place finish last year and a 49-46 record so far this season, will be guaranteed a contract at least through the remainder of this campaign. Dykes, whose Tigers were 44-52, will be taking over his sixth major league team.

This is the second Lane-DeWitt shocker of the year. On April 17, Cleveland had sent 1959 home run co-champion Rocky Colavito to the Tigers for 1959 batting champion Harvey Kuenn.

The principals in a shocking April trade: Home run co-champion Rocky Colavito (left) was sent to Detroit and batting champion Harvey Kuenn to Cleveland.

CAUGHT ON THE FLY

APRIL

The San Francisco Giants, playing before an Opening Day crowd of 42,269, christened $15 million Candlestick Park with a 3-1 victory over St. Louis.

In a startling development, Philadelphia Manager Eddie Sawyer resigned after watching his Phillies drop a 9-4 season-opening decision at Cincinnati. He was replaced by Gene Mauch.

JULY

High-kicking Juan Marichal made a spectacular major league debut for the San Francisco Giants when he allowed one hit while checking Philadelphia, 2-0, in a game at Candlestick Park.

SEPTEMBER

Milwaukee veteran Warren Spahn became a 20-game winner for the 11th time and he did it in style — with a no-hitter against Philadelphia, the first of his distinguished career.

New league expires

The new Continental League expired August 2 before it ever really got off the ground, but the new circuit got what it wanted from major league baseball — the promise of expansion.

With the eight Continental League backers concurring unanimously, the four-man expansion committee of the National and American leagues voted to recommend admission of four clubs from the new circuit into the existing major league structure. The proposed increase of the A.L. and N.L. from eight to 10 teams would be targeted for 1961, no later than 1962. No cities were mentioned, although New York would be a sure bet as a National League entry.

The Continental League, which organized in July 1959 with plans to exist as a third major circuit, was a direct result of New York's search for another team after the Giants and Dodgers had relocated to California following the 1957 season. But with numerous obstacles blocking the way — indemnification demands of minor league teams, player procurement, money raising, etc. — the franchise owners were quick to accept the expansion alternative proposal.

Ted Williams retires

Boston's Ted Williams ended his outstanding baseball career on a high note September 28 when he blasted his 521st career home run against Baltimore and promptly announced his retirement.

Williams connected for his 29th homer of the season off Jack Fisher in the eighth inning of Boston's 5-4 victory at Fenway Park. Although he had previously announced he would retire at the end of the season, he said after the game that he would forego the final three-game series against New York Yankees.

The three-time A.L. Most Valuable Player and six-time batting champion received a big ovation as he stepped to the plate for the final time. He belted Fisher's 1-1 pitch for a solo homer and then listened from the dugout as fans stood and chanted, "We want Ted." Williams refused to make a curtain call and was replaced in left field by Carroll Hardy in the ninth inning.

The 42-year-old slugger finished his career with a .344 batting average and his 521 homers rank third on the all-time list behind Babe Ruth and Jimmie Foxx.

Boston's Ted Williams finishing off his outstanding career with home run No. 521.

CASEY STENGEL

Clown, poet and managerial genius

"Casey to me was the perfect manager, in that he understood all facets of the game. He understood the players. He understood the press. He understood the fans. He understood the front office. He really had a tremendous insight into all of these facets of the game. . . . The man was absolutely in a class by himself."

Jerry Coleman, former Yankee second baseman

Dan Topping, co-owner of the New York pennant-producing machine called the Yankees, delivered the incredible news. Casey Stengel, he told a post-World Series press conference in 1960, has decided to retire as the team's manager.

Moments later, a grim-faced, straight-talking Stengel provided the audience with a different insight. "I was told my services no longer were desired," he said with detectable bitterness in his gravel voice.

The story hit New York like an earthquake, with shockwaves spreading throughout the baseball world. The man who had guided his team to 10 American League pennants and seven World Series championships in 12 years had been fired, sent packing under the auspices of a youth movement. It was like the Catholic Church firing Mother Teresa, or Metropolis telling Superman it no longer needed his crime-fighting help. Mighty

Casey, the game's most beloved character and most successful manager, had struck out.

But not before batting .623 with a winning legacy that New York fans will never forget. Stengel's 12 teams fashioned a 1,149-696 mark, matching the 1,460-867 (.627) record that Joe McCarthy's Yankees had compiled in 15-plus seasons from 1931 to '46. McCarthy's supposedly "unbreakable records" included eight pennants (Stengel won 10), seven World Series titles (Stengel matched that mark) and four straight Series championships (Stengel won five in a row). The craggy-faced, bow-legged Casey also topped the stone-faced McCarthy in two other areas — personality and flair.

Nobody expected Stengel to threaten anybody's legacy back in October 1948, when he was hired to repair a sputtering Yankee machine that had finished third under Bucky Harris. He was the surprise choice of General

A serious-looking Casey Stengel in 1949 with his Yankee managerial predecessor, Joe McCarthy, now Boston's field boss.

Manager George M. Weiss, having failed miserably in previous managerial stints with Brooklyn and the Boston Braves. Stengel's teams never had finished higher than fifth place in the eight-team National League during his nine managerial seasons.

But Stengel's biggest New York obstacle was his well-deserved reputation as a baseball clown. His antics were legendary. As a player, he once tipped his cap to a Brooklyn crowd as a sparrow flew out. Another time he hid in a center-field manhole and emerged majestically to catch a fly ball. As a manager, he was a comedian/philosopher who entertained sportswriters and broadcasters with a non-stop, stream-of-consciousness monologue filled with fractured sentences and sometimes-unintelligible thoughts. He communicated in his own colorful language known as Stengelese.

Purists abhorred the thought of this buffoon at the helm of baseball's showcase team. New Yorkers considered Stengel a smokescreen, someone to divert attention while the Yankees were rebuilding. Casey saw New York as the perfect stage to showcase both his yet-to-be-

Five World Series championships in a row — Casey's Yankee legacy.

recognized baseball genius and his considerable talent for making people smile. But the smiles would have to wait.

"Casey was serious," recalled outfielder Tommy Henrich, who was nearing the end of his outstanding Yankee career when Stengel took over. "He knew that this was his chance. Casey the clown didn't exist with the Yankees in '49."

Stengel spent most of his first season juggling lineups and overcoming 72 Yankee injuries. Even with center fielder Joe DiMaggio missing half the season and Henrich four weeks, he guided the Bronx Bombers to 97 victories and his first A.L. pennant. The Yankees finished one game ahead of Boston, beating the Red Sox in the final two regular-season games, and then buried Brooklyn in a five-game World Series.

For the next four seasons, Casey's Yankee express ran at top speed. Stengel's Bombers reeled off consecutive 98-win seasons, followed by 95 and 99-victory campaigns. Each was followed by World Series triumphs over Philadelphia (1950), the New York Giants (1951) and Dodgers (1952 and '53). Casey the clown was an amazin' 5 for 5.

"Casey to me was the perfect manager," said former Yankee second baseman Jerry Coleman, "in that he understood all facets of the game. He understood the players. He understood the press. He understood the fans. He understood the front office. He really had a tremendous insight into all of these facets of the game. . . . The man was absolutely in a class by himself."

And, unlike in Brooklyn and Boston, he had great players, such as DiMaggio, Henrich, Mickey Mantle, Yogi Berra, Whitey Ford, Allie Reynolds, Vic Raschi, Ed Lopat, Roger Maris, Elston Howard, Bill Skowron, Joe Collins, Johnny Mize, Hank Bauer, Gil McDougald, Billy Martin, Phil Rizzuto, Joe Page, Bobby Richardson, Tony Kubek and Bob Turley.

"But he was not an easy man to play for from the standpoint that you were a number," Coleman added. "I'm not talking about Mantle or Berra or

The always-colorful Stengel clowns for photographers during a Yankee rain delay.

DiMaggio or people like that. I'm talking about people like myself and the Hank Bauers and Gene Woodlings and Bobby Browns. He just used you, and there was no explanation as to why in many cases. From that standpoint, he was not lovable. He was lovable to the fans but not to the players who played for him."

The tone for Stengel's managing style was established in 1950, when he benched DiMaggio for a week without warning. DiMaggio finished the season with a .301 average, 32 home runs and 122 RBIs, but a coolness existed between the two for several years. No problem.

"So what if he doesn't want to talk to me?" Stengel said. "I'll get by and so will he. He's getting paid to play and I'm getting paid to manage."

Casey was a master at platoon baseball and ruthlessly juggled lineups with little regard for hurt feelings. He often forgot the names of his fringe players, referring to them as "that feller" or "that guy." But the Yankees kept winning and his methods were grudgingly tolerated.

As unyielding as Stengel might have seemed to some of the players, he was an absolute delight with New York's press corps, which he fondly referred to as "my writers."

Stengel, now manager of the New York Mets, enjoys a moment with former Yankee students Roger Maris (left) and Mickey Mantle.

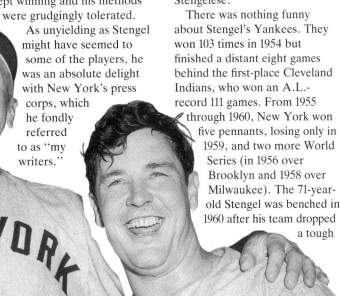

Casey's interviews were rambling, comical, confusing dissertations on anything and everything, never dull and always colorful.

"Casey could fool you," Berra said. "When he wanted to make sense, he could. But he usually preferred to make you laugh. That's why he spoke Stengelese."

There was nothing funny about Stengel's Yankees. They won 103 times in 1954 but finished a distant eight games behind the first-place Cleveland Indians, who won an A.L.-record 111 games. From 1955 through 1960, New York won five pennants, losing only in 1959, and two more World Series (in 1956 over Brooklyn and 1958 over Milwaukee). The 71-year-old Stengel was benched in 1960 after his team dropped a tough

seven-game fall classic to Pittsburgh. The Yankees outhit the Pirates, 91-60, and outscored them, 55-27, but lost the seventh game, 10-9, when Bill Mazeroski belted a ninth-inning Ralph Terry pitch over the left-field wall at Forbes Field.

Some claim the change was made because of Stengel's advanced age. Others claim Casey dug his own grave with questionable strategy in the 1960 Series. Whatever the case, Ralph Houk succeeded Stengel and produced four straight pennants and two more championships before the Yankees' four-decade dynasty (20 Series championships and nine losses in 44 years) collapsed in 1965.

Stengel came out of retirement in 1962 as the perfect manager and buffer for the expansion New York Mets, a colorful, lovable collection of misfits who lost a baseball-record 120 games in their first season. Casey lasted 3½ campaigns with the Mets, compiling a 175-404 record — a mirror image to his incredible success with the Yankees. Through the losses, he laughed and clowned and entertained, just as he had through good times and bad in a colorful baseball career that spanned more than half a decade.

A familiar sight in New York: Casey and company celebrating another championship.

☆1960☆

OCTOBER-DECEMBER

Yankees fire Stengel

New York fans, still in shock over the Yankees' sudden World Series demise four days earlier, listened in amazement October 18 to the news that the Bronx Bombers were releasing Casey Stengel as the team's manager.

"I was told that my services no longer were desired," said a grim-faced Stengel after Yankee co-Owners Dan Topping and Del Webb had instituted an age-limit program. The 71-year-old Casey had led the Yankees to 10 pennants and seven World Series championships in 12 seasons since taking the helm in 1949.

Stengel, who struggled not to show bitterness, spoke without the doubletalk and clowning that has made him famous during a 50-year baseball career. His earlier stints as manager of the Brooklyn Dodgers and Boston Braves were far removed from the success of his Yankee years.

The Yankees announced two days later that Stengel would be replaced by 41-year-old Ralph Houk, a former Army major who had served as a New York coach since 1958.

Game 1	Pittsburgh	6	New York	4
Game 2	New York	16	Pittsburgh	3
Game 3	New York	10	Pittsburgh	0
Game 4	Pittsburgh	3	New York	2
Game 5	Pittsburgh	5	New York	2
Game 6	New York	12	Pittsburgh	0
Game 7	Pittsburgh	10	New York	9

Pittsburgh Manager Danny Murtaugh with World Series hero Bill Mazeroski.

WORLD SERIES REPORT

MAZ MAKES HISTORY

Bill Mazeroski stood waving his bat as 36,683 hopeful Pirates fans sat on the edge of their seats at Pittsburgh's Forbes Field. New York Yankee righthander Ralph Terry fidgeted on the mound. The score was 9-9 in the bottom of the 10th inning of World Series Game 7 and there was no margin for error.

Terry fired and Mazeroski connected, sending a resounding smash over the left-field wall. Yankee players bowed their heads in disappointment as Maz danced around the bases to the mob of teammates that awaited him at home plate. A nation of fans rejoiced in the realization that they had just witnessed one of the classic moments in baseball history.

The 1960 World Series had been a classic even before the dramatic fireworks of Game 7. The Yankees had bludgeoned the Pirates in winning three times. The Bucs had used finesse to garner their three victories. The Yankees had outscored Pittsburgh, 46-17, and outhit them, 78-49 — yet the Series was square at three games apiece.

After the Pirates had won the opener 6-4 behind the pitching of Vern Law, the Yanks reeled off 16-3 and 10-0 drubbings, Mickey Mantle homering twice and driving in five runs in Game 2 and little second baseman Bobby Richardson hitting a grand slam and driving in a Series-record six runs in Game 3.

And so the pattern continued. Pittsburgh won the next two games, 3-2, and 5-2. New York answered, 12-0, as Whitey Ford threw his second straight shutout. Nobody knew what to expect in Game 7. But nobody was disappointed.

Pittsburgh jumped on Yankee starter Bob Turley for four runs in the first two innings, but New York's Bill Skowron hit a solo homer in the fifth and Yogi Berra's three-run homer in the sixth gave the Yanks a 5-4 lead. New York stretched the margin to 7-4 with two eighth-inning runs, but the Pirates answered with five in the bottom of the inning to take a 9-7 lead. The key blow in the rally was a three-run homer by reserve catcher Hal Smith.

Not to be denied, the Yankees scratched out two ninth-inning runs to tie the game. That set the stage for Mazeroski, who wrote the perfect ending for this confrontation and gave Pittsburgh its first Series win in 35 years.

Bill Mazeroski makes his triumphant trot home amid the Forbes Field delirium he touched off with his World Series-ending home run against the New York Yankees.

A.L. adds two teams

The American League, trying to get an expansion jump on the National League, announced October 26 that it will relocate one team and add two others — and all will play in 1961.

That announcement from New York by A.L. President Joe Cronin caught everybody by surprise. The National League had announced at its October 17 meeting in Chicago that it would add teams in New York and Houston — to begin play in 1962. Thus, for the first time since the A.L. was founded in 1900, the two leagues will present uneven alignments.

The first order of business for the A.L. was approval for Calvin Griffith's Washington Senators to move to Minneapolis-St. Paul — a move that had been contemplated for some time. With the Senators moving out of Washington, A.L. owners then approved a new team for the nation's capital and another that will play in Los Angeles.

Pressure had been building for the A.L. to place a team on the West Coast. The lucrative Los Angeles market had been grabbed in 1957 when the Dodgers relocated from Brooklyn and the Giants had snapped up the San Francisco area. Although nobody was sure where the new West Coast entry would play its games, Cronin said, "We would be silly not to move into Los Angeles."

Two important format changes will accompany the expansion to 10 teams. New York, Boston, Baltimore, Cleveland and Washington now will compete in an East Division with Minnesota, Kansas City, Chicago, Detroit and Los Angeles playing in a West Division. The league will expand its schedule from 154 to 162 games, with each team playing the other nine 18 times.

Calvin Griffith, former owner of the Washington Senators and now head of the Minnesota Twins, points to the larger-than-life painting of Walter Johnson that accompanied him on his move to Minneapolis.

" DUGOUT CHATTER "

"He's a four-letter man. He can hit, run, field and throw. You won't find many with all of those qualifications. Some have two or three, but not many have all four."

Pie Traynor

Hall of Famer, commenting on Pittsburgh right fielder Roberto Clemente

CAUGHT ON THE FLY

OCTOBER

St. Louis' George Crowe finished the season with four pinch-hit home runs, giving him a major league-record 14 for his career.

The Dodgers attracted 2,253,887 fans to the Los Angeles Coliseum, topping Milwaukee's 1957 N.L. record of 2,215,404.

DECEMBER

Charles O. Finley gained control of the Kansas City Athletics when he paid just under $2 million to acquire 52 percent of the team stock from the estate of the late Arnold Johnson.

SEASON LEADERS

	American League		National League	
Avg.	Pete Runnels, Bos.	.320	Dick Groat, Pit.	.325
HR	Mickey Mantle, N.Y.	40	Ernie Banks, Chi.	41
RBI	Roger Maris, N.Y.	112	Hank Aaron, Mil.	126
SB	Luis Aparicio, Chi.	51	Maury Wills, L.A.	50
W-L Pct.	Jim Perry, Cle. 18-10,	.643	Ernie Broglio, St. L. 21-9,	.700
ERA	Frank Baumann, Chi.	2.67	Mike McCormick, S.F.	2.70
SO	Jim Bunning, Det.	201	Don Drysdale, L.A.	246

New clubs hold draft

In a scenario unparalled in baseball history, two new American League teams came into existence December 14 as officials stocked their rosters in the first-ever expansion draft.

General Manager Fred Haney and Manager Bill Rigney represented Los Angeles interests and General Manager Ed Doherty and Manager Mickey Vernon called the shots for the new Washington club in A.L. President Joe Cronin's Boston office. The two teams paid a combined $4.5 million to the other eight clubs for the right to draft 28 names from an A.L. stockpile of 120 players.

Each of the eight existing teams had been required to submit a list of 15 players, at least seven of whom had appeared on major league rosters before August 31. Players were drafted with alternate picks by position, starting with pitchers, catchers, infielders and outfielders. Each selection cost $75,000 and both teams were given the right to pick as many as eight minor leaguers at $25,000 per player.

Los Angeles opened the draft by taking New York Yankee pitcher Eli Grba and Washington followed by taking another Yankee, veteran hurler Bobby Shantz. Among the veteran names picked were Gene Woodling, Willie Tasby, Marty Keough, Dick Donovan, Pete Burnside, Ned Garver, Ted Kluszewski and Eddie Yost.

Washington General Manager Ed Doherty announces the Senators' first pick in the A.L. expansion draft.

Mays blasts Braves

Willie Mays became the ninth player in major league history to slug four home runs in one game April 30 when he keyed an eight-homer 14-4 San Francisco victory over the Braves at Milwaukee's County Stadium.

Mays drove in eight runs with circuit blasts in the first, third, sixth and eighth innings, and advanced to the on-deck circle in the ninth, only to be denied a shot at history when Jim Davenport grounded out to end the game. Mays lined out to center in the fifth off Moe Drabowsky. The last major leaguer to accomplish the four-homer feat was Cleveland's Rocky Colavito in 1959. The last National Leaguer was Milwaukee's Joe Adcock in 1954.

Jose Pagan also hit two home runs for the Giants and Orlando Cepeda and Felip Alou added one apiece to give San Francisco a one-game record-tying eight. The Giants, who had hit five the day before, also tied a two-game major league mark of 13. Hank Aaron hit two for Milwaukee.

Mays hit his first two homers off Milwaukee starter Lew Burdette and connected later off Seth Morehead and Don McMahon. One was a three-run shot, two were two-run homers and the fourth was a solo blast.

This two-day offensive outburst was sweet revenge on Milwaukee. On April 28, the Braves' 40-year-old Warren Spahn had pitched a no-hitter against the Giants.

San Francisco's Willie Mays became the ninth player in history to hit four home runs in a single game.

College of Coaches

Vedie Himsl, a nine-year member of the Chicago organization, was named first head coach of the managerless Cubs April 6 under the innovative new system devised by Owner Philip K. Wrigley.

Himsl, one of nine coaches who will rotate through the organization's system and take turns deciding strategy for the Cubs, gets first call because of seniority. He will call the shots for the first two weeks of the season and then return to the minors.

The selection of Himsl, a Cubs pitching coach and scout since 1952, was announced after an exhibition game against the Boston Red Sox in San Antonio. The Cubs coaching staff will have a vote in starting lineups, pitching rotations and pregame strategy, but Himsl will be in control once the game begins. When Himsl steps down, another coach will rotate to the Cubs. Only four or five of the nine coaches will get head coaching shots.

Chicago's College of Coaches also includes Charlie Grimm,

Vedie Himsl, Chicago's first "head coach."

Elvin Tappe, Harry Craft, Lou Klein, Bobby Adams, Goldie Holt, Fred Martin and Rip Collins.

" DUGOUT CHATTER "

"Robinson scares me more than any other hitter in the league. I've told my pitchers they can expect an automatic fine if they hit Robinson with a pitched ball. He's tough enough at the plate without getting him riled up."

Gene Mauch

Philadelphia manager, on Cincinnati slugger Frank Robinson

Cobb dies of cancer

Ty Cobb, still holder of 16 major league records and co-holder of five more, died July 17 in Atlanta after a long battle against cancer. He was 74.

Considered by many to be the greatest player ever to put on a uniform, the Georgia Peach compiled a .367 career average over 24 seasons, 22 of which were spent with the Detroit Tigers. He played in a record 3,033 games, collected a record 4,191 hits and set more than 90 other marks during the course of his outstanding career, including his mark of nine straight American League batting championships and 12 overall.

Cobb, one of the most intense competitors ever to sharpen a pair of spikes and one of the game's most disliked players, battled his cancer the same way he used to battle pitchers on the diamond. But after more than a year and a half of painful endurance, he lost his fight.

Cobb was a charter member of baseball's Hall of Fame in 1936.

CAUGHT ON THE FLY

MAY

Baltimore first baseman Jim Gentile made baseball history when he connected for grand slams in consecutive innings of a 13-5 win at Minnesota.

JUNE

Eddie Gaedel, the midget who made one plate appearance for the St. Louis Browns in a 1951 Bill Veeck promotional stunt, died in Chicago at age 36.

JULY

The year's second All-Star Game, played at Boston's Fenway Park, ended in a 1-1 tie when heavy rain forced cancellation after nine innings.

Spahn joins 300 club

Warren Spahn became the 13th member of baseball's 300-victory club and only the third lefthander to reach the lofty plateau when he pitched a six-hit, 2-1 victory over Chicago August 11 before 40,775 fans at Milwaukee's County Stadium.

The Braves' crafty 40-year-old recorded his 12th win of the season and joined Lefty Grove and Eddie Plank as the game's only 300-win lefties. Gino Cimoli's eighth-inning home run was the deciding blow.

Spahn, a 17-year veteran and 11-time 20-game winner, was mobbed by happy teammates after he recorded the final out. He doffed his cap and blew kisses to the fans as he ran happily into the Braves dugout.

Earlier this season, Spahn recorded his 290th victory with his second career no-hitter — a 1-0 victory over San Francisco.

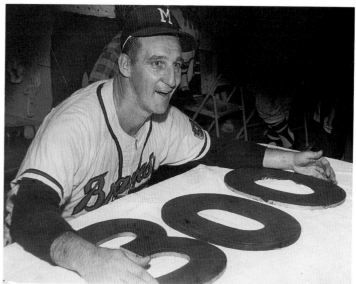

Milwaukee veteran Warren Spahn after beating Chicago for his 300th career win.

Blowing in the wind

In its 1½ seasons, San Francisco's Candlestick Park had gained a dubious reputation. The winds that whipped off San Francisco Bay often turned the stadium into an ever-changing wind tunnel and such unpredictable behavior shaped the course of many games.

So it was with some relief that the first All-Star Game of 1961 opened on a calm, sunny San Francisco day that resulted in eight well-played innings and a 3-1 National League lead, courtesy of a home run by Chicago's George Altman, two sacrifice flies and the combined one-hit pitching of Milwaukee's Warren Spahn, Cincinnati's Bob Purkey and San Francisco's Mike McCormick.

But suddenly the calm turned into a storm and late-afternoon winds turned the midsummer classic into a circus. The American League, helped when slightly-built Giants reliever Stu Miller was blown off balance in mid-delivery for a balk, scored two ninth-inning runs to tie the game.

As the wind continued to increase, so did the odd developments. The A.L. took a 4-3 lead in the top of the 10th when a throw to first by St. Louis third baseman Ken Boyer was blown into right field, allowing Chicago's Nellie Fox to score.

The N.L. came back in the bottom of the inning with, of course, a little assist from the wind. After Milwaukee's Hank Aaron had singled, advanced to second on a passed ball and scored on a double by San Francisco's Willie Mays, one of Baltimore reliever Hoyt Wilhelm's floating knuckleballs was blown into Cincinnati's Frank Robinson. Pittsburgh's Roberto Clemente followed with a game-winning single.

SEASON LEADERS

	American League		National League	
Avg.	Norm Cash, Det.	.361	Roberto Clemente, Pit.	.351
HR	Roger Maris, N.Y.	61	Orlando Cepeda, S.F.	46
RBI	Roger Maris, N.Y.	142	Orlando Cepeda, S.F.	142
SB	Luis Aparicio, Chi.	53	Maury Wills, L.A.	35
W-L Pct.	Whitey Ford, N.Y.	25-4, .862	Johnny Podres, L.A.	18-5, .783
ERA	Dick Donovan, Wash.	2.40	Warren Spahn, Mil.	3.01
SO	Camilo Pascual, Min.	221	Sandy Koufax, L.A.	269

An All-Star outfield (left to right): Roberto Clemente, Willie Mays and Hank Aaron.

The asterisk ruling

Commissioner Ford Frick threw a protective barrier around Babe Ruth July 17 when he ruled that nobody would be credited with breaking the Bambino's one-season record of 60 home runs unless he did it in a 154-game schedule.

The "asterisk ruling" was prompted by the home run derby currently being staged by New York Yankees Roger Maris and Mickey Mantle. Maris has hit 35 homers and is 19 games ahead of Ruth's 1927 pace while Mantle has 32 and is eight games ahead of Ruth. Because of expansion, all American League teams will play 162 games this year.

Frick said any player who tops the 60-homer plateau after his 154th game would get a distinctive mark in the record book to show it as a 162-game record. He said he made the formal ruling because of the unusual interest Maris and Mantle have generated.

Maris passes Babe

"Move over Babe Ruth."

So said Roger Maris, a later-edition New York Yankee outfielder, with one swing of his bat on October 1. Maris propelled a pitch from Boston rookie right-hander Tracy Stallard into the right-field bleachers at Yankee Stadium for his record-breaking 61st home run, ending his torturous season-long chase of Ruth's 60-homer ghost.

But the historic home run did not end the controversy. For a variety of reasons — such as the incredible popularity of Ruth and the unfair perception of Maris as insensitive and inconsiderate — many fans and other observers cringed at the thought of this new-era Yankee supplanting the great Bambino. And as it became obvious during the season that Maris was making a run at base-ball's most cherished record, they made that point clear, even prompting Commissioner Ford Frick to jump into the fray with his famous "asterisk ruling," which declared that a player who sought to displace Ruth in the record book would have to hit his 61st home run before his team played its 155th complete game. Ruth had set the mark in 1927 under a 154-game schedule; Maris was competing under an expanded 162-game format.

Most of the season was a fascinating home run duel between Maris and Yankee teammate Mickey Mantle. Maris, a 27-year-old lefthanded swinger, did not hit his first homer until the Yankees' 11th game — the same day Mantle hit his sixth and seventh. But Maris soon found his groove. By the end of May, Mantle had 14 and Maris 12. As June came to a close, Maris led Mantle, 27 to 25. On July 31, Maris had 40 to Mantle's 39. As August closed, Maris had 51 homers, Mantle 48.

Soon, however, Maris would be on his own. Illness would plague Mantle throughout September and he would finish with 54 homers. Maris entered the Yankees' 155th game (it would count against the asterisk because of an early-season tie) with 58. He got No. 59 off Baltimore right-hander Milt Pappas as the Yankees clinched their 26th American League pennant with a 4-2 victory. No. 60 came against Baltimore's Jack Fisher on September 26 and Maris entered the final game of the season needing one more.

He got it in the fourth inning on a 2-0 pitch from Stallard, giving the Yankees a 1-0 victory. Maris was in the record book — with an asterisk, of course.

New York Yankee Roger Maris steps on the plate to complete his record quest: 61 homers in a single season.

CAUGHT ON THE FLY

OCTOBER

Two monster seasons: San Francisco's Orlando Cepeda batted .311 and led the N.L. with 46 homers and 142 RBIs. Detroit's Norm Cash won the A.L. batting title with a .361 mark and finished with 41 homers and 132 RBIs.

NOVEMBER

Roger Maris, the Yankees' 61-homer man, captured his second straight A.L. Most Valuable Player award.

New York lefty Whitey Ford capped his spectacular 25-4 season by winning the Cy Young Award.

New York's M&M boys: Roger Maris (left) and Mickey Mantle.

Phils end skid at 23

John Buzhardt scattered nine hits and the Philadelphia Phillies brought a merciful end to their modern-era record 23-game losing streak August 20 with a 7-4 victory over Milwaukee in the second game of a doubleheader at County Stadium.

After losing its 23rd straight in the opener, 5-2, Philadelphia fought back to end its three-week record of futility. The Phillies scored twice in the fourth off Carlton Willey to take a 2-1 lead and held a 3-2 advantage when they notched four eighth-inning runs to break the game open. Buzhardt, the last Philadelphia pitcher to win a game on July 28, lifted his record to 4-13.

The victory, which snapped Milwaukee's 10-game winning streak, left the Phillies one short of the all-time record of 24 straight losses set by Cleveland in 1899. The 1906 Boston Braves had held the previous modern major league record of 20 straight losses.

New Mets hire Casey

The Old Professor is back. That was big news in New York October 2 when it was announced that former Yankee boss Casey Stengel had agreed to come out of retirement and manage the expansion New York Mets in their first National League season.

Stengel, a popular figure who is sure to attract fans to the ballpark, is known for his colorful language, fractured syntax, off-beat humor and comical behavior.

Casey will need a good sense of humor with the Mets, who figure to struggle through their formative years. It certainly will not be like it was with the Yankees, who captured 10 American League pennants and seven World Series under Stengel's 12-year leadership.

The 72-year-old Stengel, who has spent more than a half century in baseball, was dumped by the Yankees last year under the guise of a new age-limit policy.

New York Mets Manager Casey Stengel (center) with new coaches Cookie Lavagetto (left) and Solly Hemus.

" DUGOUT CHATTER "

"I figured out one day that at the rate I was hitting homers, I wouldn't catch the leaders until I was 118 years old. They aren't hiring many 118-year-old players these days, so I oughta get out now."

Hal Smith

St. Louis catcher, on why he had decided to retire from baseball

N.L. expands to 10

The National League officially grew to 10 teams October 10 when the expansion New York Mets and Houston Colt .45s selected 45 players from a draft pool of 136 as the nucleus for their first major league rosters.

The Mets picked 22 players and paid $1.8 million to the eight holdover teams while Houston grabbed 23 players at a price tag of $1.85 million. Houston General Manager Paul Richards opened the proceedings by picking San Francisco shortstop Ed Bressoud and New York General Manager George Weiss followed by taking Giants catcher Hobie Landrith.

Each club contributed 15 players to the pool, some priced at $75,000, others at $50,000. Each team had to provide two $125,000 players. The expansion teams had to select at least 16 from the $75,000 pool.

Some name players picked by the Mets were Gil Hodges, Roger Craig, Jay Hook, Don Zimmer and Gus Bell. The Colt .45s grabbed veterans Sam Jones, Norm Larker, Bobby Shantz and Ken Johnson. Shantz was the first player selected by Washington in last year's A.L. expansion draft.

WORLD SERIES REPORT

YANKEES ROLL ON

John Blanchard ignited a five-run first-inning explosion with a two-run homer and Hector Lopez contributed a three-run blast to New York's five-run fourth inning as the Yankees overwhelmed Cincinnati, 13-5, October 9 and captured their eighth World Series championship in 13 years.

The Game 5 clincher at Crosley Field was never in doubt as the Bronx Bombers, who had hit a major league record 240 home runs during the regular season, broke out to a 6-0 lead, withstood a three-run Cincinnati third inning and put the game out of reach in the fourth. The Yankees collected 15 hits off eight pitchers and got 6⅔ innings of sparkling relief from Bud Daley.

The powerful Yankees, winners of 109 regular-season games, jumped out quickly when ace Whitey Ford fired a two-hit shutout and Moose Skowron and Elston Howard hit home runs in a 2-0 Series-opening victory. After the Redlegs had rebounded for a 6-2 win, New York took control with 3-2 and 7-0 triumphs. Ford, 25-4 during the regular season, pitched five shutout innings in Game 4 to raise his Series-record scoreless-innings streak to 32.

The victory capped a successful first-season managerial debut for Ralph Houk and a 62-home run campaign for Roger Maris. The Yankee right fielder hit one in the Series after blasting a record 61 during the regular season.

Game 1	New York	2	Cincinnati	0
Game 2	Cincinnati	6	New York	2
Game 3	New York	3	Cincinnati	2
Game 4	New York	7	Cincinnati	0
Game 5	New York	13	Cincinnati	5

World Series Game 5 Yankee stars (left to right) John Blanchard, Bud Daley and Hector Lopez.

★1962★
JANUARY-SEPTEMBER

" DUGOUT CHATTER "

"He fouls off balls until he gets his pitch. We were figuring that he fouls off about 10 balls a game and he has played over 2,100 games. That makes 21,000 baseballs he has hit into the stands for souvenirs."

Danny Murtaugh

Pittsburgh manager, on Richie Ashburn, who is nearing the end of his outstanding big-league career

---

Yanks win marathon

Jack Reed's first major league home run, a two-run blast in the 22nd inning off Phil Regan, gave the New York Yankees a 9-7 victory over Detroit June 24 and brought a merciful end to the longest game (timewise) in major league history.

Reed, a utility outfielder who entered the game in the 13th inning, hit a shot into the left-field seats at Tiger Stadium, closing the curtain on the 7-hour marathon and making a winner of Jim Bou-

ton, the young Yankee right-hander who had pitched seven shutout innings. Bouton, Tex Clevenger and Bud Daley had shut out the Tigers for the last 16 frames.

Until Reed's homer, the Yankees had been shut out 19 straight innings by Jerry Casale, Ron Nischwitz, Ron Kline, Hank Aguirre and Terry Fox. New York had scored six in the first off Frank Lary and another in the second.

Jack Reed's home run in the 22nd inning, his first as a major leaguer, gave the New York Yankees a 9-7 win over Detroit.

Opening Day firsts

The Washington Senators kicked off a series of Opening Day firsts April 9 when they unveiled their $20 million D.C. Stadium and celebrated with a 4-1 victory over Detroit.

The Senators, who finished a miserable 61-101 last year as an American League expansion team, got off to a rousing start as Bob Johnson christened Washington's new home park with a two-run homer and Bennie Daniels pitched a five-hitter. U.S. President John F. Kennedy braved rainy weather to throw out the historic first ball.

Two more history-making games took place the next day.

The expansion Houston Colt .45s, playing their first National League game and the first regular-season contest in Texas, used a pair of three-run homers by Roman Mejias to pound out an 11-2 victory over the Chicago Cubs at Colt Stadium. But Los Angeles disappointed 52,564 fans at new Dodger Stadium by dropping a 6-3 decision to Cincinnati. The opening day of the Chavez Ravine facility ended the Dodgers' four-year stay in the massive Los Angeles Coliseum.

The expansion New York Mets made their major league debut April 11 in St. Louis, dropping an 11-4 verdict to the Cardinals.

Hal Smith (left), Bobby Shantz (center) and two-homer man Roman Mejias helped make Opening Day memorable for Houston's new Colt .45s.

A.L. earns a split

It was an everybody-wins, no-body-wins proposition when the dust had cleared on the two All-Star Games of 1962. The National League used pitching and speed to record a 3-1 victory in the July 10 battle at Washington's new D.C. Stadium and the American League powered its way to a 9-4 decision in the July 30 contest at Chicago's Wrigley Field.

With Los Angeles' Don Drysdale, San Francisco's Juan Marichal, Cincinnati's Bob Purkey and Milwaukee's Bob Shaw limiting the Americans to four hits, the N.L. unveiled a new offensive weapon in the first game — Maury

Wills. The Dodger shortstop, who had stolen 46 bases through the first half of the season, entered as a pinch-runner in the sixth inning.

Wills quickly swiped second and scored the N.L.'s first run on a single by Pittsburgh's Dick Groat. In the eighth, Wills singled and made two daring dashes — to third on a single to left field and home on a short fly to right field by the Giants' Felipe Alou. The Americans never recovered.

Rocky Colavito's three-run homer and four RBIs, a two-run blast by Leon Wagner and a solo shot by Pete Runnels keyed the A.L.'s second-game triumph.

Senator pitcher fans 21

Washington's Tom Cheney, a 27-year-old righthander, set a one-game major league record September 12 when he struck out 21 batters during a 16-inning 2-1 victory over the Orioles at Baltimore's Memorial Stadium.

Cheney struck out 13 Orioles in the regulation nine innings, added two in each of the 10th and 11th frames, fanned two more in the 14th and one each in the 15th and 16th. His 19th broke the modern major league record and his 20th shattered the all-time mark.

Former Cleveland ace Bob Feller and Los Angeles lefthander Sandy Koufax shared the modern nine-inning record of 18 strikeouts, Koufax having accomplished the feat for a second time in April. Two other pitchers had struck out 18 in extra-inning contests. The pre-1900 mark for a game of any duration was 19.

Cheney, who had pitched only three complete games, did not allow a hit between the eighth and 16th innings and surrendered only 10 in the game. Bud Zipfel's home run gave him his sixth victory in 14 decisions.

Washington's Tom Cheney: 21 strikeouts in 16 innings.

No-hitter craze: 5 in 3½ months

Minnesota Twins lefthander Jack Kralick, one ninth-inning walk away from the first regular-season perfect game in 40 years, pitched the fifth no-hitter in 3½ months August 26 when he stopped Kansas City, 1-0, at Metropolitan Stadium in Bloomington, Minn.

Kralick walked George Alusik with one out in the final inning to spoil his bid for perfection, but he got Billy Consolo and Bobby Del Greco to complete his no-hitter. He needed only 97 pitches to dispatch the Athletics.

Kralick's no-hitter was the fifth of a string that started on May 5, when Angels rookie lefthander Bo Belinsky defeated Baltimore, 2-0, in a game at Los Angeles. The next two came in a four-day span, Boston righthander Earl Wilson stopping the Angels, 2-0, June 26 at Fenway Park and Los Angeles lefty Sandy Koufax beating the New York Mets, 5-0, June 30 at Dodger Stadium.

Another Boston righthander, Bill Monbouquette, got into the act August 1 when he stopped Chicago, 1-0, at Comiskey Park.

It was shower time for Minnesota's Jack Kralick after his no-hitter against Kansas City.

Musial moves up on hit list

St. Louis great Stan Musial moved into second place on the all-time hit list September 2 when he singled as a pinch-hitter in a 4-3 loss to the New York Mets at Busch Stadium.

Musial, batting for pitcher Bobby Shantz in the ninth inning, delivered hit No. 3,516 off Al Jackson and moved past Tris Speaker. Musial now trails only Ty Cobb, who amassed 4,191 hits in 24 big-league seasons.

The 41-year-old Musial, playing in his 22nd campaign, holds 41 National League records, a list that has grown considerably this season. The three-time Most Valuable player will remember 1962 as a milestone year.

* On April 13, he scored his N.L.-record 1,869th run in a game against Chicago.
* On May 19, he moved past Honus Wagner into first place on the all-time N.L. hit list when he got No. 3,431 in a game against Los Angeles.
* On June 22, he became baseball's all-time total base leader, raising his career total to 5,864 in a game against Philadelphia.
* And on July 25, Musial became the N.L.'s all-time RBI leader with 1,862 in a game against the Dodgers.

CAUGHT ON THE FLY

JULY

Los Angeles lefty Johnny Podres tied the modern major league record when he struck out eight consecutive Phillies during a 5-1 conquest of Philadelphia at Dodger Stadium.

New York Yankee slugger Mickey Mantle matched a 1947 major league record set by Pittsburgh's Ralph Kiner when he exploded for seven home runs in 12 official at-bats over five games.

Minnesota set a major league record when it belted two grand slams in one inning during a 14-3 victory over Cleveland at Metropolitan Stadium. Bob Allison and Harmon Killebrew did the honors in the 11-run first frame.

★1962★

" DUGOUT CHATTER "

"Too bad we can't win a few games for that nice owner of ours over in Europe. What's her name?"

Casey Stengel

New York Mets manager, referring to Mrs. Joan Payson, owner of the team that was en route to a first-year record of 40-120

The woeful Mets

It was only fitting that New York catcher Joe Pignatano ended his season by hitting into a triple play during a 5-1 final-day loss to the Chicago Cubs. It was that kind of a year for all the Mets, the National League expansion phenomenon that lost a major league-record 120 times and finished 60½ games behind San Francisco.

The Mets were inept and lovable, horrible and marvelous. They had the perfect manager, fun-loving 73-year-old Casey Stengel, and understanding fans, 922,530 of which turned out to give them an impressive first-year bottom line. Nobody expected much and everybody accepted even less.

Numbers verify the horrible truth. The Mets were 40-120, winning 22 times at home and 18 times on the road. They finished last in the 10-team league in pitching (5.04 ERA), fielding (.967 percentage) and batting (.240 average). Five pitchers — Roger Craig (10-24), Al Jackson (8-20), Jay Hook (8-19), Craig Anderson (3-17) and Bob Miller (1-12) — accounted for 92 losses.

The Mets lost their first nine games and later suffered losing skids of 17, 13 and 11. Their frustration was compounded by the moderate success of the Houston Colt .45s, who finished in eighth place, 64-96 and six games ahead of the Cubs, in their expansion debut.

A pair of Mets: Catcher Hobie Landrith (left) and 24-game loser Roger Craig.

Desperate Giants overcome Dodgers

A desperation four-run ninth-inning rally, aided by four walks and Los Angeles' fourth error, gave San Francisco a 6-4 third-game playoff victory over the Dodgers October 3 and completed the Giants' long uphill climb to a National League pennant.

The Giants, who had teetered on the edge of elimination for more than two weeks, trailed 4-2 entering the fateful ninth. But Dodger reliever Ed Roebuck surrendered a leadoff single to Matty Alou and walks to Willie McCovey and Felipe Alou. Willie Mays hit a shot off the pitcher's hand for an infield single to score one run and Orlando Cepeda's sacrifice fly off Stan Williams tied things up. After Ed Bailey was walked intentionally to reload the bases, Williams walked Jim Davenport for the go-ahead run and another scored on second baseman Larry Burright's error.

San Francisco's 103rd victory of the season and second in the best-of-three pennant playoff, sent 45,693 Dodger Stadium fans into shock. They had watched their team blow a four-game lead with 13 to play. The Dodgers closed out their 3-10 two-week slide with a 1-0 loss to St. Louis September 30 while the Giants were edging Houston, 2-1, to force the fourth playoff in N.L. history.

San Francisco won the first contest at Candlestick Park, 8-0, behind the three-hit pitching of Billy Pierce and the two-homer salvo of Mays (his league-leading 48th and 49th), but the Dodgers rebounded in Game 2 for an 8-7 win when Maury Wills scored on Ron Fairly's ninth-inning sacrifice fly.

San Francisco became the fifth different N.L. winner in as many years. The Dodgers, who occupied first place for 111 of the campaign's 178 days and held undisputed possession from July 8 until closing day, have been involved in all four N.L. playoff series, losing three.

Billy Pierce (left) and Orlando Cepeda were key figures in San Francisco's pennant playoff victory over Los Angeles.

CAUGHT ON THE FLY

SEPTEMBER
Chicago rookie second baseman Ken Hubbs made a wild fourth-inning throw in a loss to Cincinnati, ending his major league-record errorless streak at 78 games and 418 chances.

OCTOBER
Los Angeles drew a major league-record 2,755,184 fans to new Dodger Stadium, setting the pace for an all-time big-league attendance high of 21,375,215.

NOVEMBER
The players and owners agreed to drop the second All-Star Game, an annual event since 1959.

New York Yankee Mickey Mantle, a .321 hitter with 30 homers and 89 RBIs, captured his third A.L. Most Valuable Player award.

SO-0-0-0-0 CLOSE

New York second baseman Bobby Richardson, standing in the right spot at the right time, picked off Willie McCovey's vicious line drive October 16 and preserved the Yankees' dramatic 1-0 victory over San Francisco in the seventh game of the World Series at Candlestick Park.

With 43,948 fans watching nervously from the edge of their seats, Yankee starter Ralph Terry carried a two-hit shutout into the final inning of the Series-deciding contest. He had handled the Giants easily through eight innings, but his teammates had managed only one run themselves off Giants starter Jack Sanford.

Pinch-hitter Matty Alou opened the final frame by bunting for a hit. Terry struck out Felipe Alou and Chuck Hiller, but Willie Mays slashed a double to right. Only an excellent play by right fielder Roger Maris kept Alou at third. Suddenly Terry, the man who had surrendered the Series-winning home run in 1960 to Pittsburgh's Bill Mazeroski, was facing the monstrous McCovey with the tying and winning runs in scoring position.

Disdaining a walk that would have brought Orlando Cepeda to the plate, the righthander took the count to 1-1. On his next pitch, McCovey uncoiled and hit a smash toward right field. Richardson moved slightly to his left, reached up and snared the ball, giving the Yankees their second straight World Series and 20th overall.

It was evident from the start that this would not be a typical Yankee cakewalk. It would take determination, and endurance, to stop the Giants' comeback express. Endurance would be required because of foul weather that postponed Game 5 one day and Game 6 three days, stretching the series into a 13-day marathon.

New York won the opener 6-2 behind Whitey Ford and San Francisco took the second contest, 2-0, on a three-hitter by Sanford. The victory swapping continued with the Yankees winning the third game, 3-2, the Giants prevailing, 7-3, in Game 4, the Yanks winning the fifth game, 5-3, and San Francisco the sixth, 5-2.

The Yankees won despite compiling an uncharacteristic .199 team batting average.

Game 1	New York	6	San Francisco	2
Game 2	San Francisco	2	New York	0
Game 3	New York	3	San Francisco	2
Game 4	San Francisco	7	New York	3
Game 5	New York	5	San Francisco	3
Game 6	San Francisco	5	New York	2
Game 7	New York	1	San Francisco	0

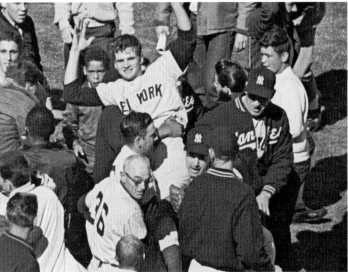

New York pitcher Ralph Terry, a World Series goat in 1960, enjoys the spoils of victory. He succeeded in shutting out San Francisco in Game 7 of the fall classic when Bobby Richardson picked off Willie McCovey's right field smash.

Dodgers' Wills steals spotlight, N.L. MVP

Maury Wills, the man who lit the offensive fuse for the Los Angeles Dodgers with a major league-record 104 stolen bases, was named the National League Most Valuable Player November 23 in a vote by the Baseball Writers' Association of America.

The speedy shortstop brought a dimension to the game that had been missing since the prime of Detroit star Ty Cobb, the man whose single-season steal record he supplanted. Wills batted .299, but his real contribution came on the basepaths, where he disrupted defenses and forced them to make costly mistakes.

Wills, the first player this century to top the 100 mark in steals, tied and broke Cobb's record September 23 in a 12-2 loss to St. Louis. He singled and swiped second in the third inning for steal No. 96 and broke the record in the seventh.

Wills' final two steals came during Game 3 of the Dodgers' pennant playoff against San Francisco. He singled in the seventh and swiped both second and third, scoring when catcher Bob Bailey's throw skipped past third baseman Jim Davenport.

That run gave Los Angeles a 4-2 lead, but the Giants scored four ninth-inning runs.

The umpire signals safe as Dodger Maury Wills slides into third with record steal No. 104 during a National League pennant playoff game against the San Francisco Giants.

SEASON LEADERS

	American League		National League	
Avg.	Pete Runnels, Bos.	.326	Tommy Davis, L.A.	.346
HR	Harmon Killebrew, Min.	48	Willie Mays, S.F.	49
RBI	Harmon Killebrew, Min.	126	Tommy Davis, L.A.	153
SB	Luis Aparicio, Chi.	31	Maury Wills, L.A.	104
W-L Pct.	Ray Herbert, Chi.	20-9, .690	Bob Purkey, Cin.	23-5, .821
ERA	Hank Aguirre, Det.	2.21	Sandy Koufax, L.A.	2.54
SO	Camilo Pascual, Min.	206	Don Drysdale, L.A.	232

" DUGOUT CHATTER "

"I've got my wife and kids to think about. And the better catcher I get to be, the better I'll be able to provide for them. There's no mystery about that."

Elston Howard

New York Yankee catcher

Marichal zeroes in

San Francisco's high-kicking Juan Marichal made his sixth straight victory and 10th of the season a memorable one June 15, holding the Houston Colt .45s without a hit in a 1-0 decision at Candlestick Park.

With 18,869 fans cheering their approval, the stylish righthander from the Dominican Republic got rookie Brock Davis on a called third strike to end the first major league no-hitter by a Latin player. Marichal, who broke into the big leagues with a one-hitter against Philadelphia three years ago, struck out five and allowed two walks while facing only 29 batters.

Marichal needed 89 pitches to outduel Houston's Dick Drott, who allowed only three hits himself. Unfortunately for Drott, two of them — back-to-back doubles by Jim Davenport and Chuck Hiller — came in the eighth inning and produced the Giants' only run.

The no-hitter was the third in the major leagues this season and the first by a Giants pitcher since Carl Hubbell in 1929. Ironically, Marichal's last loss came on May 11 — when the Giants were no-hit by the Dodgers' Sandy Koufax.

Juan Marichal waves to appreciative San Francisco fans after stopping Houston for his first career no-hitter.

Wynn captures 300th

Early Wynn's frustrating struggle to record his 300th career victory came to an end July 13 when he pitched five rocky innings in the second game of a doubleheader against Kansas City and then watched Cleveland teammate Jerry Walker close the door on his history-making triumph.

The 43-year-old righthander, the 14th member of baseball's exclusive 300 club, left the game with the Indians clinging to a 5-4 lead. Walker pitched four innings of three-hit relief to secure Cleveland's 7-4 victory.

Wynn, who joins Milwaukee's Warren Spahn as the only active 300-game winners, reached the lofty plateau on his eighth try. He had made three attempts last year with the Chicago White Sox and five since being signed last month by Cleveland. His 299th victory was recorded September 8.

Wynn, a five-time 20-game winner who began his career in 1939, yielded three runs in the fifth inning after being staked to a 5-1 lead. He walked three batters, giving him a career record total of 1,765.

Kansas City won the doubleheader opener, 6-5.

Early Wynn (left), baseball's newest 300-game winner, with Cleveland Manager Birdie Tebbetts.

Mays dominates A.L.

San Francisco's Willie Mays collected only one hit but dominated the American League in every other way possible July 9 as the National League recorded a 5-3 All-Star Game victory at Cleveland's Municipal Stadium.

Mays walked in the second inning, stole second and scored on a single by St. Louis' Dick Groat. He singled home Milwaukee's Hank Aaron in the third inning, stole second again and scored on a single by Giants teammate Ed Bailey. The center fielder drove in the Nationals' fourth run with an infield out in the fifth and made an outstanding running catch of New York Yankee Joe Pepitone's eighth-inning drive.

The A.L. scored all three of its runs in the second and third innings on singles by Los Angeles Angels pitcher Ken McBride, Boston's Frank Malzone and Minnesota's Earl Battey. Philadelphia's Ray Culp, Houston's Hal Woodeshick and Los Angeles' Don Drysdale set down the Americans on three singles over the final five innings.

The game marked the 24th and final All-Star appearance for St. Louis' Stan Musial, who is retiring at the end of the season. Musial, 0-for-1 as a pinch-hitter, completed his All-Star log with 20 hits and a record six home runs.

Goodbye Polo Grounds — again

Seven months after the Mets played their last game at the Polo Grounds, the historic New York park succumbed to the wrecking ball.

The historic Polo Grounds, home to the expansion New York Mets for the last two seasons, played host to its last major league game September 18 when Philadelphia defeated the Mets, 5-1, before a disappointing farewell crowd of 1,752.

The horseshoe-shaped home of the New York Giants for 67 years had grown old and rickety when the Mets took up residency in 1962 while waiting for their new ballpark in Flushing Meadow to be completed. New Shea Stadium will be ready when the 1964 campaign opens and the Harlem park that served as a baseball home to such names as John McGraw, Christy Mathewson, Fred Merkle, Carl Hubbell, Mel Ott, Bill Terry, Casey Stengel, Rube Marquard, Roger Bresnahan, Leo Durocher and Willie Mays will sit vacant for a second time.

The first came after the 1957 campaign, when the Giants skipped off to San Francisco. Four years went by before the Polo Grounds was given a facelift for its short tenure as the Mets' home base. That ended with the loss to the Phillies — a game played without fanfare.

Over the years, the Polo Grounds also served as a temporary home (1913-1922) for the New York Yankees and played host to 14 World Series.

CAUGHT ON THE FLY

JANUARY

Seven-time N.L. batting champion Rogers Hornsby, who compiled the highest average in baseball history (.424) for the St. Louis Cardinals in 1924, died in Chicago at age 66.

Welcome news for pitchers: The major league Rules Committee expanded the strike zone to its pre-1950 status — from the top of the batter's shoulders to the bottom of his knees.

AUGUST

Pittsburgh's Jerry Lynch became the all-time career leader in pinch-hit home runs when he connected for his 15th in a game at Chicago, breaking a tie and giving the Pirates a 7-6 victory.

Spahn, 42, ties mark

Warren Spahn, Milwaukee's 42-year-old pitching genius, became a 20-game winner for a record-tying 13th time September 8 when he scattered nine Philadelphia hits and recorded a 3-2 victory over the Phillies at Connie Mack Stadium.

Spahn tied the National League mark for 20-win seasons set by former New York Giants great Christy Mathewson. Cy Young, a winner of 511 games over 22 big-league campaigns, set the major league record with 16. Many of Young's wins were recorded in the infant American League.

Spahn, who ranks seventh on the all-time list with 347 victories over 19 seasons, shut out the Phillies for six innings before Tony Gonzalez tripled and scored on a sacrifice fly by Roy Sievers. That run tied the game, but Gene Oliver's two-run homer in the eighth helped the crafty left-hander raise his record to 20-5.

The Phillies' final run came on a solo-ninth-inning homer by Don Demeter.

Record-tying Milwaukee lefthander Warren Spahn.

Mets pitcher Craig's nightmare finally ends

Jim Hickman belted a two-out, ninth-inning grand slam off Chicago reliever Lindy McDaniel August 9 to give the New York Mets a 7-3 victory over the Cubs and end righthander Roger Craig's nightmarish losing streak one game short of the major league record.

Hickman's drive off the left-field scoreboard at the Polo Grounds snapped Craig's 18-game losing string and made him a winner for the first time since April 29. He had matched the longest losing streak in National League history and fell one short of the big-league record of 19, set in 1916 by the Philadelphia Athletics' Jack Nabors.

The Mets had carried a 3-2 advantage into the eighth. But the unlucky Craig, who had allowed solo homers to Andre Rodgers and Lou Brock, surrendered the tying run on Billy Williams' triple and Ron Santo's sacrifice fly.

The Mets loaded the bases in the ninth on Joe Hicks' single, Al Moran's double and an intentional walk to pinch-hitter Tim Harkness. Hickman belted McDaniel's 3-2 pitch to give Craig his third win against 20 defeats and only his 13th in 57 decisions over two seasons.

★1963★

Colts lose to Mets with all-rookie lineup

The New York Mets scored eight runs in the first three innings of a September 27 game at Colt Stadium and cruised to a 10-3 victory over a Houston team that played like a bunch of rookies. And with good reason. Colts Manager Harry Craft opened the matchup of National League also-rans with an all-rookie lineup.

Craft's starting unit averaged 19 years and four months with 17-year-old Jay Dahl as the starting pitcher. Fifteen first-year Houston players saw service before a veteran, Carl Warwick, entered the game. Four first-year pitchers worked before six-year veteran Dick Drott took over in the ninth.

The Colts' starting unit: Brock Davis, left field: Jimmy Wynn, center field; Aaron Pointer, right field; Rusty Staub, first base; Joe Morgan, second base; Glenn Vaughan, third base; Sonny Jackson, shortstop, and Jerry Grote, catcher.

Morgan, Staub and Davis drove in Houston's runs against New York winner Al Jackson.

Houston's all-rookie lineup included (front row, left to right): Jay Dahl, Jerry Grote; (second row) Glenn Vaughan, Sonny Jackson, Joe Morgan, Rusty Staub; (back row) Brock Davis, Aaron Pointer and Jim Wynn.

" DUGOUT CHATTER "

"I think a lot of people are staying away because they think I don't know anything about cars. And they're right. I don't."

Joe Nuxhall

Cincinnati pitcher, on the off-season filling station business he runs in Fairfield, O.

CAUGHT ON THE FLY

SEPTEMBER
San Francisco's Alou brothers, Felipe, Jesus and Matty, became the first brother trio to appear in the same lineup when they all played during a game at New York.

NOVEMBER
New York Yankee catcher Elston Howard was selected as the first black MVP in American League history. Blacks have won 11 times in the N.L.

Cincinnati second baseman Pete Rose, a .273 hitter in his first big-league season, was a runaway winner in N.L. Rookie of the Year balloting.

Dodgers take control

Los Angeles, seemingly on the verge of losing its once-safe lead to rampaging St. Louis, completed a crucial three-game Cardinal sweep September 18 that sent the Redbirds reeling and secured the Dodgers' second National League pennant in their six years on the West Coast. Ironically, the key blow in that sweep was provided by a youngster playing his first major league game.

It was showdown time when the teams met at St. Louis' Busch Stadium for the September 16 opener of the series. The Cardinals, winners in 19 of their last 20 contests, had whittled the Dodger lead to one game. The Dodgers, having won 13 of 19 themselves, were nevertheless teetering on the edge.

But lefthander Johnny Podres helped the Dodgers regain their balance, pitching a 3-1 victory that provided breathing room. Sandy Koufax was even better the next night, allowing only four hits in a 4-0 shutout — his 11th whitewash of the season. Suddenly the Cardinals were on the edge.

St. Louis fans breathed a sigh of relief September 18 when the Cardinals jumped to a 5-1 lead after three innings with Bob Gibson on the mound. But the big right-hander weakened in the eighth, permitting three runs, and the Dodgers struck dramatically in the ninth when rookie Dick Nen, just up from Spokane of the Pacific Coast League, belted a game-tying home run in his second major league at-bat.

The Dodgers, with relief ace Ron Perranoski blanking the Cardinals on three hits for six innings, pushed across a 13th-inning run for a back-breaking 6-5 victory.

Four games down and demoralized, the Cardinals dropped their next two games at Cincinnati and another at Chicago. Los Angeles cruised to a final six-game advantage.

The pennant was especially sweet for the pitching-rich Dodgers, who had collapsed down the stretch the previous season. The Big Four of Koufax (25), Don Drysdale (19), Perranoski (16) and Podres (14) accounted for 74 of the Dodgers' 99 victories.

Los Angeles rookie Dick Nen delivered a big blow to St. Louis' pennant hopes.

Musial says farewell

In an emotional conclusion to a marvelous career, Stan Musial said a pair of goodbyes to 27,576 fans at St. Louis' Busch Stadium. The greatest hitter in National League history said his first farewell over a microphone during pregame ceremonies and his second with a bat during a 14-inning 3-2 victory over Cincinnati.

The standing ovations started early when Musial was honored before his final major league game with a long series of speeches and gifts. And they continued all afternoon, as adoring St. Louis fans poured out their hearts to the greatest player in franchise history. Before the day was over Musial's No. 6 had been retired,

the first baseman-outfielder had added two hits to his N.L.-record total and he had raised his career average to .331.

"As long as I live, I will always remember this day," Musial told the crowd. "For me it is both a great joy and a great sorrow. It is a joy because of this wonderful day for me, and it is a sorrow because it is a farewell."

The 42-year-old Musial, who started his career in 1941 with a two-hit debut, singled twice off Cincinnati starter Jim Maloney — in the fourth inning and again in the sixth (career hit No. 3,630) to drive in his N.L.-record 1,951st run. He left for a pinch-runner as the crowd roared its approval.

Stan Musial says goodbye during the festivities at Busch Stadium.

SEASON LEADERS

	American League		National League	
Avg.	Carl Yastrzemski, Bos.	.321	Tommy Davis, L.A.	.326
HR	Harmon Killebrew, Min.	45	Hank Aaron, Mil.	44
			Willie McCovey, S.F.	44
RBI	Dick Stuart, Bos.	118	Hank Aaron, Mil.	130
SB	Luis Aparicio, Bal.	40	Maury Wills, L.A.	40
W-L Pct.	Whitey Ford, N.Y.	24-7, .774	Ron Perranoski, L.A.	16-3, .842
ERA	Gary Peters, Chi.	2.33	Sandy Koufax, L.A.	1.88
SO	Camilo Pascual, Min.	202	Sandy Koufax, L.A.	306

"DUGOUT CHATTER"

"Maybe the Dodgers have done us all a favor in the American League because it will prove that the Yankees can be beaten."

Gabe Paul

Cleveland general manager, after the Dodgers had swept the New Yorkers in the World Series

A REAL SHOCKER

Willie Davis drove in the lead run in the seventh inning with a sacrifice fly and Sandy Koufax made it stand up the rest of the way October 6 as the Los Angeles Dodgers defeated New York, 2-1, and completed a shocking four-game World Series sweep of the Yankees.

Koufax's six-hit, eight-strikeout victory over Yankee ace Whitey Ford at Dodger Stadium provided a fitting conclusion to a pitching-dominated fall classic. Koufax's only mistake came on a seventh-inning home run by Mickey Mantle. Ford's only mistake came on a fifth-inning blast by 6-foot-7, 250-pound Frank Howard. The Dodgers' winning run scored as a result of Yankee first baseman Joe Pepitone's three-base error.

The Big Four of Los Angeles — Koufax, Don Drysdale, Johnny Podres and Ron Perranoski — was in total control, slamming the door on the Yankees' vaunted power machine and lifting the Dodgers to their third World Series victory in 11 tries.

To say that Dodger pitchers were dominating is an understatement. Koufax started two games and recorded a 1.50 earned-run average — and he was high man. Podres at 1.08 and Drysdale and Perranoski, both unscored upon in the Series, contributed to a team 1.00 ERA (four Yankee runs in four games).

The Dodgers did not exactly pound the Yankees into submission, but they scratched and clawed for more than enough runs to support their pitching. Koufax, a 25-game winner during the regular season, struck out 15 and beat New York, 5-2, in the October 2 Series opener at Yankee Stadium. Catcher John Roseboro gave Koufax all the runs he needed with a three-run homer in the second inning.

Podres recorded a 4-1 Game 2 victory with relief help from Perranoski, and Drysdale threw a three-hit 1-0 shutout in Game 3, the only run scoring on Tommy Davis' first-inning single.

Game 1	Los Angeles	5	New York	2
Game 2	Los Angeles	4	New York	1
Game 3	Los Angeles	1	New York	0
Game 4	Los Angeles	2	New York	1

Pitcher Sandy Koufax and catcher John Roseboro celebrate Los Angeles' unlikely World Series sweep of the mighty Yankees.

☆1964☆

JANUARY-OCTOBER

No hits — and no win

A ninth-inning error by Houston second baseman Nellie Fox allowed Cincinnati to score the only run April 23 at Colt Stadium, making righthander Ken Johnson the first pitcher in history to lose a game in which he had pitched a no-hitter.

Johnson, a 30-year-old knuckleball specialist who had been selected from the Reds in the 1961 National League expansion draft, was outstanding through eight innings, walking only two batters and allowing only three balls to be hit out of the infield. But he contributed to his own demise in the ninth when, with one out, he fielded Pete Rose's bunt and threw wildly to first, allowing the rookie to reach second base. Rose moved to third on an infield out and scored when Fox booted Vada Pinson's grounder.

When Cincinnati's Joe Nuxhall retired Houston without incident in the bottom of the ninth, Johnson entered the record books on a down note. Eight pitchers had lost games after pitching nine-inning no-hitters, but all had allowed extra-inning hits.

Houston pitcher Ken Johnson held Cincinnati hitless but lost a 1-0 heartbreaker.

Koufax ties Feller

Los Angeles ace Sandy Koufax joined former great Bob Feller as the only modern major leaguers to throw three career no-hitters June 4 when he stopped the Philadelphia Phillies, 3-0, at Connie Mack Stadium.

The fireballing lefthander was in total command, walking only one and facing the minimum 27 batters. Koufax, the reigning Cy Young champion and National League Most Valuable Player, issued a pass in the fourth inning to Richie Allen, who was then caught trying to steal.

Koufax struck out 12 Phillies and allowed only four balls to be hit out of the infield. It was the 28-year-old's sixth victory in an injury-marred season.

Koufax pitched his first no-hitter against the New York Mets in 1962 and his second last year against San Francisco. Feller pitched his three no-hitters over an 11-year span. Two other pitchers, Lawrence Corcoran (1880, 1882 and 1884) and Cy Young (1897, 1904 and 1908), turned the trick three times.

Koufax got all the offensive support he needed in the seventh inning when Frank Howard belted a three-run homer off Phillies loser Chris Short.

"Three" signals Los Angeles ace Sandy Koufax after adding another no-hitter to his impressive pitching resume.

CAUGHT ON THE FLY

APRIL

The New York Mets unveiled their shiny new $25 million ballpark, but the Pittsburgh Pirates spoiled the Shea Stadium opener for 50,312 fans by posting a 4-3 victory.

JULY

Kansas City's Bert Campaneris, a 21-year-old Cuban shortstop, became the second player in baseball history to homer twice in his first major league game — an 11-inning 4-3 A's victory over Minnesota.

AUGUST

Commissioner Ford Frick officially notified the 20 major league teams that he intends to retire when this third seven-year term expires in September 1965.

The Los Angeles Angels, dissatisfied with their lease arrangement at Dodger Stadium, received A.L. permission to move to nearby Anaheim, Calif.

Young Cubs star Hubbs dies in plane crash

Ken Hubbs, the slick-fielding Chicago Cubs second baseman who won National League Rookie of the Year honors two years ago, died February 13 when the single-engine Cessna 172 he was flying crashed on a frozen lake near Provo, Utah. He was 22.

Hubbs and a companion, 23-year-old Dennis Doyle, were en route from Provo to their home in Colton, Calif., after participating in a basketball tournament at Brigham Young University, where both attended college. Hubbs, who had just secured his pilot's license two weeks earlier, took off despite bad weather and low visibility. The plane went down five miles from its point of takeoff.

Hubbs set a major league fielding record in his rookie 1962 season when he played errorless ball for 78 consecutive games while handling 418 chances. He batted .262 that year and followed with a .235 average in 1963.

Bunning writes perfect ending for Phillies' victory over Mets

Philadelphia righthander Jim Bunning, acquired last December from the Detroit Tigers, dazzled the New York Mets June 21 and became the first major league pitcher in 42 years to throw a regular-season perfect game.

Bunning, the first National Leaguer to turn the trick in 84 years and seventh major leaguer all-time, set down 27 straight Mets in a 6-0 Phillies victory in the first game of a doubleheader at New York's Shea Stadium. When the 32-year-old struck out pinch-hitter John Stephenson to end the game, he received a long ovation from appreciative Mets fans.

Bunning needed 86 pitches and two good defensive plays to carve his niche in the history books. Second baseman Tony Taylor made a diving stop and threw out Jesse Gonder in the fifth inning and shortstop Cookie Rojas made a leaping catch of Amado Samuel's line drive in the third.

Bunning is the first regular-season hurler to throw a "perfecto"

Philadelphia's Jim Bunning striking out New York Mets pinch-hitter John Stephenson to end his perfect game.

since Charles Robertson of the Chicago White Sox did it against Detroit in 1922. New York Yankees righthander Don Larsen performed the feat against Brooklyn in the 1956 World Series. Bun-

ning also is the first pitcher in the modern era to throw no-hitters in both leagues (he no-hit the Boston Red Sox in 1958). The last N.L. perfect game was thrown in 1880 by John Montgomery Ward.

Yankees clinch 5th in a row

The New York Yankees clinched their fifth straight American League pennant and 29th overall October 3 with an 8-3 victory over Cleveland. But unlike the previous four in the current streak, this one was not easy.

In matching their five-in-a-row feat of 1949-53, the Bronx Bombers, under first-year Manager Yogi Berra, had to hold off challenges from the Chicago White Sox and Baltimore Orioles in a wild stretch run. The Yankees, three games out of first as late as September 6, finally took the lead 11 days later and embarked on an 11-game winning streak that gave them their 15th pennant in the last 18 seasons.

The White Sox, who closed with a nine-game rush, finally were eliminated on the second-to-last day of the campaign and finished one game back in the final standings. Baltimore was a game behind Chicago.

" DUGOUT CHATTER "

"He was jabbering like a magpie. On the bench before the ninth, he said, 'I'd like to borrow Koufax's hummer for that last inning.' Then he's out there with two hitters to go and he calls me out and says I should tell him a joke or something, just to give him a breather."

Gus Triandos

Phillies catcher, describing Jim Bunning during his June 21 perfect game against the New York Mets

Happy National Leaguers mob Philadelphia's Johnny Callison after his dramatic game-winning All-Star homer.

Johnny on the spot

Philadelphia outfielder Johnny Callison hit the first pitch he saw from fireballing Boston reliever Dick Radatz for a dramatic two-out, three-run homer in the bottom of the ninth inning July 17 to give the National League a 7-4 victory over the American League in the All-Star Game at New York's Shea Stadium.

Callison's blast to right field capped a four-run ninth-inning rally that began with a walk to San Francisco's Willie Mays. Mays stole second and scored the tying run on Giant teammate Orlando Cepeda's bloop single and Yankee first baseman Joe Pepitone's throwing error.

After Radatz disposed of St. Louis' Ken Boyer on a foul pop and walked Cincinnati's Johnny Edwards intentionally to set up a double play, he struck out pinch-

hitter Hank Aaron. That set the stage for Callison.

The A.L. had tied the game in the sixth inning on a two-run triple by Baltimore's Brooks

Robinson and took the lead on a seventh-inning sacrifice fly by the Angels' Jim Fregosi.

The N.L. victory evened the overall All-Star series at 17-17-1.

★1964★

Phillies blow pennant

In what will be remembered as one of the great collapses in baseball history, the Philadelphia Phillies, sitting in the catbird seat with two weeks remaining in the National League pennant race, lost 10 of their final 12 games and finished in a two-way tie for second place, one game behind hard-rushing St. Louis.

The Phillies led by 6½ games over Cincinnati and the Cardinals on the morning of September 21 with San Francisco sitting another half-game back. Only 12 games remained on the schedule and the first seven would be played in front of their home fans.

But a funny thing happened on the way to the World Series. The Phillies' express was derailed by a puzzling collapse that was aided by Manager Gene Mauch's curious strategy.

The Phillies' death march started when the Reds stormed into Philadelphia and swept three games. With Milwaukee coming into town next for a four-game series, Mauch revised his pitching rotation so that aces Jim Bunning and Chris Short would work on two days rest, rather than their normal three.

The strategy backfired. Milwaukee won all four games, two of them with heartbreaking rallies in the final inning and another when Bunning was bombed in a 14-8 defeat. The snowball kept rolling and the Phillies' losing streak reached 10 when the Cardinals swept a crucial three-game set in St. Louis.

On the morning of October 1, the Phillies suddenly found themselves in third place, 2½ games behind St. Louis and 1½ behind Cincinnati. The Cardinals were riding the crest of an eight-game winning streak while Cincinnati had dropped its last two after winning nine in a row. The fourth-place Giants, 3½ games behind, had won seven of nine.

The Phillies rebounded to win their final two games against Cincinnati, but it was too little too late. The Giants were eliminated on the next-to-last day and the Cardinals, who had dropped two straight to lowly New York, clinched on the final day and avoided a three-way pennant playoff with an 11-5 victory over the Mets.

The Cardinals, 10 games behind Philadelphia at the All-Star break, ended their 18-year pennant drought with an amazing 54-29 second-half run.

Hutch dies

Fred Hutchinson's long battle with cancer ended November 12, less than a month after he had resigned as manager of Cincinnati. The 45-year-old former Detroit pitcher died in Bradenton, Fla.

The soft-hearted 6-foot-2, 240-pounder's cancer had been diagnosed last winter, but he chose to serve his sixth season as manager of the Reds. It was a difficult campaign, interrupted twice by hospital stays and a leave of absence during the hot National League pennant race. Coach Dick Sisler called the shots down the stretch and Hutchinson resigned as manager October 19.

The former righthanded hurler, 95-71 in 11 seasons with Detroit, managed the Tigers for three years and the St. Louis Cardinals for three more before taking the Reds' helm in 1959.

Hutchinson is baseball's second cancer victim this year. Houston righthander Jim Umbricht died April 8 at age 33 after compiling a 9-5 record and 3.06 earned-run average in five seasons with Pittsburgh and the Colt .45s.

Overworked Phillies Jim Bunning (left) and Chris Short.

Fred Hutchinson on his final day as Cincinnati manager.

CAUGHT ON THE FLY

OCTOBER
Minnesota outfielder Tony Oliva became the first rookie to win an A.L. batting title when he finished with a .323 mark.

NOVEMBER
Another major league attendance record: 21,280,341.

DECEMBER
Houston, ready to move into its spectacular domed stadium in 1965, officially changed its name from 'Colt .45s' to 'Astros.'

" DUGOUT CHATTER "

"It's funny, but when I'm in the bullpen in the early part of the game, I don't get excited no matter what happens. But as the game goes along, I feel myself getting worked up. When it comes time for me to warm up, I'm all worked up."

Dick Radatz

Boston Red Sox ace reliever, alias "The Monster"

SEASON LEADERS

	American League		National League	
Avg.	Tony Oliva, Min.	.323	Roberto Clemente, Pit.	.339
HR	Harmon Killebrew, Min.	49	Willie Mays, S.F.	47
RBI	Brooks Robinson, Bal.	118	Ken Boyer, St. L.	119
SB	Luis Aparicio, Bal.	57	Maury Wills, L.A.	53
W-L Pct.	Wally Bunker, Bal. 19-5, .792		Sandy Koufax, L.A. 19-5, .792	
ERA	Dean Chance, L.A.	1.65	Sandy Koufax, L.A.	1.74
SO	Al Downing, N.Y.	217	Bob Veale, Pit.	250

CARDS STUN YANKEES

Home runs by Lou Brock and Ken Boyer keyed two three-run innings and Bob Gibson made the runs stand up for a 7-5 victory that gave the St. Louis Cardinals a seven-game World Series triumph over the New York Yankees October 15 at Busch Stadium.

The Cardinals, looking for their seventh World Series championship, jumped on Yankee starter Mel Stottlemyre for three runs in the fourth and three more in the fifth and held on. Yankee slugger Mickey Mantle belted a three-run homer in the sixth to halve the lead and Gibson surrendered ninth-inning solo blasts to Clete Boyer and Phil Linz before closing out his second win of the Series.

The teams were evenly matched as they traded blows throughout an entertaining fall classic. The Cardinals struck first on October 7 with a 9-5 victory, but the Yankees answered with 8-3 and 2-1 wins, Game 3 ending when Mantle deposited a Barney Schultz ninth-inning pitch into the right-field stands at Yankee Stadium.

Undaunted by that tough loss or New York's 3-0 lead after five innings the next day, St. Louis won Game 4 when Ken Boyer nailed left-hander Al Downing for a sixth-inning grand slam. That blow stood up in a 4-3 Cardinal victory.

St. Louis jumped back into the lead with a 5-2 fifth-game triumph but the Yankees won Game 6, 8-3, behind home runs by Mantle, Roger Maris and Joe Pepitone. The stage was set for Game 7.

Mantle finished with three homers and eight RBIs while teammate Bobby Richardson batted .406 and collected a Series-record 13 hits. St. Louis catcher Tim McCarver batted .478. An exciting Series notwithstanding, the real fireworks started two days after the final out was recorded. The Yankees, winners of a record-tying five straight American League pennants but losers in three of the last five World Series, fired Manager Yogi Berra. In St. Louis, Cardinal Manager Johnny Keane announced his equally shocking resignation.

The pieces to this strange puzzle fell into place October 20 when Keane was named as the Yankees' new manager.

Game 1	St. Louis	9	New York	5
Game 2	New York	8	St. Louis	3
Game 3	New York	2	St. Louis	1
Game 4	St. Louis	4	New York	3
Game 5	St. Louis	5	New York	2
Game 6	New York	8	St. Louis	3
Game 7	St. Louis	7	New York	5

St. Louis catcher Tim McCarver, shown legging out a first-game triple, was a thorn in the New York Yankees' side throughout the seven-game World Series.

A World Series victory hug: St. Louis third baseman Ken Boyer (left) and pitcher Bob Gibson.

Atlanta gets Braves

The Braves, who broke a half century of baseball franchise stability in 1953 by moving from Boston to Milwaukee, received permission from the National League November 7 to move to Atlanta after the 1965 season.

Rumors that the Braves were heading south had run rampant since midseason and suspicions were confirmed October 21 when the team's directors voted 12-6 to ask the N.L. for permission to move to Atlanta for the 1965 campaign. A new 57,500-seat stadium already was under construction in the Georgia state capital and a lease contract had been offered to the Braves.

When legal maneuvers by Milwaukee officials complicated the issue, the N.L. dealt a killing blow to the Wisconsin city at a special meeting. The Braves were told they could move in 1966, after fulfilling the final year of their lease in Milwaukee.

The Braves, who had consistently topped 2 million in attendance in their early Milwaukee years, had dropped below the 1 million mark in recent campaigns and reported an operating loss of $500,000 in 1964.

N.L. triumphs again

An infield single by Chicago's Ron Santo drove home San Francisco's Willie Mays with the tie-breaking run in the seventh inning and the National League held on to take its first-ever lead in the All-Star Game series with a 6-5 victory over the American League July 13 at Minnesota's Metropolitan Stadium.

That run stood in contrast to the early bombing that allowed the Nationals to gain a 5-0 advantage. Mays led off the game against Baltimore's Milt Pappas with a home run, St. Louis' Joe Torre hit a two-run first-inning blast and Pittsburgh's Willie Stargell connected with a man on base in the second off Minnesota's Jim (Mudcat) Grant.

But the Americans scored a run in the fourth off Cincinnati's Jim Maloney and then hit a few shots of their own in the fifth. With two out, Maloney walked Minnesota's Jimmie Hall and Detroit second baseman Dick McAuliffe belted a home run. Baltimore's Brooks Robinson followed with a single and Minnesota's Harmon Killebrew tied the game with another long drive.

But four pitchers — Los Angeles' Don Drysdale and Sandy Koufax, Houston's Dick Farrell and St. Louis' Bob Gibson — stopped the Americans the rest of the way and lifted the N.L. All-Star ledger to 18-17-1.

All-Star Joe Torre arrives home after his two-run first-inning homer.

Houston shows off wondrous Astrodome

Houston's Harris County Domed Stadium, otherwise known as the Astrodome and the Eighth Wonder of the World, opened its gates for the first time April 9 and allowed U.S. President Lyndon B. Johnson, Texas Governor John Connally and 47,876 curious fans to gaze upon its splendor. They did so with plenty of oohs and aahs through the course of major league baseball's first indoor game — an exhibition between the New York Yankees and Houston Astros.

Let the record show that Yankee great Mickey Mantle got the park's first hit (a single to center field in the first inning) and its first home run (a 400-foot drive to right-center field in the sixth) and that the Astros won, 2-1, in 12 innings.

But the game was almost incidental. Most of the fans spent the entire game gazing in amazement at the 3½ acres of Tiffany Bermuda grass, specially imported from Georgia for this field; the 474-foot scoreboard with a half-acre surface; the massive dome that rises 208 feet — 18 stories — at its highest point and numerous other innovative wonders.

Another highlight came when the impressive scoreboard ran through its much-anticipated 45-second pyrotechnic display, which will be used to celebrate Astro home runs.

The scoreboard goes through its 45-second pyrotechnic display as Houston's Leon McFadden circles the bases after hitting a home run during an exhibition game at the wondrous new Astrodome.

1st free-agent draft

Kansas City kicked off baseball's first free-agent draft June 8 by picking Arizona State outfielder Rick Monday. The 20 major league teams picked 320 players at New York's Hotel Commodore before officials adjourned the meeting until the next day.

Under regulations adopted at last year's winter meetings, teams gain exclusive rights to negotiate with the players they select. With the clubs picking in reverse order of last year's standings, the draft should equalize the acquisition of player talent while eliminating bidding wars that have resulted in huge bonus payments to prospects.

Drafts now will be held every June and January with teams free to choose as many players as they desire. The major league teams also select talent to stock their minor league affiliates.

Monday generally was considered the best prospect available. Lefthanded high school pitcher Leslie Rohr was chosen second by the New York Mets.

MAY

Elmira scored a run in the 27th inning to defeat Eastern League-rival Springfield in the longest professional game ever played. The previous record was a 26-inning 1-1 tie between Brooklyn and Boston in 1920.

Dick Wantz, a 25-year-old rookie pitcher for the Los Angeles Angels, died after an emergency operation for a brain tumor. Wantz had worked one inning of relief in the Angels' season opener.

JUNE

Detroit youngster Denny McLain tied an A.L. record when he struck out seven straight Red Sox and 14 overall in a 6⅔-inning relief stint during a 6-5 Tigers' victory over Boston at Tiger Stadium.

Extra effort pays off

Cincinnati's Jim Maloney performed one of the more incredible pitching feats in baseball history August 19 when he fired his second 10-inning no-hitter of the season — and actually won the game at Chicago's Wrigley Field.

The hard-throwing righthander shut down the Cubs, 1-0, in one of the ugliest no-hitters ever pitched. Maloney struggled through 187 pitches, went to a three-ball count 15 times, issued 10 walks and hit one batter. He pitched out of bases-loaded jams in the third and ninth innings.

But Maloney also struck out 12 and did not allow a ball to be hit out of the infield through seven innings. Leo Cardenas rewarded him by hitting a 10th-inning home run that made a tough-luck loser of Chicago's Larry Jackson.

Maloney had not been so fortunate June 14 when he no-hit the Mets for 10 innings at New York's Shea Stadium, only to lose in the 11th when Johnny Lewis touched him for a game-winning homer. Maloney walked only one batter in that outstanding performance and struck out 18.

Cincinnati's Jim Maloney en route to his second 10-inning no-hitter of the season.

Marichal attacks Roseboro with a bat

With 42,807 fans at Candlestick Park and thousands of Los Angeles television viewers watching in horror, San Francisco pitcher Juan Marichal touched off a 14-minute brawl August 22 when, while hitting against Dodger lefthander Sandy Koufax, he suddenly attacked catcher John Roseboro with his bat.

The ugly incident occurred in the third inning of a meeting between the National League's top two teams and the circuit's most glamorous pitchers. Although both dugouts emptied onto the field, fighting was minimal. Everybody seemed horrified by the nature of the attack and the sight of blood streaming down Roseboro's face.

Marichal connected twice on Roseboro's head before Koufax and other peacemakers arrived on the scene. The catcher suffered a two-inch cut that was more ugly than dangerous and Marichal, who later was suspended for eight playing days and fined an N.L.-record $1,750, was ejected from the game. He said he attacked because Roseboro's throws back to the pitcher were coming periously close to his head.

The rest of the game (won 4-3 by the Giants on Willie Mays' three-run homer) was played in a subdued atmosphere.

Peacemakers arrive to stop San Francisco pitcher Juan Marichal's bat attack on Los Angeles catcher John Roseboro.

Stengel ends career

Casey Stengel, the colorful, lovable, irascible New York manager who went from the height of Yankee glory to the depth of Mets ineptitude, ended his 56-year baseball career August 29, announcing his retirement for health reasons at age 76.

The Old Professor, who still is recovering from a broken hip he suffered July 25, said he will turn over his managerial duties to coach Wes Westrum for the remainder of the season and perform some scouting duties for the Mets in his home state of California.

After leading the Yankees to 10 pennants and seven World Series victories in 12 years (1949-60), Stengel was forced out by management because of his age. He was hired by the expansion Mets and directed the team through an Amazin' four years. The Mets, 175-404 under Casey, were not very pretty, but they won the hearts of their fans with their bumbling and inept play.

By contrast, the machine-like Yankees were 1,149-696 under Stengel's leadership. Earlier managerial stints with Brooklyn and the Boston Braves produced a 602-767 record for an overall mark of 1,926-1,867.

MANTLE AND MAYS

Era of the Sluggers

"What speed, and what an arm! There was nobody in camp who could outrun him. Nobody even came close, and we had some pretty fast guys there."

Tommy Henrich, former Yankee star on Mickey Mantle.

"I'm not sure I know just what the hell charisma is, but I get the feeling it's Willie Mays."

Ted Kluszewski, former Cincinnati slugger

Mays (center) and Mantle (right) with Minnesota slugger Harmon Killebrew prior to the 1964 All-Star Game.

They also arrived with raw talents that bordered on the unbelievable. Baseball's greatest sluggers had always been slow-moving, muscle-bound, one-dimensional hit men, capable of belting the ball great distances but little else. Some were solid defensively with little range, while others had to be tolerated as necessary defensive liabilities. Most were station-to-station baserunners. Mantle and Mays were powerful young thoroughbreds with the five prerequisites to baseball greatness: they could hit, hit with power, run, field and throw.

"The minute I laid eyes on Willie, I knew he could do them all," said Leo Durocher, the Giants' manager in 1951.

"What speed, and what an arm," exalted former Yankee star Tommy Henrich, who coached the young Mantle. "There was nobody in camp who could outrun him. Nobody even came close, and we had some pretty fast guys there."

Indeed, the table was being set for a new breed of slugger, the athletic wonder who could steal a base or run down a 400-foot sizzler in the gap as well as blast home runs. With Mantle and Mays leading the charge, the 1950s introduced eight sluggers who would go on to reach the prestigious career 500-home run plateau, twice as many as baseball had produced in the first 30 years of the lively ball era. Ruth (714 homers), Jimmie Foxx (534) and Mel Ott (511) were early members of the club and Boston's Ted Williams was on his way to a career-ending total of 521 when Mantle and Mays made their debuts. Three other notables: Yankee first baseman Lou Gehrig finished with 493 homers in a career shortened by a fatal illness and Ralph Kiner and Hank Greenberg both fell short because of three-year military hitches during World War II.

Mantle would go on to hit 536 homers while Mays would soar to 660 in a career interrupted for two years by military duty during the Korean war. Other 500 club members who began their careers in the 1950s were Hank Aaron, who would eventually hit 755 while becoming the most prolific blaster of all time, Eddie Mathews (512), Ernie Banks (512), Frank Robinson (586), Willie McCovey (521) and Harmon Killebrew (573), a big, powerful slugger in the traditional mold. It is curious that only two players (Reggie

One hailed from a tiny northeast Oklahoma community named Commerce. The other was a product of Birmingham, Ala., the steel center of the South. When their paths first crossed in the sports-hungry metropolis of New York, Mickey Mantle and Willie Mays were fast-rising stars whose radiant talents would light the way for a new generation of sluggers.

In many ways, the Yankees' Mantle and the Giants' Mays were very different. Mantle was a white Okie with a Southwestern drawl and a take-things-as-they-come philosophy on life. He was a powerfully built switch-hitter who delighted fans with long, majestic home runs, the kind Babe Ruth had launched decades earlier into the Yankee Stadium skies. Mays, on the other hand, was a black

Southerner with a happy-go-lucky, almost bubbly personality. The righthanded hitter lit up a baseball diamond and attracted attention like a magnet. His home runs were more impersonal than Mantle's — wicked line drives to all fields.

But the two young stars also were very much alike. Both were born in 1931, both arrived on the major league scene in 1951, both played center field and both were greeted by unreasonable fan expectations that made their early big-league life difficult. Mantle arrived as the heir-apparent to the great Joe DiMaggio, who was playing his last season for the Yankees' American League pennant-producing machine. Mays was hailed as the man who would lead the Giants back to prosperity after 13 seasons without a National League pennant.

Mantle's home run trot became a familiar sight during the 1950s and '60s.

Jackson and Mike Schmidt) have reached the plateau from the following generation.

Mantle's road to the Hall of Fame was filled with potholes, courtesy of a long string of knee operations, pulled muscles and other injuries that made his journey anything but smooth. Mays performed with Hall of Fame grace and charisma in an injury-free career seemingly choreographed by the baseball Gods.

Mantle's injury problems began in Game 2 of the 1951 World Series when he caught his spikes on a Yankee Stadium drainage outlet while chasing a fly ball hit by Mays. He tore ligaments in his right knee, an injury that would plague him for the remainder of his career. When all was said and done, his most lasting legacy might have been his ability to play through pain.

"Mickey has a greater capacity to withstand pain than any man I've ever seen," Yankee trainer Joe Soares said late in Mantle's career. "Some of the things he has done while in great pain are absolutely unbelievable. Believe me, some doctors have seen X-rays of his legs and won't believe they are the legs of an athlete still active."

"He's the best one-legged player I ever saw," former Yankee Manager Casey Stengel once said. "He was always pulling a muscle because he had so many of them."

Through this spectre of physical trauma, Mantle put together an outstanding career that ended after the 1968 season. He batted .300 or better 10 times, led the league in home runs on three occasions and won three A.L. Most Valuable Player awards. After teasing New York fans for five seasons with his tape-measure home runs and glimpses of greatness, he reached superstar status in 1956 when he became the 10th modern-era player to win a league Triple Crown. He batted .353, belted 52 homers and amassed 130 RBIs.

Mantle's second most-productive season came in 1961, the amazing campaign in which he battled teammate Roger Maris in the greatest home run duel ever staged. Maris broke

Ruth's one-season home run record with 61 while Mantle finished with 54, missing the final week because of a hip abscess.

Mantle enjoyed one distinction that Mays could not come close to matching. Playing for the dominant Yankee machine of the 1950s and '60s, the Mick appeared in 12 World Series and set records for home runs (18), runs batted in (40), runs scored (42) and total bases (123).

Not that Mays had to apologize to anybody for anything. Often praised as the greatest all-round player in the history of the game, the Say Hey Kid finished his career in 1973 with his 660 home runs, second only to Ruth at the time, 3,283 hits and two MVP citations. He batted .300 or better 10 times, won four home run titles and topped the magic 50-homer plateau twice. Nobody could beat you in more ways than the talented Mays.

The greatest example was his legendary over-the-shoulder catch that robbed Cleveland's Vic Wertz of extra bases in Game 1 of the 1954 World Series, a play that gave New York momentum for its four-game sweep. Another was his four-homer effort at Milwaukee in 1961. But Willie was especially adept at showcasing his great hitting, baserunning and fielding talents in the annual All-Star Game, an honor he enjoyed 23 times. Ironically, Mays never hit a home run or batted over .300 in the four World Series he played in for the New York and San Francisco Giants and the New York Mets. "I'm not sure I know just what the hell charisma is," former big-league slugger Ted Kluszewski once said, "but I get the feeling it's Willie Mays."

And Mickey Mantle. Together they charismatically ushered in the greatest slugging era baseball ever has known.

Milwaukee's slugging duo of Eddie Mathews (left) and Hank Aaron in 1959.

The sweet swing of Mays, now performing for the Giants in San Francisco.

The pride of New York: Yankee Mickey Mantle (left) and Giant Willie Mays prior to the 1951 World Series.

★1965★

CAUGHT ON THE FLY

OCTOBER

Los Angeles lefty Sandy Koufax turned in the most prolific strikeout season in baseball history when he fanned 382, easily topping Bob Feller's 1948 record of 348.

Chicago White Sox catcher Smoky Burgess finished the season with a major league-record 115 career pinch-hits.

NOVEMBER

Playing in the wondrous new Astrodome, Houston joined the 2 million club with a team-record 2,151,470 attendance mark.

4th Koufax no-hitter has 'perfect' timing

Los Angeles lefthander Sandy Koufax, in one of the most overpowering performances ever witnessed, retired all 27 Chicago Cubs he faced September 29 and became the first major league pitcher to record four career no-hitters.

Koufax's 1-0 victory before 29,139 fans at Dodger Stadium was perfection. He allowed only seven balls to be hit to the outfield and there were no tough chances for his defense. He struck out 14, including the last six he faced and seven of the last nine. His final victim was pinch-hitter Harvey Kuenn, a former American League batting champion.

Baseball's eighth perfect game came at the expense of Chicago Cubs lefthander Bob Hendley, who retired the first 12 batters he faced and pitched a one-hitter. The Dodgers scored in the fifth inning without benefit of a hit when Lou Johnson walked, was sacrificed to second, stole third and came home on catcher Chris Krug's wild throw. Johnson later got the only hit of the game, a seventh-inning bloop double to right field.

The 29-year-old Koufax, who has pitched a no-hitter in each of the last four years, joins Philadelphia's Jim Bunning (1964) as the only modern-era National Leaguers to throw perfect games.

Lawrence Corcoran, Cy Young and Bob Feller are the other three-time no-hit pitchers.

Dodger Sandy Koufax, with a little assist from comedian Milton Berle, makes it perfectly clear that he has pitched a record four career no-hitters.

Mays caps big season

San Francisco slugger Willie Mays capped his milestone-filled season by blasting his National League-leading 52nd home run October 3 as the Giants wrapped up a second-place finish with a 6-3 victory over Cincinnati at Candlestick Park.

The fourth-inning blast off Reds starter Bill McCool set a Giants single-season record and gave Mays 505 for his outstanding career. He became the fifth member of the exclusive 500 club on September 13 at Houston's Astrodome when he connected with a Don Nottebart delivery. Mays is six home runs short of former Giant Mel Ott's National League record.

Mays had two other significant home runs. His 41st of the season on August 29 set an N.L. record for home runs in one month (17) and his 50th, on September 22, made him the second National Leaguer (after Pittsburgh's Ralph Kiner) to reach 50 twice.

He finished the season with a .317 average and 112 RBIs.

Ol' Satch delivers

Kansas City Owner Charles O. Finley brought 60-year-old Satchel Paige out of mothballs September 25 as a publicity stunt, but Ol' Satch had a surprise in store. The former Negro League great pitched three one-hit innings against the Boston Red Sox before calling it a night.

Paige, who last pitched in the major leagues for the St. Louis Browns in 1953, started the contest and allowed a two-out first-inning double to Carl Yastrzemski. He then retired the next seven hitters and gave way to Diego Segui after throwing his warmup pitches before the fourth inning.

As he left, the lights at Municipal Stadium were dimmed and matches were lit by the 10,000 fans who sang a salute to the oldest pitcher in baseball history. Paige had made his big-league debut in 1948 with Cleveland at age 42 and continued pitching in the minor leagues after 1953.

The Red Sox won, 5-2, on homers by Lee Thomas and Tony Conigliaro.

Kansas City's Satchel Paige leaves the mound after pitching three one-hit innings against Boston — at age 60.

Koufax shines again

Los Angeles ace Sandy Koufax finished off another in a growing string of outstanding seasons October 2 when he pitched a four-hit, 3-1 victory over Milwaukee that capped a brilliant Dodger stretch run and clinched their second National League pennant in the last three seasons.

Koufax, who struck out 13 and raised his record one-season strikeout total to 382, lifted his final ledger to 26-8 while capturing his fourth straight N.L. earned-run average title with a 2.04 mark. The fireballing left-hander led an outstanding staff that compiled a 2.81 ERA, lowest in the N.L. in 22 years.

That staff carried the Dodgers to their 12th pennant. The San Francisco Giants appeared sure of a World Series date with American League-champion Minnesota when they rolled off 14 consecutive victories and boasted a four-game lead over Los Angeles on September 20.

But the Dodgers answered with a 13-game streak of their own, overhauling the Giants by two games with a 15-of-16 closing run. Pitchers Koufax, Don Drysdale, Claude Osteen and Ron Perranoski were key contributors, as was journeyman outfielder Lou Johnson, who filled in for injured Tommy Davis and produced many clutch hits down the stretch.

The Dodgers batted only .245 as a team, the lowest figure for a pennant winner in N.L. history.

Los Angeles aces Sandy Koufax (left) and Don Drysdale, after Koufax had pitched the Dodgers' pennant-clinching victory over Milwaukee.

Owners pick Eckert

William D. Eckert, a 56-year-old retired lieutenant general of the United States Air Force, became baseball's fourth commissioner November 17 when he was selected to succeed the retiring Ford Frick.

Eckert, who accepted a seven-year contract, was approved unanimously by representatives of the 20 major league teams at a meeting in Chicago. The 35-year Air Force veteran, who retired in 1961, is a graduate of West Point and Harvard Business School.

Eckert will begin immediately, starting with a three-month orientation from Frick and his staff. Joe Cronin, an early candidate, accepted a contract extending his term as American League president for seven seasons.

SEASON LEADERS

	American League		National League	
Avg.	Tony Oliva, Min.	.321	Roberto Clemente, Pit.	.329
HR	Tony Conigliaro, Bos.	32	Willie Mays, S.F.	52
RBI	Rocky Colavito, Cle.	108	Deron Johnson, Cin.	130
SB	Bert Campaneris, K.C.	51	Maury Wills, L.A.	94
W-L Pct.	Mudcat Grant, Min.	21-7, .750	Sandy Koufax, L.A.	26-8, .765
ERA	Sam McDowell, Cle.	2.18	Sandy Koufax, L.A.	2.04
SO	Sam McDowell, Cle.	325	Sandy Koufax, L.A.	382

" DUGOUT CHATTER "

"I was nervous before the game. After all, this may be the end of the 13 best years of my life."

Eddie Mathews

Braves third baseman, after playing in the team's final Milwaukee game before moving to Atlanta

WORLD SERIES REPORT

DODGERS CATCH TWINS

Lou Johnson's homer and Wes Parker's run-scoring single gave Los Angeles two fourth-inning runs and the brilliant Sandy Koufax made them stand up with a three-hit, 10-strikeout performance that produced a 2-0 October 14 victory over Minnesota and the Dodgers' second World Series title in three years.

The Game 7 shutout at Minnesota's Metropolitan Stadium was Koufax's second of the Series and capped a Dodger comeback from a two-game deficit. The slugging Twins, getting home runs from Don Mincher and Zoilo Versalles and solid pitching from Jim (Mudcat) Grant, had roughed up 23-game winner Don Drysdale in an 8-2 Game 1 triumph, and then followed with a surprising 5-1 victory over 26-game winner Koufax behind the pitching of Jim Kaat.

When the Series shifted to Los Angeles, Claude Osteen shut out the Twins on five hits for a 4-0 victory, Drysdale came back strong in a 7-2 Dodger win and Koufax threw a four-hit, 10-strikeout, 7-0 victory.

Grant gave the Twins a Game 6 reprieve, pitching a six-hitter and hitting a three-run homer in a 5-1 victory, but Koufax, pitching on two days rest, was masterful in the Game 7 finale.

Game 1	Minnesota	8	Los Angeles	2
Game 2	Minnesota	5	Los Angeles	1
Game 3	Los Angeles	4	Minnesota	0
Game 4	Los Angeles	7	Minnesota	2
Game 5	Los Angeles	7	Minnesota	0
Game 6	Minnesota	5	Los Angeles	1
Game 7	Los Angeles	2	Minnesota	0

Los Angeles outfielder Lou Johnson connects for a key seventh-game World Series home run against Minnesota.

☆1966☆
JANUARY-JULY

Koufax, Drysdale sign

The unprecedented 32-day joint holdout of Los Angeles pitchers Sandy Koufax and Don Drysdale ended March 30 when the Dodgers signed their stars to a combined 1966 package worth "more than $210,000."

Dodger General Manager E.J. (Buzzy) Bavasi, flanked by his two pitchers, announced the signing at a Los Angeles news conference, but refrained from giving specific figures. It is believed, however, that Koufax received $120,000 and Drysdale $105,000, far short of their original demands but well above what they made last year (about $70,000 apiece).

The signing gives Koufax and Drysdale the distinction of becoming the highest-paid teammates in baseball history and they now rank right behind San Francisco's Willie Mays at the top of the big-league pay scale. The players would not confirm whether they intend to divide the money evenly, as they originally had said.

Koufax, a two-time Cy Young Award winner, won 26 games last season and captured his fourth straight National League earned-run average title. Drysdale was 23-12. The pair has combined for a 169-79 record over the last four seasons, Drysdale winning 85, Koufax 84.

The pitchers were quickly released from a contract they had signed with Paramount Studios to appear in the motion picture "Warning Shot."

Mets win Seaver

Young Tom Seaver as a member of the Jacksonville Suns.

The New York Mets, winners of a three-team draw for the rights to young pitching prospect Tom Seaver, signed the righthander for a bonus estimated at $50,000 and assigned him to Jacksonville of the International League.

Seaver was originally selected by Atlanta in baseball's free-agent draft and signed a $40,000 contract to play for the Braves' Richmond team in the International League. But the new Commissioner, William D. Eckert, nullified the deal because Seaver was signed after his University of Southern California team had started its season, violating major league rules.

With Atlanta no longer eligible to sign the youngster, three teams — the Mets, Philadelphia and Cleveland — put in bids for the 21-year-old Californian and the Mets won a blind draw conducted by Eckert. Under the rules, Seaver had to be signed for at least as much money as the Braves had offered.

> ## "DUGOUT CHATTER"
>
> *"He's the best young ballplayer to come into the league in the time I've been up. Players like Frank Robinson and Vada Pinson and a lot of good players have come up in that time. But he's the best. He hits a baseball like a golf ball. He can be as good as he wants to be."*
>
> **Bill White**
>
> Veteran Phillies first baseman, on young slugger Richie Allen

Atlanta celebrates arrival of Braves

The city of Atlanta officially carried the Braves across its threshold April 12, but the Pittsburgh Pirates spoiled the party by eking out a 13-inning 3-2 victory before 50,671 excited fans at the new $18 million Civic Stadium.

The festivities started with a 45-minute afternoon parade that tied up downtown traffic for hours. Banners, welcome signs and 250,000 confetti-throwing onlookers greeted the uniformed Braves players who rode in open convertibles down Peachtree Street, accompanied by marching bands and numerous floats. Pregame ceremonies included speeches from politicians, civic leaders and baseball officials.

The game, featuring an excellent pitching duel between Braves righthander Tony Cloninger and Pittsburgh lefty Bob Veale, was tied 1-1 after nine innings and carried into the 13th before Pirates slugger Willie Stargell smashed a two-run homer. Atlanta's Joe Torre hit his second solo homer in the bottom of the frame to cut the final margin to one.

The Braves were making their Atlanta debut after spending 13 seasons in Milwaukee.

Baseball arrived in Atlanta with ceremonial flair as the Braves lined up before their game against Pittsburgh.

Wills burns A.L. in St. Louis heat

Los Angeles shortstop Maury Wills drove home St. Louis catcher Tim McCarver with a 10th-inning single, giving the National League a hotly contested 2-1 All-Star Game victory over the American League July 12 in the 105-degree heat at St. Louis' new Busch Memorial Stadium.

With spectators passing out in the stands and ice packs, smelling salts and oxygen being put to good use in the dugouts, pitching dominated and the Nationals went about the business of recording their fourth straight All-Star victory. Both teams collected six hits and one extra-base blow.

The A.L. struck first against Dodger Sandy Koufax in the second inning when Baltimore's Brooks Robinson tripled and scored on a wild pitch. The N.L. tied in the fourth against Minnesota's Jim Kaat on singles by San Francisco's Willie Mays, Pittsburgh's Roberto Clemente and Chicago's Ron Santo.

Philadelphia's Jim Bunning and Giants Juan Marichal and Gaylord Perry closed the door the rest of the way on the Americans until the N.L. finally broke through in the 10th against Washington's Pete Richert.

St. Louis' Tim McCarver gets a handshake from San Francisco pitcher Gaylord Perry after scoring the winning run in the 10th inning of the All-Star Game.

Twins hit jackpot

The powerful Minnesota Twins smashed five home runs in one inning June 9 and barely missed carving a new notch in the record book when Jimmie Hall's smash hit the top of the wall, about two feet short of No. 6.

The explosion came in the seventh inning of a game against Kansas City at Minnesota's Metropolitan Stadium. The Twins trailed 4-3 and catcher Earl Battey set the stage by drawing a leadoff walk. Rich Rollins gave Minnesota the lead with a two-run shot off Catfish Hunter and Zoilo Versalles followed with another blast, knocking the righthander from the game.

After Paul Lindblad had retired Sandy Valdespino, Tony Oliva and Don Mincher belted consecutive home runs. John Wyatt re-

CAUGHT ON THE FLY

MARCH

The Major League Players Association elected 48-year-old Marvin Miller as its first full-time executive director and set up a $150,000 annual budget to operate the organization.

APRIL

Emmett Ashford became the major leagues' first black umpire when he worked Cleveland's season-opening victory over the Senators at Washington.

APRIL/MAY

California opened new Anaheim Stadium, but the Angels dropped a 3-1 decision to the Chicago White Sox. A few weeks later, St. Louis dedicated new Busch Stadium, with a 4-3 victory over Atlanta.

lieved Lindblad and Harmon Killebrew smashed his second homer of the game, giving the Twins their sixth run of the inning. Their 9-4 lead stood up.

Hall's double followed Killebrew's blast and just missed giving the Twins a major league record. Three National League teams had hit five home runs in one inning.

Cloninger 'slams' Giants

Atlanta pitcher Tony Cloninger, doing his best impression of Superman, hit two grand slams and a run-scoring single and pitched the Braves to a 17-3 victory over the Giants in a July 3 game at San Francisco's Candlestick Park.

Cloninger became only the fifth player in major league history and the first National Leaguer to hit two bases-loaded homers in the same game. The first, on a 3-2 pitch from Bob Priddy, sailed over the center-field wall and capped a seven-run Atlanta first inning. The second was an opposite-field line drive off Ray Sedecki in the fourth.

The nine runs batted in were the most ever by a pitcher, breaking the record of seven set by Vic Raschi in 1953. They raised Cloninger's season total to 19 RBIs, 18 of which have come in his last four games. He also enjoyed a two-homer, five-RBI game against New York on June 16.

The 6-foot, 200-pound righthander (9-7) did take time out from his offensive heroics to do a little pitching. He set down the Giants on seven hits.

Atlanta's pitcher-turned-slugger Tony Cloninger.

Koufax to the rescue

Sandy Koufax, working with only two days of rest in the final game of the season October 2 at Philadelphia, pitched Los Angeles to a 6-3 victory that clinched the Dodgers' second straight National League pennant and fourth in nine years on the West Coast.

Koufax allowed seven hits and struck out 10 in recording his league-leading 27th victory and helping the Dodgers become the first repeat winner in the N.L. since the 1957-58 Milwaukee Braves. The pennant was the sixth for Manager Walter Alston in his 13 years at the Dodger helm.

Alston reluctantly called on his ace lefthander when the Dodgers dropped a 4-3 decision to the Phillies in the opener of a final-day doubleheader. With second-place San Francisco already having won at Pittsburgh, the Dodger lead was only one game and a loss would have forced the Giants to play an October 3 makeup game against Cincinnati with a chance to tie. But Koufax was in full control and carried a 6-0 shutout into the ninth before the Phillies rallied for three insignificant runs.

The victory gave the Dodgers a final margin of 1½ games over the Giants with Pittsburgh three behind. The race was a three-cornered affair most of the way with the Giants using a six-game winning streak to slip past the Pirates at the end.

Koufax finished another outstanding season with a 27-9 record, a miniscule 1.73 earned-run average — his fifth straight N.L. ERA title — and 317 strikeouts.

Sandy Koufax answered an emergency call and once again pitched Los Angeles' pennant-clinching victory.

CAUGHT ON THE FLY

AUGUST
San Francisco's Willie Mays took over second place on the all-time home run list when he belted career shot No. 535 off St. Louis' Ray Washburn.

OCTOBER
Atlanta slugger Hank Aaron captured his third N.L. home run title with 44, matching his uniform number.

DECEMBER
The New York Yankees traded two-time Most Valuable Player Roger Maris, their 61-homer man, to St. Louis for third baseman Charlie Smith.

• WORLD SERIES REPORT

O'S SWEEP DODGERS

Moe Drabowsky, Jim Palmer, Wally Bunker and Dave McNally, giving the pitching-rich Los Angeles Dodgers a taste of their own medicine, fired a series of blanks at the National League champions and helped the Baltimore Orioles record a surprising four-game World Series sweep.

McNally's four-hit, 1-0 victory over Dodger righthander Don Drysdale October 9 at Baltimore's Memorial Stadium was a fitting conclusion to a quick-and-easy fall classic. The lefthander's shutout was the third straight for the Orioles and culminated a shocking and frustrating Series-record 33-inning scoreless streak for the Dodgers. Los Angeles plated its second — and last — run in the third inning of Game 1.

McNally got off to a rocky start in the opener at Dodger Stadium, giving way to Drabowsky after he had walked three straight Los Angeles hitters in the third. Drabowsky walked home a run with two out,

but pitched shutout ball the rest of the way. Back-to-back first-inning home runs by Frank Robinson and Brooks Robinson were the big blows in the Orioles' 5-2 victory.

The 20-year-old Palmer was matched against Sandy Koufax in Game 2 and the youngster made it look easy, firing a four-hit, 6-0 shutout. Koufax was victimized by a nightmarish three-error fifth inning by Dodger center fielder Willie Davis.

Paul Blair's fifth-inning home run was all Bunker needed in a 1-0 third-game triumph and McNally ended the Dodger misery in the finale with the help of Frank Robinson's fourth-inning homer.

The Dodgers set Series-record lows in runs (2), hits (17) and batting average (.142) and the four Baltimore pitchers who saw duty compiled a 0.50 earned-run average. The Orioles batted only .200 themselves, but that was more than adequate.

Game 1	Baltimore	5	Los Angeles	2
Game 2	Baltimore	6	Los Angeles	0
Game 3	Baltimore	1	Los Angeles	0
Game 4	Baltimore	1	Los Angeles	0

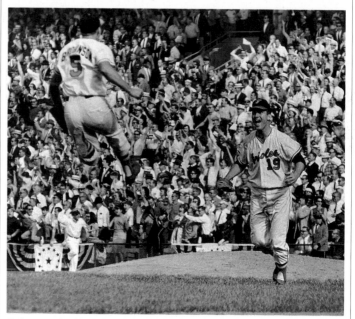

Baltimore third baseman Brooks Robinson leaps toward pitcher Dave McNally, who completed the Orioles' surprising World Series sweep of Los Angeles with a 1-0 shutout.

The end of a dynasty

It is official. The incredible New York Yankee dynasty has crumbled and, like Humpty Dumpty, it appears doubtful it can ever be put back together again.

From first place and the World Series in 1964 to last place in 1966 — the fall was quick and distressing. The Yankees lost 16 of their first 20 games this season and fired Manager Johnny Keane. Ralph Houk went from the front office back to the dugout but, confronted by injuries to key players like Mickey Mantle, Roger Maris and Whitey Ford, he could not halt the skid. The Yankees fell to 70-89, finishing a half game behind ninth-place Boston.

The realization that the Yankees are mortal comes as a shock to fans who watched them win 29 American League pennants and capture a record 20 World Series titles in a 44-year period from 1921 to '64. The Yankees, simply, were better than everybody else then and if they faltered, they simply would reload with prudent signings or one-sided trades.

But no more. The 1965 Bronx Bombers fell to sixth place and the '66 Yanks dropped the rest of the way into the basement. The *mystique* is dead.

New York Yankee Manager Johnny Keane (in uniform) made it only 20 games into the season before being replaced by General Manager Ralph Houk (right).

SEASON LEADERS

	American League		National League	
Avg.	Frank Robinson, Bal.	.316	Matty Alou, Pit.	.342
HR	Frank Robinson, Bal.	49	Hank Aaron, Atl.	44
RBI	Frank Robinson, Bal.	122	Hank Aaron, Atl.	127
SB	Bert Campaneris, K.C.	52	Lou Brock, St. L.	74
W-L Pct.	Sonny Siebert, Cle. 16-8,	.667	Juan Marichal, S.F. 25-6,	.806
ERA	Gary Peters, Chi.	1.98	Sandy Koufax, L.A.	1.73
SO	Sam McDowell, Cle.	225	Sandy Koufax, L.A.	317

" DUGOUT CHATTER "

"He's the toughest I ever caught, without a doubt. His high pitch is the hardest to handle . . . One time it sails. Another time it sinks. The next time it's straight. You never know what it's going to do. Plus the velocity."

Tim McCarver

St. Louis catcher, on what it's like working with Bob Gibson

Robinson crowned

Frank Robinson, who keyed Baltimore's first World Series championship while winning an American League Triple Crown, was unanimously selected as the circuit's Most Valuable Player November 8 becoming the first man in history to win the coveted award in both leagues.

Robinson received the maximum 280 votes from the select panel of the Baseball Writers' Association of America, leading a 1-2-3 Baltimore sweep. Third baseman Brooks Robinson finished second and first baseman Boog Powell third. Several players had won the award as many as three times, but nobody had earned the distinction in both leagues since the BBWAA took over the voting in 1931. Robinson won the N.L.'s MVP in 1961 with the Reds.

Robinson, acquired before the season from Cincinnati for Milt Pappas, Jack Baldschun and Dick Simpson, led the A.L. with a .316 average, 49 homers and 122 run

Baltimore's Triple Crown winner Frank Robinson.

batted in. The 31-year-old outfielder is baseball's 13th Triple Crown winner.

Koufax pulls shocker

Sandy Koufax, fearing that he might permanently injure his arthritic left elbow, shocked the baseball world November 18 by announcing his retirement. The amazing Los Angeles Dodger lefthander has been the most overpowering pitcher in the major leagues over the last half decade.

Appearing at a Los Angeles press conference, the talented 30-year-old said the pain has grown progressively worse in the three seasons since it began. He said he had sent a letter to the Dodgers requesting that he be put on the voluntarily retired list and added that he will forfeit his $125,000-per-year salary.

Pain or no pain, Koufax's left arm has been phenomenal. Over the last four years, he has recorded a 97-27 record, including a 27-9 ledger this year. He has won five consecutive earned-run average titles, a major league record, and three Cy Young Awards. He has pitched a record four no-hitters, including a perfect game last year, and he set a one-season strikeout mark of 382. His ERAs of 1.88 (1963), 1.74 (1964), 2.04 (1965) and 1.73 (1966) can be topped only by his 0.95 ERA in eight World Series games.

★1967★

O's no-hit Tigers, lose

In one of the ugliest and strangest endings to a classic pitching performance ever witnessed, Detroit scored two ninth-inning runs in the first game of an April 30 doubleheader and beat Baltimore, 2-1 — despite being no-hit by Oriole pitchers Steve Barber and Stu Miller.

The nine-inning no-hitter loss was only the second in major league history, as was the combined nine-inning effort. Houston's Ken Johnson dropped a 1-0 decision to Cincinnati in 1964 despite throwing a no-hitter, and three Reds pitchers combined for nine no-hit innings in 1956 before losing in the 11th.

Barber walked 10 Tigers and hit another. But still the lefthander carried a 1-0 lead into the final inning. He walked Norm Cash and Ray Oyler to open the ninth and pitcher Earl Wilson sacrificed. After Willie Horton fouled out, Barber threw a game-tying wild pitch. He walked Mickey Stanley and was replaced by Miller, who

got Don Wert to hit a ground ball. But second baseman Mark Belanger dropped the throw from shortstop Luis Aparicio on a force attempt as Oyler scored the winning run.

The Orioles managed only two hits themselves off Wilson and Fred Gladding.

Detroit could not hit Baltimore's Steve Barber, but the Tigers took advantage of his wildness for a 2-1 victory.

CAUGHT ON THE FLY

MAY
New York Yankee lefthander Whitey Ford, a 236-game winner over 16 seasons, announced his retirement after an unsuccessful battle to overcome an elbow strain.

Cincinnati switch-hitter Pete Rose saw his 25-game hitting streak end when he failed to get a hit in three at-bats against St. Louis' Dick Hughes.

JUNE
Curt Flood's N.L.-record string of 227 straight games and 568 chances without making an error ended during a game against Chicago at Busch Stadium when the center fielder dropped a fly ball.

JULY
Hall of Fame slugger Jimmie Foxx, who still ranks third on the all-time career home run list with 534, died in Miami at age 59.

Johnny Keane dies

Johnny Keane, the manager who led the St. Louis Cardinals to a 1964 World Series championship, died January 6 at his Houston home after suffering a heart attack. He was 55.

Keane took over the Cardinals midway through the 1961 season and directed them to a National League-best 93-69 record in 1964. The Redbirds won a seven-game Series against the Yankees and two days later, New York Manager Yogi Berra was fired and Keane announced his St. Louis resignation. Three days after that Keane became the new Yankee manager.

It was all downhill after that, however. The Yankees struggled to a sixth-place American League finish in 1965 and were 4-16 the next year when Keane was fired. He was a special assignments scout for California at the time of his death.

The long-time minor league third baseman and field boss is the third manager from the 1966 season to die. Former Detroit managers Chuck Dressen and Bob Swift passed away last year. Swift had replaced Dressen when he was sidelined by a heart attack.

Rohr roars in debut

Boston's Bill Rohr, a 21-year-old lefthander making his major league debut, lost his bid for baseball immortality April 14 when New York catcher Elston Howard lined a two-out, full-count, ninth-inning single to right field, breaking up the youngster's bid for a no-hitter.

The 14,375 fans who turned out for the season opener at refurbished Yankee Stadium booed Howard when he ruined Rohr's bid to become the first player to throw a first-game major league no-hitter. Rohr completed his one-hit 3-0 shutout by retiring Charley Smith on a fly ball to

right. Former St. Louis Brown Bobo Holloman had thrown a no-hitter in his first big-league start (1953), but he had made several relief appearances.

Rohr retired the first 10 Yankees before surrendering a fourth-inning walk to Bill Robinson. He went on to pass five while striking out two and needed two outstanding catches from Red Sox left fielder Carl Yastrzemski to keep the no-hitter intact.

Reggie Smith led off the game against Yankee lefthander Whitey Ford with a home run and Joe Foy connected for a two-run shot in the eighth.

Boston rookie Bill Rohr flirted with baseball immortality.

Perez ends All-Star marathon

Cincinnati's Tony Perez belted a Catfish Hunter pitch over the left-field fence with one out in the 15th inning July 12 giving the National League a 2-1 victory over the American League in the longest All-Star Game in the 35-year history of the event.

Perez's home run before 46,309 fans at California's Anaheim Stadium ended a masterful display by 12 pitchers. The N.L., which scored a second-inning run on a homer by Philadelphia third baseman Richie Allen, was held scoreless over the next 12 innings. The A.L., after tying the game on a sixth-inning homer by Baltimore third baseman Brooks Robinson, went scoreless for the next nine.

The N.L. combination of Juan Marichal, Ferguson Jenkins, Bob Gibson, Chris Short, Mike Cuellar, Don Drysdale (who got the win) and Tom Seaver allowed eight hits while striking out 17.

A.L. pitchers Dean Chance, Jim McGlothlin, Gary Peters, Al Downing and Hunter allowed nine hits while striking out 13. Perez was a replacement for Allen, meaning all three homers were hit by third basemen.

Cincinnati's Tony Perez delivering the winning blow in the All-Star Game — a 15th-inning home run.

Mantle, Mathews reach 500

Mickey Mantle and Eddie Mathews became the sixth and seventh players to reach the exclusive 500-home run plateau when they connected within a two-month period on May 14 and July 14.

Mantle crashed his 500th homer in a 6-5 New York victory over Baltimore at Yankee Stadium. With the Yankees leading 5-4 in the seventh inning, the switch-hitting center fielder connected off righthander Stu Miller, driving a solo shot into the lower right-field deck just inside the foul line. As 18,872 fans roared their approval, Mantle circled the bases for the 500th time since his career began in 1951.

Mathews, who made his debut in 1952 with the Boston Braves, hit his milestone home run exactly two months after Mantle as a member of the Houston Astros. Mathews' blow was delivered against San Francisco righthander Juan Marichal in the fourth inning of an 8-6 Houston victory at Candlestick Park.

Finley changes mind, fires Manager Dark

Controversial Kansas City Owner Charles O. Finley, on the verge of offering Manager Alvin Dark a new two-year contract, made an about-face August 20 and fired his field boss when he read a critical statement made by A's players.

The on-again, off-again relationship between Dark and Finley ended when Finley was interrupted during a meeting with his manager and told about a statement accusing him of undermining the morale of his ballclub by using informers to spy on the players. The statement was drawn up in response to Finley's August 18 suspension of pitcher Lew Krausse for conduct unbecoming a major league player.

When he saw the statement, Finley said, "This compels me to withhold the announcement of a two-year Dark contract until further consideration." That consideration led to Dark's notification that he had been fired for "losing control of his players."

Finley, who has averaged a manager per season since taking control of the A's in 1960, named coach Luke Appling as interim manager and the A's quickly drafted another statement.

"We players feel a deep personal loss at the firing of Alvin Dark," it said. The statement went on to take blame for his dismissal.

" DUGOUT CHATTER "

"Losing is no fun. When we were on top, every day used to mean something. I used to think, when I was hitting .350 and fighting Ted Williams for a batting title, that he was lucky he didn't have the pressure of the pennant race every day . . . I was wrong. It's harder to play without the pressure."

Mickey Mantle

Yankee center fielder

Kansas City Manager Alvin Dark, pre-firing, with Chicago boss Eddie Stanky.

CAUGHT ON THE FLY

SEPTEMBER

Minnesota's Walter Bond, a 29-year-old outfielder who played previously for Cleveland and Houston, died in Houston of leukemia.

Cincinnati's Bob Lee walked Dick Groat with the bases loaded in the 21st inning to give the Reds a 1-0 victory over San Francisco in a Crosley Field contest that matched the previous record for longest scoreless tie.

OCTOBER

Pittsburgh right fielder Roberto Clemente captured his fourth N.L. batting title with a .357 mark.

No-hit pitcher Dean Chance gets a happy embrace from Minnesota shortstop Zoilo Versalles.

Twins' star shines

Minnesota righthander Dean Chance overcame his wildness and an ugly first inning to pitch a no-hitter against Cleveland, recording a 2-1 victory in the second game of an August 25 doubleheader sweep that lifted the Twins into first place in the American League.

The no-hitter was Chance's second in 20 days, although the first was not officially recognized as such. He fired five perfect innings against Boston in a 2-0 rain-shortened contest.

In Cleveland, Chance walked Lee Maye and Vic Davalillo in the first inning, an error by third baseman Cesar Tovar loaded the bases and the Indians scored on a wild pitch. But the 26-year-old was in control the rest of the way, walking three more batters while striking out eight. Harmon Killebrew singled home a second-inning Minnesota run and the game-winner scored on a sixth-inning balk by Sonny Siebert.

The Twins, who won the first game, 6-5, moved a half-game ahead of Chicago and Boston. Chance lifted his record to 17-9.

From rags to riches

Carl Yastrzemski put the finishing touches on his American League Triple Crown, Jim Lonborg completed his Cy Young blitz and the Boston Red Sox wrapped up one of baseball's great rags-to-riches stories October 1 when they defeated Minnesota, 5-3, and captured their first pennant since 1946.

The end to the greatest A.L. pennant race ever staged came on the final day of the season when the Red Sox defeated the Twins at Fenway Park to break a first-place tie and Detroit split a doubleheader with California. The three teams had entered the finale bunched within a half-game of each other.

For 5½ innings, the Twins and 20-game winner Dean Chance held the pennant within their grasp. They led 2-0, but Lonborg led off the crucial sixth inning with a bunt single and suddenly the flood gates opened. Before the dust had cleared, Yastrzemski had delivered a game-tying two-run single and the Red Sox had scored three more times for a 5-2 lead. Lonborg took care of the rest, lifting his record to 22-9.

That took care of Minnesota. When the final report of the Detroit-California game arrived, fans poured into the Boston streets in a wild celebration that lasted through the night.

Boston's 92nd victory resulted in a final one-game margin over both Detroit and Minnesota with Chicago three behind. It completed the Red Sox's dramatic rise from ninth place in 1966 and ended the frustration of seven straight second-division finishes. They overcame 100-to-1 odds and Minnesota's one-game lead with two to play.

The crucial sweep was keyed by Yastrzemski, who delivered a three-run homer in a 6-4 first-game win that allowed Boston to vault a half game ahead of Detroit and tie the Twins for the lead.

The amazing Yastrzemski finished 7-for-8 in the final series. He tied Minnesota's Harmon Killebrew for the home run lead with 44 and finished first in average (.326) and RBIs (121). He is the 14th player to lead his league in all three categories.

The Big Three of Boston's Impossible Dream (left to right): Left fielder Carl Yastrzemski, Manager Dick Williams and pitcher Jim Lonborg.

Another expansion

National League owners, unhappy with the American League over what they termed "premature expansion," nevertheless voted unanimously December 1 to add two new teams by no later than 1971, agreeing to accept the A.L. decision to put franchises in Kansas City and Seattle in 1969.

The vote avoided open warfare over the A.L.'s decision to let Charles O. Finley move his Athletics to Oakland and the league's accelerated expansion program. The Athletics will compete with San Francisco for the Bay Area dollar and Seattle was considered a marketing plum.

The N.L. announcement attracted quick applications from six hungry U.S. and Canadian cities: Milwaukee, Dallas-Fort Worth, Montreal, Toronto, Buffalo and San Diego. A committee has been set up to screen the applicants.

The American League got the expansion ball rolling in October when it considered Finley's transfer request and expansion to Kansas City and Seattle in one package. Finley's stormy seven-year reign in Kansas City ended October 18 when the A.L. owners gave him permission to move to Oakland. The league also announced that expansion would occur "no later than 1971."

But when U.S. Senator Stuart Symington of Missouri threatened federal legislation, blasting Finley as "one of the most disreputable characters ever to enter the American sports scene," the timetable was accelerated to 1969. The A.L. will operate the 1969 season with two six-team divisions and a postseason championship series to determine a World Series participant.

Athletics Owner Charles O. Finley (right), during happier times in Kansas City.

" DUGOUT CHATTER "

"You know, he loves (Boston owner) Tom Yawkey so much he wants to win this thing for him more than he does for himself."

Joe Foy

Third baseman for the pennant-winning Red Sox, on A.L. Triple Crown winner and teammate Carl Yastrzemski

SEASON LEADERS

	American League		National League	
Avg.	Carl Yastrzemski, Bos.	.326	Roberto Clemente, Pit.	.357
HR	Harmon Killebrew, Min.	44	Hank Aaron, Atl.	39
	Carl Yastrzemski, Bos.	44		
RBI	Carl Yastrzemski, Bos.	121	Orlando Cepeda, St. L.	111
SB	Bert Campaneris, K.C.	55	Lou Brock, St. L.	52
W-L Pct.	Joe Horlen, Chi.	19-7, .731	Dick Hughes, St. L.	16-6, .727
ERA	Joe Horlen, Chi.	2.06	Phil Niekro, Atl.	1.87
SO	Jim Lonborg, Bos.	246	Jim Bunning, Phi.	253

WORLD SERIES REPORT

THE DREAM ENDS

St. Louis ace Bob Gibson woke the Cinderella Boston Red Sox from their "impossible dream" October 12 when he pitched a seventh-game three-hitter and belted a home run, giving the Cardinals a 7-2 victory and their eighth World Series championship.

Gibson silenced 35,188 fans at Fenway Park with a 10-strikeout effort that resulted in his third victory of the fall classic. He added a solo homer in the fifth inning off Boston ace Jim Lonborg, who also surrendered a three-run blow to second baseman Julian Javier in the sixth. It marked the second time in four years that the fireballing Gibson had won a decisive seventh World Series game.

The big righthander, who missed eight weeks of the regular season with a fractured leg, was ready when the Series opened. He pitched the Cardinals to a six-hit, 2-1 first-game victory October 4 and fired a five-hit Game 4 shutout (6-0) that gave St. Louis a three games to one advantage. But the Red Sox, ninth-place American League finishers last year, were not ready to die yet.

Lonborg, who had pitched a one-hit shutout in a 5-0 second-game victory, won the fifth game, 3-1, on a three-hitter. Then the Red Sox, under rookie Manager Dick Williams, used a pair of home runs by Rico Petrocelli and one apiece by Carl Yastrzemski and Reggie Smith to even matters with an 8-4 triumph in Game 6, setting the stage for Gibson's heroics in the seventh-game finale.

Gibson was not the only Cardinal hero. Lou Brock sizzled with a 12-hit performance that resulted in a .414 average and Roger Maris batted .385 with a homer and seven RBIs. Yastrzemski led Boston with three homers and five RBIs while batting .400.

Game 1	St. Louis	2	Boston	1
Game 2	Boston	5	St. Louis	0
Game 3	St. Louis	5	Boston	2
Game 4	St. Louis	6	Boston	0
Game 5	Boston	3	St. Louis	1
Game 6	Boston	8	St. Louis	4
Game 7	St. Louis	7	Boston	2

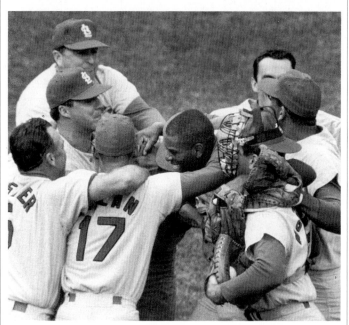

Game 7 winner Bob Gibson (without cap) is mobbed by happy Cardinals after St. Louis had popped Boston's World Series bubble.

★1968★

" DUGOUT CHATTER "

"If you could master hitting by thinking or by simply learning the technique, you'd have a lot of 50-year-old .300 hitters still around."

Joe DiMaggio

Retired baseball great

Howard muscles up

Big Frank Howard continued the most prolific home run hitting binge in baseball history May 18 when he connected twice in Washington's 8-4 victory over Detroit at Tiger Stadium, giving him 10 in six games.

That broke the six-game record of seven homers shared by former New York Yankee Roger Maris and three former New York Giants — Willie Mays, George Kelly and Walker Cooper. It also allowed him to tie the American League record of hitting homers in six consecutive games and put

him two behind Dale Long's major league mark of homers in eight straight contests.

The hulking 6-foot-7, 250-pound Senators first baseman hit his league-leading 16th homer with the bases empty in the third inning and blasted No. 17 with two on in the fifth. Both came off Tiger starter Mickey Lolich.

Howard, who has enjoyed four two-homer games during the hot streak, had already set major league records for home runs in a four-game period (7) and in five consecutive games (8).

Big Frank Howard, Washington's top hit man, went on a record home run binge in mid-May.

Catfish is perfect

Oakland's Jim (Catfish) Hunter carved his notch in the baseball record book May 8 when he shut down the powerful Minnesota Twins, 4-0, and became the ninth pitcher in major league history to throw a perfect game.

The 22-year-old righthander performed his feat before a disappointing crowd of 6,298 fans at the Oakland Coliseum. He struck out 11, allowed only five balls to be hit to the outfield and helped his own cause with three hits and three RBIs.

The four-year veteran became the first American Leaguer to perform the feat in a regular-season contest since Chicago's Charlie Robertson in 1922. New York

Yankee Don Larsen pitched the last A.L. perfect game, beating Brooklyn in the 1956 World Series. Los Angeles' Sandy Koufax (1965) was the last National Leaguer to turn the trick.

Hunter, who was 13-17 last season when the A's were in Kansas City, went to full counts on six batters and came back from a 3-0 count on two-time batting champion Tony Oliva to record a second-inning strikeout. He retired pinch-hitter Rich Reese for the final out.

Hunter is the first Athletics pitcher to throw a no-hitter since Bill McCahan stopped Washington in 1947 for the Philadelphia A's.

Oakland's Catfish Hunter delivers his perfect game-ending strikeout pitch to Minnesota pinch-hitter Rich Reese.

N.L. crosses border

Major league baseball crossed its first international boundary May 27 when Montreal was voted into the National League along with San Diego as part of a 1969 expansion package.

The vote to add a Canadian team along with a third California franchise came on the 16th secret ballot after 10 hours of discussion during a meeting in Chicago. The clubs will begin play next April, at the same time the Kansas City and Seattle expansion teams open play as members of the new 12-team American League.

San Diego was one of the favorites among the five cities actively

seeking expansion teams, but Montreal came as a shock. The hockey hotbed, which formerly served as home for the Montreal Royals of the International League, made a strong pitch by promising a domed stadium by 1971. San Diego already has a new stadium that seats 45,000.

Admission price for the new teams will be high. Each will pay $10 million, $6 million of which will purchase 30 players from the other 10 teams.

Disappointed losers in the expansion sweepstakes were Milwaukee, Buffalo and Dallas-Fort Worth.

Uniformity accepted

The American and National leagues set aside their differences July 10 and accepted the uniformity recommendations of baseball's Executive Council for their expansion 1969 seasons.

After all-day league meetings, the two circuits huddled in a 4½-minute joint session and approved everything the Executive Council had recommended two weeks ago, including the two-division, six-club format that the A.L. had already decided to use.

Other decisions included: The adoption of a 162-game schedule; a 25-week, four-day season with both leagues to begin play on April 7 and close on October 2, and a best-of-five division playoff series to determine World Series participants.

Under the new schedule format, each of the 12 teams will play 18 games against the other five teams in its own division and 12 games against each of the six clubs in the other division. Baltimore, Boston, Cleveland, Detroit, New York and Washington will compete in the A.L. East Division with California, Chicago, Kansas City, Minnesota, Oakland and Seattle in the West. The N.L. East will feature Chicago, Montreal, New York, Philadelphia, Pittsburgh and St. Louis with Atlanta, Cincinnati, Houston, Los Angeles, San Diego and San Francisco in the West.

Drysdale's scoreless streak reaches 58

Los Angeles righthander Don Drysdale streaked past Hall of Famer Walter Johnson and into the record books June 8, running his scoreless-innings count to 58 before finally surrendering a run to the Philadelphia Phillies.

Drysdale received a standing ovation from the 50,060 fans at Dodger Stadium when he edged past Johnson's 1913 record (55⅔ innings) in the third inning. He stretched the record to 58 before the Phillies finally broke through in the fifth, scoring on Tony Taylor and Clay Dalrymple singles and Howie Bedell's sacrifice fly.

That brought an end to 3½ weeks of outstanding pitching. Drysdale began his streak on May 14 against the Chicago Cubs with a 1-0 victory and then followed with shutouts against St. Louis, Houston twice, San Francisco and Pittsburgh.

Philadelphia scored a second run against Drysdale in the sixth on Bill White's home run and another in the seventh on Cookie Rojas' single. He was relieved in that inning, but still got credit for his eighth victory in 11 decisions. The 5-3 win was the Dodgers' sixth in a row.

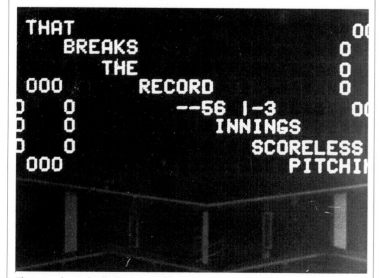

The scoreboard tells the story of Los Angeles pitcher Don Drysdale's record scoreless-innings streak.

N.L. wins 1-0 classic

Six National League pitchers made one first-inning run stand up for the circuit's sixth consecutive victory over the American League in a July 9 All-Star Game that produced three significant midsummer classic firsts — first 1-0 final, first game on artificial surface and first indoor contest.

Pitching in Houston's wondrous Astrodome, the stingy National Leaguers held the A.L. to three hits, retired 20 straight batters in one stretch and did not issue a walk. Los Angeles ace Don Drysdale pitched the first three shutout frames and received credit for the victory, which lifted his All-Star record to 2-1.

San Francisco's Juan Marichal, St. Louis' Steve Carlton, New York's Tom Seaver, Atlanta's Ron Reed and New York's Jerry Koosman were in full control after Drysdale's departure. The closest the A.L. came to scoring was when Minnesota's Tony Oliva banged a seventh-inning double off the top of the left-field fence.

Six A.L. pitchers limited the N.L. to five hits.

Los Angeles' Don Drysdale delivers the first pitch of baseball's first indoor All-Star Game at Houston's Astrodome.

CAUGHT ON THE FLY

MARCH
The expansion Kansas City franchise adopted the name "Royals," and the new Seattle club became the "Pilots."

APRIL
The Athletics played their first game in the Oakland-Alameda Coliseum and dropped a 4-1 decision to Baltimore.

JUNE
Detroit's Jim Northrup became the sixth major leaguer to hit two grand slams in the same game, connecting off Cleveland's Eddie Fisher and Billy Rohr during a 14-3 Detroit victory.

JULY
Cleveland's Luis Tiant set an A.L. record for strikeouts in a 10-inning game against Minnesota when he fanned 19, and Houston's Don Wilson tied the major league mark for a nine-inning contest when he struck out 18 Cincinnati batters.

☆1968☆

CAUGHT ON THE FLY

JULY

Washington shortstop Ron Hansen became the eighth player in big-league history to turn an unassisted triple play, performing the feat in the first inning of a 10-1 loss at Cleveland.

OCTOBER

Chicago White Sox knuckleballer Hoyt Wilhelm appeared in 72 games, bringing his record career total to 937. Before this year, Cy Young held the record with 906 appearances.

The new San Diego and Montreal clubs stocked their rosters in the N.L. expansion draft and the Kansas City and Seattle clubs followed suit the next day in the A.L. expansion lottery.

DECEMBER

In a surprising development at baseball's winter meetings, club owners asked for, and received, the resignation of Commissioner William Eckert.

McLain wins 30th

Detroit righthander Denny McLain, bidding to become baseball's first 30-game winner in 34 years, watched from the dugout September 14 as his Tiger teammates rallied for two ninth-inning runs and a 5-4 triumph over the Oakland Athletics before 44,087 fans at Tiger Stadium.

The victory lifted McLain's record to 30-5 and made the righthander the first pitcher to reach the select 30-win club since Dizzy Dean in 1934. The 24-year-old fireballer struck out 10 A's and allowed six hits, two of them homers by Reggie Jackson.

McLain was officially out of the game when Detroit started its winning rally. Diego Segui walked Al Kaline, who was pinch-hitting for McLain, and gave up a single to Mickey Stanley. Kaline scored on an error by first baseman Danny Cater and Stanley scored the winner when Willie Horton lined a one-out hit over left fielder Jim Gosger's head.

As Horton's hit fell safely, McLain raced out of the dugout and a wild celebration followed. McLain is the first 30-game winner in the American League since Philadelphia's Lefty Grove finished 31-4 in 1931.

Al Kaline (left) escorts Denny McLain out of Detroit's dugout after Willie Horton's ninth-inning single had turned the righthander into a 30-game winner.

Matching no-hitters

St. Louis righthander Ray Washburn, who watched San Francisco's Gaylord Perry no-hit the Cardinals September 17 at Candlestick Park, returned the favor the next day when he pitched another no-hitter and stopped the Giants, 2-0. It marked the first time in baseball history that pitchers had thrown back-to-back no-hitters in the same ballpark.

Perry was outstanding in his 101-pitch masterpiece that resulted in a 1-0 victory. The 30-year-old righthander struck out 10 and walked two in the 100-minute gem. Perry, 15-14, outdueled Bob Gibson in a game decided by Ron Hunt's first-inning home run.

Only 4,703 fans turned out the next day to watch the 30-year-old Washburn win his 13th game. Washburn struck out eight and threw 138 pitches, walking five. Mike Shannon doubled home one St. Louis run and Curt Flood singled home the other.

Back-to-back no-hit men: San Francisco's Gaylord Perry (left) and St. Louis' Ray Washburn.

Aaron joins 500 club

Atlanta slugger Hank Aaron belted a three-run homer off San Francisco lefthander Mike McCormick July 14 and joined seven other select stars in baseball's exclusive 500 club. Aaron's milestone blast came before 34,283 fans at Atlanta's Fulton County Stadium and gave the Braves a 4-2 victory.

The 34-year-old slugger joins active stars Willie Mays, Mickey Mantle and Eddie Mathews and former greats Babe Ruth, Jimmie Foxx, Ted Williams and Mel Ott as the only 500-home run hitters in history. His 19th homer of the season came in the third inning after Felipe Alou and Felix Millan had singled with two out.

The 400-foot blast sailed through a misty rain over the left-center field fence and provided all the runs Ron Reed needed to win his ninth game in 13 decisions. Aaron was greeted at the plate by a mob of Braves teammates and team President Bill Bartholomay, who presented him with a trophy.

Aaron has never hit more than 45 home runs in one season or less than 24 since his 1954 rookie campaign. He has won or shared four National League home run titles.

SEASON LEADERS

	American League		National League	
Avg.	Carl Yastrzemski, Bos.	.301	Pete Rose, Cin.	.335
HR	Frank Howard, Wash.	44	Willie McCovey, S.F.	36
RBI	Ken Harrelson, Bos.	109	Willie McCovey, S.F.	105
SB	Bert Campaneris, Oak.	62	Lou Brock, St. L.	62
W-L Pct.	Denny McLain, Det.	31-6, .838	Steve Blass, Pit.	18-6, .750
ERA	Luis Tiant, Cle.	1.60	Bob Gibson, St. L.	1.12
SO	Sam McDowell, Cle.	283	Bob Gibson, St. L.	268

Year of the pitcher

The Baseball Writers' Association of America put a fitting cap on the "Year of the Pitcher" in November when it handed its top four awards to Detroit's Denny McLain and St. Louis' Bob Gibson. It marked the first time that pitchers had swept the Cy Young and Most Valuable Player citations in both leagues.

The double sweep was not exactly a surprise. McLain had dominated American League headlines all season, becoming baseball's first 30-game winner since former Cardinal great Dizzy Dean in 1934. The fireballing righthander completed that quest with a 31-6 final mark and 1.96 earned-run average while leading the Tigers to an A.L. pennant. He recorded one of Detroit's four World Series victories.

The 33-year-old Gibson was equally dominant for the N.L.-champion Cardinals. He recorded a 22-9 record in an incredible regular season during which he posted the lowest ERA in N.L. history. Allowing only 38 earned runs and 198 hits in 305 innings, Gibson posted a 1.12 ERA and 13 shutouts. He also produced two powerful performances in head-to-head World Series matchups against McLain before his luck ran out in a 4-1 seventh-game loss to the Tigers.

Pitching dominated throughout the season, with American League hitters batting a collective .230 and National Leaguers .243. Boston's Carl Yastrzemski won his second straight A.L. batting title with the lowest winning mark in history — .301. No other American Leaguer reached the .300 level.

Bob Gibson, the N.L. Cy Young and Most Valuable Player award winner, with St. Louis Manager Red Schoendienst (left).

" DUGOUT CHATTER "

"That's the greatest pitching performance I've ever seen by anybody."

Denny McLain

Detroit's 31-game winner, after watching St. Louis' Bob Gibson strike out 17 Tigers in a 4-0 first-game World Series loss

WORLD SERIES REPORT

TIGERS DECK CARDS

Paunchy lefthander Mickey Lolich, lost in the massive shadow of Detroit teammate Danny McLain during the regular season, outdueled St. Louis Cardinals great Bob Gibson October 10 and recorded a 4-1 seventh-game victory that gave the Tigers their first World Series championship since 1945.

The Busch Stadium clincher was decided in the seventh inning of a scoreless game. After Norm Cash and Willie Horton had singled, Gibson induced Jim Northrup to hit a long fly ball to center field. The normally reliable Curt Flood misjudged the ball and broke in before realizing his mistake. Northrup ended up with a two-run triple and scored on Bill Freehan's double.

Lolich, a 17-game winner during the regular campaign, made the lead stand up en route to his record-tying third Series victory. The talented lefty had won the second game, 8-1, on a six-hitter and the fifth game, 5-3, on a nine-hit effort. The Game 5 win kept the Tigers alive after they had dropped three of the first four contests.

The Series opened in spectacular fashion with Gibson, who had just completed a 22-win, 1.12-ERA season, matched up against McLain, Detroit's 31-game winner. It was no contest.

Gibson struck out a World Series-record 17 Tigers and allowed only five hits in a 4-0 Cardinal victory. In a repeat matchup in Game 4, Gibson struck out 10 more Tigers and pitched another five-hitter while the Cardinals were battering McLain in a 10-1 decision.

McLain came back in Game 6, a 13-1 win keyed by Northrup and Al Kaline home runs.

Detroit became only the third team in history to win a World Series after losing three of the first four games. St. Louis' Lou Brock collected a Series record-tying 13 hits and batted .464.

Game 1	St. Louis	4	Detroit	0
Game 2	Detroit	8	St. Louis	1
Game 3	St. Louis	7	Detroit	3
Game 4	St. Louis	10	Detroit	1
Game 5	Detroit	5	St. Louis	3
Game 6	Detroit	13	St. Louis	1
Game 7	Detroit	4	St. Louis	1

St. Louis ace Bob Gibson finishing off his five-hit, 17-strikeout Game 1 performance against Detroit in the World Series.

★1969★
JANUARY-JULY

Owners avert strike

Averting the threat of a player strike, major league owners agreed to a new contract that dramatically increases player pension plan contributions while giving across-the-board improvements in other important benefits.

The sometimes-bitter negotiations ended on a high note February 25 when the executive council of the Players' Association accepted a new owners' proposal to raise pension plan contributions from $4.1 million in 1968 to $5.45 million for the next three years.

Other benefits include: the lowering of basic pension requirements from five years of major league service to four, retroactive to 1959; the lowering of the minimum age for drawing pension benefits from 50 to 45; a dental program, and improvements in life insurance coverage, widows' benefits, disability and health care benefits.

Owners tab Kuhn

New baseball Commissioner Bowie Kuhn.

In a compromise move that caught the baseball world by surprise February 4, little-known attorney Bowie Kuhn was elected Commissioner Pro Tem for a one-year term. The 42-year-old Maryland native will succeed William D. Eckert, who was forced out after fulfilling three years of his seven-year contract.

Kuhn's election at a joint major league meeting in Miami Beach, Fla., was a compromise to a stalemate that had developed between the American and National leagues. The A.L. favored New York Yankee President Michael Burke while the N.L. supported San Francisco vice president Chub Feeney.

Kuhn, a member of the New York corporate law firm of Willkie, Farr and Gallagher, is well known within baseball's inner circles. The firm has handled National League business since 1936 and Kuhn has been involved with baseball since 1950. Recently, he has served as legal counsel for the player relations committee and has been involved with baseball business ranging from franchise shifts and pension funds to Congressional hearings.

Kuhn's immediate task will be to provide leadership for a planning committee that will restructure baseball's administration.

" DUGOUT CHATTER "

"I'm glad this one's behind me, and I better enjoy it because I've got a long time to go before I catch that guy Mays."

Hank Aaron

Atlanta slugger, after moving into third place on the all-time homer list with No. 537

Ted Williams to manage Senators

New Washington Owner Bob Short pulled off a public relations coup February 21 when he lured the colorful and always controversial Ted Williams out of his eight-year retirement to manage the hapless Senators. But the Hall of Fame slugger did not come cheap.

After a week of negotiation, Williams agreed to step into his first managerial role for a five-year contract at $75,000 per season and a reported 10 percent of the team's stock. It took that kind of a package to lure the 50-year-old former Boston star away from his South Florida fishing haunts.

Unfortunately, Short does not get Williams' once-booming bat as part of the deal. The .344 lifetime hitter with 521 career home runs will try to do what no manager has been able to do since the Senators came into the American League in 1961 as an expansion franchise — produce a winner. Washington's best finish was sixth place in 1967 (76 victories).

When asked about the task that lies before him, Williams said, "I can only tell you from the heart I am happy to be here."

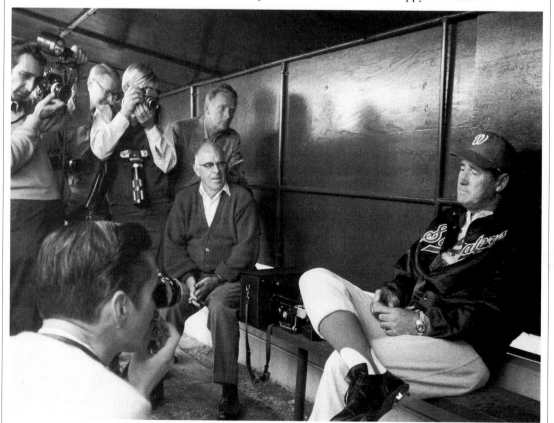

Ted Williams appeasing the press corps before his first game as Washington manager.

APRIL

The four expansion teams, Kansas City and Seattle in the A.L. and San Diego and Montreal in the N.L., all got off to rousing starts with Opening Day victories.

JUNE

The expansion Montreal Expos snapped their losing streak at 20 games with a 4-3 victory over Los Angeles at Dodger Stadium.

Mickey Mantle, who had announced his retirement before the season, was honored by 60,096 fans on a special day in his honor at Yankee Stadium. The Yankees retired Mantle's familiar No. 7.

Reggie Jackson exploded for two home runs, a double and two singles and drove in 10 runs in a 21-7 victory over Boston at Fenway Park.

No-hitters again on consecutive days

Cincinnati's Jim Maloney and Houston's Don Wilson, matching the unprecedented Gaylord Perry-Ray Washburn feat of last season, fired back-to-back no-hitters at Crosley Field April 30 and May 1, Maloney beating the Astros 10-0 and Wilson stopping the Reds 4-0.

Before San Francisco's Perry no-hit St. Louis and the Cardinals' Washburn returned the favor to the Giants last year, two pitchers had never thrown consecutive no-hitters at the same ballpark. But Maloney and Wilson made their second career no-hitters memorable ones.

The 28-year-old Maloney struck out 13 and walked five in picking up his third win in as many decisions. The fireballing right-hander needed an excellent over-the-shoulder catch by shortstop Darrel Chaney to rob Johnny Edwards of a hit and preserve his masterpiece. Maloney had beaten Chicago, 1-0, on a 10-inning no-hitter in 1965.

The 24-year-old Wilson, who pitched a no-hitter against Atlanta two years ago as a rookie, also struck out 13 while walking six and hitting another. He allowed two Reds to reach second base.

Houston's Don Wilson, one out away from completing the second no-hitter at Crosley Field in two days.

McCovey blasts A.L.

San Francisco's Willie McCovey crashed two home runs and Cincinnati's Johnny Bench added another as the National League exploded for nine runs in the first four innings and routed the American League, 9-3, in the July 23 All-Star Game at Washington's Robert F. Kennedy Stadium.

The N.L.'s seventh straight All-Star victory was decided quickly against A.L. pitchers Mel Stottlemyre (New York) and Blue Moon Odom (Oakland). After the Nationals had scored an unearned first-inning run, they struck for two more in the second on Bench's homer and five more in the third, two coming on a blast by McCovey. The Giants' big first baseman completed the N.L. scoring in the fourth with a solo shot.

The Americans also scored early. Washington's Frank Howard hit a home run in the second and Detroit's Bill Freehan homered in the third and singled home the final run in the fourth. The two A.L. homers came off St. Louis starter and winner Steve Carlton.

The game, scheduled for July 22, had to be postponed because of a downpour that soaked the Washington area. It was the first rainout in All-Star history.

Chicago's Ron Santo (10) greets San Francisco slugger Willie McCovey after his second home run of the N.L.'s 9-3 All-Star Game victory.

Baseball goes foreign

Resilient if not overly talented, the expansion Montreal Expos captured the heart of a city April 14 when they mounted a spirited rally that produced an 8-7 victory over the defending National League-champion St. Louis Cardinals in the first major league regular-season game ever contested on foreign soil.

The Expos gave 29,184 fans at Montreal's Jarry Park a taste of what to expect in the team's inaugural season. They scored six quick runs, five of them on a three-run homer and two-run triple by Mack Jones, and then helped the Cardinals to seven runs in the fourth by committing four errors. Relief pitcher Dan McGinn eventually drove in the winning run with a single in the seventh and held the Cardinals the rest of the way to pick up the victory.

More than 200 newsmen were on hand for the historic contest and the crowd was enthusiastic. Everything, from pregame introductions to lineups, was done twice — in French and English.

Montreal had been without baseball since the 1961 departure of the Montreal Royals, a long-time Triple-A farm club of the Dodgers.

SEASON LEADERS

	American League		National League	
Avg.	Rod Carew, Min.	.332	Pete Rose, Cin.	.348
HR	Harmon Killebrew, Min.	49	Willie McCovey, S.F.	45
RBI	Harmon Killebrew, Min.	140	Willie McCovey, S.F.	126
SB	Tommy Harper, Sea.	73	Lou Brock, St. L.	53
W-L Pct.	Jim Palmer, Bal.	16-4, .800	Tom Seaver, N.Y.	25-7, .781
ERA	Dick Bosman, Wash.	2.19	Juan Marichal, S.F.	2.10
SO	Sam McDowell, Cle.	279	Fergie Jenkins, Chi.	273

★1969★
AUGUST-DECEMBER

Mays hits no. 600

San Francisco center fielder Willie Mays became the second player to reach the 600-home run plateau September 22 when he blasted a two-run shot off San Diego rookie Mike Corkins, giving the Giants a 4-2 victory at Jack Murphy Stadium.

Mays joined Babe Ruth as the only player to slug 600 career homers. Batting for George Foster in the seventh inning of a 2-2 tie, Mays belted a pitch into the left-center field pavilion, helping the Giants remain a half game ahead of Atlanta in the National League West Division race.

Mays was greeted by the entire Giants bench as he stepped on the plate and the ball was retrieved and presented to him. The homer was the 13th of the season for the 38-year-old four-time N.L. home run champion.

Willie Mays, the second member of baseball's 600-homer club, acknowledges a welcome-home ovation from appreciative fans.

CAUGHT ON THE FLY

AUGUST
Baltimore lefty Dave McNally, who had tied A.L. records with 17 straight victories over two years and 15 in a row to open a season, finally lost at Minnesota, 5-2.

SEPTEMBER
San Diego pitchers Dick Kelly and Gary Ross brought an end to Los Angeles centerfielder Willie Davis' 31-game hitting streak the longest in the majors in 20 years.

OCTOBER
San Francisco outfielder Bobby Bonds finished the season as the fourth player in history to hit 30 home runs (32) and steal 30 bases (45) in the same season.

DECEMBER
Chub Feeney was a unanimous selection to succeed retiring Warren Giles as N.L. president at baseball's winter meetings in Bal Harbour, Fla.

Martin shows punch

Billy Martin, the scrappy, feisty, pugilistic manager of the Minnesota Twins, struck again August 10 — literally. Martin knocked out Twins pitcher Dave Boswell during a fight outside a Detroit restaurant after a game against the Tigers.

Boswell reportedly needed 20 stitches in facial wounds inflicted when the 41-year-old Martin landed "five or six punches in the stomach and a couple to the head." The 24-year-old righthander has a 12-9 record this season.

The incident started when Twins coach Art Fowler reported to Martin that Boswell had not run his daily laps and the manager confronted his pitcher when they met at the restaurant. Boswell stormed out of the building about 11:30 p.m., reportedly to "get that squealer Fowler."

Teammate Bob Allison followed and tried to calm him, but Boswell punched the outfielder and the players were being restrained when Martin arrived. Boswell reportedly went after Martin and hit him twice before the manager retaliated.

Martin, always a scrapper during a fight-filled playing career needed several stitches in his swollen right hand.

Carlton fans 19

St. Louis Cardinals lefthander Steve Carlton made baseball history September 15 when he struck out a major league-record 19 batters, but the amazing New York Mets continued their relentless march toward a National League championship by winning the game, 4-3.

The 24-year-old Carlton thrilled a Busch Stadium crowd of 13,806 by striking out the side in four innings, including the dramatic ninth. But he also made two critical mistakes that cost him a victory. Mets right fielder Ron Swoboda hit two-run homers in the fourth and eighth innings to wipe out a pair of one-run deficits and give the Mets a victory that lifted their N.L. West Division lead to 4½ games over Chicago.

Carlton, who shattered the one-game record of 18 strikeouts shared by Sandy Koufax, Bob Feller and Don Wilson, struck out the side in the first, second and fourth innings, but entered the final frame needing three more for the record. He got them, fanning Tug McGraw, Bud Harrelson and Amos Otis.

The 6-foot-4, 200-pounder faced 38 batters, but allowed nine hits and two walks while watching his record drop to 16-10.

St. Louis lefty Steve Carlton struck out a record 19 Mets, but the New Yorkers got the last laugh with a 4-3 victory.

Mets, O's win first Championship Series

The New York Mets worked another miracle and Baltimore continued its expected march toward a World Series championship as baseball's first Championship Series ended October 6 with a pair of three-game sweeps.

The light-hitting underdog Mets, National League East Division champions, banged out 37 hits while destroying the Atlanta Braves in 9-5, 11-6 and 7-4 triumphs. The expansion bumblers, who had finished last in the N.L. five times and ninth in their other two seasons, continued their shocking transformation by belting six homers, including three in the final game. Tommie Agee and Ken Boswell hit two apiece in the series and combined for five runs batted in during the finale at Shea Stadium.

The Orioles, 109-game winners as American League East Division champs, were methodical in their 4-3, 1-0 and 11-2 victories over Minnesota. The first game ended on Paul Blair's 12th-inning squeeze bunt and the second was decided when pinch-hitter Curt Motton's 11th-inning single concluded Dave McNally's three-hit shutout. Blair collected five hits and five RBIs in Baltimore's clincher at Minnesota.

The best-of-five Championship Series were set up to decide pennant winners under the two-division formats in each league.

Mets center fielder Tommie Agee heads home after one of his three postseason home runs.

" DUGOUT CHATTER "

"This is the summit. We're No. 1 and you just can't get any bigger than this."

Ed Charles

The New York third baseman, after the Amazing Mets had completed their climb to the top with a World Series victory over Baltimore

"I run as hard as anyone, but I just don't get there as fast."

Boog Powell

Big Baltimore first baseman

THE AMAZING METS

From expansion and ineptitude in 1962 to the top of the baseball world in 1969. From a ninth-place finish in 1968 to 100 victories and a first-place finish in the National League East Division. A three-game sweep of Atlanta in the Championship Series. A five-game victory over powerful Baltimore in the World Series.

This is the story of the Amazing Mets. They were so amazing that, when all was said and done, nobody was quite sure what they had just witnessed.

They weren't given much chance when they matched up their inoffensive lineup and young pitching staff against a Baltimore team that had won 109 regular-season games and boasted a perfect blend of pitching and power. And nobody was surprised when Baltimore's Don Buford slammed Tom Seaver's second pitch of Game 1 for a home run and the American Leaguers went on to capture a 4-1 victory behind the six-hit pitching of Mike Cuellar.

But Manager Earl Weaver and his Orioles were in for a big surprise.

With boppers Frank Robinson, Brooks Robinson and Boog Powell batting a combined .171 in the Series and the Mets making all the right plays at all the right times, logic was defied.

Jerry Koosman and Ron Taylor combined on a two-hitter in Game 2, the Mets scoring a ninth-inning run on light-hitting Al Weis' single for a 2-1 victory. Game 3 belonged to center fielder Tommy Agee, who made two outstanding catches and hit a home run to back the pitching of Gary Gentry and Nolan Ryan in a 5-0 win. Game 4 belonged to Seaver and Mets right fielder Ron Swoboda, who made a game-saving catch in the ninth inning of a 2-1, 10-inning triumph.

The Mets wrapped up their unlikely championship October 16 when they rallied from a 3-0 deficit for a 5-3 victory. Donn Clendenon's two-run sixth-inning homer, his third of the Series, and a seventh-inning blast by Weis tied the game and the Mets completed their improbable journey with a two-run rally in the eighth.

Game 1	Baltimore	4	New York	1
Game 2	New York	2	Baltimore	1
Game 3	New York	5	Baltimore	0
Game 4	New York	2	Baltimore	1
Game 5	New York	5	Baltimore	3

Relief ace Tug McGraw gets a champagne shower from Ed Kranepool after New York had disposed of Baltimore in five World Series games.

The 1970s

As the television-induced prosperity of the 1960s carried into a new decade, the economic realities of ownership suddenly became complicated.

On one hand, millions of dollars were being funneled into the owners' coffers by huge television contracts. On the other, players were becoming increasingly belligerent in their demands for a bigger piece of the television pie.

And with good reason. The once-secure reserve clause that had kept players bound and gagged for the entire century was dangling like a ready-to-burst pinata as more and more hitters stepped forward to take a whack. Well aware that collapse of the reserve clause would cut deeply into their profits, the owners watched with horror as television, their so-called benefactor, gave the players a national celebrity status and a strong power base.

As a result, 1970 ushered in a decade of litigation, strikes, free agency and escalating salaries. Discovering the power of the courtroom and organized labor unions, athletes challenged owners in every way imaginable. Facing what seemed like a never-ending stream of lawsuits

NATIONAL LEAGUE

League Batting Leaders

Average

Year	Player-Team	Avg.
1970	Rico Carty, Atl.	.366
1971	Joe Torre, St. L.	.363
1972	Billy Williams, Chi.	.333
1973	Pete Rose, Cin.	.338
1974	Ralph Garr, Atl.	.353
1975	Bill Madlock, Chi.	.354
1976	Bill Madlock, Chi.	.339
1977	Dave Parker, Pit.	.338
1978	Dave Parker, Pit.	.334
1979	Keith Hernandez, St. L.	.344

Home Runs

Year	Player-Team	HR
1970	Johnny Bench, Cin.	45
1971	Willie Stargell, Pit.	48
1972	Johnny Bench, Cin.	40
1973	Willie Stargell, Pit.	44
1974	Mike Schmidt, Phil.	36
1975	Mike Schmidt, Phil.	38
1976	Mike Schmidt, Phil.	38
1977	George Foster, Cin.	52
1978	George Foster, Cin.	40
1979	Dave Kingman, Chi.	48

RBIs

Year	Player-Team	RBI
1970	Johnny Bench, Cin.	148
1971	Joe Torre, St. L.	137
1972	Johnny Bench, Cin.	125
1973	Willie Stargell, Pit.	119
1974	Johnny Bench, Cin.	129
1975	Greg Luzinski, Phil.	120
1976	George Foster, Cin.	121
1977	George Foster, Cin.	149
1978	George Foster, Cin.	120
1979	Dave Winfield, S.D.	118

League Pitching Leaders

Winning Percentage

Year	Pitcher-Team	W-L	Pct.
1970	Bob Gibson, St. L.	23-7	.767
1971	Don Gullett, Cin.	16-6	.727
1972	Gary Nolan, Cin.	15-5	.750
1973	Tommy John, L.A.	16-7	.696
1974	Andy Messersmith, L.A.		
		20-6	.769
1975	Don Gullett, Cin.	15-4	.789
1976	Steve Carlton, Phil.	20-7	.741
1977	John Candelaria, Pit.	20-5	.800
1978	Gaylord Perry, S.D.	21-6	.778
1979	Tom Seaver, Cin.	16-6	.727

Earned-Run Average

Year	Pitcher-Team	ERA
1970	Tom Seaver, N.Y.	2.81
1971	Tom Seaver, N.Y.	1.76
1972	Steve Carlton, Phil.	1.98
1973	Tom Seaver, N.Y.	2.08
1974	Buzz Capra, Atl.	2.28
1975	Randy Jones, S.D.	2.24
1976	John Denny, St. L.	2.52
1977	John Candelaria, Pit.	2.34
1978	Craig Swan, N.Y.	2.43
1979	J.R. Richard, Hou.	2.71

Strikeouts

Year	Pitcher-Team	SO
1970	Tom Seaver, N.Y.	283
1971	Tom Seaver, N.Y.	289
1972	Steve Carlton, Phil.	310
1973	Tom Seaver, N.Y.	251
1974	Steve Carlton, Phil.	240
1975	Tom Seaver, N.Y.	243
1976	Tom Seaver, N.Y.	235
1977	Phil Niekro, Atl.	262
1978	J.R. Richard, Hou.	303
1979	J.R. Richard, Hou.	313

Most Valuable Players

Selected by BBWAA

Year	Player-Team	Pos.
1970	Johnny Bench, Cin.	C
1971	Joe Torre, St. L.	3B
1972	Johnny Bench, Cin.	C
1973	Pete Rose, Cin.	OF
1974	Steve Garvey, L.A.	1B
1975	Joe Morgan, Cin.	2B
1976	Joe Morgan, Cin.	2B
1977	George Foster, Cin.	OF
1978	Dave Parker, Pit.	OF
1979	Willie Stargell, Pit.	1B
	Keith Hernandez, St. L.	1B

Cy Young Winners

Selected by BBWAA

Year	Pitcher-Team	Thr.
1970	Bob Gibson, St. L.	R
1971	Fergie Jenkins, Chi.	R
1972	Steve Carlton, Phil.	L
1973	Tom Seaver, N.Y.	R
1974	Mike Marshall, L.A.	R
1975	Tom Seaver, N.Y.	R
1976	Randy Jones, S.D.	L
1977	Steve Carlton, Phil.	L
1978	Gaylord Perry, S.D.	R
1979	Bruce Sutter, Chi.	R

LEAGUE CHAMPIONSHIP SERIES

National League

Year	Winner	Runnerup	Games
1970	Cincinnati Reds	Pittsburgh Pirates	3-0
1971	Pittsburgh Pirates	San Francisco Giants	3-1
1972	Cincinnati Reds	Pittsburgh Pirates	3-2
1973	New York Mets	Cincinnati Reds	3-2
1974	Los Angeles Dodgers	Pittsburgh Pirates	3-1
1975	Cincinnati Reds	Pittsburgh Pirates	3-0
1976	Cincinnati Reds	Philadelphia Phillies	3-0
1977	Los Angeles Dodgers	Philadelphia Phillies	3-1
1978	Los Angeles Dodgers	Philadelphia Phillies	3-1
1979	Pittsburgh Pirates	Cincinnati Reds	3-0

American League

Year	Winner	Runnerup	Games
1970	Baltimore Orioles	Minnesota Twins	3-0
1971	Baltimore Orioles	Oakland Athletics	3-0
1972	Oakland Athletics	Detroit Tigers	3-2
1973	Oakland Athletics	Baltimore Orioles	3-2
1974	Oakland Athletics	Baltimore Orioles	3-1
1975	Boston Red Sox	Oakland Athletics	3-0
1976	New York Yankees	Kansas City Royals	3-2
1977	New York Yankees	Kansas City Royals	3-2
1978	New York Yankees	Kansas City Royals	3-1
1979	Baltimore Orioles	California Angels	3-1

Final Standings

1970

East

	W	L	Pct.	GB
Pittsburgh	89	73	.549	- -
Chicago	84	78	.519	5
New York	83	79	.512	6
St. Louis	76	86	.469	13
Philadelphia	73	88	.453	15.5
Montreal	73	89	.451	16

West

	W	L	Pct.	GB
Cincinnati	102	60	.630	- -
Los Angeles	87	74	.540	14.5
S.F.	86	76	.531	16
Houston	79	83	.488	23
Atlanta	76	86	.469	26
San Diego	63	99	.389	39

1971

East

	W	L	Pct.	GB
Pittsburgh	97	65	.599	- -
St. Louis	90	72	.556	7
Chicago	83	79	.512	14
New York	83	79	.512	14
Montreal	71	90	.441	25.5
Philadelphia	67	95	.414	30

West

	W	L	Pct.	GB
S.F.	90	72	.556	- -
Los Angeles	89	73	.549	1
Atlanta	82	80	.506	8
Cincinnati	79	83	.488	11
Houston	79	83	.488	11
San Diego	61	100	.379	28.5

1972

East

	W	L	Pct.	GB
Pittsburgh	96	59	.619	- -
Chicago	85	70	.548	11
New York	83	73	.532	13.5
St. Louis	75	81	.481	21.5
Montreal	70	86	.449	26.5
Philadelphia	59	97	.378	37.5

West

	W	L	Pct.	GB
Cincinnati	95	59	.617	- -
Houston	84	69	.549	10.5
Los Angeles	85	70	.548	10.5
Atlanta	70	84	.455	25
S.F.	69	86	.445	26.5
San Diego	58	95	.379	36.5

1973

East

	W	L	Pct.	GB
New York	82	79	.509	- -
St. Louis	81	81	.500	1.5
Pittsburgh	80	82	.494	2.5
Montreal	79	83	.488	3.5
Chicago	77	84	.478	5
Philadelphia	71	91	.438	11.5

West

	W	L	Pct.	GB
Cincinnati	99	63	.611	- -
Los Angeles	95	66	.590	3.5
S.F.	88	74	.543	11
Houston	82	80	.506	17
Atlanta	76	85	.472	22.5
San Diego	60	102	.370	39

1974

	W	L	Pct.	GB
Pittsburgh	88	74	.543	- -
St. Louis	86	75	.534	1.5
Philadelphia	80	82	.494	8
Montreal	79	82	.491	8.5
New York	71	91	.438	17
Chicago	66	96	.407	22

West

	W	L	Pct.	GB
Los Angeles	102	60	.630	- -
Cincinnati	98	64	.605	4
Atlanta	88	74	.543	14
Houston	81	81	.500	21
S.F.	72	90	.444	30
San Diego	60	102	.370	42

1975

East

	W	L	Pct.	GB
Pittsburgh	92	69	.571	- -
Philadelphia	86	76	.531	6.5
New York	82	80	.506	10.5
St. Louis	82	80	.506	10.5
Chicago	75	87	.463	17.5
Montreal	75	87	.463	17.5

West

	W	L	Pct.	GB
Cincinnati	108	54	.667	- -
Los Angeles	88	74	.543	20
S.F.	80	81	.497	27.5
San Diego	71	91	.438	37
Atlanta	67	94	.416	40.5
Houston	64	97	.398	43.5

1976

East

	W	L	Pct.	GB
Philadelphia	101	61	.623	- -
Pittsburgh	92	70	.568	9
New York	86	76	.531	15
Chicago	75	87	.463	26
St. Louis	72	90	.444	29
Montreal	55	107	.340	46

West

	W	L	Pct.	GB
Cincinnati	102	60	.630	- -
Los Angeles	92	70	.568	10
Houston	80	82	.494	22
S.F.	74	88	.457	28
San Diego	73	89	.451	29
Atlanta	70	92	.432	32

1977

East

	W	L	Pct.	GB
Philadelphia	101	61	.623	- -
Pittsburgh	96	66	.593	5
St. Louis	83	79	.512	18
Chicago	81	81	.500	20
Montreal	75	87	.463	26
New York	64	98	.395	37

West

	W	L	Pct.	GB
Los Angeles	98	64	.605	- -
Cincinnati	88	74	.543	10
Houston	81	81	.500	17
S.F.	75	87	.463	23
San Diego	69	93	.426	29
Atlanta	61	101	.377	37

1978

East

	W	L	Pct.	GB
Philadelphia	90	72	.556	- -
Pittsburgh	88	73	.547	1.5
Chicago	79	83	.488	11
Montreal	76	86	.469	14
St. Louis	69	93	.426	21
New York	66	96	.407	24

West

	W	L	Pct.	GB
Los Angeles	95	67	.586	- -
Cincinnati	92	69	.571	2.5
S.F.	89	73	.549	6
San Diego	84	78	.519	11
Houston	74	88	.457	21
Atlanta	69	93	.426	26

1979

East

	W	L	Pct.	GB
Pittsburgh	98	64	.605	- -
Montreal	95	65	.594	2
St. Louis	86	76	.531	12
Philadelphia	84	78	.519	14
Chicago	80	82	.494	18
New York	63	99	.389	35

West

	W	L	Pct.	GB
Cincinnati	90	71	.559	- -
Houston	89	73	.549	1.5
Los Angeles	79	83	.488	11.5
S.F.	71	91	.438	19.5
San Diego	68	93	.422	22
Atlanta	66	94	.413	23.5

Boston slugger Jim Rice.

and threatened work stoppages, the owners grudgingly gave ground. But it took a labor arbitrator's decision in 1975 to really open the vault doors. Peter Seitz did the honors, ruling that pitchers Andy Messersmith and Dave McNally had played out the option years of their contracts and were free to sign with any team.

As the era of free agency dawned, the once-protective owners became almost maniacal in their bidding for impact players, and mind-boggling contracts shot through the ceiling. Pete Rose, who had signed for $105,000 per year with Cincinnati in 1970, was handed an $850,000 contract by Philadelphia in 1978. Houston made Nolan Ryan a million-dollar man a year later. Nothing was sacred.

Beyond the economic maneuvering, baseball continued to grow, entertain and prosper.

The American League followed the National League's lead by placing a franchise (Toronto) in Canada, and the A.L. pioneered a new and controversial trail when it adopted the designated hitter rule. Slugger Frank Robinson blazed a trail of more historic importance when he took over at Cleveland as the game's first black manager.

On-field honors went to Oakland, which won three consecutive World Series, Cincinnati's Big Red Machine and the New York Yankees, who returned to the top in 1977 after a 15-year absence.

Memorable individual accomplishments: Atlanta's Hank Aaron became baseball's all-time home run king, St. Louis speedster Lou Brock stole a record-setting 118 bases and then broke Ty Cobb's career steal mark three years later; Pittsburgh's Rennie Stennett produced the game's first nine-inning 7-for-7 performance of the century, and Pete Rose fascinated a nation with his N.L.-record 44-game hitting streak.

But the most dramatic moment was turned in by the Yankees' Reggie Jackson, who destroyed Los Angeles with three mighty home run swings in a fascinating sixth-game conclusion to the 1977 fall classic.

WORLD SERIES

Year	*Winner*	*Pennant Winner*	*Games*
1970	Baltimore Orioles	Cincinnati Reds	4-1
1971	Pittsburgh Pirates	Baltimore Orioles	4-3
1972	Oakland Athletics	Cincinnati Reds	4-3
1973	Oakland Athletics	New York Mets	4-3
1974	Oakland Athletics	Los Angeles Dodgers	4-1
1975	Cincinnati Reds	Boston Red Sox	4-3
1976	Cincinnati Reds	New York Yankees	4-0
1977	New York Yankees	Los Angeles Dodgers	4-2
1978	New York Yankees	Los Angeles Dodgers	4-2
1979	Pittsburgh Pirates	Baltimore Orioles	4-3

HALL OF FAME Electees and Additions

1970 Lou Boudreau, Earle Combs, Jesse Haines, Ford Frick.
1971 Chick Hafey, Rube Marquard, Joe Kelley, Dave Bancroft, Harry Hooper, Jake Beckley, George Weiss, Satchel Paige.
1972 Sandy Koufax, Yogi Berra, Early Wynn, Lefty Gomez, Will Harridge, Ross Youngs, Josh Gibson, Buck Leonard.
1973 Warren Spahn, Roberto Clemente, Billy Evans, George Kelly, Mickey Welch, Monte Irvin.
1974 Mickey Mantle, Whitey Ford, Jim Bottomley, Sam Thompson, Jocko Conlan, James (Cool Papa) Bell.
1975 Ralph Kiner, Earl Averill, Bucky Harris, Billy Herman, Judy Johnson.
1976 Robin Roberts, Bob Lemon, Roger Connor, Cal Hubbard, Fred Lindstrom, Oscar Charleston.
1977 Ernie Banks, Joe Sewell, Al Lopez, Amos Rusie, Martin Dihigo, John Henry Lloyd.
1978 Eddie Mathews, Larry MacPhail, Addie Joss.
1979 Willie Mays, Hack Wilson, Warren Giles.

AMERICAN LEAGUE

League Batting Leaders

Average

Year	*Player-Team*	*Avg.*
1970	Alex Johnson, Cal.	.329
1971	Tony Oliva, Min.	.337
1972	Rod Carew, Min.	.318
1973	Rod Carew, Min.	.350
1974	Rod Carew, Min.	.364
1975	Rod Carew, Min.	.359
1976	George Brett, K.C.	.333
1977	Rod Carew, Min.	.388
1978	Rod Carew, Min.	.333
1979	Fred Lynn, Bos.	.333

Home Runs

Year	*Player-Team*	*HR*
1970	Frank Howard, Wash.	44
1971	Bill Melton, Chi.	33
1972	Dick Allen, Chi.	37
1973	Reggie Jackson, Oak.	32
1974	Dick Allen, Chi.	32
1975	Reggie Jackson, Oak.	36
	George Scott, Mil.	36
1976	Graig Nettles, N.Y.	32
1977	Jim Rice, Bos.	39
1978	Jim Rice, Bos.	46
1979	Gorman Thomas, Mil.	45

RBIs

Year	*Player-Team*	*RBI*
1970	Frank Howard, Wash.	126
1971	Harmon Killebrew, Min.	119
1972	Dick Allen, Chi.	113
1973	Reggie Jackson, Oak.	117
1974	Jeff Burroughs, Tex.	118
1975	George Scott, Mil.	109
1976	Lee May, Bal.	109
1977	Larry Hisle, Min.	119
1978	Jim Rice. Bos.	139
1979	Don Baylor, Cal.	139

Most Valuable Players

Selected by BBWAA

Year	*Player-Team*	*Pos.*
1970	Boog Powell, Bal.	1B
1971	Vida Blue, Oak.	P
1972	Dick Allen, Chi.	1B
1973	Reggie Jackson, Oak.	OF
1974	Jeff Burroughs, Tex.	OF
1975	Fred Lynn, Bos.	OF
1976	Thurman Munson, N.Y.	C
1977	Rod Carew, Min.	1B
1978	Jim Rice, Bos.	OF
1979	Don Baylor, Cal.	OF

League Pitching Leaders

Winning Percentage

Year	*Pitcher-Team*	*W-L*	*Pct.*
1970	Mike Cuellar, Bal.	24-8	.750
1971	Dave McNally, Bal.	21-5	.808
1972	Catfish Hunter, Oak.	21-7	.750
1973	Catfish Hunter, Oak.	21-5	.808
1974	Mike Cuellar, Bal.	22-10	.688
1975	Mike Torrez, Bal.	20-9	.690
1976	Bill Campbell, Min.	17-5	.773
1977	Paul Splittorff, K.C.	16-6	.727
1978	Ron Guidry, N.Y.	25-3	.893
1979	Mike Caldwell, Mil.	16-6	.727

Earned-Run Average

Year	*Pitcher-Team*	*ERA*
1970	Diego Segui, Oak.	2.56
1971	Vida Blue, Oak.	1.82
1972	Luis Tiant, Bos.	1.91
1973	Jim Palmer, Bal.	2.40
1974	Catfish Hunter, Oak.	2.49
1975	Jim Palmer, Bal.	2.09
1976	Mark Fidrych, Det.	2.34
1977	Frank Tanana, Cal.	2.54
1978	Ron Guidry, N.Y.	1.74
1979	Ron Guidry, N.Y.	2.78

Strikeouts

Year	*Pitcher-Team*	*SO*
1970	Sam McDowell, Cle.	304
1971	Mickey Lolich, Det.	308
1972	Nolan Ryan, Cal.	329
1973	Nolan Ryan, Cal.	383
1974	Nolan Ryan, Cal.	367
1975	Frank Tanana, Cal.	269
1976	Nolan Ryan, Cal.	327
1977	Nolan Ryan, Cal.	341
1978	Nolan Ryan, Cal.	260
1979	Nolan Ryan, Cal.	223

Cy Young Winners

Selected by BBWAA

Year	*Pitcher-Team*	*Thr.*
1970	Jim Perry, Min.	R
1971	Vida Blue, Oak.	L
1972	Gaylord Perry, Cle.	R
1973	Jim Palmer, Bal.	R
1974	Catfish Hunter, Oak.	R
1975	Jim Palmer, Bal.	R
1976	Jim Palmer, Bal.	R
1977	Sparky Lyle, N.Y.	L
1978	Ron Guidry, N.Y.	L
1979	Mike Flanagan, Bal.	L

Final Standings

*Defeated Boston in one-game division playoff

1970

East	W	L	Pct.	GB
Baltimore	108	54	.667	- -
New York	93	69	.574	15
Boston	87	75	.537	21
Detroit	79	83	.488	29
Cleveland	76	86	.469	32
Washington	70	92	.432	38

West	W	L	Pct.	GB
Minnesota	98	64	.605	- -
Oakland	89	73	.549	9
California	86	76	.531	12
Kansas City	65	97	.401	33
Milwaukee	65	97	.401	33
Chicago	56	106	.346	42

1971

East	W	L	Pct.	GB
Baltimore	101	57	.639	- -
Detroit	91	71	.562	12
Boston	85	77	.525	18
New York	82	80	.506	21
Washington	63	96	.396	38.5
Cleveland	60	102	.370	43

West	W	L	Pct.	GB
Oakland	101	60	.627	- -
Kansas City	85	76	.528	16
Chicago	79	83	.488	22.5
California	76	86	.469	25.5
Minnesota	74	86	.463	26.5
Milwaukee	69	92	.429	32

1972

East	W	L	Pct.	GB
Detroit	86	70	.551	- -
Boston	85	70	.548	.5
Baltimore	80	74	.519	5
New York	79	76	.510	6.5
Cleveland	72	84	.462	14
Milwaukee	65	91	.417	21

West	W	L	Pct.	GB
Oakland	93	62	.600	- -
Chicago	87	67	.565	5.5
Minnesota	77	77	.500	15.5
Kansas City	76	78	.494	16.5
California	75	80	.484	18
Texas	54	100	.351	38.5

1973

East	W	L	Pct.	GB
Baltimore	97	65	.599	- -
Boston	89	73	.549	8
Detroit	85	77	.525	12
New York	80	82	.494	17
Milwaukee	74	88	.457	23
Cleveland	71	91	.438	26

West	W	L	Pct.	GB
Oakland	94	68	.580	- -
Kansas City	88	74	.543	6
Minnesota	81	81	.500	13
California	79	83	.488	15
Chicago	77	85	.475	17
Texas	57	105	.352	37

1974

East	W	L	Pct.	GB
Baltimore	91	71	.562	- -
New York	89	73	.549	2
Boston	84	78	.519	7
Cleveland	77	85	.475	14
Milwaukee	76	86	.469	15
Detroit	72	90	.444	19

West	W	L	Pct.	GB
Oakland	90	72	.556	- -
Texas	84	76	.525	5
Minnesota	82	80	.506	8
Chicago	80	80	.500	9
Kansas City	77	85	.475	13
California	68	94	.420	22

1975

East	W	L	Pct.	GB
Boston	95	65	.594	- -
Baltimore	90	69	.566	4.5
New York	83	77	.519	12
Cleveland	79	80	.497	15.5
Milwaukee	68	94	.420	28
Detroit	57	102	.358	37.5

West	W	L	Pct.	GB
Oakland	98	64	.605	- -
Kansas City	91	71	.562	7
Texas	79	83	.488	19
Minnesota	76	83	.478	20.5
Chicago	75	86	.466	22.5
California	72	89	.447	25.5

1976

	W	L	Pct.	GB
New York	97	62	.610	- -
Baltimore	88	74	.543	10.5
Boston	83	79	.512	15.5
Cleveland	81	78	.509	16
Detroit	74	87	.460	24
Milwaukee	66	95	.410	32

West	W	L	Pct.	GB
Kansas City	90	72	.556	- -
Oakland	87	74	.540	2.5
Minnesota	85	77	.525	5
California	76	86	.469	14
Texas	76	86	.469	14
Chicago	64	97	.398	25.5

1977

East	W	L	Pct.	GB
New York	100	62	.617	- -
Baltimore	97	64	.602	2.5
Boston	97	64	.602	2.5
Detroit	74	88	.457	26
Cleveland	71	90	.441	28.5
Milwaukee	67	95	.414	33
Toronto	54	107	.335	45.5

West	W	L	Pct.	GB
Kansas City	102	60	.630	- -
Texas	94	68	.580	8
Chicago	90	72	.556	12
Minnesota	84	77	.522	17.5
California	74	88	.457	28
Seattle	64	98	.395	38
Oakland	63	98	.391	38.5

1978

East	W	L	Pct.	GB
*New York	100	63	.613	- -
Boston	99	64	.607	1
Milwaukee	93	69	.574	6.5
Baltimore	90	71	.559	9
Detroit	86	76	.531	13.5
Cleveland	69	90	.434	29
Toronto	59	102	.366	40

West	W	L	Pct.	GB
Kansas City	92	70	.568	- -
California	87	75	.537	5
Texas	87	75	.537	5
Minnesota	73	89	.451	19
Chicago	71	90	.441	20.5
Oakland	69	93	.426	23
Seattle	56	104	.350	35

1979

East	W	L	Pct.	GB
Baltimore	102	57	.642	- -
Milwaukee	95	66	.590	8
Boston	91	69	.569	11.5
New York	89	71	.556	13.5
Detroit	85	76	.528	18
Cleveland	81	80	.503	22
Toronto	53	109	.327	50.5

West	W	L	Pct.	GB
California	88	74	.543	- -
Kansas City	85	77	.525	3
Texas	83	79	.512	5
Minnesota	82	80	.506	6
Chicago	73	87	.456	14
Seattle	67	95	.414	21
Oakland	54	108	.333	34

★ 1970 ★
JANUARY - AUGUST

CAUGHT ON THE FLY

MARCH
Commissioner Bowie Kuhn returned the All-Star selection of regular players to the fans — with voting to be done on punch cards and processed by computer.

MAY
Atlanta knuckleballer Hoyt Wilhelm became the first major league pitcher to appear in 1,000 games, reaching the milestone in the Braves' 6-5 loss to St. Louis at Fulton County Stadium.

Atlanta's Rico Carty failed to hit safely in four tries against Cincinnati's Jim McGlothlin, ending his hitting streak at 31 games. Carty batted .451 during his hot spell.

JUNE
Detroit shortstop Cesar Gutierrez became the first modern major leaguer to get seven hits in one game when he singled six times and doubled once during the Tigers' 12-inning 9-8 victory at Cleveland.

Banks reaches 500

Ernie Banks, the always-enthusiastic "Mr. Cub," joined a select circle of sluggers May 12 when he hit his 500th career home run in Chicago's 11-inning 4-3 victory over the Atlanta Braves.

The 39-year-old shortstop thrilled a sparse Wrigley Field throng of 5,264 fans when he blasted a second-inning Pat Jarvis pitch into the left-field bleachers with nobody on base. The ball bounced back onto the field where it was retrieved by Atlanta's Rico Carty and delivered to the Cubs dugout. Banks doffed his cap and held the ball high as the fans roared their approval.

Banks, who hit his first major league homer in September 1953, is the ninth member of the 500-homer club and the first Chicago Cub to reach the lofty plateau. The Cubs won the game on Ron Santo's 11th-inning single after

Billy Williams had homered to tie the contest in the ninth.

Atlanta's Carty stretched his consecutive-game hitting streak to 30.

Mr. Cub, Chicago shortstop Ernie Banks, connects for career home run No. 500.

Tom Seaver fans 19

New York righthander Tom Seaver staged one of the most powerful pitching performances in baseball history April 22, striking out the last 10 San Diego Padres in succession and 19 overall during a 2-1 Mets victory at Shea Stadium.

Seaver, in winning his third straight game this year and his 13th consecutive over two seasons, tied the nine-inning major league strikeout record set last September by St. Louis lefthander Steve Carlton, who dropped a 4-3 decision to the Mets. But the 25-year-old broke the big-league mark for consecutive strikeouts (eight, shared by four players).

Seaver's 136-pitch performance was marred only by two hits — a second-inning home run by Al Ferrara and a fourth-inning single by Dave Campbell. He retired the last 16 Padres without incident, beginning his final strikeout flourish by getting Ferrara with two out in the sixth and ending the game by fanning Ferrara again.

Mike Corkins was the tough-luck loser for San Diego, allowing one run on a Ken Boswell double in the first and another on Bud Harrelson's third-inning triple. Seaver, a 25-game winner in 1969, had received his Cy Young Award in ceremonies before the game.

San Diego's Al Ferrara comes up empty on a ninth-inning swing, becoming Tom Seaver's record 10th straight strikeout victim and record-tying 19th in the game.

Seattle loses Pilots

Baseball returned to Milwaukee March 31 when a Federal bankruptcy court referee granted owners of the financially troubled Seattle Pilots permission to sell their 1-year-old franchise to interests in the Wisconsin city. Since the American League already had voted its approval for transfer of the club, the Pilots became the Milwaukee Brewers upon Sidney C. Volinn's ruling.

When Volinn decided that Milwaukee's $10.8 million offer was in order, the Pilots became the shortest-lived franchise in modern history. The 1969 expansion team, which finished 64-98 and in last place in the A.L. West

Division, reportedly lost $1 million in its only Seattle season and owners projected a $1.5 million loss for 1970. Volinn's ruling nullified a last-ditch effort by special Washington State Assistant Attorney General William Dwyer to have the case dismissed from bankruptcy court.

Baseball, American League style, returned to Milwaukee after a four-year absence on April 7 when California disappointed 37,237 fans at County Stadium by pounding out a 12-0 victory over the Brewers. The Milwaukee Braves had existed from 1953 through 1965 as a National League entry.

> "DUGOUT CHATTER"
>
> *"They say you have to be good to be lucky, but I think you have to be lucky to be good."*
>
> **Rico Carty**
>
> Atlanta outfielder

Rose crunches Fosse as N.L. rallies again

Pete Rose, playing before his home fans in Cincinnati's new Riverfront Stadium, bowled over Cleveland catcher Ray Fosse in a violent 12th-inning collision July 14 and scored the winning run in a 5-4 National League All-Star Game victory over the snakebit American League.

Rose made his mad dash from second base on a two-out single by Chicago's Jim Hickman and delivered a football-style body block as Fosse was taking a throw from Kansas City's Amos Otis. As Fosse lay dazed on his hands and knees, Rose and his teammates celebrated their eighth consecutive All-Star victory.

Through eight innings, it appeared the A.L. would end its misery. An RBI single by Boston's Carl Yastrzemski, a sacrifice fly by Fosse and a two-run triple by Baltimore's Brooks Robinson had forged a 4-1 lead and Oakland ace Catfish Hunter was on the mound.

But the N.L. magic was alive and well. San Francisco's Dick Dietz opened the ninth with a home run and New York's Bud Harrelson and Houston's Joe Morgan followed with singles. The Giants' Willie McCovey singled in one run and Pittsburgh's Roberto Clemente tied the game with a sacrifice fly.

The winning rally off California's Clyde Wright was set up on two-out singles by Rose and Los Angeles' Bill Grabarkewitz.

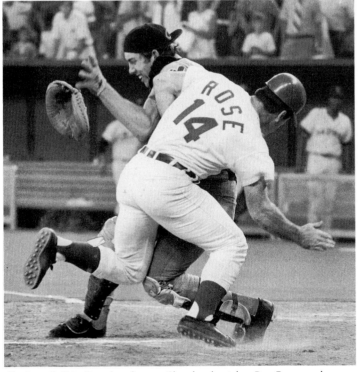

Cincinnati's Pete Rose bowls over Cleveland catcher Ray Fosse and scores the winning run in the National League's 12-inning, 5-4 All-Star Game win over the American League.

A 3,000-hit double

Atlanta's Hank Aaron and San Francisco's Willie Mays became the ninth and 10th members of baseball's 3,000-hit club — and they did it within a two-month span.

Aaron reached the milestone with a first-inning infield single off Cincinnati's Wayne Simpson in the second game of a May 17 doubleheader at Crosley Field. The 33,217 fans then watched the 36-year-old belt a two-run third-inning homer, the 570th of his career. The Reds won, 7-6, and completed a twin bill sweep.

The 39-year-old Mays got his 3,000th hit July 18 off Montreal righthander Mike Wegener in the second inning of San Francisco's 10-1 victory over the Expos at Candlestick Park. The Giants' Say Hey Kid received a standing ovation from 28,879 fans after hitting a two-out single.

Mays and Aaron, who rank second and third on the all-time home run list, are the first players to reach both the 3,000-hit and 500-homer plateaus. Mays began his big-league career in 1951, Aaron in 1954.

San Francisco veteran Willie Mays watches his 3,000th career hit roll past Montreal third baseman Coco Laboy and into left field.

> "DUGOUT CHATTER"
>
> *"I'd pitch just as I would to any other hitter, but I wouldn't be damned fool enough to let go of the ball."*
>
> **Tug McGraw**
>
> New York Mets pitcher, when asked how he would work Atlanta's Hank Aaron with the bases loaded

Flood loses 1st round

Former St. Louis center fielder Curt Flood lost the first round of his lawsuit against baseball August 12 when Federal Court Judge Irving Ben Cooper upheld the legality of the controversial reserve clause and said that any change in the system should be made through player-owner negotiations.

Flood had filed his $4.1 million antitrust suit on January 16 in New York City's Federal Court after he was traded by the Cardinals to Philadelphia. The 12-year veter-an, calling the reserve system that puts players at the mercy of the team that holds their contract a form of "slavery," retired from the game, surrendering his $90,000-per-year salary.

The trial ran for three weeks, from May 19 to June 10, and was heard by Judge Cooper without a jury. A veritable "Who's Who in Baseball" testified for both sides. Cooper's ruling likely will be only the first step. Appeals could take the case all the way to the Supreme Court.

" DUGOUT CHATTER "

"Well, I used to look like this when I was young and now I still do."

Yogi Berra

New York Mets coach, when a fan commented that he had not changed much since his playing days

"Gullett's the only guy who can throw a baseball through a car wash and not get the ball wet."

Pete Rose

Reds star, on Cincinnati's rookie fireballer Don Gullett

Umpires end strike

Major league umpires went back to work October 4 for the second games of the American League and National League Championship Series, ending their unprecedented one-day strike that included picket lines at Pittsburgh's Three Rivers Stadium.

The Major League Umpires Association, seeking higher wages for postseason games, called the strike when owners refused to meet their demands. The six umpires scheduled to work the NLCS opener at Pittsburgh between the Cincinnati Reds and the Pirates set up a picket line outside the park as four minor league arbiters worked the contest.

The strike ended quickly, with the umpires accepting a four-year agreement that gave them an escalating pay hike for all postseason and All-Star Games.

Al Barlick celebrates an end to the umpires' one-day strike by tearing up his picket sign outside Pittsburgh's Three Rivers Stadium.

A new ballpark era

The curtain dropped on three venerable baseball stages and rose on two others. Final pitches were thrown at Cincinnati's Crosley Field, Pittsburgh's Forbes Field and Philadelphia's Connie Mack Stadium while the Reds and Pirates dedicated beautiful new facilities that signaled the beginning of a new ballpark era.

Nostalgia oozed from every nook and cranny of Crosley Field June 24 when Cincinnati defeated San Francisco, 5-4, and it was more of the same four days later when Pittsburgh said goodbye to Forbes Field with a doubleheader sweep of Chicago. Connie Mack Stadium, formerly known as Shibe Park, played host to its final game October 1 when the Phillies beat Montreal, 2-1.

Shibe Park and Forbes Field had opened in 1909, setting off an explosion of ballpark construction in an era of baseball growth. Crosley was opened in 1912. Forbes was the largest of the three, seating 35,000.

On June 30, the Reds dedicated new Riverfront Stadium with an 8-2 loss to Atlanta before 51,050 curious fans. On July 16, the Reds spoiled the opening of new Three Rivers Stadium for 48,846 Pittsburgh fans with a 3-2 victory. Both parks are symmetrical facilities with AstroTurf playing surfaces — the fifth and sixth stadiums with the artificial grass.

Philadelphia's new Veterans Stadium will open next season.

Souvenir-seeking Philadelphia fans carry away uprooted seats after watching the Phillies play their final game at Connie Mack Stadium.

McLain is suspended

Detroit righthander Denny McLain, on top of the baseball world in 1968 and 1969 when he won 55 games and two American League Cy Young Awards, completed his 1970 tumble September 9 when he was suspended for the third time, the second by Commissioner Bowie Kuhn.

McLain's troubles began when Kuhn announced on April 1 that the Tiger ace would be suspended for three months because of his alleged involvement with Detroit bookmaking activities. He struggled to a 3-5 record and 4.65 earned-run average after his July 1 return and further complicated matters last week when he dumped a bucket of ice water on two Detroit sportswriters, an act that cost him another stint on the suspended list.

McLain still was serving that suspension when the commissioner announced in New York that it would continue for at least the rest of the season. Kuhn would only say that the decision concerned McLain's lack of respect toward Detroit management and information that McLain has carried a gun on occasion.

McLain, who in 1968 became the first 30-game winner in 34 years, finished that campaign with a 31-6 record and 1.96 ERA. He followed with a 24-win season.

Orioles, Reds sweep

Baseball's second Championship Series, just like its first ones in 1969, were sweeping successes — literally. Powerful Baltimore rolled to three straight victories over Minnesota and Cincinnati did the same to Pittsburgh.

For the second straight year, the best-of-five formats were broken down to the basics, with a twist. The pitching-rich Orioles, 217-game winners over the last two seasons, muscled up for six home runs during 10-6, 11-3 and 6-1 victories over the Twins. The Reds, known for their muscle, used pitching to rattle off 3-0, 3-1 and 3-2 wins over the Pirates.

Baltimore took control of the first game with a seven-run fourth inning and broke open the second with a seven-run ninth. Pitcher Mike Cuellar, Don Buford and Boog Powell hit homers in the opener while Frank Robinson and Dave Johnson connected in Game 2. Jim Palmer put the Twins out of their misery with a seven-hit performance in the finale.

Cincinnati used the committee approach as Gary Nolan and Clay Carroll set the tone in Game 1 with a combined eight-hit effort. Jim Merritt, Carroll and Don Gullett allowed only five hits in the second game and the foursome of Tony Cloninger, Milt Wilcox, Wayne Granger and Gullett spaced out 10 hits in the clincher. Bobby Tolan, Tony Perez and Johnny Bench hit solo homers for the Reds.

Baltimore second baseman Dave Johnson dodges a sliding Cesar Tovar as he completes the relay on a double play during the Orioles' A.L. Championship Series sweep of Minnesota.

ORIOLES POUND REDS

The Baltimore Orioles, wiping out a 3-0 Cincinnati lead for the third time in five games, supported the six-hit pitching of Mike Cuellar with two home runs October 15 and romped to a 9-3 victory that clinched their second World Series championship in five years.

The Reds collected four of their hits and all of their runs in the first inning off Cuellar, but the Orioles stormed back with two runs in each of the first three innings to take control of the finale at Baltimore's Memorial Stadium. Frank Robinson contributed his second Series homer and Merv Rettenmund added his first as the Orioles avenged their 1969 World Series upset loss to the New York Mets.

The Game 5 victory was similar to Baltimore's triumphs in each of the first two games. In the opener, the Reds jumped to a 3-0 advantage, two of the runs coming in the third inning on Lee May's homer. But the Orioles played a little long ball of their own, coming back on a two-run homer by Boog Powell and solo shots by Elrod Hendricks and Brooks Robinson to give Jim Palmer a 4-3 victory.

Cincinnati scored three runs in the first inning of the second game at Riverfront Stadium and increased its lead to 4-0 after three, but again the Orioles fought back. Powell's homer accounted for one run and Hendricks capped a five-run fifth inning with a two-run double as Baltimore won, 6-5. Dave McNally pitched a nine-hitter and contributed a grand slam homer to the Orioles' 9-3 third-game triumph.

The Reds pulled off a comeback of their own in the fourth game, but it was too little too late. Trailing 5-3 in the eighth, May cracked a three-run homer and Clay Carroll protected the one-run lead the rest of the way for Cincinnati's only victory.

Baltimore's Series star was third baseman Brooks Robinson, who hit two home runs, batted .429 and made several outstanding defensive plays.

Game 1	Baltimore	4	Cincinnati	3
Game 2	Baltimore	6	Cincinnati	5
Game 3	Baltimore	9	Cincinnati	3
Game 4	Cincinnati	6	Baltimore	5
Game 5	Baltimore	9	Cincinnati	3

Baltimore lefthander Mike Cuellar (right) is mobbed after pitching the Orioles to a clinching World Series victory over Cincinnati.

CAUGHT ON THE FLY

SEPTEMBER

The iron man streak of Chicago Cubs outfielder Billy Williams ended after an N.L.-record 1,117 games when he benched himself with the simple explanation that he was "pooped."

OCTOBER

California's Alex Johnson collected two final-day hits and edged Boston's Carl Yastrzemski, .3289 to .3286, in the tightest A.L. batting race since 1949.

Milwaukee's Tommy Harper became baseball's fifth 30-30 man, finishing the season with 31 homers and 38 stolen bases.

SEASON LEADERS

	American League		National League	
Avg.	Alex Johnson, Cal.	.329	Rico Carty, Atl.	.366
HR	Frank Howard, Wash.	44	Johnny Bench, Cin.	45
RBI	Frank Howard, Wash.	126	Johnny Bench, Cin.	148
SB	Bert Campaneris, Oak.	42	Bob Tolan, Cin.	57
W-L Pct.	Mike Cuellar, Bal.	24-8, .750	Bob Gibson, St. L.	23-7, .767
ERA	Diego Segui, Oak.	2.56	Tom Seaver, N.Y.	2.81
SO	Sam McDowell, Cle.	304	Tom Seaver, N.Y.	283

★ 1971 ★

Flood jumps Senators

Curt Flood, lured out of retirement by Washington Owner Bob Short over the winter, abandoned the Senators 18 games into the season and flew to Spain, apparently leaving his baseball career behind.

The controversial center fielder, who filed the ongoing 1970 lawsuit that challenges the reserve clause found in all standard player contracts, sent a 22-word telegram to Short before boarding his flight. "I tried," it said. "A year and a half is too much. Very serious problems mounting every day. Thanks for your confidence and understanding."

The 33-year-old Flood, a career .293 hitter who had sat out the 1970 campaign while living in Denmark, apparently was upset over financial problems and his inability to get back into a baseball groove. There was no problem with his $110,000 contract, half of which he already had collected, but Washington fans were not pleased with his .200 average.

The veteran center fielder, who was being used on a platoon basis by Manager Ted Williams, enjoyed 12 outstanding seasons with St. Louis before the Cardinals traded him to Philadelphia in 1969. He retired immediately and filed suit against baseball.

Baseball signs rich TV pact

Commissioner Bowie Kuhn signed the longest, richest television contract in baseball history May 6, closing a deal with the National Broadcasting Company that will net the 24 teams a reported $72 million over four years.

The new contract will run from 1972 through 1976 and include a yearly package of 10 Monday night games, 26 Saturday afternoon contests, the All-Star Game, the Championship Series and the World Series. A new provision states that all weekday World Series contests will be played at night.

The total package breaks down to $750,000 per club annually and lifts the major league's annual income from radio and television — both network and local — to about $42 million.

Negotiations also were held with the American Broadcasting Company and the Columbia Broadcasting System, but NBC came up with the winning bid.

CAUGHT ON THE FLY

FEBRUARY

As baseball's list of six-figure performers grew to 15, Boston's Carl Yastrzemski emerged as the highest paid player in history when he signed a three-year pact for $500,000.

MAY

San Francisco's Willie Mays notched another N.L. record when he scored his 1,950th career run in the first game of a doubleheader against Montreal, passing former St. Louis great Stan Musial.

JUNE

Chicago lefthander Ken Holtzman became the first modern-era Cubs pitcher to throw two career no-hitters when he blanked Cincinnati, 1-0, at Riverfront Stadium.

AUGUST

Bob Gibson, a two-time Cy Young winner and holder of virtually every St. Louis pitching record, finally notched his first career no-hitter, stopping Pittsburgh, 11-0, at Three Rivers Stadium.

" DUGOUT CHATTER "

"We were the gold dust twins. He got the gold and I got the dust."

Phil Gagliano

Boston utility man and former high school teammate of Phillies catcher Tim McCarver

Washington Owner Bob Short with new signee Curt Flood (right) at a 1970 press conference.

Aaron joins select circle with 600 homers

Atlanta slugger Hank Aaron connects for his 600th career home run.

Atlanta's Hank Aaron became the third member of slugging's inner circle April 27 when he belted a Gaylord Perry pitch for his 600th career home run during a 10-inning 6-5 loss to San Francisco at Atlanta-Fulton County Stadium.

Aaron joined Babe Ruth and Willie Mays as the only players in baseball history to hit 600 home runs and then watched as Mays singled home the Giants' winning run in the 10th inning. Aaron stroked the first pitch he saw in the third inning 350 feet over the left-field fence after Ralph Garr had reached base on an infield single. The righthanded slugger had collected his 542nd career double in his first at-bat, tying for eighth place on the all-time list.

Aaron hit his milestone homer in his 18th major league season at age 37. Ruth, the all-time career leader with 714, hit his 600th homer in his 18th big-league campaign at age 36. Mays, who has 633 career blasts, was in his 19th season at age 38.

The home run was Aaron's eighth of the season and marked his fastest start ever. His previous best total for April was seven.

" DUGOUT CHATTER "

"I'm always amazed when a pitcher becomes angry at a hitter for hitting a home run off him. When I strike out, I don't get angry at the pitcher. I get angry at myself."

Willie Stargell

Pittsburgh slugger

Wise guy ruins Reds

Rick Wise was almost perfect June 23 — in more ways than one. The Philadelphia righthander pitched his first career no-hitter, beating Cincinnati 4-0, and spiced his big effort with a pair of homers and three runs batted in.

Wise issued only a sixth-inning walk to Dave Concepcion while facing 28 batters, one over the minimum. He threw 95 pitches, struck out three and kept the powerful Reds off stride with an assortment of fastballs, curves and sliders. Saving defensive plays were turned in by his teammates shortstop Larry Bowa and third baseman John Vukovich.

Wise was guarding a 1-0 lead in the fifth inning when he took matters into his own hands, driving a Ross Grimsley pitch over the left-field wall for a two-run homer. He added a solo shot in the eighth off Clay Carroll, becoming the first hurler ever to hit two homers while pitching a no-hitter.

Ironically, Wise had won his first major league game as an 18-year-old rookie in 1964 — in the second game of a doubleheader after teammate Jim Bunning had thrown a perfect game against the New York Mets in the opener.

Philadelphia's Rick Wise doubled as a no-hit pitcher and home run hitter (right) during an amazing June performance at Cincinnati.

A.L. has a big blast

Home runs by American Leaguers Reggie Jackson, Frank Robinson and Harmon Killebrew offset a three-homer barrage by the National League as the junior circuit broke an eight-game All-Star losing streak July 13 with a hard fought 6-4 win at Detroit's Tiger Stadium.

Like two heavyweight boxers standing toe-to-toe and slugging it out, the two leagues delighted a national television audience with an unexpected power display. The fireworks started with homers by Cincinnati's Johnny Bench and Atlanta's Hank Aaron that produced three runs off Oakland's Vida Blue in the second and third innings.

But Boston shortstop Luis Aparicio led off the bottom of the third with a single and young Oakland slugger Jackson, batting for Blue, put the A.L. back on track — emphatically. Reggie connected with a delivery from Pittsburgh's Dock Ellis and hit a mammoth shot that struck a light tower on the roof in right-center field, traveling 520 feet. Jackson stood at the plate admiring his work before circling the bases.

Baltimore's Robinson added another two-run shot in the inning and Minnesota's Killebrew belted a two-run homer in the sixth. Pittsburgh's Roberto Clemente closed out the N.L. scoring with a solo blast in the eighth.

Three A.L. All-Star sluggers (left to right): Baltimore's Frank Robinson, Minnesota's Harmon Killebrew and Oakland's Reggie Jackson.

Killebrew, Robinson join 500-homer club

Minnesota's Harmon Killebrew and Baltimore's Frank Robinson became the 10th and 11th players to hit 500 career home runs, connecting a month apart in their home ballparks.

The 35-year-old Killebrew drove a first-inning pitch from Baltimore lefthander Mike Cuellar out of the park August 10 for his milestone homer and added his 501st later in the Orioles' 10-inning 4-3 victory. An excited Metropolitan Stadium crowd of 15,881 saluted the seven-time American League home run champion with a long ovation.

Robinson entered a September 13 doubleheader against Detroit with 498 home runs. He blasted his 499th in Baltimore's 9-1 first-game victory over the Tigers and then hit No. 500 in the ninth inning of the nightcap, a two-run shot off Fred Scherman that cut the Tigers' victory margin to 10-5. The 36-year-old two-time Most Valuable Player answered the chants of 13,292 Memorial Stadium fans with a cap-waving curtain call. The second homer was his 25th of the season.

★ 1971 ★

Senators go to Texas

Bob Short, owner of the financially troubled Washington Senators, received American League approval to move his franchise to the Dallas-Fort Worth area September 21, ending 71 years of major league baseball in the nation's capital.

The announcement came after a 12½-hour meeting of A.L. club owners in Boston. The vote was 10-2, with Baltimore and Chicago opposing the shift. The transfer is conditional. The stadium in Arlington, Tex., seats 22,000 and must be upgraded to 35,000 in 1972 and 45,000 in 1973. A lease must be worked out and indemnities paid to the Texas League club that now uses the ballpark.

This is the second time Washington has lost a team. The first Senators franchise moved to Minnesota in 1960 and became the Twins, but A.L. expansion brought a new Senators franchise that began play the next season.

In its long, futile history, Washington fielded only one World Series champion (1924) and two other teams (1925 and 1933) that lost in the fall classic.

Baltimore's record-tying four 20-game winners (left to right): Jim Palmer, Dave McNally, Mike Cuellar and Pat Dobson.

Four O's win 20

Baltimore's Jim Palmer pitched a three-hit shutout against Cleveland September 26 and became the record-tying fourth Oriole hurler to reach the 20-victory plateau this season.

Palmer's 5-0 victory at Cleveland's Municipal Stadium allowed him to join teammates Dave McNally (20-5), Mike Cuellar (20-9) and Pat Dobson (20-8) in a select circle that had been reached only one other time in history — by the 1920 Chicago White Sox. Urban (Red) Faber won 23 games, Lefty Williams 22 and Dickie Kerr and Ed Cicotte 21 apiece for that team. Williams and Cicotte later were banned from baseball for their parts in the infamous 1919 "Black Sox" scandal.

Palmer was overpowering as he lifted his record to 20-9 and produced Baltimore's eighth straight win and 98th overall. Cuellar's 20th victory two days earlier had clinched the Orioles' third straight American League East Division title. Palmer also contributed a run-scoring double in a three-run seventh inning that broke open a scoreless duel.

CAUGHT ON THE FLY

SEPTEMBER
Denny McLain, a 55-game winner in 1968 and '69 for Detroit, saw his 1971 Washington record dip to 10-22 when he dropped a 6-3 decision to Boston at Fenway Park.

With the Senators leading the New York Yankees 7-5 in the ninth inning, fans swarmed onto the field and began tearing up RFK Stadium, causing the final game in Washington to be declared a forfeit.

NOVEMBER
Young Oakland lefthander Vida Blue, who finished the season 24-8 with an A.L.-best 1.82 ERA, capped his big season by sweeping both the Cy Young and MVP awards.

DECEMBER
Chicago released Mr. Cub, veteran shortstop Ernie Banks, and quickly signed the popular star as a coach.

Orioles sweep again

The pitching-rich Baltimore Orioles, defending World Series champions and 318-game winners over the last three years, gave the Oakland Athletics a big dose of their Championship Series magic and swept to a third straight American League pennant.

For the Orioles, Championship Series play is as simple as 1-2-3. They won three straight games from the Minnesota Twins in 1969, followed with another sweep of the Twins last year and brushed aside the Athletics without a serious challenge this time around.

Oakland's Vida Blue carried a 3-1 lead into the seventh inning of the October 3 opener in a pitching duel against Dave McNally, but Baltimore struck for four runs, the final two coming on Paul Blair's double, and the Orioles escaped with a 5-3 victory.

Mike Cuellar pitched a six-hitter in a 5-1 second-game win keyed by two Boog Powell home runs and Jim Palmer withstood two bases-empty Reggie Jackson homers in the third game at Oakland to post a pennant-clinching 5-3 triumph.

Baltimore outfielder Paul Blair (left) gives Tom Shopay a champagne bath as the Orioles celebrate their American League Championship Series sweep of Oakland.

Robertson explodes

With the booming bat of Willie Stargell having gone strangely silent, the Pittsburgh Pirates needed a Ruthian-type lift in their National League Championship Series battle with the San Francisco Giants. They got it from first baseman Bob Robertson.

With the Pirates trailing the Giants 1-0 in the Series and 2-1 in Game 2 at Candlestick Park on October 3, Robertson, who had doubled and scored Pittsburgh's only run in the second inning, tied the game with a solo home run off John Cumberland in the fourth. He batted again in the seventh and belted a three-run homer off Ron Bryant and he completed his big day with a solo ninth-inning shot off Steve Hamilton.

Robertson's three-homer per-formance matched the postseason record set by former Yankee great Babe Ruth, who enjoyed three-homer games in both the 1926 and '28 World Series. Robertson's 14 total bases set a postseason single-game record and his five RBIs propelled the Pirates to a 9-4 victory.

The big slugger also contrib-uted a third-game homer off Juan Marichal, but third baseman Richie Hebner picked up the hero mantle with an eighth-inning blast that produced a 2-1 win. Hebner added another homer and three RBIs in Pittsburgh's 9-5 clincher at Three Rivers Stadium.

Robertson and Hebner com-bined for six homers and 10 RBIs while Stargell, a 48-homer man during the regular season, went hitless in 14 at-bats.

Pittsburgh first baseman Bob Robertson was the center of attention after his three-home run effort in Game 2 of the N.L. Championship Series.

SEASON LEADERS

	American League		National League	
Avg.	Tony Oliva, Min.	.337	Joe Torre, St. L.	.363
HR	Bill Melton, Chi.	33	Willie Stargell, Pit.	48
RBI	Harmon Killebrew, Min.	119	Joe Torre, St. L.	137
SB	Amos Otis, K.C.	52	Lou Brock, St. L.	64
W-L Pct.	Dave McNally, Bal.21-5, .808		Don Gullett, Cin.	16-6, .727
ERA	Vida Blue, Oak.	1.82	Tom Seaver, N.Y.	1.76
SO	Mickey Lolich, Det.	308	Tom Seaver, N.Y.	289

" DUGOUT CHATTER "

"(Roberto) Clemente was great, (Bruce) Kison turned the Series around, but (Steve) Blass was Mr. World Series."

Earl Weaver

Baltimore manager, commenting on his team's World Series loss to the Pittsburgh Pirates

PIRATES PREVAIL

Roberto Clemente and Jose Pagan took care of the offense and right-hander Steve Blass stymied Baltimore on four hits as the underdog Pitts-burgh Pirates recorded a 2-1 victory over the powerful Orioles October 17 in Game 7 of the World Series at Baltimore's Memorial Stadium.

Blass' second victory came in a tense duel with Baltimore lefthander Mike Cuellar, who surrendered a fourth-inning home run to Clemente and an eighth-inning run-scoring double to Pagan. The Orioles scored their only run in the bottom of the eighth on a ground out by Don Buford.

Pittsburgh's chances did not look bright when the Series opened at Baltimore. Dave McNally and Jim Palmer, half of a record-tying starting rotation that featured four 20-game winners, quickly pitched the Orioles to 5-3 and 11-3 victories.

But when the Series moved to Pitts-burgh's Three Rivers Stadium, the momentum shifted. Blass pitched the Pirates to a 5-1 victory, Bruce Kison provided stellar long relief in a 4-3 come-from-behind win and Nelson Briles fired a two-hit 4-0 shutout in Game 5. Firepower was provided by Clemente and Bob Robertson, who homered in the third and fifth games and lifted his record postseason home run total to six.

Baltimore's 10-inning 3-2 victory in Game 6 was only delaying the in-evitable. Blass was outstanding in his final-game effort that gave the Pirates their first World Series cham-pionship since 1960 and kept the Orioles from winning their second straight.

Clemente also was outstanding, closing out his second fall classic with a .414 batting average (12 for 29) and a 14-game Series hitting streak.

Game 1	Baltimore	5	Pittsburgh	3
Game 2	Baltimore	11	Pittsburgh	3
Game 3	Pittsburgh	5	Baltimore	1
Game 4	Pittsburgh	4	Baltimore	3
Game 5	Pittsburgh	4	Baltimore	0
Game 6	Baltimore	3	Pittsburgh	2
Game 7	Pittsburgh	2	Baltimore	1

Emotional Pittsburgh pitcher Steve Blass hugs teammate Bob Robertson after shutting down Baltimore in Game 7 of the World Series.

★1972★

JANUARY-OCTOBER

CAUGHT ON THE FLY

APRIL

Gil Hodges, finishing spring preparations before beginning his fifth season as New York Mets manager, suffered a fatal heart attack at West Palm Beach, Fla. He was 47.

The Texas Rangers, formerly the Washington Senators, got off to a good start in their Arlington Stadium debut, recording a 7-6 win over the California Angels before 20,105 fans.

MAY

A.L. Cy Young Award winner Vida Blue ended his holdout battle with Oakland Owner Charles O. Finley eight games into the season, signing for a reported $63,000.

JUNE/JULY

Veteran sluggers Hank Aaron of Atlanta and Willie McCovey of San Francisco both hit their 14th career grand slams, tying Gil Hodges' N.L. record.

JULY

Five days before his 49th birthday, knuckleball reliever Hoyt Wilhelm was released by the Los Angeles Dodgers. Wilhelm appeared in a major league-record 1,070 games.

Curt Flood loses suit

The United States Supreme Court extended baseball's unique exemption from the nation's antitrust laws June 19 in a 5-3 ruling that ended Curt Flood's long, frustrating legal battle against the reserve clause.

The former St. Louis center fielder had filed suit in 1970 against the system that binds a player to the team that owns his contract. The suit, sparked by Flood's trade to the Philadelphia Phillies, was supported financially by the Major League Players' Association. A lower court denied his suit because baseball had been made exempt from antitrust laws by Supreme Court decisions of 1922 and 1953, and Flood's subsequent appeals were denied.

The June 19 decision, delivered by Justice Harry A. Blackmun, upheld the previous decisions while pointing out that the system could be changed only by Congressional legislation or collective bargaining. More than 50 bills attacking baseball's antitrust status have been introduced in Congress over the last two decades, but all have failed.

Baseball is the only sport that enjoys the antitrust exemption. Other sports have gradually given players more freedom.

Mays is a big hit

Willie Mays begins life anew as a member of the New York Mets.

Willie Mays, playing in his first game as a member of the New York Mets, brought 35,505 fans to their feet at Shea Stadium May 14 when he belted a game-winning homer against his old team, the San Francisco Giants.

Mays' triumphant return to New York, where he had spent the first seven years of his fabulous career before the Giants moved to San Francisco, was a scriptwriter's dream. Traded to the Mets May 11 for a young pitcher, he batted leadoff and walked in the first inning ahead of Rusty Staub's grand slam homer.

After the Giants had tied the game with a four-run fifth inning, Mays earned a thunderous ovation by hitting a Don Carrithers pitch out of the park. The run stood up for a 5-4 New York victory.

The 41-year-old Mays, brought back to New York primarily as a public relations move, figures to be used on a spot basis and as a pinch-hitter. He probably will see most of his defensive action at first base, rather than his familiar center-field position. Generally considered one of the greatest players ever to put on a uniform, Mays entered the season with 3,178 career hits and 646 home runs, second only to Babe Ruth on the all-time list.

Baseball settles first strike

The first general strike in baseball's long history came to a merciful end April 13 when players and owners agreed to start the season without making up any of the 86 games cancelled because of the 13-day walkout.

The settlement was reached with the 24 owners gathered in Chicago and the player representatives in New York, where they had been meeting for three days. It was announced simultaneously in Chicago by Commissioner Bowie Kuhn and in New York by Marvin Miller, director of the players' association.

The issue that caused the strike, an increase in the players' pension fund, had been settled two days earlier with a compromise $500,000 raise. The dispute that

Chicago youngsters let their feelings be known midway through the 13-day strike that delayed the opening of the baseball season.

delayed the season two extra days was whether or not players would be paid for games rescheduled because of the strike.

As a result of the decision to not play the 86 games, division titles will be decided strictly on a percentage basis. All teams lost at least six games from their schedules, some as many as nine.

Padre has a blast

Nate Colbert, San Diego's five-homer man.

San Diego slugger Nate Colbert, who entered the game with a .233 batting average, lit up the Atlanta sky with a dazzling power display August 1, hitting five homers and driving in 13 runs in the Padres' 9-0 and 11-7 doubleheader sweep of the Braves.

The 6-foot-1, 200-pounder muscled up in the first game for a three-run, first-inning home run off Ron Scheuler and added a solo shot in the seventh off Mike McQueen. He also collected a pair of singles, one of which drove in a run.

But Colbert saved his best for the nightcap. First he belted a second-inning grand slam off Pat Jarvis, then he hit two-run homers off Jim Hardin in the seventh and Cecil Upshaw in the ninth.

Colbert's 13-RBI explosion set a doubleheader record and his five homers tied the twin bill mark set by Stan Musial in 1954.

Extra, extra: National Leaguers capture another All-Star Game

Lee May's ninth-inning ground out tied the game and Joe Morgan's 10th-inning single drove home the winning run as the National League rallied for a 4-3 All-Star Game victory over the American League July 25 at Atlanta's Fulton-County Stadium.

In winning for the ninth time in 10 years and the seventh time in as many extra-inning All-Star contests, the Nationals used a tried and true formula — let the A.L. players smell victory and then snatch it away at the last second.

One of the game's dramatic moments occurred in the sixth inning when Hank Aaron, who has hit 659 career home runs, excited his home fans by pounding a two-run shot that wiped away a 1-0 A.L. lead. But the Americans regained the advantage in the eighth with a two-run homer of their own — by Kansas City's Cookie Rojas, an unlikely long-ball threat.

That lead held until the ninth when Chicago's Billy Williams singled, moved to third on a single by Pittsburgh's Manny Sanguillen and scored on a ground ball by Houston's May.

Cincinnati's Morgan singled home San Diego's Nate Colbert in the 10th inning, making a winner out of New York Mets reliever Tug McGraw.

Cincinnati's Joe Morgan (8) gets a heroic welcome after driving in the All-Star Game winner for the N.L.

"DUGOUT CHATTER"

"Facing Nolan Ryan in the twilight hours is the equivalent of capital punishment."

Eddie Kasko

Boston manager, after watching California's Ryan strike out 16 Red Sox in a 6 p.m. game at Anaheim

"He's a switch-hitter. He batted .300 last year — .150 lefthanded and .150 righthanded."

Dick Williams

Oakland manager, on A's outfielder Allan Lewis

Reds topple Pirates

Pinch-runner George Foster raced home on a ninth-inning wild pitch by Pittsburgh's Bob Moose in the fifth game of the N.L. Championship Series, giving the Cincinnati Reds a 4-3 victory and a second pennant in three years.

The Reds, trailing 3-2 in the October 11 game at Riverfront Stadium, were three outs away from elimination when catcher Johnny Bench, the N.L. home run champion, led off the ninth with a home run. Tony Perez and Denis Menke followed with singles, bringing Moose out to re-place Dave Giusti. Foster, running for Perez, advanced to third on a fly ball and scored with two out when Moose bounced a pitch past catcher Manny Sanguillen.

The Pirates had blown a two games to one advantage and then failed to score in the last six innings of Game 5 off relievers Pedro Borbon, Tom Hall and Clay Carroll. Pittsburgh had won the opener, 5-1, behind Steve Blass and the third game, 3-2.

But the Reds bounced back each time, winning Game 2, 5-3, and the fourth, 7-1.

★1972★
OCTOBER-DECEMBER

A's outlast Tigers

Lefthander Vida Blue pitched four shutout innings to preserve Blue Moon Odom's 2-1 victory over Detroit October 12, giving the Athletics their first American League pennant since moving to Oakland and the franchise's first since 1931, when it was located in Philadelphia

Oakland's Game 5 triumph at frigid Tiger Stadium capped the first American League Championship Series to last more than three games.

A Game 1 pitching duel between Oakland's Catfish Hunter and Detroit's Mickey Lolich resulted in a 1-1 nine-inning tie. The Tigers took the upper hand in the top of the 11th when right fielder Al Kaline homered off A's reliever Rollie Fingers, but Oakland scored two in the bottom of

the inning, the winner coming on Kaline's throwing error, for a dramatic 3-2 victory.

When Odom fired a three-hit 5-0 shutout the next day, another sweep appeared imminent. But the Tigers had other ideas.

Detroit rebounded, 3-0, behind Joe Coleman's 14-strikeout pitching and won a 4-3 fourth-game thriller, scoring three-runs in the bottom of the 10th after the A's had scored twice in the top of the inning.

Oakland's second-game victory was spiced by a brawl after A's shortstop Bert Campaneris, who had been hit by a Lerrin LaGrow pitch, threw his bat at the Tiger righthander. Campaneris was suspended for the remainder of the Championship Series and the first seven games of the 1973 season.

Owner Charles O. Finley and shortstop Bert Campaneris celebrate Oakland's first-ever American League pennant.

SEASON LEADERS

	American League		National League	
Avg.	Rod Carew, Min.	.318	Billy Williams, Chi.	.333
HR	Dick Allen, Chi.	37	Johnny Bench, Cin.	40
RBI	Dick Allen, Chi.	113	Johnny Bench, Cin.	125
SB	Bert Campaneris, Oak.	52	Lou Brock, St. L.	63
W-L Pct.	Catfish Hunter, Oak.	21-7, .750	Gary Nolan, Cin.	15-5, .750
ERA	Luis Tiant, Bos.	1.91	Steve Carlton, Phi.	1.98
SO	Nolan Ryan, Cal.	329	Steve Carlton, Phi.	310

WORLD SERIES REPORT

TENACE, ANYONE ?

Unlikely hero Gene Tenace capped his memorable World Series with a run-scoring single and double October 22, lifting Oakland to a 3-2 seventh-game victory over Cincinnati and helping the A's win their first championship since 1930.

Tenace, a utility catcher and first baseman, singled home a first-inning run and doubled home another in Oakland's two-run sixth, making a winner of Catfish Hunter, the second of four A's pitchers. Tenace finished with a Series record-tying four home runs after hitting only five during the regular season.

He opened the fall classic at Cincinnati's Riverfront Stadium with a bang, homering in his first two Series at-bats and driving in all three Oakland runs, which Ken Holtzman, Rollie Fingers and Vida Blue made stand up for a 3-2 victory. Hunter, with

ninth-inning relief from Fingers, gave the A's a two-game advantage the next day with a 2-1 triumph keyed by a home run and spectacular catch by left fielder Joe Rudi.

The momentum shifted in Game 3 when Cincinnati pitchers Jack Billingham and Clay Carroll combined on a three-hit 1-0 shutout, but Oakland delivered a big blow in the fourth game when it strung together four consecutive ninth-inning singles that produced two runs and a 3-2 victory.

Pete Rose helped steady the ship when he led off Game 5 with a home run and then broke a 4-4 tie in the ninth with a run-scoring single. But it took a clutch throw from second baseman Joe Morgan in the bottom of the inning to cut down the tying run at the plate and preserve Cincinnati's 5-4 win. The Reds forced a seventh game with an 8-1 victory in Game 6.

Game 1	Oakland	3	Cincinnati	2
Game 2	Oakland	2	Cincinnati	1
Game 3	Cincinnati	1	Oakland	0
Game 4	Oakland	3	Cincinnati	2
Game 5	Cincinnati	5	Oakland	4
Game 6	Cincinnati	8	Oakland	1
Game 7	Oakland	3	Cincinnati	2

Oakland third baseman Sal Bando leaps on pitcher Rollie Fingers and catcher Dave Duncan after the A's Game 7 World Series victory at Cincinnati.

Carlton wins award

Lefthander Steve Carlton, the lone bright spot in Philadelphia's dismal season, was rewarded for his remarkable performance November 2 when the 24-man committee of the Baseball Writers' Association of America made him a unanimous winner of the National League Cy Young Award.

Carlton, acquired from St. Louis in an off-season trade for righthander Rick Wise, recorded a 27-10 record and accounted for 46 percent of the last-place Phillies' 59 victories. He led N.L. pitchers in eight pitching categories, including wins (27), complete games (30), innings (346), strikeouts (310) and earned-run average (1.98). The talented 27-year-old won 15 straight games from June 7 to August 17.

Carlton is the sixth unanimous choice in the 16-year history of the award, joining Sandy Koufax (1963, '65 and '66), Bob Gibson (1968) and Denny McLain (1968) in that distinction. He is the first Phillie to win the award and the first player to win it while pitching for a last-place team. The Phillies scored only 16 runs in the 10 games he lost.

Philadelphia lefthander Steve Carlton receiving his Cy Young Award.

" DUGOUT CHATTER "

"Hitting him tonight was like drinking coffee with a fork."

Willie Stargell

The Pittsburgh All-Star, after watching Philadelphia's Steve Carlton mow down the Pirates in a 2-0 victory

---

CAUGHT ON THE FLY

OCTOBER

Expos righthander Bill Stoneman pitched his second career no-hitter in the chill of Montreal, defeating the New York Mets, 7-0.

Cincinnati veteran Clay Carroll finished the season with an N.L.-record 37 saves and New York Yankee Sparky Lyle broke the A.L. mark with 35.

DECEMBER

In the most significant rules change in many years, the A.L. voted unanimously to adopt the designated hitter on a three-year experimental basis.

Hall of Fame catcher Gabby Hartnett, a stalwart with the Chicago Cubs from 1922 to '40, died in Park Ridge, Ill., at age 72.

Jackie Robinson dies

Jackie Robinson, the outstanding Brooklyn Dodgers second baseman who broke baseball's color barrier and opened the gates for blacks to enter into the major leagues, died October 24 at Stamford, Conn. He was 53.

Robinson, nearly blind from diabetes, suffered an early morning heart attack at his home and was pronounced dead upon arrival at the hospital.

In 1947, he made his debut as baseball's first modern-era black. It was not easy. He endured racial slurs from players and fans, as well as rough play, beanballs and a microscopic analysis of his every move. He took it all silently and paved the way for other blacks to join in his crusade for equality.

Robinson, a career .311 hitter, quickly developed into one of the game's great stars. A daring baserunner and excellent fielder, he also was the catalyst for a Dodger team that won six National League pennants and one World Series in his 10 seasons. Robinson won a batting championship and was named the circuit's Most Valuable Player in 1949.

Pirate slugger dies

Pittsburgh outfielder Roberto Clemente, a four-time National League batting champion and 12-time All-Star, died December 31 when a cargo plane carrying relief supplies to earthquake victims in Nicaragua crashed in the ocean moments after takeoff from San Juan International Airport.

Clemente, the most popular sports figure in the history of his native Puerto Rico, was the leader of his country's efforts to help Nicaraguan earthquake victims. He was aboard the flight because he wanted to make sure the supplies would get to those who needed them most. The DC-7, carrying a crew of three and one other passenger, crashed about a mile and a half off the coast in 100 feet of water.

The 38-year-old Clemente, a sure-bet Hall of Famer, had become the 11th major leaguer to collect 3,000 hits when he doubled off New York's Jon Matlack on September 30. His .317 career average was highest among active players and he led the Pirates to World Series championships in 1960 and '71. The 18-year veteran also was an excellent right fielder with a powerful throwing arm.

Pittsburgh right fielder Roberto Clemente joined baseball's exclusive 3,000-hit club before the tragic off-season plane crash that claimed his life.

★1973★

Historic pact okayed

Major league players and owners approved an historic three-year Basic Agreement February 25 that provides for binding arbitration in salary disputes and modifies the controversial reserve clause with a trade veto option for 10-year veterans.

Terms were revealed during a press conference that announced a March 1 opening of spring training camps. The owners, fearful of a players' strike, had refused to begin spring drills until a new Basic Agreement was reached.

Although a number of improvements were made in player benefits, Major League Players Association executive director Marvin Miller seemed especially pleased with the salary arbitration approval. In the past, a player dissatisfied with a contract offer had no recourse. Now he can submit his demand to an impartial arbitrator who will compare it to the owner's offer and make a binding decision. Arbitration cases will be heard in an 11-day period from February 11-22.

The reserve clause, which binds a player to the team that holds his contract, was modified by the new "10 and 5" rule. A player with 10 or more years of major league service, the last five of which have been spent with one club, now can reject a trade if he so desires. Previously under the reserve system, players had only one alternative when traded — retirement.

" DUGOUT CHATTER "

"Casey once told us that he didn't mind you going out with your own roommate. But he didn't want four or five of us going out together because that way everybody would want to buy one round and by the end of the night we'd all be gassed."

Ed Kranepool

New York Mets first baseman-outfielder, on former Manager Casey Stengel.

A.L. uses first DH

The great designated hitter experiment, the most significant rule change in many years, became an American League reality April 6 when New York Yankee Ron Blomberg stepped to the plate with the bases loaded in the first inning and drew a walk off Boston's Luis Tiant in a season-opening game at Fenway Park.

So began a noble experiment that is sure to alter traditional strategy while hopefully producing more offense. The rule allows each A.L. team to replace weak-hitting pitchers in the lineup with hitters who will bat without playing the field. The A.L. voted unanimously at last year's winter meetings to give the rule a three-year test before deciding whether to adopt it permanently.

Blomberg collected one hit in three at-bats as baseball's pioneer designated hitter while Boston DH Orlando Cepeda went hitless in six at-bats, even though the Red Sox pounded the Yankees, 15-5.

Fireballer Nolan Ryan, the California Angels' no-hit pitching machine.

Nolan Ryan matches no-hit feat

California fireballer Nolan Ryan joined a select circle of pitchers July 15 when he became the fourth major leaguer to throw two no-hitters in one season. The right-handed strikeout artist matched his career high by fanning 17 Tigers while beating Detroit, 6-0, before 41,411 fans at Tiger Stadium.

The 26-year-old allowed four baserunners, all on walks, in duplicating his no-hit effort of May 15 for the amazing Texan against Kansas City. Ryan struck out 12 Royals and walked only three in that 3-0 masterpiece.

Of the 10 Tigers who made contact, only Gates Brown came close to getting a hit. The big designated hitter smashed a one-out line drive that was snared by leaping shortstop Rudi Meoli in the ninth. Ryan, who retired the last 10 Tigers he faced while raising his record to 11-11, recorded his 17th and last strikeout with one out in the eighth, falling one short of the one-game American League record and two short of the major league mark. He fanned the side in the second, fourth and seventh innings.

Only Cincinnati's Johnny Vander Meer (1938), New York Yankee Allie Reynolds (1951) and Detroit's Virgil Trucks (1952) had previously thrown two no-hitters in one season.

Yankee Ron Blomberg, baseball's pioneer designated hitter.

Aaron reaches 700

Atlanta slugger Hank Aaron mounted a baseball pedestal occupied only by the immortal Babe Ruth July 21 when he connected for career home run No. 700 off Philadelphia lefthander Ken Brett during a game at Fulton County Stadium.

The 39-year-old veteran, entering the home stretch in his chase of Ruth's ghost, belted a towering 400-foot drive into the left-center field bleachers with a man aboard in the third inning. The home run gave the Braves a 4-2 lead, but the Phillies roared back to claim an 8-4 victory.

The ball was retrieved by 18-year-old Atlantan Robert Winborne, who gave it to Aaron after the game and received 700 silver dollars for his effort.

The homer pulls Aaron to within 14 of Ruth's record. Aaron was 5 months old in 1934 when the Babe connected for No. 700.

Atlanta's Hank Aaron touches home plate as the Fulton County Stadium scoreboard salutes his 700th career home run.

CAUGHT ON THE FLY

JANUARY

A 17-person group headed by Cleveland shipbuilder George Steinbrenner purchased the New York Yankees from the Columbia Broadcasting System for a surprisingly low $10 million.

MARCH

Hall of Famers Frank Frisch and George Sisler, outstanding players who spent their best seasons in St. Louis with the Cardinals and Browns, respectively, in the 1920s and '30s, died. Frisch was 74 and Sisler 80.

Denny McLain, on top of the baseball world only five years ago when he won 31 games for Detroit, was released by the Atlanta Braves, ending his stormy big-league career two days before his 29th birthday.

Mays says goodbye

The great Willie Mays, only a shell of his former self on the field, said a tearful farewell September 25 when he was honored by a sell-out crowd at Shea Stadium and saluted by old teammates, former rivals and various sports and government dignitaries.

After being lavished with costly gifts and praised by numerous speakers in ceremonies before the New York Mets-Montreal Expos game, Mays took the microphone and fought back the tears.

"In my heart, I am a sad man," he told the New York fans. "Just to hear you cheer like this for me and not to be able to do anything about it makes me a very sad man. This is my farewell. You don't know what is going on inside of me tonight."

The 42-year-old long-time New York and San Francisco Giants star, batting .211 with six home runs, had announced his retirement five days earlier, saying he no longer could handle the grind. He leaves after 22 big-league seasons with a career .302 average and 660 home runs, third on the all-time list behind Babe Ruth and Hank Aaron.

The Mets, in hot pursuit of a National League East Division title, beat the Expos, 2-1.

" DUGOUT CHATTER "

"Sex is great and playing the trumpet is out of sight, but there's no greater thrill than hitting a baseball."

Carmen Fanzone

Chicago Cubs utility man and off-season musician

N.L. continues hex

Home runs by Cincinnati's Johnny Bench, San Francisco's Bobby Bonds and Los Angeles' Willie Davis accounted for five runs and lifted the National League to an easy 7-1 All-Star Game victory over the American League July 24 at Kansas City's spectacular new Royals Stadium.

With a 12-story crown-shaped scoreboard blinking out information and colorful fountains gushing beyond the outfield walls, the Nationals pounded out their 10th victory in the last 11 years and increased their All-Star advantage to 25-18-1. After the A.L. touched St. Louis righthander Rick Wise for its only run in the second inning on a double by Oakland's Reggie Jackson and a single by Royals center fielder Amos Otis, it was all National League.

Houston's Cesar Cedeno and Atlanta's Hank Aaron singled home third-inning runs off Minnesota's Bert Blyleven and then the power display began. Bench hit a solo shot in the fourth, Bonds connected with a man aboard in the fifth and Davis belted a two-run blast in the sixth.

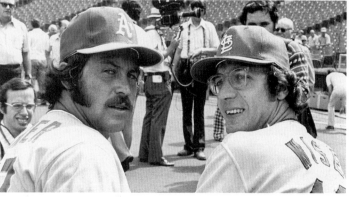

All-Star Game starting pitchers Catfish Hunter of Oakland and Rick Wise of St. Louis.

★1973★

Mets finally 'believe'

Tom Seaver and Tug McGraw combined on a seven-hitter and the New York Mets completed their "You gotta believe" pennant drive October 10 with a 7-2 victory over Cincinnati in the fifth game of the National League Championship Series.

The triumph before 50,323 fans at Shea Stadium concluded one of the most unusual pennant races in history and gave the once-lowly Mets their second pennant in five years. Nothing came easily as the Mets survived a wild sprint to the finish in the N.L. East Division race and a Game 3 Championship Series brawl to earn a World Series date against Oakland.

The New Yorkers had to win 23 of their final 32 regular-season games to capture the division title with a mediocre 82-79 record and the lowest winning percentage (.509) ever posted by a first-place team. They leapfrogged five contenders after sitting in last place as late as August 30.

Taking McGraw's "You gotta believe" slogan to heart, Yogi Berra's Mets sprinted through the final weeks as the other contenders stumbled home. When the second game of an October 1 doubleheader was canceled because of rain after the Mets had clinched the division with a 6-4 first-game victory over Chicago, the results were official. The Mets were 82-79, second-place St. Louis was 81-81, Pittsburgh 80-82, Montreal 79-83 and Chicago 77-84. St. Louis and Pittsburgh had been eliminated on the final day, Chicago and Montreal the day before.

After losing the first game of the NLCS to the Reds, 2-1, New York fought back behind Jon Matlack's two-hit pitching for a 5-0 victory and then coasted in a Game 3 brawlathon, 9-2. The main event in that contest was a shoving match between Cincinnati's Pete Rose and New York's Bud Harrelson after Rose slid hard into the shortstop while breaking up a ninth-inning double play.

After both benches had emptied and peace had been restored, Rose was greeted by flying bottles, garbage and other debris as he returned to his left-field position. Cincinnati Manager Sparky Anderson pulled his team as a delegation of New York Mets went out to plead for peace. The fans listened and the game was completed.

The Reds stormed back to win the next day, 2-1, on a 12th-inning homer by Rose, but the Mets completed their improbable journey with their Game 5 victory.

Cincinnati's Pete Rose and the Mets' Bud Harrelson (3) exchange shoves and punches during a Game 3 Championship Series incident at New York.

Right: New York's Ed Kranepool gets a pennant-winning champagne bath from relief ace Tug McGraw.

Ryan strikes out 383

California Angels fireballer Nolan Ryan stepped past Sandy Koufax in the record books September 28 when he struck out 16 Minnesota Twins in an 11-inning contest and raised his season strikeout count to 383, one more than the former Dodger great fanned in 1965.

Ryan, making his final start of the year, needed 15 strikeouts to catch Koufax. He matched the record in the eighth inning when he fanned Steve Brye, but the tie-breaker did not come easily. He failed in both the ninth and 10th innings before finally getting Rich Reese in the 11th, the same inning the Angels broke a 4-4 deadlock and handed Ryan his 21st victory.

The 26-year-old Texan was rewarded with a four-minute ovation from appreciative fans at Anaheim Stadium as the center-field scoreboard proclaimed the record-breaking news.

CAUGHT ON THE FLY

OCTOBER
Detroit bullpen ace John Hiller recorded 38 saves, a one-season major league record.

NOVEMBER
New York Mets ace Tom Seaver, 19-10 with a 2.08 ERA, became the National League's third two-time Cy Young Award winner.

DECEMBER
Chicago Cubs third baseman Ron Santo, part of a pending deal with the California Angels, became the first player to refuse a trade under the new "10 and 5" adjustment to the reserve rule.

SEASON LEADERS

	American League		National League	
Avg.	Rod Carew, Min.	.350	Pete Rose, Cin.	.338
HR	Reggie Jackson, Oak.	32	Willie Stargell, Pit.	44
RBI	Reggie Jackson, Oak.	117	Willie Stargell, Pit.	119
SB	Tommy Harper, Bos.	54	Lou Brock. St. L.	70
W-L Pct.	Catfish Hunter, Oak.	21-5, .808	Tommy John, L.A.	16-7, .696
ERA	Jim Palmer, Bal.	2.40	Tom Seaver, N.Y.	2.08
SO	Nolan Ryan, Cal.	383	Tom Seaver, N.Y.	251

Hunter steadies staggering A's in ALCS

Catfish Hunter allowed five hits and Oakland steadied its rocking ship October 11 with a 3-0 fifth-game Championship Series victory over Baltimore that secured the Athletics' second straight American League pennant.

Hunter's shutout before a disappointing crowd of 24,265 fans at the Oakland Coliseum provided a shot in the arm for the staggering A's, who had blown a 4-0 Game 4 lead while suffering a Series-tying 5-4 loss. Oakland had knocked out Jim Palmer early and appeared to be coasting when lightning struck Vida Blue in the seventh. A walk, two singles and Andy Etchebarren's three-run homer tied the score and Bobby Grich won the game for the Orioles with a solo eighth-inning shot off relief ace Rollie Fingers.

But Hunter was in control the next day and he got all the support he needed on run-scoring hits by Joe Rudi, Jesus Alou and Vic Davalillo. Hunter also pitched the A's to a 6-3 Game 2 victory that snapped Baltimore's four-year Championship Series winning streak at 10 games.

The pivotal contest was a Game 3 pitching duel between Oakland's Ken Holtzman and Baltimore's Mike Cuellar. It was decided in the 11th inning when shortstop Bert Campaneris hit a home run, giving Oakland its fourth hit and a 2-1 victory.

" DUGOUT CHATTER "

"I don't say the umpiring is bad in our league, but we'd be better off playing on the honor system."

Dick Williams
Oakland manager

WORLD SERIES REPORT

A'S OVERPOWER METS

Reggie Jackson and Bert Campaneris hit home runs to support the combined eight-hit pitching of Ken Holtzman, Rollie Fingers and Darold Knowles and lift the Athletics to a 5-2 World Series-clinching victory over the New York Mets October 21 at the Oakland Coliseum.

The seventh-game victory gave Oakland its second straight championship and dashed the Mets' hopes for an unlikely triumph in a season of surprises.

The A's got a World Series jump when Holtzman, Fingers and Knowles combined in a 2-1 opening-game victory. But New York fought back to win a wild four-hour, 13-minute second-game marathon, 10-7, in 12 innings. Aiding the Mets' four-run 12th-inning outburst were two errors by second baseman Mike Andrews, who quickly became the center of a Series storm.

Oakland Owner Charles O. Finley, never known for his tact, announced the next day that he was deactivating Andrews, in effect "firing" him. But when he tried to place the 30-year-old on the disabled list, citing a shoulder injury, Commissioner Bowie Kuhn stepped in and said no.

When the storm abated, the A's reclaimed the advantage with a 3-2 Game 3 victory at Shea Stadium. Campaneris' 11th-inning single decided the contest, which featured a 12-strikeout performance by New York's Tom Seaver. But the Mets struck back to win the next two games. Jon Matlack allowed three hits in eight innings en route to a 6-1 victory and Jerry Koosman surrendered three hits in 6⅓ innings of a 2-0 triumph. Rusty Staub homered and drove in five runs in Game 4.

The Mets were on the brink of an upset, but the A's calmly grabbed a 3-1 Game 6 victory and then used the long ball to finish off the New Yorkers. Oakland Manager Dick Williams, apparently fed up with Finley's interference, announced his resignation after Game 7.

Oakland second baseman Mike Andrews makes one of his two critical errors in Game 2 of the World Series against the New York Mets.

Oakland's Reggie Jackson punctuates his Game 7 World Series home run with an emphatic stomp on the plate.

Game 1	Oakland	2	New York	1
Game 2	New York	10	Oakland	7
Game 3	Oakland	3	New York	2
Game 4	New York	6	Oakland	1
Game 5	New York	2	Oakland	0
Game 6	Oakland	3	New York	1
Game 7	Oakland	5	New York	2

Aaron catches Ruth

Hank Aaron, answering the pressure of an unprecedented media blitz and an early season controversy involving Commissioner Bowie Kuhn, belted career home run No. 715 April 8 in his first game of the season at Atlanta-Fulton County Stadium and staked his claim as the greatest slugger in baseball history.

The record-setting blast came on a one-ball pitch from Los Angeles lefthander Al Downing in the fourth inning of a game against the Dodgers. Aaron, who had walked on his first at-bat, deposited a fastball into the Braves' left-center field bullpen with teammate Darrell Evans on base, tying the game at 3-3. As skyrockets arched over the stadium jammed with 53,775 persons, he calmly circled the bases with an escort from two over-exuberant fans and was greeted at the plate by a monster hug from his elderly mother. The game was held up for 10 minutes while fans and officials showered their praise on the new home run champion.

The historic homer, which vaulted Aaron past former New York Yankee great Babe Ruth on the all-time charts, was captured by national television cameras after a much-ballyhooed preseason media blitz that focused on the Hammer's chase of baseball's most cherished record. Aaron, whose career spans 20 seasons with the Braves in Milwaukee and Atlanta, had finished the 1973 campaign one homer short of the Bambino's career mark.

But even before Atlanta's April 4 season-opening game at Cincinnati, controversy began to swirl around Aaron and his chase for the record. First the Braves announced that their 40-year-old slugger would sit out the three-game series at Riverfront Stadium so he could begin his record assault at home. But Kuhn took exception to that strategy and issued a terse statement ordering the Braves to start Aaron in at least two of the Cincinnati contests — or face serious consequences. The Braves obliged, and Aaron showed the class that has punctuated his outstanding career.

On his first swing of the season against Reds starter Jack Billingham, Aaron rocketed a three-run homer that tied the record many had labeled unapproachable. He was swarmed by happy teammates and went to his family's box for a kiss from his wife.

Aaron failed to hit another homer in that game, sat out the Braves' second contest in Cincinnati and went hitless in the third, setting the stage for his royal homecoming.

Hank Aaron, baseball's new home run king, displays the ball he hit for milestone blast No. 715.

Right: *Hank Aaron gets a record-breaking hug from his mother.*

Arbitration begins

Minnesota righthander Dick Woodson, a 10-8 performer with the Twins in 1973 and a 32-29 pitcher in four major league seasons, made history February 11 when he became the first big leaguer to have his contract salary determined by baseball's new binding arbitration procedure.

Woodson's demand for a $29,000 contract and the Twins' offer of $23,000 were submitted to Harry H. Platt, a Detroit lawyer and labor arbitrator, in a session that lasted more than four hours. Platt, forced to choose one figure or the other without compromise, decided in Woodson's favor.

Woodson was one of 48 major leaguers who filed for arbitration before the deadline. All players and owners will plead their cases and submit their proposals to impartial third parties by February 22, although negotiations can continue right up to the time of the hearing. The process, part of the new Basic Agreement negotiated last year, gives players an alternative to costly holdouts and owners a means of keeping player demands reasonable.

CAUGHT ON THE FLY

JANUARY
Lee MacPhail was selected new American League president when Joe Cronin announced his retirement.

JUNE
Kansas City righthander Steve Busby became the first pitcher to throw no-hitters in each of his first two complete major league seasons when he stopped Milwaukee, 2-0, at County Stadium.

JULY
St. Louis righthander Bob Gibson joined former Washington great Walter Johnson as the only members of baseball's 3,000-strikeout club when he fanned Cincinnati's Cesar Geronimo during a game at Busch Stadium.

SEPTEMBER
California fireballer Nolan Ryan threw the third no-hitter of his career, stopping the Minnesota Twins, 4-0, at Anaheim Stadium.

Ryan strikes out 19, ties one-game record

California Angels righthander Nolan Ryan, picking on his favorite Boston patsies, tied the major league record for strikeouts in a single game August 12 when he fanned 19 Red Sox in a 4-2 victory at Anaheim Stadium.

The 6-foot-2 Texan walked two and allowed seven hits in his regulation performance that matched the nine-inning strikeout efforts of St. Louis' Steve Carlton (1969 against New York) and the Mets' Tom Seaver (1970 against San Diego) while breaking the 36-year-old American League record of 18 held by former Cleveland great Bob Feller. Ryan had struck out 19 Red Sox in a June 14 outing earlier this year, but he needed 13 innings to do it.

Ryan, whose fastball has been clocked in excess of 100 miles per hour, increased his major league-leading strikeout total to 260 while earning his 15th victory of the season.

The ball tells the story of Nolan Ryan's record-tying strikeout performance against the Boston Red Sox.

SEASON LEADERS

	American League		National League	
Avg.	Rod Carew, Min.	.364	Ralph Garr, Atl.	.353
HR	Dick Allen, Chi.	32	Mike Schmidt, Phi.	36
RBI	Jeff Burroughs, Tex.	118	Johnny Bench, Cin.	129
SB	Bill North, Oak.	54	Lou Brock, St. L.	118
W-L Pct.	Mike Cuellar, Bal. 22-10,	.688	Andy Messersmith, L.A.	20-6, .769
ERA	Catfish Hunter, Oak.	2.49	Buzz Capra, Atl.	2.28
SO	Nolan Ryan, Cal.	367	Steve Carlton, Phi.	240

O's streak to title

When Milwaukee's George Scott stroked a 10th-inning single to give the Brewers a 3-2 victory over New York October 1 at County Stadium, Baltimore clinched the American League East Division championship, ending one of the wildest races in years.

The three-team battle officially concluded on the second-to-last day of the season when the Yankees fell to the Brewers and Baltimore recorded a 7-6 victory in Detroit. But it technically was decided during a torrid 10-game Oriole winning streak that started August 29 at Texas and launched the Orioles on a season-ending 28-6 run. That produced a final two-game margin over New York and a seven-game advantage over late-fading Boston.

Baltimore, struggling at two games under .500, trailed the Red Sox by eight games and New York by one on the morning of August 29. But a 6-2 victory over the Rangers and a three-game sweep of Kansas City preceded an amazing run of five consecutive shutouts and a team-record 54 straight scoreless innings turned in by Ross Grimsley, Mike Cuellar, Jim Palmer and Dave McNally.

While the Orioles were sprinting home, Boston was suffering through an 8-20 stretch and the Yankees were doing a little sprinting of their own — a closing 29-12 blitz that came up just short. The Orioles took a major step toward their second straight title when they swept a three-game series at New York in mid-September.

" DUGOUT CHATTER "

"Anxiety is the edge I have on the pitcher and the catcher. I know that when I'm on base, they're filled with anxiety, and that gives me an edge."

Lou Brock

St. Louis basestealing king

Brock steals show

St. Louis outfielder Lou Brock burst into the record books September 10 when he swiped two bases in a game against Philadelphia and broke the one-season steal mark set 12 years ago by former Dodger Maury Wills.

The 35-year-old Brock singled in the first inning off Phillies starter Dick Ruthven and immediately set sail for second and his record-tying 104th steal. When he singled again in the seventh, 27,285 fans at Busch Stadium buzzed with anticipation.

They didn't have to wait long. After one pitch and two pickoff attempts, Brock took off again and catcher Bob Boone's throw was late. Steal No. 105 was greeted by confetti, firecrackers and a thundering ovation as players from both teams crowded around second base.

Brock, whose previous one-season stolen base high was 74 in 1966, was honored with an 11-minute ceremony. The two steals also made him the top National League career basestealer with 740, two more than Max Carey's former mark.

Brock went on to extend his single-season record to 118.

Single-season basestealing champion Lou Brock (left) with Hall of Famer Cool Papa Bell.

★1974★

OCTOBER-DECEMBER

Another barrier falls

The Cleveland Indians broke another baseball color barrier October 3 when they named 39-year-old Frank Robinson, a career 574-home run hitter, to succeed Ken Aspromonte as the team's 28th manager and ninth player-manager.

Robinson, who signed a one-year contract for $175,000, takes over in Cleveland 27 years after Jackie Robinson made his debut as baseball's first black player with the Brooklyn Dodgers. His appointment was announced at a crowded news conference in Municipal Stadium by the Indians' General Manager Phil

Seghi, who also read a congratulatory message from U.S. President Gerald Ford.

Robinson, who ranks fourth on the all-time homer charts, has posted a .295 average, 2,900 hits and 1,778 RBIs over 19 major league seasons. He takes over an Indians team that finished 77-85 last season, good for fourth place in the American League East Division. Cleveland picked up the two-time Most Valuable Player from California in September and used him mostly as a designated hitter, a role he probably will fill again next season as baseball's first player-manager since 1959.

Cleveland officials introduce Frank Robinson (right) as baseball's first black manager.

" DUGOUT CHATTER "

"When you play this game for 10 years, you get to bat 7,000 times or so. You get 2,000 hits and that's .286. And you know what that means? Why, you've gone 0 for 5,000."

Reggie Jackson

Oakland slugger

WORLD SERIES REPORT

A TRIFECTA

Oakland left fielder Joe Rudi belted a seventh-inning home run off iron man Los Angeles reliever Mike Marshall October 17 and Rollie Fingers made it stand up for a 3-2 victory that wrapped up the A's third straight World Series championship.

The Game 5 battle at the Oakland Coliseum was tied 2-2 entering the bottom of the seventh inning when, before Marshall could make his first pitch, unruly fans threw debris on the field, forcing a 15-minute interruption of play. When Marshall finally made his first delivery, Rudi whacked it out of the park.

The victory culminated a wild season of fighting, feuding and bickering for the A's, who somehow were able to leave their problems in the clubhouse when play began. Those problems ranged from fisticuffs — Reggie Jackson versus Bill North, Fingers versus Blue Moon Odom — to bickering among players and a collective animosity toward Owner Charles O. Finley. Catfish Hunter was on record as saying he would attempt to declare himself a free agent

after the Series unless Finley paid him the back salary he contended he had coming.

But on the field, the A's were relentless. Under the leadership of Alvin Dark, they won the American League West Division by a comfortable five games, disposed of Baltimore in a four-game Championship Series and jumped ahead in the fall classic with a 3-2 opening-game victory at Los Angeles.

After the Dodgers had evened matters, 3-2, on the pitching of Don Sutton and a two-run homer by catcher Joe Ferguson, Oakland posted 3-2 and 5-2 victories to set up the fifth-game clincher. The highlight of the Game 4 victory was a home run by winning pitcher Ken Holtzman, who had not batted during the regular season because of the designated hitter rule. Holtzman also had doubled in Game 1.

The loss brought an unhappy end to the Dodgers' 102-win regular season that was followed by a four-game waltz past Pittsburgh in the Championship Series.

Game 1	Oakland	3	Los Angeles	2
Game 2	Los Angeles	3	Oakland	2
Game 3	Oakland	3	Los Angeles	2
Game 4	Oakland	5	Los Angeles	2
Game 5	Oakland	3	Los Angeles	2

Oakland's Reggie Jackson winces under a shower of shaving cream and beer after the A's third straight World Series championship.

" DUGOUT CHATTER "

"Actually, my control wasn't that bad. I was just missing with pitches."

Harry Parker

New York Mets pitcher, after walking nine Padres in a game

"Some teams never win. They've got four or five guys who never care about anything. They don't want the grind of the full six months. As soon as things start to go bad, they crack and just go for themselves. Talent is one thing. Being able to go from spring to October is another."

Sparky Anderson

Cincinnati manager

Braves trade Aaron

The Atlanta Braves, honoring a request from their venerable slugger, traded Hank Aaron to the Milwaukee Brewers November 2, sending baseball's home run king back to the city where he started his career in 1954.

Aaron, who will turn 41 in February, asked to be dealt to the American League team so he could continue his career as a designated hitter without the strain of having to play in the outfield. Atlanta worked out a deal with the Brewers for outfielder Dave May and a player to be named later.

Aaron will leave Atlanta after nine seasons and return to the city where he hit his first 398 homers as a member of the Milwaukee Braves. He also has amassed 3,600 hits and 2,202 RBIs while compiling a lifetime average of .310. He became baseball's all-time home run king earlier this year when he passed Babe Ruth's lifetime mark of 714.

Relief ace honored

Strong-minded and rubber-armed Mike Marshall overcame his stormy relations with the press and entered the record books November 6 as the first relief pitcher ever to win baseball's coveted Cy Young Award.

The 31-year-old Los Angeles Dodger bullpen ace easily outdistanced teammate Andy Messersmith, a 20-6 performer last season, in a vote that was expected to be much closer.

While Marshall would never win a baseball popularity poll, his pitching numbers were too incredible to overlook. The big righthander appeared in a major league-record 106 games, 14 more than his own previous mark, and worked a record 208 innings in relief. At one point in late June and early July, he appeared in a record 14 straight contests and he finished the campaign with 15 victories and 21 saves.

After being informed of the award, Marshall, true to form, said he will wait until March to decide whether he will continue his career in baseball or check out other pursuits.

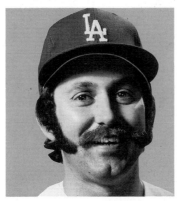

Los Angeles iron man and Cy Young winner Mike Marshall.

Yanks land Catfish

The New York Yankees concluded the most celebrated fishing expedition in American sports history with a New Year's Eve announcement that they had landed former Oakland A's pitching ace Catfish Hunter and signed him to a five-year contract calling for an estimated $3.75 million.

The 28-year-old righthander, winner of 88 games over the last four seasons and the ace of a staff that led Oakland to the last three World Series championships, became the object of an unprecedented bidding war when arbitrator Peter Seitz, agreeing with Hunter's breach of contract charge against A's Owner Charles O. Finley, declared him a free agent on December 13.

The race to sign baseball's top pitcher began in the law offices of Cherry, Cherry and Flythe in Ahoskie, N.C., near Hunter's home town. Numerous team officials paraded into the city and made their lucrative offers to the most attractive free agent in baseball history.

The Yankees landed a Catfish who finished the 1974 season 25-12 and captured the American League Cy Young Award.

Members of the Yankee delegation introduce free-agent signee Catfish Hunter to the New York media.

CAUGHT ON THE FLY

OCTOBER

Detroit right fielder Al Kaline, who became baseball's 12th 3,000-hit man when he doubled off Orioles lefty Dave McNally in September, concluded his 22-year career with 3,007 hits.

The incomparable Nolan Ryan fanned 367 batters and finished as the major league leader in strikeouts for the third straight year.

Hall of Fame outfielder Sam Rice, who batted .322 in an outstanding career with Washington and Cleveland from 1915 to '34, died in Rossmor, Md., at age 84.

NOVEMBER

Commissioner Bowie Kuhn handed a two-year suspension to George Steinbrenner after the New York Yankee owner was convicted in federal court of making illegal corporate contributions to the Presidential campaign of Richard Nixon.

★1975★

Ryan adds to resume

California's Nolan Ryan, who had tied Sandy Koufax's major league record of four career no-hitters five days earlier, came within 10 outs of adding another milestone to his impressive resume June 6 when he shut out Milwaukee, 6-0, on two hits.

Ryan was coasting in pursuit of his second consecutive no-hitter when 41-year-old Hank Aaron grounded a sharp single up the middle with two out in the sixth inning. Ryan allowed only an eighth-inning single to Bill Sharp the rest of the way in falling short of Johnny Vander Meer's 1938 consecutive no-hit feat for Cincinnati.

Ryan had thrown his fourth no-hitter June 1, defeating Baltimore, 1-0. It was a typical Ryan effort — nine strikeouts and four walks without much fanfare. When the 28-year-old righthander fanned Bobby Grich for the final out, he casually shook hands with Angels third baseman Dave Chalk, hugged catcher Ellie Rodriguez and nonchalantly strolled to the dugout. There was nothing nonchalant about the ovation he received from 18,492 fans at Anaheim Stadium.

The victory was Ryan's ninth of the season and 100th in a career that started with the New York Mets in 1966. Ryan had pitched two no-hitters in 1973 and one last year.

Robinson's big day

Frank Robinson, the first black manager in baseball history, got his new career off to a rousing start April 8 when he guided the Cleveland Indians to a 5-3 Opening Day victory over New York before a history-witnessing crowd of 56,204 at Cleveland's Municipal Stadium.

Not only did Robinson pull the managerial strings that produced a victory, he also contributed a dramatic home run while filling his part-time role as designated hitter. Robinson's 575th career homer came off Yankee starter Doc Medich with one out in the first inning. It stirred up the crowd and evoked a celebration in the Indians' dugout.

Fittingly, Rachel Robinson, the widow of Jackie Robinson, the man who broke the color barrier as a player in 1947 for Brooklyn, was accorded the honor of throwing out the historic first pitch.

Photographers surround Frank Robinson, baseball's first black manager, as he kneels in the on-deck circle during his historic debut.

Don Wilson's suicide

Houston righthander Don Wilson, a 104-game winner and author of two no-hitters in nine major league seasons, died January 5 of carbon monoxide poisoning in the garage of his Houston home, an apparent suicide victim. The 29-year-old Wilson's 5-year-old son also died and his 9-year-old daughter was rushed to the hospital in a coma.

Wilson was found in the closed garage on the passenger side of his 1972 Thunderbird with the ignition on and the car's gasoline gauge reading empty. He was sitting upright with this head back and legs crossed, a pack of cigarettes in front of him on the dashboard.

The children were found in their upstairs bedrooms, located over the adjoining garage. Wilson's wife, Bernice, was hospitalized in fair condition. She called police when she heard the car motor running and was unable to wake up her children.

There was no apparent reason for the tragedy. Wilson had completed the 1974 campaign with an 11-13 record and 3.07 earned-run average for the 81-81 Astros.

Righthander Don Wilson during his pitching days with Houston.

CAUGHT ON THE FLY

MAY

Oakland Owner Charles O. Finley ended an experiment when he released pinch-running specialist Herb Washington, a world-class sprinter who stole 31 bases in 48 attempts without ever appearing at the plate.

Lefty Grove, a career 300-game winner rated by many as the greatest lefthander of all time, died in Norwalk, O., at age 75.

Milwaukee's Hank Aaron drove in a pair of runs in a 17-3 victory over Detroit, passing Babe Ruth and moving into first place on the all-time RBI list with 2,211.

JULY

Commissioner Bowie Kuhn was elected to a new seven-year term during baseball's summer meetings in Milwaukee.

"DUGOUT CHATTER"

"If they check the upper deck, they might find Patty Hearst hiding out."

Bobby Murcer

San Francisco outfielder, on the meager crowds at Candlestick Park

Lynn goes on a tear

Boston rookie Fred Lynn had a day to remember June 18 at Detroit's Tiger Stadium. The sweet-swinging center fielder collected three home runs, a triple and a single while driving in 10 runs, one short of the American League record set 39 years ago by New York's Tony Lazzeri.

It didn't take long for the 23-year-old to get in gear against Detroit starter Joe Coleman. Lynn belted a two-run homer in the first inning and a three-run shot in the second off Coleman and a two-run triple in the third off Bob Reynolds. Lynn beat out an infield single in the eighth and completed his assault with a three-run homer off Tom Walker in the ninth. Final score: Boston 15, Detroit 1.

Lynn's RBI count was two short of the major league record set in 1924 by St. Louis' Jim Bottomley and his 16 total bases tied the A.L. mark. The 5-for-6 performance raised his average to .352 and he lifted his league-leading RBI count to 50.

Boston rookie Fred Lynn (center) is congratulated by Rick Burleson (left) and Carl Yastrzemski after one of his three home runs against Detroit.

Shea Stadium blast leaves fans in a fog

California righthander Nolan Ryan, who had allowed two hits over his last 18 innings, surrendered a two-run homer to New York's Chris Chambliss and all the Yankee runs in a 6-4 loss, but the real fireworks on this June 10 afternoon took place in the celebration that preceded the game.

The Yankees, temporarily using Shea Stadium while Yankee Stadium is being refurbished, had invited the 26th Army Band and its ceremonial gun battery from nearby Fort Hamilton to salute the U.S. Army's 200th birthday in pre-game festivities. The highlight was to be a 21-cannon salute from two 75-millimeter artillery pieces in the center-field area of the ballpark.

But the 37,793 fans, most of whom had come to watch Ryan pitch, got more than they had bargained for. When the cannons blasted their salutes, smoke filled the stadium and glass splintered everywhere. When the smoke cleared, all eyes focused on the center-field fence, which was missing three panels, and other areas of the barrier that were covered with black and white powder burns.

As it turned out, the cannons had been placed too close to the fence and reverberations from the blast caused the pieces to fall. No real damage was done, however, and the fence was repaired before the game began.

" DUGOUT CHATTER "

"It's easy to stay in the majors for 7½ years when you hit .300. But when you hit .216 like me, it's really an accomplishment."

Joe Lahoud
California outfielder

N.L. adds to its lead

Chicago's Bill Madlock drilled a two-run, ninth-inning single to break a 3-3 deadlock and Cincinnati's Pete Rose added another run with a sacrifice fly as the National League defeated the American League, 6-3, for its 12th victory in 13 All-Star Games.

The July 15 classic at Milwaukee's County Stadium looked like a cakewalk for the National Leaguers, who jumped ahead in the second inning when Los Angeles Dodgers teammates Steve Garvey and Jim Wynn hit back-to-back homers and added to their lead in the third when St. Louis speedster Lou Brock singled, moved to second base on a balk, stole third and scored on a single by Cincinnati catcher

Secretary of State Henry Kissinger bites his tongue and delivers the ceremonial All-Star Game first pitch.

Johnny Bench.

But the A.L. fought their way back in the bottom of the sixth inning when Oakland's Joe Rudi and Gene Tenace singled and Boston's veteran outfielder Carl Yastrzemski tied the score with a long homer.

The tie held until the ninth, when St. Louis' Reggie Smith singled, Pittsburgh's Al Oliver doubled and Philadelphia shortstop Larry Bowa was hit by a Goose Gossage pitch, loading the bases and setting the stage for Madlock.

★1975★

" DUGOUT CHATTER "

"He's a good manager. He might be a little selfish about some of the things he does and he may think he knows more about baseball than anybody else, but it wouldn't surprise me if he was right."

Casey Stengel

Former New York Yankee manager on current Yankee Manager Billy Martin

Four A's combine on record no-hitter

Reggie Jackson belted two home runs against California September 28, but his offensive thunder was stolen by four A's hurlers who combined for the first multi-pitcher no-hit victory in baseball history — a 5-0 decision over the Angels on the final day of the regular season at the Oakland Coliseum.

Vida Blue pitched five innings of no-hit ball as a tuneup for the upcoming American League Championship Series against Boston and Glenn Abbott (1), Paul Lindblad (1) and Rollie Fingers (2) followed with four perfect frames in the milestone contest. Only two walks by Blue, who lifted his record to 22-11, separated the A's foursome from perfection.

It marked the first time that as many as four pitchers had combined on a no-hitter and the first time that a multi-pitcher no-hitter had resulted in a victory. The last such contest occurred in 1967 when Baltimore's Steve Barber and Stu Miller combined to pitch a no-hitter against Detroit, only to drop a 2-1 decision.

Oakland relief ace Rollie Fingers (left) is congratulated by teammate Gene Tenace after completing the A's four-pitcher no-hitter.

Stennett gets 7 hits

Pittsburgh second baseman Rennie Stennett put on a stunning display September 16 when he became the first modern-era player to collect seven hits in a nine-inning game, and the Pirates made a little history of their own, pounding out a 22-0 victory at Chicago's Wrigley Field for the most lopsided shutout ever recorded.

Stennett led a 24-hit Pittsburgh barrage with four singles, two doubles and a triple while scoring five times. He tied another record by collecting two hits in two different innings — the Pirates' nine-run first and six-run fifth. Every Pittsburgh player managed at least one hit and scored at least once, and Dave Parker homered and drove in five runs.

Stennett singled and doubled in the first, singled in the third, doubled and singled in the fifth, singled in the sixth and capped his big day with an eighth-inning triple, at which point he left for a pinch-runner. He raised his average from .278 to .287.

Rookie lefthander John Candelaria coasted to his eighth victory with seven shutout innings and Cubs starter Rick Reuschel left in the first inning after surrendering six hits and two walks while retiring only one batter.

Stennett's seven-hit outburst tied the all-time record set in 1892 by former Baltimore star Wilbert Robinson.

Pittsburgh's Rennie Stennett holds up seven fingers, signaling the modern record number of hits he got in a September outburst against Chicago.

SEASON LEADERS

	American League			National League	
Avg.	Rod Carew, Min.	.359		Bill Madlock, Chi.	.354
HR	Reggie Jackson, Oak.	36		Mike Schmidt, Phi.	38
	George Scott, Mil.	36			
RBI	George Scott, Mil.	109		Greg Luzinski, Phi.	120
SB	Mickey Rivers, Cal.	70		Dave Lopes, L.A.	77
W-L Pct.	Mike Torrez, Bal.	20-9, .690		Don Gullett, Cin.	15-4, .789
ERA	Jim Palmer, Bal.	2.09		Randy Jones, S.D.	2.24
SO	Frank Tanana, Cal.	269		Tom Seaver, N.Y.	243

CAUGHT ON THE FLY

AUGUST

Los Angeles second baseman Dave Lopes set a major league record with 38 consecutive successful stolen base attempts before being caught by Montreal catcher Gary Carter.

SEPTEMBER

Colorful Casey Stengel, a former major league outfielder and the man who guided the powerful New York Yankees to seven World Series championships from 1949 to '60, died in Glendale, Calif., at age 86.

NOVEMBER

Boston center fielder Fred Lynn became the first rookie to win a Most Valuable Player award when he was voted the A.L.'s top honor in a landslide victory over Kansas City's John Mayberry.

Seitz's ruling threatens reserve system

In a ruling that could topple baseball's reserve system, labor arbitrator Peter Seitz handed pitchers Andy Messersmith and Dave McNally their unqualified free agency December 23, giving them the right to sell their services to the highest bidder.

The landmark decision puts owners in a precarious position. Twice in the last half-century they have received favorable rulings from the Supreme Court on the system that binds an athlete to his team until he is traded. But more players are testing the question and Seitz's ruling is a clear-cut victory for the Major League Players' Association.

Management has two options. It can either go to court and challenge Seitz's decision, or it can modify the system through collective bargaining with the players. Ironically, the current Basic Agreement expires in eight days.

The 31-year-old Messersmith, a two-time 20-game winner during his eight-year career with California and Los Angeles, should prosper. He instigated the decision with a suit claiming he had completed his option year with the Dodgers and should be a free agent.

McNally, a 33-year-old former star lefthander for the Baltimore Orioles, retired last year midway through his first season with the Montreal Expos.

" DUGOUT CHATTER "

"Some people breed horses. We breed hitters."

Willie Stargell

Pirates outfielder, on the secret behind Pittsburgh's success

---

WORLD SERIES REPORT

REDS SURVIVE

Ken Griffey trotted home from third base on Joe Morgan's looping ninth-inning single October 22, giving the Cincinnati Reds a 4-3 victory in Game 7 of one of the most exciting World Series ever staged.

Morgan's clutch hit at Boston's Fenway Park capped a Reds comeback from a 3-0 final-game deficit and closed the books on one of the most spellbinding Series scripts ever written. After six incredible contests, it seemed only fitting that this fall classic should be decided in the final inning of the final game.

Both teams entered the Series on a high note, Boston having swept aside Oakland in the American League Championship Series and Cincinnati having done the same to Pittsburgh in the National League playoff. The heavyweights traded punches in the first four games, Boston recording a 6-0 win in the opener behind Luis Tiant and a 5-4 triumph in Game 4 and the Reds prevailing 3-2 and 6-5 in Games 2 and 3. Game 2 was decided on a two-run ninth-inning rally and Game 3 in the 10th.

After Tony Perez's two-homer outburst had helped the Reds regain the lead with a 6-2 fifth-game victory, Mother Nature interrupted play — for 72 hours. A drenching New England rain delayed Game 6 until October 21, but the wait would be worthwhile.

Everything was normal enough through 7½ innings as the Reds built a 6-3 lead and moved within six outs of a championship. But the fireworks started in the eighth when pinch-hitter Bernie Carbo tied the game with a clutch three-run homer.

Boston was on the edge of victory in the ninth, but the Reds escaped a bases-loaded, nobody-out jam and sent the game into extra innings. The Red Sox did some escaping of their own in the 11th when right fielder Dwight Evans made a leaping catch to rob Morgan of a home run.

After Boston reliever Rick Wise escaped a two-on, one-out situation in the top of the 12th, Red Sox catcher Carlton Fisk dramatically sent the Series to a decisive seventh game with a towering drive off the left-field foul pole.

Boston catcher Carlton Fisk makes a happy homecoming after belting a 12th-inning Game 6 home run to keep the Red Sox's World Series hopes alive against Cincinnati.

Game 1	Boston	6	Cincinnati	0
Game 2	Cincinnati	3	Boston	2
Game 3	Cincinnati	6	Boston	5
Game 4	Boston	5	Cincinnati	4
Game 5	Cincinnati	6	Boston	2
Game 6	Boston	7	Cincinnati	6
Game 7	Cincinnati	4	Boston	3

Commissioner Bowie Kuhn (left) with World Series-winning Manager Sparky Anderson of Cincinnati.

A 'lifetime contract'

Atlanta Owner Ted Turner, promising that Andy Messersmith will "never be traded" and "will be a Brave as long as I am," signed the former California Angel and Los Angeles Dodger righthander to a "lifetime contract" April 10 in San Diego.

Messersmith, who became a free agent four months ago on a landmark ruling by arbitrator Peter Seitz, signed a contract believed to be in the $1.75 million range for three years, with renewal clauses to be exercised as long as the 31-year-old Messer-

smith can pitch. Turner's statement that the two-time 20-game winner would never be traded contained more than a touch of irony.

Messersmith filed suit last year because his option had run out with the Dodgers and he did not think it right that he should be bound to one team forever. The Seitz ruling that supported his free-agency contention has been upheld twice in the courtroom.

Messersmith, a 19-game winner last year for the Dodgers, was in San Diego to talk to the Padres.

Schmidt blasts four

Philadelphia third baseman Mike Schmidt blasted a tie-breaking two-run homer in the 10th inning, his record-tying fourth of the game and fourth in a row, to give the Phillies a wild 18-16 victory over Chicago April 17 at windswept Wrigley Field.

Schmidt's homer barrage, which did not begin until the fifth inning, capped a Phillies' comeback from a 13-2 deficit and allowed him to become the 10th player in history and first in 15 years to collect four round-trip-

pers in one game. He is only the fourth player to hit four in succession in the same contest and the first modern-era National Leaguer to accomplish the feat.

After Rick Monday's two-homer, two-single barrage had helped Chicago to its early lead, Schmidt began blasting away. He hit a two-run homer in the fifth, a solo shot in the seventh, a three-run blast in the eighth and his game-winner in the 10th. He finished with eight RBIs and also singled, giving him 17 total bases.

Philadelphia's Mike Schmidt watches the flight of his record-tying fourth home run during the 10th inning of a game at Wrigley Field.

A dramatic rescue

Chicago Cubs center fielder Rick Monday made the most dramatic catch of his 10-year major league career April 25 when he dashed into left field at Dodger Stadium and snatched an American flag away from two protestors who were trying to set it on fire.

The incident, which occurred before 25,167 Los Angeles fans in the fourth inning of a Sunday afternoon game, made national headlines and attracted an avalanche of praise. There were commendations from the Illinois legislature, Commissioner Bowie Kuhn, U.S. President Gerald Ford and the National League.

The Cubs set aside May 4 at Wrigley Field as Rick Monday Day.

"I saw the clowns (a man and a youth) come on the field and I thought they were out there just to prance around," Monday explained. "But they began spreading out this flag like it was a picnic blanket."

Then Monday noticed they were fumbling with a lighter and a can of fluid, so he swooped in and snatched away the flag as security officials chased down the protestors. Monday was greeted by a standing ovation and a message board citation, "Rick Monday . . . You made a great play."

Chicago outfielder Rick Monday reaches down to snatch an American flag from two protestors who were trying to set it afire.

CAUGHT ON THE FLY

JANUARY
Ted Turner, an internationally known yachtsman, purchased the Atlanta Braves in the name of Turner Communications for $12 million.

MAY
Yankee pitchers Ed Figueroa and Tippy Martinez shut out Detroit center fielder Ron LeFlore in four trips to the plate, ending his hitting streak at 30 games.

MAY
Hall of Fame outfielder Max Carey, who stole 738 bases in a 20-year career with Pittsburgh and Brooklyn from 1910 to '29, died in Miami Beach at age 86.

JUNE
A baseball oddity: A game at Houston's Astrodome was rained out when a torrential downpour flooded streets and made it difficult for people to get to the stadium.

Kuhn shocks Finley

Commissioner Bowie Kuhn, incurring the wrath of at least three team owners and Major League Players' Association director Marvin Miller, created a storm of controversy June 18 when he voided the blockbuster sale of three star players by Oakland A's Owner Charles O. Finley.

Calling his decision "in the best interests of baseball," Kuhn ordered New York to return left-handed pitcher Vida Blue to the A's and Boston to do likewise with left fielder Joe Rudi and relief ace Rollie Fingers. The Yankees had paid $1.5 million for Blue and the Red Sox had paid $1 million apiece for Rudi and Fingers.

Kuhn's action came after a hearing with the teams' executives and caught everybody by surprise. "While I am aware that there have been cash sales of player contracts in the past, there has been no instance in my judgment which had the potential for harm to our game," he said. Kuhn added that Finley's attempt to sell key players who are eligible for free agency at the end of the season would keep the once-powerful A's from competing effectively against other A.L. teams.

"I consider it sheer insanity," said Miller, who added that Kuhn had "single-handedly plunged baseball into the biggest mess it has ever seen."

Finley, who earlier traded pitcher Ken Holtzman and outfielder Reggie Jackson to Baltimore, said the commissioner "sounds like the village idiot." He promised a lawsuit against Kuhn and said he would not use the three players in Oakland games.

N.L. does it again

Cincinnati's George Foster and Houston's Cesar Cedeno hit home runs and combined for five RBIs July 13 as the National League continued its mastery of the American League with a 7-1 All-Star Game victory.

Most of the fireworks for this contest, played at Philadelphia's Veterans Stadium as part of the nation's Bicentennial celebration, were set off by N.L. players who battered four A.L. pitchers for 10 hits. Five N.L. hurlers limited the Americans to five safeties, the lone run coming on a fourth-inning homer by Boston's Fred Lynn.

By that time, the Nationals already were in control, courtesy of a two-run spurt against Detroit rookie Mark Fidrych in the first inning and Foster's two-run homer off New York's Catfish Hunter in the third. Any hopes for an A.L. comeback were erased in the eighth when Cincinnati's Ken Griffey singled home a run and Cedeno followed with a two-run homer.

San Diego starter Randy Jones picked up the win with three scoreless innings.

Cincinnati's Pete Rose jumps back to the base as Kansas City third baseman George Brett fields a grounder during the All-Star Game at Philadelphia.

" DUGOUT CHATTER "

"Either way, you wind up getting fired, so it doesn't make much difference."

Del Crandall

The former Milwaukee manager, on whether he would prefer to return as boss of an established team or an expansion club

Oakland's Joe Rudi was a member of the Boston Red Sox briefly in 1976, but never made it into a game.

Alston leaves Dodgers after 2,040 wins

Walter (Smokey) Alston, the only manager the Dodgers have known during their 19 seasons in Los Angeles, called it a career September 29 when he announced he would not return for the 1977 campaign. The 64-year-old Alston, who took over as Dodger manager in 1954 when the team still was located in Brooklyn, finishes with a career record of 2,040-1,613 over 23 seasons.

Alston, one of six managers to compile 2,000 career wins, guided the Dodgers to seven National League pennants and four World Series championships, three in Los Angeles. His greatest victory came in 1955, when he delivered Brooklyn its first Series championship after the city's frustrating string of seven losses. Alston had taken over from Chuck Dressen the year before.

The quiet Dodger leader was replaced two days after his retirement by third base coach Tom Lasorda.

YEAR OF THE BIRD

Fidrych's sensational season

"Nobody ever pulled them in the way he does — nobody. Not Feller, Newhouser, not McLain, not any of them. Everywhere we go, they ask only one thing: 'Is The Bird going to pitch?' And when he isn't, they get mad."

Hall of Famer George Kell

It was an amazing, almost mystical phenomenon, unlike anything ever before seen or experienced. It was madness, infatuation, love at first sight. It was Roy Hobbs, a summer fling, a fleeting moment of sincere and unadulterated devotion. He blew into the cynical hearts of Detroit baseball fans like a breath of fresh air and then, whoosh, he was gone. He created a 20th Century Camelot, providing that one brief shining moment during which all the problems of everyday life could be shoved mercifully into the background.

As America celebrated its bicentennial birthday in the Summer of '76, Mark (The Bird) Fidrych soared like an eagle into the lives of a hero-hungry public. He actually was more of an anti-hero, a gangling, frizzy-haired pitcher two years removed from high school and light years from the baseball establishment of millionaire superstars and unemotional mechanics.

The irreverent and unassuming Fidrych was personality, color and excitement packed into a skinny 6-foot-3, 175-pound body. Nicknamed The Bird because of his resemblance to Big Bird of *Sesame Street* fame, Fidrych lived the part, from his loping, knee-jerking gait to his fowl-like facial tics. He was a never-ending bundle of twitches, always moving, pacing, running, jumping and chattering. He was hyperactive and emotional, and the fans loved him for it.

Fidrych was a showman, unintentional and natural, who mesmerized an entire nation with his unbridled enthusiasm and eccentric behavior. The 21-year-old rookie seemed to be playing a strange kind of game on another planet in a different universe. The fans he pulled to the ballpark like a magnet brimmed with excitement at the

prospect of seeing Fidrych:
- Converse with the ball, sometimes scolding it for doing the wrong thing, other times pointing it toward the plate like a dart and telling it where to go.
- Get down on hands and knees before every inning and pat the dirt into place on the mound.
- Sprint to and from the dugout like a bird running the 100-yard dash.
- Strut around like a mad stork after every out.
- Take off his glove and applaud good defensive plays or even run around shaking the hands of his fielders.
- Win.

That, of course, was the key. Fidrych was a first-degree flake, but he also was a winner. Even though he did not make his first major league start until mid-May, the young righthander turned in a 19-9 record for a fifth-place team and led all American League starters with a 2.34 earned-run average. He was the A.L. starter in the All-Star Game and entered August with a gaudy 11-3 record and 1.80 ERA, two of the losses coming by 1-0 scores.

"He's not quite as flaky as they say," said Tiger Manager Ralph Houk. "When he's on the

mound, he doesn't know there's anyone else around. He talks to himself to help his concentration. And as a rule, we play good in the field behind him. Players like to play behind a guy who works fast and throws strikes."

At first, Fidrych's teammates were not so sure about that. Beginning only his third professional season, the rookie from Northboro, Mass., pranced around the Tigers spring training camp like a child with a new toy. Off the field, he was a care-free kid, always dressed in T-shirts and faded blue jeans. In the locker room, he was constant motion and incessant questions, a borderline annoyance. On the field, he was, well, borderline embarrassing.

A surprising addition to the Tigers' regular-season roster, Houk kept The Bird penned up through April and the first part of May, obviously unsure himself what to do with the curious youngster. He finally gave Fidrych a start against the Cleveland Indians and he responded with a 2-1 decision at Tiger Stadium. Fidrych pitched well in his next start, a 2-0 loss at Boston, and defeated Milwaukee, 5-4, at home on the last day of May. As The Bird rolled off six straight victories in the month of June, Detroit fans began flocking to the ballpark and his teammates came to several conclusions.

"He's got fantastic poise and

Detroit fans embraced their young hero with open arms and the effervescent Fidrych returned the affection.

Fidrych relaxes in the dugout with his ever-present bubblegum between starts.

great confidence," said catcher Bruce Kimm. "He's like a guy who's been around for 15 years."

"It's exhilarating being out there with him on the mound," said veteran Tigers right fielder Rusty Staub. "It's hard not to be up when he pitches. There's an electricity he brings out in everybody. Everyone can see the enthusiasm in Mark. He brings out the exuberance and youth in everybody.

"He's the most exciting thing I've seen. I've never seen a city turn on like this. I've seen Tommy Seaver go out and mow 'em down. But I've never seen anybody electrify the fans like this."

"Electrify" might have been an understatement. In one six-day period, Fidrych drew 98,887 fans to Tiger Stadium for his two starts. Through July 29, he had packed 334,123 fans into parks for his last eight appearances. For his 29 starts in 1976, Fidrych drew 899,969 fans, or 31,033 per game. The Tigers drew 605,677 when The Bird pitched.

"Nobody ever pulled them in the way he does — nobody," said Hall of Famer George Kell, a former Detroit third baseman. "Not Feller, Newhouser, not McLain, not any of them.

Everywhere we go, they ask only one thing: 'Is The Bird going to pitch?' And when he isn't, they get mad."

The game that really spread the word about The Bird was a June 28 nationally televised contest at Tiger Stadium against the East Division-leading New York Yankees. Fidrych stopped the Bronx Bombers, 5-1, and amused millions of viewers with his secretive whispers to a ball that always seemed to go exactly where he wanted it.

After the game, Detroit fans refused to leave, standing and chanting, "Bird! Bird! Bird!" for a solid 10 minutes. He returned for a curtain call, doffing his cap and enchanting the crowd further with his charismatic smile. So they started the chant all over again, forcing another curtain call which the ABC cameras delivered into living

rooms around the nation. Life would never be the same for this $19,000-per-year idol.

The rest of the summer was filled with curtain calls, lengthy autograph lines and a constant parade of gifts, letters, greeting cards, cakes, pictures, signs and banners proclaiming an undying love for The Bird. He was the talk of the baseball world, the toast of Detroit. Babies were named after him and his success was discussed on the floor of the Michigan legislature. To his credit, Fidrych handled the

The always-emotional Fidrych during one of his 1976 celebrations.

attention without ever straying from his down-to-earth persona. On the nights he wasn't pitching, fans at the ballpark could catch glimpses of him perched in a corner of the dugout, blowing giant bubbles and cheering on his teammates. Sometimes his loud screeching could be heard in the press box.

It was a wonderful dream that ended with a premature wakeup call. The next spring, Fidrych began experiencing tightness in his shoulder, a tendinitis problem that would dog him for the rest of his career. He would win only 10 more major league games in a struggling battle that ended with an unsuccessful minor league comeback in 1983. But still, the fans turned out in droves to see him pitch and even today the legend lives on.

"I've never seen anything like it in my life," said 1976 Detroit coach Dick Tracewski. "I played with Denny McLain and I roomed with Sandy Koufax for three years when he was striking out everybody and winning all those games. But nothing like that had ever happened."

Mark (The Bird) Fidrych, the toast of Detroit in 1976, bore a lovable resemblance to the Sesame Street character Big Bird.

★1976★

SEASON LEADERS

	American League		National League	
Avg.	George Brett, K.C.	.333	Bill Madlock, Chi.	.339
HR	Graig Nettles, N.Y.	32	Mike Schmidt, Phi.	38
RBI	Lee May, Bal.	109	George Foster, Cin.	121
SB	Bill North, Oak.	75	Dave Lopes, L.A.	63
W-L Pct.	Bill Campbell, Min. 17-5, .773		Steve Carlton, Phi. 20-7, .741	
ERA	Mark Fidrych, Det.	2.34	John Denny, St. L.	2.52
SO	Nolan Ryan, Cal.	327	Tom Seaver, N.Y.	235

Yankees end drought

New York first baseman Chris Chambliss belted a dramatic ninth-inning home run off Kansas City reliever Mark Littell October 14, lifting the Yankees to their first American League pennant since 1964 and touching off one of the wildest mob scenes in American sports history.

Chambliss' drive over the right-field fence leading off the ninth broke a 6-6 deadlock in the decisive fifth game of the A.L. Championship Series. As the ball flew from sight, thousands of fans rushed onto the Yankee Stadium field. By the time Chambliss reached first base, he was surrounded by spectators. When he reached second, the bag already had been removed by a souvenir collector. He never reached third and came nowhere near home, retreating to the New York club-house for his own safety.

All of the players and umpires escaped from the field without injury, but Yankee Stadium sustained $100,000 in damage.

The heavily favored Yankees had opened with a 4-1 victory at Kansas City behind Catfish Hunter, but the Royals rebounded for a Series-tying 7-3 win. The New Yorkers regained the advantage with a 5-3 triumph in Game 3, but the stubborn Royals bounced back again with a 7-4 fourth-game win.

The Yankees appeared to be in control of the finale as they entered the eighth with a 6-3 lead, but Royals third baseman George Brett dispelled that notion by blasting a game-tying three-run homer. The score remained 6-6 until Chambliss settled the issue in the ninth.

A policeman tries to protect Yankee Chris Chambliss from a delirious New York crowd after his pennant-winning homer against Kansas City.

Brett edges McRae in wild batting race

In one of baseball's most controversial conclusions to a batting race, Kansas City third baseman George Brett edged out teammate Hal McRae for the American League title October 3 amid charges that Minnesota Manager Gene Mauch had intentionally helped Brett in his final at-bat of the season.

Brett won his first championship by virtue of his 27th three-hit game, edging out McRae, .3333 to .3326. McRae, Kansas City's designated hitter, was 2 for 4 in the season finale.

The controversy arose in the ninth inning of Minnesota's 5-3 victory at Royals Stadium when Brett, who already had two doubles, hit a medium-range fly ball that fell in front of charging Twins left fielder Steve Brye and bounced over his head, allowing Brett to circle the bases for an inside-the-park homer. McRae, the next batter, grounded out and then began gesturing and yelling at the Twins' bench.

Mauch bolted onto the field and both he and McRae had to be restrained. The cause of McRae's anger was his belief that Mauch had ordered Brye to play exceptionally deep and let anything hit in front of him fall.

The National League batting race also was decided on the final day when Chicago's Bill Madlock finished with a 4-for-4 rush in an 8-2 victory over Montreal and beat Cincinnati's Ken Griffey, .339 to .336. Griffey, sitting out the Reds' finale against Atlanta with a league-leading .338 mark, was inserted into the contest when news of Madlock's late rush reached Cincinnati, but failed to hit in two at-bats. It was Madlock's second straight title.

American League batting champ George Brett.

CAUGHT ON THE FLY

OCTOBER

Milwaukee slugger Hank Aaron got an infield single in his final big-league at-bat and ended his record-breaking career with 755 home runs and 2,297 RBIs.

NOVEMBER

Seattle and Toronto, the newest members of the American League, paid $5.25 million apiece to fill their rosters with 30 players in the circuit's third expansion draft since 1960.

Cincinnati second baseman Joe Morgan became the first player to win back-to-back MVP awards since New York Yankee Roger Maris accomplished the feat in the A.L. in 1960 and '61.

DECEMBER

Danny Murtaugh, who had retired two months earlier as Pittsburgh manager, died of a heart attack in Chester, Pa., at age 59. Murtaugh compiled 1,115 wins and led the Pirates to two World Series championships in four hitches that covered 15 years.

THE BIG RED MACHINE

Johnny Bench belted two homers and drove in five runs October 21 to give the Cincinnati Reds a 7-2 victory over New York and a four-game sweep of the Yankees in the World Series. The fall classic clincher at Yankee Stadium completed the Reds' seven-game sprint through postseason play and officially established Cincinnati's finely-tuned and ever-efficient Big Red Machine as one of baseball's greatest teams.

There were rumblings of greatness as the talent-rich Reds rolled to 102 regular-season victories, but the real proof was provided by what followed. First the Reds gave the East Division-winning Philadelphia Phillies a lesson in winning baseball, taking the National League Championship Series opener, 6-3, prevailing in the second game, 6-2, and rallying for three runs in the ninth inning to win the third, 7-6. The Reds tied the final contest on back-to-back George Foster and Bench home runs and won it on Ken Griffey's single.

The World Series — the Yankees' first appearance in a fall classic since 1964 — was even easier. The Reds were not even tested.

With seven regulars hitting over .300 and Bench supplying the power, Cincinnati rolled to 5-1, 4-3 and 6-2 victories before completing its perfect postseason in style. Seven pitchers compiled a 2.00 earned-run average and the Reds batted .313 as a team.

That brought Cincinnati's two year totals to 210 regular-season victories, a 6-0 Championship Series record and wins over Boston and New York in the World Series.

Game 1	Cincinnati	5	New York	1
Game 2	Cincinnati	4	New York	3
Game 3	Cincinnati	6	New York	2
Game 4	Cincinnati	7	New York	2

Three key cogs in Cincinnati's Big Red Machine (left to right): Johnny Bench, Tony Perez and Joe Morgan.

"How can you have a much better team than this one? Good power, good baserunning, excellent pitching, very aggressive, a great bunch of guys. Who could ask for more?"

Joe Morgan

The second baseman on Cincinnati's Big Red Machine

The re-entry draft

Reggie Jackson, the 30-year-old former Oakland and Baltimore slugger, showed players and fans what it's like to really be free when he signed a five-year, $2.9 million contract November 29 with the New York Yankees. Jackson was the biggest plum in baseball's first crop of free agents.

Jackson followed in the footsteps of former Minnesota reliever Bill Campbell, who clearly demonstrated that the price of baseball talent has gone up when he signed a four-year, $1 million contract with Boston November 6, two days after the game's first free-agent re-entry draft.

Free agency became an accepted part of baseball November 4 when team owners gathered at New York's Plaza Hotel and determined bargaining rights for the 26 players who had played out their option under terms of the new Basic Agreement hammered out by Players' Association executive director Marvin Miller and owners last July. The draft allowed clubs to select players for whom they wished to bid.

Teams picked as many players as they wanted, but a particular player could only be drafted 12 times. Those players drafted by one team or none at all became free to bargain with any team. Teams that stood to loose a player could retain negotiating rights if they chose.

When the draft began, Baltimore second baseman Bobby Grich was the first player chosen, but Oakland catcher Gene Tenace was the first to be taken off the board after a dozen selections. The Chicago White Sox drafted the most players with 18 while Cincinnati refused to take part in the process.

What it all meant was that a lot of players were on the verge of getting rich quick, and the Campbell and Jackson signings officially ushered in a new era of player prosperity.

New Yankee Reggie Jackson says hello to the New York media.

"I'm going home and rest for a while and then I'm going to work like everyone else."

Ed Sprague

Pitcher recently released by the Milwaukee Brewers

"I think I throw the ball as hard as anyone. The ball just doesn't get there as fast."

Eddie Bane

Minnesota pitcher

"If I'm going to run a finishing school for managers, I want to be paid for it."

Charles O. Finley

Oakland owner on why he demanded, and received, catcher Manny Sanguillen and a reported $100,000 from Pittsburgh in exchange for Manager Chuck Tanner

★1977★
JANUARY-AUGUST

Jays soar in debut

Canada got its first taste of American League baseball April 7 when the expansion Toronto Blue Jays roared out of the gate with a 9-5 victory over Chicago before 44,649 curious fans at Toronto's Exhibition Stadium.

The Blue Jays follow the Montreal Expos, the first franchise to field a team on foreign soil. The Expos joined the National League as an expansion team in 1969.

Playing their first game on a frigid afternoon, the Blue Jays exploded for 16 hits and wiped out an early 4-1 deficit. Leading the charge was first baseman Doug Ault, who belted a solo home run in the first inning off Ken Brett, a two-run homer in the third and a run-scoring single in the eighth.

The A.L.'s other expansion club, Seattle, made its debut April 6 at Seattle's Kingdome, but did not fare as well. The Mariners were shut out, 7-0, by California lefthander Frank Tanana before 57,732 fans.

First baseman Doug Ault helped get Toronto's expansion franchise off to a fast start.

Billy versus Reggie

With a national television audience watching their every move, New York Yankee Manager Billy Martin and star right fielder Reggie Jackson nearly traded blows June 18 in a dugout confrontation after Jackson had been removed from a game at Boston's Fenway Park for "not hustling."

In an obvious expression of displeasure, Martin called his star to the dugout and replaced him with Paul Blair during the course of a sixth-inning Boston rally after Jackson had cautiously chased after a pop-fly hit by Jim Rice. Jackson entered the dugout and made a sweeping motion with his arms, Martin made some comments and Jackson answered back as coach Elston Howard jumped between them. When Jackson began walking toward the clubhouse, Martin had to be restrained from going after him.

"I only ask one thing of my players — hustle," said Martin, who has a long history of stormy relationships with both players and management in his eight years as a big-league manager.

"The man took a position today to show me up on national TV," responded Jackson, who has had stormy relations of his own with teammates and Martin since signing a $2.9 million free-agent contract with the Yankees last winter.

Yankee Manager Billy Martin (left) and Reggie Jackson had a number of run-ins, but there were a few light moments, too.

"DUGOUT CHATTER"

"I wouldn't trade Rice for anybody in baseball."

Sal Bando

Milwaukee veteran, on young Boston slugger Jim Rice

"In baseball, it took me 17 years to get 3,000 hits. I did it all in one afternoon on the golf course."

Hank Aaron

Former Braves and Brewers slugger

Vicious attack sends Lucchesi to hospital

Texas second baseman Lenny Randle, frustrated over the loss of his starting job to rookie Bump Wills, sent Rangers Manager Frank Lucchesi to the hospital March 28 with a vicious attack in front of the visitors' dugout before a spring training game at Orlando, Fla.

The 50-year-old Lucchesi was on the field in street clothes when

the 28-year-old Randle approached him during batting practice. After a short conversation, Randle suddenly lashed out with his fist, striking Lucchesi on the side of his face. With the stunned manager rendered defenseless, Randle continued his attack, hitting him at least six times and leaving him bleeding and nearly unconscious.

When several Ranger players responded to the trouble, Randle shouted an obscenity, grabbed a bat, trotted toward third base, dropped the bat and ran into the outfield, where he started doing sprints. A few minutes later, he was summoned by Rangers General Manager Dan O'Brien, who suspended him pending a hearing.

Lucchesi was rushed to a hospital, where he was treated for a concussion, a triple fracture of the right cheek bone, a lacerated hip and a back injury. He underwent surgery on his cheek bone the next day.

Randle, normally mild mannered, blamed the incident on stress over losing his job and Lucchesi calling him a "punk."

Manager for a day

Eddie Stanky, the replacement for fired Texas Manager Frank Lucchesi, guided the Rangers to a 10-8 victory over Minnesota June 22 — and then quit, returning to his home in Mobile, Ala., and his previous job as University of South Alabama baseball coach.

According to the 60-year-old Stanky, it was a simple case of homesickness. "After the excitement calmed down, I started getting lonesome and homesick," he said. So he hopped on a plane in Minneapolis and headed home, where his wife Dickie and South Alabama athletic officials welcomed him with open arms.

Stanky, affectionately known as The Brat during an 11-year big-league career as a second baseman for the Chicago Cubs, Brooklyn Dodgers, Boston Braves, New York Giants and St. Louis Cardinals, had been running the South Alabama program since 1968. He took that position after managing the Cardinals and Chicago White Sox, molding the Jaguars into a national power.

"It was a great ball game," Stanky said about his one contest as Texas manager. "Doggone, I have a great ball club — I mean they have a great ball club."

The stunned Rangers named Connie Ryan to replace Stanky on an interim basis.

Eddie Stanky: Texas manager for a day.

CAUGHT ON THE FLY

JANUARY

Commissioner Bowie Kuhn suspended Atlanta Owner Ted Turner for one year and fined him $10,000 for "tampering" with Gary Matthews, an outfielder in the 1976 re-entry draft who eventually signed with the Braves.

MARCH

Federal Judge Frank McGarr ruled that Commissioner Bowie Kuhn acted within his powers when he voided the 1976 sales of three Oakland players by Owner Charles O. Finley for $3.5 million.

APRIL

Philadelphia lefthander Steve Carlton spoiled Montreal's home opener at new Olympic Stadium, pitching the Phillies to a 7-2 victory before 57,592 curious fans.

JUNE

California's Nolan Ryan struck out 19 batters in a game for the fourth time in his career, reaching that total in the 10th inning of a contest against Toronto. The Angels eventually won in 13, 2-1.

SEASON LEADERS

	American League		National League	
Avg.	Rod Carew, Min.	.388	Dave Parker, Pit.	.338
HR	Jim Rice, Bos.	39	George Foster, Cin.	52
RBI	Larry Hisle, Min.	119	George Foster, Cin.	149
SB	Freddie Patek, K.C.	53	Frank Taveras, Pit.	70
W-L Pct.	Paul Splittorff, K.C.	16-6, .727	John Candelaria, Pit.	20-5, .800
ERA	Frank Tanana, Cal.	2.54	John Candelaria, Pit.	2.34
SO	Nolan Ryan, Cal.	341	Phil Niekro, Atl.	262

N.L. slugs A.L. again

First-inning home runs by Cincinnati's Joe Morgan and Philadelphia's Greg Luzinski put the American League in a deep hole and the National League went on to record a 7-5 All-Star Game victory July 19, its sixth straight midsummer classic win and 14th in 15 contests.

The 56,683 fans at Yankee Stadium had barely settled into their seats when N.L. leadoff man Morgan hit a pitch from Baltimore's Jim Palmer over the fence. After Pittsburgh's Dave Parker singled and Cincinnati's George Foster doubled him home, Luzinski connected and the Nationals had a 4-0 lead. A third-inning homer by Los Angeles first baseman Steve Garvey made it 5-0.

Los Angeles starter and winner Don Sutton and San Francisco's Gary Lavelle protected the lead masterfully. But the Americans dented Cincinnati's Tom Seaver in the sixth on a two-run double by Chicago's Richie Zisk and in the seventh on a run-scoring single by New York's Willie Randolph.

The N.L., however, put the game out of reach on a two-run eighth-inning single by San Diego's Dave Winfield. A two-run homer in the ninth by Boston's George Scott made the score respectable.

Brock tops Cobb's steal record

St. Louis' Lou Brock, already entrenched in the record books as the greatest one-season base thief in history, swiped second two times against San Diego August 29 and supplanted Hall of Famer Ty Cobb as the modern game's greatest basestealer.

Brock, who recorded a record 118 steals in 1974, led off the game against the Padres at San Diego by drawing a walk off Dave Freisleben. He set sail for second base on the righthander's first pitch, sliding in safely with record-tying steal No. 892. Brock advanced to third when catcher Dave Roberts' throw sailed into center field.

The Cardinals' 38-year-old left fielder got the record-breaker in the seventh when he reached first on a fielder's choice and again took off on Freisleben's first pitch, beating Roberts' wide throw. He was mobbed by happy teammates and presented with the second base bag. Brock was removed from the lineup in a game eventually won, 4-3, by the Padres.

Brock compiled his record total in 2,376 career contests. Cobb played in 3,033 games over 24 big-league seasons.

St. Louis Manager Vern Rapp gives master thief Lou Brock (20) a helping hand as he celebrates his record-setting 893rd career steal.

★1977★
SEPTEMBER-DECEMBER

" DUGOUT CHATTER "

"If you stand next to him, he smells like a drugstore."

Billy Martin

Yankee manager, on Texas pitcher Gaylord Perry, the alleged master of the greaseball

Foster muscles up

Cincinnati fell short in its bid to capture a third straight World Series championship, but nobody is pointing any fingers at left fielder George Foster. While the Reds were struggling to an 88-74 record and second-place finish in the National League West Division, their 28-year-old slugger was putting together the best offensive campaign in years.

Offensive as in 52 home runs and 149 RBIs to go with a .320 batting average. But the numbers do not stop there. Foster also topped the N.L. in runs scored (124), total bases (388) and slugging percentage (.631). He missed, by one RBI, becoming the first player since Chicago Cubs slugger Hack Wilson in 1930 to hit 50 homers and drive in 150 runs in the same season.

Even so, Foster is baseball's first 50-homer man since Willie Mays belted 52 in 1965. His home run, RBI and total base totals broke club records, as did his slugging percentage. He swatted his 52nd homer during an 8-0 win over San Diego on September 28 and then went homerless over Cincinnati's final three games.

Foster's big season follows on the heels of a .306, 29-homer, 121-RBI 1976 campaign.

George Foster, baseball's newest 50-home run man.

CAUGHT ON THE FLY

SEPTEMBER
Kansas City's 16-game winning streak, the longest in baseball in 24 years, was halted by Seattle, 4-1. The Royals lost just three times in their last 30 games en route to clinching the A.L. West title.

OCTOBER
Dusty Baker hit a home run in his final season at-bat, making Los Angeles the first team ever to boast four 30-homer hitters in the same year. Steve Garvey had 33, Reggie Smith 32 and Ron Cey and Baker 30 apiece.

NOVEMBER
New York lefthander Sparky Lyle became the first relief pitcher to win an A.L. Cy Young Award after posting 13 wins and 26 saves for the pennant-winning Yankees.

Chicago White Sox outfielder Richie Zisk jumped ship and signed a 10-year, $2.3 million free-agent contract with the Texas Rangers.

Dodgers catch Phils

Los Angeles lefty Tommy John scattered seven hits and outdueled Steve Carlton, 4-1, in a Philadelphia downpour, giving the Dodgers a four-game National League Championship Series victory over the Phillies and their second pennant in four years.

The October 8 triumph at rain-drenched Veterans Stadium, keyed by a two-run second-inning home run by Dusty Baker, completed a startling turnaround that had taken root the day before in Game 3. The Phillies appeared to be in the Series driver's seat when they carried a 5-3 lead into the ninth inning of that contest and reliever Gene Garber retired the first two batters he faced.

But suddenly, without warning, the N.L. East Division-champion Phillies came unraveled. It started innocently enough when veteran pinch-hitter Vic Davalillo beat out a drag bunt.

Another pinch-hitter, Manny Mota, doubled home Davalillo and he scored the tying run when Dave Lopes beat out a ground ball on a controversial safe call at first. Lopes eventually moved to second on an errrant pickoff throw and scored the winning run on Bill Russell's single.

The Phillies, shocked and confused, were easy pickings in Game 4.

First-year Los Angeles Manager Tom Lasorda hits his mark during a champagne celebration following the Dodgers' pennant-clinching win over Philadelphia.

Yankees rally again

The down but never out New York Yankees called upon a little Game 5 ninth-inning magic for the second year in a row and made the Kansas City Royals disappear from the American League Championship Series with a 5-3 pennant-winning victory October 9 at Royals Stadium.

As in 1976, when the Yankees needed a final-inning home run by Chris Chambliss to defeat the Royals, the two A.L. division winners had battled evenly — and bitterly — while splitting the first four games. The Royals jumped out quickly in the clincher with two first-inning runs and added another in the third for a 3-1 lead that lefthander Paul Splittorff made stand up through seven solid innings.

But the Royals' hope for a first-ever A.L. pennant began to unravel in the eighth when Reggie Jackson, benched by Yankee Manager Billy Martin because of his 1-for-14 performance through four games, stroked a pinch-hit run-scoring single and they came apart in the ninth, an inning that started with Paul Blair's bloop single off Dennis Leonard and a walk to pinch-hitter Roy White.

The big hit came when Mickey Rivers singled to right off Larry Gura, scoring Blair and tying the game. Willie Randolph's sacrifice fly and George Brett's error concluded the scoring.

Yankee reliever Sparky Lyle leaps into the arms of catcher Thurman Munson after wrapping up the Yankees' come-from-behind Championship Series victory over Kansas City.

" DUGOUT CHATTER "

"Not much money, but I no want to work so I play baseball."

Mario Soto

Cincinnati pitcher, who signed a baseball contract for $1,000 while working for a construction gang in the Dominican Republic

WORLD SERIES REPORT

REGGIE'S SHOW

Reggie Jackson, alias Mr. October, displayed his uncanny flair for the dramatic October 18 when he blasted the Los Angeles Dodgers into oblivion with three mighty swings that lifted the New York Yankees to their first World Series championship since 1962.

Jackson, signed as a free agent after playing out his option with Baltimore in 1976, had belted 32 homers and driven in 110 runs in his first New York campaign. But it was not a happy one. The 31-year-old slugger had been embroiled in a season-long squabble with Manager Billy Martin and was benched for his lethargic hitting during the Championship Series against Kansas City.

But October is showtime and the World Series is Jackson's stage. When he stepped to the plate in the fourth inning of Game 6 with the Yankees leading the fall classic three games to two, he owned a .317 career Series batting average, four home runs and 10 RBIs in 17 games (12 with Oakland). He had, in fact, homered in his last official at-bat of Game 5 and carried a .353 average into Game 6 of this Series.

On Burt Hooton's first pitch, Jackson blasted a rocket into the right-field stands for a two-run homer. With two out and Willie Randolph on base in the fifth, Jackson stroked another first-pitch homer, this time off Elias Sosa. Then, facing Charlie Hough leading off the eighth, Jackson hit a monster shot over the center-field fence — on another first pitch.

Pandemonium reigned in Yankee Stadium as 56,407 fans saluted one of the most memorable World Series performances in history. Jackson's homers, which lifted the New Yorkers to an 8-4 Series-closing victory, gave him a record five for the classic and an unprecedented four in successive official at-bats. Only one other player had hit three in one Series game and that was former Yankee showman Babe Ruth, who performed the feat twice (1926 and '28).

Taking a backseat to Jackson were righthander Mike Torrez, who won two games, including the clincher, and catcher Thurman Munson, a .320 hitter.

Game 1	New York	4	Los Angeles	3
Game 2	Los Angeles	6	New York	1
Game 3	New York	5	Los Angeles	3
Game 4	New York	4	Los Angeles	2
Game 5	Los Angeles	10	New York	4
Game 6	New York	8	Los Angeles	4

Yankee bopper Reggie Jackson, alias Mr. October, watches the flight of his second Game 6 World Series home run against Los Angeles.

★1978★

Rose reaches 3,000

Cincinnati's Pete Rose lined a sharp single to left field, his second hit of the May 5 game off Montreal righthander Steve Rogers, and became the 13th player in major league history to amass 3,000 career hits.

The 37-year-old Rose collected his milestone safety in the fifth inning of a 4-3 loss to the Expos at Riverfront Stadium and then stood at first base after a short ceremony as 37,823 fans saluted him with a rousing five-minute ovation.

The popular, always-hustling Reds third baseman had set the stage for his big moment with a third-inning chopper that was ruled hit No. 2,999 when Rogers mishandled the ball. The official scorer received a standing ovation for his decision.

Rose, a 10-time National League All-Star and co-record holder for 200-hit seasons (nine), reached the plateau faster than any player in history. The last to get 3,000 hits was former Detroit outfielder Al Kaline in 1974.

McCovey belts 500th

Big Willie McCovey uncoiled his 40-year-old body into a two-strike pitch from lefthander Jamie Easterly June 30 and crashed a towering drive over the left-field wall at Atlanta's Fulton County Stadium for his 500th career home run, putting him in select company with 12 former sluggers.

The San Francisco first baseman reached the milestone in the second inning of a doubleheader opener against the Braves. Despite McCovey's blast and four other homers by his teammates, the National League West Divi-sion-leading Giants dropped both games to the lowly Braves, 10-9 and 10-5.

"It was more of a relief than a thrill, to get it over with," said McCovey. "I was anxious to get the homer behind me so we can concentrate on the more important thing — the pennant race."

McCovey, who began his illustrious career with San Francisco in 1959, spent two-plus seasons with San Diego and the end of 1976 with Oakland before rejoining the Giants. He hit 52 of his homers in a Padres uniform.

San Francisco slugger Willie McCovey gets a warm reception after hitting his 500th career home run.

N.L. stars roll on

The National League spotted its snakebit American League counterparts a three-run lead July 11 before roaring back for its seventh straight All-Star Game victory, a 7-3 runaway at San Diego Stadium.

When Kansas City's George Brett doubled home a run and scored himself in the first inning and then hit a sacrifice fly in the third, it appeared the A.L. might finally be on the right track. But Baltimore's Jim Palmer came unraveled in a three-run National third and the senior circuit added four runs in the eighth to close out its 15th victory in 16 games.

Philadelphia's Larry Bowa opened the N.L. third with a single and moved around to score as Palmer walked Cincinnati's Joe Morgan and George Foster and the Phillies' Greg Luzinski in succession. Los Angeles first baseman Steve Garvey tied the game with a two-run single.

That score held until the bottom of the eighth when the Nationals prospered against New York Yankee relief ace Goose Gossage. Garvey opened the decisive inning with a triple and the Phillies' Bob Boone contributed a key two-run single.

Chicago's Bruce Sutter pitched 1⅔ scoreless innings to gain credit for the victory.

All-Star Game MVP Steve Garvey and wife Cindy after the N.L.'s 7-3 victory at San Diego.

" DUGOUT CHATTER "

"If I had done everything I was supposed to up to now, I'd be leading in homers, have the highest batting average, have given $10,000 to the cancer fund and married Marie Osmond."

Clint Hurdle

Kansas City player, on being one of the most heralded rookies in baseball history

Martin resigns

The love-hate relationship between Billy Martin and New York Owner George Steinbrenner took two strange twists in late July when the Manager submitted a tearful resignation to the Yankees and then resurfaced five days later as the team's manager of the future at a Yankee Stadium Old-Timers Day game.

Martin announced his resignation July 24 on a balcony at Kansas City's Crown Center Hotel. He delivered his tearful goodbye and then wished the Yankees luck in their American League pennant quest under new Manager Bob Lemon.

Martin's action came in the wake of his Chicago quip about Yankee star Reggie Jackson, who was coming off a five-game suspension, and Steinbrenner, who had served a two-year suspension after being convicted of making illegal political campaign contributions. "The two of them deserve each other," Martin said. "One's a born liar, the other's convicted."

The most shocking development in this bizarre case came July 29 at the Old-Timers Day festivities when it was announced to a packed house that Martin would return to manage in 1980. Ironically, Martin had been hired to replace then-manager Bill Virdon on Old-Timers Day in 1975.

A tearful Billy Martin during a Kansas City press conference to announce his resignation as New York Yankee manager.

" DUGOUT CHATTER "

"It means No. 51 is next."

Gaylord Perry

San Diego pitcher, when asked the significance of his 50th career shutout

CAUGHT ON THE FLY

MARCH

San Diego officials pulled a shocker when they fired Manager Alvin Dark 17 days before the Padres were to open their N.L. season. It was believed to be the earliest managerial firing in modern history.

APRIL

The U.S. Court of Appeals upheld a lower-court decision and ruled against Charles O. Finley in his suit that claimed Commissioner Bowie Kuhn had overstepped his authority in cancelling the Oakland owner's 1976 sales of three star players.

MAY

Wayne Garland, Cleveland's $10 million free agent signee who went 13-19 in his first season, made only six 1978 starts before undergoing career-threatening rotator cuff surgery.

JUNE

Cincinnati righthander Tom Seaver, who had lost three no-hit bids in the ninth inning, finally recorded his first career gem when he throttled the Cardinals in a 4-0 victory at Riverfront Stadium.

Former Cleveland star Larry Doby, baseball's second black player, became the sport's second black manager when he replaced fired Chicago White Sox boss Bob Lemon.

AUGUST

Amateur umpires worked the 13 scheduled games as major league umps staged a one-day strike for better benefits. They returned the next day when a Federal judge granted restraining orders and ordered them back to work.

Bostock gunned down

California right fielder Lyman Bostock, a four-year major leaguer with a career .311 average, was killed September 23 by an errant shotgun blast while riding in a car in Gary, Ind.

The 27-year-old, who had signed a five-year free-agent contract with the Angels during the off-season after three years with Minnesota, was riding with two women in a 1976 Buick driven by his uncle, Edward Turner, when the estranged husband of the woman sitting in the back seat with Bostock pulled alongside the car and fired a single shotgun blast through the window. Bostock was hit in the temple and Barbara Smith ended up in the hospital with facial wounds.

Bostock, one of the Angels' most popular players, was batting .296 with 70 RBIs at the time of his death. He always went to Gary, 35 miles southeast of Chicago, to visit Turner when the Angels played the White Sox.

Braves stop Rose

Cincinnati third baseman Pete Rose failed to get a hit in four official at-bats against Atlanta rookie Larry McWilliams and veteran reliever Gene Garber August 1 and saw his National League record-tying 44-game streak come to an end, 12 games short of Joe DiMaggio's all-time mark.

The 31,159 fans at Fulton County Stadium enjoyed watching their Braves pound out a 16-4 victory, but they were more interested in seeing Rose inch closer to DiMaggio's legendary 56-game record, set in 1941. The Reds' veteran had tied Willie Keeler's 81-year-old N.L. record by hitting in his 44th straight contest July 31.

Rose, facing McWilliams, walked in the first inning and hit a second-inning line drive that was picked off ankle high by the pitcher. He grounded out on his third at-bat and lined into a double play in the seventh facing Garber.

When Rose stepped to the plate in the ninth for what obviously would be his last at-bat, the crowd gave him a long ovation. He bunted Garber's first offering foul, took two balls, fouled off the fourth pitch and finally went down swinging.

Over the streak that began June 14, Rose batted .385 and collected 70 hits.

With his 44-game hitting streak nearing an end, a disappointed Pete Rose walks away from home plate after striking out against Atlanta reliever Gene Garber.

CAUGHT ON THE FLY

OCTOBER

The Los Angeles Dodgers became the first major league team to break the 3 million attendance barrier, finishing with 3,347,845.

Pittsburgh right fielder Dave Parker batted .334 and earned his second straight National League batting crown en route to league MVP honors.

Houston's J.R. Richard finished the season with 303 strikeouts, the most ever recorded by an N.L. righthander.

Royals tumble again to Yankees in ALCS

Graig Nettles and Roy White belted fourth-game home runs to support the combined seven-hit pitching of Ron Guidry and Goose Gossage as the New York Yankees recorded a 2-1 victory over Kansas City and handed the Royals their third American League Championship Series loss in as many years.

The Yankees' third straight pennant was a welcome conclusion to an exhausting season. Guidry surrendered a game-opening triple to George Brett and an RBI single to Hal McRae before settling down to outduel Kansas City ace Dennis Leonard, who finished with a four-hitter.

The pivotal game of the series was the third at Yankee Stadium after the teams had split the first two at Kansas City. The Royals got a three-homer effort from third baseman Brett in that contest, but the Yankees rallied to win, 6-5, on a two-run eighth-inning homer by Thurman Munson.

Brett hit solo shots in the first, third and fifth off Catfish Hunter.

Kansas City's George Brett rounds third after one of his three homers in the Royals' 6-5 Game 3 Championship Series loss at New York.

The Yankee express

Light-hitting shortstop Bucky Dent stunned the Boston Red Sox with a three-run, seventh-inning blast over the left-field wall at Fenway Park and the New York Yankees went on to punctuate their incredible comeback story with a 5-4 victory October 2 in a one-game playoff to decide the American League East Division championship.

Dent's surprising homer off Boston's Mike Torrez, his fifth of the season, wiped out a 2-0 Red Sox advantage and sent shock-waves through 32,925 Boston fans. The Yankees added another run in the inning and increased their lead to 5-2 on Reggie Jackson's eighth-inning homer before the Red Sox mounted a last-ditch rally. But Goose Gossage came on to save starter Ron Guidry's 25th win and give the Yanks their third straight division title.

The victory capped a frantic Yankee comeback that began under the always-intense Billy Martin and ended under the laid-back leadership of Bob Lemon, who had been fired as Chicago White Sox manager on June 30. The Yankees appeared hopelessly out of the division race on July 19, buried 14 games behind the first-place Red Sox.

But the Yankees, under typical Bronx Zoo conditions, battled through distractions, egos, suspensions and clubhouse bickering to pull off the greatest comeback in A.L. history. They won five straight games before Martin was forced into a tearful resignation and never missed a beat under Lemon, winning 52 of 73 contests down the stretch to catch the sputtering Red Sox.

The Yankees actually pulled even for the first time over the weekend of September 7, 8, 9 and 10 when they staged the infamous Boston Massacre at Fenway, out-scoring the Red Sox, 42-9, and outhitting them, 67-21, in the four-game series. The teams played even the rest of the way and finished with 99-63 records, forcing the first division playoff in baseball history.

Yankees Roy White (6) and Chris Chambliss (10) greet Bucky Dent after his three-run seventh-inning home run during a one-game divisional playoff victory over Boston.

" DUGOUT CHATTER "

"Basically, I think they're telling the truth."

Dave Parker

Pittsburgh outfielder, when told he had been voted the N.L.'s best all-round player in a poll of general managers

Guidry gets reward

Ron Guidry, the New York Yankees' Louisiana Lightning, was named unanimous choice of the Baseball Writers' Association of America for the American League Cy Young October 31 after completing one of the most overpowering seasons in history.

Guidry was phenomenal in posting a 25-3 record, 1.74 earned-run average, nine shutouts and 248 strikeouts for the World Series-champion Yankees. The 28-year-old lefthander posted the highest winning percentage in major league history (.839) for a 20-game winner and the second lowest ERA in A.L. history.

The skinny 5-foot-11, 160-pounder with the 96-mph fastball becomes only the seventh unanimous selection and second in the A.L. Detroit's 31-game winner Denny McLain swept the first-place votes in 1968. Guidry, who won his first 13 decisions, is the second straight Yankee to win the award, following in the footsteps of reliever Sparky Lyle.

The National League Cy Young choice was San Diego veteran Gaylord Perry, who compiled a 21-6 record and 2.72 ERA. Perry, the 1972 Cy Young winner for Cleveland, is the first pitcher to win the award in both leagues.

Yankee lefty Ron Guidry capped his spectacular 25-3 campaign with an A.L. Cy Young Award.

Phillies pick a Rose

Pete Rose's jet-propelled promotional tour closed down operations December 5 when the 16-year Cincinnati star signed a four-year, $3.2 million free-agent contract with Philadelphia.

The winner of the Rose sweepstakes was announced at a packed news conference in Orlando, Fla., site of baseball's winter meetings. It concluded an innovative sales job by the 37-year-old veteran, who jetted around the country and invited offers from various major league teams. Those offers

reportedly reached as high as $1 million per year from Atlanta and similar amounts from the New York Mets, Pittsburgh and Kansas City.

But Rose opted for Philadelphia, which had dropped out of the bidding a week earlier, only to jump back in with a revised offer. The Phillies get a .310 career hitter who will help them with his hustling style and clubhouse leadership.

The contract makes Rose the highest-paid player in baseball.

YANKS WHIP DODGERS

Light-hitting Bucky Dent and Brian Doyle combined for five runs batted in and slugger Reggie Jackson added a two-run homer October 17 as the New York Yankees defeated Los Angeles, 7-2, in the decisive sixth game of the World Series.

The victory at Dodger Stadium completed a four-straight blitz by the Yankees after Los Angeles had won the first two contests by 11-5 and 4-3 scores. It also completed the Yankees' season of comebacks in fitting style.

Dent, the hero of New York's one-game division playoff victory over Boston, singled three times and drove in three runs and Doyle collected two

singles, a double and two RBIs to lead the sixth-game charge. Doyle finished the Series with a team-leading .438 average and Dent checked in at .417.

The Dodgers, who belted four home runs in the first two games, scored only eight runs in the final four in losing to starters Ron Guidry, Jim Beattie and Catfish Hunter and reliever Goose Gossage. Again stepping to the offensive forefront was Jackson, Mr. October, who homered twice and drove in eight runs.

The championship was the Yankees' record 22nd overall and second straight after a 14-year dry spell.

Game 1	Los Angeles	11	New York	5
Game 2	Los Angeles	4	New York	3
Game 3	New York	5	Los Angeles	1
Game 4	New York	4	Los Angeles	3
Game 5	New York	12	Los Angeles	2
Game 6	New York	7	Los Angeles	2

Little Brian Doyle batted .438 as an unlikely hero in New York's six-game World Series triumph over Los Angeles.

SEASON LEADERS

	American League		National League	
Avg.	Rod Carew, Min.	.333	Dave Parker, Pit.	.334
HR	Jim Rice, Bos.	46	George Foster, Cin.	40
RBI	Jim Rice, Bos.	139	George Foster, Cin.	120
SB	Ron LeFlore, Det.	68	Omar Moreno, Pit.	71
W-L Pct.	Ron Guidry, N.Y.	25-3, .893	Gaylord Perry, S.D.	21-6, .778
ERA	Ron Guidry, N.Y.	1.74	Craig Swan, N.Y.	2.43
SO	Nolan Ryan, Cal.	260	J.R. Richard, Hou.	303

Umpire strike ends

Order returned to major league baseball May 19 as 52 umpires went back to work after a bitter work stoppage that resulted in the first six weeks of the season being played under the sometimes wild and crazy dictates of amateur and minor league arbiters.

An agreement was hashed out May 17 after a 14-hour negotiating session in New York. The umpires, represented by Richie Phillips, unanimously approved a contract that will give them an average $7,000 salary increase, raise the maximum salary from $40,000 to $50,000 after 20 years, provide for a two-week vacation during the season and strengthen their health and pension benefits.

The vacation concession, a major breakthrough for the umpires, forces the American and National leagues to hire an extra crew of four umpires. A.L. President Lee MacPhail and N.L. boss Chub Feeney immediately filled their expanded staffs with so-called "scab umpires," those minor league arbiters who worked as crew chiefs while the regulars were walking "informational picket lines" outside of ballparks throughout the country.

It was the spotty work of the substitute umpires that turned the tide and forced the leagues to re-open dialogue. As patience began to wear thin among players and managers, the cease-and-desist orders to protect the amateur umpires were ignored and arguments and sticky disputes became more commonplace.

In an April 24 game between New York and San Francisco at Shea Stadium, the substitute umpires consulted amid bitter argument for 28 minutes and changed their minds twice before making a compromise decision. Mets Manager Joe Torre and Giants Manager Joe Altobelli both filed protests. Then on May 9, the argument-weary substitutes ejected four managers, five players and a coach amid a flurry of controversy and chaos.

The three-month dispute started at the beginning of spring training and lasted through 45 days of the season.

The four umpires working the Yankee-Red Sox game in Boston acknowledge the cheers of appreciative fans who welcomed them back from their six-week strike with a standing ovation.

An 11-homer slugfest

Aided by an 18-mph wind blowing out at cozy Wrigley Field, Philadelphia and Chicago batters pounded helpless pitchers into submission May 17 in an 11-home run, 50-hit slugfest that resulted in a 23-22 Phillies victory over the Cubs.

The outcome of this wild and crazy marathon was not decided until the 10th inning when Phillies' third baseman Mike Schmidt hit a Bruce Sutter pitch out of the park for his second home run of the game. That left Schmidt one behind Dave Kingman, who belted three for Chicago.

The 45 combined runs fell four short of the major league record set by the same two teams at Wrigley Field in 1922. The Cubs won that game, 26-23. The 11 home runs tied a record accomplished five times and the 50 total hits were two short of the National League record for an extra-inning contest.

The Phillies scored seven runs in the first inning and eight in the third while building a 17-6 advantage. Chicago scored six in the first, seven in the sixth and finally caught the Phillies at 22-22 with a three-run eighth.

Bob Boone drove in five runs for the Phillies while Chicago got seven RBIs from Bill Buckner and six from Kingman. Rawley Eastwick, the Phillies' fifth pitcher, fired two shutout innings for the victory.

Dave Kingman, Chicago's three-homer man.

CAUGHT ON THE FLY

FEBRUARY
Seven-time A.L. batting champion Rod Carew, entering the option year of his contract and unable to reach agreement with the Minnesota Twins, was traded to California for pitchers Brad Havens and Paul Hartzell, outfielder Ken Landreaux and infielder-catcher Dave Engle.

APRIL
Houston righthander Ken Forsch held Atlanta hitless in a 6-0 victory at the Astrodome and joined St. Louis righthander Bob Forsch as the only brother combination to throw major league no-hitters.

JUNE
California's Nolan Ryan fanned 16 Tigers in a 9-1 win over Detroit, passing the 15-strikeout barrier for the record 21st time in his career.

JULY
Philadelphia's Del Unser set a major league record when he belted home runs against St. Louis, New York and San Diego in consecutive pinch-hitting appearances.

AUGUST
Walter O'Malley, long-time owner of the Dodgers and the man who moved them from Brooklyn to Los Angeles in 1958, died in Rochester, Minn., at age 75.

Munson dies in crash

Thurman Munson, the 32-year-old catcher and captain of the New York Yankees, died August 2 when the plane he was piloting crashed short of the runway while he was trying to land at the Akron-Canton Airport in Ohio.

Munson, the American League's Rookie of the Year in 1970 and its Most Valuable Player in 1976, was trying to land his Cessna Citation twin-engine jet when it clipped the tops of some trees, crashed just off a road and came to rest about 200 feet from the runway. The plane lost its wings and burst into flames.

David Hall and Jerry D. Anderson, two passengers with Munson, survived the crash and were reported in fair condition. The men tried to rescue Munson, but the intense flames thwarted their efforts. Munson was a native of Canton and often flew home during the season to be with his wife and three children.

The 5-foot-11, 190-pounder was an intense competitor. He owned a .292 career average and topped the .300 mark five times. He helped lead the Yankees to three pennants and two World Series titles during his 10-year career.

Police and other officials look over the wreckage of a plane that crashed and killed New York Yankee catcher Thurman Munson.

Promotion goes awry

Master promoter Bill Veeck watched helplessly July 12 as Disco Demolition Night at Chicago's Comiskey Park turned into a riotous romp for unruly fans, forcing the White Sox to forfeit the second game of a doubleheader against Detroit.

The promotion, organized by rock-and-roll disc jockey Steve Dahl of radio station 98 WLUP-FM, attracted more than 50,000 fans, many of them teens who brought disco records and gained entrance to the park for 98 cents. The records were to be burned in a bonfire between games of the twin-bill.

But the first contest, won 4-1 by the Tigers, was interrupted several times when fans began slinging records, Frisbee-style, onto the field. When the first game ended, the bonfire was built and more than 7,000 fans raced out of the stands, refusing to leave the field as the starting time approached for the second contest. An appeal from White Sox Owner Veeck fell on deaf ears.

One hour and 16 minutes after the nightcap was scheduled to begin, umpire-in-chief Dave Phillips deemed the field unplayable. He turned the matter over to American League President Lee MacPhail, who later awarded a forfeit to Detroit.

" DUGOUT CHATTER "

"He was one of those guys who worked hard at refusing to let people think he was a nice fellow."

Gabe Paul

Cleveland President, on former Yankee catcher Thurman Munson, who was killed in a plane crash

N.L. wins on walk

New York's Lee Mazzilli tied the score with an opposite-field home run in the eighth inning and then drew a bases-loaded walk in the ninth as the National League continued its incredible hex over the American League July 17 with a 7-6 All-Star Game victory at Seattle's Kingdome.

The N.L.'s eighth straight All-Star win and 16th in 17 games was achieved in an ugly ninth inning during which Texas reliever Jim Kern walked the bases loaded and New York's Ron Guidry issued the two-out walk to Mazzilli. The Mets center fielder had delivered his game-tying homer as a pinch-hitter off Kern.

The N.L. struck for two first-inning runs against California's Nolan Ryan, but the A.L. answered with three runs against Phillies ace Steve Carlton, two scoring on a homer by Boston's Fred Lynn.

The teams traded leads the rest of the way, with Seattle's Bruce Bochte giving the A.L. a 6-5 advantage with a sixth-inning single. Two potential A.L. runs were cut down at third and home by outstanding throws from Pittsburgh right fielder Dave Parker.

A Disco Demolition Night promotion at Chicago's Comiskey Park was ruined by the riotous romp of unruly fans.

★ 1979 ★
SEPTEMBER - DECEMBER

Yaz joins 3,000 club

Boston veteran Carl Yastrzemski ended three nights of frustration September 12 when he grounded an eighth-inning single into right field for career hit No. 3,000, joining 14 other greats in that exclusive club.

Yaz broke an 0-for-10 slump against New York righthander Jim Beattie, who was only 6 years old in 1961 when the 19-year veteran got his first major league hit. Beattie was pitching in relief of Yankee righthander Catfish Hunter, a 9-2 loser in his final career outing at Fenway Park. Hunter, who is retiring at the end of the season, received a standing ovation from 34,337 fans when he left in the fifth inning.

But the biggest ovation was reserved for Yastrzemski, who becomes the first American Leaguer to garner 3,000 hits and 400 home runs in his career. The 40-year-old joins former National League stars Hank Aaron, Willie Mays and Stan Musial in that distinction.

When Yastrzemski collected his milestone hit, streamers flowed down from the stands, teammates rushed out to congratulate him and a microphone was set up near first base where a 15-minute ceremony took place.

Brock's milestones

St. Louis speedster Lou Brock, who had become the 14th member of baseball's 3,000-hit club 41 days earlier, earned his niche as the game's undisputed all-time leading basestealer September 23 when he passed Billy Hamilton on the career list during a game at New York's Shea Stadium.

The 40-year-old Brock, who is retiring at the end of the season, stole second base in the fifth inning of St. Louis' 7-4 victory over the Mets, giving him 938 stolen bases in his 19-year career. Hamilton was credited with 937 from 1890 to 1901, but his total was in-

flated by rules of an era that granted steals any time a runner advanced a base. Brock became the modern basestealing king in 1977 when he passed Ty Cobb's career total of 892.

Brock's 3,000th hit, an infield single, was collected August 13 in a 3-2 Cardinal victory over Chicago at Busch Stadium. With 44,457 fans chanting, "Lou, Lou, Lou," Brock lined a fourth-inning pitch off the hand of righthander Dennis Lamp and scampered safely to first, where he was honored in a brief ceremony that drew a thunderous ovation.

St. Louis' Lou Brock (20) gets a warm welcome to the 3,000-hit club.

Keough ends long skid

Center fielder Dwayne Murphy homered and drove in four runs September 5, but the attention after Oakland's 6-1 conquest of Milwaukee focused on pitcher Matt Keough. Champagne corks popped and everybody celebrated the righthander's first victory of the season after 14 losses.

Keough allowed five hits and struck out five in winning for the first time since September 1, 1978. The 14 losses had tied a major league record for defeats to open a season (set in 1906 by Joe Harris of the Boston Red Sox) and his 18 straight setbacks over two campaigns was one short of the American League record.

Murphy had a lot to do with Keough's breakthrough victory, adding two outstanding catches to his offensive heroics. It was Murphy who had called a pre-game meeting, urging the A's to try a little harder for the youngster.

They did, and with the sparse crowd of 1,172 fans at the Oakland Coliseum chanting, "Keough, Keough," the 24-year-old responded by handcuffing the Brewers and thwarting Mike Caldwell's bid for his ninth straight triumph.

Oakland A's hard-luck righthander Matt Keough.

" DUGOUT CHATTER "

"I learned a lot, but I don't want to learn it again."

Matt Keough

Oakland pitcher, after winning his first game in more than a year and snapping a personal 18-game losing streak

"Baseball should be played on natural grass. It's nice and soft and it grows and you don't get hurt. Artificial turf is reincarnated dinosaurs. It's petroleum. We're wasting a non-renewable resource by making artificial turf. Cut a hole in it and let the sunshine in."

Bill (Spaceman) Lee

Montreal lefthander and philosopher

SEASON LEADERS

	American League		National League	
Avg.	Fred Lynn, Bos.	.333	Keith Hernandez, St. L.	.344
HR	Gorman Thomas, Mil.	45	Dave Kingman, Chi.	48
RBI	Don Baylor, Cal.	139	Dave Winfield, S.D.	118
SB	Willie Wilson, K.C.	83	Omar Moreno, Pit.	77
W-L Pct.	Mike Caldwell, Mil. 16-6, .727		Tom Seaver, Cin. 16-6, .727	
ERA	Ron Guidry, N.Y.	2.78	J.R. Richard, Hou.	2.71
SO	Nolan Ryan, Cal.	223	J.R. Richard, Hou.	313

Martin fired again

New York Yankee Manager Billy Martin, who split the lip of a Minnesota marshmallow salesman five days earlier in a Bloomington barroom fight, was fired October 28 by Owner George Steinbrenner for the second time in 15 months.

The ever-tempestuous Martin decked 52-year-old Joseph W. Cooper October 23 in a one-punch altercation, causing a badly cut lip that required 20 stitches. Martin denied the charge, saying Cooper had fallen, but witnesses told a different story. Martin re-portedly landed his punch after Cooper had taken a swing at him.

Steinbrenner did not waste much time, firing Martin and replacing him with former Yankee player and coach Dick Howser. It marked the fifth time that Martin has lost a managerial job. He served one season in Minnesota, three in Detroit, one and a half with Texas and just short of three in his first stint with the Yankees.

Howser takes over a Yankee team that finished 89-71 last season, good for fourth place in the American League East Division.

CAUGHT ON THE FLY

SEPTEMBER

Philadelphia's Pete Rose singled in a 7-2 loss to St. Louis, becoming a 200-hit man for the record 10th time in his career. Ty Cobb had held the record with nine.

Atlanta's Phil Niekro raised his record to 20-20 with a 9-4 victory over Houston and brother Joe, a 20-game winner for the Astros.

OCTOBER

The Oakland Athletics, 54-108 and last in the American League West Division, finished with a disappointing home attendance of 306, 763.

WORLD SERIES REPORT

A FAMILY AFFAIR

Willie Stargell crashed a two-run homer and relievers Grant Jackson and Kent Tekulve combined for 4⅓ hitless innings as the Pittsburgh Pirates completed their startling comeback from a three-games-to-one World Series deficit with a 4-1 seventh-game victory over Baltimore.

The October 17 clincher at Baltimore's Memorial Stadium was orchestrated by the 38-year-old Stargell, known affectionately in the Pirates' clubhouse as "Pops." It seemed only fitting that the game-deciding blow off Orioles starter Scott McGregor, wiping out a 1-0 deficit, should be provided by the un-official head of Pittsburgh's "family" and the glue that had pulled every-one together during the season when the chips were down.

They couldn't have been more down following Game 4 at Pitts-burgh, after the Orioles had wiped out a 6-3 deficit with a six-run out-burst in the eighth inning. That 9-6 Oriole victory and 3-1 Series advan-tage would provide a serious test to the Pirates' family structure.

The Pirates, who had not been challenged at all in a quick-and-easy National League Championship Series sweep of Cincinnati, pulled to-gether and came up with a 7-1 fifth-game victory behind the combined six-hit pitching of Jim Rooker and Bert Blyleven. They pulled even two days later at Baltimore when John Candelaria and Tekulve combined on a seven-hit 4-0 shutout. Jim Bibby, Don Robinson, Jackson and Tekulve outdueled McGregor in Game 7, which remained 2-1 until the Pirates scored twice in the ninth. Baltimore had managed only two runs in the final 28 innings of the Series.

"Pops," of course, was the offen-sive ringleader, batting .400 and hit-ting three home runs, but four other Pirates (Dave Parker, Phil Garner, Omar Moreno and Tim Foli) col-lected 10 or more hits. And Pirate pitchers, who were supported by a .323 team batting average, held the Orioles to a .232 mark.

It was celebration time for the Pittsburgh Pirates after disposing of Baltimore in a seven-game World Series.

Game 1	Baltimore	5	Pittsburgh	4
Game 2	Pittsburgh	3	Baltimore	2
Game 3	Baltimore	8	Pittsburgh	4
Game 4	Baltimore	9	Pittsburgh	6
Game 5	Pittsburgh	7	Baltimore	1
Game 6	Pittsburgh	4	Baltimore	0
Game 7	Pittsburgh	4	Baltimore	1

'Family' leader Willie Stargell gets a hug from Omar Moreno after hitting a two-run Game 7 World Series homer.

The 1980s

Amazingly, the essence of the game being played in the 1980s by millionaire athletes in high-tech stadia remained similar to early-century baseball played under less desirable and rewarding conditions.

No matter how hard they tried, owners and players could not mess up a good thing.

And try they did. While owners raised ticket prices to support their indiscriminate spending, fluff and showmanship, players fought them for money, filed lawsuits, went on strike, jumped teams and cleansed their physical indiscretions in drug and alcohol rehabilitation clinics. Both sides tested the patience of their fans in every way imaginable and pushed them to the brink of revolt. Still they came.

Despite a 50-day midseason strike in 1981, despite the 1985 Pittsburgh trials that exposed widespread player drug abuse, despite unending courtroom battles and threatened work stoppages, despite the astronomical salaries . . . they poured through the turnstiles. And baseball prospered, to the tune of billion-dollar television contracts and almost yearly attendance records.

That's because baseball, as distasteful as it often was off the field, was

NATIONAL LEAGUE

League Batting Leaders

Average

Year	Player-Team	Avg.
1980	Bill Buckner, Chi.	.324
1981	Bill Madlock, Pit.*	.341
1982	Al Oliver, Mon.	.331
1983	Bill Madlock, Pit.	.323
1984	Tony Gwynn, S.D.	.351
1985	Willie McGee, St. L.	.353
1986	Tim Raines, Mon.	.334
1987	Tony Gwynn, S.D.	.370
1988	Tony Gwynn, S.D.	.313
1989	Tony Gwynn, S.D.	.336

Home Runs

Year	Player-Team	HR
1980	Mike Schmidt, Phil.	48
1981	Mike Schmidt, Phil.	31
1982	Dave Kingman, N.Y.	37
1983	Mike Schmidt, Phil.	40
1984	Mike Schmidt, Phil.	36
	Dale Murphy, Atl.	36
1985	Dale Murphy, Atl.	37
1986	Mike Schmidt, Phil.	37
1987	Andre Dawson, Chi.	49
1988	Darryl Strawberry, N.Y.	39
1989	Kevin Mitchell, S.F.	47

RBIs

Year	Player-Team	RBI
1980	Mike Schmidt, Phil.	121
1981	Mike Schmidt, Phil.	91
1982	Dale Murphy, Atl.	109
	Al Oliver, Mon.	109
1983	Dale Murphy, Atl.	121
1984	Gary Carter, Mon.	106
	Mike Schmidt, Phil.	106
1985	Dave Parker, Cin.	125
1986	Mike Schmidt, Phil.	119
1987	Andre Dawson, Chi.	137
1988	Will Clark, S.F.	109
1989	Kevin Mitchell, S.F.	125

Most Valuable Players

Selected by BBWAA

Year	Player-Team	Pos.
1980	Mike Schmidt, Phil.	3B
1981	Mike Schmidt, Phil.	3B
1982	Dale Murphy, Atl.	OF
1983	Dale Murphy, Atl.	OF
1984	Ryne Sandberg, Chi.	2B
1985	Willie McGee, St. L.	OF
1986	Mike Schmidt, Phil.	3B
1987	Andre Dawson, Chi.	OF
1988	Kirk Gibson, L.A.	OF
1989	Kevin Mitchell, S.F.	OF

League Pitching Leaders

Winning Percentage

Year	Pitcher-Team	W-L	Pct.
1980	Jim Bibby, Pit.	19-6	.760
1981	Tom Seaver, Cin.	14-2	.875
1982	Phil Niekro, Atl.	17-4	.810
1983	John Denny, Phil.	19-6	.760
1984	Rick Sutcliffe, Chi.	16-1	.941
1985	Orel Hershiser, L.A.	19-3	.864
1986	Bob Ojeda, N.Y.	18-5	.783
1987	Dwight Gooden, N.Y.	15-7	.682
1988	David Cone, N.Y.	20-3	.870
1989	Scott Garrelts, S.F.	14-5	.737
	Sid Fernandez, N.Y.	14-5	.737

Earned-Run Average

Year	Pitcher-Team	ERA
1980	Don Sutton, L.A.	2.21
1981	Nolan Ryan, Hou.	1.69
1982	Steve Rogers, Mon.	2.40
1983	Atlee Hammaker, S.F.	2.25
1984	Alejandro Pena, L.A.	2.48
1985	Dwight Gooden, N.Y.	1.53
1986	Mike Scott, Hou.	2.22
1987	Nolan Ryan, Hou.	2.76
1988	Joe Magrane, St. L.	2.18
1989	Scott Garrelts, S.F.	2.28

Strikeouts

Year	Pitcher-Team	SO
1980	Steve Carlton, Phil.	286
1981	Fernando Valenzuela, L.A.	
		180
1982	Steve Carlton, Phil.	286
1983	Steve Carlton, Phil.	275
1984	Dwight Gooden, N.Y.	276
1985	Dwight Gooden, N.Y.	268
1986	Mike Scott, Hou.	306
1987	Nolan Ryan, Hou.	270
1988	Nolan Ryan, Hou.	228
1989	Jose DeLeon, St. L.	201

Cy Young Winners

Selected by BBWAA

Year	Pitcher-Team	Thr.
1980	Steve Carlton, Phil.	L
1981	Fernando Valenzuela, L.A.	L
1982	Steve Carlton, Phil.	L
1983	John Denny, Phil.	R
1984	Rick Sutcliffe, Chi.	R
1985	Dwight Gooden, N.Y.	R
1986	Mike Scott, Hou.	R
1987	Steve Bedrosian, Phil.	R
1988	Orel Hershiser, L.A.	R
1989	Mark Davis, S.D.	L

LEAGUE CHAMPIONSHIP SERIES

National League

Year	Winner	Runnerup	Games
1980	Philadelphia Phillies	Houston Astros	3-2
1981	Los Angeles Dodgers	Montreal Expos	3-2
1982	St. Louis Cardinals	Atlanta Braves	3-0
1983	Philadelphia Phillies	Los Angeles Dodgers	3-1
1984	San Diego Padres	Chicago Cubs	3-2
1985	St. Louis Cardinals	Los Angeles Dodgers	4-2
1986	New York Mets	Houston Astros	4-2
1987	St. Louis Cardinals	San Francisco Giants	4-3
1988	Los Angeles Dodgers	New York Mets	4-3
1989	San Francisco Giants	Chicago Cubs	4-1

American League

Year	Winner	Runnerup	Games
1980	Kansas City Royals	New York Yankees	3-0
1981	New York Yankees	Oakland Athletics	3-0
1982	Milwaukee Brewers	California Angels	3-2
1983	Baltimore Orioles	Chicago White Sox	3-1
1984	Detroit Tigers	Kansas City Royals	3-0
1985	Kansas City Royals	Toronto Blue Jays	4-3
1986	Boston Red Sox	California Angels	4-3
1987	Minnesota Twins	Detroit Tigers	4-1
1988	Oakland Athletics	Boston Red Sox	4-0
1989	Oakland Athletics	Toronto Blue Jays	4-1

Final Standings

Defeated Los Angeles in one-game division playoff †Split season; Montreal defeated Philadelpnia, 3-2, and Los Angeles defeated Houston, 3-2, in division playoffs

1980

East	W	L	Pct.	GB
Philadelphia	91	71	.562	--
Montreal	90	72	.556	1
Pittsburgh	83	79	.512	8
St. Louis	74	88	.457	17
New York	67	95	.414	24
Chicago	64	98	.395	27

West	W	L	Pct.	GB
*Houston	93	70	.571	--
Los Angeles	92	71	.564	1
Cincinnati	89	73	.549	3.5
Atlanta	81	80	.503	11
S.F.	75	86	.466	17
San Diego	73	89	.451	19.5

1981

East	W	L	Pct.	GB
St. Louis	59	43	.578	--
†Montreal	60	48	.556	2
Philadelphia	59	48	.551	2.5
Pittsburgh	46	56	.451	13
New York	41	62	.398	18.5
Chicago	38	65	.369	21.5

West	W	L	Pct.	GB
Cincinnati	66	42	.611	--
†Los Angeles	63	47	.573	4
Houston	61	49	.555	6
S.F.	56	55	.505	11.5
Atlanta	50	56	.472	15
San Diego	41	69	.373	26

1982

East	W	L	Pct.	GB
St. Louis	92	70	.568	--
Philadelphia	89	73	.549	3
Montreal	86	76	.531	6
Pittsburgh	84	78	.519	8
Chicago	73	89	.451	19
New York	65	97	.401	27

West	W	L	Pct.	GB
Atlanta	89	73	.549	--
Los Angeles	88	74	.543	1
S.F.	87	75	.537	2
San Diego	81	81	.500	8
Houston	77	85	.475	12
Cincinnati	61	101	.377	28

1983

East	W	L	Pct.	GB
Philadelphia	90	72	.556	--
Pittsburgh	84	78	.519	6
Montreal	82	80	.506	8
St. Louis	79	83	.488	11
Chicago	71	91	.438	19
New York	68	94	.420	22

West	W	L	Pct.	GB
Los Angeles	91	71	.562	--
Atlanta	88	74	.543	3
Houston	85	77	.525	6
San Diego	81	81	.500	10
S.F.	79	83	.488	12
Cincinnati	74	88	.457	17

1984

	W	L	Pct.	GB
Chicago	96	65	.596	--
New York	90	72	.556	6.5
St. Louis	84	78	.519	12.5
Philadelphia	81	81	.500	15.5
Montreal	78	83	.484	18
Pittsburgh	75	87	.463	21.5

West	W	L	Pct.	GB
San Diego	92	70	.568	--
Atlanta	80	82	.494	12
Houston	80	82	.494	12
Los Angeles	79	83	.488	13
Cincinnati	70	92	.432	22
S.F.	66	96	.407	26

1985

East	W	L	Pct.	GB
St. Louis	101	61	.623	--
New York	98	64	.605	3
Montreal	84	77	.522	16.5
Chicago	77	84	.478	23.5
Philadelphia	75	87	.463	26
Pittsburgh	57	104	.354	43.5

West	W	L	Pct.	GB
Los Angeles	95	67	.586	--
Cincinnati	89	72	.553	5.5
Houston	83	79	.512	12
San Diego	83	79	.512	12
Atlanta	66	96	.407	29
S.F.	62	100	.383	33

1986

East	W	L	Pct.	GB
New York	108	54	.667	--
Philadelphia	86	75	.534	21.5
St. Louis	79	82	.491	28.5
Montreal	78	83	.484	29.5
Chicago	70	90	.438	37
Pittsburgh	64	98	.395	44

West	W	L	Pct.	GB
Houston	96	66	.593	--
Cincinnati	86	76	.531	10
S.F.	83	79	.512	13
San Diego	74	88	.457	22
Los Angeles	73	89	.451	23
Atlanta	72	89	.447	23.5

1987

East	W	L	Pct.	GB
St. Louis	95	67	.586	--
New York	92	70	.568	3
Montreal	91	71	.562	4
Philadelphia	80	82	.494	15
Pittsburgh	80	82	.494	15
Chicago	76	85	.472	18.5

West	W	L	Pct.	GB
S.F.	90	72	.556	--
Cincinnati	84	78	.519	6
Houston	76	86	.469	14
Los Angeles	73	89	.451	17
Atlanta	69	92	.429	20.5
San Diego	65	97	.401	25

1988

East	W	L	Pct.	GB
New York	100	60	.625	--
Pittsburgh	85	75	.531	15
Montreal	81	81	.500	20
Chicago	77	85	.475	24
St. Louis	76	86	.469	25
Philadelphia	65	96	.404	35.5

West	W	L	Pct.	GB
Los Angeles	94	67	.584	--
Cincinnati	87	74	.540	7
San Diego	83	78	.516	11
S.F.	83	79	.512	11.5
Houston	82	80	.506	12.5
Atlanta	54	106	.338	39.5

1989

East	W	L	Pct.	GB
Chicago	93	69	.574	--
New York	87	75	.537	6
St. Louis	86	76	.531	7
Montreal	81	81	.500	12
Pittsburgh	74	88	.457	19
Philadelphia	67	95	.414	26

West	W	L	Pct.	GB
S.F.	92	70	.568	--
San Diego	89	73	.549	3
Houston	86	76	.531	6
Los Angeles	77	83	.488	11.5
Cincinnati	75	87	.463	17
Atlanta	63	97	.394	28

Atlanta slugger Dale Murphy.

as charming and invigorating as ever between the white lines. Like George Brett flirting with the magic .400 average. Rookie Fernando Valenzuela, a moon-faced Mexican pitcher, capturing the heart of a nation. Rickey Henderson's flying feet breaking every basestealing record. Nolan Ryan's bionic arm piling up no-hitters and strikeouts. Pete Rose breaking Ty Cobb's all-time hit record. Len Barker, Mike Witt and Tom Browning throwing perfect games. Roger Clemens striking out 20 batters in one contest. Orel Hershiser pitching 59 straight scoreless innings. And Bo Jackson earning acclaim in two sports.

The decade began with Philadelphia, one of the original 16 teams when World Series play began, ending 77 years of frustration by claiming its first fall classic. It ended with Oakland sweeping San Francisco in a World Series that was memorable because of a devastating earthquake that almost brought it to a premature conclusion. In between, Kansas City (1985) and Minnesota (1987) won their first championships and the New York Mets captured their second (1986) with a near-miraculous comeback.

There were sad notes. A tradition passed in Chicago when Wrigley Field, the last bastion of daytime baseball, lit up for the first time, and a legend was tarnished in Cincinnati when Rose was banned from baseball for his alleged gambling activities. Baseball lost a commissioner to a heart attack when A. Bartlett Giamatti passed away — eight days after announcing his decision on Rose.

But through it all, the game has never lost its zest or its penchant for the absurd. Like the Baltimore Orioles starting a season 0-21, or a salary structure that has spiraled beyond any player's wildest fantasy. Consider that Reggie Jackson, one of the original free agents in 1976, accepted a five-year, $2.9 million deal with the New York Yankees. Fifteen years later, free agent Bobby Bonilla signed a five-year, $29 million contract with the New York Mets.

WORLD SERIES

Year	Winner	Pennant Winner	Games
1980	Philadelphia Phillies	Kansas City Royals	4-2
1981	Los Angeles Dodgers	New York Yankees	4-2
1982	St. Louis Cardinals	Milwaukee Brewers	4-3
1983	Baltimore Orioles	Philadelphia Phillies	4-1
1984	Detroit Tigers	San Diego Padres	4-1
1985	Kansas City Royals	St. Louis Cardinals	4-3
1986	New York Mets	Boston Red Sox	4-3
1987	Minnesota Twins	St. Louis Cardinals	4-3
1988	Los Angeles Dodgers	Oakland Athletics	4-1
1989	Oakland Athletics	San Francisco Giants	4-0

HALL OF FAME Electees and Additions

- 1980 Al Kaline, Duke Snider, Chuck Klein, Tom Yawkey.
- 1981 Bob Gibson, Johnny Mize, Rube Foster.
- 1982 Hank Aaron, Frank Robinson, A.B. (Happy) Chandler, Travis Jackson.
- 1983 Brooks Robinson, Juan Marichal, George Kell, Walter Alston.
- 1984 Luis Aparicio, Harmon Killebrew, Don Drysdale, Rick Ferrell, Pee Wee Reese.
- 1985 Hoyt Wilhelm, Lou Brock, Enos Slaughter, Arky Vaughan.
- 1986 Willie McCovey, Bobby Doerr, Ernie Lombardi.
- 1987 Billy Williams, Catfish Hunter, Ray Dandridge.
- 1988 Willie Stargell.
- 1989 Johnny Bench, Carl Yastrzemski, Al Barlick, Red Schoendienst.

AMERICAN LEAGUE

League Batting Leaders

Average

Year	Player-Team	Avg.
1980	George Brett, K.C.	.390
1981	Carney Lansford, Bos.	.336
1982	Willie Wilson, K.C.	.332
1983	Wade Boggs, Bos.	.361
1984	Don Mattingly, N.Y.	.343
1985	Wade Boggs, Bos.	.368
1986	Wade Boggs, Bos.	.357
1987	Wade Boggs, Bos.	.363
1988	Wade Boggs, Bos.	.366
1989	Kirby Puckett, Min.	.339

Home Runs

Year	Player-Team	HR
1980	Reggie Jackson, N.Y.	41
	Ben Oglivie, Mil.	41
1981	Tony Armas, Oak. Dwight Evans, Bos. R. Grich, Cal. Eddie Murray, Bal.	22
1982	Reggie Jackson, Cal.	39
	Gorman Thomas, Mil.	39
1983	Jim Rice, Bos.	39
1984	Tony Armas, Bos.	43
1985	Darrell Evans, Det.	40
1986	Jesse Barfield, Tor.	40
1987	Mark McGwire, Oak.	49
1988	Jose Canseco, Oak.	42
1989	Fred McGriff, Tor.	36

RBIs

Year	Player-Team	RBI
1980	Cecil Cooper, Mil.	122
1981	Eddie Murray, Bal.	78
1982	Hal McRae, K.C.	133
1983	Cecil Cooper, Mil.	126
	Jim Rice, Bos.	126
1984	Tony Armas, Bos.	123
1985	Don Mattingly, N.Y.	145
1986	Joe Carter, Cle.	121
1987	George Bell, Tor.	134
1988	Jose Canseco, Oak.	124
1989	Ruben Sierra, Tex.	119

Most Valuable Players

Selected by BBWAA

Year	Player-Team	Pos.
1980	George Brett, K.C.	3B
1981	Rollie Fingers, Mil.	P
1982	Robin Yount, Mil.	SS
1983	Cal Ripken, Bal.	SS
1984	Willie Hernandez, Det.	P
1985	Don Mattingly, N.Y.	1B
1986	Roger Clemens, Bos.	P
1987	George Bell, Tor.	OF
1988	Jose Canseco, Oak.	OF
1989	Robin Yount, Mil.	OF

League Pitching Leaders

Winning Percentage

Year	Pitcher-Team	W-L	Pct.
1980	Steve Stone, Bal.	25-7	.781
1981	Pete Vuckovich, Mil.	14-4	.778
1982	Pete Vuckovich, Mil.	18-6	.750
	Jim Palmer, Bal.	15-5	.750
1983	Rich Dotson, Chi.	22-7	.759
1984	Doyle Alexander, Tor.	17-6	.739
1985	Ron Guidry, N.Y.	22-6	.786
1986	Roger Clemens, Bos.	24-4	.857
1987	Roger Clemens, Bos.	20-9	.690
1988	Frank Viola, Min.	24-7	.774
1989	B. Saberhagen, K.C.	23-6	.793

Earned-Run Average

Year	Pitcher-Team	ERA
1980	Rudy May, N.Y.	2.47
1981	Steve McCatty, Oak.	2.32
1982	Rick Sutcliffe, Cle.	2.96
1983	Rick Honeycutt, Tex.	2.42
1984	Mike Boddicker, Bal.	2.79
1985	Dave Stieb, Tor.	2.48
1986	Roger Clemens, Bos.	2.48
1987	Jimmy Key, Tor.	2.76
1988	Allan Anderson, Min.	2.45
1989	Bret Saberhagen, K.C.	2.16

Strikeouts

Year	Pitcher-Team	SO
1980	Len Barker, Cle.	187
1981	Len Barker, Cle.	127
1982	Floyd Bannister, Sea.	209
1983	Jack Morris, Det.	232
1984	Mark Langston, Sea.	204
1985	Bert Blyleven, Cle.-Min.	206
1986	Mark Langston, Sea.	245
1987	Mark Langston, Sea.	262
1988	Roger Clemens, Bos.	291
1989	Nolan Ryan, Tex.	301

Cy Young Winners

Selected by BBWAA

Year	Pitcher-Team	Thr.
1980	Steve Stone, Bal.	R
1981	Rollie Fingers, Mil.	R
1982	Pete Vuckovich, Mil.	R
1983	LaMarr Hoyt, Chi.	R
1984	Willie Hernandez, Det.	L
1985	Bret Saberhagen, K.C.	R
1986	Roger Clemens, Bos.	R
1987	Roger Clemens, Bos.	R
1988	Frank Viola, Min.	L
1989	Bret Saberhagen, K.C.	R

Final Standings

**Split season; New York defeated Milwaukee, 3-2, and Oakland defeated Kansas City, 3-2, in division playoffs*

1980

East	W	L	Pct.	GB
New York	103	59	.636	- -
Baltimore	100	62	.617	3
Milwaukee	86	76	.531	17
Boston	83	77	.519	19
Detroit	84	78	.519	19
Cleveland	79	81	.494	23
Toronto	67	95	.414	36

West	W	L	Pct.	GB
Kansas City	97	65	.599	- -
Oakland	83	79	.512	14
Minnesota	77	84	.478	19.5
Texas	76	85	.472	20.5
Chicago	70	90	.438	26
California	65	95	.406	31
Seattle	59	103	.364	38

1981

East	W	L	Pct.	GB
Milwaukee	62	47	.569	- -
Baltimore	59	46	.562	1
*New York	59	48	.551	2
Detroit	60	49	.550	2
Boston	59	49	.546	2.5
Cleveland	52	51	.505	7
Toronto	37	69	.349	23.5

West	W	L	Pct.	GB
*Oakland	64	45	.587	- -
Texas	57	48	.543	5
Chicago	54	52	.509	8.5
Kansas City	50	53	.485	11
California	51	59	.464	13.5
Seattle	44	65	.404	20
Minnesota	41	68	.376	23

1982

East	W	L	Pct.	GB
Milwaukee	95	67	.586	- -
Baltimore	94	68	.580	1
Boston	89	73	.549	6
Detroit	83	79	.512	12
New York	79	83	.488	16
Cleveland	78	84	.481	17
Toronto	78	84	.481	17

West	W	L	Pct.	GB
California	93	69	.574	- -
Kansas City	90	72	.556	3
Chicago	87	75	.537	6
Seattle	76	86	.469	17
Oakland	68	94	.420	25
Texas	64	98	.395	29
Minnesota	60	102	.370	33

1983

East	W	L	Pct.	GB
Baltimore	98	64	.605	- -
Detroit	92	70	.568	6
New York	91	71	.562	7
Toronto	89	73	.549	9
Milwaukee	87	75	.537	11
Boston	78	84	.481	20
Cleveland	70	92	.432	28

West	W	L	Pct.	GB
Chicago	99	63	.611	- -
Kansas City	79	83	.488	20
Texas	77	85	.475	22
Oakland	74	88	.457	25
California	70	92	.432	29
Minnesota	70	92	.432	29
Seattle	60	102	.370	39

1984

	W	L	Pct.	GB
Detroit	104	58	.642	- -
Toronto	89	73	.549	15
New York	87	75	.537	17
Boston	86	76	.531	18
Baltimore	85	77	.525	19
Cleveland	75	87	.463	29
Milwaukee	67	94	.416	36.5

West	W	L	Pct.	GB
Kansas City	84	78	.519	- -
California	81	81	.500	3
Minnesota	81	81	.500	3
Oakland	77	85	.475	7
Chicago	74	88	.457	10
Seattle	74	88	.457	10
Texas	69	92	.429	14.5

1985

East	W	L	Pct.	GB
Toronto	99	62	.615	- -
New York	97	64	.602	2
Detroit	84	77	.522	15
Baltimore	83	78	.516	16
Boston	81	81	.500	18.5
Milwaukee	71	90	.441	28
Cleveland	60	102	.370	39.5

West	W	L	Pct.	GB
Kansas City	91	71	.562	- -
California	90	72	.556	1
Chicago	85	77	.525	6
Minnesota	77	85	.475	14
Oakland	77	85	.475	14
Seattle	74	88	.457	17
Texas	62	99	.385	28.5

1986

East	W	L	Pct.	GB
Boston	95	66	.590	- -
New York	90	72	.556	5.5
Detroit	87	75	.537	8.5
Toronto	86	76	.531	9.5
Cleveland	84	78	.519	11.5
Milwaukee	77	84	.478	18
Baltimore	73	89	.451	22.5

West	W	L	Pct.	GB
California	92	70	.568	- -
Texas	87	75	.537	5
Kansas City	76	86	.469	16
Oakland	76	86	.469	16
Chicago	72	90	.444	20
Minnesota	71	91	.438	21
Seattle	67	95	.414	25

1987

East	W	L	Pct.	GB
Detroit	98	64	.605	- -
Toronto	96	66	.593	2
Milwaukee	91	71	.562	7
New York	89	73	.549	9
Boston	78	84	.481	20
Baltimore	67	95	.414	31
Cleveland	61	101	.377	37

West	W	L	Pct.	GB
Minnesota	85	77	.525	- -
Kansas City	83	79	.512	2
Oakland	81	81	.500	4
Seattle	78	84	.481	7
Chicago	77	85	.475	8
California	75	87	.463	10
Texas	75	87	.463	10

1988

East	W	L	Pct.	GB
Boston	89	73	.549	- -
Detroit	88	74	.543	1
Milwaukee	87	75	.537	2
Toronto	87	75	.537	2
New York	85	76	.528	3.5
Cleveland	78	84	.481	11
Baltimore	54	107	.335	34.5

West	W	L	Pct.	GB
Oakland	104	58	.642	- -
Minnesota	91	71	.562	13
Kansas City	84	77	.522	19.5
California	75	87	.463	29
Chicago	71	90	.441	32.5
Texas	70	91	.435	33.5
Seattle	68	93	.422	35.5

1989

East	W	L	Pct.	GB
Toronto	89	73	.549	- -
Baltimore	87	75	.537	2
Boston	83	79	.512	6
Milwaukee	81	81	.500	8
New York	74	87	.460	14.5
Cleveland	73	89	.451	16
Detroit	59	103	.364	30

West	W	L	Pct.	GB
Oakland	99	63	.611	- -
Kansas City	92	70	.568	7
California	91	71	.562	8
Texas	83	79	.512	16
Minnesota	80	82	.494	19
Seattle	73	89	.451	26
Chicago	69	92	.429	29.5

★1980★
JANUARY - OCTOBER

An American disaster

A sixth-inning error by New York second baseman Willie Randolph allowed the winning run to score and the National League held on for a 4-2 All-Star Game victory over the American League in the July 6 classic at Dodger Stadium, extending its winning streak to nine.

Continuing its amazing hex and winning for the 17th time in 18 games, the N.L. fought back after being retired without a hit by Baltimore's Steve Stone and New York's Tommy John for 4⅔ innings and falling behind on a two-run fifth-inning homer by Boston's Fred Lynn.

The Nationals' first hit was a solo homer by Cincinnati's Ken Griffey in the bottom of the fifth and they tied in the sixth on singles by Cincinnati's Ray Knight, Pittsburgh's Phil Garner and St. Louis' George Hendrick. Garner scored the game-winner when Randolph failed to come up with a smash by San Diego slugger Dave Winfield.

Dodger Jerry Reuss pitched one inning for the victory while Chicago reliever Bruce Sutter, winner of both the 1978 and '79 midsummer classics, pitched two innings for a save.

Cincinnati's Ken Griffey gave the N.L. a jump start with a fifth-inning homer that triggered a 4-2 All-Star Game victory at Dodger Stadium.

" DUGOUT CHATTER "

"Some days you tame the tiger and some days the tiger has you for lunch."

Tug McGraw

Philadelphia pitcher, on the peaks and valleys of life as a relief pitcher

"I can only repeat what Dave McNally once said about Earl. That is, 'The only thing he knows about pitching is that he couldn't hit it.' "

Jim Palmer

Baltimore pitcher, on Orioles manager Earl Weaver

Strike is averted

The major league season, on the verge of being interrupted for the first time in history by a players' strike, got a reprieve only 10 hours before the walkout was to begin May 23 when the players and owners agreed to defer a settlement of the troublesome free-agent compensation issue until next January.

With a players' strike scheduled to start with an afternoon game in Chicago, the two sides reached agreement at 5 a.m. in New York. Everything was settled except a dispute involving the system that allows players to become free agents after six years of major league service. The owners want to increase the compensation teams receive after losing a free agent and the players feel such a modification would dilute the system. Unable to solve the problem, the parties decided to put it off until next year.

The agreement, which will last four years if the free-agent issue can be resolved, came after six months of negotiations that included a player boycott during the last week of spring training. The players agreed to play the first six weeks of the season, setting the May 23 deadline for reaching an accord.

Houston ace Richard hospitalized by stroke

Fireballing Houston ace J.R. Richard, a 20-game winner in 1976, underwent successful surgery for a blocked artery in his neck July 30, hours after suffering a stroke during a workout at the Astrodome.

The 6-foot-8 Richard, despite compiling an impressive 10-4 record this season, had been complaining for several months of a fatigued arm. Team doctors sent him to the hospital in mid-July for four days of tests, but the results were negative. Rumors had begun circulating that Richard's problems were emotional rather than physical.

That obviously was not the case. The big righthander with the blazing fastball and 90-mph slider suddenly became dizzy and collapsed while playing catch. He was rushed to the hospital where a blood clot was detected behind his right collarbone in a main artery that provides circulation for the upper limbs. That caused the stroke.

Richard, who had pitched the first two innings for the National League in the July 6 All-Star Game, has a career record of 107-71 with a 3.15 earned-run average and 1,493 strikeouts in seven-plus seasons. It is not known whether he will be able to pitch again.

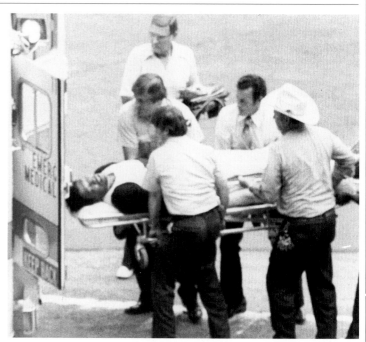

Houston pitching ace J. R. Richard is lifted into an ambulance after suffering a stroke during a workout at the Astrodome.

Astros regroup, beat Dodgers in playoff

First baseman Art Howe drove in four runs and knuckleballer Joe Niekro earned his 20th victory with a six-hitter as the Houston Astros avoided one of baseball's great collapses October 6 with a 7-1 victory over Los Angeles in a one-game playoff to decide the National League West Division championship.

The clutch victory before 51,127 pennant-hungry fans at Dodger Stadium came on the heels of a near-disastrous season-closing sweep that allowed the desperate Dodgers to pull even on the final day. The confident Astros, sporting a three-game lead, had arrived in Los Angeles October 3 for a three-game showdown against the Dodgers needing only one victory to clinch the first division title since the club was formed in 1962. But it never happened — at least not as choreographed by Houston players and fans.

The Dodgers won the first game, 3-2, on Joe Ferguson's 10th-inning home run, won the

second, 2-1, on Steve Garvey's fourth-inning homer and won the third, 4-3, on Ron Cey's two-run shot in the eighth inning. The shellshocked Astros, who blew a 3-0 lead in the finale, would have to regain their composure — and fast.

They did. Houston struck quickly with two unearned runs in the first inning of the playoff against Dodger starter Dave Goltz and Howe's two-run homer, which he celebrated with an exuberant hand-clapping jaunt around the bases, increased the lead in the third. Howe singled home two more runs in a three-run fourth inning that made life easy for Niekro, who allowed only one unearned run in his complete-game performance.

The Astros, well aware that a playoff loss would have linked them historically with such collapsing teams as the 1951 Dodgers, the 1964 Philadelphia Phillies and the 1978 Boston Red Sox, will meet Philadelphia in the

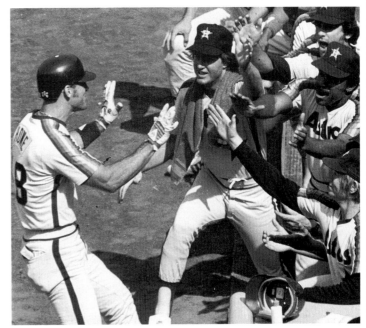

Houston's Art Howe gets a hero's welcome after blasting a two-run homer during the Astros' N.L. West Division playoff victory over Los Angeles.

upcoming N.L. Championship Series. The Phillies edged Montreal by a single game in the N.L. East Division race, clinching the

title on October 4 when Mike Schmidt delivered a dramatic two-run, 11th-inning homer in a 6-4 win over the Expos.

Kuhn is overruled

Arbitrator Raymond Goetz, a law professor at the University of Kansas, overturned the Commissioner-imposed suspension of Texas pitcher Ferguson Jenkins September 22, handing baseball's highest authority its first-ever such reversal.

Commissioner Bowie Kuhn had suspended Jenkins September 8 when the talented right-hander refused to cooperate with investigators and answer questions about his August 25 arrest for drug possession in Toronto. Customs officials had discovered cocaine, marijuana and hashish in Jenkins' suitcase.

When the 36-year-old right-hander, a winner of more than 250 big-league games, was suspended for the remainder of the season, the Major League Players' Association filed a grievance. Marvin Miller, executive director of the players' association, and Ray Grebey, director of the owners' player relations committee, split their votes as the other two members of the arbitration panel, leaving Goetz to decide the issue.

The decision indicates that the

Commissioner's authority over players is not as all-encompassing as it is over owners. Jenkins, a Canadian citizen, is scheduled to be tried December 18.

Texas Rangers pitcher Ferguson Jenkins and wife leaving a Brampton, Ontario, courthouse.

CAUGHT ON THE FLY

MAY
Chicago White Sox first baseman Mike Squires caught the final inning of an 11-1 loss to Milwaukee, becoming the first lefthanded backstop since the Chicago Cubs' Dale Long in 1958.

Baltimore lefthander Scott McGregor stopped Minnesota's Ken Landreaux four times in an 11-1 Oriole victory, ending the outfielder's hitting streak at 31 games.

JUNE
Fred Patek, California's miniature 5-foot-4 shortstop, muscled up and belted three homers while driving in seven runs in a 20-2 Angels' victory at Boston.

JULY
Houston fireballer Nolan Ryan fanned Cincinnati's Cesar Geronimo during an 8-1 loss to the Reds, becoming the fourth pitcher to reach the 3,000-strikeout plateau.

AUGUST
The Seattle Mariners fired Darrell Johnson and made former Los Angeles shortstop Maury Wills the third black manager in major league history.

☆1980☆

OCTOBER-DECEMBER

Phillies win classic

Philadelphia's Garry Maddox doubled home the winning run in the 10th inning October 12 and the Phillies escaped with an 8-7 victory over Houston, ending a tense, topsy-turvy National League Championship Series that was full of comebacks, clutch performances and extra-inning heroics.

If this wasn't the greatest League Championship Series ever played, it had to be close. The Game 5 finale at the Houston Astrodome was a classic by itself. The Phillies wiped out a 5-2 deficit with a five-run eighth-inning rally, the Astros scored two in the bottom of the inning to tie and Philadelphia broke through for its game-winner in the 10th. Dick Ruthven, the last of six Phillies' pitchers, made the lead stand up with his second shutout inning and Philadelphia had its first pennant since 1950.

That was the fourth extra-inning game of the Series. Only the opener, won 3-1 by Philadelphia behind Steve Carlton and Tug McGraw, was decided in regulation. Greg Luzinski provided the

offensive spark in that contest with a two-run homer.

The fireworks really started when Houston scored four 10th-inning runs in Game 2 and escaped with a 7-4 victory. The Astros moved within one game of their first N.L. pennant two days later with a pulsating 1-0 victory in 11 innings. Joe Niekro (10 innings) and Dave Smith combined on the seven-hitter that was decided by Joe Morgan's triple and Denny Walling's sacrifice fly.

The fourth game featured a near-triple play controversy in the fourth inning that delayed the contest 20 minutes. When play resumed, the Phillies wiped out a 2-0 deficit with three eighth-inning runs, Houston tied in the bottom of the inning and Philadelphia won in the 10th on RBI doubles by Luzinski and Manny Trillo.

Houston starter Nolan Ryan coasted through seven innings of Game 5 before being routed in the Phillies' five-run eighth. Three pitchers followed with Frank LaCorte finally surrendering Maddox's winning double.

Garry Maddox gets a victory ride from his Philadelphia teammates after supplying the pennant-winning hit against Houston.

Royals break through

Kansas City third baseman George Brett blasted the New York Yankee jinx into oblivion October 10 and the Royals completed a stunning three-game Championship Series sweep of their hated rivals with a 4-2 victory that secured the franchise's first American League pennant.

Brett provided the Game 3 dramatics when he connected with a Goose Gossage fastball and sent a towering three-run shot into the upper tier at Yankee Stadium. The seventh-inning blast wiped away a 2-1 Yankee lead, made a winner of relief ace Dan Quisenberry and avenged ALCS losses to the Yankees in 1976, '77 and '78.

Brett, coming off a .390 regular

season, also homered in Game 1, a 7-2 Kansas City victory at Royals Stadium. Frank White, Willie Wilson and Willie Aikens drove in two runs apiece to support Larry Gura's 10-hit pitching.

Wilson's two-run triple keyed a three-run third inning and set up a 3-2 victory in Game 2. The pivotal play of the Series occurred in the eighth inning of that contest when Yankee Willie Randolph was cut down at the plate by a Brett relay while trying to score the tying run on a Bob Watson double.

The heavily-favored Yankees had posted baseball's best record, 103-59, while edging Baltimore by three games in the A.L. East Division race.

After enduring playoff losses to New York in 1976, '77 and '78, Kansas City third baseman George Brett had reason to celebrate after the Royals' Championship Series sweep of the Yankees.

" DUGOUT CHATTER "

"Some people are only superstars statistically, but you are a .400 hitter as a person. When I grow up, I want to be just like you."

Joe Morgan

Houston second baseman's tribute to Pittsburgh veteran Willie Stargell on Willie Stargell Day at Three Rivers Stadium

"They don't have a father-son game here because the kids would get lost."

Graig Nettles

Yankee third baseman, on the long infield grass at Detroit's Tiger Stadium

OCTOBER

A National League first: All 12 teams topped the 1 million attendance mark in the same season.

Oakland left fielder Rickey Henderson finished the season with 100 stolen bases, four more than the A.L.-record 96 Ty Cobb swiped in 1915 for Detroit.

Philadelphia lefthander Steve Carlton rolled to a 24-9 record and 2.34 ERA while earning his record-tying third N.L. Cy Young Award.

DECEMBER

Dave Winfield became the highest-paid player in team sports history when he joined the New York Yankees from San Diego as a free agent, signing a 10-year deal worth at least $16 million.

THE FUTILITY ENDS

Mike Schmidt drilled a two-run single and Steve Carlton and Tug McGraw pitched Philadelphia to a 4-1 victory over Kansas City October 21, clinching the first World Series championship in the long, futile history of the Phillies franchise.

The Game 6 clincher at Veterans Stadium ended 97 years of frustration for the long-time National League patsy, which had won only two previous pennants — in 1915 and 1950. Carlton, a 24-game winner during the regular season and a Game 2 Series victor, carried a 4-0 final-game lead through seven innings before giving way to McGraw, who closed out the historic victory.

The Phillies jumped out quickly, handing the Royals come-from-behind 7-6 and 6-4 losses in the first two contests at Philadelphia. But Kansas City rebounded for 4-3 and 5-3 wins at Royals Stadium and held a 3-2 lead in the ninth inning of Game 5, only to see the Phillies rally for a 4-3 triumph. Philadelphia carried that momentum into Game 6.

Schmidt batted .381 and hit a pair of home runs, but the Royals claimed top offensive honors. Amos Otis batted .478 with three homers and seven RBIs, Willie Aikens blasted four homers and drove in eight runs and George Brett batted .375, despite spending time in the hospital between Games 2 and 3 battling an embarrassing case of hemorrhoids.

Game 1	Philadelphia	7	Kansas City	6
Game 2	Philadelphia	6	Kansas City	4
Game 3	Kansas City	4	Philadelphia	3
Game 4	Kansas City	5	Philadelphia	3
Game 5	Philadelphia	4	Kansas City	3
Game 6	Philadelphia	4	Kansas City	1

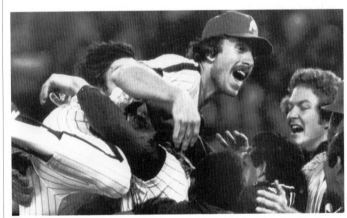

Mike Schmidt was on top of the world after helping Philadelphia beat Kansas City in a six-game World Series.

Brett's dream season

Kansas City third baseman George Brett, who compiled the highest one-season batting average since Ted Williams hit .406 in 1941, was named American League Most Valuable Player November 18, capping a season that ran the gamut from despair to ecstasy.

The 1980 campaign started slowly, with Brett struggling for hits and fighting nagging injuries. And just when the talented left-handed hitter heated up in early June with a 34-for-76 tear, he suffered ligament damage in his foot and missed 26 games.

But there was nothing frustrating about the rest of the regular season. Brett compiled a 30-game hitting streak, flirted with the magic .400 mark until late September and led the Royals to the A.L. West Division title while working under a media microscope and capturing the imagination of an entire nation. He finished his dream season with a .390 average, 24 home runs and 118 RBIs in 117 games.

Brett went on to hit a dramatic Championship Series-winning home run off New York relief ace Goose Gossage and he batted .375 in the Royals' World Series loss to Philadelphia.

Kansas City's George Brett flirted with the magic .400 mark, but settled for a not-too-shabby .390.

SEASON LEADERS

	American League		National League	
Avg.	George Brett, K.C.	.390	Bill Buckner, Chi.	.324
HR	Reggie Jackson, N.Y.	41	Mike Schmidt, Phi.	48
	Ben Oglivie, Mil.	41		
RBI	Cecil Cooper, Mil.	122	Mike Schmidt, Phi.	121
SB	Rickey Henderson, Oak.	100	Ron LeFlore, Mon.	97
W-L Pct.	Steve Stone, Bal.	25-7, .781	Jim Bibby, Pit.	19-6, .760
ERA	Rudy May, N.Y.	2.47	Don Sutton, L.A.	2.21
SO	Len Barker, Cle.	187	Steve Carlton, Phi.	286

★1981★
JANUARY-AUGUST

CAUGHT ON THE FLY

JANUARY

Frank Robinson, the man who broke the managerial color barrier with Cleveland in 1975, was named field boss of the San Francisco Giants.

APRIL

Two new members of baseball's elite 3,000-strikeout club: Cincinnati righthander Tom Seaver and Philadelphia lefty Steve Carlton.

The Oakland A's set a major league record when they opened the season with 11 consecutive victories, eight of which came on the road.

MAY

New York Yankee righthander Ron Davis set a record for consecutive strikeouts by a reliever when he fanned the last eight batters in a 4-2 victory over the California Angels.

Texas infielder Bill Stein set an A.L. record when he collected seven consecutive pinch-hits.

Barker is perfect

Fireballing righthander Len Barker, pitching in the cold and mist at Cleveland's Municipal Stadium, retired all 27 Toronto Blue Jays he faced May 15 while pitching the major leagues' first perfect game in 13 years.

Barker's 3-0 victory was quick and easy. He threw 103 pitches and struck out 11 Blue Jays before a sparse crowd of 7,290. He needed a good play from shortstop Tom Veryzer on a first-inning ground ball, but otherwise set the Jays down without any close calls.

The 25-year-old ended the game by retiring Rick Bosetti on a foul pop, striking out pinch-hitter Al Woods and getting pinch-hitter Ernie Whitt on a fly ball.

It was the 10th perfect game in major league history and the first since Oakland's Catfish Hunter beat Minnesota in 1968. It was the second no-hitter in five days, following Montreal righthander Charlie Lea's gem against San Francisco.

Len Barker, Cleveland's Mr. Perfect.

Red Sox lose Fisk

The unintentional dismantling of the Boston Red Sox's offensive machine continued February 12 when a labor arbitrator declared star catcher Carlton Fisk a free agent because of a front-office blunder.

Arbitrator Raymond Goetz, a law professor at the University of Kansas, ruled that the Red Sox had violated the Basic Agreement between players and owners by mailing a new contract to Fisk two days beyond the specified deadline. As a result, the six-time All-Star becomes free to sell his services to any team.

Fisk and Fred Lynn, Boston's hard-hitting center fielder, both had claimed negligence on the Red Sox's part and took their cases to arbitration over the winter, insisting they should be freed from their contracts. Boston officials, afraid of losing Lynn without compensation, hastily arranged a trade with California, sending him with pitcher Steve Renko to the Angels for pitchers Frank Tanana and Jim Dorsey and outfielder Joe Rudi. Lynn signed a four-year California deal and agreed to drop his arbitration case.

But the 33-year-old Fisk, a .285 career hitter, pushed his to completion and now appears to have a rich future.

It's Fernandomania

"Fernandomania" continued to grip Los Angeles April 27 as lefthander Fernando Valenzuela, a 20-year-old Mexican wunderkind, enhanced his growing mystique by pitching his fourth shutout of the season and fifth straight complete game in a 5-0 whitewash of San Francisco before 49,478 roaring fans at Dodger Stadium.

Valenzuela, an awkward-looking youngster with a moon face, a winning smile and a devastating screwball, has taken the city by storm. Fans are pouring through the turnstiles to see him perform and so far he is drawing rave reviews. Fernando, who doesn't even speak English, broke into the big leagues late last year with 17⅔ scoreless innings in 10 relief appearances and he has allowed one earned run (April 14 to the Giants) in five starts this year. His ERA is a miniscule 0.20 in 1981, 0.14 in 62⅔ career innings. He is working on a scoreless string of 28⅔ innings.

But that talented left arm is only part of the story. Valenzuela, the youngest player in the National League, also can swing a bat, as evidenced by the seven hits he has collected in his last 11 at-bats. He was 3 for 4 against the Giants and singled in the Dodgers' four-run fourth inning.

Los Angeles lefthander Fernando Valenzuela was nothing short of amazing in early 1981.

"DUGOUT CHATTER"

"If someone threw him a resin bag, he'd get a double."

Gene Mauch

California manager, after watching Seattle's Tom Paciorek during a 17-for-38 spree

50-day strike ends

Montreal's Gary Carter belted two solo home runs and Philadelphia's Mike Schmidt hit a two-run shot in the eighth inning August 9 to give the National League its 10th straight All-Star Game victory over the American League. But the N.L.'s 5-4 victory at Cleveland's Municipal Stadium had a more serious undertone — it was the kickoff to baseball's "second season" after a 50-day strike that shut down ballparks and short-circuited pennant races while labor negotiators argued about dollars and sense.

The longest strike in American sports history came to a merciful end July 31 when those negotiators reached agreement on the sticky free-agent compensation issue that had halted the season seven weeks earlier. With the season fast approaching the point of no return, Marvin Miller, head of the Major League Players' Association, hammered out agreement on a complicated pooling system with Ray Grebey, the owners' chief negotiator. The owners also restored service credit to the players for strike time in exchange

for an extra year on the Basic Agreement that was signed in 1980 without resolution of the compensation problem.

The strike, which began on June 12, forced cancellation of 706 games (38 percent of the schedule) and cost players an estimated $28 million in salaries. The owners' losses were estimated at $116 million, although strike insurance cut that deficit by more than a third.

With the cancellation of so many games, a plan was formulated to divide the season into halves. Teams in first place through games of June 11 were declared first-half division winners and will meet teams that finish in first over the second half in a best-of-five divisional playoff to decide League Championship Series participants. Oakland (A.L. West), New York (A.L. East), Philadelphia (N.L. East) and Los Angeles (N.L. West) already have qualified as first-half champions.

The second season officially opened with the All-Star Game (scheduled for July 14) and teams began play the next day.

With an end to the long baseball strike nowhere in sight, many players, such as Yankee pitcher Ron Davis (right), tried their hands at regular jobs.

" DUGOUT CHATTER "

"It's like when your mother tells you to do something and you don't want to do it. Then she tells you, 'There are lots of things in life you don't want to do, but you have to do them.' That's the way I feel about this."

Don Cooper

Minnesota rookie pitcher heading into baseball's 50-day strike

Pawtucket wins longest game ever played

Two months and 33 innings after it started, the longest professional baseball game ever played ended in just 18 minutes on June 23. The Pawtucket Red Sox scored the first time they batted in the continuation of an April 18 marathon and defeated the Rochester Red Wings, 3-2.

The International League teams had battled to a 2-2 tie through 32 innings of their 8-hour, 7-minute April encounter in Pawtucket, R.I., when league President Harold Cooper ordered the game halted. It was 4:07 on the morning of April 19 and only 20 of the original 1,470 fans remained in the stands.

The game, scheduled for completion on Rochester's next trip to Pawtucket, generated national headlines. The attention was magnified because of the protracted players' strike that had shut down major league ballparks around the country. When the contest was resumed, 54 newspaper representatives, three tele-

vision networks and numerous radio crews were crammed into little McCoy Stadium along with 5,756 fans. Broadcasters came from as far away as Great Britain and Japan.

Amid all the hoopla, Pawtucket's Bob Ojeda retired the Red Wings without incident in the top of the 33rd. But the Red Sox loaded the bases with nobody out in the bottom of the inning and Dave Koza's single brought in Marty Barrett, ending the most publicized minor league game in history.

The previous longest professional game was a 29-inning Florida State League contest between Miami and St. Petersburg in 1966.

Pawtucket Red Sox hero Dave Koza (left), who stroked the winning hit in the 33rd inning, hugs winning pitcher Bob Ojeda after the completion of the longest game in baseball history.

Ryan takes the fifth

Nolan Ryan, Houston's always ready for prime time righthander, thrilled a national television audience September 26 when he fired his major league-record fifth career no-hitter, beating Los Angeles, 5-0, in a game at the Astrodome.

The 34-year-old Texan walked three and struck out 11 in moving past former Dodger great Sandy Koufax, the only other pitcher with four career no-hitters. The no-hitter was the first in the National League for Ryan, who had pitched his previous four during the mid-1970s as a member of the A.L.'s California Angels.

The big fireballer struggled through the first three innings, throwing 65 pitches, constantly falling behind on the count and yielding all three of his walks. But after pitching coach Mel Wright walked to the mound at the beginning of the fourth inning and told his pitcher to stop overstriding, Ryan settled down and retired the last 19 Dodgers in order.

He struck out pinch-hitter Reggie Smith to open the ninth and retired Ken Landreaux and Dusty Baker on easy ground balls.

Houston's Nolan Ryan got carried away after firing his record-breaking fifth no-hitter.

" DUGOUT CHATTER "

"The thing I got most excited about was forming the world's only Q-initialed battery with Jamie Quirk."

Dan Quisenberry

Kansas City reliever, after a game against Toronto

"Jimmy Carter lost, but the University of Georgia was the national football champion and I got into the Hall of Fame. Two outta three ain't bad."

Johnny Mize

A native Georgian and former baseball great

'Extra' playoffs end

Major league baseball officially ended its regular season October 11 when three division champions were crowned in fifth games of special playoffs that were set up as the result of the seven-week mid-season players' strike.

Los Angeles, Montreal and the New York Yankees emerged from the playoff quagmire with fifth-game victories over divisional opponents and joined the Oakland A's in the League Championship Series rounds. Oakland had swept through its American League West Division series against Kansas City.

The playoffs were set up as a result of the "two seasons" forced by the 50-day strike and cancellation of 706 games from June 12 to August 10. Division leaders through games of June 11 were declared first-half champions and teams that finished on top from games of August 10 to the end of the regular schedule became second-half champs. The two "half champions" met in a five-game playoff to determine final division winners.

The prize for perseverance went to the Dodgers, who fell behind Houston two games to none and then beat the Astros three straight times to claim the National League West. The pitching of starters Burt Hooton, Fernando Valenzuela and Jerry Reuss in 6-1, 2-1 and 4-0 victories put the Dodgers over the top in the final three contests at Dodger Stadium.

The Montreal Expos qualified for their first-ever Championship Series by defeating Philadelphia in an exciting N.L. East matchup. Ace righthander Steve Rogers twice outdueled Phillies top gun Steve Carlton, posting a six-hit, 3-0 victory in the decisive fifth game at Veterans Stadium.

Like the Dodgers, Milwaukee recovered from a two-games-to-none deficit in their A.L. East series against the Yankees. But unlike the Dodgers, the Brewers fell short in the finale when Reggie Jackson, Oscar Gamble and Rick Cerone belted home runs and lifted New York to a 7-3 triumph.

The Royals were easy marks for Oakland pitchers Mike Norris, Steve McCatty and Rick Langford, who reeled off 4-0, 2-1 and 4-1 victories to decide the A.L. West.

Catcher Gary Carter hugs winning pitcher Steve Rogers after Montreal's N.L. East Division playoff victory over Philadelphia.

Monday burns Expos

Rick Monday's ninth-inning home run over the center-field fence at Montreal's Olympic Stadium gave Los Angeles a 2-1 victory over the Expos and secured the Dodgers' third National League pennant in five years.

Monday's October 19 blast came off Montreal ace Steve Rogers in Game 5 of the N.L. Championship Series and dashed the Expos' hopes for a first-ever appearance in the World Series. Rogers was pitching in relief of starter Ray Burris, who had dueled Dodger lefthander Fernando Valenzuela evenly for eight innings on a cold, rainy afternoon.

Rogers, coming off a 4-1 Game 3 victory, had permitted just two runs in his last 42 innings. Valenzuela got ninth-inning help from Bob Welch to close out the victory.

The teams split the first two games at Los Angeles, the Dodgers winning the opener 5-1 and Montreal rebounding for a 3-0 win behind the five-hit pitching of Burris. Rogers brought the Expos to within one game of the World Series with his Game 3 triumph, but Steve Garvey's two-run homer keyed Burt Hooton's second NLCS win, a 7-1 Game 4 decision.

Los Angeles' Rick Monday connecting for the dramatic home run that sank Montreal's N.L. pennant hopes.

CAUGHT ON THE FLY

AUGUST

Philadelphia's Pete Rose became the N.L.'s career hit leader when he singled off Mark Littell in a 7-3 loss to St. Louis. Rose's 3,631st hit moved him into third on the all-time list, ahead of former Cardinal Stan Musial.

SEPTEMBER

The Minnesota Twins, scheduled to move into a new domed stadium in 1982, said goodbye to Metropolitan Stadium with a 5-2 loss to Kansas City. The Met had been the Twins' home since their move to Minnesota in 1960.

Fingers pulls sweep

Milwaukee's Rollie Fingers entered the record books November 25 when he became the first relief pitcher to win American League Most Valuable Player honors and the first to win both his league's MVP and Cy Young awards in the same season.

Fingers compiled a 6-3 record, 1.04 earned-run average and 28 saves in baseball's strike-shortened season. He was phenomenal in the second half, compiling a 5-1 record, 16 saves and a 0.72 ERA.

Fingers outdistanced Oakland outfielder Rickey Henderson, 319-308, in the MVP vote and easily beat out A's righthander Steve McCatty for the Cy Young.

Los Angeles phenom Fernando Valenzuela became the first rookie to win a Cy Young Award when he edged Cincinnati's Tom Seaver in the National League voting. The 21-year-old Mexican finished 13-7 with a 2.48 ERA, eight shutouts and a league-leading 180 strikeouts.

WORLD SERIES REPORT

THE ARTFUL DODGERS

Pedro Guerrero drove in five runs with a homer, triple and single and the Los Angeles Dodgers wrapped up their fifth World Series championship October 28 with a 9-2 sixth-game thumping of New York at Yankee Stadium.

A stunned crowd of 56,513 watched the Dodgers complete their four-game blitz of the Bronx Bombers after falling behind two games to none.

Bob Watson's three-run, first-inning home run in the opener had keyed Ron Guidry's 5-3 win over Los Angeles, and Tommy John and Goose Gossage had combined on a four-hit, 3-0 victory in Game 2. But the rest of the Series belonged to the Dodgers.

Ron Cey provided a three-run homer and Fernando Valenzuela struggled to a 5-4 third-game triumph at Dodger Stadium; the Dodgers fell behind 6-3 in Game 4 but rallied for an 8-7 victory that pulled them even; Jerry Reuss' five-hit pitching and back-to-back seventh-inning homers by Guerrero and Steve Yeager off Guidry gave the Dodgers a 2-1 verdict in Game 5, and Burt Hooton and Steve Howe combined for the sixth-game victory.

Yankee reliever George Frazier was tagged with a Series record-tying three losses.

Game 1	New York	5	Los Angeles	3
Game 2	New York	3	Los Angeles	0
Game 3	Los Angeles	5	New York	4
Game 4	Los Angeles	8	New York	7
Game 5	Los Angeles	2	New York	1
Game 6	Los Angeles	9	New York	2

Los Angeles' World Series heroes (left to right): Pedro Guerrero, Steve Yeager and Ron Cey.

SEASON LEADERS

	American League		National League	
Avg.	Carney Lansford, Bos.	.336	Bill Madlock, Pit.	.341
HR	Tony Armas, Oak.	22	Mike Schmidt, Phi.	31
	Dwight Evans, Bos.	22		
	Bobby Grich, Cal.	22		
	Eddie Murray, Bal.	22		
RBI	Eddie Murray, Bal.	78	Mike Schmidt, Phi.	91
SB	Rickey Henderson, Oak.	56	Tim Raines, Mon.	71
W-L Pct.	Pete Vuckovich, Mil.	14-4, .778	Tom Seaver, Cin.	14-2, .875
ERA	Steve McCatty, Oak.	2.32	Nolan Ryan, Hou.	1.69
SO	Len Barker, Cle.	127	Fernando Valenzuela, L.A.	180

Braves start fast

Cincinnati righthanders Bruce Berenyi and Tom Hume combined on a six-hitter April 22 and the Reds handed the sizzling Atlanta Braves their first loss after a modern major league-record 13 straight victories with a 2-1 decision at Atlanta's Fulton County Stadium.

The 13 wins to open a season broke the 1-year-old record of 11 set by Oakland but fell far short of the all-time mark of 20 set in 1884 by St. Louis of the Union Associa-tion. The Braves had defeated Houston six times, Cincinnati five and San Francisco twice.

Atlanta starter Bob Walk held a 1-0 lead through four innings, but the Reds gained the edge in the fifth on run-scoring singles by Wayne Krenchicki and Berenyi. The Braves loaded the bases with one out in the seventh against Berenyi, but Hume came on and retired Glenn Hubbard on a short fly ball and Claudell Washington on a grounder.

" DUGOUT CHATTER "

"We didn't expect to go 162-0."

Chris Chambliss

Atlanta first baseman, after the Braves' 13-game season-opening winning streak came to an end

---

Perry wins No. 300

Aging righthander Gaylord Perry, a man without a team only a few months earlier, pitched the Seattle Mariners to a 7-3 victory over New York May 6 and became the 15th hurler in major league history to record 300 career wins.

The 43-year-old Perry, a self-acknowledged master of the spit-ball, allowed nine hits and four walks while rewarding 27,369 Kingdome fans who buzzed with anticipation throughout the game. His young teammates made it easy, rocking Yankee starter Doyle Alexander for five third-inning runs on RBI hits by Terry Bulling, Manny Castillo, Todd Cruz and Al Cowens.

Perry, a 21-game winner for San Diego in 1978 and the National League Cy Young Award recipient at age 40, was released by Atlanta at the end of last season, three wins short of 300. Seattle, his seventh team, was the only one to offer him a contract.

Ironically, the talented right-hander had won his 299th game on April 30 at the expense of the Yankees. Alexander also started that contest. Perry is the first pitcher to join the 300 circle since Early Wynn made it in 1963.

Seattle's Gaylord Perry, baseball's newest 300-game winner, walks from the Kingdome field after beating the New York Yankees, 7-3.

Rose passes Aaron

Philadelphia first baseman Pete Rose took another big step up the milestone ladder June 22 when he drilled a third-inning double against St. Louis and moved past former Atlanta and Milwaukee great Hank Aaron into second place on the all-time hit list.

Rose, who had become the fifth player in baseball history to play in 3,000 games two nights earlier, collected his 3,772nd hit off the Cardinals' John Stuper during a 3-2 loss at Busch Stadium. He now trails only Ty Cobb.

"I should make it sometime before the All-Star Game in 1984," Rose said, referring to the former Detroit great's all-time record of 4,191 hits.

The 41-year-old Rose, a three-time N.L. batting champion and the league's 1973 Most Valuable Player, tied Aaron's mark with two hits against St. Louis on June 21. He managed only one hit in four at-bats against Stuper, but that record-setter drove in a run.

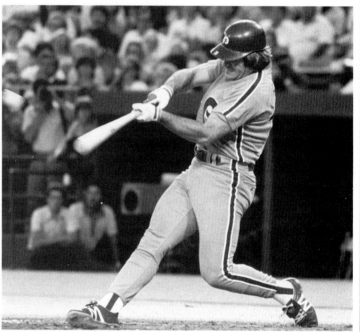

Philadelphia's Pete Rose connects for career hit No. 3,772, a double against St. Louis that moved him into second place on the all-time list.

CAUGHT ON THE FLY

APRIL

Jim Kaat, St. Louis' 43-year-old lefthander, set a longevity record when he pitched in his 24th major league season.

Seattle spoiled the party for 52,279 Minnesota fans, who got their first look at the new Hubert H. Humphrey Metrodome and watched the Mariners beat the Twins in an 11-7 Opening Day slugfest.

MAY

Chicago Cubs righthander Ferguson Jenkins became the seventh member of the 3,000-strikeout club when he fanned San Diego shortstop Garry Templeton during a 2-1 loss to the Padres.

JUNE

Satchel Paige, generally considered the greatest pitcher in Negro League history and one of the most colorful characters ever to wear a baseball uniform, died in Kansas City at age 75.

" DUGOUT CHATTER "

"He's fat, he has pimples all over his face, he can't speak English and he's ugly. We're glad to have him back."

Jay Johnstone

Los Angeles outfielder, on the return of pitcher Fernando Valenzuela after a spring holdout

"I know winning isn't everything, but with (Twins Owner) Calvin Griffith, winning isn't anything."

Ron Davis

Yankee reliever, after being traded to Minnesota

N.L. wins 11th in row

The National League took its All-Star act to another country July 13 with the same old result. The American League fell for the 11th straight year and 19th time in 20 games, losing on the Canadian soil of Montreal's Olympic Stadium, 4-1.

The Americans jumped out quickly against Montreal's Steve Rogers when Oakland's Rickey Henderson led off the game with a single and came around to score on a sacrifice fly by California's Reggie Jackson. But that was all she wrote offensively for the junior circuit as Rogers, Philadel-

phia's Steve Carlton, Cincinnati's Mario Soto, Los Angeles' Fernando Valenzuela, San Francisco's Greg Minton, Dodger Steve Howe and the Reds' Tom Hume combined to allow only six hits the rest of the way.

The Nationals, meanwhile, scored all the runs they needed off Boston starter Dennis Eckersley. The big blow was a two-run second-inning homer by Cincinnati shortstop Dave Concepcion. Philadelphia's Pete Rose added a third-inning run with a sacrifice fly and Montreal's Gary Carter singled home a run in the sixth.

Cincinnati shortstop Dave Concepcion gets a big greeting from his N.L. teammates after hitting a second-inning All-Star Game home run.

Rickey passes Brock

Oakland left fielder Rickey Henderson sped past former St. Louis great Lou Brock and into uncharted territory August 27 when he swiped four bases during a game at Milwaukee and claimed baseball's one-season basestealing record.

Henderson's record-breaking 119th steal came in the third inning of a 5-4 Oakland loss after he drew a two-out walk from Doc Medich. The Brewers' right-hander made four throws to first and then threw a pitchout as Henderson took off for second base. Ted Simmons' throw was on target, but Henderson slid under the tag and was called safe.

As members of both teams surrounded Henderson, he pulled the base out of the ground and held it high in a triumphant gesture. The 41,600 fans at County Stadium stood and applauded as American League President Lee MacPhail and Brock, who was on hand for the historic moment, went onto the field for a brief ceremony.

But Henderson, who set the record in 127 games, 26 fewer than Brock needed to steal 118 bases in 1974, didn't stop there. He stole second in the sixth and he swiped second and third in the eighth, bringing his total to 122. He went on to finish the season with 130.

Oakland's Rickey Henderson, having eclipsed the one-season record of 118 steals set by former St. Louis Cardinals great Lou Brock (left), holds court in Milwaukee's County Stadium.

Youngblood journeys into record books

Joel Youngblood made an unusual entry into the major league record books August 4 when he became the first player to collect hits for two teams on the same day. Youngblood carried his distinction even further by pulling off his feat in two different cities against pitchers with combined

career totals of more than 500 victories and 6,000 strikeouts.

Youngblood's day began in Chicago, where he started in center field for the New York Mets in a game against the Cubs. The 30-year-old righthanded hitter delivered a two-run single in the third inning off Ferguson Jen-

kins, helping the Mets to a 7-4 victory.

But Youngblood was not around to see the end of that game. He had received word after his third-inning hit that he had been traded to Montreal and quickly headed for the airport to catch a flight for Philadelphia,

where the Expos were getting ready to play. He arrived in the third inning of that contest, was inserted into right field in the sixth and singled in his only at-bat off Philadelphia lefthander Steve Carlton, who went on to earn his 15th victory of the season with a 5-4 decision.

★1982★

SEASON LEADERS

	American League		National League	
Avg.	Willie Wilson, K.C.	.332	Al Oliver, Mon.	.331
HR	Reggie Jackson, Cal.	39	Dave Kingman, N.Y.	37
	Gorman Thomas, Mil.	39		
RBI	Hal McRae, K.C.	133	Dale Murphy, Atl.	109
			Al Oliver, Mon.	109
SB	Rickey Henderson, Oak.	130	Tim Raines, Mon.	78
W-L Pct.	Pete Vuckovich, Mil.	18-6, .750	Phil Niekro, Atl.	17-4, .810
	Jim Palmer, Bal.	15-5, .750		
ERA	Rick Sutcliffe, Cle.	2.96	Steve Rogers, Mon.	2.40
SO	Floyd Bannister, Sea.	209	Steve Carlton, Phi.	286

Brewers win ALCS

Milwaukee first baseman Cecil Cooper delivered a two-run seventh-inning single and the Brewers completed an unprecedented comeback in the American League Championship Series October 10 with a pennant-clinching 4-3 victory over California at County Stadium.

Cooper's bases-loaded single capped the Brewers' rally from a 3-1 Game 5 deficit and a 2-0 Series deficit, a comeback feat never before accomplished. The Angels had rolled to 8-3 and 4-2 victories, but could not close the door on the franchise's first World Series berth.

Milwaukee's road to its first A.L. pennant started with a 5-3 win in Game 3 behind Don Sutton. The Brewers evened the Series in Game 4, thanks to a 3-for-4, three-RBI performance by seldom-used Mark Brouhard in a 9-5 victory. The Angels built their Game 5 lead on two RBI singles by Fred Lynn and one by Bob Boone, but Bruce Kison and Alex Sanchez could not hold the Brewers.

Despite the loss, top offensive honors went to a pair of Angels. Lynn batted an incredible .611 (11 for 18) and Don Baylor, who keyed California's first-game win with five runs batted in, finished with 10 RBIs in the Series.

Ecstatic Brewer players celebrate Milwaukee's first-ever A.L. pennant.

Milwaukee survives

Milwaukee's booming bats came alive against the rampaging Baltimore Orioles October 3, just in time to rescue the Brewers' fading American League pennant hopes, and San Francisco second baseman Joe Morgan handed the Atlanta Braves their first National League West Division title in 13 years with a dramatic final-day home run against the Los Angeles Dodgers.

When the smoke from the regular season-ending fireworks had cleared, Milwaukee was king of the A.L. East Division for the first time in its history and Atlanta ruled the N.L. West for the first time since 1969 — the inaugural year for divisional play. The Brewers earned their title with a 10-2 victory that broke a first-place deadlock with the Orioles and the Braves clinched when Morgan's three-run homer gave the Giants a 5-3 victory and spoiled the Dodgers' chance to force a playoff.

The Brewers, who led by 7½ games on August 19, entered their season-closing four-game series against Baltimore with a three-game advantage and needed only one win to clinch. But the Orioles, who recorded a 33-10 record down the stretch, swept a Friday night doubleheader, 8-3 and 7-1, and forced a tie with an 11-2 Saturday victory. Baseball's top offensive team had been outhit, 46-24, and outscored, 26-6, in the three games.

But the Brewers turned it around in the finale, hitting four home runs and pounding three-time Cy Young Award winner Jim Palmer. Shortstop Robin Yount connected twice and Cecil Cooper and Ted Simmons once each to support the 10-hit pitching of Don Sutton and Bob McClure.

The Braves lost their final game at San Diego, 5-1, but watched the final moments of the Giants-Dodgers contest on a clubhouse television. By that time, Morgan had already wrecked the Dodgers' pennant hopes with his seventh-inning blast.

The Braves had led the Dodgers by 10½ games on July 30, but finished one game ahead of them with San Francisco one game further back.

Joe Morgan acknowledges the cheers of San Francisco fans after sinking Dodger pennant hopes.

CAUGHT ON THE FLY

OCTOBER

Unlucky Minnesota righthander Terry Felton finished his second big-league season with an 0-13 mark, bringing his total to 0-16 and setting a record for consecutive losses to begin a career.

The major league season ended without a no-hitter, the first time that had happened since 1959 and only the 14th time since the turn of the century.

NOVEMBER

Steve Carlton, 23-11 with a 3.10 ERA for Philadelphia, captured his unprecedented fourth N.L. Cy Young Award.

IN THE CARDS

Sixth-inning singles by Keith Hernandez and George Hendrick drove in three runs and gave the St. Louis Cardinals a lead they never relinquished en route to a 6-3 World Series-clinching victory over Milwaukee October 20 at Busch Stadium.

Hernandez's two-run blow wiped out a 3-1 Brewer lead and Hendrick's single put the Cardinals ahead in the Game 7 thriller. The Redbirds added a pair of eighth-inning insurance runs and Bruce Sutter pitched two hitless innings in relief of Joaquin Andujar to close out St. Louis' first Series championship since 1967.

Not only did the Cardinals win on the scoreboard, they also triumphed in a battle of contrasting styles. The Series pitted St. Louis' speed, defense and pitching against Milwaukee's raw power. When the classic opened in St. Louis, it appeared Whitey Herzog's Cardinals might be overwhelmed.

With Paul Molitor banging out a Series-record five hits, Robin Yount hitting safely four times, Ted Simmons drilling a home run against his former teammates and Mike Caldwell pitching a three-hitter, Milwaukee pounded out a 10-0 victory. The onslaught was witnessed by 53,723 stunned Cardinal fans.

But the determined Redbirds shook off that embarrassment and rebounded to win the next two games, 5-4 and 6-2. Center fielder Willie McGee provided the Game 3 spark with two home runs and a pair of outstanding catches.

When Harvey's Wallbangers, so named because they had hit a record 216 regular-season home runs for Manager Harvey Kuenn, bounced back to post 7-5 and 6-4 decisions at Milwaukee's County Stadium, the Cardinals answered with a 13-1 bombardment in a rain-delayed marathon at St. Louis, forcing a Game 7. Hernandez homered and drove in four runs in support of John Stuper's four-hit pitching.

The World Series victory was the National League-leading ninth for the Cardinals, who rank second to the American League's New York Yankees (22).

Fireworks signal victory as St. Louis fans pour onto the Busch Stadium field after the Cardinals' seventh-game World Series win over Milwaukee.

Game 1	Milwaukee	10	St. Louis	0
Game 2	St. Louis	5	Milwaukee	4
Game 3	St. Louis	6	Milwaukee	2
Game 4	Milwaukee	7	St. Louis	5
Game 5	Milwaukee	6	St. Louis	4
Game 6	St. Louis	13	Milwaukee	1
Game 7	St. Louis	6	Milwaukee	3

" DUGOUT CHATTER "

"Normalcy has returned. Owners again are chasing the commissioner."

Bowie Kuhn

Baseball Commissioner, when asked why he had taken up jogging

Commissioner Bowie Kuhn.

Owners vote Kuhn out of office

Bowie Kuhn's sometimes-stormy 14-year career as commissioner ended abruptly November 1 when five National League club owners voted not to renew his contract during a meeting in Chicago.

Kuhn, the game's fifth commissioner, received a favorable 11-3 vote from American League owners but managed only a 7-5 margin from bosses in the N.L. A commissioner cannot be hired or re-elected without receiving nine of 12 votes in the N.L. and 10 out of 14 in the A.L.

The revolt surfaced last August in San Diego and Kuhn forces managed to postpone the election while campaigning for votes. It did not make any difference. The N.L. opposition was led by New York's Nelson Doubleday and St. Louis' August A. Busch and those owners drew support from Atlanta's Ted Turner, Houston's John McMullen and Cincinnati's William Williams. New York Yankee boss George Steinbrenner, Texas' Eddie Chiles and Seattle's George Argyros reportedly cast the no votes in the A.L.

The reasons for Kuhn's ouster vary, from personal vendettas to a call for a commissioner with stronger business ties. Busch drew up a compromise plan that would have provided for a new operating officer to handle the office's business affairs, but could not get the needed support.

Kuhn will remain in office until his term expires next August.

★1983★
JANUARY-AUGUST

" DUGOUT CHATTER "

"They both show a lot, but not everything."

Toby Harrah

Cleveland third baseman, comparing statistics to a girl in a bikini

More drug problems

St. Louis Cardinals outfielder Lonnie Smith left the team June 11 and checked into a rehabilitation center, becoming the third major league player to seek substance-abuse treatment this season.

Cardinals Manager Whitey Herzog called an impromptu news conference before his team's game in Chicago and announced that Smith had departed for three weeks of therapy at an undisclosed clinic. Herzog said Smith had come to him before the Cardinals' June 9 game in Philadelphia and admitted he had a drug problem. After discussion with a doctor, all parties agreed on Smith's course of action.

Smith, who is hitting .311, joins Los Angeles reliever Steve Howe and Cubs pitcher Dickie Noles as players who have sought help this year. Howe, who underwent off-season treatment for drug and alcohol problems, was readmitted to a center recently. Noles underwent treatment for alcohol problems earlier this season and returned to the team this week.

San Diego outfielder Alan Wiggins, Montreal outfielder Tim Raines, Los Angeles outfielder Ken Landreaux and former Kansas City catcher Darrell Porter, now with St. Louis, have undergone treatment in the last three years.

CAUGHT ON THE FLY

JANUARY

Unpredictable New York Owner George Steinbrenner moved Yankee Manager Clyde King into a front-office position and replaced him with Billy Martin, the man he had fired on two previous occasions.

FEBRUARY

Los Angeles lefthander Fernando Valenzuela became the first player to win a $1 million salary award through the controversial arbitration process.

MAY

Yankee Owner George Steinbrenner, fined $50,000 by Commissioner Bowie Kuhn for his comments about umpires, was suspended for a week by A.L. President Lee MacPhail after another outburst against the men in blue.

JUNE

A new addition to the 3,000-strikeout club: Milwaukee righthander Don Sutton.

New York Mets veteran Rusty Staub tied a major league record when he collected eight consecutive pinch-hits.

JULY

Kansas City's Gaylord Perry became the fourth major leaguer to record 3,500 career strikeouts during a 5-4 win over Cleveland.

The strikeout race

In a race that probably will not be won or lost for several years, Houston's 36-year-old Nolan Ryan and Philadelphia's 38-year-old Steve Carlton passed the great Walter Johnson on baseball's all-time strikeout list and began battling each other for "King of the K" honors.

Ryan, the fireballing right-hander with five career no-hitters and a record five seasons of 300 or more strikeouts, was the first to move past Johnson, the former Washington Senator who retired in 1927. Ryan fanned five Expos in Houston's 4-2 victory at Montreal on April 27 and finished the day with 3,509, one more than Johnson.

Ryan's record-tying and record-breaking strikeouts came consecutively in the eighth inning when he got Tim Blackwell swinging and pinch-hitter Brad Mills looking on a 1-2 curve. Johnson set his strikeout mark in 21 seasons and 5,923 innings and Ryan broke it in his 16th full campaign covering 3,357 innings.

Carlton, fast approaching the career 300-victory plateau, passed Johnson and closed within 10 of Ryan on May 20 during a 5-0 loss to San Diego. The big lefthander struck out four and raised his career total to 3,511 in 19 big-league seasons.

St. Louis outfielder Lonnie Smith.

A really big deal

The 26 major league teams reaped a financial bonanza April 7 when networks ABC and NBC agreed to share a six-year television contract that will pay baseball $1.2 billion.

Each team will receive about $7 million per year under the contract that takes effect next season. That is more than three times the $1.9 million they got from the previous pact with the two networks. The new contract calls for ABC to pay about $575 million and NBC $550 million, giving baseball an annual average payoff of $180 million.

ABC will get a regular-season prime-time package with a few Sunday afternoon games and NBC will broadcast 30 Saturday afternoon contests. The networks will continue to alternate coverage of the League Championship Series, World Series and All-Star Game through 1989.

Phils' strikeout artist Steve Carlton.

The pine tar game

In an unexciting conclusion to one of the most controversial major league games ever played, Kansas City officially posted a 5-4 victory over New York August 18 — 25 days after the first 8⅓ innings of the contest had been played at Yankee Stadium.

There was nothing unusual about the July 24 game through the first eight innings. The Yankees held a 4-3 lead as Kansas City batted in the ninth with two out and nobody on base. But a single by U.L. Washington brought up George Brett, who promptly deposited a Goose Gossage fastball into the right-field stands for a home run — or so everybody thought.

After Brett had circled the bases, Yankee Manager Billy Martin protested that the Royals third baseman had used an illegal bat. The umpires examined the bat, conferred, measured the stick against home plate and conferred again before Tim McClelland thrust his arm in the air and signaled "out."

Brett flew out of the dugout in a rage and charged McClelland,

only to be intercepted and grabbed around the neck by umpiring crew chief Joe Brinkman. In the confusion that followed, Kansas City pitcher Gaylord Perry sneaked out and swiped the bat, only to have security men retrieve it before it could be secreted away.

The point in question was a sticky substance called pine tar, used by many players to enhance their grip. The rule book allows the substance to extend 18 inches up the bat from the handle, a distance that clearly was violated by Brett. But the Royals protested to A.L. President Lee MacPhail on the basis of intent, arguing that the substance does not enhance a player's hitting ability. MacPhail agreed and ruled four days later that the game would have to be resumed from the point of stoppage, with the Royals leading.

Resumption of the game occurred on an open date for both teams. With 1,245 fans on hand, Kansas City's Hal McRae made the final out in the top of the ninth and the Yankees went down in order in the bottom of the inning.

Umpire Joe Brinkman restrains an enraged George Brett after the Kansas City third baseman's ninth-inning game-winning homer at Yankee Stadium had been disallowed because of an illegal bat.

Lynn slams N.L. jinx

California slugger Fred Lynn capped a record seven-run third inning with the first-ever grand slam home run in All-Star Game history and propelled the American League to a 13-3 victory over the National League, ending the junior circuit's embarrassing 11-game losing streak in the midsummer classic.

The first A.L. victory since 1971 came on the 50th anniversary of the showcase event, which was staged on the same field where it was originally contested in 1933 — Chicago's Comiskey Park. The American Leaguers won that game, too, but not with the sort of vengeance they showed July 6 in

their record 13-run onslaught.

After spotting the N.L. an unearned first-inning run, the A.L. tied the game in the bottom of the inning, took the lead in the second and exploded against San Francisco lefthander Atlee Hammaker in the third.

Boston's Jim Rice led off the inning with a solo homer and two more runs scored before Hammaker issued a two-out intentional walk to Milwaukee's Robin Yount to load the bases for Lynn. On a 2-2 pitch, Lynn drove a ball into the right-field bleachers. The A.L. added two runs in both the eighth and ninth innings to complete the scoring.

California's Fred Lynn raises a triumphant fist as he circles the bases after hitting the first grand slam in All-Star Game history.

" DUGOUT CHATTER "

"I'm not going to wear it too much. I might wind up minus a finger and a ring."

Willie McGee

St. Louis outfielder, after getting his World Series ring valued at $1,200

"I know I'm old, fat and ugly, but I am still Ted Williams."

The 65-year-old Splendid Splinter when a security guard failed to recognize him at a Red Sox benefit for stroke victim Tony Conigliaro

★1983★

" DUGOUT CHATTER "

"Steve is the kind of guy who, for laughs, does impersonations of Tom Landry."

Jay Johnstone

Chicago Cubs outfielder, on former Los Angeles teammate Steve Garvey

Garvey streak ends

San Diego first baseman Steve Garvey, who dislocated his thumb in the first game of a July 29 doubleheader against Atlanta, sat out the nightcap and ended his National League-record consecutive-games streak at 1,207.

Garvey, who ranks third on the all-time iron man list behind former New York Yankees Lou Gehrig (2,130) and Everett Scott (1,307), suffered his injury in the first inning of a 2-1 Padres loss at San Diego's Jack Murphy Stadium. He reached first base on an infield single, moved to third on

Ruppert Jones' single and attempted to score on a wild pitch by Atlanta's Pascual Perez. He was thrown out and jammed his thumb on the slide.

The 34-year-old Garvey, the long-time Los Angeles star who signed a free-agent contract over the winter with the Padres, had broken the N.L. record of former Chicago outfielder Billy Williams (1,117) April 16 on his first trip back to Dodger Stadium. He had not missed a game since 1975.

Garvey, who is batting .292, will be sidelined for three weeks.

Carlton gets 300

Philadelphia's Steve Carlton joined baseball's select "300 club" September 23 when he pitched the National League East Division-leading Phillies to their eighth straight victory, a 6-2 decision over the St. Louis Cardinals at Busch Stadium.

The 38-year-old Carlton worked eight innings, allowed seven hits and struck out 12 batters in becoming the 16th pitcher to record 300 career victories. The milestone win came against the team that traded him in 1972 and before 27,266 fans in his former home park. He raised his career mark against the Cardinals to 37-12.

The Phillies, who now boast a three-game lead over Pittsburgh with eight to play, made life easy for their talented lefthander with a 17-hit attack against three St. Louis pitchers. Carlton even got in on the act, singling home Philadelphia's first run in the second inning.

The slide that dislocated San Diego first baseman Steve Garvey's thumb and ended his iron man streak at 1,207 games.

Winfield's birdie

New York Yankee outfielder Dave Winfield.

New York center fielder Dave Winfield, arrested by Canadian police August 4 after the Yankees' 3-1 victory over Toronto, received good news the next day when a senior Crown Attorney announced that he would seek to have a criminal charge of cruelty to animals dropped.

Winfield's problems began in the middle of the fifth inning when he threw a warmup ball to a ball boy near the Yankee bullpen in right-center field. The ball skipped on the artificial surface and hit a snoozing seagull on the head, killing it instantly. Seagulls are frequent visitors to Exhibition Stadium, which is located near the edge of Lake Ontario.

The ball boy returned with a towel to remove the dead bird and Winfield stood with his cap over his heart, obviously not realizing that the seagull is on Canada's endangered species list. Fans in the outfield stands began tossing debris and obscenities at the 6-foot-6 slugger.

When the game ended, Winfield was arrested by plainclothes officers, who charged him with a crime punishable by up to a $500 fine and six months in jail. He posted a $500 bond and was told to return August 12.

Crown Attorney Norman Matusiak decided to have the charges dropped after talking with Winfield and determining that the bird's death was accidental.

3 Royals sentenced

United States Magistrate J. Milton Sullivant, noting a professional athlete's "special place in our society," sentenced three members of the 1983 Kansas City Royals to a three-month prison sentence for attempting to purchase cocaine.

Willie Wilson, Willie Aikens and Jerry Martin became the first active baseball players ever to be sent to prison November 17 and the Federal judge also announced maximum fines of $5,000 for Wilson and Aikens and $2,500 for Martin. Sullivant later pronounced the same sentence and fine on former Royals pitcher Vida Blue, who pleaded guilty to possession of cocaine in the same case.

Wilson, Aikens and Martin all pleaded guilty after being caught trying to buy the drug during an investigation centered in Kansas City. Martin and Blue have been released by the Royals and Aikens was traded to Toronto for Jorge Orta. The 28-year-old Wilson, the Royals' starting center fielder and a former American League batting champion, still is a member of the organization.

Baseball Commissioner Bowie Kuhn followed the convictions by issuing one-year suspensions against the players. They will be eligible for a review hearing May 15.

Kansas City center fielder Willie Wilson.

CAUGHT ON THE FLY

SEPTEMBER

St. Louis righthander Bob Forsch became the first pitcher in Cardinal history to throw two career no-hitters when he blanked Montreal, 3-0, at Busch Stadium.

OCTOBER

Kansas City submariner Dan Quisenberry shattered John Hiller's 10-year-old major league save record (38) in September and finished the season with 45.

DECEMBER

Dr. Bobby Brown, a former major league infielder-turned-Texas cardiologist, was elected to succeed retiring A.L. President Lee MacPhail.

SEASON LEADERS

	American League		National League	
Avg.	Wade Boggs, Bos.	.361	Bill Madlock, Pit.	.323
HR	Jim Rice, Bos.	39	Mike Schmidt, Phi.	40
RBI	Cecil Cooper, Mil.	126	Dale Murphy, Atl.	121
	Jim Rice, Bos.	126		
SB	Rickey Henderson, Oak.	108	Tim Raines, Mon.	90
W-L Pct.	Rich Dotson, Chi.	22-7, .759	John Denny, Phi.	19-6, .760
ERA	Rick Honeycutt, Tex.	2.42	Atlee Hammaker, S.F.	2.25
SO	Jack Morris, Det.	232	Steve Carlton, Phi.	275

O'S WASTE PHILLIES

Baltimore slugger Eddie Murray, held to two hits in 16 at-bats through the first four games of the World Series, belted a pair of homers and drove in three runs October 16 as the Orioles closed out Philadelphia with a 5-0 victory and claimed their first championship since 1970.

While Murray was breaking out of his slump with a vengeance, left-hander Scott McGregor was disappointing 67,064 fans at Veterans Stadium with a nifty five-hit shutout. The victory was sweet for McGregor, an 18-game regular-season winner who suffered Baltimore's lone defeat in the fall classic, a tough-luck 2-1 decision in Game 1.

With that game tied 1-1 entering the top of the eighth, McGregor took his warmups and then waited . . . and waited. Television held up the contest for five minutes, first to interview President Ronald Reagan, then for commercials. When McGregor finally delivered his first pitch, Garry Maddox hit it out of the park and the Phillies held on for the victory.

But that was the only high point of the Series for Philadelphia. With slugger Mike Schmidt struggling through a 1-for-20 drought, the Phillies dropped consecutive 4-1, 3-2 and 5-4 decisions to set up the Game 5 clincher. Baltimore rookie right-hander Mike Boddicker pitched a three-hitter in Game 2 and second baseman Rich Dauer sparked the Game 4 triumph with three hits and three RBIs.

The Orioles rallied for two seventh-inning runs off Steve Carlton to win Game 3, but the big story of that contest was Philadelphia Manager Paul Owens' benching of first baseman Pete Rose. Baseball's 3,990-hit man had gone 1 for 8 in the first two games.

The World Series victory was a nice finish to Baltimore's 98-win regular season and four-game victory over Chicago in the American League Championship Series. Philadelphia, a 90-game winner, had defeated Los Angeles in a four-game N.L. Championship Series.

Game 1	Philadelphia	2	Baltimore	1
Game 2	Baltimore	4	Philadelphia	1
Game 3	Baltimore	3	Philadelphia	2
Game 4	Baltimore	5	Philadelphia	4
Game 5	Baltimore	5	Philadelphia	0

The Baltimore Orioles had reason to celebrate after disposing of Philadelphia in a five-game World Series.

★1984★

CAUGHT ON THE FLY

MARCH

Charley Lau, an 11-year major league catcher who won greater renown as a batting coach for Kansas City, the New York Yankees and the Chicago White Sox, died in Key Colony Beach, Fla., at age 50.

JUNE

Montreal's Pete Rose played in his 3,309th major league game, passing the all-time record of former Boston great Carl Yastrzemski. Rose set the mark during a 7-3 conquest of Cincinnati, his former team.

JULY

Another 3,000-strikeout man: New York Yankee knuckleballer Phil Niekro.

AUGUST

Toronto veteran Cliff Johnson connected for his 19th career pinch-hit home run off Baltimore's Tippy Martinez, eclipsing the record held previously by former Pittsburgh and Cincinnati star Jerry Lynch.

An 8-hour marathon

Chicago's Harold Baines hit a home run with one out in the bottom of the 25th inning May 9, giving the White Sox a 7-6 victory over Milwaukee and ending baseball's first eight-hour game.

The 8-hour, 6-minute Comiskey Park marathon, which actually started the previous night and was suspended at 1:05 a.m. after 17 innings because of the American League curfew, resumed before the regularly scheduled game of May 9. It tied the major league record for a game played to a decision (25 innings) and it easily topped the longest previous game in time — a 23-inning 1964 contest that lasted 7 hours and 23 minutes.

The game featured 43 hits and several critical rallies. Chicago scored twice in the ninth to tie the score 3-3 and force extra innings and the White Sox rallied for three runs in the bottom of the 21st after Milwaukee's Ben Oglivie had hit a three-run homer in the top of the inning.

Chuck Porter, Milwaukee's sixth pitcher, surrendered Baines' home run and Tom Seaver, Chicago's eighth hurler, received credit for the victory.

Ueberroth elected

New Commissioner Peter V. Ueberroth.

Baseball's 26 owners elected Peter V. Ueberroth as the game's sixth commissioner March 3, ending a long search for a successor to Bowie Kuhn. The 46-year-old Ueberroth will not begin his five-year term until October 1, after his work as president of the Los Angeles Olympic Organizing Committee has been completed.

Until then, Kuhn will remain in the job he has held for the last 15 years. The 57-year-old attorney was deposed in November 1982 when five National League owners blocked his re-election. Since last August, when his second term officially ended, Kuhn has agreed three times to delay his departure.

Ueberroth, a Californian who directed a small travel agency into a $300 million business, had said all along he was interested in the job only if the commissioner's role was strengthened. At his insistence, a series of changes were made in the sport's bylaws.

The most significant change was in the controversial re-election procedure. The bylaw was amended so that a simple majority of clubs in each league was needed instead of the three-fourths majority that had doomed Kuhn.

N.L. regains its lost momentum

Montreal's Gary Carter and Atlanta's Dale Murphy hit home runs and five pitchers combined on a seven-hitter as the National League defeated the American League, 3-1, in the July 10 All-Star Game at San Francisco's Candlestick Park.

The Nationals, winning for the 20th time in 22 midsummer classics, scored a first-inning run off Toronto starter Dave Stieb. After Kansas City's George Brett had tied the score with a second-inning homer, the N.L. regained the lead in the bottom of the frame on Carter's blast. Murphy closed out the scoring in the eighth and the pitchers took care of the rest.

The highlight of the game was a fourth and fifth-inning strikeout exhibition by Los Angeles' Fernando Valenzuela and New York rookie Dwight Gooden. Valen-

High fives were in order after a second-inning All-Star Game home run by Montreal catcher Gary Carter (center).

zuela struck out A.L. sluggers Dave Winfield, Reggie Jackson and Brett in succession and Gooden followed in the next inning by getting Lance Parrish, Chet

Lemon and Alvin Davis. The six consecutive strikeouts broke the 50-year-old record of five set by New York Giants lefthander Carl Hubbell.

The brawl game

In an ugly, brawl-filled game reminiscent of the rough-and-tumble baseball played at the turn of the century, the Atlanta Braves duked their way to a 5-3 victory over the San Diego Padres August 12 at Fulton County Stadium.

The game included two bench-clearing brawls, some serious head-hunting by pitchers on both teams and 13 ejections — four pitchers, five players, the two managers and two replacement managers. The brawls also involved fans, five of whom were arrested, and the game ended with cleared benches and policemen stationed on the top of both dugouts.

The fun began early, when Braves starter Pascual Perez hit the first batter in the game, San Diego's Alan Wiggins, in the back with a pitch. When Perez batted in the second inning, a pitch from Padres starter Ed Whitson sailed behind his head. Perez made a threatening motion toward Whitson and both benches emptied, but no punches were thrown and home plate umpire Steve Rippley issued a warning to Whitson and both managers.

When Perez batted again in the fourth, Whitson knocked him down with a high inside pitch. Whitson and Padres Manager Dick Williams were automatically ejected. Perez was knocked down again in the fifth and pitcher Greg Booker and replacement manager Ozzie Virgil were banished. The big brawl erupted in the eighth inning when Perez was hit by a Craig Lefferts pitch.

When all was said and done, nine more players and managers were ejected, both benches were cleared of non-playing personnel and policemen were used to control a crowd that was becoming increasingly hostile. Under these unusual conditions, the game was completed without further incident.

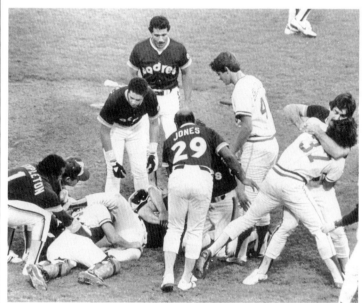

Braves and Padres players try to break up the main event brawl as a side skirmish breaks out on 'Fight Night' in Atlanta.

" DUGOUT CHATTER "

"I look at Michael Jackson, who has to wear dark sunglasses and have bodyguards around him the rest of his life, and I think I ought to be able to get by with the problems I've got."

Mike Schmidt

The two-time MVP of the Phillies, on life as a public figure

" DUGOUT CHATTER "

"We usually sit around and whittle or do needlepoint. Whatever old people do."

Tommy John

41-year-old California pitcher, when asked how it felt being the oldest player on baseball's oldest team

Reds get their Rose

Pete Rose, in hot pursuit of Ty Cobb's record of 4,191 hits, returned to his hometown Cincinnati August 16 as player-manager of the Reds, the team he helped lead to four National League pennants as a player in the 1970s.

The 43-year-old switch-hitter, who needs 130 hits to become baseball's all-time career leader, will replace Vern Rapp as Reds manager. Cincinnati management hopes that some of Rose's enthusiasm and hustle will rub off on a team that stands 50-70 and fifth in the N.L. West Division. Rose, who had signed a free-agent contract with Montreal before this season, was acquired from the Expos for a minor league player to be named later.

Rose, a Cincinnati native, captured three N.L. batting championships and a Most Valuable Player citation during his 16 years with the Reds. He was one of the stars of the Big Red Machine that rolled to World Series championships in 1975 and '76 and he later played on a Series winner during his five-year stay in Philadelphia. The veteran has played irregularly this season because of a sore arm.

But he did thrill Expos fans April 13 when he picked up his 4,000th career hit at Olympic Stadium. The milestone came in the fourth inning of a 5-1 victory over his old team, the Phillies, when he doubled off lefthander Jerry Koosman. The hit came on the 21st anniversary of his first big-league safety and made him only the second player to reach the 4,000 plateau. The crowd gave their aging star a three-minute standing ovation.

Rose does not figure to play regularly for the Reds, but he will pinch-hit and start occasionally at first base.

Pete Rose meets the Cincinnati press in his new role as Reds player-manager.

Jackson hits 500th

California slugger Reggie Jackson punctuated his sometimes-stormy but always-exciting career September 17 when he drilled a towering shot into the right-field seats at Anaheim Stadium for his 500th home run.

Baseball's Mr. October provided the only thrill of the night for 28,862 Angels fans who watched the Kansas City Royals pound out a 10-1 victory and regain sole possession of first place in the American League West Division. The 38-year-old left-handed hitter belted Bud Black's first pitch of the seventh inning and then spoke briefly during a short ceremony.

Jackson, who has played in five World Series and 11 A.L. Championship Series during an 18-year career with Oakland, Baltimore, New York and California, is the 13th player to reach the 500-homer milestone and the first since San Francisco's Willie McCovey in 1978.

The loss dropped California 1½

Reggie Jackson acknowledges the cheers of California fans after circling the bases on his 500th career home run.

games behind the first-place Royals and a half-game behind second-place Minnesota.

CAUGHT ON THE FLY

SEPTEMBER
St. Louis relief ace Bruce Sutter matched the 1-year-old record of Kansas City's Dan Quisenberry when he recorded his 45th save in a 10-inning 4-1 victory at Chicago.

Joe Cronin, a Hall of Fame shortstop, pennant-winning manager and president of the A.L. 1959-73, died in Osterville, Mass., at age 77.

OCTOBER
Walter Alston, the Hall of Fame manager who guided the Brooklyn and Los Angeles Dodgers to seven N.L. pennants and four World Series championships, died in Oxford, O., at age 72.

NOVEMBER
A clean sweep: Detroit relief ace Willie Hernandez captured both the A.L. Cy Young and Most Valuable Player awards.

Striking umps return

Major league umpires, agreeing to let Commissioner Peter V. Ueberroth arbitrate their dispute over postseason pay, ended their one-week strike October 7 and worked the final game of the National League Championship Series at San Diego's Jack Murphy Stadium.

Ueberroth, who began his five-year term as commissioner October 1, stepped into the dispute between the umpires and the two leagues and talked both parties into accepting binding arbitration. The umpires, who had been paid $10,000 for working the playoffs and $15,000 for the World Series, were demanding a pool of $340,000, which would be distributed to all 60 umpires, including those not selected for postseason assignments.

A condition of the agreement was that the umpires begin immediately and a crew was rounded up quickly to work the decisive fifth game of the N.L. Championship Series between Chicago and San Diego. The American League Championship Series had ended two days earlier when Detroit swept Kansas City.

Amateur umpires, mostly from the college ranks, were used in the early LCS games. The World Series would have been worked by former major league umpires.

The perfect ending

California's Mike Witt brought down the curtain on the 1984 season in grand style September 30 when he became the 11th pitcher in major league history to throw a perfect game.

The 6-foot-7 righthander was masterful in setting down 27 straight Texas Rangers in a 1-0 season-closing victory at Arlington Stadium. He needed just 94 pitches, 70 of which were strikes. He went to three balls on only one batter and struck out 10.

Only 8,975 fans witnessed the masterpiece, the first nine-inning perfect game since Cleveland's Len Barker beat Toronto in 1981. Witt struck out Tommy Dunbar to open the ninth inning and then got pinch-hitters Bobby Jones and Marv Foley on grounders.

The Angels scratched out their only run in the seventh when Doug DeCinces singled and eventually scored on Reggie Jackson's grounder. Witt ended the season with a 15-11 record.

California catcher Bob Boone gives Mike Witt a 'perfect' victory hug.

Padres tame Cubs

San Diego's Tony Gwynn doubled home two runs during a four-run seventh-inning blitz against Rick Sutcliffe and the Padres went on to complete their stunning National League Championship Series comeback against Chicago with a 6-3 Game 5 victory October 7 at Jack Murphy Stadium.

The Padres, who had trailed two games to none in the Series and 3-0 in the finale, tied the game on an error by Cubs first baseman Leon Durham and grabbed the lead one batter later when Gwynn's smash took a wild hop over the shoulder of second baseman Ryne Sandberg. Steve Garvey singled home the final run to make a winner of Craig Lefferts, one of four pitchers who combined for 7⅔ innings of shutout relief.

The Cubs appeared primed to end their 39-year World Series famine when they won the opener, 13-0, behind Sutcliffe (a 16-1 regular-season performer) and the second game, 4-2, behind Steve Trout and Lee Smith. Gary Matthews belted two first-game homers and Bob Dernier, Ron Cey and Sutcliffe added one apiece.

But the Padres, given up for dead, turned the tables at San Diego. Kevin McReynolds homered and drove in three runs in a 7-1 Game 3 victory and the Padres won Game 4 when Garvey belted a two-run ninth-inning homer off Smith for a 7-5 decision.

Steve Garvey (facing camera), pitcher Goose Gossage (54) and catcher Terry Kennedy jump for joy after San Diego's pennant-winning victory over Chicago.

" DUGOUT CHATTER "

"Did I know it was a homer? I had a good idea. I've thrown so many to other hitters I recognized the sound."

John Candelaria

Pittsburgh pitcher, after hitting his first home run in 566 major league at-bats

---

SEASON LEADERS

	American League		National League	
Avg.	Don Mattingly, N.Y.	.343	Tony Gwynn, S.D.	.351
HR	Tony Armas, Bos.	43	Mike Schmidt, Phi.	36
			Dale Murphy, Atl.	36
RBI	Tony Armas, Bos.	123	Gary Carter, Mon.	106
			Mike Schmidt, Phi.	106
SB	Rickey Henderson, Oak.	66	Tim Raines, Mon.	75
W-L Pct.	Doyle Alexander, Tor.	17-6, .739	Rick Sutcliffe, Chi.	16-1, .941
ERA	Mike Boddicker, Bal.	2.79	Alejandro Pena, L.A.	2.48
SO	Mark Langston, Sea.	204	Dwight Gooden, N.Y.	276

TIGERS DOMINATE

Kirk Gibson wrote the perfect ending for Detroit's dream season October 14 when he belted a pair of majestic upper-deck home runs at Tiger Stadium to close out a five-game World Series blitz of the Cinderella San Diego Padres.

Gibson's three-hit, five-RBI performance keyed an 8-4 victory that wrapped up the Tigers' first fall classic victory since 1968. One of his blasts came in the first inning and staked Detroit to a 3-0 lead — a typical position in a season of domination.

The 1984 Tigers were quick-strike artists who liked to bury the opposition in deep holes. They jumped out of the gate faster than any team in history, winning 35 of their first 40 games, and finished with 104 wins while leading the American League East Division from first day to last. That momentum continued into the postseason as they swept Kansas City in the A.L. Championship Series before putting down the Padres. In four of the World Series games, two San Diego starters failed to get through the first inning, one could not make it past the second and another could not survive the third.

The only Padre starter to last more than three was Mark Thurmond, who pitched five innings in the opener and dropped a 3-2 decision to Detroit's Jack Morris. The first Series game contested in San Diego was decided by a two-run fifth-inning homer by Larry Herndon.

The Tigers knocked Ed Whitson out of Game 2 with a three-run first, but Padre relievers Andy Hawkins and Craig Lefferts pitched brilliantly and San Diego rebounded for a 5-3 victory. That was it, however, for the Padres. The Tigers won the third game, 5-2, won the next day, 4-2, and finished off their romp in Game 5.

Game 1	Detroit	3	San Diego	2
Game 2	San Diego	5	Detroit	3
Game 3	Detroit	5	San Diego	2
Game 4	Detroit	4	San Diego	2
Game 5	Detroit	8	San Diego	4

Detroit got two final-game World Series home runs from the ever-emotional Kirk Gibson.

★1985★

2 milestones reached

Tom Seaver and Rod Carew, two of the game's most exciting and consistent performers since their major league debuts in 1967, reached career milestones during August 4 games played a continent apart in New York and Anaheim.

Seaver, the Chicago White Sox's 40-year-old righthander, became baseball's 17th 300-game winner when he pitched a six-hitter and stopped New York, 4-1, at Yankee Stadium. The three-time National League Cy Young Award winner, who had spent 12 seasons as a member of the Mets organization, thrilled a near-capacity crowd of 54,032 howling New Yorkers with his milestone

effort five nights after winning his 299th game, 7-5, at Boston.

While New York was celebrating the triumphant return of its prodigal son, 41,630 fans at Anaheim Stadium were doing a little celebrating of their own. The spotlight belonged to the 39-year-old Carew, who became the 16th member of baseball's 3,000-hit club when he drove a third-inning single off Minnesota's Frank Viola. Carew, ironically, had spent the first 12 years of his career with the Twins.

The lefthanded-hitting Carew, a seven-time American League batting champion, was hitless in four other at-bats during the Angels' 6-5 victory.

Chicago's Tom Seaver en route to his 300th career victory.

California's Rod Carew collecting his 3,000th career hit.

All-Star hex resumes

Five National League pitchers combined on a five-hitter and the snakebit American Leaguers fell for the 21st time in 23 All-Star Games July 16, dropping a 6-1 decision at Minnesota's Hubert H. Humphrey Metrodome.

The A.L. scored an unearned first-inning run against San Diego's LaMarr Hoyt, but that was it. Houston's Nolan Ryan, Los Angeles' Fernando Valenzuela, Montreal's Jeff Reardon and San Diego's Goose Gossage followed Hoyt to the mound and shut down the A.L.'s big bats.

The Nationals, meanwhile,

were chipping away at seven A.L. pitchers. They scored a second-inning run against Detroit starter Jack Morris, added a run in the third on a single by Padre Steve Garvey and two more in the fifth on a single by Philadelphia catcher Ozzie Virgil. St. Louis center fielder Willie McGee doubled home the final two runs in the ninth inning.

The only A.L. run scored when New York's Rickey Henderson singled, stole second, advanced to third on a bad throw and came home on a sacrifice fly by Kansas City's George Brett.

" DUGOUT CHATTER "

"The greatest feeling in the world is to win a major league game. The second greatest feeling is to lose a major league game."

Chuck Tanner

The always bubbly Pittsburgh manager

Two-day strike ends

After nine months of disagreement, major league players and owners settled their differences August 7 and ended the second midseason baseball strike in five years.

But whereas the 1981 work stoppage stretched over 50 days and forced cancellation of 706 games, this strike lasted two days and resulted in the cancellation of 25 contests, all of which will be made up on open dates or as parts of double-headers. The settlement came when owners decided to drop their demand for an arbitration salary cap and the players also agreed to extend the arbitration eligibility requirement from two years of

service to three years.

The formal announcement of a new five-year agreement came at 10:45 p.m. Teams were instructed to resume play August 8 with the New York Mets and Los Angeles leading the two National League divisions and Toronto and California leading in the American League.

Other points in the settlement: the abolishment of the re-entry draft, giving free agents the right to negotiate with any team, raising of the minimum salary from $40,000 to $60,000 and continuation of the League Championship Series under the best-of-seven formats.

SEASON LEADERS

	American League		National League	
Avg.	Wade Boggs, Bos.	.368	Willie McGee, St. L.	.353
HR	Darrell Evans, Det.	40	Dale Murphy, Atl.	37
RBI	Don Mattingly, N.Y.	145	Dave Parker, Cin.	125
SB	Rickey Henderson, N.Y.	80	Vince Coleman, St. L.	110
W-L Pct.	Ron Guidry, N.Y.	22-6, .786	Orel Hershiser, L.A.19-3, .864	
ERA	Dave Stieb, Tor.	2.48	Dwight Gooden, N.Y.	1.53
SO	Bert Blyleven, Cle.-Min.	206	Dwight Gooden, N.Y.	268

Rose tops hit mark

When Cincinnati player-Manager Pete Rose uncoiled into a 2-1 pitch from San Diego righthander Eric Show at 8:01 on the night of September 11 and lined a single into left field, a dream was fulfilled. With that flick of his wrists, Rose collected career hit No. 4,192 and ended his long, relentless chase of a ghost.

Rose's record-breaking moment was a glowing tribute to the spirit of former Detroit great Ty Cobb, who had retired 57 years ago to the day with 4,191 career hits. The 44-year-old Rose rounded first base with his usual vigor and paused as flashing cameras turned Riverfront Stadium into a light show. He returned to the bag and pandemonium broke loose.

Rose's 15-year-old son Petey led the surge from the dugout as teammates and opponents gathered to congratulate him. A red Corvette with license plate "PR 4192" was presented to Rose by Reds Owner Marge Schott, who hugged and kissed him.

Suddenly, Rose found himself standing alone as the ovation began to vibrate through the stadium. Tears streamed down his face. When the game resumed, the 23-year veteran and three-time National League batting champion went on to score both runs and hit a triple in the Reds' 2-0 victory.

Pete Rose salutes cheering Reds fans after collecting his record-breaking 4,192nd career hit.

" DUGOUT CHATTER "

"This place stinks. It's a shame that a great guy like HHH had to be named after it."

"If you ask my 4-year-old granddaughter what grandpa does, she says, 'He kicks dirt on umpires.' "

Billy Martin

Yankee manager, on playing at the Hubert H. Humphrey Metrodome in Minneapolis and life on the homefront

CAUGHT ON THE FLY

FEBRUARY
A salary arbitration record: Montreal outfielder Tim Raines received an award of $1.2 million.

APRIL
He-e-e's Ba-a-ck: New York Owner George Steinbrenner hired Billy Martin for the fourth time as Yankee manager, replacing Yogi Berra.

JULY
Houston's Nolan Ryan stepped into uncharted territory when he fanned Danny Heep of the New York Mets for career strikeout No. 4,000.

AUGUST
New York Yankee Don Baylor earned a dubious distinction when he was hit by a pitch for the 190th time in his career, passing the A.L. record of 189 held by Minnie Minoso. Baylor was plunked by California's Kirk McCaskill.

Niekro gets 300th

New York Yankee veteran Phil Niekro, who had failed on four previous attempts to record his 300th career win, abandoned his bread-and-butter knuckleball on the final day of the regular season and pitched a four-hit, 8-0 victory over Toronto at Exhibition Stadium.

The 46-year-old Niekro, who became the oldest pitcher in history to throw a complete-game shutout, baffled a young Blue Jay lineup with an assortment of sinking fastballs, curves and blooper pitches en route to becoming the 18th member of the elite 300-win circle. He did not throw a knuckleball until Tony Fernandez doubled with two out in the ninth inning and then he threw three straight to strike out Jeff Burroughs.

Niekro was facing a reserve-filled lineup, the result of Toronto having clinched the American League East Division championship the day before. He allowed one hit through the first six innings — a single by Cecil Fielder.

The 22-year veteran lifted his season record to 16-12 and his career mark to 300-250. Twenty of those seasons were spent with the Milwaukee and Atlanta Braves.

Players testify

Curtis Strong, a central figure in the Pittsburgh trials of seven alleged drug dealers, was found guilty September 20 by a Federal jury on 11 counts of selling cocaine to major league players between 1980 and 1983.

The verdict ended a sensational 14-day trial that centered around testimony from players about drug use throughout the National Pastime. Among the witnesses granted immunity from prosecution were the New York Mets' Keith Hernandez, Kansas City's Lonnie Smith, Cincinnati's Dave Parker, San Francisco's Jeffrey Leonard and the New York Yankees' Dale Berra.

They mesmerized the jury and courtroom spectators with their descriptions of widespread drug use among the major league player fraternity and they implicated others who were not scheduled to appear in court.

Strong, a 39-year-old Philadelphia caterer, was one of seven men indicted. Further revelations about player drug involvement could be made as the other six cases are resolved.

Cincinnati outfielder Dave Parker leaves the Pittsburgh Federal Court building after testifying in the trial of alleged drug dealer Curtis Strong.

PETE ROSE

 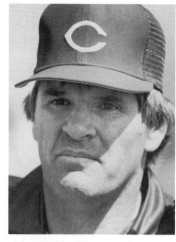

The life and times of 'Charlie Hustle'

Rose always was the first player to the ballpark and last to leave. He hated days off because they messed up his timing. Getting him out of the lineup or away from the batting cage was like trying to remove Moby Dick from a bathtub.

From the top of the baseball mountain to the depths of despair and humiliation, Pete Rose has fallen a long way, baby. It wasn't supposed to work this way. According to his well choreographed schedule, Rose figured to be enshrined in baseball's Hall of Fame by now. He expected writers to be mentioning his name in the same breath with the game's great players. He wanted respect and the undying adulation accorded such former stars as Babe Ruth, Ty Cobb, Willie Mays and Hank Aaron.

What Rose got instead was Shoeless Joe Jackson, scandal, banishment from baseball for alleged gambling activities and rejection as a Hall of Fame candidate, no matter how worthy. He also got a five-month prison sentence for income tax evasion.

"I think I'm perceived as a very aggressive, arrogant type of individual," an apologetic Rose said after his July 1990 sentencing. "But I want people to know that I do have emotion, I do have feelings and I can be hurt like everybody else."

Love him or hate him, Pete Rose spent most of his 24-year major league career stirring emotions in others. He was baseball's classic blue-collar player, a down-and-dirty, head-first-sliding hustler who gave every ounce of energy in every inning of every game he ever played. And he played in a major league-record 3,562 of them.

The man called "Charlie Hustle" by his contemporaries was like a waterbug skittering around the field, always moving and always looking for a weakness in his opponent. Rose's trademark was his mad dash to first base after drawing a walk, as if he was afraid the umpire might change his mind. But he also sprinted back and forth from the dugout to his position, ran the bases with abandon and charged the outfield wall without concern for his or its well being. His never-waning aggressiveness, whether swinging a bat, running the bases or pacing the dugout between innings, made up for a lot of his minor deficiencies.

"I saw the first scouting report on me after my first two months in the minor leagues in Geneva, N.Y.," he said in 1978, his 16th season with the Cincinnati Reds. "It said I couldn't hit lefthanded, I couldn't run, I couldn't throw. . .

"It's true I can't throw well, but I do get the ball there. I can't run well, but I'm one of the best runners in the game. I always take the extra base and I'm the only player in the history of the National League to have led it in doubles for three straight years. And during the 1977 season, having batted lefthanded more than right, I broke Frank Frisch's record for more hits than any switch-hitter in the history of baseball."

Dave Bristol, Cincinnati's manager from 1966 to '69 and Rose's first boss in 1962 at Macon of the South Atlantic League, remembered seeing the crew-cut second baseman for the first time: "I kind of sat back and watched him running all the time to everywhere. I asked myself, 'Is he putting me on with all this razzmatazz, or is he real?' Well, he was. He never gave up all year — not once on anything."

Rose's hustling style triggered the inevitable "hot dog" labels from his opponents, but the youngster smiled all the way to the major leagues. After a .330 season at Macon, he started for the Reds in 1963 and batted .273, earning N.L. Rookie of the Year honors.

After a .269 second season, Rose embarked on a nine-year string of .300 campaigns that would produce three batting titles and undying praise as the heart and soul of Cincinnati's vaunted Big Red Machine of the mid-1970s. The Reds of that period had such stars as Johnny Bench, Joe Morgan, Ken Griffey and George Foster, but Rose was the straw that stirred the drink.

He was arrogant, cocky and never met a pitcher he couldn't hit. He was fiery, hated to lose and had an amazing ability to stay focused on an immediate goal. But more than anything else, baseball was fun for Rose and he loved to play the game. "It doesn't take much to get me up for baseball," he said in 1981. "Once the national anthem plays, I get chills."

Rose always was the first player to the ballpark and last to leave. He hated days off because they messed up his timing. Getting him out of the lineup or

Two key cogs in Cincinnati's 1976 Big Red Machine: Rose (left) and second baseman Joe Morgan.

away from the batting cage was like trying to remove Moby Dick from a bathtub. "There are players with better bodies than Pete's got and there are players with more natural ability, but the big difference is that Rose has his act together up here," said former Reds Manager Sparky Anderson, pointing toward his head.

Rose, ever brash and goal-oriented, could recite every record he considered within his power to break. He relished 200-hit seasons and set his sights on Cobb's record of nine. He wanted to play more games, bat more times and score more runs than any player. He especially wanted to top Cobb's incredible mark of 4,191 career hits and he boldly predicted in 1967 that he would become baseball's first $100,000 singles hitter, a prophecy he fulfilled three years later.

Like the legions of fans who flocked to N.L. parks to watch Rose play, writers viewed him with mixed emotions. He was charming, glib and always

available, a story that would write itself. But he also could be sharp-tongued, ambivalent and overbearing, traits that often showed up on the baseball field.

In 1970, Rose ran over Cleveland catcher Ray Fosse in a celebrated home plate collision that ended the All-Star Game and nearly ended Fosse's professional career. He was both praised for his take-no-prisoners style and criticized for his action in a meaningless game. In 1973, he exchanged blows with Mets shortstop Bud Harrelson after sliding hard into second base during N.L. Championship Series action at Shea Stadium, earning the wrath of New York fans. "I play hard. That's the only way I know how to play," Rose said. "I get paid $100,000 a year to play the way I do."

With Rose playing the way he did and earning All-Star selection at three different positions (second and third base and left field), Cincinnati appeared in four World Series in the 1970s, winning in 1975 and '76. It was no coincidence that longtime doormat Philadelphia captured its first-ever World Series championship in 1980, the year after Rose signed a free-agent contract to play first base for the Phillies. He collected his 3,000th career hit in 1978 with Cincinnati, his 4,000th in 1984 with Montreal and the Cobb record-breaker, No. 4,192, as player-manager of the Reds in 1985. Although Rose already had his own private section of the record book when he retired as an active player in 1986, the latter was his coup de grace (he finished with 4,256), the one Rose thought would insure immortality.

But baseball immortality was cheated by the human side of Pete Rose, the one that

Rose left Cincinnati to play first base in the greener pastures of Philadelphia in 1979.

succumbed to a gambling addiction. After months of legal maneuvering amid accusations that Rose had consorted with bookmakers while betting on baseball games, Commissioner A. Bartlett Giamatti declared a lifetime ban against the game's all-time hit leader in 1989 — subject to appeal on an annual basis. Like Joe Jackson after the 1919 Black Sox scandal, Rose was threatened with the prospect of spending the rest of his days like a little boy peering lustfully through a Hall of Fame knothole.

The baseball Gods could not have devised a worse torture.

The record-breaker: Hit No. 4,192 in September 1985.

K.C. catches Jays

Jim Sundberg's bases-loaded triple keyed a four-run sixth inning October 16 and Kansas City went on to record a 6-2 victory over Toronto in the seventh game of the American League Championship Series. The pennant-clinching triumph at Exhibition Stadium completed the Royals' comeback from a three games to one deficit.

That comeback was possible only because the Championship Series in both leagues had been extended from best-of-five to best-of-seven formats earlier in the year. The Blue Jays recorded 6-1 and 6-5 victories at Toronto to open the Series and split the next two contests at Royals Stadium, losing 6-5 and winning 3-1.

But the Royals rolled off a 2-0 victory behind Danny Jackson's eight-hit pitching and prevailed 5-3 in the sixth game, the winning run eventually coming on George Brett's third home run of the Series and his record ninth in Championship Series play. That put Kansas City in position to win its second pennant and the Royals battered Toronto ace pitcher Dave Stieb in Game 7.

Stieb had been outstanding in the Blue Jays' first-game victory, allowing only three hits in eight innings. The Jays won Game 2 in dramatic fashion, scoring two 10th-inning runs after the Royals had tied the game in the ninth on Pat Sheridan's homer and taken the lead in the top of the 10th.

Brett homered twice, collected four hits and drove in three runs in the Royals' third-game win.

Clark's blast destroys Dodgers

St. Louis first baseman Jack Clark sent shockwaves through Dodger Stadium October 16 when he crushed a three-run, ninth-inning homer off Los Angeles reliever Tom Niedenfuer, giving the Cardinals a 7-5 victory in the decisive sixth game of the National League Championship Series.

Clark's pennant-winning blast completed the Cardinals' comeback from a two-game Series deficit and 4-1 deficit in the final game. It came with Willie McGee on third, Ozzie Smith on second and first base open, leading second-guessers to wonder why Dodger Manager Tom Lasorda did not walk the hard-hitting Clark and pitch to Andy Van Slyke.

Whatever the answer, Clark's blow provided a nightmarish ending for the Dodgers, who appeared to be World Series-bound a few days earlier. They had opened the N.L.'s first best-of-seven Championship Series by posting 4-1 and 8-2 victories behind the pitching of Fernando Valenzuela and Orel Hershiser and the timely hitting of Bill Madlock and Pedro Guerrero.

But when the Series shifted to St. Louis, the Cardinals speeded up their attack. Vince Coleman, Willie McGee and Tommy Herr ran and hit the Cardinals to a 4-2 win in Game 3 and Tito Landrum, filling in for injured leadoff man Coleman, collected four hits and three RBIs in a 12-2 Game 4 rout.

The Cardinals won Game 5 dramatically when Smith, the switch-hitting shortstop who had never hit a lefthanded home run in eight seasons, drove a Niedenfuer pitch over the right-field fence, breaking a 2-2 ninth-inning tie.

The Dodgers built a 4-1 lead in Game 6, only to have the Cardinals rally for three seventh-inning runs against Hershiser. Mike Marshall's eighth-inning homer gave Los Angeles a 5-4 advantage and set the stage for Clark.

The entire St. Louis team greets Jack Clark at home plate after his ninth-inning pennant-winning home run against Los Angeles.

" DUGOUT CHATTER "

"It was the first game in major league history where everyone in the stands got a foul ball."

Dave LaPoint

San Francisco pitcher, on a crowd of 1,632 fans at Candlestick Park

CAUGHT ON THE FLY

OCTOBER

St. Louis speedster Vince Coleman became the third N.L. player and fourth overall to steal 100 or more bases in a season, finishing his rookie campaign with 110.

Cincinnati lefthander Tom Browning became the first rookie since 1954 to win 20 games.

New York Yankee Manager Billy Martin was fired by George Steinbrenner for the fourth time.

DECEMBER

Roger Maris, the man who broke Babe Ruth's single-season home run record when he hit 61 for the New York Yankees in 1961, died in Houston at age 51.

Kansas City's George Brett was an inviting champagne target after the Royals' pennant-winning triumph over Toronto.

A ROYAL COMEBACK

Darryl Motley keyed Kansas City's 14-hit attack with a two-run homer and Bret Saberhagen pitched a five-hit shutout October 27 as the Royals pounded out an 11-0 seventh-game victory over cross-state rival St. Louis and claimed the franchise's first World Series championship.

The victory capped an amazing postseason run for the Royals, who fell behind three games to one in both the American League Championship Series against Toronto and the World Series before storming back for dramatic victories.

St. Louis carried a three games to two advantage into the key sixth game of the fall classic and the Royals' Charlie Leibrandt and the Cardinals' Danny Cox matched zeroes for seven tense innings. St. Louis broke through for what appeared to be the Series-winning run in the eighth when Brian Harper, pinch-hitting for Cox, blooped a single to center that scored Terry Pendleton.

With Cardinal relief ace Todd Worrell on to protect the 1-0 lead, the Royals' ninth inning opened when pinch-hitter Jorge Orta hit a grounder to first baseman Jack Clark, who tossed to Worrell dashing for the bag. Television cameras showed

Worrell definitely beat Orta, but umpire Don Denkinger thought otherwise. The Cardinals argued vehemently . . . and then unraveled.

Clark inexplicably let Steve Balboni's foul pop-up drop and Balboni singled to left. Jim Sundberg bunted into a forceout, but Cardinal catcher Darrell Porter's passed ball advanced the runners. Hal McRae was walked intentionally, bringing on pinch-hitter Dane Iorg. The former Cardinal singled home the tying and winning runs.

The Cardinals still were fuming the next night when the Royals struck quickly and often. Manager Whitey Herzog and pitcher Joaquin Andujar were ejected during a stormy fifth-inning argument — an inning in which the Royals scored six times.

The Cardinals had gained their early momentum on two outstanding performances by seventh-game loser John Tudor, who pitched them to a 3-1 first-game victory and a 3-0 Game 4 triumph. St. Louis earned its other victory by scoring four times in the ninth inning for a 4-2 Game 2 decision.

Saberhagen kept Kansas City alive with a 6-1 win in Game 3 and Danny Jackson did likewise with a 6-1 Game 5 triumph.

Kansas City catcher Jim Sundberg scores the winning run in the Royals' Game 6 World Series-tying victory over St. Louis.

Game 1	St. Louis	3	Kansas City	1
Game 2	St. Louis	4	Kansas City	2
Game 3	Kansas City	6	St. Louis	1
Game 4	St. Louis	3	Kansas City	0
Game 5	Kansas City	6	St. Louis	1
Game 6	Kansas City	2	St. Louis	1
Game 7	Kansas City	11	St. Louis	0

" DUGOUT CHATTER "

"Two hits a day keeps the doctor away, and in this case the doctor is George Brett."

Wade Boggs

Boston third baseman, locked in a hot duel with Kansas City's Brett for the A.L. batting title

Young hurlers sweep

New York Mets righthander Dwight Gooden, three days short of his 21st birthday, became the youngest player in history to win a Cy Young Award November 13 when he swept all 24 first-place votes cast by a panel of writers. He also joined 21-year-old American League winner Bret Saberhagen of Kansas City in a youthful sweep of the game's most prestigious pitching honor.

Gooden recorded a 24-4 record, a 1.53 earned-run average and 268 strikeouts. The young fireballer led the major leagues in all three categories, the first such sweep since Los Angeles' Sandy Koufax turned the trick in 1966. Gooden lost only one decision over the last four months of the campaign.

Gooden outpointed St. Louis lefthander John Tudor, who opened the season 1-7 and then won 20 of his last 21 decisions to finish 21-8. Tudor fashioned a 1.93 ERA and led the N.L. with 10 shutouts.

Saberhagen, Kansas City's World Series hero, was 20-6 with a 2.87 ERA.

Young and talented N.L. Cy Young winner Dwight Gooden.

CAUGHT ON THE FLY

JUNE

Former Yale University President A. Bartlett Giamatti was elected to a five-year term as N.L. president, succeeding Chub Feeney, who retired after 17 years at the helm.

AUGUST

Minnesota's Bert Blyleven became the 10th member of baseball's 3,000-strikeout fraternity.

Veteran lefthander Steve Carlton, now pitching for San Francisco, joined Nolan Ryan as the only pitchers to record 4,000 career strikeouts.

SEPTEMBER

Houston lefthander Jim Deshaies set a major league record when he struck out the first eight Los Angeles Dodgers he faced en route to a two-hit, 4-0 triumph at the Astrodome.

Sutton reaches 300

Don Sutton, a career grinder with only one 20-victory season to his credit, joined the elite circle of 300-game winners June 18 when he pitched California to a 5-1 win over Texas before 37,044 fans at Anaheim Stadium.

The 41-year-old righthander, who has been churning out double-figure victory totals for 20-plus seasons with five teams, pitched a complete-game three-hitter, nine days after shutting out Chicago, 3-0, on a two-hitter for win No. 299. The 15-year Los Angeles Dodger star had not pitched two complete games in a season since 1983, when he did it for Milwaukee.

Sutton, the 19th pitcher to record 300 victories and the fifth to reach the milestone in the 1980s, needed only 85 pitches to set down Texas on two Ruben Sierra singles and a Pete Incaviglia home run. Angel fans gave him a rousing ovation as he took the mound for the ninth inning

California righthander Don Sutton, a newly ordained 300-game winner.

and he responded by getting Scott Fletcher and Oddibe McDowell on fly balls and Gary Ward on strikes.

The Rocket explodes

Boston righthander Roger Clemens, known around the American League as the Rocket, put his turbo-charged fastball into high gear April 29 when he blew away 20 Seattle Mariners and set a major league single-game strikeout record during the Red Sox's 3-1 victory at Fenway Park.

Using an overpowering fastball clocked as high as 98 mph, Clemens lived up to his nickname and broke the modern nine-inning mark shared by Steve Carlton (St. Louis, 1969), Tom Seaver (New York Mets, 1970) and Nolan Ryan (California, 1974). The 23-year-old fireballer, who had undergone shoulder surgery eight months earlier, threw 138 pitches and did not walk a batter.

Clemens struck out every hitter in the Seattle starting lineup at least once and fanned Phil Bradley four times. Eight batters took called third strikes and Clemens punched out the side in the first, fourth and fifth innings. He also matched the A.L. record of eight consecutive strikeouts from the fourth to the sixth.

Bradley became his 20th victim with two out in the ninth, after Spike Owen had struck out to lead off the frame. The Mariners, who managed only three hits, scored their only run on a seventh-inning Gorman Thomas homer.

Flame-throwing Roger (the Rocket) Clemens, on his way to a major league-record 20 strikeouts during a game against Seattle, gets a glad hand from a Boston teammate.

7 players suspended

Commissioner Peter Ueberroth, trying to find the antidote for a rapidly growing drug problem, handed out one-year suspensions February 28 to seven players, all of whom he said had used drugs themselves or facilitated the spread of drugs in baseball.

The New York Mets' Keith Hernandez, the Yankees' Dale Berra, Oakland's Joaquin Andujar, Cincinnati's Dave Parker, San Francisco's Jeffrey Leonard, Kansas City's Lonnie Smith and Los Angeles' Enos Cabell all were suspended without pay. But Ueberroth did offer an alternative for them to consider.

The players can have their suspensions lifted if they agree to certain conditions, including contribution of 10 per cent of their salaries this year to drug-prevention programs, a willing submission to drug tests for the remainder of their careers and participation in up to 200 hours of community service over the next two years.

All of the seven either testified or were implicated last year during the Pittsburgh trials of seven men charged with cocaine distribution.

The commissioner also handed out lesser penalties to 14 other players for drug-related transgressions.

The American way

Two second basemen, Detroit's Lou Whitaker and Kansas City's Frank White, drilled home runs and American League pitchers allowed only five National League hits as the junior circuit broke through for its second All-Star Game victory in 15 years, a 3-2 decision July 15 at Houston's Astrodome.

The A.L. headliner for this contest was Boston righthander Roger Clemens, who entered the All-Star break with an outstanding 15-2 record. Clemens did not disappoint, pitching three perfect innings, and Milwaukee's Ted Higuera, Texas knuckleballer Charlie Hough, New York's Dave Righetti and Baltimore's Don Aase shut down N.L. hitters the rest of the way. The Nationals scored both of their runs off Hough in the eighth inning, primarily because Boston catcher Rich Gedman had trouble handling his dancing deliveries.

The A.L. broke through in the second when Whitaker hit a two-run shot off New York Mets righthander Dwight Gooden and added to its lead in the seventh when White connected against Houston's Mike Scott.

Horner blasts Expos

Atlanta's Bob Horner became the 11th player in major league history to blast four home runs in a single game July 6, but the slugging first baseman's record-tying performance went for naught as the Braves dropped an 11-8 decision to the Montreal Expos.

Horner, the first player in 10 years to accomplish the feat and the first since 1961 to do it in the regulation nine innings, connected for solo homers off Expos starter Andy McGaffigan in the second and fourth innings and added a three-run shot off McGaffigan in the fifth. He completed his rampage with a solo blast off Montreal reliever Jeff Reardon with two out in the ninth.

Horner received a standing ovation from the 18,153 Atlanta-Fulton County Stadium fans, who then watched Reardon retire the final batter. Mitch Webster was the Expos' offensive star, collecting five hits and three RBIs. Montreal scored eight of its runs in the first four innings off Zane Smith.

Philadelphia's Mike Schmidt had been baseball's last four-homer man, turning the trick in a 10-inning 1976 win over Chicago.

Bo becomes Royalty

Bo Jackson, possibly the greatest physical specimen ever to put on a baseball uniform, completed his first season October 5 with mediocre numbers and great expectations. That was fine with the Kansas City Royals who literally stole this budding superstar from other officials who had assumed he would take his Heisman Trophy-winning talent to the National Football League.

With everybody thinking Jackson would snap up the $7.6 million contract that awaited him as the No. 1 selection by Tampa Bay in the NFL draft, baseball teams bypassed him in the early stages of the June draft before the Royals finally took a shot on the fourth round. The former Auburn University football star shocked everybody by opting for a three-year, $1.066 million contract to play the sport he "likes best."

He certainly has the tools: a rifle arm, world-class speed and power. But he showed quickly that his talent is raw, batting .277 with seven homers and 81 strikeouts in 53 games with the Royals' Class-AA Memphis team. And despite flashes of brilliance, he struggled through his September debut in Kansas City.

Jackson batted .207 with two homers while striking out 34 times as a major leaguer. But one of those home runs was a 475-footer off Seattle's Mike Moore — the longest ever hit at Royals Stadium.

Atlanta slugger Bob Horner is greeted by Manager Chuck Tanner (center) and catcher Ozzie Virgil after the second of his four July 6 home runs.

" DUGOUT CHATTER "

"When it rains, it pours, and I'm about to drown. Even my wife was booing out there. My little boy can't even talk, but he was trying to boo."

Pete Rose

Cincinnati manager, after an ugly loss to the Montreal Expos

"The weight of the world is on policemen, firemen and teachers who are raising families and not getting paid enough. This is easy."

Ken Harrelson

Director of operations for the Chicago White Sox

"The only way I'm going to get a Gold Glove is with a can of spray paint."

Reggie Jackson

California slugger

Bo Jackson spent the first part of his rookie professional season playing for the Class-AA Memphis Chicks.

Red Sox stun Angels

Anaheim Stadium was rocking as 64,223 fans warmed up for the celebration that would accompany the California Angels' first American League pennant. Twenty-six years of frustration was about to be wiped away by one pitch from reliever Donnie Moore, who had a 1-2 count on Boston's Dave Henderson.

The Angels owned a three games to one lead over the sputtering Red Sox in the A.L. Championship Series and a 5-4 advantage in Game 5. Boston's faint hopes were in the hands of Henderson, who was down to one swing with a man on base.

Moore's next pitch was low for ball two. The crowd gasped. With the Angels players poised on the top step of the dugout, ready to rush the field, Moore delivered again. Foul ball. Another delivery, another foul. Moore took a deep breath, the crowd gasped again and Henderson took his best rip at another fastball. He connected. As the stunning two-run homer sailed out of sight over the left-field fence, thousands of dreams went up in smoke.

The Angels fought back to tie in the bottom of the ninth on Rob Wilfong's run-scoring single, but the Red Sox finally won 7-6 in the 11th — on Henderson's sacrifice fly. Boston, given a last-second reprieve, made short work of the demoralized Angels in the next two contests at Boston, recording 10-4 and 8-1 victories that secured a most unlikely pennant.

It was the Red Sox who appeared demoralized through the first four games. Roger Clemens, a 24-4 performer during the regular season, was pounded by the Angels, 8-1, in the opener and then failed to hold a 3-0 lead that he took into the ninth inning of Game 4. The Angels pulled off a shocking comeback of their own, tying the game on a Doug DeCinces home run, two singles, a run-scoring double by Gary Pettis and a run-scoring hit batsman by reliever Calvin Schiraldi. The Angels won in the 11th on a Bobby Grich single.

The Red Sox had won the second game, 9-2, behind Bruce Hurst and California had recorded a 5-3 third-game win behind John Candelaria and Moore. Clemens, getting home run support from Dwight Evans and Jim Rice, wrapped up Boston's first pennant since 1975 in Game 7.

Boston savior Dave Henderson (right) gets a hug from teammate Bill Buckner after his Game 5 Championship Series homer.

A special no-hitter

Houston righthander Mike Scott joined a multitude of major league pitchers who have thrown no-hitters when he shut down San Francisco, 2-0, September 25. But there was something out of the ordinary about Scott's gem, which was performed before 32,808 fans at the Astrodome.

Scott's no-hitter clinched the National League West Division championship for the Astros, marking the first time in history that a division title or pennant had been clinched in that manner. The division title, with Cincinnati running a distant second, was the first for Houston since 1980 and the shutout was the third straight by a Houston pitcher.

The 31-year-old Scott, who turned his career around by mastering the split-finger fastball, struck out 13 Giants and needed only 102 pitches to post his 18th victory against 10 losses.

Houston ace Mike Scott en route to his no-hitter and N.L. West Division-clinching victory.

CAUGHT ON THE FLY

SEPTEMBER
Hall of Fame slugger Hank Greenberg, a two-time Detroit MVP who once hit 58 home runs in a single season, died in Beverly Hills, Calif., at age 75.

OCTOBER
New York lefthander Dave Righetti saved both ends of the Yankees' doubleheader sweep of Boston, giving him a major league-record 46 for the season.

NOVEMBER
Boston's Rocket Man, Roger Clemens, capped his 24-4, 2.48-ERA season by sweeping the A.L. Cy Young and Most Valuable Player awards.

A survival of fittest

The New York Mets scored three runs in the top of the 16th inning and held on for dear life in the bottom of the frame to wrap up their first National League pennant since 1973 with a dramatic 7-6 victory over Houston at the Astrodome.

The Mets' October 15 triumph in the sixth game of the Championship Series was a memorable conclusion to an exciting classic. The Astros struck for three runs against Mets starter Bob Ojeda in the first and New York tied the game in the ninth with a three-run rally against Astros lefthander Bob Knepper and reliever Dave Smith. When the Mets took the lead with a 14th-inning run, the Astros' Billy Hatcher answered with a tying home run.

The Mets, 108-game winners during the regular season, broke through in the 16th, but again Houston rallied, scoring twice and getting the tying and winning runs on base. Jesse Orosco ended the game by striking out Kevin Bass.

Houston won the Series opener, 1-0, and the fourth game, 3-1, behind Mike Scott. Two of

New York pitchers Bob Ojeda (left) and Jesse Orosco after the Mets' 16-inning pennant-clinching victory over Houston.

New York's first three wins were decided in the Mets' final at-bats — Game 3 on Lenny Dykstra's two-run ninth-inning homer (6-5) and Game 5 on Gary Carter's 12th-inning single (2-1).

" DUGOUT CHATTER "

"The wind always seems to blow against catchers when they are running."

Joe Garagiola

NBC broadcaster and former major league catcher

"Ever notice the vampires when they see a crucifix? That's the way I am when I see scales."

Tom Lasorda

The portly Los Angeles manager

SEASON LEADERS

	American League		National League	
Avg.	Wade Boggs, Bos.	.357	Tim Raines, Mon.	.334
HR	Jesse Barfield, Tor.	40	Mike Schmidt, Phi.	37
RBI	Joe Carter, Cle.	121	Mike Schmidt, Phi.	119
SB	Rickey Henderson, N.Y.	87	Vince Coleman, St. L.	107
W-L Pct.	Roger Clemens, Bos.	24-4, .857	Bob Ojeda, N.Y.	18-5, .783
ERA	Roger Clemens, Bos.	2.48	Mike Scott, Hou.	2.22
SO	Mark Langston, Sea.	245	Mike Scott, Hou.	306

METS PULL DOWN SOX

Darryl Strawberry and Ray Knight cracked home runs and Keith Hernandez delivered a key two-run single as the New York Mets, having arisen from the dead in Game 6, recorded an 8-5 seventh-game victory over Boston and captured their first World Series championship since 1969.

Hernandez's sixth-inning single brought the Mets back from a 3-0 deficit in the October 27 clincher at Shea Stadium and Knight's solo blast gave them a 4-3 lead. Strawberry's eighth-inning blow expanded a lead that Jesse Orosco protected with two shutout innings of relief.

The Mets were still alive by virtue of their sixth-game resiliency in an amazing and most improbable 10-inning 6-5 victory. The Red Sox, having bolted to a three games to two advantage behind the pitching of Bruce Hurst, were on the verge of giving starved Boston fans their first championship since 1918.

Roger Clemens, a 24-game winner during the regular season, was on the mound for Game 6 and the big righthander left after seven innings with the Red Sox leading, 3-2. But the Mets quickly tied the score in the eighth against reliever Calvin Schiraldi.

Dave Henderson put Boston back on top in the 10th with a homer and the Red Sox added another run on Marty Barrett's single. Boston fans prepared to party when Schiraldi retired the first two Mets in the bottom of the inning.

But singles by Gary Carter and Kevin Mitchell delayed the celebration and Knight followed with a two-strike single to center, scoring Carter and moving Mitchell to third. Now it was up to Mookie Wilson, facing new pitcher Bob Stanley.

Wilson worked the count to 2-2 and began fouling off pitches. Stanley's seventh delivery was wild and Mitchell scored the tying run. Wilson finally hit Stanley's 10th pitch fair — and right through the legs of first baseman Bill Buckner. Knight bolted home with the winning run.

Game 1	Boston	1	New York	0
Game 2	Boston	9	New York	3
Game 3	New York	7	Boston	1
Game 4	New York	6	Boston	2
Game 5	Boston	4	New York	2
Game 6	New York	6	Boston	5
Game 7	New York	8	Boston	5

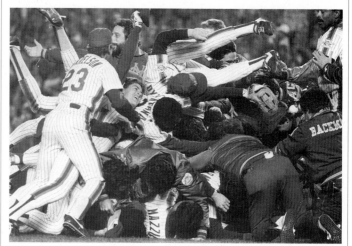

There are bodies, bodies everywhere as the New York Mets celebrate their seven-game World Series victory over the Boston Red Sox.

Bo knows football

Just three months after reaffirming his intention of having a baseball-only career, Bo Jackson shocked Kansas City officials and fans by signing a five-year contract to play with the Los Angeles Raiders of the National Football League.

But that does not mean Bo is suddenly changing careers. The former Heisman Trophy winner from Auburn is simply adding "a hobby" to get him through those cold winter months.

Jackson's two-sport plan, announced July 14, calls for him to join the Raiders as soon as Kansas City's baseball season is over. That would be October 4 if the Royals do not make the playoffs, the end of October if they go to the World Series. That would give him about half a football season.

For those eight or so games, he will earn approximately $500,000 to go with a $1 million signing bonus. He is making approximately $300,000 in his first full season with the Royals and entered the All-Star break batting .254 with 18 home runs and 45 RBIs.

Jackson spurned a $7.6 million offer from Tampa Bay last year to sign with Kansas City.

Kansas City pitcher Mark Gubicza (right) prepares to receive a pass from Bo Jackson in the Royals' dugout. Jackson signed a contract earlier in the week to double as a running back for the Los Angeles Raiders.

Schmidt hits No. 500

Philadelphia third baseman Mike Schmidt wrote a storybook ending to his quest for 500 career home runs April 18 when he smashed a dramatic three-run, ninth-inning shot over the left-field fence at Pittsburgh's Three Rivers Stadium to give the Phillies an 8-6 victory over the Pirates.

Schmidt's milestone blast came on a 3-0 pitch from Don Robinson and gave the Phillies only their third victory in 11 games. When the three-time Most Valuable Player reached the plate, he was mobbed by delirious teammates and saluted by 19,361 Pittsburgh fans. He received another standing ovation when he returned to his third base position.

The 37-year-old Schmidt, the National League's home run champion eight times during his 15-year career, became the 14th player to reach the prestigious 500 plateau.

" DUGOUT CHATTER "

"Someday he's going to manage and he'll be a good one. He'll have Wade Boggs as his hitting instructor and me as his pitching coach."

Roger Clemens

Boston pitcher, on heady second baseman Marty Barrett

"I heard that Billy Buckner tried to commit suicide over the winter. He stepped in front of a car, but it went through his legs."

Billy Gardner

Kansas City manager, on the Red Sox first baseman whose World Series misplay helped the New York Mets win the 1986 championship

Campanis speaks out

Al Campanis, the 70-year-old vice president in charge of player personnel for the Los Angeles Dodgers, resigned under fire April 8 in the wake of a national storm caused by his comments on the April 6 segment of "Nightline," an ABC news program.

Campanis, appearing on a show honoring the 40th anniversary of Jackie Robinson breaking baseball's color barrier, was asked by host Ted Koppel why the major leagues had no black managers, general managers or owners.

"I truly believe that they may not have some of the necessities to be, let's say, a field manager or perhaps a G.M.," replied Campanis, who had played as a minor leaguer with Robinson 41 years ago. When Koppel asked Campanis if he really believed that, the Dodger executive responded, "Well, I don't say that all of them, but they are short. How many quarterbacks do you have, how many pitchers to you have, that are black."

A moment later, Campanis added, "Why are black men or black people not good swimmers? Because they don't have any buoyancy."

The comments unleashed a storm of controversy and forced Campanis into an apology. He steadfastly maintained that his statements were misconstrued and that he does not believe that blacks are less intelligent than whites.

Los Angeles Dodger vice president Al Campanis (backseat) is spirited away from cameramen in the wake of his controversial statements on ABC's Nightline television show.

Howser is dead

Kansas City Manager Dick Howser, frail from off-season surgery for brain cancer, tried unsuccessfully to make a comeback during spring training.

Dick Howser, the soft-spoken manager who led Kansas City to its first World Series championship in 1985, died June 17 in a Kansas City hospital after a year-long battle with brain cancer. He was aged 51.

Howser had entered St. Luke's Hospital early this month when his condition worsened after his third operation. The cancerous tumor had been diagnosed during the All-Star Game break in July 1986, when he was managing the American League team to a 3-2 victory.

Howser's major league career began in 1961 when he captured A.L. Rookie of the Year honors as a shortstop for the Kansas City Athletics. He went on to play eight years for the A's, Cleveland Indians and New York Yankees, compiling a .248 career average. He coached 10 years after his retirement for the Yankees and went on to manage the Bronx Bombers to an A.L. East Division title in 1980 and the Royals to A.L. West titles in 1984 and '85.

His 1985 Kansas City team came back from three games to one deficits in both the A.L. Championship Series against Toronto and the World Series against St. Louis.

CAUGHT ON THE FLY

FEBRUARY

San Diego's LaMarr Hoyt, a former A.L. Cy Young winner, was suspended by Commissioner Peter V. Ueberroth for the entire season following his release from prison, where he had served 38 days for Federal drug violations.

APRIL

New York Mets righthander Dwight Gooden, the N.L.'s 1985 Cy Young Award winner, entered a drug abuse program in New York after testing positive for cocaine use.

JUNE

The 25-game hitting streak of Boston third baseman Wade Boggs came to an end during a game in which the New York Yankees rallied from a 9-0 deficit for a 10-inning, 12-11 victory over the Red Sox.

Philadelphia relief ace Steve Bedrosian set a major league record by recording saves in 13 consecutive appearances.

JULY

When Boston's Don Baylor was plunked by a pitch from New York's Rick Rhoden during a game at Yankee Stadium, it marked the 244th time he had been struck and moved him past career record-holder Ron Hunt.

Mattingly goes wild

New York Yankee first baseman Don Mattingly hit a 2-0 pitch from Texas righthander Jose Guzman over the left-center field fence at Arlington Stadium July 18, tying a 31-year-old major league record that many felt would never be matched. The blast gave Mattingly home runs in eight consecutive games, tying the 1956 mark set by Pittsburgh's Dale Long. .

The fourth-inning homer was inconsequential to the final score, a 7-2 Rangers victory, but it was the reason many of the 41,871 fans had come to the ballpark. A long ovation followed the homer and Mattingly was pushed out of the dugout for a curtain call.

The home run was Mattingly's 10th in a stretch that began July 8 against Minnesota's Mike Smithson. The 26-year-old had broken the American League record the day before when he connected against Texas' Paul Kilgus.

Mattingly's homer was his 18th of the season and he added a single to lift his average to .340.

N.L. Raines on All-Star parade

Montreal's Tim Raines drilled a two-run, 13th-inning triple to left-center field July 14, breaking up the greatest pitching duel in All-Star Game history and giving the National League a 2-0 victory over the American League at the Oakland Coliseum.

Raines, who collected three of the N.L.'s eight hits, connected with two out off Oakland reliever Jay Howell, the last of seven A.L. pitchers. Kansas City's Bret Saberhagen, Detroit's Jack Morris, Seattle's Mark Langston, Milwaukee's Dan Plesac, New York's Dave Righetti and Toronto's Tom Henke had worked 11 scoreless innings.

The A.L. missed a scoring opportunity in the ninth when New York's Dave Winfield was cut down at the plate in a collision with Atlanta catcher Ozzie Virgil, but otherwise the eight-man N.L. staff of Mike Scott (Houston), Rick Sutcliffe (Chicago), Orel Hershiser (Los Angeles), Rick Reuschel (Pittsburgh), John

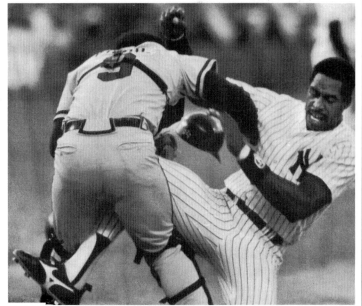

New York Yankee Dave Winfield crashes into Atlanta catcher Ozzie Virgil in the ninth inning of the All-Star Game at Oakland. Virgil tagged Winfield out, forcing the game into extra innings.

Franco (Cincinnati), Steve Bedrosian (Philadelphia), Lee Smith (Chicago) and Sid Fernandez (New York) was in control,

allowing only six hits.

Eight All-Star Games have gone extra innings and the N.L. has won all of them.

★1987★

CAUGHT ON THE FLY

SEPTEMBER

The Toronto Blue Jays blasted a major league-record 10 home runs in a game against Baltimore. Ernie Whitt (three), George Bell and Rance Mulliniks (two apiece) and Lloyd Moseby, Rob Ducey and Fred McGriff all connected in the 18-3 rout of the Orioles.

OCTOBER

San Diego's Benito Santiago was handcuffed by Los Angeles' Orel Hershiser, ending the longest hitting streak ever compiled by a rookie or a catcher at 34 games.

Oakland first baseman Mark McGwire obliterated the rookie record for home runs when he blasted 49, 11 more than former stars Wally Berger and Frank Robinson hit in their debut seasons.

Billy Martin, fired as New York Yankee manager for the fourth time after the 1985 season, was hired by George Steinbrenner for a fifth term, replacing Lou Piniella.

Molitor streak ends

Cleveland rookie John Farrell won the battle but got a no-decision in the war. The 25-year-old righthander stopped Paul Molitor's 39-game hitting streak August 26, but he was not around in the 10th inning when pinch-hitter Rick Manning delivered a two-out single to give Milwaukee a 1-0 victory.

Farrell allowed only three hits through nine innings of the game at County Stadium, striking out Molitor in the first and getting him to hit ground balls in the third, sixth and eighth. The Milwaukee designated hitter reached base in the eighth when first baseman Pat Tabler bobbled a throw that clearly would have recorded the out, and he was waiting in the on-deck circle in the 10th when Manning singled off reliever Doug Jones to make a winner of Brewer lefthander Ted Higuera.

During his streak, the fifth longest in modern major league history, Molitor collected 68 hits in 164 at-bats for a .415 average. It was the longest major league streak since 1978 when Cincinnati's Pete Rose hit in 44 straight games and it was the longest in the American League since 1941, when Yankee Clipper Joe DiMaggio compiled his record 56-game skein.

Milwaukee streaker Paul Molitor.

Tigers catch Jays

Detroit lefthander Frank Tanana pitched a six-hitter and the Tigers completed a stunning season-closing sweep of Toronto October 4 with a 1-0 victory that decided the American League East Division title.

The victory before 51,005 fans at Tiger Stadium, Detroit's fourth in a row and third straight over the Blue Jays, gave the Tigers a final 98-64 record and a two-game bulge in the A.L. East standings. Toronto, which had won its 96th game on September 26, lost its final seven in one of baseball's all-time great collapses.

The Blue Jays owned a 3½-game bulge with seven to play when they inexplicably stopped hitting, dropping a 13-inning, 3-2 decision to Detroit and three straight to Milwaukee before traveling to Detroit with a one-game advantage. They fell to the inspired Tigers, 4-3, on October 2 and 3-2 in 12 innings the next day.

That set up the final-game showdown with the Blue Jays now hoping to force a division playoff. Tanana and Larry Herndon, who belted a second-inning homer off hard-luck loser Jimmy Key, took care of that.

Detroit players had reason to celebrate after a 1-0 final-day victory that completed a sweep of Toronto and secured the A.L. East Division championship.

" DUGOUT CHATTER "

"I broke a bat on the first hit, took a half swing on the second. The third was a 53-hopper up the middle and the last a ground ball double to second."

Wade Boggs

Boston third baseman, describing his 4-for-5 performance on the artificial surface at Kansas City's Royals Stadium

NO PLACE LIKE HOME

The Minnesota Twins, a living tribute to the adage that there's no place like home, waved their magic hankies and powerful bats at the St. Louis Cardinals October 24 and 25 and made them disappear from a seven-game World Series that had baseball purists mumbling to themselves.

Playing in the cozy Hubert H. Humphrey Metrodome, the Twins won the first two indoor games in World Series history, lost the next three in St. Louis and captured the final two in Minnesota. That was similar to the script they had followed in posting a mediocre 85-77 record en route to winning the American League West Division — an outstanding 56-25 mark at home, a 29-52 ledger on the road. They also won both games of the A.L. Championship Series (a five-game triumph over Detroit) contested in Minnesota.

The Cardinals, 95-67 while winning the National League East, got their first taste of the Metrodome's teflon roof, bad lighting, ear-splitting acoustical problems and trash bag-lined walls October 17. And the combination of the Twins' batting power (Dan Gladden hit a homer and drove in five runs) and the hanky-waving fans' lung power resulted in a 10-1 defeat. Minnesota followed the next night with an 8-4 triumph.

But the bats that had produced four home runs in the first two games went silent when the scene shifted to massive Busch Stadium and the Cardinals rolled off 3-1, 7-2 and 4-2 victories.

Trailing 5-2 in Game 6, the Twins turned the power back on. Don Baylor hit a three-run homer in the fifth, Kent Hrbek hit a grand slam in the sixth and Minnesota recorded an 11-5 win.

The Game 7 clincher came when Frank Viola pitched eight strong innings and Minnesota overcame two runners being thrown out at the plate for a 4-2 victory.

Game 1	Minnesota	10	St. Louis	1
Game 2	Minnesota	8	St. Louis	4
Game 3	St. Louis	3	Minnesota	1
Game 4	St. Louis	7	Minnesota	2
Game 5	St. Louis	4	Minnesota	2
Game 6	Minnesota	11	St. Louis	5
Game 7	Minnesota	4	St. Louis	2

Cards trip up Giants

The St. Louis Cardinals, on the brink of National League Championship Series elimination after losing Game 5 to San Francisco, stormed back behind successive shutout efforts by John Tudor and Danny Cox to claim their third pennant in six years.

With the Giants one step away from their first World Series appearance since 1962 after a 6-3 victory at Candlestick Park, Tudor shut them down for 7⅓ innings in Game 6 and relievers Todd Worrell and Ken Dayley took care of the rest in a 1-0 victory. Then Cox scattered eight hits in a 6-0 seventh-game triumph that featured a stunning three-run homer by light-hitting Jose Oquendo.

St. Louis' comeback spoiled outstanding performances by Giants' lefthander Dave Dravecky and left fielder Jeffrey Leonard. Dravecky pitched a two-hit, 5-0 shutout in Game 2 after St. Louis had won the opener, 5-3, and he was the tough-luck loser in Game 6, a contest decided by Oquendo's sacrifice fly.

Leonard batted .417 and smashed a playoff record-tying four home runs, one in each of the first four games. His Game 3 blast came in a 6-5 loss and his fourth-game homer with a man aboard sparked a 4-2 triumph.

San Francisco's Game 5 win featured a home run by Kevin Mitchell and five innings of one-hit relief by Joe Price.

St. Louis wizard Ozzie Smith makes a double play relay over sliding San Francisco catcher Bob Brenly during the Cardinals' seventh-game Championship Series conquest of the Giants.

Celebration time for the Minnesota Twins, who recorded a 4-2 victory over St. Louis in Game 7 of the World Series.

SEASON LEADERS

	American League		National League	
Avg.	Wade Boggs, Bos.	.363	Tony Gwynn, S.D.	.370
HR	Mark McGwire, Oak.	49	Andre Dawson, Chi.	49
RBI	George Bell, Tor.	134	Andre Dawson, Chi.	137
SB	Harold Reynolds, Sea.	60	Vince Coleman, St. L.	109
W-L Pct.	Roger Clemens, Bos.	20-9, .690	Dwight Gooden, N.Y.	15-7, .682
ERA	Jimmy Key, Tor.	2.76	Nolan Ryan, Hou.	2.76
SO	Mark Langston, Sea.	262	Nolan Ryan, Hou.	270

O-21: An Oriole legacy

Nobody was overly shocked when Baltimore opened the season with two losses to Milwaukee and four more to Cleveland. But the reaction from Oriole management to fire Manager Cal Ripken Sr. after only six games and replace him with Frank Robinson caught everybody by surprise.

And so did what transpired over the next two weeks as the once-proud Orioles sank into the lower reaches of the American League East Division standings with an embarrassing thud.

Now under the direction of Robinson, the Orioles lost three straight home games to Kansas City and three more to the Indians. When they lost their 13th straight game two days later at Milwaukee, the Orioles broke the major league record for most consecutive losses to open a season. But they were just getting started.

Two more losses to the Brewers and three at Kansas City raised the count to 18 and threatened the A.L. record for futility — 20 straight losses. Three more at Minnesota broke that mark and now they were approaching the longest losing streak ever — 23, by Philadelphia in 1961.

But with a nation watching with morbid fascination, the Orioles rose up and belted the White Sox, 9-0, in Chicago April 29, ending the nightmare. Well, almost. They lost two more to Chicago and staggered home with a 1-23 record.

" DUGOUT CHATTER "

"He's still ugly, he's still tall and he still can pitch."

Dave Parker

Oakland slugger, after New York Yankee pitcher and former Pittsburgh teammate John Candelaria had shut out the A's on a two-hitter

Steinbach lifts A.L.

Oakland catcher Terry Steinbach, maligned by the media as an unworthy All-Star Game starter, drove in both American League runs with a homer and sacrifice fly July 12 and eight pitchers made them stand up for a 2-1 victory over the National League at Cincinnati's Riverfront Stadium.

Steinbach, voted into the starting lineup despite a .217 average and a long stint on the disabled list, drove a pitch from New York Mets starter Dwight Gooden over the right-field wall in the third inning and hit his bases-loaded sacrifice fly off Houston's Bob Knepper in the fourth.

The Nationals managed only five hits and one fourth-inning run off Minnesota's Frank Viola, Boston's Roger Clemens, Kansas

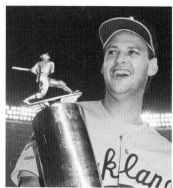

Oakland catcher Terry Steinbach, A.L. offensive hero and All-Star Game MVP.

City's Mark Gubicza, Toronto's Dave Stieb, Texas' Jeff Russell, Cleveland's Doug Jones, Milwaukee's Dan Plesac and Oakland's Dennis Eckersley.

The bumbling Orioles tested the patience of Baltimore Manager Frank Robinson (foreground) and his coaches in the early days of the 1988 campaign.

Seven players freed

Detroit slugger Kirk Gibson, declared a new-look free agent a week earlier by a labor arbitrator, signed a three-year, $4.5 million contract January 29 with the Los Angeles Dodgers. The 30-year-old outfielder was one of seven players freed by arbitrator Thomas Roberts, who had ruled in September that owners acted in collusion against free agents after the 1985 season.

Joining Gibson on the free-agent market were Detroit's Tom Brookens, Chicago White Sox catcher Carlton Fisk, Minnesota pitcher Joe Niekro, California's Butch Wynegar and Donnie Moore and Toronto's Juan Beniquez, all of whom have until March 1 to shop their talents without relinquishing their existing contracts. After March 1, they have to declare their intention to remain with their team or continue as free agents.

This remedy was the result of the first of three conspiracy actions brought against the 26 teams by the Major League Players Association. The players claimed the owners had violated their labor agreement by acting in collusion to restrict the movement of free agents and to hold down salaries.

" DUGOUT CHATTER "

"It's a great testimony to what sports fans are supposed to be. This is their only team, and they are showing their support. It's easy to get 50,000 when you win 20 in a row. I think every franchise in baseball could take a lesson from it."

Bobby Valentine

Texas manager, on the tremendous reception the Orioles received from Baltimore fans after returning home with a 1-23 record

MAY

Cincinnati Manager Pete Rose was handed a stiff 30-day suspension by N.L. President A. Bartlett Giamatti after a shoving incident with umpire Dave Pallone.

JUNE

Out again: New York Yankee Manager Billy Martin was fired for the fifth time and replaced by the man he had replaced — Lou Piniella.

Baltimore shortstop Cal Ripken Jr. became the sixth major leaguer to reach the 1,000 plateau in consecutive games played during a 10-3 Oriole loss to Boston.

JULY

Lee Weyer, an N.L. umpire since 1963, died of a heart attack in San Francisco after working a Chicago Cubs-Giants game at Candlestick Park. He was 51.

AUGUST

Philadelphia submariner Kent Tekulve joined Hoyt Wilhelm as the only pitchers to appear in 1,000 major league games when he worked two innings in the Phillies' 7-5 victory over San Francisco.

SEPTEMBER

Baseball's second and third 300-save men: The Chicago Cubs' Goose Gossage and Atlanta's Bruce Sutter.

Wrigley lights up

The sun set on day-only baseball August 9 when the Chicago Cubs defeated the New York Mets, 6-4, in the first official night game at Chicago's Wrigley Field — the last bastion of a time-honored au naturel tradition. It was treated as a gala occasion, but there was mixed emotion among the 36,399 fans and more than 500 media representatives who witnessed the 74-year-old park's first explosion of artificial light.

Most of the ceremony and clamor actually occurred on August 8, the scheduled day of the memorable event. History was made when a 91-year-old Chicago fan flipped the switch, turning on the 540 lights resting in six banks on the park's roof. But the Cubs and Philadelphia Phillies managed to play only 3½ innings before the game was postponed by a heavy thunderstorm.

The decision to light Wrigley was made in February after years of fighting among community groups, politicians and traditionalists. It also was a matter of Cubs management facing economic reality. Permission was granted with a hitch — the Cubs were limited to 18 night games per year.

Harry Grossman, a 91-year-old diehard Chicago Cubs fan, hits the switch and turns on Wrigley Field to the wonder of night baseball.

Ruling stuns owners

Major league owners were stunned for the second time in less than a year when labor arbitrator George Nicolau ruled August 31 that they were guilty of collusion against the 1986 class of free agents in violation of the sport's collective bargaining agreement.

In an 81-page opinion formed during 39 days of hearings over seven months, Nicolau ruled that the owners had acted in concert to restrict the movement of free agents, refusing to make offers to those coveted by their previous clubs. His opinion was more severe and pointed in identifying specific examples of violations than the one handed down last September by arbitrator Thomas Roberts.

Nicolau, not wanting to disrupt pennant races at midseason, withheld remedy until after the campaign, but it is almost certain that a number of players will be granted new-look free agency and that the players will be handed a huge damage reward. Lawyers estimate that Roberts and Nicolau could award damages in the area of $75 million.

The end of a baseball tradition: lights at Chicago's Wrigley Field.

Giamatti is selected to replace Ueberroth

National League President A. Bartlett Giamatti, the former president of Yale University, was elected to succeed Peter V. Ueberroth as baseball's seventh commissioner September 8 in Montreal.

The former professor of Renaissance literature received unanimous approval from the 26 team owners. He will begin his five-year term April 1, six months before the scheduled end of Ueberroth's five-year term.

Ueberroth had announced earlier that he would not consider a second term and Giamatti's election was expected. National League owners had been impressed with his law-and-order style and strong disciplinary approach to the game during his two-year stint as N.L. boss. The only questions surround his business acumen, a quality Ueberroth brought to the office when he was hired in 1984. Ueberroth's prime directive had been to straighten out baseball's financial problems while strengthening its economic base.

The 50-year-old Giamatti said he plans to hire a strong businessman to complement him in areas where he might be short on experience.

★1988★

Close, but no cigar

Toronto righthander Dave Stieb watched in horror September 30 as a blooper hit by Baltimore pinch-hitter Jim Traber cleared first baseman Fred McGriff's glove by about two feet and fell for a single, ruining his no-hit bid with two out in the ninth inning. It was a shocking feeling of deja vu.

Six days earlier at Cleveland, Stieb had carried a no-hitter and 1-0 lead into the ninth-inning of a game against the Indians. He retired the first two batters before inducing Julio Franco to hit a routine grounder. But as second baseman Manny Lee prepared to make the play that would seal the first no-hitter in Blue Jays history, the ball took a wild hop over his head and Stieb was forced to settle for a one-hit shutout.

Undaunted, Stieb faced the minimum 26 Orioles through 8⅔ innings of his next start. But he had to settle for another one-hitter and a 4-0 victory that lifted his record to 16-8.

" DUGOUT CHATTER "

"Harmon told me never to chew gum at the plate. He said it makes your eyeballs bounce up and down."

Charlie Manuel

Cleveland batting coach, on a tip he once received from Hall of Fame slugger Harmon Killebrew

---

Browning is perfect

Cincinnati lefthander Tom Browning snapped baseball's ninth-inning no-hit jinx September 16 when he recorded the 12th perfect game in major league history, beating Los Angeles, 1-0, before 16,591 fans at Riverfront Stadium.

Browning was in total command as he set down the Dodgers on 102 pitches without going to a three-ball count. The 28-year-old recorded first-pitch strikes on 22 of the 27 men he faced and struck out seven. No above-average defensive plays were needed.

Browning's effort snapped a string of 1988 near-miss no-hitters. Six pitchers, including Reds teammate Ron Robinson, had taken no-hit attempts into the ninth, only to have them spoiled.

Browning, who had watched the Reds score the game's only run on a sixth-inning throwing

Cincinnati lefty Tom Browning lets out a yell after finishing off his perfect effort against Los Angeles.

error, got Rick Dempsey on a fly ball and Steve Sax on a grounder to open the ninth. He ended the game by striking out pinch-hitter Tracy Woodson.

L.A.'s Orel surgeon

Los Angeles ace Orel Hershiser completed one of the most dazzling pitching displays in baseball history September 28 when he worked 10 shutout innings in a game at San Diego and broke former Dodger Don Drysdale's 20-year-old record for consecutive scoreless innings.

Hershiser was not the pitcher of record in the 16-inning contest eventually won by the Padres, 2-1. But he was around long enough to stretch his scoreless streak to 59 innings, one more than Drysdale managed during his 1968 streak.

The 30-year-old righthander was virtually unhittable over the last month and finished with 23 victories, a 2.26 ERA and eight shutouts. His incredible stretch run began on August 30 when he pitched scoreless baseball over the final four innings of a 4-2 victory at Montreal.

In his next start, Hershiser shut out Atlanta, 3-0. He followed with a 5-0 victory over Cincinnati,

Orel Hershiser, the Los Angeles Dodgers' Mr. Shutout.

a 1-0 win over Atlanta, a 1-0 triumph at Houston and a 3-0 win at San Francisco, setting the stage for his record-breaking effort against San Diego.

SEASON LEADERS

	American League		National League	
Avg.	Wade Boggs, Bos.	.366	Tony Gwynn, S.D.	.313
HR	Jose Canseco, Oak.	42	Darryl Strawberry, N.Y.	39
RBI	Jose Canseco, Oak.	124	Will Clark, S.F.	109
SB	Rickey Henderson, N.Y.	93	Vince Coleman, St. L.	81
W-L Pct.	Frank Viola, Min.	24-7, .774	David Cone, N.Y.	20-3, .870
ERA	Allan Anderson, Min.	2.45	Joe Magrane, St. L.	2.18
SO	Roger Clemens, Bos.	291	Nolan Ryan, Hou.	228

CAUGHT ON THE FLY

OCTOBER

Boston's Wade Boggs, en route to his fourth straight A.L. batting championship (.366), became the first player in history to reach the 200-hit plateau in six consecutive seasons.

Young Oakland slugger Jose Canseco became baseball's first 40-40 man when he finished the season with 42 home runs and 40 stolen bases.

The Minnesota Twins became the first A.L. team to top 3 million in one-season attendance.

NOVEMBER

Hall of Fame lefthander Carl Hubbell, the outstanding screwball artist who compiled a 253-154 record in 16 seasons with the New York Giants, died in Mesa, Ariz., at age 85.

Dodgers shock Mets in comeback series

Orel Hershiser pitched a five-hit shutout and Steve Sax drove in a pair of runs to lead underdog Los Angeles to a 6-0 victory over the Mets October 12 in the seventh game of a comeback-filled National League Championship Series at Dodger Stadium.

The Mets set the comeback pattern in the first game when they scored three ninth-inning runs against Hershiser and Dodger relief ace Jay Howell to claim a 3-2 triumph. After the Dodgers had rebounded for a 6-3 win in Game 2, the New Yorkers did it again,

wiping out a 4-3 Game 3 deficit with a five-run eighth-inning rally and claiming an 8-4 win.

But L.A. catcher Mike Scioscia hit a dramatic two-run homer off Dwight Gooden to tie Game 4 in the ninth and Kirk Gibson hammered a 12th-inning blast off

Roger McDowell to give Los Angeles a Series-tying 5-4 win.

The Dodgers took the lead with a 7-4 fifth-game win as Tim Belcher claimed his second victory, but David Cone kept the Mets alive in Game 6 with a five-hit, 5-1 victory.

AN UPSET SPECIAL: DODGERS SHOCK A'S

Game 1	Los Angeles	5	Oakland	4
Game 2	Los Angeles	6	Oakland	0
Game 3	Oakland	2	Los Angeles	1
Game 4	Los Angeles	4	Oakland	3
Game 5	Los Angeles	5	Oakland	2

Orel Hershiser capped his amazing late-season drive with a four-hit, 5-2 victory over Oakland October 20, giving Los Angeles a five-game World Series upset of the powerful A's and wrapping up the Dodgers' first championship since 1981.

Hershiser's victory at the Oakland Coliseum was the perfect ending for an incredible stretch run. The right-hander finished the season with a record 59-inning scoreless streak, pitched the seventh-game clincher in the Dodgers' National League Championship Series victory over New York and won two Series contests, including the decisive Game 5. Mickey Hatcher and Mike Davis made life easy for Hershiser in the finale by drilling two-run homers.

The Cinderella Dodgers were big underdogs to Oakland, which had powered its way to 104 regular-season victories and a four-game sweep of Boston in the American League Championship Series. And, true to form, the Series opened at Dodger Stadium with Jose Canseco's second-inning grand slam giving the A's a 4-2 lead. The advantage was 4-3 entering the ninth when Manager Tony LaRussa turned matters over to reliable relief ace Dennis Eckersley, who quickly recorded two outs.

But Davis worked the righthander for a walk and Dodger Manager Tom Lasorda sent a limping Kirk Gibson to the plate as a pinch-hitter. The lefthanded swinger appeared overmatched as he winced in obvious pain with every swing.

Gibson worked the count to 2-2 and Davis stole second on ball three. Wearing a pained expression, the Dodger outfielder stepped back into the box for the full-count pitch. Giving everything he could muster, the intense Gibson swung hard and

Orel Hershiser gets a lift after pitching the Los Angeles Dodgers to a clinching fifth-game World Series win over Oakland.

connected — hitting the first final-inning, come-from-behind home run in World Series history. Gibson limped around the bases and the A's limped away as 5-4 losers.

Game 2 was all Hershiser, who pitched a three-hitter, and Mike Marshall, who homered in a 6-0 Dodger victory. After Mark McGwire gave Oakland hope with a ninth-inning Game 3 homer that produced a 2-1 win, the Dodgers grabbed a 4-3 fourth-game triumph. Hershiser took care of the rest.

A welcome-home committee greets Kirk Gibson (23) as he prepares to step on the plate after his dramatic Game 1 World Series homer against Oakland.

★1989★

SkyDome unveiled

Toronto's SkyDome, the ballpark for the fan who wants everything, opened June 5 with the Milwaukee Brewers recording a 5-3 victory over the Blue Jays. But the score was incidental to the state-of-the-art spectacle that bedazzled 48,378 curious fans.

The SkyDome is a ballpark — and much more. It has the world's largest scoreboard, a built-in hotel in center field, four McDonald's, a health club, a Hard Rock Cafe, a theater, a miniature golf course, a swimming pool and an 800-seat restaurant. It also has a retractable roof, meaning fans can enjoy baseball, regardless of the weather.

The stadium, only a few blocks from Lake Ontario in downtown Toronto, took three years and more than $425 million to build. It required eight acres of concrete and steel paneling. The scoreboard, four stories tall and 115 feet wide, is built into the hotel and utilizes 420,000 lights that produce a movie screen-quality picture.

The SkyDome is the first new stadium to open since 1982, when the Metrodome was unveiled in Minneapolis.

Toronto's wondrous and spectacular new SkyDome.

Dravecky sidelined

San Francisco's Dave Dravecky, who had made a remarkable comeback from cancer surgery 10 months earlier, crashed to the turf at Montreal's Olympic Stadium August 15 after throwing a sixth-inning pitch that broke his arm.

The 33-year-old lefthander, who said later that he felt a sharp, painful pop in his pitching arm, went down like he was shot after delivering a pitch to Tim Raines. Teammates rushed from the dugout and Dravecky, writhing in pain and gripping his left arm, was rushed to a hospital, where it was determined he had suffered a stress fracture of the humerus, the largest bone between the elbow and shoulder.

The injury ended Dravecky's courageous comeback from surgery to remove a cancerous tumor from his arm last October. His rehabilitation included three complete-game victories on the minor league level and an inspirational 4-3 win over Cincinnati August 10 at Candlestick Park. He carried a three-hit shutout into the sixth inning at Montreal.

The Giants won the game, 3-2, and Dravecky finished his short season 2-0.

Revitalized A.L. wins All-Star Game — again

Kansas City's Bo Jackson and Boston's Wade Boggs hit back-to-back home runs leading off the game and the American League went on to record its second straight All-Star victory July 11, a 5-3 decision over the National League at California's Anaheim Stadium.

The Jackson-Boggs double, an All-Star first, came at the expense of San Francisco starter Rick Reuschel and wiped out a 2-0 N.L. lead. The Americans added a single run in the second on Jackson's grounder and two more in the third on run-scoring hits by Texas' Ruben Sierra and Chicago's Harold Baines.

Eight A.L. pitchers combined to take care of the rest. First-inning singles by San Francisco's Kevin Mitchell and the New York Mets' Howard Johnson produced runs off Oakland starter Dave Stewart and Philadelphia's Von Hayes singled home an eighth-inning run against Texas reliever Jeff Russell. Jackson, the fifth player to lead off a midsummer classic with a homer, also singled and stole a base in his first All-Star appearance.

The victory, the A.L.'s third in four years, marked the first time since 1957-58 that the junior circuit had won back-to-back All-Star Games.

Kansas City's Bo Jackson gets a high five from Boston's Wade Boggs after his first-inning homer in the All-Star Game.

CAUGHT ON THE FLY

JANUARY
Commissioner Peter V. Ueberroth, who had signed a four-year, $1.06 billion contract with CBS-TV in December, announced a four-year, $400 million cable package with ESPN and a four-year CBS-Radio tieup worth $50 million.

FEBRUARY
Former All-Star first baseman Bill White became the highest ranking black executive in the history of professional sports when he was elected to succeed A. Bartlett Giamatti as N.L. president.

MARCH
Nick Bremigan, an A.L. umpire since 1974, died of a heart attack in Garland, Tex., at age 43.

APRIL
New York Yankee Tommy John, a 45-year-old lefthander, set a major league record on Opening Day when he appeared in his 26th season.

JULY
After stealing a major league-record 50 straight bases over two seasons, St. Louis' Vince Coleman was nailed by Montreal catcher Nelson Santovenia.

Bionic man Ryan gets 5,000th strikeout

Rubber-armed Nolan Ryan, the Texas Rangers' 42-year-old bionic man, passed into uncharted territory August 22 when he fired a 96-mile-per-hour fastball past Oakland's Rickey Henderson and became the first pitcher in baseball history to record 5,000 career strikeouts.

The much-anticipated milestone was reached in front of 42,869 fans at Arlington Stadium. The big Texan, who entered the contest needing six strikeouts, fanned Jose Canseco in the first inning, Dave Henderson and Tony Phillips in the second and Rickey Henderson and Ron Has-sey in the third. The crowd roared its approval when Ryan got Henderson for the second time and the righthander responded by doffing his cap.

The Rangers went on to lose, 2-0, but Ryan allowed only five hits and finished the night with 5,007 strikeouts. He has fanned 1,066 different batters in his 23 seasons, including 17 enshrinees in the Hall of Fame.

Ryan's strikeout record should stand for many years. Lefthander Steve Carlton, who retired last year, is second on the all-time list with 4,136. Nobody else has reached the 4,000 plateau.

" DUGOUT CHATTER "

"When I see him in the pitching probables, I don't exactly hurry to the ballpark."

Terry Francona

Milwaukee first baseman, on Texas fireballer Nolan Ryan

Oakland's Rickey Henderson swings and misses, becoming Texas righthander Nolan Ryan's record 5,000th strikeout victim.

Giamatti hands Rose lifetime suspension

Commissioner A. Bartlett Giamatti concluded baseball's biggest gambling controversy since the 1919 Black Sox scandal August 24 when he announced at a nationally televised press conference that Pete Rose, Cincinnati's manager and the game's all-time hits leader, had accepted a lifetime suspension from any involvement with the National Pastime.

Saying he believed Rose had bet on baseball games, including those of his Reds, Giamatti told a packed room of reporters at the New York Hilton Hotel that Rose had accepted his decision, acknowledged that he was treated fairly by the Commissioner, waived his right to a hearing and agreed not to challenge his banishment. Baseball's all-time top hit man (4,256) also agreed to dismiss a civil suit filed against Giamatti.

Giamatti, who had replaced former Commissioner Peter V. Ueberroth April 1, had spent much of his five months in office directing an investigation into the gambling activities of Rose, one of the game's top personalities for three decades. Rose in turn had used a series of legal maneuvers to block Giamatti's efforts.

But Rose, buried under a mountain of evidence that chronicled his gambling activities and associations with known bookmakers, finally struck a deal whereby he signed a carefully-worded agreement in which he accepted punishment without admitting guilt. It gave Giamatti the suspension he wanted, reaffirmed the authority of his office and allowed Rose to continue denying allegations publicly.

The document also stipulated that Rose could apply for reinstatement after a year, but did not issue any guarantee. Giamatti stated at the news conference that he believed Rose had bet on baseball games and the former Reds manager, at his own nationally televised session in Cincinnati, denied it. Rose is the 15th major leaguer to receive a lifetime ban.

Baseball's Charlie Hustle, who spent 24 productive seasons with Cincinnati, Philadelphia and Montreal before returning to the Reds in 1984 as player-manager, finished his career in 1986 with a .303 lifetime average. He played in four World Series with the Reds and two with the Phillies.

" DUGOUT CHATTER "

"It's like Humpty-Dumpty. If it's true, all the king's horses and all the king's men can't put Humpty back together again."

Johnny Bench

Former Cincinnati catcher, on the gambling allegations swirling around one-time teammate Pete Rose

Pete Rose spent five months fending off reporters and photographers before being handed a lifetime suspension.

★1989★

CAUGHT ON THE FLY

OCTOBER

Boston third baseman Wade Boggs recorded his record seventh straight 200-hit season.

Major league baseball established a regular-season attendance record for the fifth straight year and seventh in the last eight, finishing with a combined total of 55,173,096.

SEASON LEADERS

	American League		National League	
Avg.	Kirby Puckett, Min.	.339	Tony Gwynn, S.D.	.336
HR	Fred McGriff, Tor.	36	Kevin Mitchell, S.F.	47
RBI	Ruben Sierra, Tex.	119	Kevin Mitchell, S.F.	125
SB	Rickey Henderson, N.Y.-Oak.	77	Vince Coleman, St. L.	65
W-L Pct.	Bret Saberhagen, K.C.	23-6, .793	Scott Garrelts, S.F. 14-5, .737 Sid Fernandez, N.Y.	14-5, .737
ERA	Bret Saberhagen, K.C.	2.16	Scott Garrelts, S.F.	2.28
SO	Nolan Ryan, Tex.	301	Jose DeLeon, St. L.	201

Giamatti dies at 51

Former baseball Commissioner A. Bartlett Giamatti.

Commissioner A. Bartlett Giamatti, the 51-year-old former Renaissance scholar and president of Yale University, died of a heart attack at his summer cottage in Massachusetts September 1, eight days after handing baseball great Pete Rose a lifetime ban for his alleged gambling activities.

Giamatti had replaced former Commissioner Peter V. Ueberroth April 1 after serving two years as National League president. He spent much of his five months in office directing an investigation into the gambling activities of Rose, baseball's all-time hits leader (4,256) and one of the game's top personalities since 1963.

The end came suddenly when Giamatti collapsed at his summer home on Martha's Vineyard and was discovered unconscious, in full cardiac arrest. He was pronounced dead several hours later at Martha's Vineyard Hospital.

Giamatti's roots were academia, but his secret passion was baseball. He served as Yale's 19th president from 1978 to '86, a post he gave up to become president of the National League. When Ueberroth announced last year that he would not seek a second term as commissioner, Giamatti was elected unanimously as his replacement.

Giamatti is only the second commissioner to die in office, the first since Kenesaw Mountain Landis, the original high priest of the sport.

Vincent elected

Fay Vincent Jr., the assistant hired to bring business sense to baseball's highest office, was unanimously elected as the sport's eighth commissioner September 13, replacing former boss A. Bartlett Giamatti.

Vincent will serve the 4½ years remaining in the first term of Giamatti, who died September 1 of a heart attack. Giamatti, in need of someone to provide the business expertise he lacked, had hired the 51-year-old Vincent as baseball's first deputy commissioner and chief operating officer.

Vincent, an attorney by way of Williams College and Yale, came to baseball from a business and legal background. He practiced corporate law for 15 years in Washington and New York before working briefly for the Securities and Exchange Commission. He later was appointed chairman and chief executive of Columbia Pictures, a position he held until 1988 when he returned to private law practice.

Gwynn, Puckett win batting titles

San Diego's Tony Gwynn became the first player in 37 years to win three consecutive National League batting titles when he zipped past San Francisco's Will Clark in a season-closing confrontation, and Minnesota's Kirby Puckett held off Oakland's Carney Lansford to capture his first American League title.

The lefthanded-hitting Gwynn successfully defended his crown when he collected three hits in four at-bats during the Padres' 3-0 victory over the Giants October 1. Gwynn finished at .336 while Clark, 1 for 4, closed at .333. The Giants' hard-hitting first baseman entered the game with a slim advantage, .3339 to .3333.

Gwynn became the first N.L. player to win three straight titles since seven-time St. Louis batting champion Stan Musial from 1950 to '52. Clark was trying to become the Giants' first batting champ since Willie Mays in 1954.

Puckett, Minnesota's fireplug

Four-time N.L. batting champion Tony Gwynn.

center fielder, finished with a 2-for-5 flourish in the Twins' 3-1 loss to Seattle, raising his final average to .339. Lansford, 0-for-3 in the A's 5-3 win over Kansas City, closed at .336. Puckett ended the four-year A.L. reign of Boston's Wade Boggs.

THE QUAKE SERIES

Rickey Henderson led off the game with a homer and Terry Steinbach drove in three runs to help Oakland close out its Bay Area World Series sweep of San Francisco October 28 with a 9-6 victory at Candlestick Park.

The A's final-game romp was a fitting conclusion to an unexciting fall classic. The powerful A's, who had blitzed Toronto in a five-game American League Championship Series, never trailed in their four-game cruise past the Giants and they never left any doubt about their determination to avenge their 1988 Series upset loss to Los Angeles and claim Oakland's first championship since 1974.

But while this Series lacked the classic moments and drama of past fall classics, it may go down in history as the most unforgettable ever. Mother Nature's intervention saw to that at 5:04 p.m. on October 17, just moments before the start of Game 3.

The crowd of 60,000-plus was in a festive mood when Candlestick suddenly started shaking and electric power stopped. Fans and players remained remarkably calm as reports circulated that the Bay Area had been hit by an earthquake measuring 7.1 on the Richter scale.

Commissioner Fay Vincent reacted quickly to the news, postponing the game and clearing the park before darkness could set in. The mood, generally light immediately following the earthquake, turned somber as reports of death and destruction circulated.

That death and destruction eventually would total 67 lives and billions of dollars. As Californians dug through the rubble and counted their blessings in the ensuing days, winning and losing baseball games became low priority. Vincent postponed the Series indefinitely and repairs were made to the ballpark. Finally, amid some calls for cancellation, the Commissioner and San Francisco Mayor Art Agnos endorsed October 27 as the resumption date. The 10-day postponement and 12-day gap in games were the longest in Series history and marked the first interruption for anything other than weather.

For the record, the A's recorded 5-0, 5-1, 13-7 and 9-6 victories. Dave Stewart and Mike Moore were two-game winners and Stewart was Series MVP.

Players, officials and fans at San Francisco's Candlestick Park shortly after the Bay Area earthquake.

Oakland players mill around the Candlestick Park field and try to locate loved ones after the earthquake.

Game 1	Oakland	5	San Francisco	0
Game 2	Oakland	5	San Francisco	1
Game 3	Oakland	13	San Francisco	7
Game 4	Oakland	9	San Francisco	6

Billy Martin dies in Christmas Day crash

Billy Martin, the combative former player and manager whose association with baseball spanned 39 years, died on Christmas Day when a pickup truck in which he was a passenger crashed near his home in Binghamton, N.Y. He was 61.

Martin was riding in the truck driven by longtime friend William Reedy. The vehicle skidded off the road, plunged 300 feet down an embankment and stopped at the foot of Martin's home driveway. Martin was pronounced dead at the hospital and Reedy, who was cited for driving while intoxicated, sustained a broken hip and several broken ribs.

Martin, who fought with players, owners and fans throughout his stormy career, played for seven teams as a second baseman, but his heart and soul belonged to the New York Yankee organization he served for the first seven of his 11 big-league seasons. He also managed five teams, but he will be remembered as the man Yankee Owner George Steinbrenner hired and fired five times. Martin was working as a member of the Yankee front office at the time of his death.

Martin compiled a .257 average as a player and 1,209 wins as a manager. He played in five World Series (batting .333) and managed the Yankees to a 1977 championship.

" DUGOUT CHATTER "

"That's the first time in my career I ever went 0 for a city in three games."

Mike Greenwell

Boston outfielder, after an 0-for-14 slump at Arlington, Tex.

The 1990s

If the 1980s signaled the arrival of the million-dollar superstar, the 1990s signaled the arrival of the big-money part-timer.

As the salaries of the low-profile players spiraled, those of the top guns skyrocketed. Three players became $7 million men with Barry Bonds' paycheck going right through the stratosphere. The San Francisco Giants agreed to pay the former Pittsburgh Pirates outfielder $43.75 million for six years while the Detroit Tigers put Cecil Fielder and the Chicago Cubs put Ryne Sandberg in a league all their own.

The new decade also ushered in a period of confusion, disenchantment and finger-pointing as both players and owners jockeyed for position in the ever intensifying race for big bucks and fan support.

Five teams changed ownership in a 12-month period and the San Francisco Giants tried to become the St. Petersburg (Fla.) Giants, only to be rebuffed by other National League owners. Those same owners did approve the creation of franchises in Denver and Miami that brought their number to 14 teams, matching the American League for the first time since 1977.

Padres third baseman Gary Sheffield.

Mets slugger Bobby Bonilla.

NATIONAL LEAGUE

League Batting Leaders

Average

Year	Player-Team	Avg.
1990	Willie McGee, St. L.	.335
1991	Terry Pendleton, Atl.	.319
1992	Gary Sheffield, S.D.	.330

Home Runs

Year	Player-Team	HR
1990	Ryne Sandberg, Chi.	40
1991	Howard Johnson, N.Y.	38
1992	Fred McGriff, S.D.	35

RBIs

Year	Player-Team	RBI
1990	Matt Williams, S.F.	122
1991	Howard Johnson, N.Y.	117
1992	Darren Daulton, Phi.	109

Most Valuable Players

Selected by BBWAA

Year	Player-Team	Pos.
1990	Barry Bonds, Pit.	OF
1991	Terry Pendleton, Atl.	3B
1992	Barry Bonds, Pit.	OF

League Pitching Leaders

Winning Percentage

Year	Pitcher-Team	W-L	Pct.
1990	Doug Drabek, Pit.	22-6	.786
1991	John Smiley, Pit.	20-8	.714
	Jose Rijo, Cin.	15-6	.714
1992	R. Tewksbury, St. L.	16-5	.762

Earned-Run Average

Year	Pitcher-Team	ERA
1990	Danny Darwin, Hou.	2.21
1991	Dennis Martinez, Mon.	2.39
1992	Bill Swift, S.F.	2.08

Strikeouts

Year	Pitcher-Team	SO
1990	David Cone, N.Y.	233
1991	David Cone, N.Y.	241
1992	John Smoltz, Atl.	215

Cy Young Winners

Selected by BBWAA

Year	Pitcher-Team	Thr.
1990	Doug Drabek, Pit.	R
1991	Tom Glavine, Atl.	L
1992	Greg Maddux, Chi.	R

Final Standings

1990

East	W	L	Pct.	GB
Pittsburgh	95	67	.586	--
New York	91	71	.562	4
Montreal	85	77	.525	10
Chicago	77	85	.475	18
Philadelphia	77	85	.475	18
St. Louis	70	92	.432	25

West	W	L	Pct.	GB
Cincinnati	91	71	.562	--
Los Angeles	86	76	.531	5
S.F.	85	77	.525	6
Houston	75	87	.463	16
San Diego	75	87	.463	16
Atlanta	65	97	.401	26

1991

East	W	L	Pct.	GB
Pittsburgh	98	64	.605	--
St. Louis	84	78	.519	14
Philadelphia	78	84	.481	20
Chicago	77	83	.481	20
New York	77	84	.478	20.5
Montreal	71	90	.441	26.5

West	W	L	Pct.	GB
Atlanta	94	68	.580	--
Los Angeles	93	69	.574	1
San Diego	84	78	.519	10
S.F.	75	87	.463	19
Cincinnati	74	88	.457	20
Houston	65	97	.401	29

1992

East	W	L	Pct.	GB
Pittsburgh	96	66	.593	--
Montreal	87	75	.537	9
St. Louis	83	79	.512	13
Chicago	78	84	.481	18
New York	72	90	.444	24
Philadelphia	70	92	.432	26

West	W	L	Pct.	GB
Atlanta	98	64	.605	--
Cincinnati	90	72	.556	8
San Diego	82	80	.506	16
Houston	81	81	.500	17
S.F.	72	90	.444	26
Los Angeles	63	99	.389	35

LEAGUE CHAMPIONSHIP SERIES

National League

Year	Winner	Runnerup	Games
1990	Cincinnati Reds	Pittsburgh Pirates	4-2
1991	Atlanta Braves	Pittsburgh Pirates	4-3
1992	Atlanta Braves	Pittsburgh Pirates	4-3

American League

Year	Winner	Runnerup	Games
1990	Oakland Athletics	Boston Red Sox	4-0
1991	Minnesota Twins	Toronto Blue Jays	4-1
1992	Toronto Blue Jays	Oakland Athletics	4-2

WORLD SERIES

Year	Winner	Pennant Winner	Games
1990	Cincinnati Reds	Oakland Athletics	4-0
1991	Minnesota Twins	Atlanta Braves	4-3
1992	Toronto Blue Jays	Atlanta Braves	4-2

HALL OF FAME   Electees and Additions

1990	Joe Morgan, Jim Palmer.
1991	Rod Carew, Fergie Jenkins, Tony Lazzeri, Gaylord Perry, Bill Veeck.
1992	Rollie Fingers, Tom Seaver.
1993	Reggie Jackson.

But instability and turbulence continued to plague the National Pastime. New York Yankee Owner George Steinbrenner was banned from the game for activities thought to be "not in the best interests of baseball" and the man who sent him to the sideline, Commissioner Fay Vincent, was deposed two years later by a combination of unhappy owners who forced him into early retirement. The decade opened with a 32-day spring training lockout and Pete Rose, one of the game's greatest superstars, serving a five-month prison sentence for income tax evasion.

But all was not bleak. Several players delivered milestone performances, several teams rose from the dead to championship heights and several new ball parks, Camden Yards at Baltimore and New Comiskey in Chicago, signaled a return to the traditional, natural way the game was played in yesteryear.

Texas' Nolan Ryan continued to capture headlines with two more no-

hitters (his record sixth and seventh), his 300th career victory and more and more and more strikeouts. Baltimore's Cal Ripken finished the 1992 season with 1,735 consecutive games played, moving ever closer to Lou Gehrig's all-time record. Rickey Henderson became baseball's all-time top basestealer, Dennis Martinez pitched a perfect game and venerable stars Robin Yount and George Brett joined baseball's 3,000-hit club.

One of the more interesting stories was the 1991 rise of the Minnesota Twins and Atlanta Braves from last place to first place in their divisions and a scintillating performance in the "Worst to First" World Series, captured in a thrilling Game 7 by the Twins. But a more significant first was recorded in 1992, when the Toronto Blue Jays finally ended their postseason jinx and defeated the Braves in a six-game Series, bringing Canada its first championship and the first ever for a team playing on foreign soil.

Twins center fielder Kirby Puckett.

Oakland first baseman and power hitter Mark McGwire.

Atlanta Braves lefthander Tom Glavine.

AMERICAN LEAGUE

League Batting Leaders

Average

Year	Player-Team	Avg.
1990	George Brett, K.C.	.329
1991	Julio Franco, Tex.	.341
1992	Edgar Martinez, Sea.	.343

Home Runs

Year	Player-Team	HR
1990	Cecil Fielder, Det.	51
1991	Cecil Fielder, Det.	44
	Jose Canseco, Oak.	44
1992	Juan Gonzalez, Tex.	43

RBIs

Year	Player-Team	RBI
1990	Cecil Fielder, Det.	132
1991	Cecil Fielder, Det.	133
1992	Cecil Fielder, Det.	124

Most Valuable Players

Selected by BBWAA

Year	Player-Team	Pos.
1990	Rickey Henderson, Oak.	OF
1991	Cal Ripken, Bal.	SS
1992	Dennis Eckersley, Oak	P

League Pitching Leaders

Winning Percentage

Year	Pitcher-Team	W-L	Pct.
1990	Bob Welch, Oak.	27-6	.818
1991	Scott Erickson, Min.	20-8	.714
1992	Mike Mussina, Bal.	18-5	.783

Earned-Run Average

Year	Pitcher-Team	ERA
1990	Roger Clemens, Bos.	1.93
1991	Roger Clemens, Bos.	2.62
1992	Roger Clemens, Bos.	2.41

Strikeouts

Year	Pitcher-Team	SO
1990	Nolan Ryan, Tex.	232
1991	Roger Clemens, Bos.	241
1992	Randy Johnson, Sea.	241

Cy Young Winners

Selected by BBWAA

Year	Pitcher-Team	Thr.
1990	Bob Welch, Oak.	R
1991	Roger Clemens, Bos.	R
1992	Dennis Eckersley, Oak.	R

Final Standings

1990

East	W	L	Pct.	GB
Boston	88	74	.543	--
Toronto	86	76	.531	2
Detroit	79	83	.488	9
Cleveland	77	85	.475	11
Baltimore	76	85	.472	11.5
Milwaukee	74	88	.457	14
New York	67	95	.414	21

West	W	L	Pct.	GB
Oakland	103	59	.636	--
Chicago	94	68	.580	9
Texas	83	79	.512	20
California	80	82	.494	23
Seattle	77	85	.475	26
Kansas City	75	86	.466	27.5
Minnesota	74	88	.457	29

1991

East	W	L	Pct.	GB
Toronto	91	71	.562	--
Detroit	84	78	.519	7
Boston	84	78	.519	7
Milwaukee	83	79	.512	8
New York	71	91	.438	20
Baltimore	67	95	.414	24
Cleveland	57	105	.352	34

West	W	L	Pct.	GB
Minnesota	95	67	.586	--
Chicago	87	75	.537	8
Texas	85	77	.525	10
Oakland	84	78	.519	11
Seattle	83	79	.512	12
Kansas City	82	80	.506	13
California	81	81	.500	14

1992

East	W	L	Pct.	GB
Toronto	96	66	.593	--
Milwaukee	92	70	.568	4
Baltimore	89	73	.549	7
Cleveland	76	86	.469	20
New York	76	86	.469	20
Detroit	75	87	.463	21
Boston	73	89	.451	23

West	W	L	Pct.	GB
Oakland	96	66	.593	--
Minnesota	90	72	.556	6
Chicago	86	76	.531	10
Texas	77	85	.475	19
California	72	90	.444	24
Kansas City	72	90	.444	24
Seattle	64	98	.395	32

Ripken passes Scott

Baltimore shortstop Cal Ripken Jr. moved into second place on baseball's all-time iron man list June 12 when he played in his 1,308th consecutive game, passing former New York Yankee shortstop Everett Scott and setting his sights on former Yankee first baseman Lou Gehrig.

Catching Gehrig, however, will be no easy task. The Yankees' Iron Horse played in 2,130 straight games 1925-39 and Ripken would have to extend his streak into 1995. Ripken has not missed a game since May 20, 1982.

Since playing in his 1,000th straight game in 1988, Ripken has passed Joe Sewell (1,103), Billy Williams (1,117), Steve Garvey (1,207) and Scott. The 29-year-old slugger had his streak of 8,243 consecutive innings snapped in 1987 when he was pulled from a game in the eighth.

Baltimore won the contest against Milwaukee at Memorial Stadium, 4-3 in 10 innings.

Baltimore shortstop Cal Ripken, the No. 2 iron man in baseball history.

CAUGHT ON THE FLY

MAY

The incredible two-season errorless streak of Chicago's Ryne Sandberg ended after 123 games, the most ever for a second baseman, during the Cubs' 7-0 victory at Houston.

Oakland's Rickey Henderson became the most prolific basestealer in A.L. history when he swiped No. 893, passing former Detroit star Ty Cobb, during a 2-1 loss to Toronto.

JUNE

N.L. officials announced plans for expansion from 12 to 14 teams in the 1993 season.

JULY

Minnesota turned an unprecedented two triple plays during a 1-0 loss to Boston, both coming on ground balls that went from third baseman Gary Gaetti to second baseman Al Newman to first baseman Kent Hrbek.

Baltimore's Cal Ripken Jr. bobbled a ground ball during a contest against Kansas City, ending his major league-record string of errorless games for a shortstop at 95.

The no-hitter craze

Texas righthander Nolan Ryan, defying age like no pitcher before him, hurled the record sixth no-hitter of his career June 11. But no-hit fever reached epidemic proportions 18 days later when Oakland's Dave Stewart and Los Angeles' Fernando Valenzuela pitched the fourth and fifth hitless games of the season.

Ryan, who had thrown his record fifth no-hitter in 1981 as a member of the Houston Astros, struck out 14 A's and walked two while pitching the Rangers to a 5-0 victory at Oakland. The 43-year-old, making his second start since coming off the disabled list with a bad back, became the oldest pitcher to throw a no-hitter and the first to do it for three different teams. Ryan pitched four in the 1970s for California.

But the June 29 spotlight belonged to Stewart and Valenzuela. First the A's righthander struck out 12 and walked three in pitching Oakland to a 5-0 victory at Toronto's SkyDome. Then the lefthanded Valenzuela struck out seven and walked three in Los Angeles' 6-0 win over St. Louis at Dodger Stadium. It marked the first time two no-hitters had been pitched on the same day.

Earlier 1990 no-hitters had been thrown by California's Mark Langston and Mike Witt, who combined for a 1-0 April 11 victory over Seattle, and Mariners lefthander Randy Johnson, who beat Detroit, 2-0, on June 2.

32-day lockout ends

Players and owners hammered out an agreement during a 12-hour negotiating session in New York March 18, ending the second longest shutdown in baseball history and clearing the way for spring training to begin.

The owners' 32-day lockout of spring camps ended when the parties agreed on a four-year contract and cleared the way for the regular season to open on April 9. That one-week delay will result in games being made up over the course of the campaign on open dates and as parts of doubleheaders. Spring camps officially opened March 20, although many players reported a day earlier.

The issue that led to the owners' February 15 spring lockout was salary arbitration. A compromise was reached when the owners agreed to grant eligibility to 17 percent of players with between two and three years of major league service. The owners also agreed to increase contributions to the players' pension fund while raising the minimum salary to $100,000.

Tired negotiators explain the four-year contract they hammered out during the marathon talks that ended the owners' 32-day player lockout of spring training camps.

Steinbrenner out

Commissioner Fay Vincent banned controversial George Steinbrenner from further involvement with the management of the New York Yankees July 30 because the team's principal owner had acted in a manner "not in the best interests of baseball."

Vincent took surprisingly severe action against Steinbrenner after determining that he had maintained a three-year association with Howard Spira, a "known gambler," and paid Spira $40,000 to uncover unfavorable information about Dave Winfield, the Yankee outfielder with whom Steinbrenner had engaged in a long-running feud. Vincent said Steinbrenner could remain only as a limited partner and could not participate in the operation of the team.

Vincent said he was "able to evaluate a pattern of behavior that borders on the bizarre" after conducting a two-day interview with Steinbrenner. Many fans, players and associates had felt that way throughout Steinbrenner's stormy 17½-year reign as keeper of "the Bronx Zoo."

Under his leadership, the Yankees did win four American League pennants and two World Series, but the team was constantly in turmoil.

Former New York Yankee boss George Steinbrenner during happier times.

A no-hitter — a loss

New York righthander Andy Hawkins pitched baseball's sixth no-hitter of the season July 1, but a bizarre two-out, eighth-inning rally by Chicago netted four runs and gave the White Sox a 4-0 victory over the hapless Yankees.

As a result, Hawkins joined former Houston righthander Ken Johnson as the only pitchers in history to throw complete-game no-hitters — and lose. Johnson fell to Cincinnati, 1-0, in 1964.

Hawkins was locked in a scoreless duel with Chicago lefthander Greg Hibbard when disaster struck in the eighth. With two out, Chicago's Sammy Sosa reached first on a throwing error by third baseman Mike Blowers and Hawkins walked Ozzie Guillen and Lance Johnson, loading the bases. Robin Ventura hit a fly ball to left field that rookie Jim Leyritz dropped for a two-base error, allowing three runs to score. Right fielder Jesse Barfield added to Hawkins' misery by dropping Ivan Calderon's fly for another run-scoring error.

"I'm stunned," said Hawkins, whose record dropped to 1-5. "When you pitch a no-hitter, you expect jubilation."

The 30-year-old Hawkins struck out three and walked five. The Yankees, at 28-44, have the worst record in baseball.

" DUGOUT CHATTER "

"I'll live forever as the answer to a trivia question. It's a strange, strange feeling. Once people get over the shock of my losing, they realize it was a no-hitter. I did throw a no-hitter."

Andy Hawkins

New York Yankee pitcher, after no-hitting Chicago and losing, 4-0

" DUGOUT CHATTER "

"He winds up just like Nolan Ryan, but he throws about as hard as I do."

Charlie Hough

42-year-old Texas knuckleballer, after watching his son pitch in a Little League game

"I'm supposed to be the guru of pitching and I ain't gururing worth a damn right now."

Roger Craig

San Francisco manager, on his club's pitching woes

Franco sparks A.L.

Texas second baseman Julio Franco doubled home two seventh-inning runs and six pitchers combined on a record-low two-hitter as the American League won its third straight All-Star Game with a 2-0 decision over the National League July 10 at Chicago's Wrigley Field.

Franco delivered his game-winner off Cincinnati fireballer Rob Dibble, who was facing his first batter after a 68-minute rain delay. Cleveland's Sandy Alomar Jr. and California's Lance Parrish scored on the drive to right field.

That was all the A.L. needed. Oakland starter Bob Welch allowed a first-inning single to San Francisco's Will Clark and Oakland's Dennis Eckersley surrendered a ninth-inning single to Philadelphia's Len Dykstra. In between, Toronto's Dave Stieb, Kansas City's Bret Saberhagen, Chicago's Bobby Thigpen and California's Chuck Finley allowed only two baserunners, both on walks. A.L. pitchers retired 16 straight batters at one point.

Texas second baseman Julio Franco gave the A.L. an All-Star lift.

" DUGOUT CHATTER "

"Sitting in the dugout at Candlestick is like being at the bottom of a toilet. All the tissue comes in and nobody flushes."

Whitey Herzog

St. Louis manager, on conditions at San Francisco's windswept ballpark

Stieb gets no-hitter

Toronto righthander Dave Stieb, overcoming an eerie ninth-inning jinx that had spoiled four previous no-hit bids, fired the major leagues' record ninth no-hitter of the season September 2, defeating the Indians, 3-0, at Cleveland.

The 33-year-old Stieb opened the ninth by retiring Cleveland's Chris James on a fly ball and then made Candy Maldonado his ninth strikeout victim before walking Alex Cole and getting Jerry Browne on a line drive to right. That wrapped up his 17th victory and the first no-hitter in Blue Jays history — one the unlucky Stieb thought never would come.

In September 1988, he took a no-hitter against Cleveland into the ninth inning and retired the first two batters. That effort was spoiled by a bad-hop grounder. Then, six days later, he lost a no-hit bid against Baltimore, again with two out in the ninth.

Stieb was one out away from a perfect game on August 4, 1989, when the Yankees' Roberto Kelly doubled. He lost another 1989 no-hit bid in the ninth and pitched his fifth one-hitter in less than a year.

Happy Toronto players congratulate Dave Stieb after the righthander had finally broken his no-hitter jinx.

Ryan joins elite club

Texas righthander Nolan Ryan, baseball's strikeout and no-hitter king over a fantastic 24-year career, reached another milestone July 31 when he became the 20th major league pitcher to win 300 games.

Ryan struck out eight and allowed three runs over 7⅔ innings of the Rangers' 11-3 victory at Milwaukee's County Stadium. A capacity crowd of 55,097 cheered him to victory almost 29 years after former Braves lefthander Warren Spahn had earned his 300th career triumph on the same mound.

Ryan, who had failed in his first attempt to gain the historic win, achieved his milestone at age 43 years and 6 months, making him the game's fourth-oldest 300-game winner behind Phil Niekro, Gaylord Perry and Early Wynn. Ryan left the game in the eighth when the Brewers pulled to within 5-3, but Julio Franco's ninth-inning grand slam sparked a six-run Texas rally to put the contest out of reach.

Texas star Nolan Ryan tips his cap to Milwaukee fans after winning his 300th game.

SEASON LEADERS

	American League		National League	
Avg.	George Brett, K.C.	.329	Willie McGee, St. L.	.335
HR	Cecil Fielder, Det.	51	Ryne Sandberg, Chi.	40
RBI	Cecil Fielder, Det.	132	Matt Williams, S.F.	122
SB	Rickey Henderson, Oak.	65	Vince Coleman, St. L.	77
W-L Pct.	Bob Welch, Oak. 27-6, .818		Doug Drabek, Pit. 22-6, .786	
ERA	Roger Clemens, Bos.	1.93	Danny Darwin, Hou.	2.21
SO	Nolan Ryan, Tex.	232	David Cone, N.Y.	233

Rose begins sentence

Pete Rose, baseball's all-time hits leader and one of the game's top players and personalities for almost three decades, completed his fall from grace August 8 when he reported to a Federal work camp at Marion, Ill., to begin serving a five-month sentence for cheating on his income taxes.

The 49-year-old "Charlie Hustle," who was handed a lifetime ban from baseball a year ago because of his alleged gambling activities, was sentenced July 20 by U.S. District Judge S. Arthur Spiegel after pleading guilty to two counts of income tax evasion. Rose was cited for failing to report more than $350,000 from autograph signing and baseball memorabilia sales.

Rose began his term at the Southern Illinois prison camp two days before his court-ordered deadline and is scheduled for release January 7. The start of his sentence was delayed to allow him to recover from knee surgery. Warden John Clark said Rose will not be accorded special privileges and he will be matched to one of 35 available prison jobs.

Cecil Fielder hits 51

Cecil Fielder, the former Toronto backup first baseman who spent the 1989 season in Japan, closed his first campaign as a Detroit Tiger with a two-home run salvo that moved him into select company. Fielder became the first player in 13 years and 11th overall to hit 50 homers in a season.

The heavyweight slugger hit No. 50 in the fourth inning off New York's Steve Adkins and received a long ovation from the Yankee Stadium crowd. Fielder connected for his 51st in the eighth, a three-run shot off Alan Mills.

Fielder, signed in the off-season as a free-agent, is the first player to reach the 50 plateau since Cincinnati's George Foster belted 52 in 1977. He is the second Tiger, joining former first baseman Hank Greenberg (58 in 1938).

Other closing-day notes:

* Boston defeated Chicago, 3-1, and clinched its third American League East Division title in five years.

* Kansas City's George Brett managed a pinch-hit single in a 5-2 loss at Cleveland and captured his third A.L. batting title. Brett (.329) is the first player to win crowns in three different decades.

* Willie McGee closed out his second National League batting title (.335) while playing for an A.L. team. McGee, traded by St. Louis to Oakland August 29, had accumulated enough at-bats to qualify for the N.L. crown.

Detroit heavyweight slugger Cecil Fielder.

" DUGOUT CHATTER "

"Pudge is so old, they didn't have history class when he went to school."

Steve Lyons

Chicago utility man, on 42-year-old White Sox catcher Carlton Fisk

CAUGHT ON THE FLY

AUGUST

The Griffeys, 20-year-old Ken Jr. and 40-year-old Ken Sr., became the first father-son duo to play together in the major leagues and both singled in the first inning of a Seattle victory over Kansas City at the Kingdome.

SEPTEMBER

Comiskey Park, the oldest active stadium in the major leagues, played host to its final game, a 2-1 Chicago White Sox victory over Seattle. The Sox will move into new Comiskey Park, being built across the street, in 1991.

OCTOBER

Chicago White Sox reliever Bobby Thigpen finished with a whopping 57 saves, breaking the major league record by 11.

WORLD SERIES REPORT

A SWEEPING SUCCESS

Cincinnati righthander Jose Rijo, getting two-out relief from Randy Myers, pitched a two-hitter and Hal Morris drove in the go-ahead run with an eighth-inning sacrifice fly as the Reds posted a 2-1 victory over Oakland October 20 and completed their stunning four-game World Series sweep.

The Reds' triumph at the Oakland Coliseum doomed a powerful A's team that had entered the fall classic as a heavy favorite to duplicate its four-game Series sweep of San Francisco a year earlier. The A's had a lot of everything that wins championships — power, speed, pitching and defense. They also had three straight American League pennants and were coming off a 103-win regular season and a sweep of Boston in the A.L. Championship Series.

But with Rijo, Rob Dibble and Myers combining on an opening-game shutout and Cincinnati hitters battering Oakland ace Dave Stewart in a 7-0 victory, the Reds set the tone for their upset. They followed with a 10-inning 5-4 win and an 8-3 third-game triumph.

Eric Davis blasted a homer and Chris Sabo delivered a pair of runs with a single in the opener and Joe Oliver ended Game 2 at Riverfront Stadium with a 10th-inning single. Sabo hit two homers and drove in three runs to support Tom Browning's pitching in Game 3.

With Oakland's aura of invincibility now shattered, Cincinnati delivered the final blow in Game 4 with a two-run eighth-inning rally that required only one hit. The tying run scored on Glenn Braggs' grounder, the winner on Morris' fly ball.

Dibble and Myers, two of Cincinnati's "Nasty Boys," combined for 7⅔ scoreless innings in the Series while Billy Hatcher batted .750 and Sabo .563.

Game 1	Cincinnati	7	Oakland	0
Game 2	Cincinnati	5	Oakland	4
Game 3	Cincinnati	8	Oakland	3
Game 4	Cincinnati	2	Oakland	1

The Cincinnati Reds had reason to celebrate after their shocking four-game World Series sweep of the Oakland Athletics.

★1991★
JANUARY-JULY

New Comiskey opens

As a new era of baseball began April 18 in Chicago's new Comiskey Park, a funeral was taking place across the street. Many of the 44,702 fans who entered the shiny new $135 million structure to see the White Sox play host to Detroit first filed past old Comiskey, pausing momentarily in a sort of funeral procession to say a heart-felt goodbye to a piece of their past.

As the wrecking ball was busy knocking out chunks of baseball memories at the old park, new Comiskey began making a few of its own. The first ones were un-fortunate, courtesy of Detroit's four-home run, 16-0 bombing of the White Sox. But the new ballpark was of more interest on this day, anyway.

What the curious fans saw was a symmetrical all-grass field with a three-deck grandstand, an old-time facade complete with arches and an exploding scoreboard in the old Comiskey tradition. The park, which has 90 skyboxes and suites, is the first baseball-only facility to open since Kansas City's Royals Stadium in 1973.

The ballpark it replaces was built in 1910.

Chicago's new Comiskey Park; almost ready for Opening Day festivities.

Ryan does it again

Amazing Nolan Ryan, pitching what he called the most dominating game of his 25-year career, fired his record seventh no-hitter May 1, shutting down hard-hitting Toronto on "Arlington Appreciation Night" at Arlington Stadium.

Ryan, who has 12 one-hitters to go with his no-hit legacy, struck out 16 and walked two in the 3-0 victory over Toronto, the best-hitting team in the major leagues (.276). Mesmerizing the Blue Jays with a nasty assortment of 96-mph fastballs, curveballs and changeups, the 44-year-old Ryan was in full command and did not allow a hard-hit ball.

With the crowd of 33,439 fans chanting "No-lan, No-lan," Ryan retired Manny Lee and Devon White on ninth-inning ground balls and struck out Roberto Alomar to end the game. Baseball's all-time strikeout king fanned at least one batter in each inning of his 305th career win and reached the 15-strikeout plateau for the 26th time.

Ryan, who became the oldest pitcher to throw a no-hitter last year when he notched his sixth, also has lost five no-hit bids in the ninth inning.

CAUGHT ON THE FLY

FEBRUARY
Two-time Boston Cy Young Award winner Roger Clemens became the highest paid player in history when he signed a four-year contract worth $21.5 million.

MAY
Philadelphia stars Lenny Dykstra and Darren Daulton were seriously injured in an early-morning one-car accident after attending a bachelor party for teammate John Kruk. Dykstra was charged with drunk driving.

JULY
Total team effort: Baltimore pitchers Bob Milacki, Mike Flanagan, Mark Williamson and Gregg Olson combined on a 2-0 no-hit victory at Oakland.

Steve Palermo, an A.L. umpire since 1977, was paralyzed from the waist down when he was shot once in the back while trying to break up a robbery attempt outside a Dallas restaurant.

White Sox sign Bo

The Chicago White Sox agreed to a share-the-risk contract with Bo Jackson April 3, reviving the sagging baseball fortunes of the two-sport star after Kansas City had released him 16 days earlier because of a football hip injury.

The 28-year-old Jackson, a worldwide celebrity because of his prowess as a football running back, a baseball outfielder and the subject of popular television commercials, was injured during the Los Angeles Raiders' January 13 playoff victory over Cincinnati. The Royals, based on a report by their orthopedist that Jackson would not be able to play baseball this year and maybe never again, released him and paid a termination price of $391,484.

The remaining 25 teams could have picked him up on waivers, along with his bulky salary, but all passed. The White Sox, believing Jackson's injury was not as bad as reported, decided Bo was worth a gamble.

The incentive-spiced contract calls for a guaranteed salary of $700,000 this year, whether Jackson plays or not, and two option years. The $700,000 is the minimum Jackson could earn.

Bo Jackson, now sporting the colors of a Chicago White Sox uniform.

Henderson sets mark

Oakland speedster Rickey Henderson dove head-first into the record books May 1 when he swiped third base against the New York Yankees and passed former basestealing king Lou Brock on baseball's all-time list.

Henderson's 939th stolen base was officially recorded in the fourth inning of the A's 7-4 victory at the Oakland Coliseum. Henderson, on second base as Harold Baines came to the plate, took off on Tim Leary's first pitch and dove safely into third ahead of Matt Nokes' hurried throw. Nokes had thrown out Henderson in the first inning when he tried to steal second.

Henderson lifted his arms in triumph, pulled the base from its moorings and held it high above his head as the crowd of 36,139 saluted him. He then greeted his mother, Bobbie Henderson, with a long hug.

The game was halted for eight minutes as Brock came onto the field and praised Henderson as the game's greatest basestealer. Brock reached his record total in 19 seasons with the Chicago Cubs and St. Louis Cardinals, Henderson in 13 campaigns with the A's and Yankees. Henderson had broken Brock's one-season mark of 118 steals when he swiped 130 bases in 1982.

New stolen base king Rickey Henderson (right) and Lou Brock, the man he passed on the all-time list.

" DUGOUT CHATTER "

"I'd rather have a Mercedes, but I guess a Porsche makes a nice summer car."

Rickey Henderson

Oakland left fielder, after the team gave him a Porsche for breaking Lou Brock's career stolen base record

Expansion winners

Miami and Denver were declared winners of the six-city expansion race June 10 when a National League committee recommended they be given the two new franchises that will begin play in 1993. Commissioner Fay Vincent called approval by N.L. team owners a formality.

The selection, which extends baseball's geographic map to the Rocky Mountains and South Florida, ends a six-year contest among the six finalists. Washington, Buffalo and the Florida sites of St. Petersburg-Tampa and Orlando were the losers.

The ownerships will pay $95 million to join the league, which has operated with 12 clubs since 1969. The American League expanded to 14 teams in 1977, when the Toronto and Seattle franchises were added.

Ripken's star rises

Baltimore shortstop Cal Ripken Jr. belted a three-run homer in the third inning and American League pitchers made it stand up for the circuit's fourth straight All-Star Game victory, a 4-2 decision over the National League July 9 at Toronto's SkyDome.

Ripken connected off Montreal righthander Dennis Martinez after Oakland's Rickey Henderson and Boston's Wade Boggs had reached base on singles. The only other A.L. run came on a seventh-inning sacrifice fly by Oakland's Harold Baines.

Seven A.L. pitchers combined on a 10-hitter and limited the N.L. to three or less runs for the sixth straight year. The senior circuit, which rolled up an 11-game winning streak and won 19 of 20 All-Star classics from 1963 to '82, has managed only six runs and two extra-base hits in the last four midsummer games.

Both of the extra-base blows came in this contest. Chicago's Ryne Sandberg stroked a one-out double in the third inning off winning pitcher Jimmy Key (Toronto) and teammate Andre Dawson connected for a fourth-inning homer off Boston righthander Roger Clemens. The N.L. scored its other run in the first when Pittsburgh's Bobby Bonilla hit a smash off the ankle of Minnesota's Jack Morris, driving home San Diego's Tony Gwynn.

Chicago catcher Carlton Fisk tags out San Francisco's Will Clark during All-Star Game action at Toronto.

THE TEXAS FIREBALLER

Nolan Ryan

"When Nolan came up with the Mets and I was managing Cincinnati, he was always in the mid-90s or higher. Guys would come back to the dugout and say, 'I'm glad he's not wild tonight.' "

Detroit Manager Sparky Anderson

On the surface, Nolan Ryan is your average, everyday, 46-year-old pitcher. You can pick him out of the twenty and thirtysomething company he keeps by his aging facial features and balding head. But don't let that good ol' boy smile fool you. Hidden beneath his Texas Rangers uniform is a young and still vigorous body with a bionic arm, nerves of steel and a heart of gold.

It is the type of body that just keeps going . . . and going . . . and going, no batteries needed. He just winds himself up and fires a 95-mile per hour fastball that still jumps and whooshes past intimidated hitters. That fastball is Nolan Ryan's concession to age. He used to deliver it at 100 mph.

"When Nolan came up with the Mets and I was managing Cincinnati, he was always in the mid-90s or higher," said Detroit boss Sparky Anderson. "Guys would come back to the dugout and say, 'I'm just glad he's not wild tonight.' "

Now they return to the dugout just shaking their heads, wondering how an arm that has thrown by some estimates a quarter of a million pitches can still work with such efficiency. "I guess I've thrown more pitches than anybody else," Ryan admitted after the 1990 season.

"That's bull," responded then Detroit pitcher Jack Morris. "Nolan has thrown twice as many pitches as any man alive."

And, entering the 1993 campaign, he had accumulated 25 years worth of numbers to prove it. Such as the 50 major league, American League and National League records he either held or shared. Such as his 319-287 lifetime record and career 3.17 earned-run average. Such as seven career no-hitters. Such as one, two, three, the simple formula he needed to record every one of his record 5,668 career strikeouts.

The strikeouts, no-hitters and longevity are Ryan trademarks, his someday tickets into the Hall of Fame. The 319 victories (12th on baseball's all-time list) probably would get him there, too, but not without reservations. His 287 losses rank third on the all-time charts and Ryan was criticized throughout his early career as a .500 pitcher with a million-dollar arm.

"The most frustrating thing in my career was being on bad teams," said Ryan, who has pitched for the New York Mets, California Angels, Houston Astros and the Rangers in a career that started with a two-game trial in 1966. "I lost a lot of real close games. Under different circumstances, I would have been pitching to win 'em. That was frustrating."

Through 1992, Ryan's teams had won 83 games or less 18 times while averaging fewer than four runs per outing. During his prime with the Angels from 1972-79, Ryan averaged 273 innings and 304 strikeouts but posted an average season record of only 17-15. The 6-foot-2, 212-pound righthander has played on only one World Series champion (the 1969 Mets) and three division winners.

"When I sit around dreaming, I think about how nice it would have been if I could have pitched for one of those Oakland clubs in the early '70s or for the Big Red Machine (Cincinnati) in the mid-'70s," Ryan admitted.

But the big Texan, baseball's oldest active player, has masked his frustration well — with an unending stream of strikeouts and no-hitters. His feats are legendary and fans flock to the ballpark knowing that he is a no-hit threat any time he steps on the mound.

His first two no-hitters came with the Angels in 1973 and he tied Los Angeles lefty Sandy Koufax's career record by throwing his third in 1974 and fourth the next season. No. 5 came as a member of the Astros in 1981 and his sixth and seventh were pitched in a Rangers uniform in 1990 and '91. The last two, at ages 43 and 44, gave him the distinction of pitching at least one in three different decades. He punctuated his 1991 effort with 16 strikeouts in an overpowering 3-0 victory

Ryan's sixth no-hitter in 1990 was the first of two with the Texas Rangers.

The scoreboard flashes the magic number as California's Ryan walks off the mound as baseball's one-season strikeout king in 1973.

Career no-hitter No. 3 was followed by a big smile in 1974.

"It's a matter of proper mechanics and work ethics," he said. "I don't know how many pitchers are going to have that drive and discipline that it takes. Believe me, there are plenty of days I don't want to. But I can't deviate. I have to do it."

And that, perhaps, is where Ryan enjoys his greatest edge. The work ethic he learned as a youngster growing up in Alvin, Tex., nags, tugs and pulls at him, telling him not to get beat by somebody who is in better shape. That work ethic has paid off in seven All-Star Game selections in a career that borders on the unbelievable.

Although he has won 20 or more games only twice, he has failed to reach double figures in victories only twice since 1971, his fourth and last season with the Mets and 1992. Most of the writers who once criticized Ryan as an underachiever and undeserving candidate for the Hall of Fame, now are predicting a quick and easy victory when he becomes eligible five years after retirement. If, that is, he ever retires.

Former Los Angeles pitcher Don Drysdale thinks baseball should get its priorities straight. "They ought to send him to the Smithsonian before they send him to Cooperstown," he said.

Ryan pitched his fifth no-hitter for the Houston Astros.

over hard-hitting Toronto.

"I had the best command of all three pitches," Ryan said after the game. "This is the best. This is my most overpowering night."

The seven no-hitters say plenty, but to put Ryan's career into perspective consider that he also has lost five no-hit bids in the ninth inning while pitching 12 career one-hitters, 19 two-hitters and 30 three-hitters. He has allowed less than seven hits per nine innings throughout his career.

And then there are the strikeouts. Ryan's name is sure to dominate that section of the record books for years, perhaps decades, to come.

He is the only pitcher to record more than 5,000 in his career and he now is more than halfway to 6,000. He has fanned 19 batters in a game four times, 18 once, 17 three times, 16 eight times and 15 on 10 occasions. His 9.59 strikeouts per nine innings ranks first in baseball history and he has led his league in whiffs 11 times. He has topped the 300-strikeout plateau six times and holds the one-season record of 383 (1973). Ryan fanned 203 in 1991, despite spending 36 days on the disabled list, and

averaged a strikeout per inning in an injury-plagued 1992 season.

"I think a lot of people think I really tried to strike out people, and that's not the case," Ryan said. "I was just a strikeout-style pitcher . . . My really high totals come when hitters are looking for my fastball and I'm getting my breaking ball over the plate. I'm going to have more strikeouts than other pitchers do because of my breaking ball."

Ryan also added a changeup to his repertoire in the early 1980s, helping to lengthen his career. But the real key to his longevity is good, old-fashioned hard work — and luck.

"I've been very fortunate over the years in regard to injuries," Ryan said. "I've been on the disabled list a few times, but mostly because of pulled muscles in my legs. I've only had to undergo surgery once, in 1975, and that was minor for bone chips in my elbow."

Ryan credits much of his good fortune to weight conditioning (as opposed to weight lifting), which he discovered in 1972 with the Angels. Now he is dedicated to a workout routine that would demoralize less dedicated performers.

★1991★
JULY-DECEMBER

Martinez is perfect

Montreal righthander Dennis Martinez made it perfectly clear who was boss July 28 when he retired all 27 Los Angeles batters he faced in a 2-0 victory at Dodger Stadium. Baseball's 13th perfect game was witnessed by 45,560 fans less than 48 hours after the Expos' Mark Gardner had pitched nine no-hit innings against the Dodgers, only to lose the game, 1-0, in the 10th.

The 36-year-old Martinez (11-6) was masterful while striking out five, pitching his fourth shutout and lowering his National League-leading earned-run average to 2.05. The perfecto was the first since Cincinnati's Tom Browning accomplished the feat against the Dodgers in 1988.

Neither team managed a baserunner until Montreal catcher Ron Hassey led off the sixth with a single. The Expos broke through for two runs in the seventh on two errors and Larry Walker's triple.

Martinez, a former Baltimore Orioles star and a 16-year major league veteran, retired Mike Scioscia on a fly ball to open the ninth, struck out pinch-hitter Stan Javier and got pinch-hitter Chris Gwynn on a fly ball.

Montreal righthander Dennis Martinez (facing camera) being mobbed by teammates after his perfect-game effort in Los Angeles.

CAUGHT ON THE FLY

AUGUST

Chicago White Sox lefthander Wilson Alvarez, making only his second major league start, pitched a 7-0 no-hitter against the Baltimore Orioles.

OCTOBER

St. Louis righthander Lee Smith finished the season with an N.L.-record 47 saves.

The Toronto Blue Jays completed their season with a major league-record attendance mark of 4,001,527.

New York Mets righthander David Cone tied an N.L. record on the final day of the season when he struck out 19 Philadelphia hitters in a 7-0 victory.

Leo Durocher, the feisty former infielder who recorded 2,010 victories and captured three pennants as the manager of four N.L. teams, died in Palm Springs, Calif., at age 86.

SEASON LEADERS

	American League		National League	
Avg.	Julio Franco, Tex.	341	Terry Pendleton, Atl.	.319
HR	Jose Canseco, Oak.	44	Howard Johnson, N.Y.	38
	Cecil Fielder, Det.	44		
RBI	Cecil Fielder, Det.	133	Howard Johnson, N.Y.	117
SB	Rickey Henderson, Oak.	58	Marquis Grissom, Mon.	76
W-L Pct.	Scott Erickson, Min.	20-8, .714	Jose Rijo, Cin.	15-6, .714
			John Smiley, Pit.	20-8, .714
ERA	Roger Clemens, Bos.	2.62	Dennis Martinez, Mon.	2.39
SO	Roger Clemens, Bos.	241	David Cone, N.Y.	241

A Braves new world

Atlanta righthander John Smoltz pitched a six-hitter and the Braves used three first-inning runs to propel them past Pittsburgh, 4-0, in Game 7 of the National League Championship Series October 17.

Atlanta's pennant was secured at the expense of Pirates starter John Smiley, who surrendered a two-run homer to Brian Hunter and failed to survive the opening inning. Relievers Bob Walk, Roger Mason and Stan Belinda limited the Braves to one run the rest of the way, but Smoltz was in command as he beat the Pirates for a second time and extended Atlanta's scoreless-innings streak against Pittsburgh to 22.

Most of the Series belonged to the pitchers, with only Atlanta's 10-3 third-game victory breaking the pattern. Pittsburgh's Doug Drabek was a 5-1 victor in the opener at Pittsburgh and 21-year-old Steve Avery combined with Alejandro Pena for a six-hit 1-0 second-game win for Atlanta. The only run scored on Mark Lemke's bad-hop double off Zane Smith in the sixth inning.

After the Braves routed Smiley in Game 3 with a three-home run explosion (Ron Gant, Greg Olson and Sid Bream), the Pirates fought back for a 3-2 victory that was decided in the 10th inning on Mike LaValliere's single. Pittsburgh gained the advantage with a 1-0 decision in Game 5 behind Smith and Mason, but the Braves evened matters two days later when Avery and Pena turned the tables for their second combined 1-0 victory of the Series.

The key to Atlanta's victory was its ability to control Pittsburgh's Big Three of Barry Bonds, Bobby Bonilla and Andy Van Slyke. Bonds batted .148 and did not drive in a run. Bonilla managed only one RBI, Van Slyke a homer and two RBIs.

Braves catcher Greg Olson and pitcher John Smoltz celebrate Atlanta's NLCS Game 7 victory over Pittsburgh.

" DUGOUT CHATTER "

"The first time I came into a game there, I got into the bullpen car and they told me to lock the doors."

Mike Flanagan

Veteran Toronto lefthander, on playing in New York

Puckett helps Twins shoot down Blue Jays

Kirby Puckett continued his hot hitting in Game 5 of the Championship Series with a home run and two singles as the Minnesota Twins captured their second American League pennant in five years with an 8-5 triumph over Toronto.

The October 13 win at Toronto's SkyDome completed Minnesota's incredible run from last place in the A.L. West Division last season to the championship this year.

Six of Puckett's nine ALCS hits and both of his homers came during the Twins' Series-closing 9-3 and 8-5 romps. Starter Jack Morris was the winner in Game 4 while relievers David West, Carl Willis and Rick Aguilera turned in five shutout innings in the finale after Kevin Tapani had been hammered for all five Toronto runs.

The Twins had opened the Series with a 5-4 win at the Metrodome and the Blue Jays answered with a 5-2 victory. Mike Pagliarulo set the stage for Toronto's exit when he belted a 10th-inning homer off Mike Timlin to give the Twins a 3-2 win in Game 3.

" DUGOUT CHATTER "

"I'm a lefthander trapped in a righthander's body."

Roger McDowell

Los Angeles reliever, on his reputation as a prankster

Minnesota's Dan Gladden slides safely under the tag of Toronto catcher Pat Borders in the final game of the A.L. Championship Series.

WORLD SERIES REPORT

WORST TO FIRST

Pinch-hitter Gene Larkin's 10th-inning single over a drawn-in outfield gave Jack Morris and the Minnesota Twins a stirring 1-0 victory over Atlanta October 27 in the seventh game of the "worst-to-first" World Series.

Larkin hit the first pitch he saw from Braves reliever Alejandro Pena and drove in Dan Gladden with the run that gave the Twins their second championship and settled the battle of teams that had risen from last-place division finishes in 1990 to pennants. Gladden, who had doubled to lead off the inning and was sacrificed to third, danced down the line with the run that ended one of the most intense and exciting Series ever played.

The timely hit delighted a loud Metrodome crowd and ended an outstanding pitching duel between Morris, who worked all 10 innings, and Atlanta's John Smoltz, who left after 7⅓. It also settled a Series that duplicated the Twins' 1987 triumph over St. Louis: four wins at the Metrodome, three losses on the road.

The Twins continued their Metrodome magic in Games 1 and 2, recording a 5-2 decision behind Morris and a 3-2 victory when light-hitting Scott Leius blasted an eighth-inning home run.

But the Braves fought back, sweeping to 5-4 (12 innings), 3-2 and 14-5 victories at Atlanta. Second baseman Mark Lemke drove in the Game 3 winner with a 12th-inning single and scored the Game 4 winner after hitting a one-out triple in the ninth.

Twins center fielder Kirby Puckett stepped into the Game 6 spotlight, keying Minnesota's 4-3 victory with an RBI triple, a sacrifice fly, an outstanding leaping catch and a decisive 11th-inning homer. That set the stage for a seventh game that lived up to every expectation.

Both teams had scoring chances, but neither could break through. The Braves missed a golden opportunity when Lonnie Smith, on base with a leadoff eighth-inning single, failed to score because he hesitated at second after losing sight of Terry Pendleton's double off the left-center field wall. Smith was stranded at third when Morris got an infield out and a double-play grounder from Sid Bream.

Game 1	Minnesota	5	Atlanta	2
Game 2	Minnesota	3	Atlanta	2
Game 3	Atlanta	5	Minnesota	4
Game 4	Atlanta	3	Minnesota	2
Game 5	Atlanta	14	Minnesota	5
Game 6	Minnesota	4	Atlanta	3
Game 7	Minnesota	1	Atlanta	0

Atlanta's David Justice (right) scores the winning run in Game 3 of the World Series.

★1992★

O's open new home at Camden Yards

Camden Yards, new home of the Baltimore Orioles.

With 44,568 fans and President George Bush watching the festivities, Baltimore unveiled new Oriole Park at Camden Yards April 6 and free-agent signee Rick Sutcliffe provided the capper with a five-hit 2-0 shutout of the Cleveland Indians.

The new stadium, a throwback to the ballparks of yesteryear, provides fans with all the modern amenities while maintaining an old-time flavor. Camden Yards is a homey, intimate park with irregular dimensions, a city skyline looming beyond its center-field fence, a 94-year-old brick warehouse beyond right field and a 25-foot scoreboard built into the right field wall.

The new facility played to rave reviews and so did the young Orioles. After President Bush had bounced his ceremonial first pitch to the plate, Sutcliffe, who pitched last season for the Chicago Cubs, settled into his Opening Day assignment and fired his first shutout and complete game since 1989.

A.L. continues roll in All-Star Game

Eight of the American League's first nine batters singled in a four-run first inning and Seattle's Ken Griffey Jr. and Texas' Ruben Sierra added home runs in a 13-6 pounding of the National League, the A.L.'s fifth straight All-Star Game triumph.

The July 14 contest at San Diego's Jack Murphy Stadium was a nightmare for Atlanta lefthander Tom Glavine, who retired Toronto's Roberto Alomar to open the game. But Boston's Wade Boggs, Minnesota's Kirby Puckett, Toronto's Joe Carter, Oakland's Mark McGwire, Baltimore's Cal Ripken, Griffey and Cleveland's Sandy Alomar Jr. stroked successive singles to open a 4-0 lead.

After the A.L. added a single run in the second, Griffey connected off Chicago's Greg Maddux with nobody on in the third, thus combining with Ken Sr. to become the only father-son combination ever to hit All-Star homers. Sierra hit a two-run homer in a four-run sixth inning that stretched the A.L.'s advantage to 10-0.

The N.L. did fight back for six runs, three coming on San Francisco first baseman Will Clark's eighth-inning home run, but it was too little too late. A.L. Manager Tom Kelly used 10 pitchers, nobody working more than one inning.

Minnesota's Kirby Puckett crosses the plate with a first-inning run during the All-Star Game in San Diego.

Boston's Matt Young fires no-hitter, loses

Boston Red Sox lefthander Matt Young joined Houston righthander Ken Johnson (1964) and New York Yankee righthander Andy Hawkins (1990) as the only pitchers in major league history to lose complete-game, regulation no-hitters April 12 when he dropped a 2-1 decision to Cleveland in the first game of a double-header at Municipal Stadium.

Young, who even fell short of gaining official credit for a no-hitter because he pitched only eight innings (Cleveland did not have to bat in the ninth), allowed seven walks and three of them contributed to Cleveland's runs. Kenny Lofton walked to lead off the first, stole second and third and scored on an error by shortstop Luis Rivera. Mark Lewis and Lofton walked to open the third and Lewis eventually scored on a ground out.

Charles Nagy pitched seven innings for the victory and Brad Arnsberg worked two for the save. Aside from Johnson and Hawkins, two Baltimore pitchers (Steve Barber and Stu Miller) combined on a no-hit loss in 1967.

As if to make amends for Young's disappointment, Boston righthander Roger Clemens followed with a two-hit, 3-0 victory in the nightcap. Cleveland's two-hit doubleheader set a major league record, breaking the old mark of three.

Vincent resigns

Deposed baseball Commissioner Fay Vincent.

Fay Vincent, acting "in the best interests of baseball," gave up his fight to keep his job in the wake of an overwhelming no-confidence vote by major league owners and resigned September 7 as the game's eighth commissioner.

Vincent, who had vowed three weeks earlier that "I will not re-sign ever," made his decision after a weekend at his vacation home in Harwich Port, Mass. It came after Thursday's 18-9 vote (with one abstention) by the owners urging him to quit.

"I've concluded that resigna-tion — not litigation — should be my final act as commissioner," Vincent wrote in a three-page let-ter to the owners. The resignation came six days before completion of his third year in the office he took in 1989 when A. Bartlett Giamatti died of a heart attack.

The ownership group seeking his ousting, headed by the Chicago White Sox's Jerry Reins-dorf, Milwaukee's Bud Selig, the Chicago Cubs' Stanton Cook and Los Angeles' Peter O'Malley, was upset with Vincent's order to re-align the National League and his stance on superstations and col-lective bargaining.

Yount gets 3,000th hit

Milwaukee's 3,000-hit man, Robin Yount.

Robin Yount, who has built a legacy of quiet consistency for 19 seasons in Milwaukee, became the 17th big-league player to col-lect 3,000 hits September 9 when he drove a seventh-inning pitch from Cleveland's Jose Mesa into right-center field during a 5-4 Brewers loss at County Stadium.

With a crowd of 47,589 roaring its approval, Yount was hoisted on to the shoulders of happy teammates near the first base bag as the scoreboard's video screen flashed "3,000." Then, as Yount stood alone, the board showed a retrospective of his career and flashed the names of his predeces-sors in the 3,000-hit club.

Yount, the third youngest player to achieve the milestone, is a week shy of his 37th birthday. The Brewers' outfielder began his career in 1974 as an 18-year-old shortstop and collected all of his hits and both of his American League Most Valuable Player awards in a Milwaukee uniform. He is the first player to reach 3,000 hits since Rod Carew in 1985.

Yount, who hit an 0-1 pitch, was hitless in his previous three at-bats.

CAUGHT ON THE FLY

APRIL
Texas righthander Nolan Ryan tied Tommy John's record for longevity when he started the Rangers' season-opener against Seattle, thus pitching in his 26th major league campaign.

MAY
California Manager Buck Rodgers and first baseman Alvin Davis were the most seriously injured Angels when a team bus swerved off the New Jersey Turnpike and crashed into a grove of trees about 20 miles from Philadelphia. Rodgers, who injured an elbow, a knee and a rib, will miss at least two months of the season following surgery and Davis was sent home with a bruised kidney. Ten other Angels sustained injuries.

AUGUST
Seattle second baseman Bret Boone joined his father, Bob, and grandfather, Ray, both former major league players, to form the first three-generation family trio in big-league history. Young Bret went 1 for 4 in his debut.

The Milwaukee Brewers set an American League record when they tattooed the Toronto Blue Jays pitchers for 31 hits (26 of them singles) in a 22-2 victory.

"DUGOUT CHATTER"

"If this keeps up, I'm going to look like Don Knotts and Telly Savalas rolled into one."

Pirates Manager Jim Leyland after 14 one-run games and five two-run games in a 27-game span.

"You can bet Pendleton won't be asked to play the lead in 'The Darryl Strawberry Story'."

Braves announcer Don Sutton on third baseman Terry Pendleton's leadership and willingness to play with pain.

"If Otis makes that catch in the World Series, they don't even show Willie Mays' catch anymore."

Braves coach Jim Beauchamp on an over-the-wall, game-saving catch by Atlanta outfielder Otis Nixon.

Athletics trade Jose Canseco to Rangers

The Oakland Athletics, sitting atop the American League West Division and apparently heading for a postseason playoff date, shocked everybody August 31 when they traded controversial slugger Jose Canseco to Texas for three players and cash.

The 28-year-old Canseco, one of the game's top sluggers and the

A.L.'s 1988 Most Valuable Player, was pulled from a game against Baltimore in the first inn-ing and informed that he had been dealt for an outfielder Ruben Sierra and pitchers Bobby Witt and Jeff Russell. The two-time A.L. home run champion had battled injuries throughout the 1992 campaign and was hitting

.246 with 22 homers and 72 runs batted in.

In Sierra, the A's pick up a player who is battling the chicken pox and will not be available for about a week. Sierra, who will become a free agent after the sea-son, was hitting .278 with 14 homers and 70 RBIs, while Witt, a righthanded starter, was 9-13

with a 4.46 earned-run average. Russell, a righthanded reliever, has 28 saves and a 1.91 ERA.

Canseco is in the second year of a five-year contract. He has been a constant source of controversy, ranging from his clubhouse demeanor to his off-field domestic problems and arrests for speeding violations.

★1992★
SEPTEMBER-DECEMBER

CAUGHT ON THE FLY

SEPTEMBER

Philadelphia second baseman Mickey Morandini became the ninth player in history to turn an unassisted triple play and the first in the N.L. since 1927 when he grabbed a liner by Pittsburgh's Jeff King, stepped on second to force Andy Van Slyke and tagged Barry Bonds, the runner on first. The Pirates won the game, 3-2.

Cincinnati's Bip Roberts tied a 95-year-old N. L. record with 10 consecutive hits before grounding out during the Reds' 3-0 victory over Los Angeles. Roberts became the eighth player to tie Ed Delahanty's mark (1897) and the first since 1943. The major league record is 12.

OCTOBER

Don Baylor became baseball's fourth current minority manager when he was hired by the expansion Colorado Rockies. Baylor, an African American, joins Toronto's Cito Gaston, Kansas City's Hal McRae and Montreal's Felipe Alou.

NOVEMBER

Baseball's owners, in a move that is sure to spark a series of lawsuits, rejected a $115 million deal to move the San Francisco Giants to St. Petersburg, Fla., even though the monetary package was $15 million more than the best offer to keep the team on the West Coast.

Baseball conducted its first expansion draft since 1976 when two new N.L. franchises, the Colorado Rockies and Florida Marlins, selected players off the rosters of the other 26 major league teams.

Brett reaches 3,000

Kansas City's George Brett drove a hard ground ball past second baseman Ken Oberkfell for his fourth hit of a September 30 game against California and became the 18th member of baseball's 3,000-hit club.

Brett, who had sat out the previous two games with a sore shoulder, needed four hits in his final five contests of the 1992 season. He returned with a vengeance, slicing a first-inning double to left, hitting a ground ball through the right side of the infield in the second, lining a single to center in the fifth and collecting his milestone hit on the first pitch of the seventh. The four-hit game was the 59th of an outstanding 19-year career during which Brett became the only player in history to win batting titles in three decades — in 1976, 1980 and 1990.

The 39-year-old Brett, who was mobbed by happy teammates, reached first on an error in the ninth inning of the Royals' 4-0 victory.

Braves catch Pirates

The Braves' backup catcher Francisco Cabrera, who had collected only three major league hits in the 1992 regular season, delivered a two-out, two-run, pinch-hit single in the bottom of the ninth inning October 14, giving Atlanta a dramatic come-from-behind 3-2 seventh-game victory over Pittsburgh in the National League Championship Series finale at Atlanta.

Cabrera's single off Pirates reliever Stan Belinda capped a three-run rally that wiped out a 2-0 Pittsburgh advantage and made a tough-luck loser of Doug Drabek, the first pitcher ever to drop three decisions in a Championship Series. Drabek had allowed only five hits through eight innings, but Atlanta's Terry Pendleton opened the ninth with a double.

The next batter, Dave Justice, hit a ground ball that was bobbled by second baseman Jose Lind, who had made only six errors during the regular season, and an exhausted Drabek walked Sid Bream to load the bases. Belinda came on to retire Ron Gant on a sacrifice fly, he walked Damon Berryhill to reload the bases and he retired Brian Hunter on a check-swing popup. Cabrera worked the count to 2-1. He then lined a drive to left field that scored Justice and Bream, who barely beat the throw from Barry Bonds.

The Braves won three of the first four games, two behind the pitching of John Smoltz and the other behind Steve Avery. Atlanta won the first game, 5-1, and then routed the Pirates 13-5 in a Game 2 victory that featured Gant's grand slam homer. Otis Nixon keyed a 6-4 Game 4 win with four hits.

The Pirates, who had won the third game, 3-2, behind the give-hit pitching of rookie knuckle-baller Tim Wakefield, rebounded for 7-1 and 13-4 wins in Games 5 and 6. Wakefield was the sixth-game winner as Bonds, Jay Bell and Lloyd McClendon hit home runs.

N. L. Championship Series hero Francisco Cabrera gets a well-deserved champagne bath.

Atlanta's Sid Bream (bottom of pile) is mobbed by teammates after scoring the Championship Series-winning run in Game 7 against Pittsburgh.

Blue Jays end jinx

Joe Carter belted a two-run first-inning homer and Candy Maldonado added a three-run shot in the third October 14 as Toronto broke its American League Championship Series jinx with a 9-2 victory over Oakland and gave Canada its first pennant.

The Blue Jays, three-time losers in Championship Series play since 1985, made quick work of the Athletics and starter Mike Moore in the Game 6 finale to earn their first World Series berth. They had a 7-0 advantage after five innings, at which point starter Juan Guzman had not allowed a hit, and cruised the rest of the way as a jubilant SkyDome crowd of 51,355 celebrated.

The A's, winners of three of the last four ALCS, opened with a 4-3 victory at Toronto but then watched as the Jays won the next three, 3-1, 7-5 and 7-6. Game 4 was pivotal as the A's blew a 6-1 lead and the Blue Jays pounded relief ace Dennis Eckersley, who had led the major leagues with 51 saves in the regular season.

The Jays managed two run-scoring singles off Eckersley in a three-run eighth and Roberto Alomar delivered a dramatic two-run ninth-inning homer to tie the game, 6-6. The Jays won in the 11th on Pat Borders' sacrifice fly.

Oakland got a temporary reprieve when Dave Stewart pitched a 6-2 victory in Game 5.

Toronto second baseman Roberto Alomar (right) is greeted at the plate after tying Game 4 of the ALCS with a dramatic ninth-inning home run.

SEASON LEADERS

	American League		National League	
Avg.	Edgar Martinez, Sea.	.343	Gary Sheffield, S.D.	.330
HR	Juan Gonzalez, Tex.	43	Fred McGriff, S.D.	35
RBI	Cecil Fielder, Det.	124	Darren Daulton, Phi.	109
SB	Kenny Lofton, Cle.	66	Marquis Grissom, Mon.	78
W-L Pct.	Mike Mussina, Bal. 18-5, .783		Bob Tewksbury, St. L.	16-5, .762
ERA	Roger Clemens, Bos.	2.41	Bill Swift, S.F.	2.08
SO	Randy Johnson, Sea.	241	John Smoltz, Atl.	215

O, CANADA

Dave Winfield, a 41-year-old free-agent pickup, grounded a double just inside the third base bag with two out in the 11th inning October 24, driving in two runs and allowing the Toronto Blue Jays to become baseball's first Canadian World Series winner with a 4-3 victory at Atlanta.

Winfield's Game 6 blow off Braves lefthander Charlie Leibrandt ended a tense duel that almost was decided in regulation. The Blue Jays carried a 2-1 lead into the ninth behind the pitching of David Cone and four relievers and were within one strike of victory when Atlanta's Otis Nixon poked a game-tying single to left off relief ace Tom Henke. After the Jays regained the lead in the 11th, the Braves scored one run and had the potential tying run on third, but Nixon bunted to pitcher Mike Timlin for the final out.

The victory went to Jimmy Key, the Jays' sixth pitcher of the night and a two-time Series winner. Key had recorded a 2-1 Game 4 decision that followed 5-4 and 3-2 Toronto victories (both credited to reliever Duane Ward) after the Braves had won the opener, 3-1, in Atlanta.

Tom Glavine was masterful in his four-hit first-game effort and catcher Damon Berryhill took hero honors with a three-run homer. But the Jays captured Game 2 and then won a tense third-game duel that marked the first World Series game on Canadian soil.

Kelly Gruber smashed a game-tying homer in the eighth inning and Candy Maldonado decided the outcome in the ninth with a one-out single off Jeff Reardon.

After Key had shackled the Braves for 7⅔ innings in his Game 4 victory, the Braves fought back in Game 5 behind John Smoltz's pitching and a grand slam home run by Lonnie Smith for a 7-2 triumph. That victory set the table for Winfield's final-game heroics.

Game 1	Atlanta	3	Toronto	1
Game 2	Toronto	5	Atlanta	4
Game 3	Toronto	3	Atlanta	2
Game 4	Toronto	2	Atlanta	1
Game 5	Atlanta	7	Toronto	2
Game 6	Toronto	4	Atlanta	3

Jubilant Toronto fans pour onto the SkyDome field as fireworks signal the Blue Jays' victory over Atlanta in Game 6 of the World Series.

CAREER STATS

Taken from *The Sporting News Complete Baseball Record Book*

* Asterisks denote current players active in 1992 or 1993

BATTING

Average
at least 10 years or 1,000 hits

Player	Avg.
Ty Cobb	.367
Rogers Hornsby	.358
Joe Jackson	.356
Pete Browning	.354
David Orr	.352
Dan Brouthers	.349
Frank O'Doul	.349
Ed Delahanty	.346
Willie Keeler	.345
Tris Speaker	.345
Billy Hamilton	.344
Ted Williams	.344
Jake Stenzel	.344
Jesse Burkett	.342
Harry Heilmann	.342
Babe Ruth	.342
Bill Terry	.341
Lou Gehrig	.340
Tip O'Neill	.340
George Sisler	.340
Cap Anson	.339
Napoleon Lajoie	.339
*Wade Boggs	.338
Riggs Stephenson	.336
Sam Thompson	.336
Bill Lange	.336
Mike Donlin	.334
John McGraw	.334
Al Simmons	.334
Eddie Collins	.333
Paul Waner	.333
Denny Lyons	.331
Stan Musial	.331
Hugh Duffy	.330
Heinie Manush	.330
Honus Wagner	.329
Rod Carew	.328
*Tony Gwynn	.327
Earle Combs	.325
Roger Connor	.325
Joe DiMaggio	.325
Bob Fothergill	.325
Jimmie Foxx	.325
Edd Roush	.325

Hits

Player	Hits
Pete Rose	4,256
Ty Cobb	4,191
Hank Aaron	3,771
Stan Musial	3,630
Tris Speaker	3,515
Honus Wagner	3,430
Carl Yastrzemski	3,419
Eddie Collins	3,309
Willie Mays	3,283
Napoleon Lajoie	3,252
Paul Waner	3,152
Cap Anson	3,081
Rod Carew	3,053
*Robin Yount	3,025
Lou Brock	3,023
Al Kaline	3,007
*George Brett	3,005
Roberto Clemente	3,000
Sam Rice	2,987
Sam Crawford	2,964
Willie Keeler	2,955
Frank Robinson	2,943
Jake Beckley	2,930
Rogers Hornsby	2,930
Al Simmons	2,927
Zack Wheat	2,884
Frank Frisch	2,880
Mel Ott	2,876
Babe Ruth	2,873
Jesse Burkett	2,872
*Dave Winfield	2,866
Brooks Robinson	2,848
Charley Gehringer	2,839
George Sisler	2,812
Vada Pinson	2,757

Singles

Player	1B
Pete Rose	3,215
Ty Cobb	3,052
Eddie Collins	2,639
Willie Keeler	2,534
Honus Wagner	2,426
Rod Carew	2,404
Tris Speaker	2,383
Napoleon Lajoie	2,354
Cap Anson	2,330
Jesse Burkett	2,301
Hank Aaron	2,294
Sam Rice	2,272
Carl Yastrzemski	2,262
Stan Musial	2,253
Lou Brock	2,247
Paul Waner	2,243
Frank Frisch	2,171
Roger Cramer	2,163
Luke Appling	2,162
Nellie Fox	2,161
Roberto Clemente	2,154
Jake Beckley	2,142
George Sisler	2,122
Richie Ashburn	2,119
Luis Aparicio	2,108
Zack Wheat	2,104
Sam Crawford	2,102
*Robin Yount	2,101
Lafayette Cross	2,077
Fred Clarke	2,061
Al Kaline	2,035
Lloyd Waner	2,032
Brooks Robinson	2,030
Rabbit Maranville	2,020
Max Carey	2,018
George Van Haltren	2,008
George Davis	2,007

Doubles

Player	2B
Tris Speaker	793
Pete Rose	746
Stan Musial	725
Ty Cobb	724
Napoleon Lajoie	652
Honus Wagner	651
Carl Yastrzemski	646
*George Brett	634
Hank Aaron	624
Paul Waner	605
Charley Gehringer	574
*Robin Yount	558
Harry Heilmann	542
Rogers Hornsby	541
Joe Medwick	540
Al Simmons	539
Lou Gehrig	534
Cap Anson	530
Al Oliver	529
Frank Robinson	528
Dave Parker	526
Ted Williams	525
Willie Mays	523
Joe Cronin	516
Ed Delahanty	508
Babe Ruth	506
Tony Perez	505
Goose Goslin	500

Triples

Player	3B
Sam Crawford	312
Ty Cobb	298
Honus Wagner	252
Jake Beckley	246
Roger Connor	227
Tris Speaker	222
Fred Clarke	219
Dan Brouthers	212
Paul Waner	191
Joe Kelley	189
Eddie Collins	186
Jesse Burkett	185
Harry Stovey	185
Sam Rice	184
Ed Delahanty	182
John McPhee	180
Buck Ewing	179
Rabbit Maranville	177
Stan Musial	177
Goose Goslin	173
Zack Wheat	172
Elmer Flick	170
Tommy Leach	170
Rogers Hornsby	169
Joe Jackson	168
Edd Roush	168
George Davis	167
Bill Dahlen	166
Sherry Magee	166
Roberto Clemente	166
Jake Daubert	165

Home Runs

Player	HR
Hank Aaron	755
Babe Ruth	714
Willie Mays	660
Frank Robinson	586
Harmon Killebrew	573
Reggie Jackson	563
Mike Schmidt	548
Mickey Mantle	536
Jimmie Foxx	534
Ted Williams	521
Willie McCovey	521
Eddie Mathews	512
Ernie Banks	512
Mel Ott	511
Lou Gehrig	493
Stan Musial	475
Willie Stargell	475
Carl Yastrzemski	452
Dave Kingman	442
*Dave Winfield	432
Billy Williams	426
Darrell Evans	414
*Eddie Murray	414
Duke Snider	407
*Andre Dawson	399
Al Kaline	399
*Dale Murphy	398
Graig Nettles	390
Johnny Bench	389
Dwight Evans	385
Frank Howard	382
Jim Rice	382
Orlando Cepeda	379
Tony Perez	379
Norm Cash	377
*Carlton Fisk	375
Rocky Colavito	374
Gil Hodges	370
Ralph Kiner	369
Joe DiMaggio	361
Johnny Mize	359
Yogi Berra	358
Lee May	354
Dick Allen	351

Runs Scored

Player	Runs
Ty Cobb	2,245
Babe Ruth	2,174
Hank Aaron	2,174
Pete Rose	2,165
Willie Mays	2,062
Stan Musial	1,949
Lou Gehrig	1,888
Tris Speaker	1,881
Mel Ott	1,859
Frank Robinson	1,829
Eddie Collins	1,816
Carl Yastrzemski	1,816
Ted Williams	1,798
Charley Gehringer	1,774
Jimmie Foxx	1,751
Honus Wagner	1,740
Willie Keeler	1,720
Cap Anson	1,712
Jesse Burkett	1,708
Billy Hamilton	1,690
Mickey Mantle	1,677
John McPhee	1,674
George Van Haltren	1,650
Joe Morgan	1,650
Jim Ryan	1,640
Paul Waner	1,627
Al Kaline	1,622
Fred Clarke	1,620
Lou Brock	1,610
Roger Connor	1,607
Jake Beckley	1,601

Total Bases

Player	TB
Hank Aaron	6,856
Stan Musial	6,134
Willie Mays	6,066
Ty Cobb	5,862
Babe Ruth	5,793
Pete Rose	5,752
Carl Yastrzemski	5,539
Frank Robinson	5,373
Tris Speaker	5,103
Lou Gehrig	5,060
Mel Ott	5,041
Jimmie Foxx	4,956
Honus Wagner	4,888
Ted Williams	4,884
Al Kaline	4,852
Reggie Jackson	4,834
*Dave Winfield	4,821
*George Brett	4,801
Rogers Hornsby	4,712
Ernie Banks	4,706
Al Simmons	4,685
Billy Williams	4,599
*Robin Yount	4,558
Tony Perez	4,532
Mickey Mantle	4,511
Roberto Clemente	4,492
Napoleon Lajoie	4,478
Paul Waner	4,478
Dave Parker	4,405
Mike Schmidt	4,404
Eddie Mathews	4,349
Sam Crawford	4,328
Goose Goslin	4,325

Runs Batted In

Player	RBI
Hank Aaron	2,297
Babe Ruth	2,204
Lou Gehrig	1,990
Ty Cobb	1,960
Stan Musial	1,951
Jimmie Foxx	1,921
Willie Mays	1,903
Mel Ott	1,861
Carl Yastrzemski	1,844
Ted Williams	1,839
Al Simmons	1,827
Frank Robinson	1,812
*Dave Winfield	1,710
Reggie Jackson	1,702
Tony Perez	1,652
Ernie Banks	1,636
Goose Goslin	1,609
Mike Schmidt	1,595
Harmon Killebrew	1,584
Al Kaline	1,583
Rogers Hornsby	1,578
*Eddie Murray	1,562
Tris Speaker	1,562
Willie McCovey	1,555
Harry Heilmann	1,551
Willie Stargell	1,540
Joe DiMaggio	1,537
*George Brett	1,520
Mickey Mantle	1,509

Stolen Bases

Player	SB
*Rickey Henderson	1,042
Lou Brock	938
Billy Hamilton	937
Ty Cobb	892
Walter Latham	791
Harry Stovey	744
Eddie Collins	743
Max Carey	738
*Tim Raines	730
Honus Wagner	720
Tom Brown	697
Joe Morgan	689
*Willie Wilson	660
Bert Campaneris	649
George Davis	632
*Vince Coleman	610
William Hoy	605
John Montgomery Ward	605
John McPhee	602
Hugh Duffy	597
Bill Dahlen	587
Maury Wills	586
John Doyle	560
Dave Lopes	557
Herman Long	554
Cesar Cedeno	550
Michael Griffin	549
*Ozzie Smith	542
George Van Haltren	537
Patrick Donovan	531
Fred Clarke	527
Curtis Welch	526
Willie Keeler	519
Tommy McCarthy	506
Luis Aparicio	506

PITCHING

Games

Pitcher	Yrs.	G.
Hoyt Wilhelm	21	1,070
Kent Tekulve	16	1,050
Lindy McDaniel	21	987
Rollie Fingers	17	944
Gene Garber	19	931
*Goose Gossage	20	926
Cy Young	22	906
Sparky Lyle	16	899
Jim Kaat	25	898
Don McMahon	18	874
Phil Niekro	24	864
Roy Face	16	848
Tug McGraw	19	824
*Jeff Reardon	14	811
*Charlie Hough	23	803
Walter Johnson	21	802
*Nolan Ryan	26	794
*Lee Smith	13	787
Gaylord Perry	22	777
Don Sutton	23	774
Darold Knowles	16	765
Tommy John	26	760
Ron Reed	19	751
Warren Spahn	21	750
Tom Burgmeier	17	745
Gary Lavelle	13	745
Willie Hernandez	13	744
Steve Carlton	24	741
*Dennis Eckersley	18	740
Ron Perranoski	13	737
Ron Kline	17	736
Clay Carroll	15	731
Mike Marshall	14	723
Johnny Klippstein	18	711
Greg Minton	16	710
Stu Miller	16	704
Joe Niekro	22	702
Bill Campbell	15	700

Earned-Run Average

3,000 or more innings to qualify

Earned Run Average as a statistic was only accepted after 1911 in N.L., 1912 in A.L.

Pitcher	IP	ERA
x-Walter Johnson	4,195	2.37
y-Grover Alexander	4,822	2.56
Whitey Ford	3,171	2.74
Tom Seaver	4,782	2.86
Jim Palmer	3,947⅓	2.86
Stan Coveleski	3,071	2.88
Juan Marichal	3,506	2.89
Wilbur Cooper	3,482	2.89
Bob Gibson	3,885	2.91
Carl Mays	3,022	2.92
Don Drysdale	3,432	2.95
Carl Hubbell	3,591	2.98
Lefty Grove	3,940	3.06
Warren Spahn	5,246	3.08
Gaylord Perry	5,352	3.10
Eppa Rixey	4,494	3.15
Urban Faber	4,087	3.15
*Nolan Ryan	5,321	3.17
Steve Carlton	5,216⅓	3.22
Dolf Luque	3,221	3.24
Bob Feller	3,828	3.25
Dutch Leonard	3,220	3.25
Don Sutton	5,281⅔	3.26
Catfish Hunter	3,449	3.26
Vida Blue	3,344	3.26
Jim Bunning	3,759	3.27
Billy Pierce	3,305	3.27
Luis Tiant	3,485⅔	3.30
William Walters	3,104	3.30
Claude Osteen	3,459	3.30

x-*Does not include 1,729 innings pitched 1907-12.*

y-*Does not include 367 innings pitched in 1911.*

Victories

Pitcher	W.	L.	Pct.
Cy Young	511	313	.620
Walter Johnson	416	279	.599
Christy Mathewson	373	188	.665
Grover Alexander	373	208	.642
Warren Spahn	363	245	.597
Kid Nichols	361	208	.634
Pud Galvin	361	309	.539
Tim Keefe	342	225	.603
Steve Carlton	329	244	.574
John Clarkson	327	176	.650
Don Sutton	324	256	.559
*Nolan Ryan	319	287	.526
Phil Niekro	318	274	.537
Gaylord Perry	314	265	.542
Tom Seaver	311	205	.603
Hoss Radbourn	308	191	.617
Mickey Welch	307	209	.595
Eddie Plank	305	181	.628
Lefty Grove	300	141	.680
Early Wynn	300	244	.551
Tommy John	288	231	.555
*Bert Blyleven	287	250	.534
Robin Roberts	286	245	.539
Tony Mullane	285	213	.572
Ferguson Jenkins	284	226	.557
Jim Kaat	283	237	.544
Red Ruffing	273	225	.548
Burleigh Grimes	270	212	.560
Jim Palmer	268	152	.638
Bob Feller	266	162	.621
Eppa Rixey	266	251	.515
Jim McCormick	265	215	.552
Gus Weyhing	262	226	.537
Ted Lyons	260	230	.531
Urban Faber	254	212	.545
Carl Hubbell	253	154	.622
Bob Gibson	251	174	.591

20-Victory Seasons

Pitcher	Years
Cy Young	16
Christy Mathewson	13
Warren Spahn	13
Walter Johnson	12
Kid Nichols	11
Pud Galvin	10
Grover Alexander	9
Hoss Radbourn	9
Mickey Welch	9
John Clarkson	8
Lefty Grove	8
Jim McCormick	8
Joe McGinnity	8
Tony Mullane	8
Amos Rusie	8
Jim Palmer	8
Charlie Buffinton	7
Clark Griffith	7
Ferguson Jenkins	7
Tim Keefe	7
Bob Lemon	7
Eddie Plank	7
Gus Weyhing	7
Victor Willis	7
Mordecai Brown	6
Steve Carlton	6
Bob Caruthers	6
Bob Feller	6
Wes Ferrell	6
Juan Marichal	6
Robin Roberts	6
Jack Stivetts	6
Jesse Tannehill	6

Shutouts

Pitcher	Games
Walter Johnson	110
Grover Alexander	90
Christy Mathewson	83
Cy Young	76
Eddie Plank	64
Warren Spahn	63
*Nolan Ryan	61
Tom Seaver	61
*Bert Blyleven	60
Don Sutton	58
Ed Walsh	58
Pud Galvin	57
Bob Gibson	56
Steve Carlton	55
Jim Palmer	53
Gaylord Perry	53
Juan Marichal	52
Mordecai Brown	50
Rube Waddell	50
Victor Willis	50
Don Drysdale	49
Ferguson Jenkins	49
Luis Tiant	49
Early Wynn	49
Kid Nichols	48
Tommy John	46
Jack Powell	46
Guy White	46
Charles Adams	45
Whitey Ford	45
Addie Joss	45
Phil Niekro	45
Robin Roberts	45
Red Ruffing	45

Strikeouts

Pitcher	SO
*Nolan Ryan	5,668
Steve Carlton	4,136
*Bert Blyleven	3,701
Tom Seaver	3,640
Don Sutton	3,574
Gaylord Perry	3,534
Walter Johnson	3,508
Phil Niekro	3,342
Ferguson Jenkins	3,192
Bob Gibson	3,117
Jim Bunning	2,855
Mickey Lolich	2,832
Cy Young	2,819
*Frank Tanana	2,657
Warren Spahn	2,583
Bob Feller	2,581
Jerry Koosman	2,556
Tim Keefe	2,538
Christy Mathewson	2,505
Don Drysdale	2,486
Jim Kaat	2,461
Sam McDowell	2,453
Luis Tiant	2,416
Sandy Koufax	2,396
Robin Roberts	2,357
Early Wynn	2,334
Rube Waddell	2,310
Juan Marichal	2,303
*Jack Morris	2,275
Lefty Grove	2,266
Tommy John	2,245
Jim Palmer	2,212
Grover Alexander	2,198
Vida Blue	2,175
*Charlie Hough	2,171
Camilo Pascual	2,167
*Dennis Eckersley	2,118
Eddie Plank	2,112
Bobo Newsom	2,082
Dazzy Vance	2,045
Rick Reuschel	2,015
Catfish Hunter	2,012

Saves

Saves as a statistic were only accepted from 1969.

Pitcher	Saves
*Jeff Reardon	357
*Lee Smith	355
Rollie Fingers	341
*Goose Gossage	308
Bruce Sutter	300
*Dave Righetti	251
Dan Quisenberry	244
*Dennis Eckersley	239
*John Franco	226
Sparky Lyle	222
*Tom Henke	220
Gene Garber	218
*Dave Smith	216
*Bobby Thigpen	200
*Steve Bedrosian	184
Kent Tekulve	184
Tug McGraw	179
Mike Marshall	178
*Doug Jones	164
*Jay Howell	153
Greg Minton	150
*Roger McDowell	149
Willie Hernandez	147
*Mitch Williams	143
*Rick Aguilera	142
Dave Giusti	140
Gary Lavelle	136
*Dan Plesac	133
Bob Stanley	132
*Randy Myers	131
*Gregg Olson	131
Ron Davis	130
*Todd Worrell	129
Terry Forster	127
Bill Campbell	126
*Bryan Harvey	126
Dave LaRoche	126

INDEX

Page references in italic refer to illustrations